MW00831241

William Wilberforce recorded many intimate details about his spiritual life, and thanks to Michael McMullen's painstaking work, many of them are published here for the first time. This book is an inestimable treasure – it draws back the curtain on Wilberforce's struggles and rejoicings in his own words as he wrestled both with himself and all that God had called him to be and do.

Eric Metaxas
Author of *Amazing Grace: William Wilberforce and the Heroic Campaign to End Slavery*
Host of the nationally syndicated Eric Metaxas Radio Show

In my efforts to educate this generation about the impactful life of William Wilberforce, Dr McMullen has travelled across the country each year to share his knowledge about the man, his life, and more importantly, why he is still relevant.

The spiritual journals synthesized by Dr McMullen provide timeless applications for the young men I work with who seek to impact their own culture. I am always challenged by Dr 'Mc's' insights and admonitions.

TIM ECHOLS
Vice-chairman, Georgia Public Service Commission
Creator of TeenPact
Co-founder of the Wilberforce Fellowship

William Wilberforce, the leader of the campaign for the abolition of the slave trade, was a devoted Evangelical Christian. His spiritual journals between 1785 and 1833 open a window on the inward life of this public man. He was frank, self-critical and conscious of his constant dependence on the God of mercy. Michael McMullen has transcribed all the journals and added helpful explanatory notes so as to make this detailed record of Wilberforce's Christian journey available for the first time.

DAVID BEBBINGTON
Emeritus Professor of History, University of Stirling, Scotland

These remarkable journals of William Wilberforce, all carefully edited and some published here for the first time, allow us to chart the spiritual life of perhaps the most consequential shaper of practical Christianity since the Reformation.

Here is an evangelical paradigm of *ora et labora*, a pattern of devotion in the royal service of Christ.

TIMOTHY GEORGE
Distinguished Professor of Divinity, Beeson Divinity School,
Samford University, Birmingham, Alabama

Despite the numerous demands and pressures of parliamentary business, social contacts and family commitments on his time, Wilberforce consistently set aside over an hour each day, and many more on Sundays, for personal and family Bible reading, prayer and meditation. The depth of his commitment to such daily priorities is a challenge to us all, most of whom have nothing like his demanding schedule and responsibilities. His Journal illustrates clearly how he took to heart the teaching and example of Jesus, that *the night cometh when no man can work.*

It is a tremendous service to have this Journal transcribed and a bonus to have the excellent introductions to each section.

MARYLYNN ROUSE
Founder Director, the John Newton Project
Honorary Visiting Fellow, Leicester University, England

Wilberforce has fascinated and confused biographers and historians for centuries – how did this hilarious, spontaneous, chaotic and conspicuously gracious man change the world? Christians have delighted in his attachment to their gospel and have hoped that the silver stream of world-changing inspiration was divine. And now at last, in these pages, Wilberforce can speak for himself – and the conclusion is luminous: Jesus Christ once said that people would be fruitful as they abide in him. In these pages we see a man, an undeniably fruitful man, abiding in Christ. Believers will find a brother travelling the path that they have known, and will be inspired to press on, rejoicing by faith in the One who brings fruit into sight. I can't think of a more thrilling or important publication from the last ten years.

BEN VIRGO
Director, Christian Heritage London

Michael McMullen's detailed labour of love for the first time makes widely accessible the inspiring and fascinating inner spiritual life of one of the greatest public figures of the later Hanoverian era.

JOHN WOLFFE
Professor of Religious History, The Open University

William Wilberforce has long been regarded as the classic example of evangelical activism in the long eighteenth century. His tenacious fight against the barbarous inhumanity of the slave trade and slavery have made him an iconic hero for many in our day. But what is often not remembered is the spiritual matrix out of which Wilberforce drew the resources to wage his indomitable battle for justice and social righteousness. Prof McMullen has put us all in his debt by editing these previously-unpublished diaries of this great human being. They reveal that Wilberforce's love for the African people was intimately tied to his ardent Christian spirituality. Wilberforce was a man who lived life *coram deo*. May the reading of these diaries inspire many in our day to do likewise and attempt great things for God.

MICHAEL A. G. HAYKIN
Chair and Professor of Church History,
The Southern Baptist Theological Seminary, Louisville, Kentucky

William Wilberforce was a man marked by a wonderful integrity between the private and the public. Now more than ever, integrity amongst all who bear the name of Jesus is needed. William Wilberforce has so much to teach the church today, and Michael McMullen has performed a significant task in making this possible by transcribing and explaining Wilberforce's journals. As the rector of the church where Wilberforce once worshipped, I am deeply grateful for Michael's work.

JAGO WYNNE
Rector of Holy Trinity Clapham, London

William Wilberforce

His Unpublished
Spiritual Journals

Ed. Michael D. McMullen

CHRISTIAN
FOCUS

Published in 2021
by
Christian Focus Publications Ltd,
Geanies House, Fearn, Ross-shire,
IV20 1TW, Great Britain.

www.christianfocus.com

Cover design by
Daniel van Straaten

Cover image by Henry Pether – A Moonlit View of the Houses of
Parliament from the Thames
Contributor: Artiz / Alamy Stock Photo

Printed and bound by Bell & Bain

Contents

To Amy

William Wilberforce:
Reflections and Assessments

I have not allowed myself to forget that the abolition of the Slave-trade by Great Britain, was agitated a hundred years before it was a final success; that the measure had its open fire-eating opponents; its stealthy 'don't-care' opponents; its dollar and cent opponents; its inferior race opponents ... But I have also remembered that though they blazed, like tallow-candles for a century, at last they flickered in the socket, died out, stank in the dark for a brief season, and were remembered no more, even by the smell. School-boys know that Wilberforce, and Granville Sharp helped that cause forward; but who can now name a single man who labored to retard it?

Abraham Lincoln (1809–1865)
16ᵗʰ US President

William Wilberforce has served as an example for me, Mr Speaker, and I commend him to all Members of Congress concerned with changing our times for the better ... Wilberforce's life was animated by his deeply held personal faith, by a sense of calling, by banding together with like-minded friends, by a fundamental belief in the power of ideas and moral beliefs to change the culture through public persuasion ... let us reflect on this anniversary of the passing of the great abolitionist William Wilberforce, and may we each of us in this Chamber always be inspired by his example and may we always aspire to those words he most assuredly heard 168 years ago: 'Well done, good and faithful servant.'

Mike Pence (1959–)
Former US Vice-President, Speech given in Congress 2001

It is well worth the enquiry by what system of self-treatment these happy fruits had been matured. They were not merely the results of a naturally cheerful temper leavened with religious feeling: they resulted from close and systematic discipline. He kept a most strict watch over his heart. He still recorded by a set of secret marks the results of frequent and close self-examination under a number of specific heads. He used every help he could devise for keeping always on his soul a sense of the nearness and the goodness of God.

Robert and Samuel Wilberforce (1802–57 and 1805–1873)
Sons and biographers

Wilberforce's deep trust in Christ, persistence, courage and determination to transform the lives of many is a wonderful example that should inspire us all today to make a difference.

Dr John Sentamu (1949–)
97th Archbishop of York

… the wittiest man in England, and the most religious.

Madame de Stael (1766–1817)
Woman of letters and historian

[As] pure and virtuous a man as ever lived.

The York Herald

He was also a most cheerful Christian. His harp appeared to be always in tune; no 'gloomy atmosphere of a melancholy moroseness' surrounded him; his sun appeared to be always shining: hence he was remarkably fond of singing hymns, both in family prayer and when alone. He would say, 'A Christian should have joy and peace in believing. It is his duty to abound in praise.'

Rev. Joseph Brown, Rector of Christ Church, Blackfriars Rd., London
Sermon preached in London on occasion of Wilberforce's death

I never saw any other man who seemed to enjoy such a perpetual serenity and sunshine of spirit. In conversing with him, you feel assured that there is no guile in him; that if ever there was a good man and happy man on earth, he was one.

Robert Southey (1774–1843)
British Poet Laureate 1813–1843

As he walked about the house he was generally humming the tune of a hymn or Psalm as if he could not contain his pleasurable feelings of thankfulness and devotion.

Joseph John Gurney (1788–1847)
Quaker and banker, comments after staying for a week with Wilberforce

Being himself amused and interested by everything, whatever he said became amusing or interesting ... His presence was as fatal to dullness as to immorality. His mirth was as irresistible as the first laughter of childhood.

James Stephen (1758–1832)
Lawyer and M.P.

[Wilberforce] had the greatest natural eloquence of any man I ever knew.

William Pitt the Younger (1759–1806)
British Prime Minister 1783–1801 and 1804–06

I saw what seemed a mere shrimp mount upon the table, but as I listened, he grew and grew, until the shrimp became a whale.

James Boswell (1740–1795)
Lawyer, diarist and biographer

If I were called upon to describe Wilberforce in one word, I should say he was the most 'amusable' man I ever met with ... Instead of having to think what subjects will interest him, it is perfectly impossible to hit on one that does not ... When he was in the House of Commons, he seemed to have the freshest mind of any man there. There was all the charm of youth about him. And he is quite as remarkable in this bright evening of his days as when I saw him in his glory many years ago.

Sir James Mackintosh (1765–1832)
M.P. and Judge

In person ... Wilberforce was slightly deformed ... [He] usually carried an inkstand in his coat pocket ... He invariably wore black clothes, sometimes till they became quite dingy, for he ignored the outer man ... He was quite unconscious of the notice which his personal appearance attracted ... Few men have been so little influenced by the distracting passions of ambition, avarice, vanity and resentment.

John Shore (1796–1885)
1st Baron Teignmouth

[Wilberforce was] naturally a person of great quickness and even subtlety of mind, with a lively imagination, approaching a playfulness of fancy; and hence he had wit in an unmeasured abundance ... His nature was mild and amiable beyond that of most men. His eloquence was of the highest order.

Henry Brougham (1778–1868)
1st Baron Brougham and Vaux, Lord Chancellor

William Wilberforce was a great man who impacted the Western world as few others have done. Blessed with brains, charm, influence and initiative, much wealth … he put evangelism on Britain's map as a power for social change, first by overthrowing the Slave Trade almost single-handed and then by generating a stream of Societies for doing good and reducing evil in public life … To forget such men is foolish.

J. I. Packer (1926–2020)
Anglican theologian and author

It's difficult to escape the verdict that William Wilberforce was simply the greatest social reformer in the history of the world. The world that he was born into in 1759 and the world he departed in 1833, were as different as lead and gold. William Wilberforce presided over a social earthquake that rearranged the continents and whose magnitude we are only now beginning to fully appreciate.

Eric Metaxas (1963–)
Author and biographer of Wilberforce

On the very night on which we were successfully engaged in the House of Commons in passing the clause of the Act of Emancipation … the spirit of our friend left the world. The day which was the termination of his labors was the termination of his life.

Sir Thomas Fowell Buxton (1786–1845)
M.P.

Wilberforce became a national hero and it was the government that requested he be buried here in Westminster Abbey. His coffin, carried by two Royal Dukes, the Lord Chancellor, the Speaker of the House of Commons and four Peers of the Realm, was followed into this Abbey by members of both Houses of Parliament.

Rev. Tony Kyriakides
Priest Vicar, Sermon in Westminster Abbey 2017

The world 'will not look upon his like again'.

Robert Southey (1774–1843) British Poet Laureate 1813–1843
comments upon Wilberforce's retirement from Parliament in 1825

Wilberforce modeled a combination of Christian principle and tactical genius as relevant in the twenty-first century as in his own time.

William Jefferson Hague (1961–)
Baron Hague of Richmond, Life Peer, former M.P.,
and biographer of Wilberforce

Acknowledgements

I never envisaged the mammoth project that this volume eventually became, and as such I have many that I would like to thank, being very much aware that I am certain to forget some, and for that I am truly sorry.

I wish to begin by thanking Mr Colin Harris and his wonderful staff at the Bodleian Library at Oxford University, who provided me with every courtesy and helpfulness in all my pilgrimages to consult the Wilberforce Manuscripts.

Thanks are also due to particular individuals who provided timely encouragement during this project: Kevin Belmonte, biographer of Wilberforce and lead script and historical consultant for the movie 'Amazing Grace', who has been very kind with all his assistance, including the very kind Foreword he generously contributed; to Marylynn Rouse, John Newton scholar, who not only welcomed me into her home and furnished me with invaluable help on Newton's relationship with Wilberforce, but who also kindly made several invaluable suggestions on the present text; and to Dr Timothy Whelan, Professor of English at Georgia Southern University, who has been a very good friend and constant encourager.

I would also like to express my thanks to Dr John Coffey of Leicester University, General Editor of the Wilberforce Diaries Project in the UK. Having completed this present volume, I was kindly invited to join the UK project as an editor with him and several other scholars. This next multi-volume project with OUP, seeks to bring to publication the complete Diaries of Wilberforce, which number in total almost one million words.

Sincere appreciation too goes to Tim Echols, vice-chairman of the Georgia Public Service Commission, creator of TeenPact, and co-founder of the Wilberforce Fellowship, a weekend devoted to energizing and equipping young Christian students and leaders in the spirit of William Wilberforce and his campaign to make goodness fashionable. The event involves valuable teaching and mentoring from seasoned executives and national ministry leaders from across America.

I would also like to record my very real thanks to the administration and trustees of Midwestern Baptist Theological Seminary, for the generous granting of a Sabbatical to complete this volume. Appreciation goes too to all the students I have had the honor and privilege to teach and mentor, and especially those who gladly and maybe nervously, took up my challenge to grapple with some selections of Wilberforce's handwriting. Many of them found themselves like me at the conclusion of their adventure, blessed and challenged, not so much with the difficulty of the transcription, but with the very real impact the life, words and witness of Wilberforce had on their own lives.

I am thankful too to Willie Mackenzie of Christian Focus Publications for his constant encouragement and patience; and to Rosanna Burton and Stephen Greenhalgh for their invaluable help in guiding and editing this volume, and helping it look so good.

I would also like to record my great thanks to my remaining siblings, to Kevin, Sue and Rick for all the help and encouragement I was blessed to receive from them during this project, including the valuable time spent at Rick and Katherine's gorgeous 'British' house in rural Virginia, where I was finally able to complete this volume. I should note here too that my brother Rick was a student at the very same Hull Grammar School that Wilberforce attended.

Lastly I would like to record the privilege it has been to receive such incredibly kind and thoughtful reflections from both Richard and William Wilberforce. It was several years ago that I originally met Richard at Ripon Castle tea rooms, and he has been a source of real encouragement and blessing to me in this endeavor. I will forever be in the debt of both men and their incredible words will follow these acknowledgements.

Foreword

Pertinacity. It was a word William Wilberforce liked to use, and a word we ought to know better today. It is word that expresses the virtue of one who is tenacious, resolute, and capable of holding fast to a purpose or design.

Wilberforce modeled pertinacity in his own life when he resolved to undertake the very considerable task of keeping a spiritual diary. It was no little or cursory commitment. He invested great thought, care, and reflection in writing it. It was an ongoing expression of his faith, setting out hopes, consolations, his sense of his own shortcomings, and his great desire to learn and grow in Christian teachings. He wrote of his indebtedness to many exemplars of faith, and how he tapped the renewing springs of belief present in their writings. Written with genuine humility and a forthright pen, he was introspective and contemplative, yet a pilgrim who found places of blessed assurance and abiding peace. The world has long needed a book which traces the many steps of his spiritual journey. This book helps greatly to meet that need.

And here it must also be said that we owe a profound debt to Wilberforce himself.

That might seem self-evident, but one need only consider the press of demands on his time to understand what he achieved in writing a spiritual diary over so many years. From 1780 to 1825 he served as a Member of Parliament; and from 1784 to 1812, as M.P. for the entire County of Yorkshire: some twenty-eight years in all, serving one of the most important constituencies in all England. For twenty years, 1787–1807, he led the parliamentary struggle to abolish the British slave trade, during which time he was threatened with murder, had to travel for a time with an armed bodyguard, and suffered what appears to have been two nervous breakdowns. Physically, he suffered from bouts of poor eyesight, increasing curvature of the spine, and debilitating episodes of ulcerative colitis. Add in his responsibilities as a husband and father of a family of six, and the also ever-present need to maintain a crushing load of parliamentary correspondence, to say nothing of personal letters, and one begins to see just how significant Wilberforce's commitment writing a spiritual diary was. At the same time, one understands the kind of importance he placed upon it. It was a central part of his life.

So this said, the commitment of Christian Focus Publications to publish *William Wilberforce: His Unpublished Spiritual Journals* is a rare and noteworthy endeavor. And there is no one better suited to undertake the task of gathering and editing this collection of Wilberforce's spiritual reflections than Michael McMullen. I, and many others, owe a great debt to him for his scholarship, pertinacity, and vision in bringing this book to completion. It will aid the ongoing pursuit of Wilberforce studies, a worthy goal indeed, and be a book that offers riches of spiritual insight and pilgrimage for those who share Wilberforce's faith.

May this book find a wide, well-deserved, and ongoing readership.

Kevin Belmonte

Reflections on this Volume

by Richard William Wilberforce

'Let them boldly assert the cause of Christ in
an age when so many who bear the name of
Christians are ashamed of him.'

William Wilberforce was a man of great talent and charm but ever conscious of his frailties. Poor health and eyesight affected him throughout his life and as a young man he was no different to any other in wishing to enjoy the pleasures of his wide social life.

With a discipline that belied his young years he carried out regular self-appraisal in the search for a better way to lead his life. This he found through his faith and as a practical Christian he sought a way to 'please' God and be useful. He writes of his being involved 'by accident' in the campaign to Abolish the Slave Trade. That the trade was an offence against humanity was clear, but it was also an affront to his Christian principles. Its Abolition in 1807 brought him huge political success and fame but he did not use this to accept honour nor reward. He had shown that he could practice the principles of a Christian life and be successful in the political world. It is this aspect of his life which earned him a place in history as not only a great reformer but Friend of Man.

Many were inspired by his example and writing. It is my hope that the efforts of Michael McMullen in transcribing these personal journals will result in others continuing to derive inspiration.

Richard W. Wilberforce
great-great-great-grandson of William Wilberforce

Reflections on this Volume

by William Wilberforce

William Wilberforce is a man I have known my whole life. First as a child as a portrait, or as an accompanying story to a trinket or other old possession of his I had stumbled across around the house. Then in history lessons or a trip to London; and later as a man, in books and accounts, as intrigue pushed me to open a biography or two and expand my knowing of him beyond family lore. Wilberforce has always been a presence in my life, a feeling at the back of my mind that pushed me to favor empathy and understanding, to see possibility in challenge. But it also brought pressures.

History does strange things to the achievements of men and women. His memory in many senses has become a creed in and of itself, not just in my family or on a personal level, but for anyone anywhere who sees in his actions a parable of struggle and triumph. I have to say that I have, in the past, been uncomfortable with the adulation Wilberforce receives, often feeling that he has become a poster boy for the collective soothing of a society's guilty conscience. That the true essence of his story has been lost in and amongst the narrative of relief and moral victory. For me, his story is one of cooperation, of monotony and tenacity, of rejection and humiliation, but also of extremity and prescription. Society forgets that great deeds are seldom the consequence of one person, and are rarely glamorous in their commission. We celebrate the outcome, but often discard the variables that, although were vital to the story, are inconvenient or lackluster to acknowledge. I have often wondered, who was he as a man? Would he be comfortable with how history has portrayed him?

One thing is clear. To Wilberforce, faith was his great facilitator. It gave him a framework and lens through which he could look at the world. It gave him a zeal that accompanied him on the countless hours and miles he traveled in pursuit of a dream. Faith gave him a reason to feel the way he did and it allowed him to contextualize these feelings for those who might not share them. Grounding what was considered an extremist position in a religious philosophy gave it a palatability, even though that was often nowhere near enough for people to take him seriously. Faith nurtured him in desperate hours and fostered lifelong friendships. Without the strength that his piety gave him, there would be no story.

Even if you acknowledge the spinning of the yarn, accept the poetic license and embrace the Wilberforce that popular history depicts, what is still so beautiful is how one man's piety and love can transcend time and place. That his faith can inspire and provoke centuries after his death. Even those without religious inclinations can observe and benefit from the actions that faith provoked in Wilberforce; his fortitude and unwavering commitment to the idea of something better. In this sense, in an increasingly godless age, stories like Wilberforce's show that faith can continue to work, long after the person whose conviction it was has passed.

What a wonderful thought.

Thank you, Michael, for this window into his mind.

William Wilberforce
great-great-great-great-grandson of William Wilberforce

Chronology

William Wilberforce: Born August 24, 1759, Kingston-Upon-Hull

Age

8   (1767–8) Attended Hull Grammar School.

9   (1768) Death of father. William sent to Nottingham then London.

9-12 (1768–71) Attended Chalmer's School, Putney.

12   (1771) Returns to Hull.

12-16 (1771–76) Attended Pocklington School.

17   (1774) His grandfather William Wilberforce dies.

17   (1776) Student at Cambridge University, meets Pitt.

18   (1777) Uncle William dies, inherits wealth.

21   (1780, Sept. 11) Elected Member of Parliament for Hull.

24   (1783, Sept. 3) Visits France with Pitt and Eliot, meets Franklin and Lafayette.

24   (1784) Elected Member of Parliament for Yorkshire.

25   (1784, October-Feb. 1785) European trip, discusses Doddridge.

26   (1785, Autumn-Dec.) European trip, reads Greek New Testament. Meets Newton.

26-27 (1785, Nov.-1786, Oct.) Religious Journal for this period missing.

28   (1787, Oct. 28) The 2 Great Objectives recorded in Journal.

29   (1789, May 12) First Abolition Speech lasts 3.5 hrs.

31   (1791, April) Introduces first Bill for Abolition, defeated 163-88.

33   (1793) Moves Abolition, defeated.

35   (1795) Moves Abolition, defeated.

36   (1796) Moves Abolition, defeated.

37   (1797) Publishes his book, *A Practical View*. Moves for Abolition, defeated.
      Marries Barbara Spooner (May 30), she dies 1847.

38   (1798, July 21) First child, William born, dies 1879.
      Moves Abolition, defeated.

39   (1799, July 21) Second child, Barbara born, dies 1821.
      Moves Abolition, defeated.

41   (1801, Jan. 19) Third child, Elizabeth born, dies 1832.

42   (1802, Dec. 19) Fourth child, Robert born, dies 1857.

44   (1804) Moves Abolition, defeated.

45   (1805, Sep. 7) Fifth child, Samuel born, dies 1873.
      Moves Abolition, defeated.

46   (1806) General resolution for Abolition passes both Houses.

47   (1807, Mar. 25) Abolition Act receives Royal Assent.
      Publishes Letter on Abolition.

48   (1807, Sep. 22) Sixth child, Henry born, dies 1873.

53   (1812) Elected Member of Parliament for Bramber.

61   (1821) Relinquishes leadership of Abolition campaign to Buxton. Daughter, Barbara dies.

63   (1823) Publishes his *An Appeal to the Religion, Justice and Humanity of the Inhabitants of the British Empire on Behalf of the Negro Slaves in the West Indies.*

65   (1825, Feb. 22) Retires from Parliament.

72   (1832) Daughter, Elizabeth dies.

73   (1833, July 26) 3rd Reading of Slavery Bill passes.

73   (1833, July 29) Death of William Wilberforce.

Introduction to the Life, Spirituality and Journals of William Wilberforce

I was Born Augt. 24, 1759 at Hull; probably at about 7 attended the Grammar School with Satchell on my shoulder, having all my meals at home. When I had been at School about a year I believe, Joseph Milner succeeded therein in Hull School. I used occasionally to go to my Grandfather at Ferriby, 8 Miles off by the Humber side. In May 1768 a general Election in which my Father supported Mr. Weddell, who elected with Lord Rt. Manners. Soon after the Election my Father died & some months after, my Mother had a most long & dangerous Fever. In the Autumn I went with my aunt Smith to Nottingham & afterwards with their eldest Son to London to live with my Uncle Wilberforce my Father's elder & only Brother & his Lady, John Thornton's Sister – never any Children.[1]

It is now more than a decade since I began this labor of love. Having had my interest in William Wilberforce reawakened, my particular concern was to discover whether any of his diaries were still extant and if so, were they published, as surely they must be. That began an investigative quest and labor of love that has lasted from that day till this. For what I was shocked to discover, was that only very selective excerpts from Wilberforce's diaries had ever been published, and that really only by his two sons in their five-volume hagiographic biography of their father, published five years after his death.

Certainly since that time, much additional material has been published on Wilberforce and on the group which came to be known

---

1. This was how William Wilberforce began his autobiography, published here for the first time.

as the 'Clapham Circle.' Most of this happened as a consequence of
the renaissance of interest generated by the Slave Trade's Abolition
bicentennial celebrations in 2007. However, even with the abundance
of material which appeared then and since, very little if any of it has
had any serious interaction with the extant, though as yet unpublished,
Wilberforce manuscripts.[2] The suspicion held by the present writer,
is that those who may have been tempted to have even a cursory
investigative glance at those documents, were somewhat shocked at the
legibility, and quickly gave up any further thoughts of transcribing.
If that was indeed the case, then they should have had the privilege
(and challenge) as the present writer did have, of working on the extant
manuscripts of Jonathan Edwards (1703–58) for example.

The result is then, that I have spent much of the past decade, researching
the extent of what remains unpublished from those manuscripts held in
the Bodleian Library, Oxford, and in the original home of Wilberforce
in the High Street of Kingston-upon-Hull. Years have then been spent in
painstakingly deciphering Wilberforce's hand as found in his Spiritual
Journals particularly, but also in his unpublished Autobiography and
in other manuscripts too. Having worked on manuscripts from the
Wesley family, Andrew Fuller and several other Christian giants, I find it
interesting that in his Spiritual Journals, Wilberforce uses no real code or
shorthand. The only temptation to such things that I discovered, was his
occasional tendency to transpose some words and names into Hebrew
and Greek letters, in what one assumes was a basic means to keep less
educated eyes from completely understanding certain entries.

Wilberforce was born in Hull in 1759; I was born in the same city
200 years later, so it has been an especial honour and privilege working
with Richard Wilberforce, William's great-great-great-grandson, in
seeking to bring those manuscripts, or at least a small but significant
portion of them, to publication. Sadly, we can calculate from a list of
Wilberforce's diaries compiled by his son Robert, that almost half of the
volumes listed, consisting of both journals and diaries, are missing. This
is all the more tragic as one of those missing religious journals, listed
as 'Book 2, Nov 1785–Oc 1786', covers the period of his conversion, his
meetings with John Newton, and the first days of his newly-awakened
evangelical faith. The other missing volumes include two volumes of his
diaries, 'Book 3, Decem: 1791–Sept 1793', and 'Book 6, Aug 5 1802–April
1808', and one other religious journal, 'Book 9, Oc 1800–1804'.

Whilst much therefore of what is included in this volume will be
taken directly from Wilberforce's unpublished Journals, I also draw
on Robert and Samuel's five-volume biography of 1838, as some of the
manuscripts the sons used are no longer extant. One result of this will be
to demonstrate how the sons 'edited' their father's Journal entries, as one
is able to compare their words with the extant manuscripts. One suspects

---

2. The one work which displays clear evidence of substantial research into Wilberforce's
manuscripts is Anne Stott's volume, *Wilberforce Family and Friends* (New York: Oxford University
Press, Inc., 2012).

that they did this, both to show their father in the best possible light, and somewhat sadly it might be argued, to reduce Thomas Clarkson's footprint in the campaign for, and the achievement of, Abolition.

My love and admiration for all Wilberforce achieved, especially in the face of very real adversities, has only grown and deepened over these years the more I have come to know him. Yet at the same time, I recognize both that it is much more a matter of what God did in and through Wilberforce, and that Wilberforce really was one among many as he fought for Abolition and to reform the so-called 'manners' of Britain in the early nineteenth century. I have been humbled recently, by being appointed a Fellow of the Wilberforce Fellowship, an annual weekend conference based in Georgia, that exists to encourage millennials who are in political office, law, business, and non-profits, to utilize Wilberforce as their role-model as they seek to live out the Gospel in such positions. In a similar way, and because there is no lack of material that seeks to tell the story of Wilberforce, the intention of this present volume is rather to look at Wilberforce's personal spiritual formation, and draw out from his discipleship, spiritual lessons for our own. For it is the view of this writer, that it was Wilberforce's spirituality which drove him to pursue all that he did: Abolition, a radical change in Britain's moral outlook, and the conversion of those around him.

So, by way of introduction, and in the quote we began with from Wilberforce's unpublished Autobiography, he gives glimpses of several incidents in his life which are of especial interest to us, in charting the course of the development of his spirituality. William Wilberforce was born into a very wealthy family, who could afford to send him to the local Grammar School, adjacent to the beautiful Holy Trinity Church in which he was baptized, and close enough to his home in the center of the old Town of Hull, that he could enjoy lunch at home every day. He tells us he had been there about one year, when Joseph Milner became Head of the school, and that through the influence of Wilberforce's very wealthy grandfather, also named William and for whom the young Wilberforce was named. Wilberforce senior had himself held political office having twice held the office of Mayor of Hull.

By this appointment and by countless others, it is very easy to see the hand of God at work in the young Wilberforce's life. For example, it would be Isaac Milner, Joseph's brother, who would be directly instrumental in at least the spiritual awakening, if not the evangelical conversion itself, of Wilberforce. Indeed it must be regarded as somewhat ironic, that the very man who made the very real threat that his grandson would never see a penny of the family fortune if he became a 'Methodist' (a synonym at that point for an evangelical), is the same man who brought about the very means for Wilberforce to experience such an evangelical conversion, by using his undoubted influence as mentioned earlier, in having Joseph Milner appointed to the Grammar school, and who then brought his brother Isaac as his assistant.

In his Autobiography, Wilberforce also mentions his father's interest in the 1768 General Election, something which will obviously also become central in his own life, as he will go on to represent three different Parliamentary constituencies. He then follows those brief comments, with a note concerning his father's untimely death and his mother's dangerous fever, events that necessitated his own removal from the family home in Hull whilst still only nine years old. He is sent first to Nottingham to spend a week at the Abel Smiths, and then on to London, into the care of his Uncle William and Aunt Hannah. In the few years he spends there, he is not only exposed to and greatly influenced by these very committed evangelicals, but it is where begins his relationship with John Newton. Wilberforce also makes the comment that they never had children of their own, which will later result in his inheriting their substantial wealth, including the home in which he had stayed in as a young boy. He will later not only use this house as a base while serving in Parliament, but will set aside space for William Pitt the Younger to stay, as he will frequently do.

As Wilberforce is allowed to speak for himself through his Spiritual Journals, Autobiography and Reflections on Psalm 40, one should begin to acquire a more accurate, complete picture of him. This will be especially true of his spirituality, as one will now not be so dependent as previously, on a rather limited and somewhat edited number of previously published Journal and Diary extracts. The increased availability of the Journals should also help in another beneficial way, for as John Pollock, an acknowledged expert on Wilberforce, points out in his masterful biography,

> 'In printing them [entries in Wilberforce's journals and diaries] by the yard five years after his death, his sons gave the public a view of their father which lacked perspective, for none of the playfulness of his letter writing obtruded into the diary, nor the exuberance and joyousness which delighted his friends.'[3]

To be clear, it is not being argued here that the Spiritual Journals suddenly and radically transform our understanding of Wilberforce into some superficially happy or wildly exuberant individual. Wilberforce went through so much and endured so much for that to ever be true, but what one does discover through these newly brought to light entries, is something of the very real joy that filled Wilberforce's heart and life. We discover, in fact, a Wilberforce that is noticeably absent in the previously published material. In another published piece, Pollock went further in his criticism of the sons' published *Life* of their father, further than the present writer probably would, but the conclusion he came to as to their motives and agenda is surely correct,

> Throughout the twenty-year campaign for Abolition, Wilberforce showed himself a masterly politician. Indeed, it is as a statesman,

---

3. John Pollock, *Wilberforce* (London: Constable and Co., 1977), p. 45.

empowered and directed by faith in Christ, that he stands or falls, and not, as his sons tried to make out in their dreary five volume biography, as a religious person who happened to be in politics (and as their religious views no longer coincided with their father's when they wrote, they sought to fashion him into something other than he had been, and the real, delightful, many-sided Wilberforce disappeared for nearly 140 years).[4]

That joy that many have remarked on as being so characteristic of the later Wilberforce, flowed from the rekindling of his spiritual life, something for which Isaac Milner was so instrumental. It occurred as the two men journeyed to Europe together, especially as Milner introduced Wilberforce to Doddridge's *Rise and Progress of Religion in the Soul*, (referred to by some as the last great Puritan spiritual autobiography), and also as Milner witnessed to Wilberforce through the Greek New Testament. Such was the impact, that even whilst still on the Continent, both Wilberforce's inward and outward behavior began to be noticeably affected. Wilberforce soon then records how he had started to rise early each day to pray, how he was sensing great guilt for the many years spent neglecting his spiritual life, and even noting how he found himself in a deep, depressed state as a result. He soon also begins the first of many Spiritual Journals, which he saw as a vital means to keep him, 'humble and watchful'.

If it is true as a number of scholars have argued, that journaling did for evangelicals what the confessional had done for the medieval church, that seems to be just how Wilberforce approached his entries. He also began a regimen of serious Scripture and devotional reading, with his early mornings consisting of private devotions, meditation, and family prayer. A major development took place in December 1785, when he reacquainted himself with John Newton, and whose wise counsel would become vitally significant in helping Wilberforce set the future course of his whole life. In this vein for example, Wilberforce records that, 'He [Newton] told me that he had always entertained hopes that God would sometime bring me to him. When I came away I found my mind in a calm, tranquil state, more humbled, and looking more devoutly up to God.'

One question in regards to such comments, is whether, as Newton here hints at, that Wilberforce was maybe not converted in the years he spent at Wimbledon with his Aunt and Uncle, but only merely religiously inclined? I do not follow Furneaux's conclusion on this, in his 1974 volume on Wilberforce, that Wilberforce actually experienced two conversions. His argument is that it was, 'eleven years later, in 1785' that Wilberforce 'experienced a second and permanent conversion.' Considering the various factors, the present writer is much more inclined to agree with John Pollock's assessment, that Wilberforce's

---

4. https://www.christianitytoday.com/ct/1978/april-21/little-abolitionist-william-wilberforce.html.

adult experience was 'perhaps a re-dedication to the Christ of his boyhood faith.' Even Furneaux himself feels obliged to say, for example, that as a preteen Wilberforce was 'already, a devout and surprisingly mature Methodist.' One also has the evidence of the letters which Wilberforce wrote whilst in exile in London as that preteen, and which he then continued to write for several years after his mother 'rescued' him from such 'poisonous evangelical influences'. Added to this, we also have his own grandfather's threat, evidencing even in the backwaters of Ferriby in Yorkshire, that he too was well aware of something similar 'untoward' happening to his grandson. Wilberforce himself later reflected, that 'the religious impressions which I had gained at Wimbledon continued for a considerable time after my return to Hull, but my friends spared no pains [under the direct orders of his own mother one suspects] to stifle them.' Surely it is worth noting that Wilberforce does not say, that they succeeded in killing or eradicating them entirely, simply that they merely stifled them. We also have his own recollection, that when 'rescued' at the age of twelve or thirteen, he wasn't sure of the age, he considers himself already by then to have been 'completely a Methodist.'

Whether converted evangelically as a young boy, or later as a young man, what is clear as evidenced throughout his Journals, is that his spirituality became something very rich, complex and winsome. If one tries to identify the main influences on his developing spirituality, the early ones must include his uncle William and aunt Hannah, John Newton and John Thornton, the latter being not simply Wilberforce's uncle, but regarded by some as the founder of the evangelical movement.[5] We then have the impact of those he met later, including both Isaac Milner and his ongoing friendship with him, together with the renewed influence and mentoring of Newton.

As the avid reader one discovers Wilberforce to be, one also encounters the authors and works he particularly came to love and appreciate. Philip Doddridge's work both on the spiritual life, and on the spiritual rules and regulations life should be lived by, became so embedded and influential in Wilberforce's thought and practice, that this writer would argue that it was Doddridge who was of central importance in the form Wilberforce's spirituality took. This was true even from his earliest days and practices, with the various spiritual disciplines he consistently employed. There were, of course, other influencers that his Journals reveal as having played a not insignificant role too. One such was the seventeenth-century German evangelical Anthony Horneck, again done through his particular emphasis on utilizing spiritual *Rules*. Isaac Watts, more usually known for his contribution to hymnody, should also be recognized as another influential figure in Wilberforce's spiritual development. Wilberforce discovered clear patterns to follow

---

5. See Ford K. Brown, *Fathers of the Victorians: The Age of Wilberforce* (Cambridge: Cambridge University Press, 1961).

and organize his spiritual life around in Watts' 1729 volume for example, *Discourses of the Love of God and The Use and Abuse of the Passions in Religion, with a Devout Meditation suited to each Discourse. To which is prefix'd, A plain and particular Account of the Natural Passions, with Rules for the Government of them.* Though again there is no copy of this in the current library collection of Wilberforce House, yet there is a copy of Watts' *Concise History of the Bible.*

In his 1957 work, 'Philip Doddridge: His Influence on Personal Religion,' James[6] argues correctly, I believe, that Doddridge's use and promotion of specific spiritual disciplines, came from his own studies of the Puritans. In other words, one could argue that Wilberforce's spirituality was heavily influenced by Doddridge's distillation of Puritan spiritual practice. That being the case, it is little wonder that Wilberforce himself had such a love of the Puritans, evidenced to some degree by the books still held in Wilberforce's library. In view of such an argument, maybe it is more than a little surprising then however, that there is no copy of Doddridge's *Rise and Progress* in his library today. One possible answer, however, is as the Museum itself acknowledges, that what was his and what then became his family's library, was broken up in the early twentieth century, with the result that they are unable to say with any certainty, how many volumes were actually in his original library. There is still an 1807 copy of Doddridge's *Life of James Gardiner*; a copy of Job Orton's *Memoirs of the Life, Character and Writings of Doddridge* (1804); as well as the five volumes of Doddridge's *Family Expositor*. As for Puritan influences, there is an 1823 edition of Richard Baxter's *A Call to the Unconverted*; another as yet unidentified 1671 volume by Richard Baxter; a 1721 edition of *Sermons by John Owen*; and an 1820 copy of William Orme's, *Memoirs of the Life, Writings, and Religious Connexions of John Owen D.D.* Some theological volumes Wilberforce records in his Journals as having read, especially a number written by those he counts as among his favorite authors, but for which we have no examples in his library as it is today, include surprisingly Horneck, Jonathan Edwards, John Newton, John Venn and Thomas A Kempis.

Wilberforce's spiritual development was surely significantly influenced too by the preachers he was regularly exposed to, including John Venn and Thomas Scott, together with those he loved to hear when he could, including men such as Rowland Hill. John Venn, for example, was not only the very active rector of Clapham, chaplain to the Clapham Circle itself, but he also helped found and finance several of the Societies Wilberforce was also involved with. This included Venn financially supporting several local schools, with the unusual result for the day that every child in his parish enjoyed free schooling. He once lamented that one drawback of being in Heaven would be the lost opportunities

---

6. A. T. S. James, 'Philip Doddridge: His Influence on Personal Religion,' in *Philip Doddridge 1702–1751; His Contribution to English Religion*, pp. 36-38.

to do good. The circle of men surrounding Wilberforce, the so-called Clapham Circle, together had an incredible impact on the moral and spiritual life of Britain,

> It was a remarkable fraternity – remarkable above all else, perhaps, in its closeness, its affinity, It not only lived for the most part in one little village; it had one character, one mind, one way of life. They were mostly rich, living in large roomy houses; but they were all generous givers to the poor. Thornton indeed gave away as much as six-sevenths of his income till he married, and after that at least a third of it. They could mostly have been gentlemen of leisure; but they all devoted their lives to public service. They were what Wilberforce meant by 'true Christians.'[7]

Their biographical details are given in the later endnotes and so will not be detailed here, except to agree with another biographer, that, 'William Wilberforce is proof that a man can change his times, though he cannot do it alone.'[8]

As for the Spiritual Disciplines Wilberforce exercised, they point consistently and certainly to his being of an evangelical spirituality, and a spirituality that he practiced until the end of his life, as opposed to what some commentators have recently tried to argue. In the early mornings his spirituality consisted of extended periods of prayer, personal and family devotions, together with Scripture reading and meditation. He also tried to set aside what he regarded as his increasingly precious Sundays, as well as certain other days when he could, for extended periods of prayer, Scripture and devotional reading, and Scripture Memorization. In 1798, for example, he notes down, 'I had bo't a testament which had not the common Dress of one, on purpose. Got 2 or 3 St. Paul's Epistles by Heart, when otherwise quite idle, & had rather resolv'd to get by Heart much of Scripture in this way, rememberg old Venn's Comfort from it.' A decade later he reflects, ' My Sundays are so precious to me in these weeks of bustle.'

As for the Scriptures, Wilberforce particularly loved the Psalms, and so not surprisingly we discover it to be not only the most quoted Bible book in his Journals, but he also records being drawn to memorize and pray them often. It is in this particular discipline, that he seems to have been quite unique amongst the other members of the Clapham Circle. 'I am reading the Psalms just now', he recorded in 1803, 'What wonderful compositions! What a decisive proof of the Divine origin of the religion to which they belong! There is in the world nothing else like them!' Almost twenty years later he records, 'Walked from Hyde Park Corner, repeating the 119th Psalm, in great comfort.' Dr. Henry Van Dyke, when describing how the Psalms have played a central role in the lives of the people of God throughout history, wrote,

---

7. Sir Reginald Coupland, *Wilberforce A Narrative* (Oxford: The Clarendon Press, 1923), p. 251.

8. John Pollock, *William Wilberforce: A Man Who Changed His Times* (London: The Trinity Forum, 2010), p. 86.

St. Chrysostom, fleeing into exile; Martin Luther, going to meet all possible devils at Worms; George Wishart, facing the plague at Dundee; Wycliff, on his sick bed, surrounded by his enemies; John Bunyan, in Bedford goal; William Wilberforce, in a crisis when all his most strenuous efforts seemed in vain, and his noble plans were threatened with ruin – all stayed their hearts, and renewed their courage, with verses from the Psalms.[9]

Fasting and solitude were also important to Wilberforce's spirituality, though due to his poor health, his fasting would be tailored as best he could to his digestive issues, caused probably by what would be diagnosed today as ulcerative colitis.

Wilberforce sought to commit each of his days to God and to living for Him, but constantly ends up berating himself for how badly he believes he has missed the mark in keeping his resolutions, both in thought and deed. 'With Grief & Shame I take up my pen to record my own Guilt & my Breaches of the most solemn & deliberate Resolutions. I desire now to renew them, & to turn to thee O God from lying Vanities.' He chastises himself for never regularly rising early enough, and for not being enough concerned for the spiritual good of his family, servants, friends, and colleagues. 'How little have I observed my peculiar Character. How vain glorious in truth. How little Solicitous for friends' Spirit[l.] Good. How secretly malicious, Oimoi.' [Sept 23, 1798] He even records how he sinfully rejoiced in the tragic experiences of others, even those of his own beloved wife Barbara, as he does on February 18, 1798, 'sometimes even secret unkindness to my dearest <u>B</u>. Alas, Alas! how deceitful & corrupt is my Heart!' In June of that same year, he was again most self-critical due to his response upon witnessing the pain from toothache she experienced, 'I fear I am secretly pleas'd that the Pain B. suffers is not mine. O the Uncleanness of this defil'd Heart. <u>Renew</u> it O God.'

From the very early days of Wilberforce's spiritual development, journaling as a spiritual discipline held a significant place in Wilberforce's life. As early as 1787, he resolved,

> To be in Bed always if possible & well by 11 & be up by 6 oClock, in general to reform according to my so often repeated Resolutions. These are now made in the presence of God, & will I would humbly hope be adhered to. I will every night note down whether have been so or not, & not being scrupulous in minute Points, I will at the end of every Week set down on this paper Whether in the Course of it I have in any Instance clearly transgressed.

This is very likely the reason, that the majority of his Spiritual Journal entries will be made on midweek and Sunday evenings, as he reflected on the week gone by. His Journals also reveal how Wilberforce made much use of Resolutions, it was a constant spiritual exercise for him,

---

9. Dr Henry Van Dyke (1852–1933), *The Story of the Psalms* (New York, 1887).

especially as he also writes that almost as soon as he made them, he broke them. He even had a favorite word he used when he sensed how spiritually negligent he had been, 'Oimoi, Oimoi', a term similar to 'Woe, Woe', echoing the cry of a woman's lament at funerals in classical Greece.

The manuscripts also reveal how much he utilizes the spiritual discipline of Journaling itself, as an aid to his self-reflection and self-examination. In August 1793 for example, he recorded, 'I propose to draw up some Hints & Observations for my Conduct &c. & a Statement of some of the most remarkable particulars of my Life &c. in order to help Self-examination, & enable me to avoid the Temptations & obtain the advantages of my peculiar Situation.' He then proceeds to detail how he intends to examine those events in his life that speak of how Providence has been active throughout his life. He is going to list the 'Chief Mercies of my Life', the 'Events & Turns' of his life, and the 'Chief Goods of my Condition'. He then turns his attention to the 'Evils & Sufferings' of his life, including his 'chief Defects', his 'general Duties', 'Temptations', and then the 'Chief Sins of my Life'. Having done this, he moves on to record what his response must now consist of,

> My Chief Proper Objects of Endeavor both in Spiritually & intellectually. Friends list &c. Hints for Conduct, throughout. Diff^t. Employments for diff^t States of Mind. Understanding Improvem^t. Hints & Plan forming. Observations, both Relig^s & Moral & Political. Examine yourself what Studies Books &c. &c. you have in fact found more useful, both in Religion & other Pursuits. O how my Time, & all my faculties & Powers have been wasted. Let me now begin in earnest to press towards the Mark of my High Calling, & to endeavor to improve my faculties to the Glory of my God & the advancement of his Cause in y^e World.

He then concludes the entry by stating that he needs to draw up, 'A List of Subjects of Meditation &c. as God, Xt. &c. Examine how I may glorify God more by my Talents, <u>Fortune</u>, Connections, &c. &c. Love of X^t how to improve in it. How to cultivate a Taste for Heaven & its enjoy$^{ts.}$.'

As common as his Resolutions, or possibly even more so, are the Spiritual Rules Wilberforce established and sought seriously to follow, the most regular being those for moderating his eating and drinking, believing he always overindulged. Such Rules did not exist for him simply for the sake of it, but so that he would have better use of his body, that he would be ready to talk to others and witness, and that he might experience more spiritual and physical strength in his various campaigns. Wilberforce's generosity, his charity to others in the giving of both time and treasure, were at the heart too of his spirituality. It is well documented that he gave away much of his personal wealth. Estimates are that he regularly gave away at least one quarter of his yearly income, some years giving away considerably more. As for his time, obviously his family and the cause of Abolition took much of that, but he was also very active pursuing the second of his Great Objects, impacting society with the Gospel, for example, 'It has been calculated that three-quarters of all voluntary charitable organizations in existence in England in 1850 were evangelical in character and control.'[10]

Wilberforce was an active creator, member, leader or supporter of at least sixty-nine very active societies, including being V.P. of twenty-nine, on the Committees of five, Governor of five, and Treasurer of one. He campaigned for the poor, for chimney sweeps, for prisoners, prison conditions and penal reform, the uneducated, and for children in mines and factories. He helped found the Church Missionary Society, the British and Foreign Bible Society, and the London Missionary Society (which would send Eric Liddle to China and Livingstone to Africa). He sacrificially supported dozens of evangelical and humanitarian institutions including fever hospitals, asylums, infirmaries, and prisons. He founded schools for the deaf and the blind, lending libraries and schools for the poor. He helped to found the School for the Blind in York, the National Gallery in London, the Royal Society for the Prevention of Cruelty to Animals, and the Royal National Lifeboat Institution, all four of which are still flourishing. He financially supported the artist William Blake; Patrick Bronte through school; Mrs. Charles Wesley in her widowhood; and many missionary and ministry candidates who were too poor to finance their own training.

One final aspect of his Wilberforce's life and spirituality was that of the importance he attached to sharing his evangelical faith, something he would do primarily through his 'Friends Papers' – his use of 'Launchers.' Wilberforce could easily spend an hour preparing these 'launchers', openers that he could use to move the conversation to more 'relevant' matters in his mind. We learn that among Wilberforce's manuscripts was discovered one such 'Friends' document that he had marked 'to be looked at each Sunday.' On the sheets he had listed thirty of his friends, and written aside each of the names he had attached thoughts of how he could personally help each of them toward Christ.[11]

Interestingly though, it appears to have been common knowledge amongst many of his friends and acquaintances, that this indeed was Wilberforce's plan, but so attractive as a potential guest was he viewed by them, that no one thought anything of it. Indeed so much so, that one contemporary recorded that, 'when the little man came in late to a dinner party, bristling, maybe, with "launchers", every face lighted up with pleasure at his entry.' Wilberforce's concern for evangelism was seen too in his active, wider support of both domestic and foreign missions, including the Baptist missions associated with Andrew Fuller and William Carey.

---

10. Ian Bradley, *The Call to Seriousness: The Evangelical Impact on the Victorians* (New York: Macmillan Publishing Co. Inc, 1976).

11. See Garth Lean, *God's Politician: William Wilberforce's Struggle* (London: Darton, Longman and Todd, 1980), p. 121.

Transcribing and Editing the
Spiritual Journals

The aim of this volume has been to make available in print for the first time, all the extant Spiritual Journals of William Wilberforce. Wilberforce has actually left us recorded entries in two forms: those he wrote in his general Diaries and those that form his 'Religious' Journals. The latter will usually be referred to in this volume, as his 'Spiritual' Journals, as the latter word seems to more closely align with his understanding of 'religious,' being somewhat differently used today. Sadly, we know from a list that his son Robert drew up in c.1835, that we are missing volumes from both forms. However we should note that to have any of his manuscripts at all is a great thing, with family members often acting on instructions to destroy such materials upon the death of the creator. The one particular Journal that appears to leave the greatest gap, is the one that covered the period he referred to as his 'Great Change,' 1785 to 1786. We can only hope that at some point, that one together with the others will be discovered.

All of Wilberforce's Journals are housed in the Bodleian Library in Oxford, together with the majority of his known Diaries, the only exception being the Diary volume kept at the Wilberforce Museum in Hull. While it is correct to refer to Wilberforce's Diaries and Journals as being quite distinct, there is great overlap between the two forms too. The Diaries are replete with spiritual reflection, demonstrative of Wilberforce's evangelical spirituality, and the Journals likewise are a treasure-trove of his general life too, including the events of the time, people he met, places he travelled to, and some of the many books he read. This is borne out by the inclusion of the thousands of annotated endnotes, provided to help the reader appreciate and understand something of an amazingly busy life Wilberforce lived, despite massive opposition and ongoing physical and medical challenges. Where it was not possible to identify someone or something, then again a note has been included to that effect. Wilberforce directly or indirectly referred to dozens of Scripture texts, and much effort has been used to identify as many of these as possible, so that it might easily be seen how much a part the Bible played in his mind and heart.

The extant Journals form a relatively small proportion of the overall word count of his entries, at c.65,000 words from a total of c.900,000. There are five sources of the extant Journals, all identified in the appropriate endnotes in this volume, as coming from 'MS Wilberforce' in the Bodleian system, followed by their particular volume identifiers, and then the folio markers. MS Wilberforce c. 4 and c. 42 are both composed of loose leaves that Wilberforce used, intending them to be inserted into the Journal volumes at a later date. Respectively they cover 1787 to 1790, and August to October, 1800; and then August to November 1806, and October 1826. C.40 consists of a 92 page journal, that is blank after page 82, and covers August 1791 to October 1793. C.41 is a larger journal consisting of 188 leaves, blank after p.140. It covers a longer period, that from November 1793 to April 1800. The last volume e. 24, has 136 pages, but sadly is blank after only page 16. It covers the period of December 1815 to 1818, and October 1826. In essence what is extant then in the Spiritual Journals are entries that mainly cover the period from 1787 to 1800, with some material covering parts of 1806, 1811, 1815–16, and 1826.

Just three years after Wilberforce's death, his sons Robert and Samuel, published a five-volume *Life* of their father, and it is that work which has usually formed the source for most later biographers of Wilberforce. For what the sons did was to draw from their father's manuscripts, and publish extracts from both the Diaries and Journals to illustrate their biography. What can be clearly seen now, is that they had access to volumes that are no longer extant. The decision was taken that where it appears they have reproduced extracts from those Journals now missing, those have also been included in this volume. There will also be some extracts included here from the *Life*, that the sons most likely though not certainly at this point, drew from the general Diaries; they appear here too if it was deemed that they shed some particular light on Wilberforce's spiritual life and development. The Journal entries in his manuscripts have been carefully compared with any extracts that his sons chose to publish, and where there are differences between the two versions, that has been noted to reveal what they decided to change from the actual manuscripts.

Apart from his Journals, two other documents are also published here for the first time. The first is Wilberforce's Autobiography, referred to as MS Wilberforce c. 43, which speaks of events from 1759 to 1792, thereby covering the period of the 'Great Change' that we lack in his Journals. We cannot say with certainty when this was composed, though we know from some internal evidence that it could not have been before 1807. The Autobiography covers 35 leaves and was dictated by Wilberforce and is in the hand of an amanuensis.

The last piece included here, again a previously unpublished piece, is MS Wilberforce c. 63, a relatively brief document written by

Wilberforce in 1828, consisting of his own 'Exposition of Psalm 40.' The Psalms were surely Wilberforce's favourite section of the Bible, he spoke of them often, memorized a number of them including the incredibly long Psalm 119, and were the most-often-quoted Bible texts in the Journals.

The aim in publishing Wilberforce's Spiritual Journals, is that we have even greater opportunity to hear from Wilberforce himself, especially in very personal words and thoughts, never foreseeing that they would ever appear publicly in print for everyone to read. As was said earlier, very few biographers have made any real attempt to get to grips with his manuscripts, and consequently we have been dependent to a large extent on the carefully chosen extracts the sons published. The one major exception has to be the incredible research undertaken by Anne Stott and published in her 2012 volume, *Wilberforce Family and Friends*. Stott has wrestled with many of Wilberforce's manuscripts, and produced a work that relies heavily on the detail unearthed in many of his unpublished writings. While her work has to be admired, one may well not agree entirely with her conclusions, especially those here which she described and then attempted to account for what she read, though with difficulty,

> His 'religious journal,' which ran parallel with the Diary, is easier to read and though less detailed, is even more revealing. Neither manuscript enhances Wilberforce's reputation, as they both show a man in his mid-thirties going through a personal crisis in which he demonstrates an extreme emotional immaturity. Yet his frequently bizarre and selfish behaviour can be explained as the consequence of the strains of his childhood and adolescence; the almost exclusively male environment in which he functioned; the ever-present tensions of his political life; the medication he was taking to counteract his ill-health; and above all his voracious need for love and affection.[1]

While it is true for example, that Wilberforce did experience several crises during his life, including the early death of his father; his evangelical conversion; sustained and serious opposition to many of his campaigns; serious and sometimes critical health episodes; and the premature deaths of some of his own children, it is not the opinion of this writer that any of them resulted in a life characterized either by extreme emotional immaturity, or by bizarre and selfish behaviour. It is hoped and believed that his Journals especially let the reader see a man in his relationship with his Savior, as he wrestles with a powerful sense of his own unworthiness and sinfulness, as he contemplates the greatness of the task he believes absolutely, that God has called him to. So there is much heart-searching, much self-examination and judgment, a great deal of wonder that God could use such a weak servant as he discovered himself to be – especially in light of the two great objects – but all the

---

1. Anne Stott, *Wilberforce Family and Friends* (New York: OUP, 2012), p. 66.

while he confirms that though he is never equal to the task, the One who called him is. These are obviously very different assessments to those made earlier, but surely those that come through the pages of his Journals presented here.

Wilberforce first recorded his intention to keep a spiritual journal in which he would reflect much on his inward life and outward behavior, on the evening of Sunday, January 19, 1794, while staying at Battersea Rise; the following entry is taken directly from his manuscript,

> I proceed to frame a kind of plan for a Journal of my interior & exterior conduct, in which I propose almost daily to examine myself, with a view to progress in Holiness, Tenderness of Conscience, & that watchfulness which my situation in life so abundant in snares, particularly requires. This scheme is to be drawn up with a view to my most besetting sins and temptations.

His sons also published that extract in their *Life* but added their own thoughts,

> these times of self-examination are regularly recorded in a plan which extends through this and five succeeding years; with such persevering diligence did he watch over his heart, and so strictly painstaking and practical was his personal religion.[2]

William Hague, himself an M.P. as he published his own biography of Wilberforce, rightly assesses that Wilberforce's inner life became one of agonizing struggle, filled with relentless self-criticism as he harshly judged his own spiritual life, his self-perceived bad use of time, his constant over-indulgence, consequent lack of control, as well as how he believed he related so badly to others.[3]

It is noteworthy that for a person of the stature of Wilberforce his Journals and Diaries have for the most part, remained unpublished for so long. There are many factors that have contributed to this: the relative inaccessibility of the manuscripts themselves, having been in various private hands until relatively recently; the incredible difficulty of actually deciphering much of what Wilberforce wrote, especially true with the Diaries; but there is also the factor that Wilberforce has been generally ignored by academia, mainly due to his having been an evangelical. Much of academic scholarship, uncomfortable with Wilberforce's pious evangelicalism, something oddly reminiscent of the views of many in his own day, has acknowledged Wilberforce's significance within the cause for Abolition, but has neglected to pursue him in anything like the depth many of his contemporaries have.

The Wilberforce Museum in Hull for example, when commenting on their particular portion of his Diary that they hold, covering the

---

2. R. I. and S. Wilberforce, *Life of William Wilberforce*, 5 vols. (London, 1838), Vol. ii, p. 48.
3. William Hague, *William Wilberforce: The Life of the Great Anti-Slave Trade Campaigner* (London: Harcourt, 2008), pp. 207-10.

ycars 1814 to 1823, states quite rightly that Wilberforce used it to record his thoughts and feelings on his personal and political life. The Museum then promotes a very personal and intimate extract from his thoughts recorded in March 1819, wherein he disapproves of his eldest son's friends, 'His soft nature makes him the sport of his companions, all the wicked and idle naturally attach themselves like dust.'[4]

The Museum's webpage then adds the following comment, suggesting what one might gain from reading Wilberforce's entries,

> … we understand William Wilberforce better on a personal level, as a loving husband and father. They also give a unique insight into his opinions in Parliament, and his constant battle with ill health.[5]

Interestingly absent from those comments is any real mention, at least at that point, of the absolute importance to Wilberforce of his evangelical faith, a fact revealed constantly by him in that very same Diary.

It has been a constant concern of this volume to confirm as many of the details of Wilberforce's life as possible, to fact-check as it were and whenever possible, the oft-repeated details given in the numerous biographies already available. The fact that some anecdotes appear quite often, obviously does not thereby mean that they have a solid basis in fact. One such anecdote emerges from Wilberforce's teenage years, how that at the age of fourteen of thereabouts, he penned a letter to the editor of the 'Yorkshire Gazette,' in which he clearly condemned the practice of slavery. Some biographers, when recounting this story, have even suggested that such a letter was good evidence of the early effect of Newton's sermons, initiating in the young Wilberforce this anti-slavery stance. However it is difficult to confirm the historicity of this account. The date always given places the incident in or about the year 1773, the problem here is that the 'Yorkshire Gazette' did not begin publication until 1819. The one other possible periodical, 'The York Gazetteer,' also could not be the one, as it was only published from 1740 to 1752. Stott too notes this story, adding it may well have originated with a contemporary pupil colleague of Wilberforce at Pocklington, who claimed he knew of the letter.[6] What may have happened subsequently is that further details were added, including the supposed newspaper's name, without actually verifying the story.

Just as the aim of publishing the Spiritual Journals has been to let Wilberforce speak for himself in a greater way than ever before – so too in the introductions provided there is a similar objective. They contain a number of quotes from primary sources including his manuscripts, that seek to allow Wilberforce, as it were, to reflect on many of the events that are being related, hopefully complementing the volume as a whole.

As one scholar stated earlier, the Spiritual Journals are on the whole easier to read than Wilberforce's general Diaries. What that does not

---

4. http://museumshull.blogspot.com/2016/03/the-wilberforce-library.html.
5. http://museumshull.blogspot.com/2016/03/the-wilberforce-library.html.
6. Stott, *Wilberforce*, p. 14.

mean, however, is that they presented no significant challenges in the work of transcribing. Wilberforce used abbreviations constantly, and he regularly differed in how he employed those abbreviations, especially as he got older. Thankfully he did not use a specific form of shorthand, as many other Diarists chose to do, but he did have his own method which was simply to shorten as many different words as possible, and in an interesting variety of ways. He would also use the older 'ye' in place of 'the' encouraging modern readers to continue to believe it should be pronounced, as is done incorrectly in some movies and other such contexts, as Ye Olde Tea Shoppe, etc. Whereas in actuality it is nothing more than an older form of 'the' in pronunciation. Where he did use 'ye' that has usually been retained, as have most of his abbreviations and contractions. The most common involved contracting words that ended with -ing, where he would often simply omit as many letters as he was able before the final 'g,' while still retaining some possibility of his recognizing the word at some later date. The following occur as the most common of his contractions: 'g' (in place of -ing); 'B.' (his wife Barbara's name); 'Xt.' and associated contractions ('Christ'); 'Ld.' and 'Ly.' (Lord and Lady); 'Sr.' (Sir); Bp. (Bishop); 'Evg.' (Evening); and 'Recd.' (Received).

Wilberforce was also never consistent with the style of his dates for his Journal entries. Sometimes he will give the full date, including day, month and time, together with the place at which he is residing as he records his entry. Other times he only records the date or day. Nothing has been changed in how he wrote the entry headings, except where he would sometimes and for no apparent reason, underline some of them, as was done too by a later hand. For those reasons, the underlining has not been reproduced. In a number of entries Wilberforce will transliterate English letters into Greek ones, in an attempt, one imagines, to at least keep some subject matter confidential. Where he has done that in the entries, it will be footnoted.

Throughout his Journal entries, Wilberforce makes copious use of dashes, especially it appears to indicate the start of a new paragraph, and these have usually been retained. He also seems to employ them in place of commas, colons or periods. Where this appears to have been clearly meant, some helpful punctuation has been added, including the use of a period at the conclusion of each diary entry. He also capitalized much more frequently than is current practice, and often in seemingly random places, with no intention to emphasize. Most of those have been retained too, so that there is not constant intervention in his style, and so that one gets as accurate portrayal of his writing as possible. Where Wilberforce has marked through a word or two, if it was felt important enough, a note to that effect has been given; generally however, no indication of words crossed out will appear. There were a number of instances where even with much time expended, it proved impossible to identify certain words with any degree of certainty. Where that occurred, a note has been made, sometimes indicating what it is believed that word might be.

The Spiritual Reflections
of
William Wilberforce

1759–1786

William Wilberforce 1759–1786

As was noted earlier in the introduction to transcribing, the Journal volume containing entries for the period November 1785 to October 1786 tragically is missing, especially so with its having been the volume that covered the events associated with Wilberforce's 'Great Change.'

One branch of Wilberforce's descendants still live at Markington Hall in Yorkshire, a house that had earlier belonged to William Wilberforce. On their website they have posted a detailed account of both the family's origins and of the Wilberforce name itself. The following is an extract,

> The Wilberforce family originally came from Wilberfoss near York, which was on the outskirts of the ancient forest of Galtres. The forest was occupied by herds of wild boar, from which the village got its name Wild Boar Foss, which later became Wilberfoss and the family name went from Wilberfoss to Wilberforce. The family tree dates back to Ilger, son of Osbert of Eggleston who at the Battle of Alnwick in 1174 fought under the banner of William de Kynme (Lord Wilberfoss). Ilger of Eggleston was of Saxon descent, and there is a family tradition that his great-grandfather was the man responsible for Harold Hardrada's overthrow at the Battle of Stamford Bridge in 1066. Eggleston launched a swill-tub and sailing beneath the bridge thrust his spear upwards to kill the giant Norseman. There are probably few people in modern times who realize that it was a Wilberforce antecedent who wielded the fatal spear![1]

This first period of Wilberforce's life as presented here, covers events from his birth in 1759 through to the year 1786. By friends and family young William was always addressed as Billy, and even as an adult he was never referred to as William, but always as Wilber. George III began his relatively long reign as British monarch a little over a year after Billy was born, reigning until 1820. William Wilberforce was

---

1. http://markingtonhall.co.uk/the-wilburforces.

born August 24, 1759, at 25 High Street, Hull. He was the third child and only son of Robert and Elizabeth (Bird), with only his sister Sarah (Sally) living to adulthood. Both his father and grandfather had become wealthy through trading in the Baltic, with his grandfather William, for whom he was named, having set an example in public office, by twice occupying the position of Mayor of Hull.

Wilberforce is enrolled at the nearby Hull Grammar School, with interesting details added by Wilberforce in his Autobiography included in its entirety later in this volume. He began at the school at a very providential time, for both Joseph and Isaac Milner had recently been appointed to work there, the former as Headmaster and his brother as a simple usher. It would be during this brief period, that Isaac Milner remembered Wilberforce being hoisted onto desktops in the school to read as an example to the other scholars. Isaac Milner, whose life story is almost as amazing as Wilberforce's, having recently been described as a man who though, 'not unknown to students of evangelical history ... his figure is a shadowy one.'[2]

While so much that is interesting about Isaac Milner cannot be related here, some detail will help as he will become significant in Wilberforce's life. Coming from a Yorkshire working-class background, Milner went from being a simple school usher to later hold the following positions: a Fellow of the Royal Society, the Jacksonian Professor of Natural Philosophy, the Lucasian Professor of Mathematics (a Chair previously held by Sir Isaac Newton and subsequently by Stephen Hawking), President of Queen's College and later Vice-Chancellor, each position being held at Cambridge University, and concluding with his appointment as Dean of Carlisle Cathedral. When one appreciates all of this, it appears all the more remarkable to learn that upon later reflection Wilberforce was certain he would have not chosen Milner as his travelling companion to Europe, had he known Milner's evangelical sentiments. This will be examined in greater detail later.

As a young child, Wilberforce not only had to cope with bodily frailty then, but his weak constitution will cause him to suffer throughout his life with various illnesses, some of which became severe. In 1768 his father Robert, aged only forty, passed away quite unexpectedly. His sister Elizabeth had died a little earlier, and then on top of everything, his mother who was expecting another child contracted a fever and became gravely ill. It was agreed that the young Wilberforce, possibly to protect him, would be sent away to stay with family members for an indefinite period. He went first to Nottingham and then to his uncle and aunt, William and Hannah Wilberforce in London. The couple were wealthy with an attractive townhouse in St. James' Place, London, as well as enjoying Lauriston House, a fine villa in nearby Wimbledon. Tragically, Wilberforce's sister Ann, born after the death of her father, would also pass away prematurely in August 1773.

---

2. Barbara J. Melaas-Swanson, 'The Life and Thought of the Very Reverend Dr Isaac Milner and his contribution to the Evangelical Revival in England,' Ph.D. Thesis, Durham University, 1993, Abstract.

It was during his stay with his evangelical aunt and uncle in London, that things began to develop quickly for Wilberforce. If not converted at the young age of ten or thereabouts, as this present writer believes him to have been, he was certainly and markedly exposed to and affected by evangelical sentiments. This happened especially through the influence of John Newton, who along with several other leading evangelicals, including George Whitefield, were close friends and regular visitors to the Wilberforce home in Wimbledon. John and Polly Newton lived and ministered in Olney, and the extended Wilberforce family from London would occasionally travel to Olney to visit their good friends and fellowship with them,

> I was much with them. My aunt was an admirer of Whitfield's preaching, and kept up a friendly connection with the early Methodists; and I often accompanied her and my uncle to church and to chapel. I was warmly attached to them both. They had no children, and I was to be their heir. Under these influences my mind was, even in these early days, much interested and impressed by the subject of religion. In what degree these impressions were genuine I can hardly determine, but at least I may venture to say that I was sincere.[3]

During his stay in London, Wilberforce attended Chalmer's School in nearby Putney, an experience he later reflected on quite humorously,

> I was sent to a school in Putney, near London, when I was about twelve years old. It was a very indifferent school, where there was a little of geography, a little of classics, a little of everything taught.[4]

He later also spoke of a Scottish usher employed at the school, 'a dirty disagreeable man,' and that 'the things which we had for breakfast which were so nasty that I could not swallow them without sickness.'[5] While still in London, William and Hannah arranged for their beloved eleven year old nephew, the child they had never had and who had very quickly become their heir, to have his portrait painted. John Russell, one of the eighteenth century's foremost pastel portraitists, was commissioned to undertake the work. He had already painted many of the day's leading evangelicals, including Whitefield and Rowland Hill. The things Russell and Wilberforce have that link them, apart from the portrait sitting, are quite remarkable. Russell has also left behind numerous Diaries that similarly recorded an ongoing concern for his own spiritual welfare. As the incredibly popular and respected painter that he was, he would also be invited to many social occasions, but frequently would either make an apology and not attend, or would leave early, always concerned that the behaviour at such gatherings would affect his spiritual walk. He too, like Wilberforce, especially treasured his Sundays, with Russell refusing

---

3. John S. Harford, *Recollections of William Wilberforce, Esq.* 2nd edition (London: Longman, Green, Longman, Roberts & Green, 1865), p. 197.

4. Ibid.

5. MS Wilberforce e. 11, fo. 122 and d. 56, fo. 4.

to paint at all on them. He also had a link with Hull though a sad one, suffering a fatal typhus attack there in 1806. His portrait of Wilberforce, without which we would have no real idea of what Wilberforce looked like as a child, is housed today in London's National Portrait Gallery. He was dressed in a fashionable blue Van Dyck costume with a lace collar and a crimson sash over his left shoulder. He appears as a slight, delicate-looking child with large dark eyes, a high forehead, and a serious face gazes out thoughtfully at the viewer; he seems preoccupied with his inner life and looks ill-suited to the rough and tumble of a boys' school and the vagaries of eccentric teachers.[6]

Wilberforce came not just to love William and Hannah as if they were his own parents, but he clearly imbibed their faith too. So much so that his letters and occasional visits home caused real alarm to the Yorkshire Wilberforces, confirming their worst fears that he had indeed been influenced by evangelicals, necessitating in their minds his 'rescue' and retrieval back to the relative safety of Hull, 'From the tenor of my letters, some of which are still in existence, my friends in Yorkshire became alarmed with the idea that I was in danger of becoming a Methodist ... The apprehensions I have mentioned brought her up to town to fetch me away.'[7] After consulting with her father-in-law Alderman Wilberforce, Billy's mother rushed to London, and retrieved her charge, 'Before I should imbibe what she considered was little less than poison, which indeed I at that time had done. Being removed from my uncle and aunt affected me most seriously. It almost broke my heart, I was so much attached to them.'[8]

One suspects with some justification, that his mother's actions were not done for entirely theological reasons, but also from a very real fear of the threat of Billy's grandfather. For he had made it clear that her son would be cut out of his substantial inheritance, if no intervention occurred to distract his grandson from what he viewed as such radical views and influences. Mother and son arrived back in Hull in October 1771, a few weeks after his twelfth birthday. Wilberforce often later reflects on the very real pain and sadness the sudden parting caused him, 'I very deeply felt the parting from my uncle and aunt, whom I loved as if they had been my parents; indeed, I have scarcely ever felt more pain of mind than from this separation.'[9] Just one month after his forced separation, Wilberforce pens two letters to his much-missed family members in London, even going so far as to sign them, 'Your Dearest Son.'[10] In the letter he addressed to his aunt Hannah he wrote, 'Oh how happy are those who can fly to Jesus in trouble who have got such a mighty Deliverer,' and to his uncle William,

---

6. Stott, *Wilberforce*, p. 11.
7. Harford, *Recollections*, pp. 197-8.
8. MS Wilberforce e. 11, fo. 123.
9. Harford, *Recollections*, p. 198.
10. MS Wilberforce c. 51, fo. 100.

> Oh my Dearest, sometimes I have sweet communion with the blessed Jesus: then I can truly say He is the Chief among ten thousand ... Comfort yourself you Dearest that they who are in Jesus must suffer Persecution & it is just as it should be; if we suffer with him we shall also reign with him.[11]

The pain and sadness were obviously real, but later when he was again reflecting on these days in his Journal, he seemed to weigh things a little differently,

> How eventful a life has mine been, & how visibly I can trace the Hand of God, guiding & leading me by ways which I knew not. I don't think I ever before remarked, that probably my Mother's taking me from my Uncle's when about 12 or 13, & then completely a Methodist, probably has been the means of my becoming useful in life, connected with political men &c. If I had staid with my Uncle, I should probably have been a bigotted, despised Methodist, yet to come to what I am, thro' so many years of vice & folly as those which elapsed between my last year at Pocklington, & 1785, 6 is wonderful. O the depth of the Counsels of God. What cause have I for Gratitude and Humiliation.[12]

Upon his return to the supposed safety of Yorkshire, nothing was spared in seeking to prepare the young Wilberforce for a life of respectable privilege, and he was constantly exposed to the rich and varied upper-class social life that Hull then amply provided, much of it clearly planned with ulterior motives,

> My religious impressions continued for some time after my return to Hull, but no pains were spared by my friends to stifle them, by taking me a great deal into company and to places of amusement. I might almost venture to say that no pious parent ever laboured more to impress a beloved child with sentiments of religion than my friends did to give me a taste for the world and its diversions ... Hull was then one of the gayest places out of London. The theatre, balls large suppers and card parties, were the delight of the principal merchants and their families.[13]

He was also not sent back to study at the Grammar School, for it was clear to everyone that Joseph Milner was also now identifying openly as an evangelical. So Billy was sent instead to the school in Pocklington, a village about eight miles from York, very close to where the original family name of Wilberfoss originated. It was also the School where his grandfather William had attended, and where one assumes, his close family believed he could best be secreted away from any further 'Methodist' influence. As had been the case at the school in Putney, William here too was afforded special privileges, 'The Master was a good sort of man and rather an elegant scholar but the boys were a sad lot ... I did nothing at all there.'[14] Pocklington School, still operating

---

11. MS Wilberforce c. 51, fos. 96-9.
12. MS Wilberforce c. 41, fos. 106-7, 'Good Friday, April 14th, Bath, 1797.'
13. Harford, *Recollections*, p. 198.
14. MS Wilberforce e. 11, fo. 124.

today, is rightly proud of their former pupil, 'Our former pupil William Wilberforce devoted his life to abolishing slavery. We must never be complacent.'[15]

He remained at Pocklington from 1771 to 1776, during which time his grandfather died setting the stage for young Wilberforce to soon inherit great wealth, while in the wider world the American War of Independence had begun. Wilberforce will later as an independent Member of Parliament not support the use of military force against the Americans in an effort to retain the Colony. The same year the Declaration of Independence was signed, William went up to Cambridge to begin his undergraduate studies at St. John's College. It was at Cambridge where he will have his initial encounter with the man who will later become his close friend, William Pitt the Younger. Wilberforce himself later regretted that he was not a serious student while there, but he was a popular one, always having 'a great Yorkshire pie' on hand, with lots of students always eager to share in his feasts. He later recorded,

> The first night I arrived at Cambridge I supped with my tutor and was introduced to two of the most gambling vicious characters perhaps in all England. There was also a set of Irishmen of this sort to whom I was introduced. There I used to play at cards a great deal and do nothing else and my tutor who ought to have repressed this disposition ... rather encouraged it: he never urged me to attend lectures and I never did.[16]

Wilberforce readily admitted that his successful graduation was really only accomplished because of his love of classical literature, enabling him to sit and successfully pass the University examinations. After just one year there, his Uncle William from Wimbledon passed away, making the young Wilberforce heir of his substantial fortune too.

In 1779 Wilberforce sets out from Cambridge to meet Thomas Cookson, William Wordsworth's uncle in the Lake District, an area of England that he would always especially love and which would become a place of solace and escape for him in the many visits he made to the area. Wilberforce kept a Diary during the tour, and it has become the only Diary volume that has been published. Interestingly it was edited for publication by Wilberforce's great-great-grandson, Cuthbert E. Wrangham, but due to his untimely death was completed by his widow Jean Wrangham and published as *Journey to the Lake District from Cambridge 1779: A diary written by William Wilberforce, Undergraduate of St. John's College, Cambridge.*

As a wealthy young man with no real responsibilities, Wilberforce decided to run for political office as the Parliamentary member for Hull. Many of Hull's electors were employed in London, and as it was expected that freemen would be financially courted for their votes, so

---

15. https://twitter.com/pockschool/status/1185140541937332224.
16. MS Wilberforce e. 11, fo. 126.

Wilberforce traveled to London to do exactly that. It was at this point that he would regularly meet Pitt in the public gallery of the House of Commons, and their friendship became lifelong and closer than ever. He won the Parliamentary election for Hull in September 1780, due in no small part to the more than £8,000 that he had spent for that very purpose. One imagines, however, that his campaign was helped too by his family name, his grandfather having blazed a political trail he built upon. He was seated in Parliament three months before Pitt, and only two weeks over the minimum age of twenty-one that was required for Parliament. He was also very honest in his later reflections concerning what he had achieved in his first term as an M.P., believing that he had done nothing to any purpose during his first years, except that which promoted his own distinction. He won the next election for Hull on March 31, 1784, but only a week later was chosen, against all the odds, as the representative for the highly coveted, and much more prestigious and powerful seat of Yorkshire.

In September 1783, and accompanied by Pitt and Edward Eliot, Wilberforce undertook a visit to France, where they not only met Benjamin Franklin and Lafayette, but were also presented to the French king and queen at Fontainebleau. By December of that same year, Pitt became the youngest Prime Minister of Britain. His Continental tour was followed by two further ones in 1784 and 1785, though he will make those journeys with family members and one traveling companion, his usher from school Isaac Milner. These European tours will also be different to the first, in that they will have inestimable consequences both for Wilberforce and for the world, especially when the newly converted M.P. became the champion for Abolition.

As will easily be recognized, Wilberforce often used his Journals to reflect on the goodness of God to him, especially as he looked back at past events, recognizing the providential hand of God at work. At one such time he reflected,

> Notables in my Life for which I sho'd return Thanks or be humbled or be suitably affected: The singular accident as it seemed to me of askg Milner to go abroad with me in 1784, havg first asked Burgh who refused, which first bro't me acquainted with the Truth as it is in Jesus. If M[nr.] had been as ill as afterw[ds.] if I had known his char[r.] probably certainly we should not have gone together.[17]

In a later reflection on the same events, Wilberforce's sentiments remained the same, especially those about Milner not being his first choice as a traveling companion, and also that had he been aware of Milner's evangelicalism, he would not have been asked him at all. But these reflections, with the additional detail that is given, give us an even greater insight into Wilberforce's view of how miraculous the course of events were, that led to Milner being asked,

---

17. MS Wilberforce c. 41, fo. 94 'Sunday September 4[th.] 1796.'

When I engaged him as a companion in my tour, I knew not that he had any deeper principles. The first time I discovered it, was at the public table at Scarborough. The conversation turned on a Mr. Stillingfleet and I spoke of him as a good man, but one who carried things too far. 'Not a bit too far,' said Milner; and to this opinion he adhered, when we renewed the conversation in the evening on the sands. This declaration greatly surprised me; and it was agreed that at some future time we would talk the matter over. Had I known at first what his opinions were, it would have decided me against making him the offer; so true is it that a gracious hand leads us in ways that we know not, and blesses us not only without, but even against, our plans and inclinations.[18]

Wilberforce's evangelical conversion would come none too soon, as it was probably by this point in his life that he had imbibed some at least, of the unorthodox Unitarianism of Theophilus Lindsey. Wilberforce would occasionally attend Lindsey's Essex Street Chapel when he was in London. Stillingfleet on the other hand was an active player in the evangelical wing of the Anglican church.

Wilberforce with his mother, sister Sally, two cousins, and Milner set off from Dover to Calais on 20 October 1784 for their grand tour of Europe. As they traveled through France to Lyons Wilberforce wrote about many of the beautiful scenes in nature he witnessed. The party then sailed the Rhone to Avignon, Marseilles and Toulon, reaching Nice – a favorite for British in the winter – by the end of November 1784. As they traveled, Wilberforce found himself arguing with Milner about Christianity, often ridiculing those he knew to have evangelical views, even including his beloved aunt Hannah and her half-brother John Thornton. Milner responded, 'Wilberforce, I don't pretend to be a match for you in this sort of running fire. But if you really wish to discuss these topics in a serious and argumentative manner I shall be most happy to enter on them with you.'[19]

Wilberforce there received a letter from Pitt, pleading with him to return to London for urgent Parliamentary business. It was agreed that the ladies would stay and enjoy themselves, with the men making the return journey alone. Wilberforce 'happened' to see a book which Bessy Smith had brought with her and he asked Milner's opinion on the little volume, Philip Doddridge's *Rise and Progress of Religion in the Soul*. Milner responded, 'It is one of the best books ever written. Let us take it with us and read it on our journey.' Wilberforce later recorded about that book and it, 'having so Providentially fallen in my way whilst abroad.'[20] Doddridge later became one of Wilberforce's favourite authors, with him making repeated entries in his Journals referring to several of his works.

Once they were able Wilberforce and Milner returned to the continent and rejoined the ladies in Genoa. From there they began the journey

18. *Life*, i. p. 75.
19. Harford, *Recollections*, p. 206.
20. MS Wilberforce c. 41, fo. 94 'Sunday, September 4th, 1796.'

home together, traveling through Switzerland to Spa, arriving back in London on 10 November, 1785. On this leg of the journey, Wilberforce and Milner studied the Greek New Testament together. This would be the start of his evangelical conversion or of a very real rededication of his life to Christ, the 'Great Change' as he would often refer to it. Even by October of that year, Wilberforce had already started to rise earlier each day, so that he might have time to pray and write in his Journals. He recorded sensing very real guilt and grief for the many years he had wasted, especially spiritually. He became deeply troubled at that time, and began recording very personal thoughts, especially about his spiritual life. The aim of this writing he stated, was to keep him 'humble and watchful.'

> Began three or four days ago to get up very early. In the solitude and self-conversation of the morning had thoughts, which I trust will come to something. As soon as I reflected seriously upon these subjects, the deep guilt and black ingratitude of my past life forced itself upon me in the strongest colors, and I condemned myself for having wasted my precious time, and opportunities, and talents.[21]

As was suggested earlier, Wilberforce really did approach Journaling in such a way, that the spiritual discipline of it was doing for him as an evangelical, what the Confessional had done for the Medieval Church. Even though his sons Robert and Samuel moved away in later life from many of their father's theological positions, they did state that their father's Journals and his constant self-examination became central to his spiritual life,

> It is well worth the enquiry by what system of self-treatment these happy fruits had been matured. They were not merely the results of a naturally cheerful temper leavened with religious feeling; they resulted from close and systematic discipline. He kept a most strict watch over his heart. He still recorded by a set of secret marks the results of frequent and close self-examination under a number of specific heads. He used every help he could devise for keeping always on his soul a sense of the nearness and of the goodness of God.[22]

One of the great turning points in Wilberforce's life happened once he started to seriously contemplate meeting his old friend and mentor, John Newton. As early as 30 November, 1785, Wilberforce recorded that he had been struggling with the thought of having such a meeting, 'I thought seriously this evening of going to converse with Mr. Newton.' Two days later he was still self-debating as he would so often do, 'Resolved again about Mr. Newton. It may do good; he will pray for me. Kept debating in that unsettled way.' Later that very same day, Wilberforce himself took the following private and very revealing note to Newton, seeking an imminent confidential meeting,

---

21. *Life*, i. p. 88.
22. *Life*, iv. p. 342.

Sir ... I wish to have some serious conversation with you, and will take
the liberty of calling on you for that purpose, in half an hour; when,
if you cannot receive me, you will have the goodness to let me have a
letter put into my hands at the door, naming a time and place for our
meeting, the earlier the more agreeable to me. I have had ten thousand
doubts within myself, whether or not I should discover myself to you;
but every argument against doing it has its foundation in pride. I am
sure you will hold yourself bound to let no one living know of this
application, or of my visit, till I release you for the obligation ... p.s.
Remember that I must be secret, and that the gallery of the House is
now so universally attended, that the face of a member of Parliament
is pretty well known.[23]

The meeting was agreed to in one week's time, but even up to the very
moment of rekindling their relationship in person, Wilberforce was
still struggling,

After walking about the Square once or twice before I could persuade
myself, I called upon old Newton – was much affected in conversing
with him – something very pleasing and unaffected in him. He told me
he always had hopes and confidence that God would sometime bring
me to Him ... When I came away I found my mind in a calm, tranquil
state more humbled and looking more devoutly up to God.[24]

But if Wilberforce was looking for confirmation from Newton that the
Christian ministry was now to be Wilberforce's calling, then Newton
thankfully did not give such. Instead Newton clearly told him that
he should remain in the place God had placed him, and later wrote
to Wilberforce, 'It is hoped and believed that the Lord has raised you
up for the good of his Church and the good of the nation.'[25] He also
began to have regular times with Wilberforce, times that he would use
to mentor Wilberforce in the Faith, 'Great subjects to discuss, great
plans to promote, great prospects to contemplate will always be at hand.
Thus employed, our hours when we meet, will pass away like minutes.'[26]
After much prayer, soul-searching and counselling, Wilberforce was
able to record the following, 'It is evident we are to consider our peculiar
situations, and in these to do all the good we can. Some men are thrown
into public, some have their lot in private life ... It would merit no
better name than desertion ... if I were thus to fly from the post where
Providence has placed me.'[27]

The above quote is often used and quite rightly, to illustrate something of the early struggles Wilberforce was having, as he wrestled
with his future course of life as a newly-converted, eighteenth century,
evangelical M.P. But it is the context from where that quote is taken

---

23. *Life*, (New edition, abridged, London, 1843), p. 47.
24. *Life*, i. p. 95.
25. Ibid., i. p. 48.
26. MS Wilberforce c. 49, fo. 4.
27. *Life*, i. pp. 105-6.

from that is usually left unaddressed, which for our purposes is of particular interest. For it is a brief extract from a lengthy letter that he wrote to his mother, quite soon after word of his evangelical conversion was becoming more widely known. He appears to be writing to allay any fears she might have that he has gone completely and fanatically mad,

> What I have said will, I hope, be sufficient to remove any apprehensions that I mean to shut myself up either in my closet in town, or in my hermitage in the country. No, my dear mother, in my circumstances this would merit no better name than desertion; and if I were thus to fly from the post where Providence has placed me, I know not how I could look for the blessing of God upon my retirement … What humbles me is, the sense that I forego so many opportunities of doing good; and it is my constant prayer, that God will enable me to serve him more steadily, and my fellow-creatures more assiduously.[28]

His friendship with Newton continued to grow all the deeper over the next twenty years, as Newton confirmed himself as Wilberforce's true friend, supporter, encourager, pastor and intercessor. As Wilberforce himself later reflected, 'Mr. Newton, whom, after reverencing him as a parent when I was a child, I valued and loved him for more than twenty years.'[29] It is little wonder therefore, that some biographers have seen their relationship as very similar to that Wilberforce had with his uncle William and aunt Hannah, that he became the beloved son none of them personally had. Once the Great Change had occurred, Wilberforce also wrote to Pitt, informing him of what had transpired, and though Pitt not a Christian himself, responded by encouraging Wilberforce not to turn his back on politics as a result, 'Surely the principles as well as the practice of Christianity are simple, and lead not to meditation only but to action.'[30]

As we do not possess any manuscript Journals for this period of Wilberforce's life, we are entirely dependent on the Journal and Diary entries that Wilberforce's sons extracted when they had access to the originals, and which they published in their *Life* of their father.

---

28. *Life*, i. pp. 105-7.
29. Harford, *Recollections* 1864, p. 218.
30. *The Private Papers of William Wilberforce*, collected and edited by Anna M. Wilberforce. (London: T. F. Unwin, 1897), p. 13.

Began three or four days ago to get up very early. In the solitude and self-conversation of the morning had thoughts, which I trust will come to something. As soon as I reflected seriously upon these subjects, the deep guilt and black ingratitude of my past life forced itself upon me in the strongest colors, and I condemned myself for having wasted my precious time, and opportunities, and talents.

William Wilberforce, 1785

1785

Tuesday, October 25th. 1785

Began three or four days ago to get up very early. In the solitude and self-conversation of the morning had thoughts, which I trust will come to something. As soon as I reflected seriously upon these subjects, the deep guilt and black ingratitude of my past life forced itself upon me in the strongest colors, and I condemned myself for having wasted my precious time, and opportunities, and talents.[1]

Thursday, November 10th. 1785

It was not so much the fear of punishment by which I was affected, as a sense of my great sinfulness in having so long neglected the unspeakable mercies of my God and Savior; and such was the effect which this thought produced, that for months I was in a state of the deepest depression, from strong convictions of my guilt. Indeed nothing which I have ever read in the accounts of others, exceeded what I then felt.[2]

Thursday, November 24th. 1785

Heard the Bible read two hours, Pascal[3] one hour and a quarter, meditation one hour and a quarter, business the same. If ever I take myself from the immediate consideration of serious things, I entirely lose sight of them, this must be a lesson to me to keep them constantly in view. Pitt[4] called, and commended Butler's Analogy.[5] Resolved to write to him, and discover to him what I am occupied about: this will save me much embarrassment, and I hope give me more command both of my time and conduct.[6]

Friday, November 25th. 1785

Up at six, private devotions half an hour, Pascal three quarters, to town on business. I feel quite giddy and distracted by the tumult, except when in situations of which I am rather ashamed, as in the stage coach: the

---

1. Wilberforce, Robert Isaac and Samuel, *The Life of William Wilberforce*, 5 vols. (London: John Murray, 1838). Hereafter, *Life*. As here, *Life*, i. p. 88.

2. *Life*, i. p. 89.

3. Blaise Pascal (1623–1662), a French mathematician, writer and Catholic philosopher, remembered especially for his unfinished *Pensées*.

4. William Pitt the Younger (1759–1806), son of William Pitt 'the Elder', the latter having been 1st Earl of Chatham, and who like his son, also served as British Prime Minister, though his son retains the distinction at twenty-four, as having been the youngest ever to hold the Office. A close friend of Wilberforce from their Cambridge days, Pitt was influential both in Wilberforce's remaining an M.P. after his conversion, and also in the cause for Abolition. As Prime Minister, Pitt's administration contended with several major events, including the Revolution in France and the subsequent Napoleonic Wars. He is buried close to Wilberforce in Westminster Abbey.

5. Joseph Butler (1692–1752), theologian, philosopher, Bishop of Bristol and then Durham. He is especially remembered for his *Analogy of Religion, Natural and Revealed* (1736), regarded as one of the ablest attacks on Deism and defenses of orthodox Christianity.

6. *Life*, i. p. 90.

shame, pride; but a useful lesson. St. Antholyn's.[7] Mr. Forster's.[8] Felt much devotion, and wondered at a man who fell asleep during the Psalms, during the sermon I fell asleep myself. Walked, and stage coach, to save the expense of a chaise.[9]

Sunday, November 27th. 1785

Up at six, devotions half an hour, Pascal three quarters, Butler three quarters. Church, read the Bible, too ramblingly, for an hour. Heard Butler, but not attentively, two hours. Meditated twenty minutes. Hope I was more attentive at church than usual, but serious thoughts vanished the moment I went out of it, and very insensible and cold in the evening service. Some very strong feelings when I went to bed. God turn them to account, and in any way bring me to himself. I have been thinking I have been doing well by living alone, and reading generally on religious subjects; I must awake to my dangerous state, and never be at rest till I have made my peace with God. My heart is so hard, my blindness so great, that I cannot get a due hatred of sin, though I see I am all corrupt, and blinded to the perception of spiritual things.[10]

Monday, November 28th. 1785

I hope as long as I live to be the better for the meditation of this evening; it was on the sinfulness of my own heart, and its blindness and weakness. True, Lord, I am wretched, and miserable, and blind, and naked. What infinite love, that Christ should die to save such a sinner, and how necessary is it he should save us altogether, that we may appear before God with nothing of our own! God grant I may not deceive myself, in thinking I feel the beginnings of gospel comfort. Began this night constant family prayer, and resolved to have it every morning and evening, and to read a chapter when time.[11]

Tuesday, November 29th. 1785

I bless God I enjoyed comfort in prayer this evening. I must keep my own unworthiness ever in view. Pride is my greatest stumbling-block; and there is danger in it in two ways, lest it should make me desist from a Christian life, through fear of the world, my friends, etc.; or if I persevere, lest it should make me vain of so doing. In all disputes on religion, I must be particularly on my guard to distinguish it from a zeal for God and his cause. I must consider and set down the marks whereby they may be

---

7. St Antholyn's or St. Antholin's in Budge Row, Watling Street, was a church destroyed in the Great Fire of London, 1666. Sir Christopher Wren designed the new church, which was itself demolished in 1874.

8. Wilberforce may be referring here to Henry Foster (1745–1814), a minister-friend of John Newton, one of the original four in Newton's 'Eclectic Society'. If that is indeed the case, as would fit the circumstances elsewhere that his sons record, it would mean that they here had his name recorded slightly wrong, being Foster and not Forster. This is borne out by Wilberforce's Diary entry on Tuesday 20 December 1785, recorded in MS Don e. 164, where two entries are clearly 'Foster' by Wilberforce himself.

9. *Life*, i. p. 90.

10. Ibid.

11. Ibid., p. 91.

known from each other. I will form a plan of my particular duty, praying God to enable me to do it properly, and set it before me as a chart of the country, and map of the road I must travel. Every morning some subject of thought for the hours of walking, lounging, etc. if alone.[12]

Wednesday, November 30th. 1785

Was very fervent in prayer this morning, and thought these warm impressions would never go off. Yet in vain endeavored in the evening to rouse myself. God grant it may not all prove vain; oh if it does, how will my punishment be deservedly increased! The only way I find of moving myself, is by thinking of my great transgressions, weakness, blindness, and of God's having promised to supply these defects. But though I firmly believe them, yet I read of future judgment, and think of God's wrath against sinners, with no great emotions. What can so strongly show the stony heart? O God, give me a heart of flesh![13] Nothing so convinces me of the dreadful state of my own mind, as the possibility, which, if I did not know it from experience, I should believe impossible, of my being ashamed of Christ. Ashamed of the Creator of all things! One who has received infinite pardon and mercy, ashamed of the Dispenser of it, and that in a country where his name is professed! Oh, what should I have done in persecuting times? (Forgot to set down that when my servants came in the first time to family prayer, I felt ashamed.) I thought seriously this evening of going to converse with Mr. Newton,[14] waked in the night, obliged to compel myself to think of God.[15]

Friday, December 2nd. 1785

Resolved again about Mr. Newton. It may do good, he will pray for me; his experience may enable him to direct me to new grounds of humiliation, and it is that only which I can perceive God's Spirit employ to any effect. It can do no harm, for that is a scandalous objection which keeps occurring to me, that if ever my sentiments change, I shall be ashamed of having done it: it can only humble me, and, whatever is the right way, if truth is right I ought to be humbled, but, sentiments change! Kept debating in that unsettled way to which I have used myself, whether to go to London

---

12. Ibid., pp. 91-92.

13. Ezekiel 36:26.

14. John Newton (1725–1807), minister at Olney and St. Mary Woolnoth, London. His mother died when he was no older than six and he was then brought up by his father, a merchant navy captain. At the age of eleven, John would go on the first of several voyages with his father. In 1744 Newton was press-ganged into service with the Royal Navy. After serving on the slave ship *Pegasus*, Newton ended up on the trader *Greyhound*, on which during a severe storm in March 1747 he was converted. After serving one voyage as First Mate on the *Brownlow*, and then three as Captain of the slave traders, including the *Duke of Argyle* and *The African*, he finally left the Sea in November 1754. The following year he bean working as Tide Surveyor in Liverpool, and began an informal home fellowship group on Sunday evenings, together with some occasional preaching. He had begun ministering at Olney even before he was ordained a deacon and then priest for Olney in 1764. His period of ministry at St. Mary Woolnoth in London began in 1779. Wilberforce would meet Newton as a child when Newton would visit Wilberforce's aunt and uncle's home, and later as here, Wilberforce would revisit Newton, to seek his advice as to his future course as a Christian.

15. *Life*, i. p. 92.

or not, and then how, wishing to save expense, I hope with a good motive, went at last in the stage to town. Inquired for old Newton, but found he lived too far off for me to see him. Lingered till time to go to Mr. Forster's. Much struck with the text, 2 Chron. xv. 2.[16] Afterwards walked home.[17]

I got Pitt's answer, much affected by it, to see him in the morning. It was full of kindness. Nothing I had told him, he said, could affect our friendship; that he wished me always to act as I thought right. I had said that I thought when we met we had better not discuss the topics of my letter. 'Why not discuss them?' was his answer; 'let me come to Wimbledon tomorrow, to talk them over with you.' He thought that I was out of spirits, and that company and conversation would be the best way of dissipating my impressions.[18]

Saturday, December 3rd. 1785

I had prayed to God, I hope with some sincerity, not to lead me into disputing for my own exaltation, but for his glory. Conversed with Pitt near two hours, and opened myself completely to him. I admitted that as far as I could conform to the world, with a perfect regard to my duty to God, myself, and my fellow-creatures, I was bound to do it; that no inward feelings ought to be taken as demonstrations of the Spirit being in any man, (was not this too general? 'witnesseth with one Spirit,' etc.) but only the change of disposition and conduct. He tried to reason me out of my convictions, but soon found himself unable to combat their correctness, if Christianity were true. The fact is, he was so absorbed in politics, that he had never given himself time for due reflection on religion. But amongst other things he declared to me, that Bishop Butler's work raised in his mind more doubts than it had answered. Had a good deal of debate with myself about seeing Newton, but the rather right if I talk upon the subject with those who differ from me, as I am so new to it myself.[19]

Sunday, December 4th. 1785[20]

To the Rev. John Newton.

December 2, 1785.

Sir,

There is no need of apology for intruding on you, when the errand is religion. I wish to have some serious conversation with you, and will take the liberty of calling on you for that purpose, in half an hour; when, if you cannot receive me, you will have the goodness to let me have a letter put into my hands at the door, naming a time and place for our meeting, the earlier the more agreeable to me. I have had ten thousand

---

16. 'And he went out to meet Asa, and said unto him, Hear ye me, Asa, and all Judah and Benjamin; The Lord is with you, while ye be with him; and if ye seek him, he will be found of you; but if ye forsake him, he will forsake you.'

17. *Life*, i. p. 93.

18. Ibid., p. 94.

19. Ibid., p. 95.

20. Wilberforce composed a letter to Newton, which he took with him on Sunday, December 4, 1785, and he records, 'Delivered it myself to old Newton at his church.' *Life* i. p. 95.

doubts within myself, whether or not I should discover myself to you; but every argument against doing it has its foundation in pride. I am sure you will hold yourself bound to let no one living know of this application, or of my visit, till I release you from the obligation.[21]

P.S. Remember that I must be secret, and that the gallery of the House is now so universally attended, that the face of a member of Parliament is pretty well known.[22]

Tuesday, December 6[th.] 1785

After walking about the Square once or twice before I could persuade myself, I called upon old Newton. Was much affected in conversing with him. Something very pleasing and unaffected in him. He told me he always had entertained hopes and confidence that God would some time bring me to Him. That he had heard from J. Thornton[23] we had declined Sunday visits abroad. On the whole he encouraged me, though got nothing new from him, as how could I, except a good hint, that he never found it answer to dispute, and that it was as well not to make visits that one disliked over agreeable. When I came away I found my mind in a calm, tranquil state, more humbled, and looking more devoutly up to God.[24] This very day, accordingly as I promised, I went to Pitt's. Sad work. I went there in fear, and for some time kept an awe on my mind. My feelings lessened in the evening, and I could scarce lift up myself in prayer to God at night.[25]

Wednesday, December 7[th.] 1785

At Holwood.[26] Up early and prayed, but not with much warmth. Then to the St. John's at Beckenham.[27] In chaise opened myself to _____[28] who had felt much four years ago when very ill. He says that H. took off his then religious feelings, but query, what did he give him in the room of them? Rather tried to show off at the St. John's, and completely forgot God. Came away in a sad state to town, and was reduced almost

---

21. The remainder of the letter up to the postscript, including the signature, has been torn off.

22. *Life*, i. p. 95.

23. John Thornton (1720–1790), active evangelical, wealthy merchant and a great philanthropist. Thornton was the son of Robert Thornton, a merchant who became a Director of the Bank of England. He financially supported many evangelical ministries, including that of John Newton at Olney, later offering him the living of St. Mary Woolnoth in London.

24. Wilberforce's sons say that it was part of Newton's counsel, that he should not hastily form new connections, nor widely separate from his former friends, *Life*, i. p. 95.

25. *Life*, i. p. 95.

26. Holwood House in Keston, Kent, which Pitt purchased in 1785 for £8,950, was subsequently demolished and rebuilt between 1823 and 1827. The present house, purchased in 2016 for £12 million by the Crabb and Puddephatt family, has in its grounds, a public footpath and stone seat bearing an inscription commemorating the 'Emancipation Oak' tree, where Wilberforce was urged by Pitt, to put forward a motion in the House of Commons for abolition. Wilberforce later recorded the following entry in his 1787 diary, 'I well remember after a conversation with Mr. Pitt in the open air at the root of an old tree at Holwood, I resolved to give notice in the House of Commons of my intention to bring forward the abolition of the slave trade.'

27. Beckenham was a small village near London, today it is a post town and district of London in the Borough of Bromley. Its rapid growth began in 1773, when John Cator built Beckenham Place and became Lord of the Manor, and much expansion began soon after.

28. Wilberforce does not identify this person.

to wish myself like others when I saw the carriages and people going to court, etc. With what different sensations of confidence and comfort did I come away from Newton and Beckenham! The one was confidence in myself, the other in God. Got out of town, but instead of mending when alone, as I dismissed all caution, I grew worse, and my mind in a sad state this evening. Could scarcely pray, but will hope and wait on God.[29]

Thursday, December 8th. 1785
Very cold all day, and dead to religious things, could not warm myself in prayer or meditation; even doubted if I was in the right way: and all generals: no particular objection. O God, deliver me from myself! When I trust to myself I am darkness and weakness.[30]

Friday, December 9th. 1785
God I hope has had mercy on me, and given me again some spark of grace. Dined at Mrs. Wilberforce's.[31] Mr. Thornton there. How unaffectedly happy he is, oh that I were like him. I grow hardened and more callous than ever. A little moved in prayer, but when I leave my study I cannot keep religious thoughts and impressions on my mind.[32]

Sunday, December 11th. 1785
Heard Newton on the 'addiction' of the soul to God. 'They that observe lying vanities shall forsake their own mercy.'[33] Excellent. He shows his whole heart is engaged. I felt sometimes moved at church, but am still callous.[34]

Monday, December 12th. 1785
More fervent, I hope, in prayer, resolved more in God's strength; therefore, I hope, likely to keep my resolutions. Rather shocked at Lady L's, these people have no thought of their souls.[35]

Tuesday, December 13th. 1785
I hope I feel more than I did of divine assistance. May I be enabled to submit to it in distrust of myself. I do not know what to make of myself; but I resolve, under God, to go on. Much struck in Mr. Newton's Narrative,[36] where he says he once persevered two years, and went back again. Oh may I be preserved from relapse! and yet if I cannot stand now, how shall I be able to do it when the struggle

---

29. *Life*, i. pp. 97-98.

30. Ibid., p. 98.

31. His aunt.

32. *Life*, i. pp. 98-99.

33. Jonah 2:8.

34. *Life*, i. p. 99.

35. Ibid.

36. John Newton (1725–1807) published his life story entitled *Authentic Narrative* in August 1764, *An Authentic Narrative of some Remarkable and Interesting Particulars in the Life of ******** Communicated in a Series of Letters, to the Reverend Mr. Haweis, Rector of Aldwinckle, Northamptonshire; and by him (at the Request of Friends) now made Public* (London, 1764).

comes on in earnest? I am too intent upon shining in company, and must curb myself here.[37]

Tuesday, December 20[th.] 1785
More enlarged and sincere in prayer. Went to hear Romaine.[38] Dined at the Adelphi:[39] both before and afterwards much affected by seriousness. Went to hear Forster, who very good, enabled to join in the prayers with my whole heart, and never so happy in my life, as this whole evening, enlarged in private prayer, and have a good hope towards God.[40]

Wednesday, December 21[st.] 1785
Got up Wednesday morning in the same frame of mind, and filled with peace, and hope, and humility; yet some doubts if all this real, or will be lasting. Newton's church, he has my leave to mention my case to my aunt[41] and Mr. Thornton. Not quite so warm, but still a good hope. I trust God is with me, but he must ever keep beside me for I fall the moment I am left to myself. I staid in town to attend the ordinances, and have been gloriously blest in them.[42]

Friday, December 23[rd.] 1785
I do not find the use of keeping a diary in this way, I will therefore try how I go on without it. I think it rather makes me satisfied with myself, by leading me to compare the number of hours I spend seriously with those others do, when all depends on doing it to good purpose. Was strengthened in prayer, and trust I shall be able to live more to God, which determined to do. Much affected by Doddridge's directions for spending time,[43] and

---

37. *Life*, i. p. 99.

38. William Romaine (1714–1795), a noted Hebrew Scholar, Professor of Astronomy, and popular evangelical Calvinistic Anglican preacher, a chaplain of the Countess of Huntingdon. Romaine, though friendly with both John and Charles Wesley, was criticized by John Newton for influencing many to become antinomians through his high Calvinistic theology. Remembered especially for his trilogy on Christian spirituality, *The Life of Faith* (1763), *The Walk of Faith* (1771), and *The Triumph of Faith* (1795).

39. Adelphi is a small area in Westminster, London, named after the Adelphi Buildings, 24 neoclassical terraced houses built between 1768–1774 by the Adam brothers. Dr Johnson, David Garrick and Lady Hamilton were amongst the fashionable residents of the Adelphi.

40. *Life*, i. p. 101.

41. Hannah Wilberforce, née Thornton (1724–1788), wife of William Wilberforce (1721–1777) of Wimbledon, and aunt of William Wilberforce (1759–1833). Hannah was the daughter of Robert Thornton (1692–1748), of the wealthy Thornton family. On the death of his father, William was sent to London to stay with his evangelical aunt and uncle, and a great bond was established, with William becoming their heir. Hannah especially would attempt to have him sit under the preaching of John Newton and George Whitefield at every opportunity.

42. *Life*, i. p. 101.

43. Philip Doddridge (1702–1751), a leading nonconformist minister, author, hymn writer, and Academy principal in Northamptonshire, one of William Wilberforce's favourite writers. Doddridge laid great emphasis on cultivating the spiritual life through following directions and rules for godly living. It would be these 'rules' that Wilberforce would refer to constantly in his Journal entries. See for example, Philip Doddridge *Some more particular Directions for maintaining continual Communion with God, or being in his Fear all the day long'*, Works vol. 1.See also volumes such as, *Important Directions How to Spend Every Day, and particularly the Lord's Day. Chiefly collected from the Rev. Mr. Baxter and Dr. Doddridge, with Prayers for the Morning and Evening in the Closet and in the Family* (London, 1748).

hope to conform to them in some degree: it must be by force at first, for I find I perpetually wander from serious thoughts when I am off my guard.[44]

Saturday, December 24th. 1785

Up very early, and passed some hours tolerably, according to my resolutions; but indolence comes upon me. Resolved to practice Doddridge's rules, and prayed to God to enable me. I wish to take the sacrament tomorrow, that it may fix this variable, and affect this senseless heart, which of itself is dead alike to all emotions of terror and gratitude in spiritual things.[45]

1786

Undated

I go off sadly. I am colder and more insensible than I was. I ramble. O God, protect me from myself. I never yet think of religion but by constraint. I am in a most doubtful state. To Newton's, but when he prayed I was cold and dead; and the moment we were out of his house, seriousness decayed. Very wretched, all sense gone. Colder than ever, very unhappy. Called at Newton's, and bitterly moved, he comforted me.[46]

Wednesday, January 11th. 1786

To town and Woolnoth,[47] after church, brought Mr. Newton down in chaise. Dined and slept at Wimbledon. Composure and happiness of a true Christian: he read the account of his poor niece's death, and shed tears of joy.[48]

Thursday, January 12th. 1786

Newton staid. Thornton Astell[49] surprised us together on the common in the evening. Expect to hear myself now universally given out to be a Methodist: May God grant it may be said with truth.[50]

Sunday, June 18th. 1786

In how sad a state is my soul today! Yesterday when I had company at Wimbledon, I gave the reins to myself, sometimes forgetting, at others

---

44. *Life*, i. 101.

45. Ibid., p. 102.

46. Ibid., pp. 100-101. The final two sentences here are from Wilberforce's manuscript entry for Monday 2 January 1786, recorded in MS. Don e. 164.

47. St. Mary Woolnoth in London has been a site of Christian worship for almost two millennia, with the present church at least the third on the site, dating from 1727. John Newton was incumbent there from 1780 to 1807.

48. *Life*, i. p. 104 . This 'account' was of Eliza Cuningham and may be read at www.johnnewton. org/eliza.

49. William Astell (formerly Thornton – 1774–1847), M.P., Director and Chairman of the East India Co., Director and Chairman of the Russia Co., and of the Great Northern Railway. Thornton changed his name to Astell in 1807 to inherit the estate of his maternal great-uncle, in compliance with the will of the latter's widow, Hannah Pownall, after his uncle, William Thornton Astell, had died without issue. His family were related to the Thorntons of Hull and Clapham, and William Wilberforce was an uncle by marriage. He was an ardent supporter of evangelical missions in India.

50. *Life*, i. p. 104.

acting in defiance of God. If Christ's promise, that he will hear those who call upon him, were less direct and general, I durst not plead for mercy, but should fall into despair; and from what I perceive of the actual workings of my soul, the next step would be an abandoning of myself to all impiety. But Christ has graciously promised that he will be made unto us not redemption only but sanctification.[51] O! give me a new heart, and put a right spirit within me, that I may keep thy statutes and do them.[52] This week has been sadly spent; I will keep a more strict watch over myself by God's grace.[53]

Wednesday, June 21st. 1786

To endeavor from this moment to amend my plan for time, and to take account of it, to begin tomorrow. I hope to live more than heretofore to God's glory and my fellow-creatures' good, and to keep my heart more diligently. Books to be read: Locke's Essay,[54] Marshall's Logic, Indian Reports. To keep a proposition book with an index; a friend's book; a commonplace book, serious and profane; a Christian-duty paper. To try this plan for a fortnight, and then make alterations in it as I shall see fit. To animate myself to a strict observance of my rules by thinking of what Christ did and suffered for us; and that this life will soon be over, when a Sabbath will remain for the people of God.[55]

Thursday, June 22nd. 1786

Near three hours going to and seeing Albion Mill.[56] Did not think enough of God. Did not actually waste much time, but too dissipated when I should have had my thoughts secretly bent on God. Meditation, 'What shall I do to be saved?'[57]

Friday, June 23rd. 1786

Thought too faintly. Meditation, 'Heart deceitful above all things.'[58]

Sunday, June 25th. 1786

I this day received the sacrament: I fear too hastily; though I thought it right not to suffer myself to be determined by my momentary feelings. I do not think I have a sufficiently strong conviction of sin; yet I see plainly that I am an ungrateful, stupid, guilty creature. I believe that Christ died that all such, who would throw themselves on him, renouncing every claim of their own and relying on his assurance of free pardon, might be reconciled to God, and receive the free gift of his Holy Spirit to renew

---

51. 1 Corinthians 1:30.

52. Psalm 51:10.

53. *Life*, i. pp. 115-116.

54. John Locke (1632–1704), *Essay Concerning Human Understanding* (1689).

55. *Life*, i. pp. 116-117.

56. Albion Mills was the first steam-powered commercial flour mill in Britain. It was built by Matthew Boulton and had just been completed in Southwark, London, when Wilberforce visited, but it would only last five years, being completely gutted by fire in just two hours in 1791.

57. Acts 16:30; *Life*, i. p. 117.

58. *Life*, i. p. 117.

them after the image of God in righteousness and true holiness; and I hope in time to find such a change wrought by degrees in myself, as may evidence to me that he has called me from darkness to light, and from the power of Satan unto God.[59] I wander dreadfully at church. [60]

Sunday, July 2nd. 1786

I take up my pen because it is my rule; but I have not been examining myself with that seriousness with which we ought to look into ourselves from time to time. That wandering spirit and indolent way of doing business are little if at all defeated, and my rules, resolved on with thought and prayer, are forgotten. O my God, grant that I may be watchful, and not mistake that disapprobation which cannot but arise in me when I look into myself and recollect all my advantages, and my first sensations and resolutions, and how little the event is answerable. Let me not mistake this for that contrition and repentance which operates upon the mind with a settled force, and keeps the whole man, if not always, yet for the most part, waiting and anxiously looking for God.[61]

Sunday, July 30th. 1786

At church, I wander more than ever and can scarce keep awake, my thoughts are always straying. Do Thou, O God, set my affections on purer pleasures. Christ should be a Christian's delight and glory. I will endeavor by God's help to excite in myself an anxiety and longing for the joys of heaven, and for deliverance from this scene of ingratitude and sin. Yet, mistake not impatience under the fatigues of the combat for a lawful and indeed an enjoined earnestness for, and anticipation of the crown of victory. I say solemnly in the presence of God this day, that were I to die, I know not what would be my eternal portion. If I live in some degree under the habitual impression of God's presence, yet I cannot, or rather I will not, keep true to him; and every night I have to look back on a day misemployed, or not improved with fervency and diligence. O God! do Thou enable me to live more to Thee, to look to Jesus[62] with a single eye,[63] and by degrees to have the renewed nature implanted in me, and the heart of stone removed.[64]

Friday, August 4th. 1786

My chief temptations against which to guard this week particularly, are, first, my thoughts wandering when reading or doing anything. Secondly, losing sight of God in company and at meals. This often begins by an affected vivacity. Thirdly, I am apt to favor my wandering temper by too

---

59. Acts 26:18.
60. *Life*, i. p. 117.
61. Ibid., pp. 117-118.
62. Hebrews 12:2.
63. Matthew 6:22.
64. Ezekiel 36:26; *Life*, i. pp. 119-120.

short and broken periods of study. To form my plan as carefully as I can to prevent these. Think how to serve these you are in the house with, in the village, your constituents. Look to God through Christ. How does my experience convince me that true religion is to maintain communion with God, and that it all goes together. Let this be a warning. Contempt of this world in itself, and views constantly set upon the next. Frequent aspirations. To call in at some houses in the village. To endeavor to keep my mind in a calm, humble frame, not too much vivacity. To put my prayers into words to prevent wandering. Consider always before you take up any book what is your peculiar object in reading it, and keep that in view. Recollect all you read is then only useful when applied to purify the heart and life, or to fit you for the better discharge of its duties. To recapitulate verbally, discutiendi causa.[65] Let me try by prayer and contemplation to excite strong desires for future heavenly joys, to trust less to my own resolutions and more to Christ.[66]

Sunday, August 13th. 1786

I see plainly the sad way in which I am going on. Of myself I have not power to change it. Do Thou, O Thou Saviour of sinners, have mercy on me, and let me not be an instance of one who having month after month despised Thy goodness and longsuffering, has treasured up to himself wrath against the day of wrath.[67] The sense of God's presence seldom stays on my mind when I am in company and at times I even have doubts and difficulties about the truth of the great doctrines of Christianity.

With God nothing is impossible.[68] Work out then thy own salvation.[69] Purify thy heart, thou double-minded,[70] labor to enter into that rest.[71] The way is narrow;[72] the enemies are many,[73] to thee particularly, rich, great, etc.;[74] but then we have God and Christ on our side: we have heavenly armor; the crown of everlasting life,[75] and the struggle how short, compared with the eternity which follows it! Yet a little while, and he that shall come will come, and will not tarry.[76]

Thursday, August 24th. 1786

On this day I complete my twenty-seventh year. What reason have I for humiliation and gratitude! May God, for Christ's sake, increase my

---

65. Latin: in order to investigate.
66. *Life*, i. pp. 122-123.
67. Romans 2:5.
68. Luke 1:37.
69. Philippians 2:12.
70. James 4:8.
71. Hebrews 4:11.
72. Matthew 7:14.
73. Psalm 3:1.
74. Revelation 3:17.
75. James 1:12.
76. Hebrews 10:37; *Life*, i. pp. 120-121.

desire to acquire the Christian temper and live the Christian life, and enable me to carry this desire into execution.[77]

Sunday, September 3rd. 1786

I am just returned from receiving the sacrament. I was enabled to be earnest in prayer, and to be contrite and humble under a sense of my unworthiness, and of the infinite mercy of God in Christ. I hope that I desire from my heart to lead henceforth a life more worthy of the Christian profession. May it be my meat and drink to do the will of God, my Father. May he daily renew me by his Holy Spirit, and may I walk before him in a frame made up of fear, and gratitude, and humble trust, and assurance of his fatherly kindness and constant concern for me.[78]

Sunday, October 8th. 1786

Remember to pray to God that I may be cheerful without being dissipated. Remember your peculiar duties arising out of your parliamentary situation, and wherever you are, be thinking how you may best answer the ends of your being, and use the opportunities then offered to you. Above all, let me watch and pray with unremitting fervency; when tempted, recollect that Christ, who was also tempted, sympathizes with thy weakness, and that he stands ready to support thee, if thou wilt sincerely call on him for help.[79]

Saturday, November 18th. 1786

I am too apt to be considering how far I may advance towards sin, in animal indulgences particularly; not remembering that a Christian's life is hid with Christ in God,[80] that he ought to have more satisfaction in offering the little sacrifices God requires, as the willing tribute of a grateful heart, than in gratifying fleshly appetites; and that he should look for his happiness in fellowship with God, and view with jealousy whatever tends to break in on this communion. I am apt to be thinking it enough to spend so many hours in reading, religious service, study, etc. What a sad sign is this!

How different from that delight in the law and service of God in the inner man, which St. Paul speaks of,[81] and which was so eminent in David! O my God, for the sake of Thy beloved Son, our propitiation, through whom we may have access to the throne of grace, give me a new heart, give me a real desire and earnest longing for one. I have got a trick of congratulating myself when I look at my watch, or the clock strikes, 'Well, one hour more of this day is gone.' What ingratitude is

---

77. *Life*, i. p. 121.
78. Ibid., pp. 121-122.
79. Hebrews 4:15; *Life*, i. p. 123.
80. Colossians 3:3.
81. Ephesians 3:16; 2 Corinthians 4:16.

this to God, who spares this cumberer of the ground from day to day, to give him time for repentance![82]

Undated, 1786

Walk charitably wherever you are be on your guard, remembering that your conduct and conversation may have some effect on the minds of those with whom you are, in rendering them more or less inclined to the reception of Christian principles, and the practice of a Christian life. Be ready with subjects for conversation, for private thought, as Watts[83] and Doddridge recommend. This week to find opportunities for opening to M. B. and to endeavor to impress her deeply with a sense of the importance of the one thing needful,[84] and to convince her that the loose religion and practice of common professors is not the religion and practice of the Bible.[85]

---

82. *Life*, i. pp. 127-128.

83. Isaac Watts (1674–1748), prolific and popular hymn-writer (credited with 750 hymns), and theologian, nicknamed 'The Father of English hymnody'. Having learned several languages by the age of thirteen, including Greek and Hebrew, Isaac followed his father into nonconformity, by studying at a nonconformist academy in London. He worked as a Pastor for several years, but resigned due to mental stress. Apart from his incredible output of hymns, he also wrote almost thirty theological volumes, pieces on psychology, astronomy philosophy; volumes of sermons; and the first hymnal for children. Though John Wesley referred to Watts as a genius, Watts believed that Charles Wesley's 'Wrestling Jacob', was equal in value to all of his hymns. In Wilberforce's personal library, now held at the Wilberforce House Museum in Hull, there is a copy of Isaac Watts's *A New and Concise History of the Bible* (1793).

84. Luke 10:42.

85. *Life*, i. p. 128.

The Spiritual Journals
of
William Wilberforce

1787–1792

William Wilberforce 1787–1792

> My walk I am sensible is a public one; my business is in the world, and
> I must mix in assemblies of men, or quit the post which Providence
> seems to have assigned me.[1]

In this second period of the Journals covering the relatively brief time
between the years 1787 to 1792, Wilberforce continues to wrestle with
the consequences of his Great Change. He has met with Newton and
also informed Pitt of what he has experienced, as well as what that might
mean for any future political career. On May 12, 1787 Wilberforce has
his famous Oak Tree rendezvous with Pitt. There is a path that leads
south from Keston Common, past Pitt's home at Holwood House
towards Downe. The path passes what is now a dead oak tree and a
seat, it is that tree now known as the 'Wilberforce Oak,' that the two
men met and discussed Wilberforce's possible future plans, and where
at Pitt's strong encouragement Wilberforce committed to pursue the
cause for Abolition.

> When I had acquired so much information I began to talk the matter
> over with Pitt and Grenville. Pitt recommended me to undertake its
> conduct, as a subject suited to my character and talents. At length, I
> well remember, after a conversation in the open air at the root of an old
> tree at Holwood just above the steep descent into the vale of Keston, I
> resolved to give notice on a fit occasion in the House of Commons of
> my intention to bring the subject forward.[2]

It was on Sunday, October 28 of that same year, that Wilberforce
recorded what became synonymous with his life, that God had laid
before him two great objects, the suppression of the Slave Trade and
the Reformation of Manners. Indeed his whole life will be spent in
pursuing those two incredible ends, that of ending the Slave Trade with
the accompanying aim of full emancipation, together with making

---

1. *Life,* i. p. 187, entry in 1788.
2. *Life* i. pp. 150-1.

an impact on Britain's culture for good. Wilberforce became involved in several evangelical networks, one of which met at the home of Sir Charles and Lady Middleton at Barham Court in Teston. It was Middleton who initially approached Wilberforce, as early as 1786, to encourage the young M.P. to take the lead in the Parliamentary campaign for Abolition. It was at a dinner a year later, with Thomas Clarkson and others, that Wilberforce first announced his plan to accept Middleton's proposal.

That same year Wilberforce also became active in two newly created societies, the first of which he himself conceived of. It was to work toward accomplishing the second of his great objects, namely that of positively impacting the moral behavior of Britain. Once the support of the Crown was obtained, the Society for the Suppression of Vice was created, with a Royal Proclamation describing the society's aims, 'the encouragement of piety and virtue; and for the preventing of vice, profaneness, and immorality.' The second organization, the Society for the Abolition of the Slave Trade, became the engine to achieve his first great object. Clarkson would be the driving force behind what became an incredibly effective campaign, that of influencing public opinion in regard to how slavery was then viewed. Local branches were also established across the country, and Josiah Wedgwood designed and created the very popular logo for the campaign.

On 12 May, 1789 Wilberforce stood up in the House of Commons and delivered his maiden speech, it had the horrors of slavery as well as his call for its abolition as its subject, and he spoke passionately for three and a half hours. He concluded with the words, 'Having heard all of this, you may choose to look the other way, but you can never again say that you did not know!' It was a very challenging address from a very gifted orator, and he did surprise the other members, but the prospects for real success could hardly have been worse. How could Parliament be persuaded to support a course of action that would seemingly have as its consequence, the undermining of what laid at the very foundation of the British economy. Wilberforce's chief opponent in the House was the member for Liverpool, Sir Banastre Tarleton, who fiercely attacked the cause for Abolition. Tarleton was none other than 'Bloody Tarleton' as many Americans referred to him, the man whose life became the basis for the evil Col. Tavington in Mel Gibson's movie of 2000, 'The Patriot.' Though Gibson has Tavington being skewered on an American flag at the conclusion of his movie, the real leader of 'Tarleton's Raiders,' lived to become the M.P. representing the very wealthy slave-trading port of Liverpool, who would obviously thereby be committed to opposing Wilberforce. Tarleton would not be alone in such work. It is interesting to note that Tarleton lived in St. James' Place, London, the self-same street in which Wilberforce had inherited the house from his Uncle William, and in which he often stayed while in London.

Wilberforce was physically assaulted by an irate sea captain, received numerous serious death threats, received a challenge to a duel, and survived at least two actual assassination attempts. As a direct consequence of how things were rapidly developing, he traveled with an armed bodyguard. He was also mercilessly attacked in the newspapers. It was even believed that the great national hero, Admiral Lord Nelson, had written that he would stand and fight as long as he had breath, against the position taken by Wilberforce and his hypocritical allies. Very recent research is arguing, however, that the said Letter containing that declaration is actually a forgery. But the real opposition became so fierce and focused, that a friend told Wilberforce that one day he fully expected to read that he had been broiled, barbecued and eaten.

The truth is that Wilberforce, convinced that he was pursuing those objects that God had set before him, was actually very naïve concerning what that pursuit would involve. From various sources one discovers that Wilberforce had little doubt Abolition would be achieved relatively quickly,

> As early as 1789, he and Clarkson managed to have 12 resolutions against the slave trade introduced – only to be outmaneuvered on fine legal points. The pathway to abolition was blocked by vested interests, parliamentary filibustering, entrenched bigotry, international politics, slave unrest, personal sickness, and political fear.[3]

As time passed and opposition to Abolition only seemed to grow, it became more obvious that victory would not be achieved as quickly as he had assumed. In the midst of such opposition, manifested in numerous attacks and defeats, Wilberforce was sent an incredible letter of encouragement by John Newton, in which his pastor attempted to bring real help and consolation,

> The situation of the slaves, and your exertions for their relief, are, if I may so say, palpable subjects—they are felt by all, where sordid interest has not benumbed—and therefore your name will be revered by many, who are little affected by the love of the Great Philanthropist. If therefore you meet with some unkind reflections and misrepresentations, from men of unfeeling and mercenary spirits, you will bear it patiently, when you think of Him, who endured the contradiction of sinners against Himself.[4]

In that same year 1789, Wilberforce also recorded the first of several entries in which he detailed accidents he had experienced, most of which occurred as he was traveling by coach. Wilberforce was always very careful as a result, to thank God for preserving him from them being more serious than they were. 'Had two or three narrow escapes, drunken postilion nearly driving into Ashborne Water, carriage spring broken, etc. Through God's mercy, got safe to Buxton.' The following year he records another narrow escape from what could have been a really

---

3. www.christianitytoday.com/history/people/activists/William-wilberforce.html
4. MS Wilberforce c. 49, fos. 43-4, Letter from Newton dated 4 August 1792.

serious accident, when his carriage actually overturned in the village of Bessingby, near Bridlington, 'How little have I thought of my deliverance the other day, when the carriage was dashed to pieces! How many have been killed by such accidents, and I unhurt! Oh let me endeavor to run to Thee.' The third such accident that he recorded took place on Tuesday, October 25, 1803. This time he was not traveling, but instead was enjoying what he termed 'a charming day' as he walked 'with pencil and book' on the banks of the River Avon. He writes how he sat in a portable chair,

> ... when suddenly,' with his back to the River, 'it struck me that it was not quite safe. Writing, I might be absent, and suddenly slip off, etc. I moved therefore a few yards, and placed my stool on the grass, when in four or five minutes it suddenly broke, and I fell flat on my back, as if shot. Had it happened five minutes sooner, as I cannot swim, I must, a thousand to one, have been drowned, for I sat so that I must have fallen backwards into the river. I had not the smallest fear or idea of the seat's breaking with me, and it is very remarkable, that I had rather moved about while by the river, which would have been more likely to break it, whereas I sat quite still when on the grass. A most providential escape. Let me praise God for it.'

The final accident he wrote of happened on October 29, 1806, 'I have also been preserved from all accidents. One narrow escape, night before last, from a wagon heavy loaded & going opposite way to my Chaise L & in the dark, & grazed very hard.'

It was in April 1791, that Wilberforce's parliamentary crusade to have an Abolition Bill passed took concrete shape with the introduction of his first Bill. Though it was defeated, the vote tally of 163 to 88 gave him real hope that it would indeed be achieved in the not too distant future. As he said in his speech to the House at the time, 'Never, never will we desist until we extinguish every trace of this bloody traffic.'

As one considers the Journals he composed during this limited period of time, Wilberforce certainly reflected on a number of interesting and varied topics. He began by reflecting over his recent conversion but then he quickly became highly self-critical at his own perceived lack of progress since the great change occurred,

> It is now a year and three quarters since I began to have a serious concern about my soul; and little did I then think that this time would have passed to no better purpose, or that I should now be no further advanced in the Christian walk. Two sessions of Parliament gone over, yet nothing done for the interests of religion. My intellectual stores not much increased, and I am less able in debate than formerly, which is highly criminal, considering the weight to be derived from credit for eloquence in this country.[5]

He recorded many entries that described how he planned to live and order his life, the organization of his times and days that he might benefit the most from the limited time as well as the vast responsibilities he appreciated he now had. He constantly sought to live by various rules

---

5. Undated entry by Wilberforce in 1787.

and regulations that he found in different authors, including Doddridge and Horneck, but almost without exception he later recorded how he believed he failed in keeping them. In July of 1788 for example he wrote,

> I will now form and note in my pocket-book such resolutions for this week's regulation, as are best adapted to my present circumstances and do Thou, O God, enable me to keep them. My general object, during my stay at this place, should be to guard against habits of idleness, luxury, selfishness, and forgetfulness of God, by interlacing as much as I can of reading, and meditation, and religious retirement, and self-examination. Let me constantly view myself in all my various relations as one who professes to be a Christian, as a member of Parliament, as gifted by nature and fortune, as a son, brother, paterfamilias, friend, with influence and powerful connexions.[6]

His desire to be serious in keeping the rules and regulations he set for himself (regls. he usually abbreviated the word to in the Journals), is seen not just in the content of his entries, but at one point in 1789 where he entered into a financial penalty agreement with Isaac Milner,

> M. and I made an agreement to pay a guinea forfeit when we broke our rules, and not to tell particulars to each other. I hope this will be an instrument under divine grace to keep me from excess. When once a settled habit is formed less rigid rules will be necessary. Exceeded, and determined to pay forfeit. Went on rather better, yet by no means up to the strictness of my plan.[7]

In February of that same year, he recorded visiting John Wesley at his house, very possibly at City Road in London, affectionately referring to him as 'a fine old , fellow.'[8] In July Wilberforce visited Bath in order to partake of the waters there, something the family will do quite often. Bath became a favorite destination for both William and Barbara, especially with her local family connections there. But the Bath Waters too, with their hoped-for healing properties were for many a very popular draw. While in the area, Wilberforce also took the opportunity to visit the Cheddar area,

> After breakfast to see Cheddar. Intended to read, dine, etc. amongst the rocks, but could not get rid of the people; so determined to go back again. The rocks very fine. Had some talk with the people, and gave them something, grateful beyond measure, wretchedly poor and deficient in spiritual help. I hope to amend their state.[9]

This desire to do a work amongst the poor and needy of the Cheddar area was later accomplished through the activities of Hannah More and her sisters, through their establishing schools and providing practical help to the local families, with Wilberforce himself financially supporting them. The fruit of such work is seen in one example entry he recorded three years later,

---

6. Entry dated July 1788.
7. Undated entry in 1789.
8. Journal entry, Tuesday, 24 February, 1789.
9. Journal entry, Friday, 21 August, 1789.

Accompanied the Miss Mores to Shipham, Hounswick, Axbridge, and Cheddar. God seems indeed to prosper their work, both amongst young and old are those who are turning to him. Near a thousand children in all. One mere child had Brought all his father's household to family prayers.[10]

Wilberforce also detailed a number of the books he was reading during this period, the list is quite amazing especially for one as busy as Wilberforce. In December 1789 he has 'Lear, Othello, Hamlet, Macbeth, Twelfth Night, Ferguson, Bible, Johnson's Lives, and Doddridge's Sermons.' A little while later, he's now engrossed in Reading, Bible, English History, Fenelon's Characters, Horace, by heart, Cicero de Oratore, Addison's Cato, Hume, Hudibras, Pilgrim's Progress, Doddridge's Sermons, Jonathan Edwards, Owen, Letters.[11]

At the dawn of 1790 he again uses the opportunity as he does often, of the arrival of the new year to reflect on the course of his life to that point, and it's not good. Newton is coming to eat with his family on New Year's Day and he knows that to be a real blessing. Wilberforce's health is not good either, and with all that lies ahead of him, one can sense something of the stress and pressure he is experiencing,

> How should I be humbled by seeing the little progress I have made since 1786! Poor Newton dines with me today, on whom I then called. He has not dined from home on new-year's day for thirty years. I shall now form a set of rules, and by God's help adhere to them. My health is very bad, a little thing disorders me, at thirty and a half I am in constitution sixty. 'The night cometh when no man can work.' Oh may divine grace protect and support me throughout the ensuing campaign, preserve me from the world's mistaken estimate of things, and enable me to be a Christian indeed, and to glorify God by my life and conduct.[12]

As one reads through his Journals, one quickly becomes aware of several recurrent issues or themes, this period is no different. He recorded for example, his sincere thankfulness for Sundays, where he had the opportunity to take time to rest a little, to attend church, to meet with family and friends for fellowship and relaxation, 'Blessed be God for the Sunday.' He spoke too of his ongoing pain and the bodily struggles he continually faced through all his various illnesses. Very often he noted the great difficulty he had in seeing properly, a symptom of his inherited eye disease. While his eyes will progressively deteriorate as time passed, even at this relatively early point in his life his eyesight was becoming a real issue, especially for one so dependent on the ability to read and write to accomplish his aims. In a series of entries Wilberforce gives us a glimpse of his struggle,

---

10. Journal entry, Sunday, 26 August, 1792.
11. Journal entry, Sunday, February 13, 1781.
12. Journal entry, Friday, 1 January, 1790.

'My eyes bad & therefore I cannot write,' 'My eyes being bad, I cannot write by Candlelight yet let me take up a pen for one moment to record my own sad failures,' 'My eyes indifferent & therefore cannot write,' 'Eyes too weak to allow of night writing therefore but one word,' 'It is too late & my eyes are too indifferent to allow me to write at large,' and 'My eyes are bad, I can't write, but I humbly resolve to amend my ways & turn to the Lord with my whole heart.'[13]

One also sees the way Wilberforce lived, in that he clearly loved to travel to the homes of his family and friends, and stay with them, sometimes for extended periods. Thankfully he often recorded the name of the actual place where he stayed when he dated the entries, something sadly that the sons did not do in their published extracts. In just the few years this period of his Journal covered, he stayed at Cowslip Green (Hannah More's), Bath, Stevenage near London, London itself, Temple Rothley, Bristol, Hamels, Forncett, Yoxall Lodge, Clapham, Keston, Battersea Rise and Walmer Castle, as well as a number of other locations.

Wilberforce will utilize not just the dawn of a new year for serious reflection, he did that too with a number of his birthdays, as he reflects over the course of his life including any progress or lack of it. He does just that here on his thirty-third birthday, not being introspective just for the sake of it though, but always as a means to challenge and remind himself that though he does fail and often, God is faithful,

I am now entering my 34th year, about the Half of my Life is spent & I have not yet begun to live. I should despair of doing better & sink into utter languor or sensuality but that God holds forth in X\. to all on this side the Grave Assurances of Grace & Strength if they are applied for heartily & perseveringly, & this Sincerity & Perseverance He will also grant to our petitions. Relying then on his Help & using all the means which my own Reflection & Experience of others suggest, I will press forward, first to secure my Eternal Salvation, & next to qualify myself for the Discharge of the Duties of Life with ability, 'Give an account of thy Stewardship, for thou mayest be &c.' O may I never forget this aweful address which will one Day be made to me. How thankful ought I to be that notwithstanding the past shameful misapplication both of my Intellectual & Bodily Powers, they are still left me.[14]

---

13. Journal entries, 1792.
14. Journal entry, Friday, 24 August 1792, Bath.

So enormous, so dreadful, so irremediable did the trade's wickedness appear that my own mind was completely made up for abolition. Let the consequences be what they would; I from this time determined that I would never rest until I had effected its abolition.

William Wilberforce, 1789

1787

Undated, 1787

God has set before me as my object the reformation of (my country's) manners.[1] By God's help I will set vigorously about reform. I believe one cause of my having so fallen short is my having aimed no higher. Lord Bacon[2] says, great changes are easier than small ones. Remember, thy situation abounding in comforts requires thee to be peculiarly on thy guard, lest when thou hast eaten and art full thou forget God.[3]

It is now a year and three quarters since I began to have a serious concern about my soul; and little did I then think that this time would have passed to no better purpose, or that I should now be no further advanced in the Christian walk. Two sessions of Parliament gone over, yet nothing done for the interests of religion. My intellectual stores not much increased, and I am less able in debate than formerly, which is highly criminal, considering the weight to be derived from credit for eloquence in this country. But the heart is the worst of all. Oh let not, Lord, my compunction be so transitory as it has been before, when Thou hast impressed me with a conviction of my danger, but may it be deeply worked into my heart, producing a settled humility, and an unremitting watchfulness against temptation, grounded on a consciousness of my own impotence and proneness to offend.[4]

Sunday, October 28th. 1787

God, God Almighty has set before me two great objects, the suppression of the slave trade and the reformation of manners.[5]

Novr. 30th. 1787

After dining with Pitt, tete-a-tete - Time after time I have been giving Way to the temptations of the table, against the sharpest Convictions of the Criminality of the Compliances, for little as they might seem, what Sins are they seeing they disqualify me for every useful purpose in Life, waste my time, impair my Health, fill my mind with Tho't's of Resistance before & Self-Condemnation afterwards, & so by both, take one off from being absorbed with the love of those objects which alone are worthy of my Regard - Sometimes tis an excess in Wine &c. sometimes in eating, or in dessert as today.

May God almighty forgive me - I see Bob Smith[6] who is influenced by inferior considerations, I see Pitt too, & others of my friends practicing

---

1. *Life*, i. p. 130.

2. Sir Francis Bacon (1561–1626), Viscount Saint Alban, philosopher, politician and Lord Chancellor of England (1618–1621).

3. *Life*, i. p. 139.

4. Ibid., pp. 139-140.

5. Ibid., p. 149.

6. Robert Smith (1752–1838), 1st Baron Carrington, M.P., banker, Captain of Deal Castle, and the third son of Abel Smith a member of the wealthy Smith banking family. His family home, Hamels, was in Hampstead, London. As a slave owner of several hundred slaves, he received a substantial payment from the British Government after 1833.

Self-denial & Restraint in these respects, & if they exceed tis at Seasons of Jollity, whereas I do it merely from the Brutal Sensuality of animal gratification. I trust I shall better keep than I have done my Resolutions of Temperance that I make at this moment. No Dessert - No Tastings - One thing in fruit, one in second Course – Simplicity - In quantity moderate - As little Thought about my Eating & drinking as possible either before or after - Never more than 6 glasses of wine, my Common allowance 2 or 3 - to resolve the number & the sort of dinner beforehand & keep to determination -

To be[7] in Bed always if possible & well by 11 & be up by 6 oClock - in general to reform according to my so often repeated Resolutions. These are now made in the presence of God, & will I would humbly hope be adhered to. I will every night note down whether have been so or not, & not being scrupulous in minute Points, I will at the end of every Week set down on this paper Whether in the Course of it I have in any Instance clearly transgressed. The Effect on my Health sho'd be attended to, a full diet good for me, but that a simple one, no meat, no rich things, no mixtures.[8]

Dec[r.] 9[th.] Sunday 1787

I thank God I have been enabled to keep my Resolutions rather better than I have sometimes done, tho' not well - I have however enjoyed today a degree of Happiness that this World cannot afford, & I trust the Resolution of it will stimulate me to that more active & vigorous discharge of my duty towards God & man. O may the Spirit of Xt. fill me with all Joy & Peace in believing,[9] & whilst that Temper & Frame of Soul are gradually forming within me which may fit me for that better world which is reserv'd for them who by <u>patient continuance</u> in well doing &c. May I so comport myself as to bring Religion into Credit & promote throughout Mankind the Glory of God & the Cause of the Gospel. Duty tow[ds]. _____[10] Pitt &c. &c - Apportionment of time Subjects of conversat[n]. tho't[s] &c. &c.[11]

1788

July, 1788

The life I am now leading is unfavorable in all respects, both to mind and body, as little suitable to me considered as an invalid, under all the peculiar circumstances of my situation, as it is becoming my character and profession as a Christian. Indolence and intemperance are its capital features. It is true, the incessant intrusion of fresh visitors, and

---

7. One or two words crossed out before 'be'.
8. MS Wilberforce c. 4, fos. 1-3.
9. Romans 15:13.
10. Word illegible.
11. MS Wilberforce c. 4, fo. 4.

the constant temptations to which I am liable, from being always in company, render it extremely difficult to adhere to any plan of study, or any resolutions of abstemiousness, which last too it is the harder for me to observe, because my health requires throughout an indulgent regimen. Nothing however can excuse or palliate such conduct, and with the sincerest conviction of its guilt, I pray to that gracious God whose ways are not as our ways, to have mercy upon me, to turn the current of my affections, to impress my mind with an awful and abiding sense of that eternity which awaits me, and finally to guide my feet into the way of peace. And though I have so often resolved and broken my resolutions, that I am almost ready to acquiesce in the headlong course which I am following; yet as thus to acquiesce would be to consign myself to irreversible misery, I must still strive to loose myself from this bondage of sin and Satan, calling on the name of the Lord, who alone can make my endeavors effectual.

I am this week entering on a scene of great temptation, a perpetual round of dissipation and my house overflowing with guests; it is the more necessary for me to live by the faith of the Son of God. Do Thou then, Thou blessed Saviour and Friend of sinners, hear and have mercy on me. Let Thy strength be magnified in my weakness. But whatever be the issue of this residence at Rayrigg,[12] may it be a useful lesson to teach me to form my plans hereafter with greater caution and circumspection, and not to run myself into temptations, from the evil of which he who voluntarily exposes himself to them cannot reasonably expect to be delivered.

I will now form and note in my pocket-book such resolutions for this week's regulation, as are best adapted to my present circumstances and do Thou, O God, enable me to keep them. My general object, during my stay at this place, should be to guard against habits of idleness, luxury, selfishness, and forgetfulness of God, by interlacing as much as I can of reading, and meditation, and religious retirement, and self-examination. Let me constantly view myself in all my various relations as one who professes to be a Christian, as a member of Parliament, as gifted by nature and fortune, as a son, brother, paterfamilias, friend, with influence and powerful connexions.

1. To be for the ensuing week moderate at table.
2. Hours as early as can contrive. Redeeming the time.[13]

Burford Sunday 5th. Octr.
Alas! Alas! on a sober & impartial Review of myself, & of all the Circumstances of my Situation, what Reason have I not to adore the longsuffering

---

12. Wilberforce leased Rayrigg Hall, a small manor house on the shore of Lake Windermere in the Lake District, from 1780–1788. He would occasionally use his 'summer house' as he referred to it, as a base for walking and boating on the lake. In 1788, Wilberforce wrote of Rayrigg, 'I never enjoyed the country more than during this visit, when in the early morning I used to row out alone, and find an oratory under one of the woody islands in the middle of the Lake.' *Life*, i. p. 180.

13. *Life*, i. pp. 18-21.

of God, who has so long permitted me to cumber the ground neglecting & abusing his innumerable mercies, whilst I have been compromising with him as it were by the performance of some Duties for the Neglect of others & have almost deceived myself into an opinion that I am endeavouring to live to his Glory, when in Truth I am given up to my own Heart's Lusts. For all in me is false & hollow. I want that true principle of Obedience, the Love of God, that Charity which fixing its Views & Desires on him, accounts all other things subordinate & inconsiderable, which shews its Zeal & Sincerity, by an active, constant & universal conformity to his Will, which relinquishes sensual Gratifications not out of a Principle[14] of fear, but because they tend to divert the Soul from its true Source of Happiness, to seduce its affections & thoughts from Heavenly to earthly things, & to weaken the Intimacy of that Communion with God, which is the vital Principle of its Being - "Our Life is hid with X^t. in God."[15] - O! what a change must be wrought in me before I am brought into this happy State, yet let me not despair - That would be to distract from the power of God's Grace, & the Efficacy of his Son's Atonement - If "by my own power or Strength or Holiness it were required of me to effect this mighty Renovation,"[16] as well indeed might I expect the Cripple to recover the Use of his Limbs at my bidding, but the name of Jesus thro' faith in his name, is as able to produce in me mental, as it was bodily Soundness in the man who sat at the beautiful Gate of the Temple. "Repent & be converted that your Sins may be blotted out."[17] The address is made to one as properly as it then was to the Jews. God has promis'd that he will give his holy Spirit to them that ask him, he encourages nay commands us to be incessant & importunate. Let us urge our Suit in the Temper of Jacob, "I will not let thee go until thou bless me."[18] "He that spared not his own Son but delivered him up for us all, how shall he not with him also freely give us all things."[19] "Whatever ye shall ask in my name I will do it, that the Father may be glorified in the Son."[20] The Promise was made to the Disciples, but all they are X^t's Disciples, who do the Will of his Father which is in Heaven.

Come then in prayer to God thro' Christ, who died for thy Sins, who is now on the Right Hand of God interceding for his people,[21] who "having receiv'd of the Father the Gift of the Holy Ghost," (Acts:2:33), sheds it abundantly into the Hearts of those who earnestly seek for & depend on its Influence. "Without me ye can do nothing!"[22] But with thee, O Thou Prince & Savior, we can do all - Quicken me by thy free Spirit. Fill me with that true Love of thee & of God which may inspire

---

14. 'Out of a Principle' is inserted here above two crossed out words.
15. Colossians 3:3.
16. Acts 3:12.
17. Acts 3:19.
18. Genesis 32:26.
19. Romans 8:32.
20. John 14:13.
21. Romans 8:34.
22. John 15:5.

DIARY 1787–1792

me with a new & living Principle of universal Holiness. Make me desire to devote to thee all my powers both of Soul & Body, to find my Happiness in the Consciousness of Communion with thee on Earth & in the blessed Hope of everlasting Life with thee in Heaven.

I am about to take a Survey of all the Circumstances of my Situation, that I may be the better able to discover wherein I may make my feeble Powers subservient to their great purpose, & avail myself of every opportunity that is afforded me of promoting the Glory of God, remembering always that it is to be the sole End of all my actions, small & great. "Whether you eat or drink or whatsoever you do,"[23] &c. and because general Resolutions are ill-suited to the State of one who is assail'd by the, "Sins that do most easily beset him,"[24] at Times when there is neither Leisure or Calmness for Reflection, I will form particular ones, & adhere to them in their Spirit, without binding myself an overscrupulous & rigid observance of them. Let me consider too what are the faults to which I am most prone, the Duties to which most averse & by an honest & constant Self-examination Labor daily to correct the one, & clear away the impediments which obstruct me in the performance of the other. The infirm State of my Health requires great Indulgencies, much Relaxation, but let me act faithfully by myself in a Concern of this infinite Importance, & if the Eye be single, the whole Body will be full of Light. Sermon on the Nature of Angels, a most unprofitable discourse. A Sunday spent in solitude spreads and extends its fragrance; may I long find the good effects of this.[25]

Wednesday, October 31st. 1788, Stevenage

At night. I have been transgressing in every Way whilst in Town, but chiefly in that my affections are mainly set on carnal & not on spiritual things. In the mens:[26] <u>sad Work</u>, which is particularly culpable considering I am just come from Bath.[27] Here at least I wo'd hope a Reform is practicable & I now resolve on it in the most solemn manner. Let me endeavor at one too universally. Assist me O God, tho' I have so

---

23. 1 Corinthians 10:31.

24. Hebrews 12:1.

25. *Life*, i. p. 185.

26. Wilberforce often records how badly he fears he acted at mealtimes, both in the amount he ate and drank, and the form of what he ate particularly. Desserts caused him significant digestive problems, but as he will often record, they were something he often succumbed to, and would later regret. When he recorded his failures at table he would often use the Latin word for table, 'mensa', sometimes abbreviating as here, simply to 'mens.' He suffered from what is thought to be ulcerative colitis, and treatment at that time was minimal at best. He sought to follow the directions of Doddridge and others, in seeking to live a somewhat ascetic life, though as he would record, this was hampered ironically by his ailments.

27. The city of Bath was a very popular destination for the Wilberforces, often prompted by his desire to take of the mineral waters available there, hoping they might help when he was especially ill. They also traveled there in 1821, that their eldest daughter Barbara might also partake, as she was seriously ill with tuberculosis. It had similarly been just such a destination for the Spooners, as they sought any healing properties for Barbara's father, Isaac. Bath probably held a special place for Wilberforce too, in that he both met his future wife there and then married there. He would also purchase an estate close by. Wilberforce returned to the city in May 1833 when he himself was obviously dying. He did regain some strength, if only temporarily, beginning the return journey to London less than two weeks before he would pass away.

long & so repeatedly abused thy long Suffering that I dare scarce call on thee for Help.[28]

Sunday, November 9[th.] 1788, Wilford[29]

With Grief & Shame I take up my pen to record my own Guilt & my Breaches of the most solemn & deliberate Resolutions. I desire now to renew them, & to turn to thee O God from lying Vanities. Particularly in the mens: & in the Redeeming of Time let me Reform, there at least the change is not difficult if the Heart be really willing & the Intention sincere. How different am I now from what I was when at this place 2 years ago, how much less spiritually minded, less interested for the Salvation of others, less diligent, less humble minded, less circumspect, watchful & fearful of the Effects of my own Corruption & of my great Enemies. O may these Considerations rouze me to Exertion, & thro' the power of divine Grace, may my Exertions be active, constant & universal.[30]

Sunday Evening, November 9[th.] 1788

Even today not quite right quoad mens. I will make some positive Rules for the Week ensuing.[31]

Sunday, November 16[th.] 1788, Bath

I have little Reason to be better satisfied with this Week than the preceding ones, no diligence & nimia[32] indulgent & not mens: Resolves attended to.[33]

Wednesday, November 19[th.] 1788, London

All my mens: Rules sadly violated again & again. The Meetg. of Parl[t.] tomorrow.[34]

1789

New Year, 1789

Received the Sacrament. Thought over my future plan of conduct and resolutions. I resolve to endeavor henceforth to live more to the glory of God, and the good of my fellow-creatures, to live more by rule, as in the presence of him by whom I shall finally be judged. For the ensuing week I resolve to begin the day with meditation or reading Scripture,

---

28. MS Wilberforce c. 4, fo. 4.
29. Samuel Smith (1754–1834), a cousin of Wilberforce. Smith was a wealthy banker and M.P. like many others in his family, including his father and four of his brothers. He had Wilford Hall in Wilford (now part of Nottingham), built for him in 1781, where Wilberforce stayed in the summer of 1786. Still standing, the Hall was designed by William Henderson, and is used today as office accommodation.
30. MS Wilberforce c. 4, fo. 4.
31. Ibid.
32. Latin: excessive; great.
33. MS Wilberforce c. 4, fo. 4.
34. Ibid.

to pray thrice, constant self-examination, table rules, Horneck's rules,[35] and my other rules, an account of time also.[36]

Undated, 1789

How long, alas, have I been a cumberer of the ground! How little have I availed myself of the opportunities of usefulness, which have been so abundantly afforded me! Be more diligent and watchful for the future. The night cometh when no man can work.[37] Let this consideration quicken my exertions. I am about to enter upon keeping a regular account of my time, from which it will be in my power to derive many advantages. My health requires me to live indulgently in all respects; my station and sphere of action call me much into company. Let me deal faithfully with myself, and not give way further or more frequently than really shall be necessary, but strive to redeem the time as one who works for eternity. Bless this work, O God, I beseech thee. Gross account of time. N. B. Never to harass myself or spend the present time, in considering needlessly under what head to enter any portion of what is past. Squandered, waste or misappropriation, all unnecessary meals, or bed time. House of Commons, business, etc. into this is brought all time spent in going to and from public offices, letters of business, reading for business, consulting, etc. Relaxation sua causa.[38] Here meal times when alone or quite at liberty, etc. the more this head can be reduced the better. Dressing, etc. all that is frittered away, all which I forget how to account for. Requisite company, going from place to place, waiting for people. Minor application, study, reading for entertainment, or with no great attention, familiar common letters, etc. Major application: study, reading for use, composing, getting by heart. Serious, private and family devotions, etc. Remember my rules and hints respecting the employment of odd half hours, and of thoughts in company or alone, riding, walking, providing store of thoughts, etc. etc.[39] Surely these are not little things, health depends upon them, and duty on health. They are not little things if my health and power of serving God be a great one.[40]

M. and I made an agreement to pay a guinea[41] forfeit when we broke our rules, and not to tell particulars to each other. I hope this will be

---

35. Anthony Horneck (1641–1697), was a German evangelical minister and scholar working in England. His works are mainly devotional and went through several editions, being republished through the mid-19th century. In his, *The Life of the Reverend Anthony Horneck* (1698), Richard Kidder (1633–1703) gives Horneck's 'Rules for the Religious Society' on page 13. They will constitute a large part of Wilberforce's spirituality and so are given in Appendix A. In a similar vein, Horneck also published, *The Happy Ascetick; or the Best Exercise … to which is added, A Letter to a Person of Quality concerning the Holy Lives of the Primitive Christians,* (1681).

36. *Life*, i. p. 193.

37. John 9:4.

38. Latin: relaxation for its own sake.

39. *Life*, i. pp. 195-196.

40. Wilberforce's sons make the comment that their father's Journal affords many instances of contentions with himself, upon which he entered not without some indignation at discovering their necessity, *Life*, i. p. 196.

41. A Guinea was the first British machine-struck coin, made of approximately one quarter ounce of gold, and minted in Great Britain from 1663 to 1814, after which it was recalled. It was worth

an instrument under divine grace to keep me from excess. When once a settled habit is formed less rigid rules will be necessary.[42] Exceeded, and determined to pay forfeit. Went on rather better, yet by no means up to the strictness of my plan.

I have lately been ill, and by the mercy of God have recovered; yet instead of devoting my renewed strength to him, I am wasting it, particularly by exceeding my rules. I re-resolve, humbly imploring pardon for Christ's sake. Considering my constitution, resolutions, and opinions, how far am I from perfect temperance. This brings on unfitness for communion with God; averseness from him; alienated affections; a body unequal to business; an antinomian[43] and self-righteous spirit, too easily forgiving myself for the past, and looking for comfort to better performances in future. I am hurt and ashamed at myself; yet looking to God for strength, I resolve through him to amend; and, as the only way of being safe, (licitis perimus)[44] to adhere to my strict rules. May this have an effect in other things.

Nothing is to be resisted more than the disposition which we feel when we have been long striving unsuccessfully for any particular grace or against any habitual infirmity, to acquiesce in our low measure of that grace, or in the presence of that infirmity, so as not to feel shame, humiliation, and compunction. We are not to cast off the hope of getting better of the one and attaining to the other. This is the very state in which we are to work out our own salvation with fear and trembling.[45] The promise is sure in the end. Therefore though it tarry wait for it; it will surely come, it will not tarry.[46]

1789[47] - Jany 1st.

Next to my advancement & growth in grace, Objects are

1st. The establishment of my Health

2dly. Improvement of Intellectual Powers, & acquisition of Knowledge. Discute &c -

3 Victory over that fatal Habit of trifling away time Which being long indulged has so got the mastery over me -

---

£1.1 shilling at the time when £1 comprised 20 shillings. Once made of gold from Guinea, guineas used to be the regular currency for buying horses. Hence the title of the 2,000 Guineas race - that being the amount in the prize fund in 1809. Tattersalls, the blood stock auctioneer, founded in 1766, still conducts its bidding in guineas as it has done since it began. The shilling was the auctioneer's cut and Tattersalls still takes 5pc commission. From 1717 to 1816, the Guinea's value was officially fixed at twenty-one shillings, but after Britain adopted the gold standard, the term Guinea became a colloquial or specialized term.

42. Wilberforce's sons state that as their father perceived his difficulties in life arose from carelessness as much as self-indulgence, he sought to counteract it by laying down a set of rules, which they believed too minutely practical to be inserted into their biography. They added that while not content with recording against himself every infraction of these severe regulations, Wilberforce had recourse to another expedient to keep his vigilance awake, *Life*, i. p. 196.

43. Antinomianism, literally 'against law', is the notion within theology that because of faith being salvific, the law does not apply to Christians; it is often based on the idea that because Christians are no longer under law but grace, the laws of ethics and morality no longer apply.

44. Latin: We perish through lawful pursuits.

45. Philippians 2:12.

46. Habakkuk 2:3; *Life*, i. p. 197.

47. In the loose sheets of the diary as here, Wilberforce did not always number them consecutively, and as here sometimes duplicates the numbers at the head of the pages.

For the rest - vide[48] my other Books & Papers - I have made frequent & serious Resolutions, but they have been forgotten almost as soon as made, O may God's Grace enable me to keep them better for the time to come. I am in a Situation of Life wherein I have Opportunities of Usefulness long & abundant; let me not be wanting to it, but remember always that to whom much is given of him will <u>much be required</u>.[49]

I hope to spend this year better than the preceding. Eliot[50] breakfasted with me, and I went with him to the Lock,[51] received the sacrament. Dined at home. Thought over future plan of conduct. Called at Pitt's. Last night the Speaker put off the House by a note in Warren's[52] hand-writing, after he had sent word he had passed a good night, we suspect a trick.[53]

Thursday Evg. 1ˢᵗ· Jany.

I receiv'd the Sacrament this morning, at the Lock. O may God enable me to live henceforth more to his Glory - I have been reading poor Johnson's Diary & Prayers[54] & in the Defects of his Character how exactly we agree! Like him, I resolve and reresolve & forget my Resolutions as soon as made, but by God's Blessing I would humbly hope to keep them better for the time to come, & I thank the mercy of God in Xᵗ· that has not yet given me wholly over to a reprobate mind.[55] Whilst I have any feeling left, let me be faithful to it; whilst the Day is continued to me let me work, the night cometh when no man can work[56] – T.O.[57]

Saturday Morg 3ᵈ Jany

In spite of all my solemn Resolutions, yesterday at Dinner at Lord Chatham's I exceeded mens in all ways, chiefly dessert sweets Tea & Coffee &c. that after coming from my aunt's funeral, hearing of Speaker Cornwall's sudden death, & everything that ought to have impress'd me with seriousness. How strange & mad is this Conduct. How merciful is God in having spared me when others more likely than myself for Life have been suddenly cut off. O may I profit from this forbearance & seek the Lord whilst he is to be found. The Bible assures us that his Ear is not heavy,[58] 'tis our Iniquities that separate.

---

48. Latin: look, see.

49. Luke 12:48.

50. Edward James Eliot (1758–1797), Lord of the Treasury, brother-in-law and close friend of William Pitt the Younger. After his wife Harriot died soon after childbirth in September 1786, Eliot was brought to Christ by Wilberforce, and moved to Clapham and later served in Pitt's Cabinet.

51. The London Lock Hospital in Grosvenor Place, near Hyde Park Corner, opened in 1747, becoming the first of several Lock Hospitals, originally established for the treatment of syphilis. Thomas Scott (1747–1821), an influential preacher, author, friend of both Wilberforce and Newton, and founding secretary of the Church Missionary Society, was hospital chaplain from 1785–1803. Wilberforce would often worship at the Lock's chapel.

52. John Warren (1730–1800), Bishop of Bangor, see later note.

53. *Life*, i. p. 199.

54. Samuel Johnson (1709–1784), author and lexicographer. *Prayers and Meditations, Composed by Samuel Johnson, LL.D. and Published from his Manuscripts* by George Strahan, 2ⁿᵈ ed. (London, 1785).

55. Romans 1:28.

56. John 9:4.

57. MS Wilberforce c. 4, fo. 3.

58. Isaiah 59:1.

Have mercy on me, Have mercy on me O God for X[t's] Sake. Deliver me from this unaccountable Infatuation which makes me sacrifice my Health, & opportunities of Usefulness to the lowest & most debasing of all gratifications.

Did Ld. C., Lady C. or B.[m]. act so sottishly, yet I with my View full fix'd on Eternity could deliver myself from these beastly Sensualities - I am now set free from the Effects of these Extravagancies, having had a sad night. O God have mercy on me & enable me to keep my Resolves better for time to come - The one probable Hope of success lies in my binding myself tight up.[59]

Tuesday Morng – 6th Jany -

Yet again, yesterday at Ld. Camden's[60] broke all Mens. Reg. I am now suffering from the Effects of my Excess. How dare I resolve or even apply for mercy, yet to despair were to perish - Once more let me hope to do better for the time to come - I have every motive to stimulate me. The Consideration of the high Character however falsely wholly unjustly that I have in the World. The Observation of others, who do not profess Religion, yesterday Lady Bayham &c. &c. &c. - I observe that all my Regls go together therefore let me be particularly guarded ag[t] the first transgression & rather bind myself too tight for the present, that I may more thoroughly get the mastery - I can never suffer more from manition than I am now doing from Excess, even in Body, & then <u>for the Mind</u> - O may this be the last record against me.[61]

Tuesday Evg. 13th Jany:

3 or 4 times have I most grievously broke my Resolutions anew. I last took up my pen - Alas! Alas! how miserable a Wretch am I! How infatuated, how dead to every better feeling - Yet – yet – yet - May I O God, be enabled to repent & turn to thee with my whole Heart - I am now flying from thee - Thou hast been above <u>all measure</u> gracious & forgiving: nor durst I hope to ever to amend even in these little things but that thou hast promised to hear our prayers - Great Changes as Ld. Bacon – Henceforth.[62]

Friday Morng 16th Jany

Yet once more - at Home - when intendg do Business, vide duty. I <u>will</u> endeavour yet again in spite of feeling & try as rigid an adherence to Rules as proper.[63]

Sunday Evg 18th Jany. 1789

I exceeded some Regls. yesterday admens.[64] Bp of Salisbury.[65] But alas! the grand Evil is that my Heart is not right before God, my Affections are

59. MS Wilberforce c. 4, fo. 4.

60. Charles Pratt (1714–1794), 1st Earl Camden, M.P., Attorney General, Chief Justice of the Common Pleas, and Lord Chancellor. His town house was in Hill Street, Berkeley Square, London.

61. MS Wilberforce c. 4, fo. 5.

62. Ibid.

63. Ibid.

64. Latin: at table.

65. Shute Barrington (1734–1826), was Bishop of Salisbury at the time of this entry. He was transferred from Llandaff (1769–1782), and was then translated to Durham (1791–1826).

set on temporal things, & I grow daily more conformed to this World. Late Hours at night & morning have produced bad Effects, prevent my performing properly, or enjoying my devotions. Here I will make a thorough Reform. 8 Hours Bed at least seems to be good for me, but let me try if I can to be in bed before 11, & to read or think over some passage of Scripture or religious Book. Sursum Corda.[66] Have mercy on me O God.[67]

Sunday Morg before Bkfast 25[th.] Jany.

Repeatedly have I transgress'd my Mens: Rules this last Week & never more than yesterday at Mr. Braithwaite's.[68] This surely is the worst species of Insanity. O God, restore me to my senses. I cannot tell how it is that I am so sottishly hurrying on to Destruction, giving Way to the very lowest species of temptations, & with long motive to restrain me: Was anyone yesterday so inconsistent as myself. Was not I the very Fool Gen[l]. Vernon[69] contended could not exist who was continually denying his God & acknowledging him again. My Heart is so far sunk in Vice, my affections are so deprav'd, the Image of God is so defac'd in my Soul, that to repair all this mischief & to restore me but to the State in which I once was, will be a Work of difficulty in the Extreme. But in these mens: particulars, in earl. Hours hard 'tis not impossible - None fail here but the most grossly stupid & beastly - For the next week therefore devotions more constant & earl. Hours: Mens Regls.[70]

Sunday Morng after Church 25[th.] Jany.

Mr. Woodd,[71] Except the Lord had left a Remnant, we had been like Sodom &c.[72] O how do these Words reproach me with my Hypocrisy. Instead of being one who is drawing down on his Country the Blessing of God, I am bringing on it his righteous Indignation yet he is ever merciful when I have not ruined beyond.[73]

Remembered for his criticism and rebuke of George Whitefield, Barrington had something of a difficult relationship with evangelicals, though he became Wilberforce's leading episcopal patron after Beilby Porteus's death. He denounced slavery in sermons and Wilberforce regarded his support as highly significant in the cause for Abolition.

66. A Latin phrase meaning 'lift up your hearts', which is taken from Lam. 3:41, and a phrase that Wilberforce not surprisingly uses on a number of occasions, as he would have been exposed to it on a regular basis from its use in the communion service of the Anglican Prayer Book.

67. MS Wilberforce c. 4, fo. 6.

68. Probably John Braithwaite, slave-owner and parliamentary agent for the Barbados assembly.

69. Charles Vernon (1719–1810), army officer (as Wilberforce records here, a General, a rank he attained in 1783) and M.P. There is no record of Vernon ever having spoken in the House.

70. MS Wilberforce c. 4, fo. 6.

71. Basil Woodd (1760–1831), hymn writer, Anglican minister and successful in establishing schools through his ministry at the Bentinck Chapel, London. At least three thousand children passed through his schools. He was also actively involved in many Christian societies, including the Church Missionary Society, The Society for Promoting Christian Knowledge, and the British and Foreign Bible Society.

72. Romans 9:29.

73. MS Wilberforce c. 4, fo. 6.

Monday, January 26th. 1789

Till near six, slave business all the evening, with only biscuit and wine and water. Nervous in the night, and dreamed about slavery, without referring it to blacks.[74]

Sunday, February 8th. 1789

Eliot and Henry Thornton.[75] Lock. Scott[76] excellent on St. James v. 7, 8. Much affected with the discourse. Oh blessed be God who hath appointed the Sabbath, and interposes these seasons of serious recollection. May they be effectual to their purpose; may my errors be corrected, my desires sanctified, and my whole soul quickened and animated in the Christian course. The last week has been spent little, if at all, better than the preceding; but I trust God will enable me to turn to him in righteousness. Write, I beseech Thee, Thy law in my heart, that I may not sin against Thee.[77] I often waste my precious hours for want of having settled beforehand to what studies to betake myself, what books to read. Let me attend to this for the time to come, and may my slave business, and my society business, be duly attended to.[78]

Monday, February 9th. 1789

Went to Pitt's to talk on slave trade. King[79] much better, thank God.[80]

Sunday, February 15th. 1789

Morning Lock. Scott. Eliot much affected. Called Gordon's,[81] who ill, in pain, etc. Much affected all day with a sense of heavenly things. Westminster Abbey[82] in the afternoon. Once more I thank God for the intervention of the Sabbath, and I pray that I may be enabled to make a due use of it.[83]

---

74. *Life*, i. p. 202.

75. Henry Thornton (1760–1815), like his father John, was a highly successful merchant banker, but was also an M.P., a leading director of the Sierra Leone Company, and grandfather of the writer, E. M. Forster. Wilberforce and Henry were cousins, and shared a house as bachelors in Clapham for five years. Following their marriages, both men lived as neighbors, and it was around them that the Clapham Circle eventually formed. It is recorded that Henry gave away seven-eighths of his income before marriage and three-quarters afterwards.

76. Rev. Thomas Scott (1747–1821), Anglican minister at Olney, chaplain at the London Lock Hospital, prolific writer and biblical scholar. He was already a minister when he experienced an evangelical conversion, which he describes in his spiritual autobiography *The Force of Truth* (1779). A friend of both Wilberforce and John Newton, Scott helped found the Church Missionary Society in 1799. He is remembered especially for his *Commentary on the Bible*, 4 vols., (1788–1792).

77. Psalm 119:11.

78. *Life*, i. pp. 203-204.

79. George III (1738–1820), King of Great Britain and Ireland (United Kingdom 1801–1820) from 1760 to 1820, was the 3rd British monarch of the House of Hanover. He suffered much in his later life from recurrent and eventually permanent mental illness, possibly due to porphyria.

80. *Life*, i. p. 204.

81. Wilberforce may here be referring to Alexander Gordon (1743–1827), 4th Duke of Gordon, Keeper of the Great Seal of Scotland (1794–1806, 1807–1827), Chancellor of King's College, Aberdeen (1793–1827), and Lord Lieutenant of Aberdeenshire (1794–1808). Later he does refer to the Duchess of Gordon, see later notes.

82. Benedictine monks first came to the site that is now Westminster Abbey, in the middle of the tenth century, establishing a tradition of daily worship which continues to the present day. The Abbey has been the coronation church since 1066 and is the final resting place of seventeen monarchs. The present church was begun by Henry III in 1245. The Abbey is also the place where at least 3,300 of Britain's great and good are either buried or commemorated.

83. *Life*, i. p. 204.

Wednesday, February 18[84] 1789

Stephen[84] and Eliot, breakfasted. Ditto evening. Slave business till near bed, and slept ill, as I commonly do when my mind is occupied before bedtime, nervous, and tossing, haunted by thoughts about trifles.[85]

Tuesday, February 24th 1789

I called on John Wesley,[86] a fine old fellow. The bustle and hurry of life sadly distract and destroy me. Alas, alas, I must mend, may God enable me.[87]

Wednesday, February 25th 1789

Sub-committee. Bishop of Salisbury's. Dined at Lord Salisbury's, large party, nothing in conversation worth remembering. Pitt showed me the King's excellent letter, long conversation, in which he inquired after everybody. On full conviction from experience that it is impossible for me to make myself master of the slave subject, and to go through my other various occupations, except I live more undistractedly, I determine scarce ever to dine out in parties, and in all respects to live with a view to these great matters, till the slave business is brought to some conclusion. May God bless the work and my endeavors. My health very indifferent. Milner[88] at Kew,[89] he comes in and gives me the extraordinary account, all surprise and astonishment. Bulletin, 'Free from complaint.' Walked to the Observatory[90] and back. There Milner saw him, and at night in the circle.[91]

Thursday, February 26th 1789

Slave committee breakfasted with me, then out, calls, etc. House, business went off, no questions asked. Dined at home, Milner and I had some serious talk.[92]

---

84. James Stephen (1758–1832), a newspaper reporter, brilliant lawyer, M.P., Master of Chancery, and great-grandfather of Virginia Woolf. After witnessing the horrific treatment of slaves on Barbados, he became actively involved in the Abolitionist cause. He married Wilberforce's sister, Sarah, in 1800. He became a council member of the London Abolition Committee, the African Institution, and the Anti-Slavery Society. Stephen provided the legal advice needed in the drafting of the 1807 Slave Trade Bill, and his, 'An Address to the People and Electors of England' (1826), paved the way for the Abolition Bill of 1833, though he did not live to see its successful passing. Two of Stephen's sons, however, remained active in the Abolitionist cause.

85. *Life*, i. p. 204.

86. John Wesley (1703–1791). Leader along with his brother Charles, of the 18th century Evangelical Revival and a founder of Methodism.

87. *Life*, i. p. 206.

88. Isaac Milner (1750–1820), a leading, influential evangelical of his day, and influential in the conversion of Wilberforce. He began an incredibly distinguished career as a lowly usher at Hull Grammar School, where his brother Joseph had been appointed as Headmaster. After an early display of his genius, he would later go on to become President of Queen's College, Cambridge; Dean of Carlisle; the Lucasian Professor of Mathematics at Cambridge; and a great supporter of Wilberforce and the abolitionist cause.

89. Kew is a suburban district in the London Borough of Richmond upon Thames, and is the location of the Royal Botanic Gardens, usually referred to simply as 'Kew Gardens'. Successive monarchs, including Tudor, Stuart and Georgian, maintained links with Kew. In 1721, for example, the future George III moved into the White House at Kew. Kew is also home to a palace built in 1631.

90. The Royal Observatory in Greenwich is known especially for being the location of the prime meridian. It was commissioned in 1675 by Charles II, with John Flamsteed being appointed as the first Astronomer Royal. The area that includes the Observatory has seen many significant buildings, including Greenwich Palace, the birthplace of Henry VIII, and Greenwich Castle, which actually stood on the site on which the Observatory was later built.

91. *Life*, i. p. 206.

92. Ibid.

Sunday, March 1st. 1789

Eliot breakfasted and Lock. Scott. Called Lord Chatham's about politics (a work of real necessity). Strongly and deeply affected by an examination of myself, I would hope to good purpose, and resolved to change my habits of life. This perpetual hurry of business and company numbs me in soul if not in body. I must make a thorough reform. More solitude and earlier hours, diligence, proper distribution and husbandry of time, associating with religious friends; this will strengthen my weakness by the blessing of God.

On an impartial examination of my state, I see that the world is my snare; business and company distract my mind, and dissipate those serious reflections which alone can preserve us from infection in such a situation of life as mine, where these antidotes are ever wanted to prevent our falling victims to this mortal contagion. My error hitherto has been, I think, endeavoring to amend this and the other failing, instead of striking at the root of the evil. Let me therefore make a spirited effort, not trusting in myself, but in the strength of the Lord God. Let me labor to live a life of faith, and prayer, and humility, and self-denial, and heavenly-mindedness, and sobriety, and diligence. Let me labor this week in particular, and lay down for myself a course of conduct. Yet let not this be mainly on my mind, but the fear and love of my Maker and Redeemer. Oh that the blessed day may come, when in the words of St. Paul, I may assert of myself that my conversation is in heaven; that the life I now lead in the flesh, I live by faith in the Son of God, who loved me and gave himself for me![93]

I trust I can say in the presence of God that I do right in going into company, keeping up my connections, etc. Yet as it is clear from a thorough examination of myself that I require more solitude than I have had of late, let me henceforth enter upon a new system throughout. Rules. As much solitude and sequestration as are compatible with duty. Early hour's night and morning. Abstinence as far as health will permit. Regulation of employments for particular times. Prayer three times a day at least, and begin with serious reading or contemplation. Self-denial in little things. Slave trade my main business now.[94]

Sunday, March 8th. 1789

I did not think it prudent to go to church, so within all day. Bates[95] and Frewen. I made it too little of a Lord's Day; it is better to spend it chiefly alone, for one at least so much in company as myself; yet I resolve to amend. Alas, my sluggish spirit grovels in the carnal enjoyments, and my deceitful heart loses itself in the vain pursuits, of the world. Do Thou, O God, quicken me by Thy blessed Spirit. Bring home the wanderer. Fix my misplaced affections on Thee. Oh strive to enter in at the strait gate.[96]

---

93. Galatians 2:20.
94. *Life*, i. pp. 206-207.
95. Ely Bates (m. 1788, d.c. 1813), subscriber to the African Institution, see later note.
96. Matthew 7:13; *Life*, i. pp. 208-209.

Wednesday, April 8th 1789
I resolve to live with a view to health. Slave business, attention to my rules, no waste of eyesight, and may God bless the work: may my religion be more vital from this retirement.[97]

Easter Sunday, April 12th 1789
I am going to renew the dedication of myself to thee at thy table, O Lord. Be thou made unto me, O Jesus, wisdom and sanctification.[98] Enlighten my understanding, renew my heart, purify my affections; guide and guard me through this vain world, and conduct me to those heavenly mansions where faith shall be lost in sight, and where secure from change thy people shall live forever in thy presence.[99]

Sunday, May 31st 1789
Received the sacrament, much affected. May this day be the beginning of a new life with me, the great rule, 'Set your affections on things above.'[100]

Sunday, July 5th 1789
Burgh and I had some most serious conversation, he read his book against Lindsey.[101] Then to Newton's church, rambling, but fervently devout. Called at H. Thornton's, and then Newton for an hour.[102]

Saturday, July 18th 1789
Came off to Teston, to see the Middletons[103] and Mrs. Bouverie.[104] How much better is this society! I will endeavor to confine myself more to those who fear God.[105]

Thursday, July 30th 1789
Began the waters. Resolved to lead a new life, adhering more steadfastly to my resolutions. Do Thou, O God, renew my heart, fill me with that love of Thee which extinguishes all other affections, and enable me

---

97. Ibid., pp. 213-214.

98. 1 Corinthians 1:30.

99. *Life*, i. p. 214.

100. Colossians 3:2; *Life*, i. p. 223.

101. William Burgh would write two volumes against the ideas of Theophilus Lindsey, copies of which are both currently in the Wilberforce library in Wilberforce House, Hull.

102. *Life*, i. p. 227.

103. Sir Charles Middleton (1726–1813), 1st Baron Barham after 1805 and Lord of the Admiralty, lived at Barham Court, a manor house in Teston, four miles from Maidstone, Kent. It had once been the home of Randall Fitz Urse, one of the knights who murdered Thomas Beckett in 1170. The Middletons were evangelicals, and Hannah More and Wilberforce would visit them often. It was here, in 1786, that the Middletons urged Wilberforce to champion the cause for Abolition in Parliament. Wilberforce also stayed here 1815–1816, when he persuaded Henry Thornton, who was then dying with TB, to stay at his Kensington Gore residence, for the believed fresher air of that area. Barham Court still stands, but has been converted into office and residential accommodation.

104. Mrs Harriet Bouverie, born Harriet Fawkener (1750–1825), was the daughter of Sir Everard Fawkener, silk merchant and diplomat, and Harriet, daughter of Lieutenant General Charles Churchill, a nephew of the 1st Duke of Marlborough. On 30 June, 1764, Harriet married the Honourable Edward Bouverie of Delapre Abbey in Northamptonshire, at St. George's in Hanover Square, London. Harriet Bouverie actively campaigned for the Whig party, and entertained lavishly at her house, guests including Charles James Fox. She had three daughters, Harriet Elizabeth, Jane and Diana Juliana Margaretta, and three sons, Edward, John and Henry Frederick Bouverie.

105. *Life*, i. p. 234.

to give Thee my heart, and to serve Thee in spirit and in truth. In the evening my sister arrived; at twelve o'clock at night H. Thornton came. Read Barrow's[106] sermon on love of God, and much affected by it, yet I get insensibly into a sluggish state of mind. I must amend. A continual sense of God's presence is the best preservative.[107]

Friday, August 21st. 1789

After breakfast to see Cheddar.[108] Intended to read, dine, etc. amongst the rocks, but could not get rid of the people; so determined to go back again. The rocks very fine. Had some talk with the people, and gave them something, grateful beyond measure, wretchedly poor and deficient in spiritual help. I hope to amend their state.[109]

Sunday, August 23rd. 1789

Resolved to think seriously today for tomorrow, my birthday, on which I shall be much more disturbed. Cowslip Green,[110] birthday eve. Tomorrow I complete my thirtieth year. What shame ought to cover me when I review my past life in all its circumstances! With full knowledge of my Master's will, how little have I practiced it! How little have I executed the purposes I formed last summer at Rayrigg! Wherein am I improved even in my intellectual powers? My business I pursue but as an amusement, and poor Ramsay (now no more) shames me in the comparison. Yet is there hope in God's mercy through Christ. May He give constancy and vigor to my resolutions. May I look ever forward to that day of account to which I am hastening; may I act as in his sight, and preserving the deepest

---

106. Isaac Barrow (1630–1677), theologian and mathematician, usually credited with for his early role in the development of infinitesimal calculus. Isaac Newton, one of his students, later developed calculus in a modern form. For the sermon Wilberforce here mentions, see *Of the love of God and our neighbour, in several sermons* , vol. 3, by Isaac Barrow (London, 1680).

107. *Life*, i. p. 236.

108. The area of Cheddar in Somerset has, according to archeological discoveries, been inhabited since prehistoric times. Cheddar comes from an Old English word meaning deep cavity. The village of Cheddar itself has been of importance both during the Roman and the Saxon periods, having a royal palace during the latter period. The area, known throughout the world as the origin of Cheddar Cheese, had several mines and watermills. When Wilberforce picnicked there in 1789, he recorded that he saw much local poverty, that instead of eating he began to organize food, clothing and later along with Hannah More and her sisters, even established schools in the area. (See his entry for 21 August, 1789). On the day Wilberforce returned to Hannah More's home at Cowslip Green, he was asked how he liked the cliffs? He replied that they were very fine, but that the poverty and distress of the people was dreadful. In the unpublished Journal of Mrs. Martha More we then have the following insight, 'He retired to his apartment and dismissed even his reader. I said to his sister and mine, I feared Mr. W. was not well. The cold chicken and wine put into the carriage for his dinner were returned untouched. Mr. W. appeared at supper, seemingly refreshed with a higher feast than we had sent with him. The servant at his desire was dismissed, when immediately he began, "Miss Hannah More, something must be done for Cheddar." He then proceeded to a particular account of his day, of the inquiries he had made respecting the poor; there was no resident minister, no manufactory, nor did there appear any dawn of comfort, either temporal or spiritual. The method or possibility of assisting them was discussed till a late hour; it was at length decided in a few words, by Mr. W.'s exclaiming, "If you will be at the trouble, I will be at the expense."' *The Life of William Wilberforce* by R.I. and S. Wilberforce (abridged edition, 1843), 119. The area with the Gorge also became a popular tourist destination, especially with the advent of the railways in 1869.

109. *Life*, i. pp. 238-239.

110. Cowslip Green, now Brook Lodge, is a small thatched cottage in Somerset, that Hannah More called her 'sweet retirement'. Wilberforce used this for his honeymoon and would later often stay here himself.

self abasement, may my light so shine before men, that they may see my good works, and glorify my Father which is in heaven.[111]

Monday, August 24th. 1789

Left Cowslip Green for Bristol.[112] Spent half an hour with Sir James Stonhouse,[113] seventy-four; under many bodily tortures, yet patient and cheerful, much pleased with him. He recommended 12th of Hebrews, and 3rd of Lamentations. Spoke in the highest terms of Dr. Doddridge, and related the circumstances of his own conversion, when he belonged to a deistical[114] club.[115]

Saturday, September 5th. 1789

Found that I had few acquaintance here, Archbishop of Canterbury[116] and family, etc. For the last week at Sir R. Hill's.[117] He is indeed a good man: but how much time does one waste even in such a house. Let me as often as possible retire up into the mountain, and come down only on errands of usefulness and love. Oh may God enable me to fix my affections mainly on him, and to desire to glorify him, whether in life or death; looking unto Jesus,[118] and continuing constant in prayer.[119]

Saturday, September 12th. 1789

Condemned my going on, (read, read, read,) and resolve to endeavor at a new plan of thought, etc. and to keep the account plus and minus. To get much by heart and recapitulate. Long walk with the Archbishop.[120]

October, 1789

Had two or three narrow escapes, drunken postilion nearly driving into Ashborne Water,[121] carriage spring broken, etc. Through God's mercy, got safe to Buxton.[122]

---

111. Matthew 5:16; *Life*, i. pp. 240-241.

112. Bristol is a city in south-west England on the River Avon. The transatlantic slave trade brought great prosperity to the city, Edmund Burke was M.P. Population in 1801 at the time of the first census was numbered at 66,000, which quintupled through the rest of the century.

113. Sir James Stonhouse (1716–1795), 11th Baronet, physician, Anglican minister, hospital founder and religious writer. A close friend of Philip Doddridge, through whom he was converted.

114. Sir James Stonhouse had before his conversion been a deist. Deism involved a belief in God but rejected the core tenets of orthodox Christianity. It was highly popular among the upper class in the 18th and 19th centuries. Hannah More would refer to Stonhouse as the one who awakened her religious sense, and she would subsequently compose his epitaph in 1792.

115. *Life*, i. p. 243.

116. John Moore (1730–1805), Archbishop from 1783 to 1805.

117. Sir Richard Hill (1733–1808), second baronet, M.P., evangelical debater, brother of the evangelical preacher Rowland Hill, and an ardent supporter of the British and Foreign Bible Society. Wilberforce was not always positive in his comments on Hill's lifestyle or spirituality, as seen in some of the journal entries.

118. Hebrews 12:2.

119. *Life*, i. p. 244.

120. Ibid.

121. Ashborne (now Ashbourne) is a market town in the Dales of Derbyshire, and known as the 'Gateway to the Peak District'. It was granted a Charter for a market in 1257, and was a popular rest stop for religious pilgrims heading for shrine in Dunstable, Bedfordshire. St. Oswald's Church in Ashbourne dates from 1220. The poet, Sir Brooke Boothby, and Catherine Booth, the 'Mother of the Salvation Army,' were both born in the town. The population in 1801 was approximately 3,800.

122. *Life*, i. p. 245.

Sunday, October 25th. 1789

Saw a poor and very religious man, much affected by his meek piety. Oh may God enable me to turn to him henceforth. Buxton is in a sadly neglected state.[123]

Undated, 1789

I went I think in 1786 to see her,[124] and when I came into the room Charles Wesley[125] rose from the table, around which a numerous party sat at tea, and coming forwards to me, gave me solemnly his blessing. I was scarcely ever more affected. Such was the effect of his manner and appearance, that it altogether overset me, and I burst into tears, unable to restrain myself.[126]

Tuesday, October 27th. 1789

Off after breakfast for R. where a large party at dinner, B. the philosopher, etc. Played at cards evening and supped. S. how little of St. Paul. F. an old man. Alas! Alas! Sat up too late, and strong compunctions.[127]

Friday, October 30th. 1789

At Wilford, seven little children; two of them poor Mrs. Manning's. To aim at eight hours: minor business, business, and serious, added together, and keep an accurate account. May God enable me to live more to his glory. Oh how difficult it is to keep alive in the soul any spark of the true spirit of religion! 'Quicken me, O Lord.'[128] Form in me daily that new creature which is made after thy likeness. May I be endeavoring in all things to walk in wisdom to them that are without, redeeming the time;[129] laboring for the spiritual improvement of others; mortifying the flesh, and living soberly, righteously, and godly in this present world. For the ensuing week let it be my main care to exterminate a sensual spirit rather by substituting better regards in its place, than by attacking it directly; yet being moderate in all enjoyments, and looking through them to the gracious Author of all good. Sober-mindedness, good-nature, plan for time, etc. Topics for conversation and study. Looking unto Jesus.[130]

Tuesday, November 17th. 1789

Resolved with difficulty to start for Cookson's,[131] and then to my many and great matters in town. Miss L. Smith[132] very seriously disposed.

---

123. Ibid.

124. Wilberforce's sons state that their father formed a personal acquaintance with the Wesley family at the home of Hannah More.

125. Charles Wesley (1707–1788), the renowned Christian hymn writer, and leader along with his brother John, in the 18th century Evangelical Revival and a founder of Methodism. Upon Charles' death, Wilberforce would provide his widow with a pension for the remainder of her life.

126. *Life*, i. p. 248.

127. Ibid., pp. 249-250.

128. Psalm 119:107.

129. Colossians 4:5.

130. Hebrews 12:2; *Life*, i. p. 250.

131. Wilberforce could here be referring to the Cookson family in Leeds, or the Cooksons in Forncett.

132. Abel Smith (1717–1788), M.P., and the founder of the Nottingham Smith's Bank. In 1745 he married Mary Bird (1724–1780), whose younger sister Elizabeth Bird would become William

Had I looked for them, doubtless I had found many opportunities of serious conversation and mutual edification. May God forgive my neglected occasions, and enable me to profit more from them in future.[133]

Sunday, November 29th. 1789

On an inquiry I think it right to stay here for a while, God willing, rather than to remove as yet. To form my plan and keep to it by God's blessing. Try at eight hours at least of all sorts. Topics ready for discussion and conversation. Moderation, early hours, relaxation regulated, and as I stay here may I employ my leisure well, and try to walk as remembering God's eye is ever over me. Books, reading, commonplaces, etc.[134]

Sunday, December 6th. 1789

Had some very serious thoughts and strong compunctions, from which I hope good will result. Remember, O my soul, that if thou availest not thyself of these warnings, the greater will be thy condemnation. May I be enabled to place my happiness in communion with God, and may I be found in the spotless robe of Christ's righteousness, covering my iniquities from the pure eyes of a holy God. When B. dined here I was too vain and talkative (humility should be joined to cheerfulness). At night a long and earnest conversation with my host upon religion. May God bless it to both of us.[135]

Sunday, December 13th. 1789

I have been too sedentary for my health this last week. I must take more air, and be satisfied with eight hours' reading, if I find more too much. This last week: Letters, Lear, Othello, Hamlet, Macbeth, Twelfth Night,[136] Ferguson,[137] Bible, Johnson's Lives,[138] Doddridge's Sermons,[139] a topic daily henceforth. Recapitulation.[140]

Wilberforce's mother. Abel and Mary had eight children, five of the sons following their father into Parliament, and Lucy possibly being the Miss L. Smith Wilberforce refers to in the entry.

133. *Life*, i. p. 251.

134. Ibid.

135. Ibid., pp. 251-252.

136. As recorded here by the variety of Shakespeare's works Wilberforce records, what seems to be clear is that Shakespeare's writings were clearly amongst some of his most favorite readings.

137. Wilberforce was most likely referring here to Adam Ferguson (1723–1816), philosopher and historian, for in a later entry Wilberforce refers to Ferguson's *Roman Republic* (1783).

138. Samuel Johnson (1696–1772), writer and lexicographer, published his *Lives of the Most Eminent English Poets* between 1779 to 1781. The work is composed of short biographies and Johnson's critical appraisals of 52 mostly 18th century poets, including John Milton (1608–1674), Alexander Pope (1688–1744), Joseph Addison (1672–1719), and Jonathan Swift (1667–1745).

139. See for example, *Sermons And Religious Tracts of the late Reverend Philip Doddridge, D.D., Now first collected together, in three volumes* (London, 1761).

140. *Life*, i. p. 252.

1790

Friday, January 1st. 1790

Lock. Scott, with Henry Thornton, 'These forty years in the Wilderness',[141] received the sacrament. Most deeply impressed with serious things, shame from past life, and desire of future amendment. I have been receiving the sacrament after an excellent sermon of Scott's, and with the deepest humiliation I look up for mercy, through Christ, to that God whose past mercies I have so often abused. I resolve by God's help to mortify the flesh with the affections and lusts, so far as my very infirm health will permit me, and to labor more and more to live the life I now live in the flesh, in the faith of the Son of God.[142]

How should I be humbled by seeing the little progress I have made since 1786! Poor Newton dines with me today, on whom I then called. He has not dined from home on new-year's day for thirty years. I shall now form a set of rules, and by God's help adhere to them. My health is very bad, a little thing disorders me, at thirty and a half I am in constitution sixty. 'The night cometh when no man can work.'[143] Oh may divine grace protect and support me throughout the ensuing campaign, preserve me from the world's mistaken estimate of things, and enable me to be a Christian indeed, and to glorify God by my life and conduct.[144]

Sunday, January 31st. 1790

Alas! With how little profit has my time passed away since I came to town! I have been almost always in company, and they think me like them rather than become like me. I have lived too little like one of God's peculiar people. Hence come waste of time, forgetfulness of God, neglect of opportunities of usefulness, mistaken impressions of my character. Oh may I be more restrained by my rules for the future; and in the trying week upon which I am now entering, when I shall be so much in company, and give so many entertainments, may I labor doubly by a greater cultivation of a religious frame, by prayer, and by all due temperance, to get it well over.[145]

Undated, 1790

The confusion of a canvass, and the change of place, have led me lately to neglect my resolution. But self-indulgence is the root of the evil: with idleness it is my besetting sin. I pray God to enable me to resist both of them, and serve him in newness of life. How little have I thought of my deliverance the other day, when the carriage was dashed

---

141. Deuteronomy 2:7.
142. Galatians 2:20.
143. John 9:4.
144. *Life*, i. pp. 253-254.
145. Ibid., p. 257.

to pieces! How many have been killed by such accidents, and I unhurt! Oh let me endeavor to turn to Thee.[146]

I have been thinking too much of one particular failing, that of self-indulgence, whilst I have too little aimed at general reformation. It is when we desire to love God with all our hearts, and in all things to devote ourselves to his service, that we find our continual need of his help, and such incessant proofs of our own weakness, that we are kept watchful and sober, and may hope by degrees to be renewed in the spirit of our minds.[147] Oh may I be thus changed from darkness to light! Whatever reason there may be for my keeping open house in Palace Yard,[148] certain it is, that solitude and quiet are favorable to reflection and to sober-mindedness; let me therefore endeavor to secure to myself frequent seasons of uninterrupted converse with God.[149]

Thursday, May 27th. 1790

Being much in company on my birthday, and on account of Henry Thornton's illness not being able to retire and spend it in private, that anniversary passed over with too little recollection. Oh may I from this time cultivate heavenly affections by mortifying the flesh, and living much in the view of unseen things, and may the Spirit of the Lord sanctify me wholly! I have been spending much time lately with W. Hey. May I profit from the example of that excellent man.[150]

Next Week – Sunday 25th. July 25

Bus^s Letters when Eyes &c. Slave Plan. Private accounts – Eyes. Notables Eyes - Scripture perlord: Eyes. Plan of work. Vide Paper alm^l daily. Clericou &c. daily &c. Hearg or composg.

Walkg Ridg & Relax^n. Compn^y &c. Recapi: Proper Readg. Serious & Prophane. Recapi: Scripture &c.

Time: Bed 8 Hours most if well. Bed as early, & up as early as can. Dinner try not more than 2 Hours from down sittg. Bft - not more than ¾.

Selfishness: Talkg of self Thinkg of self. Sensuality - Mens: Regl. Peevishness. Truth. Laus Deo - What not receivd. Candor. 4 main Ideas – Gold. 5 Selfishness – Ease, from Pain &c. Prayer &c. Doddridge's Rules daily. Self-debatg.

---

146. In his private Diary, Wilberforce reviews the time which he had spent in this canvass, and records his narrow escape from a serious accident, when his carriage overturned in the village of Bessingby, near Bridlington, *Life*, i. p. 271.

147. Ephesians 4:23.

148. Palace Yard, or Old Palace Yard, referred to a block of houses that stood directly opposite the Sovereign's Entrance to the House of Lords in Westminster. Wilberforce lived at number 4 from 1786–1808, when Henry Thornton bought the remainder of the lease. Most of the houses were demolished in 1896, except for numbers 6-7, which are now part of the Parliamentary Estate.

149. These reflections were recorded a few days after the previous entry, *Life*, i. pp. 271-272.

150. Ibid., p. 275. The sons have here as elsewhere, combined several different entries into one, and entries covering quite a broad period as evidenced from Wilberforce's reference here to his birthday.

Bus[s] Catechisms - Historical Proposition. Roman chiefly. Autent military.

Mens. Regl - Try abstaining a Course as Health will allow for a week. Health, eat very slow - Try vegetables. Try gentle meds. No dis, Vin: 4 or 5½ with ½ witht. aqu. twiselfr: mane[151] &c. To try if figl for Beers an Hour after dinnr & with that quanty to stick permanently.[152]

Sunday, October 10th 1790, Yoxall Lodge

Time: Try 10 hours. Ser[s] MB and MB people, one day with another, except Salies oetat. Try 1¾ Dinner and 1¼ night. Up about ½ past 6, bed 10¾. Sers: Scripture daily - Prayers before Supp[r] fere. Rising & Bed going tho'ts. The serious Readg of y[e] Day. Self-Exam[n] Short, once a day. Mens. Regl: As before. Simple. Mod. No dis ferms resolv: twi. Selpmane. Enjoy good thing with grateful Heart. After every meal ask yourself how &c. Eat by eye, & seem finished, have done. No picking.

Chf. Bus Letters & accts. Slaves. Tract occasionally hints. Ser[s] Reading &c. &c: Scripture with aspiration. Practice Book. Slowly. Relax[n] Tho'ts & Conversation: Walking out &c. As on com[g] out of comp[y] Set down per notables. Recap. Readings, or per notables, or get perlord when eyes &c. Topics for talk of all kinds reading always. Set down per notables. Mind to be impressed: Love of X[t] constrains &c. Satan, but God &c. God's eye &c. Golden Rule all around: Do good to & daily ask what good &c. &c.

Faults to be chiefly watch'd: Sensuality: (by Substitution) Mens Tho'ts &c. Peevishness. Heat in argument &c. Conduct: Mature tho'ts & Conduct. Humility, with Shame. Love of God, & solacing with tho'ts of becomg holy & happy. Set down main faults &c: Set down day particulars once p[r] Day, &c. Strengthen: Sensuality mortify. Feufeuassioxinus nisalus.[153] You can give Pleasure to God, or grieve him. Recreation: Cowper.[154] Shakespeare.[155] Biography. Stewart.[156] Sers: Occasionally think of own faults, & cultivate Love of God (Barrow).[157]

---

151. Latin: in the morning.

152. MS Wilberforce c. 4, fo. 23.

153. It is uncertain exactly what Wilberforce meant here, possibly 'fire, fire ...'

154. William Cowper (1731–1800), poet and hymn-writer. The stress of appearing at the bar of the House of Lords for a possible clerkship, had a chronic impact on Cowper's mental health, resulting in attempted suicide and his being sent to a private lunatic asylum. But it was while there that through the Holy Spirit's revelation of the meaning of Romans 3:25, he experienced an evangelical conversion. He lived in Olney at the time John Newton was minister there, and after several years the two men together published a collection of their hymns known as *Olney Hymns* in 1779. Even though some of the hymns had been published individually, part of the reason for publishing a collection was that other people had been publishing the two men's hymns under their own name. In Wilberforce's personal library in Hull there is a copy of Cowper's *Poems* (1786).

155. Based simply on the quantity and variety Wilberforce mentions, the writings of William Shakespeare (c. 1564–1616), were clearly amongst some of his most favorite readings.

156. Dugald Stewart (1753–1828), FRSE FRS, Scottish philosopher, professor at Edinburgh University, and mathematician.

157. MS Wilberforce c. 4, fo. 20.

Monday, November 1st. 1790

Havg rather hurt my Health by working too hard, I must somewhat reduce my MB &c. Hours, perhaps to 9 or at the most 10, Cetera as before.[158] Minor Regls. Face fear. Eti, Regl[s.] of faults when Eyes permit. Avoid peevish or arrogant Spirit &c. Solace with God &c.[159]

Tuesday, November 9th. 1790

Heard this evening that on Sunday morning, at Bath, died what was mortal of John Thornton. He was allied to me by relationship and family connection. His character is so well known that it is scarcely necessary to attempt its delineation. It may be useful however to state, that it was by living with great simplicity of intention and conduct in the practice of a Christian life, more than by any superiority of understanding or of knowledge, that he rendered his name illustrious in the view of all the more respectable part of his contemporaries. He had a counting-house in London, and a handsome villa at Clapham.[160] He anticipated the disposition and pursuits of the succeeding generation. He devoted large sums annually to charitable purposes, especially to the promotion of the cause of religion both in his own and other countries. He assisted many clergymen, enabling them to live in comfort, and to practice a useful hospitality. His personal habits were remarkably simple. His dinner hour was two o'clock. He generally attended public worship at some church or Episcopalian chapel several evenings in the week, and would often sit up to a late hour, in his own study at the top of the house, engaged in religious exercises. He died without a groan or a struggle, and in the full view of glory. Oh may my last end be like his![161]

---

158. *Life*, i. p. 287 has amended the entry to read, 'New Testament, Psalms, slave business with Dickson and Whitaker, attacked evidence, etc. Continued to work very hard at the evidence all the week. Slept ill, not being well, partly through working too much.'

159. MS Wilberforce c. 4, fo. 21.

160. Clapham is a district of southwest London in the Boroughs of Lambeth and Wandsworth. It began as a Saxon village, and is recorded in the Domesday Book as Clopeham. By the late 1600s it became a refuge from both the Plague and the Great Fire of London, and by the 1800s had become a fashionable place for the wealthy to live, being close to London yet still retaining a rural setting. Many famous people have made Clapham their home, including Samuel Pepys (1633–1703), Benjamin Franklin, Elizabeth Cook (Captain James Cook's widow), Charles Barry (1795–1860) the architect of Parliament, and the various members who came to be known as the Clapham Circle. These included John Thornton (1720–1790); Henry Thornton (1760–1815) influential banker and M.P., of Battersea Rise on the south side of Clapham Common; John Venn (1759–1813) the minister of Clapham; the leading lawyer and M.P. James Stephen (1758–1832); Granville Sharp (1735–1815) influential barrister and chairman of the Abolition Committee; Charles Grant (1746–1823) Director of the East India Co. and M.P; Zachary Macaulay (1768–1832) a lawyer and M.P; Thomas Babington (1758–1837) M.P; William Smith (1756–1835) M.P. and as a Unitarian, the only non-evangelical; and Lord John Shore Teignmouth (1751–1834) Governor-General of India. Wilberforce also lived in Clapham until he was forced to move closer to Parliament through his failing health. The population of Clapham in 1801 was 3,864.

161. *Life*, i. pp. 283–284.

Sunday Nov[r.] 14[th.]

As to future, chiefly: Solace with God & give him pleasure. Others' Spiritual Good. Time, less sittg up night. Sensualy, fewer Heart & Practice. Humbly think of own faults. Conversat[n.] Topics readg.[162]

Sunday, December 13[th.] 1790

Sunday. Lock. Scott, 'God forbid that I should glory,' etc.[163] Thought much on it, and I hope with benefit. I have been lately tempted to vanity and pride. Many symptoms occur to my recollection. Pleased with flattery. To Pitt's, where a great circle of House of Commons chiefly on taxes, etc. Oh how foolish do they seem so to neglect heavenly things![164]

1791

Sunday, February 13[th.] 1791

Blessed be God for the Sunday. Scott, an excellent sermon, very serious thoughts. Held forth to my family as now usual on Sunday night.[165]

Monday, March 7[th.] 1791

I have lived much in company for the last fortnight, and kept late hours. My devotions have been much curtailed thereby; my business a labor to me. Never was I more busy; besides the daily examinations of the Slave Trade witnesses, there are public and private letters, county matters, etc. Pray for me that I may preserve a sober mind and a single eye[166] amidst all my distractions. I have lately heard of the deaths of many who seemed far more likely to live than I did. May these events be a warning to me. May I labor to do the work of my heavenly Father whilst it is day. My Parliamentary and London winter should now begin as from a new era. Let me press forward with renewed alacrity. May the love of Christ constrain me.[167]

Friday, August 5[th.] 1791

To be as diligent whilst here as I can be, consistently with health, and to cultivate in prayer, and reading Scripture, through the help of the Spirit of Christ, the graces of the Christian temper. It pleased God to give me this morning an affecting sense of my own sinfulness, and a determination to live henceforth, by his grace, more to his glory.

---

162. MS Wilberforce c. 4, fo. 21.
163. Galatians 6:14.
164. *Life*, i. p. 285.
165. Ibid., p. 287.
166. Matthew 6:22.
167. *Life*, i. p. 288, the second entry is undated.

Cold at first, yet moved afterwards by a sense of heavenly things, and determined to go to the important work of self-examination, and to set about a thorough change. Henceforth I purpose, by God's grace, to employ my faculties and powers more to his glory; to live a godly, diligent, useful, self-denying life. I know my own weakness, and I trust to God alone for strength.[168]

Undated, 1791

Reading. Bible, English History, Fenelon's Characters,[169] Horace, by heart. Cicero de Oratore,[170] Addison's Cato,[171] Hume,[172] Hudibras,[173] Pilgrim's Progress,[174] Doddridge's Sermons, Jonathan Edwards,[175] Owen,[176] Letters.[177]

---

168. *Life*, i. pp. 311-312.

169. François de Fénelon (1651–1715) is remembered especially for *The Adventures of Telemachus* (1699).

170. Marcus Tullius Cicero (106 B.C.–43 B.C.), Consul of the Roman Republic, remembered as one of Rome's greatest orators, as well as a poet and philosopher. Significantly influential on both the development of Latin language and literature, and also on leading Enlightenment thinkers such as John Locke, David Hume and Edmund Burke. His *Catiline Orations* mentioned here by Wilberforce, were speeches by Cicero given in 63 B.C., to expose to the Senate of Rome, the plot to overthrow the Roman government.

171. Addison's *Cato*, a play written in 1712 by Joseph Addison (1672–1719), with a prologue by Alexander Pope (1688–1744), was first performed the following year, and soon became popular internationally. Based in Roman history, the Tragedy touches on themes such as individual liberty versus government tyranny, Republicanism versus Monarchism, and maybe not surprisingly, is regarded as almost certainly playing some part in the American Revolution. Addison was an M.P., as well as an essayist and playwright, being remembered particularly for his co-founding of 'The Spectator' magazine.

172. David Hume (1711–1776), Scottish philosopher and historian, remembered especially for his influential thinking on empiricism, skepticism, naturalism and his attack on the Teleological Argument for God's existence. His writings include, *A Treatise of Human Nature* (1739–40); *Abstract of a Book lately Published* (1740); *Essays, Moral and Political* (1741–42, 1777); *A Letter from a Gentleman to his Friend in Edinburgh* (1745); *An Enquiry concerning Human Understanding* (1748, 1777); *An Enquiry concerning the Principles of Morals* (17:10, 1777); *Political Discourses* (1752, 1777); *Four Dissertations* (1757, 1777); *Essays and Treatises on Several Subjects* (1758, 1777); *Essays and Treatises on Several Subjects*, vol. 1 (1777); *Essays and Treatises on Several Subjects*, vol. 2 (1777); *My Own Life* (1777); *Of Suicide & Of the Immortality of the Soul* (1777, 1755); and *Dialogues concerning Natural Religion* (1779).

173. *Hudibras* by Samuel Butler (1613–1680), was a very popular satirical polemic upon Roundheads, Presbyterians, Puritans and many other factions involved in the English Civil War, published in three parts between 1663 and 1678. Butler was pro-Royalist and this is clearly reflected in his ridicule of the Parliamentarian side.

174. *The Pilgrim's Progress from This World to That Which Is to Come; Delivered under the Similitude of a Dream* (1678), by John Bunyan (1628–1688), a highly significant work in English literature, translated into more than 200 languages.

175. Jonathan Edwards (1703–1758), Congregational minister, revival preacher and regarded by many as the greatest philosopher America has ever produced.

176. John Owen (1616–1683), M.P., English Puritan theologian, and Vice-Chancellor of Oxford University. He has been called one of the greatest European Reformed theologians of his day, and possibly the finest theological mind that England has produced. Knowing the genre of writings Wilberforce was interested in reading, he was probably referring to Owen's *The Mortification of Sin in Believers: The 1. Necessity, 2. Nature, and 3. Means of it. With a Resolution of sundry Cases of Conscience thereunto belonging* (London, 1656). In Wilberforce's personal library, now held at the Wilberforce House Museum in Hull, there is a copy of John Owen's *Sermons* (1721).

177. *Life*, i. p. 312.

Temple Rothley[178] August 28[th.] Sundy Evg 1791

My Eyes being indifferent I cannot note down at large the particulars of my State as to Heart & L, but it may be useful thro' God's Blessing to put down a few Hints, & short mementos, to which from time to time I may recur. Alas! could I now write at large I should have only to record my own Disgrace. What advantages have I possess'd, how shamefully have I abused them. I scarce dare believe myself a Child of God, for though I don't give into many practices of worldly men, though I abstain from gross vice, how little can I say I have the renewed mind. Doddridge describes in his 3[d] Sermon on Regeneration how little of true Love to God, and Xt. O that I could say with the Psalmist, There is none upon Earth I desire in Comparison with thee.[179] Yet mercy is held forth in the Gospel to the vilest Sinner. O lead me & I will run after thee.[180] O may he who was exalted to be a Prince & a Savior, give to me Repentance, may he be made unto me Wisdom & Righteousness & Sanctification & Redemption,[181] Amen! Amen!

My besetting Sin seems to be a Volatility of mind which (like the Stony Ground Hearers) makes me soon forget & become insensible to the most serious Impressions. O may I quicken those things that are ready to die.[182] Again, I suffer much from a carnal sensual Disposition, much time is lost thro' Want of Temperance, my Health is impair'd, my Peace of Conscience disturb'd, thy Holy Spirit griev'd & the Usefulness of my Example lessen'd. I purpose here as thorough a Reform as my Health, (which absolutely requires rather an indulgent Course) will allow. Also, I have been sadly inattentive when engag'd in Study. Let me henceforth be not slothful in Business, fervent in Spirit, serving the Lord.[183] In S, may I labor henceforward, whether I eat or drink or whatever I do, to do all to the Glory of God,[184] <u>Looking unto Jesus</u>, the Author and finisher

---

178. Rothley Temple, more correctly Rothley Preceptory, was a religious establishment dating from 1231, operated by the Knights Templar and Hospitallers, in Rothley, Leicestershire. It was dissolved by Henry VIII in 1540, with the Lordship of Rothley Manor passing to the Babington family from 1565 to 1845. When Thomas Babington (1758–1837), a close friend of William Wilberforce and an active member of the Clapham Circle, inherited the estate, the two men would meet regularly at Rothley to draft their anti-slavery bill, and to analyze the Select Committee's enquiries into the slave trade. Babington also played a major part in rescuing his wife's younger brother, Zachary Macaulay (1768–1838), from the mental anguish he suffered, after having served as an overseer on a slave plantation in Jamaica. Babington would bring Macaulay to Rothley to recuperate successfully, whereupon Zachary became a Christian and an active, lifelong supporter of abolition. He would, like Wilberforce, return often to Rothley, and on one such visit in 1800, his wife gave birth to historian, poet and politician Thomas Babington Macaulay, 1st Babington Macaulay (1800–1859). A stone monument and plaque have been erected on the estate to commemorate both Rothley's and Babington's part in the abolition of slavery.

179. Psalm 73:25.

180. Song of Solomon 1:4.

181. 1 Corinthians 1:30.

182. Revelation 3:2.

183. Romans 12:11.

184. 1 Corinthians 10:31.

of our Faith.[185] O may I bc cnabled to say from my Heart, Come quickly, O L[d.] Jesus![186]

Henry Thornton returned to us from Wales. Prayed this evening with some earnestness. Religious conversation with B. he is an excellent man, and far more sober-minded than I am. [187]

Monday, August 29[th.] 1791

In pain all today. Thought too much of my sufferings, and am not thankful enough to God for all his mercy. My sister and friends kind and tender in the extreme. I find when I am ill that I cannot attend to serious things: this should be a warning to me to work whilst it is day. Oh may I still press forward! Religion is still too much a toil to me, and not enough of a delight. I am shortly going into a scene of great temptation: oh may I be preserved from infection, and so conduct myself as to glorify my Father which is in heaven.[188]

Sunday Rothley – 11[th.] Sept[r.]

Alas! Alas! I find myself no better yet hoping still to amend. My Eyes bad & therefore I cannot write: But many of the same sins & Infirmities have predominated over me since my last Record, particularly - God forgetting, & Coldness in my Affections - Sensual frame, Indolence. O may God for Xt's Sake, yet deliver me.[189]

Rothley Sunday 18[th.] Sept[r.]

(I have gone on but ill) this last week, particularly (- quoad)[190]

A. Forgetfulness of God & X[t.] & losing Sight of them particularly in compy. &c.

B. Too Sensual a Mind, & too earthly -

C. Mens: Regl: Freq[t.]

D. Inattentive in Study

E. Peevish tow[ds.] Inferiors -

F. Not kind enough to Mother & Sally[191] –

G. Not thoughtful for friends Spiritual Good, & in general too selfish

H. Vain & conceited & captious in Compy.

J. Evil Speaking –

K. Wandering in Prayer - particularly at family Devotions: & little Seriousness in reading Scripture

---

185. Hebrews 12:2.

186. Revelation 22:20.

187. *Life*, i. p. 313.

188. Matthew 5:16; *Life*, i. 313.

189. MS Wilberforce c. 40, fo. 4.

190. Latin: as.

191. Sarah (Sally) Wilberforce (1758–1816), sister of William Wilberforce, married James Stephen (1758–1832), of whom she wrote, 'Stephen is an improved and improving character, one of those whom religion has transformed and in whom it has triumphed by conquering some natural infirmities.'

L. Little or no Gratitude to God for my many Comforts, (at meals prosecution) friends &c. &c.

May God for X[ts] Sake renew me in the Spirit of my Mind. O may I learn to live by faith in the Son of God,[192] & to <u>look to Jesus</u>[193] for Wisdom & Righteousness & Sanctification & Redemption.[194] I am shortly going into a Scene of great Temptation. O may I be preserv'd from Infection, & so conduct myself as to glorify my Father which is in Heaven[195] (my Eyes but poorly I must desist).[196]

Friday, September 23[rd.] 1791

Read Witherspoon's sermon upon the World crucified to Believers,[197] and much affected by it. Oh may it be to some purpose. But how soon do good impressions evaporate! How have I been at times intoxicated by the external comforts of the scene around me, instead of feeling thankful that I am not exposed to them![198]

Sunday Night Sept[r.] 25[th.] 1791, Hamels[199]

My eyes being bad, I cannot write by Candlelight yet let me take up a Pen for one moment to record my own sad failures, Alas! Alas! how weak am I! How carnal! Tho' in Mens. Regl. I have been rather better, yet not with[t] too much thought about it, & many wandering of mind towards sensual Comforts & Indulgences. Today also I have gone to the Extreme of the Bounds of temperance too far for Sunday, too far to allow me to relish spiritual Things, and then how must I reproach myself with having fail'd last week in Nos A B E F G H J K L; & how have I been at times intoxicated by the External Comforts of the Scene around me, not feeling thankful that I am not Expos'd to them.

O may God for X[ts] Sake enable me to amend my ways, & to turn to him with my whole Heart. This Week I will endeavor by his Grace to attend particularly to the Faults noted down in the preceding page, & I go now to address him in humble prayer to strengthen my weakness by his Spirit for X[ts] Sake. Let me often review Witherspoon's fine Sermon on the believers being crucified to the World, Amen, Amen.[200]

---

192. Galatians 2:20.

193. Hebrews 12:2.

194. 1 Corinthians 1:30.

195. Matthew 5:16.

196. MS Wilberforce c. 40, fo. 5.

197. John Knox Witherspoon (1723–1794), evangelical Church of Scotland minister, President of the Presbyterian College of New Jersey in Princeton, New Jersey, and a signer of the Declaration of Independence for New Jersey. Witherspoon was a long-standing member of the Continental Congress almost continually from 1776 to 1782. He served on more committees (over 100), than any other member of that Congress. See *The Works of John Witherspoon: containing essays, sermons, &c., on important subjects, together with his lectures on moral philosophy, eloquence and divinity, his speeches in the American Congress, and many other valuable pieces, never before published in this country* (1815).

198. *Life*, i. p. 313.

199. Hamels was the Hampstead home of Robert Smith (1752–1838), 1st Baron Carrington.

200. MS Wilberforce c. 40, fo. 6.

Sunday Noon Oct[r.] 9th 1791, Forncett

My Eyes bad, I cannot write: Alas! I have but too much Reason to be dissatisfied with the Retrospect, & to resolve to press forward with renewed vigor & watchfulness. The same faults or most of them, have reigned with little Control & I have also discover'd from this Business of Williams's[201] that I am less deliver'd than I hoped from Love of the World's applause & fear of Unpopularity.

May God enable me for X[t's] Sake, to set my affections on things above[202] & have my Life hid with X[t.] in God.[203] O how apt also I am to tire in running the Race that is set before me.[204] Behav[g.] with too little Respect towards Dr. Oliver, & being too <u>polemic</u> in arguing points of Divinity & Morality with him & Bob, too little serious & humble Desire to serve them, too much Desire of Victory in Debate. Remember the Character of the Wisdom that is from above, pure, peaceable, gentle &c. &c.[205] Before and this morning much serious talk with Cookson.[206] He laments the deadness of his parish, seems truly bent on his important work. God bless and prosper him. I encourage him to persevere with renewed alacrity, and to hope for the best in God's good time. They attend him better at church than his neighbors. Spent much time in discussing with him; meaning to make only a short stay with him, and coming for this very purpose.[207]

Sunday Noon Oct[r.] 16[th.] Kings Arms Y[d.208]

I have been going on ill (this last week), too sensual, too little thought of God, or for Man. O were God no more careful of & attentive to me than I of & to him, what would become of me! I renew my pious Resolutions and by the Help of his Spirit in & thro' X[t.] Jesus, I hope yet to amend. Let me endeavor to strengthen the main Principle. In nature the Tree good, & his fruit Good.[209] My most marked failures have been in Losing[210] Sight of God & X[t.], Languid Devotions, Sensuality & Selfishness, Gratitude at meals,[211] little tho't for others, too much Regard for worldly praise. Inattention in Study. Vanity &c.[212]

---

201. The lack of specific source information makes it difficult to identify with certainty, the particular issue Wilberforce here refers to.

202. Colossians 3:2.

203. Colossians 3:3.

204. Hebrews 12:1.

205. James 3:17.

206. Rev. Dr William Cookson (1754–1820), Anglican Rector of Forncett, Norfolk (1788–1804) and Canon of Windsor (1792–1820). His sister Anne was the mother of William Wordsworth.

207. *Life*, i. p. 315.

208. Wilberforce occasionally stayed at 6, King's Arms Yard, London, the home of John Thornton and his sons, Samuel and Henry. Another abolitionist and lawyer, Sir George Stephen (1794–1879), who was also a witness to a Copy lease and marriage settlement and abstract of the settlement relating to property of Wilberforce in May 1797, lived at 17, King's Arms Yard.

209. Matthew 12:33.

210. In left margin is written, 'Faults'.

211. '_____ at meals' inserted here in left margin.

212. MS Wilberforce c. 40, fo. 7.

Sunday Oct[r.] 30[th.] Yoxall Lodge

Alas! Alas! how little satisfactory is the Review of my past Time, Even here, when so many Advantages so few Temptations, yet let me not slacken in my Exertions nor despair of Help from above - By <u>Grace</u> we are saved - God of his great Mercy, even when we were dead in Sins, hath quicken'd us together with X[t] &c.[213] This only is my Hope! & relying on this, I will still struggle with my Corruptions. O that I were <u>really</u> more desirous of Victory. My Eyes bad, so I can't write - my faults the same as before, &c.[214]

Sunday Nov[r.] 6[th.] Yoxall Lodge

My Eyes indiff[f.] & therefore cannot write (no time between Church & dinner, & soon dark when come home after Church aftn). But alas! much Reason for deep Humiliation on the Review of the last week, yet I renew my Resolves, praesertim,[215] meaning thro' X[ts] help to labor after.God:

1. Sense of God's Presence & X[t's.] & redeem'd with a Price so not our own &c.[216] <u>Looking to Jesus</u>[217] internal.

Self:

2. Less Volatility & more internal Self Possession in Company with gay Exterior - Conversation Regls - rat[l.] & improvg.

3. More Gratitude at meals & when enjoying other Comforts; Mind friends, recreational conveniences &c.

4. More fixedness in Devotion, (family) readg Scripture - & Self Examin[n.] by these Reg.

5. Mens: Regls: Try a plan of greater temp[ce.] (yet so as not to injure Health) both in food & ferms & in genl. less Sensual in tho't & act - little Self Denials with[t] much tho't.

6. Less Vanity & Captiousness in Compy others.

7. Evil Speaking care -

8. Kinder & more respectful to mater & Sali -

9. Kindness & Mildness to Inferiors

10. Concern for friends Spiritual Good; think for each of them –

11. General Kindness & Mildness

12. Truth strictly to be observed.

O may God for X[t's] Sake enable me to serve him from a genuine principle of evangelical obedience. May I walk worthy of him who hath call'd me to his Kingdom & Glory,[218] & quickening those things

---

213. Ephesians 2:5.
214. MS Wilberforce c. 40, fo. 8.
215. Latin: chiefly.
216. 1 Corinthians 6:20.
217. Hebrews 12:2.
218. Colossians 1:10-13.

that are ready to die,[219] may I press towards the mark &c. &c.[220] Amen - Mondy chiefly fail'd.[221]

Sunday 13th. Novr.

I thank God that for the most part I was much impressed with a sense of serious things, and resolved anew; yet how weak am I in performance! May God, for Christ's sake, enable me to serve him from a genuine principle of evangelical obedience. I will labor after a sense of God's presence, and a remembrance that I have been redeemed, and so am not my own.[222] More fixedness in devotion, reading Scripture, and self-examination, greater self-restraint in lawful things, both in thought and act. Little secret self-denials, without much thought. More real gratitude to God at meals, and when enjoying other comforts, kind friends, and all external conveniences.

In company, rational conversation and innocent mirth. Topics prepared, what good can I do or get, draw out others when I can without feeding their vanity, above all aim at their spiritual good, think for each of them. Truth to be observed strictly. General kindness and mildness, especially towards inferiors, beware of vanity and evil speaking. Frequent aspirations in solitary relaxation, recapitulate or revolve topics, or at least avoid rambling, wandering thoughts. In everything, according to its measure, you may please or displease God.[223] Though the Retrospect fills me with Shame, yet I fly for Refuge to Xt. I reresolve & see that all but God's favor is but loss in comparison - Eyes bad.[224]

Sunday 20th. Novr. Yoxall Lodge

The last Week affords me much Cause for deep Humiliation. O blessed be God for his Kindness in giving these Seasons of Recollection. I am all unclean! There is no Health in me,[225] yet "Arise & wash away thy Sins calling on the name of the Lord,"[226] & "Seek those things that are above &c. &c."[227] What Reason have I to be thankful also for those many comforts that surround me. O may I at length awake to Righteousness,[228] & press forward in earnest! Two & thirty years & 3 months of my Life are now past, & that is equivalent to 5 & 40 years of a strong man - It is high time to awake &c. Look to Jesus![229]

---

219. Revelation 3:2.
220. Philippians 3:14.
221. MS Wilberforce c. 40, fos. 8-9.
222. 1 Corinthians 6:20.
223. Life, i. pp. 317-318.
224. MS Wilberforce c. 40, fo. 9.
225. Psalm 38:3.
226. Acts 22:16.
227. Colossians 3:1.
228. 1 Corinthians 15:34.
229. Hebrews 12:2.

I have been reading Sir M^w. Hale's[230] *Life*, What a man was he! & why might not I love God as well & <u>render</u> to X^t. as gratefully (Look not to man's applause[231] & remember God seeth the heart[232]). Williams's Incident teaches me how much I am a slave to the opinion of the world - may it teach me to glory only in y^e. Cross of X^t.[233] For the ensuing week attend to,

1. Heavenly Mindedness & seeing God in & thro' X^t.
2. Mens: Regl: & meal Cond^t. Gratitude &c. Monday baddish
3. Compy Regl - Monday bad
4. Truth Strictness.
5. Mildness & Kindness My bad -
6. Conversatn. Regl - My forgot.
7. Diligence & Bus^s. Regl: settling beforehand.
8. Aspirations - My – bad -
9. Humility - My – bad –

Fail'd in all, this last week – Oimoi - 27th Nov. particy. 2, 3, 5, 9.[234]

Sunday, November 27th. 1791

Sunday. Cold at first rising, afterwards earnest – serious thoughts and fervent prayer; and now I most seriously resolve to turn to God with my whole heart. I have been reading Doddridge's *Life*.[235] What a wonderful man! Yet I may apply to the same Savior. I propose henceforth to try at eleven hours of all sorts of business one day with another whilst in the country; nine hours of which to be exclusive of 'serious'.[236]

Sunday 27th. Novr. Yoxall Lodge

My Eyes are too indiff^t to allow me to write, or I should rather largely. Last week has gone on but little better than preceding ones if at all, & much in Reliance on God's Help thro' X^t. by his Spirit, reresolve the above Resolutions & add to them:

10. Friends Spiritual Good.
11 Selfishness –
12. Golden Rule –

---

230. Sir Mathew Hale (1609–1676), M.P., Chief Baron of the Exchequer and later, Lord Chief Justice of England and writer. A close friend of Richard Baxter, he is remembered especially for his integrity, and for his *The History of the Pleas of the Crown*. See Gilbert Burnet, *The Life and Death of Sir Mathew Hale, Knt.* (1682).

231. Galatians 1:10.

232. 1 Samuel 16:7.

233. Galatians 6:14.

234. MS Wilberforce c. 40, fos. 10–11.

235. See for example, *Memoirs of the Life, Character and Writings Of the late Reverend Philip Doddridge , D.D. of Northampton* (Salop, 1766, 2nd ed.).

236. *Life*, i. p. 319.

13. <u>Devotion</u> & Self Exam[n]

I will particularly attend this week to 1, 2, 3, 4, 5, 6, 7, 8, 9, 10, 11, 12, & 13.

I have been reading Doddridge's *Life*. What a man he was, yet X[t.] is the <u>same</u> yesterday, today & forever.[237] O may I be enabled to press forward. I mean to try if (Health being attended to, & living pretty well) I cannot contrive to get one day with another 10 ½ Hours of all sorts. The night cometh. My Eyes prevent my creating a design I had of forming a list of duties faults, friends &c. &c. but alas! I have lain apt to lay too much Stress on those things; yet let me now set down a few notes for Self-examination on loose paper that I may carry it about &c. &c. 27th. Nov[r.238]

Yoxall Lodge 4[th.] Dec[r.] 1791 - Sunday

It has pleased God to visit me with a most trying Embarrassment of a most delicate kind. O may I be enabled to Conduct myself in it in a manner becoming my high & holy calling. I think I can say I desire this & I pray to God in X[t.] for Help & Succour.[239]

Sunday Aftn -

Alas! Alas! This whole week & this Day, this blessed & spiritual Day also I have been giving Way to my habitual Propensity to Excess at table; & perhaps my constant failure here may have caused God to hide his face, to withdraw his preventing Spirit, & renewing grace from me! I desire to humble myself throughout '<u>for there is no Health in me</u>"[240] – "<u>any little Fruit of Holiness God knoweth</u> & <u>I record it as my fix'd opinion</u> it is all unsound, yet O X[t.] have mercy upon me. Enable me to repent of all my evil ways, & "putting on the Breastplate of faith & love, & for an Helmet the Hope of Salvation,"[241] may I thro' God's Grace conquer all my Spiritual Enemies. Res[n.] I here, humbly, & conscious of my own Weakness (but he is strong) I here resolve to begin once more a Life of Holiness to the Lord, rememberg it is that to which he hath called us & not to Uncleanness.[242]

Let me during the ensuing week particularly attend to the Duties & failings before noted down & be more particularly watchful ~~against~~ ab[t.] Sensuality & Selfishness <u>Mens: Regl</u> &c. Comp[y] Regl. Conv[n] &c. Heavenly-mindedness, volatility, aspirations &c. Friends' &c. spirit[l] Good. Doddridge's Day Rules, mainly. Bo't with a Price.[243] Humility. Vanity & captiousness.[244]

---

237. Hebrews 13:8.
238. MS Wilberforce c. 40, fos. 11-12.
239. MS Wilberforce c. 40, fo. 12.
240. Psalm 38:3
241. 1 Thessalonians 5:8.
242. 1 Thessalonians 4:7.
243. 1 Corinthians 6:20.
244. MS Wilberforce c. 40, fo. 13.

Sunday Evening, December 4th 1791

I have been too inattentive to the Duties of Charity &c. & by God's Help will attend more to them.[245]

Sunday 18th Dec[r] 1791, King's Arms Yard
Sunday 11th at Wilford

O what Cause have I to praise the Long Suffering & forbearance of God, & to deplore my own exceeding Unworthiness. Being call'd suddenly away from the Lodge (<u>perhaps by the preventing grace of God</u> vide) I have not consider'd my Plan of Life for y[e] Winter, as I meant to do before I came to London or its neighborhood, but I will do so soon. Meanwhile may God for X[ts] Sake pardon all that is past, & enable me henceforth to walk in newness of Life, <u>looking unto Jesus</u>,[246] <u>& relying on his Help</u>.

In addition to my former principal Cares & objects, let me now put down: Avoidg Self-Debatings &c. Reliance on God's protection. Making y[e] most of my peculiar advantages. My Eyes are very indiff[t] or I Should write more. Grant[247] & Henry both ag[st] Resolutions, I believe they are right, let me try rather to Strengthen in me those things that are ready to die,[248] yet observg Of Resolutions those Rules, <u>in the main</u>, which I have made but not <u>thinking much on them</u> but on - The love of X[t] constraineth us &c.[249]

Sunday Night, December 18th 1791

This very day having fasted for dinner till rained, I exceeded needed temperance so as not to enjoy Newton's Evg Sermon, violate purity of Conscience &c. I am now cold & heartless. This has been on the whole but a very poor Sunday with me. God Help me to amend.[250]

1792

Sunday Jany 1st 1792 Palace Yard

Return'd Home today havg been at H. Thornton's Kgs Arms Yd for a fortnight. O with what Shame & Sorrow ought I to be fill'd on looking back over the last year, & how little do I now find myself in the State of a true & lively Xtian. My Eyes are indiff[t] so I will not injure them by writing, but deeply humbling myself for all that is past, will repair to the

---

245. Ibid.

246. Hebrews 12:2.

247. Charles Grant (1746–1823), M.P. and Chairman of the Directors of the East India Company. After the deaths of two children to smallpox, Grant was converted to evangelical Christianity, and lived for a time in a house on Henry Thornton's estate at Battersea Rise. Grant was very active in the work of the Clapham Circle, working with them, to have a 'Missionary Clause' inserted into the Company's Charter renewal in 1813.

248. Revelation 3:2.

249. 2 Corinthians 5:14. MS Wilberforce c. 40, fos. 14-15.

250. MS Wilberforce c. 40, fo. 15.

Throne of Grace for mercy & forgiveness. O spare me, sparc me. I have been receivg the Sacrament & I desire now to be enabled to purpose steadfastly to lead a new Life &c.

I have been in a Hurry of Business since I have been in Town, indulging Sensual Inclin[ns] & Mens: Reg. Infractions constantly. Short & cold and wandering Devotions &c. & I am now in a sad frame of settled Stupidity, yet I feel in some Degree my miserable Condition, & tho' I am convinc'd by abundant Experience that in myself is no Health or Strength, yet I would hope that even I may look to him who is able to save to the Uttermost.[251] I come like the Returng Prodigal, Father &c. I am not worthy[252] yet receive me accordg to thy Mercy. I am sure that all my Resolutions with[t] his Help must be vain, yet relying on it & laboring to Strengthen the main principle (tis here I have been most deficient) I will also strive to keep such Mens: & other Regls. as seen in my Situation to be proper to adhere to, but not trusting to them nor being too strict about them. God help me for X[ts] Sake.[253]

Jany 4[th.] 1792

I thank God I have been in rather a more watchful Sober frame of mind[254] than for some time past. I pray God it may continue. O how much Room still for more Watchfulness. Yet I trust that I am mending. I feel my own Weakness daily & proneness to fall. I yesterdy mens: forg[t.] des. & exced. Ferms, yet I trust saw rather in a mending way. It seems to assist that whilst in y[e.] streets I expect & then contre with W.[255]

Sunday Jany 8[th.] 1792 Palace Yard

I have been hearing a most excellent Sermon at the Lock from Mr. Scott on Procrastination. I was yesterday & this morng very cold & sluggish & declining in spiritual affections & views but I hope this discourse has warm'd me &c. O may I be enabled to put in practice these most important admonitions. My Eyes are indiff[t] & I must desist. I have much Cause for Humiliation in y[e.] last week, fail'd as to mens: Regl. &c. yet I think I go on better in my own House than at Henry's from more quiet &c. & I humbly resolve to press forward & to apply diligently & perseveringly to the Throne of Grace, that X[t.] my be made unto me Wisdom & Righteousness & Sanctification & Strength.[256]

---

251. Hebrews 7:25.

252. Luke 15:19.

253. MS Wilberforce c. 40, fos. 15-17. *Life*, i. p. 325 has, 'Came to Palace Yard today, having been at H. Thornton's, King's Arms Yard a fortnight. A better Sunday than some past. I trust that I have been sincerely affected. Cecil's in the evening, and went over the sermon afterwards to my family. I have been today receiving the sacrament, and looking back upon the last year, and I desire now to be enabled to purpose steadfastly to lead a new life. I have been in a hurry of business since I came to town, and short in my devotions. All my resolutions for the future must be vain without the help of God; yet relying on it; and laboring to strengthen the main principle, I will strive to keep such rules as seem proper in my situation.'

254. 'Of mind' published here in entry dated, January 4th, 1792 in *Life*, i. pp. 325-326.

255. MS Wilberforce c. 40, fo. 17.

256. 1 Corinthians 1:30; MS Wilberforce c. 40, fo. 17. *Life*, i. p. 326 has, 'I have been hearing a most excellent sermon from Mr. Scott on procrastination I was very cold and sluggish in spiritual

Sunday Evg Jany 15th. 1792

The last week has gone on worse than the preceding one. I din'd out in Compy at Home every day but Monday, & always rather exceeded, sometimes greatly particularly in ferms. I have Reason to adore the Goodness of God in letting me see my Evil ways, & not hardening my Heart. O may I be enabled to turn to him with my whole Soul, & to devote myself altogether to his Service, laboring to adorn the Gospel &c.[257] If this public Company keepg Life cannot be made consistent with a heavenly frame of Mind (owing to my extreme weakness) I should think I ought to retire more. But let me strive agst. my Corruptions more, & particularly not straiten Prayer before God. Both my Body & my mind have suffer'd from my last week's operations. My chief faults have been all those to which I am particularly prone (vide Paper) together with in general, Forgetfulness of God's Rules, of Xt. Devotions shorten'd &c. Oimoi. O may I endeavor in God's Strength to quicken those things that are ready to die[258] & labor after universal Holiness, Amen.

Let me Particularly attend to Seriousness of Mind under Gaiety:

1. God's Eye & Consciousness.
2. God & Xt. frequent aspiratns.
3. Diligence & attention in Study, work &c.
4. Devotions more serious &c. -
5. Temperance – Meals Gratitude &c. -
6.. Humility
7. Meekness & Kindness -
8. Steadiness of Mind, no Self-debatings
9. No Trifling Thots indulg -
10. Regls observg – conary Bus: Recr. &c. &c. Compy -
11. Friends spiritual good -
12. Truth, & avoidg Evil Speakg - Pleasure in Religion.

I have been exceedingly idle this last week, have trifled over my Work &c. & by way of keepg this in my view, I will renew my account of time. O how should I condemn in another, & him a professing Xtian, all the Idleness Unprofitableness Ungodliness Sensuality Selfishness Hardness of Heart &c. of which I am conscious. God be merciful to me a Sinner![259] Let me not deceive myself by believg what others say

---

affections both yesterday and this morning but I hope this discourse has roused me may I be enabled to put in practice these most important admonitions I have cause for humiliation in the past week yet I think go on better in my own house than in Henry Thornton's from having more quiet and I humbly to press forward and apply diligently to the throne of grace that Christ may be made to me wisdom righteousness and sanctification and redemption.'

257. Titus 2:10.
258. Revelation 3:2.
259. Luke 18:13.

118

of me, who know not my Heart or see really into my Conduct. O that
I were in Harriet's[260] state.[261]

Tuesday Evg 17[th.] Jany

Yesterday I did rather better than sometimes but today I have most
foolishly & unprovokedly been offendg ag[t.] the Rules of temperance,
whence I am now feeling indiff[t.] in Body & Soul griev'd & asham'd
in mind. God Help me. It is not in this Particular only, but in all that
I have been offendg. Alas! Alas! Forgetfulness of God & want of due
Faith & Love are the foundations of y[e.] Evil. O let me strengthen those
things that are ready to die,[262] ere it be too late.[263]

Undated, 1792

Both my body and mind suffer from over-occupation. My heart is now
in a cold and senseless state, and I have reason to adore the goodness of
God in not hardening me. I have been short, and cold, and wandering
in private devotions. Habit and the grace of God preventing me have
kept me in a decent observance of external duties, but all within is
overgrown with weeds, and every truly Christian grace well-nigh
choked. Yet, O Thou all-merciful Father, and Thou Saviour of sinners,
receive me yet again, and supply me with strength.

Oh let me now quicken the things that are ready to die![264] My
worldly connections certainly draw me into temptations great and
innumerable, yet I dare not withdraw from a station in which God
has placed me. Still let me deal honestly with myself in this matter,
and if, on further trial, I find reason to believe I ought to lead a more
sequestered life, may I not dread the imputation of singularity. If
from my extreme weakness this public company-keeping life cannot
be made consistent with a heavenly frame of mind, I think I ought
to retire more. Herein and in all things may God direct me; but let
me strive more against my corruptions, and particularly not straiten
prayer. I find myself confiding in my resolutions; let me universally
distrust myself, but let me throw myself at the feet of Christ as an
undone creature, distrusting yea despairing of myself, but firmly
relying upon him. 'Him that cometh unto Me I will in no wise cast
out.'[265] 'They that wait on the Lord shall renew their strength.'[266]

Sunday Night 22[d.] Jany

The last week has been a sad one. Mens: Regls. Freq: & all of them
little attended to. I have been extremely affected by Miss More's account

---

260. Harriet Bird.
261. MS Wilberforce c. 40, fos. 18-19.
262. Revelation 3:2.
263. MS Wilberforce c. 40, fo. 20.
264. Revelation 3:2.
265. John 6:37.
266. Isaiah 40:31; *Life*, i. pp. 328-329.

of Harriet's Death bed scene, as how can I but be so, particularly her Illumination, & the followg Agony, just before she was taken into Glory. I have felt these things I would humbly hope, not in vain. She prayed for me on her Death Bed. O what a Wretch have I been like to! How does her Progress shame me. I am behind, back behind, all of them. My Eyes compel me to desist. May God for X$^{t's}$ Sake cause my Tears not to flow in vain. I fly to him for pardon, pleadg the Blood of Jesus. Amen.[267]

Sunday Night 5$^{th.}$ Feby. Palace Yard

The last 10 or 12 days, particularly the last week, have gone on sadly, Oimoi, & my Heart is now in a sad cold senseless frame. My practice has been Universally bad. Mens. Regls. Forgot. Compy d$^{o.}$ & all others D$^{o.}$ Time fritter'd away &c. &c. I observe what Doddridge says, laying the foundation of these spiritual decays in closet duties omission, Breach, & tis most true that I have of late been sadly negligent in private devotions, sometimes scarce any at night, & in the morng, short & cold. O let me now quicken the things that are ready to die &c.[268] as Owen well says (mortification stinks).[269] The cure must be radical, the war universal. X$^{t.}$ must dwell in the Heart by faith. Let me endeavor more to turn to God in X$^{t.}$ & labor to be made a new Creature.[270]

Sunday 12$^{th.}$ Feby 2 oClock – PalYd

The last week has gone on little if for the last two or three days, at all better than preceding ones. Yesterday & the day before, dining out, I found too much Reason to believe from what pass'd, that I am not consider'd as one who has resolv'd to live no longer to the Lusts of the flesh but to the Will of God.[271] Even Lady St. John[272] seemed ignorant I had assum'd a new Character. This surely strongly at least confirms what Milner told me, that it was thought I had once a turn to Methodism,

---

267. MS Wilberforce c. 40, fo. 20. *Life*, i. p. 329 has, 'Saw the astonishing letter from Miss More containing an account written inter moriendum of Harriet Bird's death at six o clock on Wednesday morning. Oh may my latter end be like hers. Strongly affected may it be deeply. I have been extremely affected by Miss More's account of Harriet's death bed scene how can I but be so particularly her illumination and the following agony just before she was taken to glory. I have felt these things I humbly hope not in vain. She prayed for me on her death bed. How does her progress shame me. I am behind far behind all of them. But my eyes will not allow me to write, many tears to day from mental struggles have injured them. May God for Christ's sake cause them not to flow in vain. I fly to Him for pardon pleading the blood of Jesus. Though I almost despair yet Christ is mighty to save. I have been looking over letters written to me by Milner Pitt &c. when I first entered upon a religious profession. How little have I corresponded to the outset. Yet it is not too late. But I am apt to take comfort after writing thus as though the business was done. Let me dismiss all vain confidence and build upon the sure foundation.'

268. Revelation 3:2.

269. The work Wilberforce here refers to was John Owen's *Of the Mortification of Sin in Believers* (London, 1656).

270. MS Wilberforce c. 40, fos. 20-21.

271. 1 Peter 4:2.

272. Lady St. John here probably refers to Susanne Louise Simond, the daughter of Peter Simond and Susanne Groteste de la Buffiere. She married John St. John, 12th Baron St. John of Bletso, son of John St. John, 11th Baron Saint John of Bletso and Elizabeth Crowley, on 13 December, 1755, and from that date her married name became St. John.

but was now come round again, & tho' a decent moral man, was no wise particular in my notions or over rigid - X^t· says thro' his Apostle, Be not conformed to this world.[273] O do thou teach me the true limits of Conformity to the World, O change my Heart that I may in deed & in Truth not in word only, be a Xtian. I seem to myself much like Dr. Johnson, resolving & resolving & all to no purpose. I yield daily to my Lusts & evil affections when the moment of Temptation arrives, I forget my Resolutions, & lose all Sense of the Presence of God. O let me probe the wound to the Bottom. Let me come anew to Jesus, & strengthen the foundation. Tis this alone, can enable me to reform, & I here humbly pray to be enabled to believe in him, to follow him, to take him for my Prophet, Priest & King, to devote myself to his Service, & to live henceforth to his glory. I find I have all to begin again, yet let me not despair tho' I have been so sad a Backslider, The invitation is general. Ho! Every one that thirsteth &c. &c.[274] X^t· is able to save to the Uttermost &c. &c.[275] At this moment I find myself ready to grow indolent & dull & inactive, but may God for X$^{t's}$ Sake & thro' his Spirit stir me up & quicken me.

Laboring therefore to look to Jesus as the Alpha & Omega, the Beginner & Finisher of our faith.[276] Let me strive ag$^{st·}$ my besettg Sins with more Vigor, & rely on his Help if I steadily watch & pray for it: Volatility & forgettg Resoluts. Forgetfulness of God & Self-Dependence. Intemperance & Indolence. Vanity, & Pride & Love of applause. Too little thought for others, spiritual good protection. Inattention in & to Business. God help me to amend radically, really to find my Joy & Comfort & delight in him, really to love him & seek his face. Above all, neglect of private devotions, & careless readg of Scripture.[277]

Sunday Night Feby 19$^{th·}$ Palace Yard

Alas. Alas! How little have all my Resolutions been remember'd during the last week, & how like has it gone on to the preceding. My Plan however was the right one. Nothing but X^t· I will pray to be enabled to do better in future. The insincerity of my Heart has been shamefully evinced to me today, when I can hardly bring myself to resolve to do my duty & please God at the Expence (if, as I suspect it will turn out on consideration) of my cordiality with Pitt or rather his with me, my worldly good & Popularity &c &c But my Eyes will not allow me to write, many tears today from mental struggles &c have injur'd them.

I must go on with my Plan, tho' I almost despair, yet X^t· is mighty to save to the Uttermost.[278] I have been looking over Letters written to me by Milner, Pitt &c. when I first enter'd on a Religious Profession.

---

273. Romans 12:2.
274. Isaiah 55:1.
275. Hebrews 7:25.
276. Hebrews 12:2.
277. MS Wilberforce c. 40, fo. 21.
278. Hebrews 7:25.

How little have I corresponded & Habitual, the truth seems to be that like Halyburton,[279] whose Life I am reading. I was in some degree wounded by Sin, but had not a true holy hatred of it, & never really fled to Christ as my only Hope & Refuge, & sincerely gave him my whole Heart. O may I do so now. It is not yet too late, but I am apt to take Comfort after writing this as tho' the Business was done. Let me dismiss all vain Confidences & build on the sure foundation, the Rock of ages. Amen.[280]

Sunday 26th· Feby 1792, Clapham

Alas! Alas! In what a State do I find myself: I have a Name to live, but in Truth I am dead,[281] except in refraining from gross internal acts of Vice, & from these a Sense of Consistency would preserve me. I differ but little from the worldly & profane. No love to God & X[t·] No delight in his Ordinances or Service, no sense of the Perfections of his Character or desire to imitate them. Little or no thought ab[t] him, alas, alas. Sensual, Indolent, Selfish, negligent of friends good, Morose, Tyrannical. I yield on the first occurrence of temptatns, particularly my habit[l] Sensuality Mens: & volatility, whenever they occur. The only thing that affords me any Comfort is that I see my wretched State, & am thoroughly resolv'd by divine Grace to make a vigorous effort to escape. The effort must be universal. I have of late been particularly negligent wandering, formal &c. in respect of private Prayer. Let me here mainly apply the Exertions. Watch & pray. God may punish my Carelessness herein by suffering me to fall a prey to my Mens: Lusts &c. &c. whereby my Health, Time, Talents &c. are so squander'd away. O may he enable me to cast myself on the mercy of X[t·] desiring to forsake my Sins thro' his Grace, & to obtain from his fulness, Wisdom, Righteousness, Sanctification.[282]

O what a Hypocrite am I. O if the world knew me as God knows me, how little could I bear the face of men: yet Blessed be the forbearance & longsuffering of God who still allows me space for Repentance. X[t·] is able to save to the Uttermost.[283] Things are come to a point with me, I must now break the chain of my lusts or I shall be bound for ever. May God for X[t's] Sake support me in this hard conflict, & havg been so long mensa nominal, may I now be a real Xtian. My Worldly Connections certainly draw me into Temptations great & innumerable, yet I find myself givg into Sin, alone & in my Chamber, if less in act, yet in affections & I dare not withdraw from a Station wherein God has placed me, yet let me deal honestly with myself in this matter, & if in another trial I find Reason to

---

279. Thomas Halyburton (1674–1712), Scottish divine, Professor of Divinity in St. Andrews and remembered especially for his richly theological, deeply experimental and yet very practical writings. See his autobiography, *Memoirs of the Life of the Reverend, Learned and Pious Mr. Thomas Halyburton* (Edinburgh, 1715).

280. MS Wilberforce c. 40, fos. 23-24.

281. Revelation 3:1.

282. 1 Corinthians 1:30.

283. Hebrews 7:25.

believe I ought to lead a more sequester'd life may I be supported so as not to dread the Imputation of Singularity. Herein & in all things may God direct me like Halyburton.

I find myself confiding in my Resolutions &c. &c. Let me universally distrust myself. But let me throw myself at the feet of X[t.] as an undone Guilty Creature, believing his declaration, He that comes to me I will in no wise cast out. This is the main, as assistant means I purpose by divine Grace: More attention to Secret Devotions. More sense of God's & X[t's] Presence. Less Volatility. Mortify y[e.] flesh, Mens. Regls. &c. &c. Meal times Gratitude &c. &c. Compy & Conversat[n.] Regl. Others' spiritual good. Less Peevishness, Selfishness &c. & more meek & kind & forgiving in <u>Heart</u>. Self-Diffidence & Reliance on X[t.] Scott's Regl. & Doddridge's Plan. God for X[t's] Sake strengthen me, I proceed to pray for help: Humility from Sense of past miscarriages. Self-Examination has been quite neglected, I now purpose to practice it daily, & as being necessary to secure me quiet Hours of devotion &c. I purpose to try at Earlier Hours.[284]

Sunday Noon Clapham March 4[th.] 1792

I have gone on but little better if at all this last week than before, yet I am sure there is no other way, & by God's Grace I hope to be yet enabled to conquer in some measure my Corruptions, & be in some degree conform'd to his Image. My Eyes being very indiff[t.] I cannot write. Lord save me, I perish.[285] The fear of the Lord is the Beginng of Wisdom,[286] this leads to a discovery of our own Vileness, Indigence & Weakness, which drives us to X[t.] & there only can we find Peace & Holiness.[287]

Sunday Night, March 11[th.] 1792, Palace Yard

My eyes bad, therefore I cannot write. Last week has gone on no better, or at least but little. O may I amend! I have chiefly offended as before in a general failure of Spiritual frame, & in yielding to the temptations to my besettg Sins which have occurr'd to me, neglect of devotions &c. &c. O may I know reform & repent thoroughly. My great Business is coming on again, may God enable me to be animated in the Performance of it by a sincere Love of him & desire to promote his Glory.[288]

Sunday Night 18[th.] March 1792 Clapham

I have not amended my ways, or kept my Heart since my last recording. But all has gone wrong with me. The main has been alienation of Heart from God, & Deadness of Spiritual Things, but this has prepar'd the way for my givg into every Temptation that has presented itself, more particularly my besetting Sin, Sensuality. Yesterday havg Company I

---

284. MS Wilberforce c. 40, fo. 27.
285. Matthew 14:30.
286. Proverbs 9:10.
287. MS Wilberforce c. 40, fo. 27.
288. MS Wilberforce c. 40, fo. 28.

fell insensibly, I scarce know how, into intemperance, & my devotions today have been cut out by wandering thoughts &c. & foolish idle Self-debatings, Oimoi. Let me pray to God thro' X^t· to renew me in the Spirit of my mind that only can be effectual. I will strive to press forward. I heard the alternative is eternal misery.[289]

Good Friday Night, April 6$^{th.}$ 1792, Palace Yard

Eyes too weak to allow of night writing therefore but one Word. O how much have I been trying the forbearance & Long suffering of God, every Day receivg fresh Instances of his Bounty, yet every day falling into a State of greater aversation from him neglecting devotions, indulging in Excesses, forgetting him altogether sometimes, & almost livg without him in the World. Excessive flurries of Business & seeking for Refreshment from these not in the Enjoyment of his presence but in sensual Indulgences. And today how sadly have I squander'd away a golden opportunity in as extreme a Self-debating humor (ab^t· whether I should stay in Town or go to Clapham) as I ever before gave into. In this Season of solemn Recollection, let me look into my Heart & consider my Ways, & pray to God to enable me to repent & forsake my Sins & bring forth fruits meet for Repentce, & as with my Piety, all Zeal for the good or Happiness of others has gone off. O let me be watchful & quicken those things that are ready to die.[290] Let me strive to go to the Root of the Evil & mend first there, make the Tree good & his fruit good &c.[291]

In particular let me attend to: my Secret devotions & Self Exam^n· Sense of God's Presence &c. Love of X^t constraining. Mortify flesh & mealtimes Gratitude. Company & Conversation Regls. Others' spiritual good. Less Peevishness &c. & mildness to all. Truth stricter. Make God your Delight & Solace. Mortify Vanity & cultiva$^{te.}$ Humility. Live above y^e· World. Self-debatg cure.[292]

Easter Sunday, April 8$^{th.}$ 1792, R^t· Thornton's[293] Clapham

Yesterday I most foolishly wasted the whole morning by my self-debatg weakness, & at dinner broke Mens: Regl. & was every way to blame, & today I have been little alive to spiritual Things. My mind has been running over worldly ones & taking up with a name instead of the Substance of Religion. Thinking ab^t· where to find myself &c. &c. in moments of true worship &c. My devotions both at night & morng (as they have been for some time) most indistinct & vague. In short, I am in a sad State altogether. I have a name to live whilst in fact I am altogether dead.[294] O let me quicken those things that are ready to die.[295] With me, all has gone together. Seeking the

289. Ibid.
290. Revelation 3:2.
291. Matthew 12:33.
292. MS Wilberforce c. 40, fos. 29-30.
293. Robert Thornton (1759–1826), M.P. and Director of the East India Company.
294. Revelation 3:1.
295. Revelation 3:2.

favor & looking for the presence of God, Self-denial or even moderation in myself, & active Zeal for the good of my fellow-creatures. Habit &c. &c. & the Grace of God ever preventing us tho' long & much abus'd, have kept me in a decent observance of worldly & exterior duties, but all within is overgrown with Weeds & Thorns & Briars & every truly Christian Grace & Temper is choked & destroyed.

But O, thou all-merciful Father & thou Saviour of Sinners, receive me yet again, & supply me with Strength & power & ability. I am weak, but thou art Strong. O protect me from the Wiles of Satan & the Corruptions of my own Heart & may I yet live to experience in myself the Efficacy of thy renewing Grace, & to adorn in the sight of others, the Gospel of God, my Saviour in all things.[296] Watch & Pray[297] as for particular Sins &c. to be avoided, vide my Bodily passion. God help me for X^{t's} Sake.[298]

Sunday Afternoon, April 15th. 1792, Palace Yard
Alas! Alas! I have gone on ill indeed this week. Perhaps a little more attentive to my devotions, but yet little thinking of God's Presence & favor. Not mortifying flesh but Mens: excds. & that even today, when no Temptation. Compy & Convers^{n.} Regl. & friends Good forgot, & this morng sadly a Prey to Self-debatg, Oimoi, Oimoi. My Eyes are bad from dust I must therefore lay aside my Pen. But tho' with a cold dead Heart, I will proceed to pray for more Grace & Strength & tho this next fortnight or three weeks will be a sad hurryg one I will hope by God's Help to amend at least in some things. Make the tree good.[299] Look to Jesus.[300] All other modes are vain.[301]

Sunday Evening, June 3rd. 1792, Palace Yard[302]
It is too late & my Eyes are too indifferent to allow me to write at large. I have for some Time gone on sadly as to Spiritualy & have little if at all amended in any of the particulars wherein I have been us'd most to offend. I thank God that he is yet so gracious to me as to excite in me a deep Sense of the Evil of my Ways, of the Corruption of my Heart & I humbly hope some Practical Conviction that my Sanctification must be the Work of his Spirit. But O How little if at all do I feel anything of the Reverence & love & spirit of obedience which ought to fill my mind.

May God enable me for X^{t's} Sake to begin anew from this Day. May I attend to the Root of the Matter. His Grace is sufficient for me,[303] none need despair. Let him that is athirst come.[304] Father I am wholly unworthy

---

296. Titus 2:10.
297. Matthew 26:41.
298. MS Wilberforce c. 40, fo. 32.
299. Matthew 12:33.
300. Hebrews 12:2.
301. MS Wilberforce c. 40, fo. 32.
302. MS Wilberforce c. 41, fos. 85-86.
303. 2 Corinthians 12:9.
304. Revelation 22:17.

to be call'd thy Son, but there is forgiveness with thee.[305] Surely he that spared not his Son &c. &c.[306] therefore I will press forward, distrusting yea despairing of <u>myself</u> but firmly relying on <u>him</u>. They that wait on the Lord shall renew their Strength.[307] What I ought now principally to attend to in the way of duties vide Page 30 & accompanying Pages, & Diligence for I have of late been indolent. O what a hypocrite I am, how I have a Name to live whilst in truth I am dead.[308] But, ho! <u>Everyone</u> that thirsteth etc.[309] And though your sins be as scarlet &c. &c.[310]

Sunday 3 oClock, June 10th. 1792, Keston

Alas! Alas! How carnally minded I am! How little have I of the mind of Xt. How little are my affections set on heavenly Things![311] What can I do but prostrate myself at the footstool of God's Throne, despairg of myself & expecting & seeking all from a crucified Redeemer. I now humbly beseech him to enable me to come to him & devote myself to his Service. I am now a very hypocrite, Sensual, Indolent, proud vain envious, volatile, fond of the Praise of men, given to Evil Speakg, falsehood. O my God do thou cleanse me, make in me a <u>new Heart</u>. Take away the Heart of Stone[312] & grant that havg liv'd so long to the Lusts of the flesh, I may live henceforth to the Will of God.

The beginning of a long Recess draws near, I will endeavor to consecrate it to God by a Day of solemn Prayer, & fasting such as may not disorder my Body & I will labor to lay aside every weight & the Sin that does most easily beset me,[313] to remember we are to adorn the Doctrine of God our Saviour,[314] to follow peace with all men, & Holiness,[315] & above all, to love the Lord our God with all our Heart & Soul & Strength,[316] & even here to put on Xt. to have ye. Mind & Spirit of Xt.[317] O strengthen me by thy Grace for I am very Weakness, cleanse me for I am all corruption.[318] After writing thus, I am apt to go away tolerably easy. Ease begets Carelessness. I grow remiss &c. &c. & so go on as ill as before. May it now be different. <u>May I be clothed with Humility.</u> <u>May I fear always.</u> May I be practically habitually constantly conscious of my own Proneness to folly of the Watchfulness of the Devil, of the Snares which surround me & lay in my Path, & may I therefore ever be

---

305. Psalm 130:4.
306. Romans 8:32.
307. Isaiah 40:31.
308. Revelation 3:1.
309. Isaiah 55:1.
310. Isaiah 1:18.
311. Colossians 3:2.
312. Ezekiel 36:26.
313. Hebrews 12:1.
314. Titus 2:10.
315. Hebrews 12:14.
316. Luke 10:27.
317. Romans 13:14.
318. 2 Corinthians 12:9.

looking up to him, who will never fail them that put their trust in him, for he shall feed his flock like a Shepherd.[319] Seek & ye shall find[320] Rest unto your Soul &c.[321] Amen. Amen.[322]

Sunday, June 24[th.] 1792 (Interrupted)
Sunday ¼ past 7 oClock Evening, July 8[th.] 1792, Kgs Arms Yd

Alas, Alas. With too much reason may I repeat all I wrote down on the 10th June. Still do I find myself in the same miserable State, a very Hypocrite, fair indeed to men, but God searcheth the Heart & trieth the Reins[323] & he thus convicteth me of a sensual worldly frame. I know that to be carnally minded is Death.[324] O may God help me to become spiritually minded. X[t.] has declared that he came to seek & save that which was lost.[325] To him let me apply at this moment whilst I see my deplorable State, my Heart is so hard that I cannot be said to feel it. O may X[t.] give me the Heart of flesh[326] & enable me yet to live to his Glory. I have gone off even in diligence. Let me aim at a Radical Reform. Vain tampering does but nurture the Disease. Lord have mercy upon me. From attempting too much by Rules, I have of late neglected them altogether. Let me now note down a few Heads for Self-examination, which may assist me in watching over my ways. These Heads to be look'd over daily if convenient. I mean to make my Health an object of great attention that if it may please God, I may yet recover Strength for his Service.

1. Sense of God's Presence & Sobermindedness, aspir[ns.] Spirit[l.] frame & Dependence on divine Influences. Less Volatility Xtian's peculiar Char[r.] rememb[d]: rather better but bad, bad from aftn. 3 Baddish 4 Worse 5 bad 6 Bad.

2. Looking to Jesus & Love of him, vide 2 Cor 5: bad – bad 3 bad[sh.] 4 [Wor]se

3. Devotions more serious (very distracted of late) & Self-Examination: rather better but bad. Bad at night 3 middg, 4 Midd.

4. Temperance & meals Gratitude, & Self Denial oppos'd to Selfishness. Mens: Regl: Baddish but rather better 3 middg, 4 bad[sh.]

5. Humility less Vanity, shewing off &c: Bad, Bad 3 4.

---

319. Isaiah 40:11.
320. Matthew 7:7.
321. Matthew 11:29.
322. MS Wilberforce c.40, fos. 34-35. *Life*, i. pp. 352-353 has, 'The beginning of a long recess draws near and I will endeavor to consecrate it to God by a day of solemn prayer and fasting I will labor to lay aside every weight and the sin which doth so easily beset me and to adorn the doctrine of God my Savior to follow peace with all men and above all to love the Lord my God with all my heart O strengthen me Lord by Thy grace for I am very weakness cleanse me for I am all corruption and since ease begets carelessness may I be clothed with humility and may I fear always.'
323. Revelation 2:23.
324. Romans 8:6.
325. Luke 19:10.
326. Ezekiel 36:26.

6. Pleasure in Religion Joy in believg: 2 forgot 3 & 4 forgot
7. Less Peevishness, & more meekness &c prosecution Lewis &c.
8. Evil speaking Care. Pride Tillotson: Forgot, forgot 3
9. Others spirit$^{l.}$ Good: forgot, forgot 3 & 4 forgot
10. Truth, more strictly
11. Compy & Conv$^{n.}$ Regls. Observg: forgot, forgot 3 & 4 forgot
12. Relaxat$^{n.}$ Tho'ts Recape: forgot 2, better 3 & 4 Middg
13. Diligence so far as Health. No Self Debatg. Procrastination care
14. Health Regls. Viz Early Hours. Frictions &c vide Plan
15. Time Plan, vide, Paper & Business.

B Schemes mainly. Nothing is small when done from the right motive.
Whether we eat or drink or whatever we do, we should do all to the
Glory of God.[327] Add: Constant Sense of Satan's Watchfulness, forgot,
forgot 3 & 4 forgot. Doddridge's Day Regl. I mean to allot rather less
time than last Summer to general Readg, Study &c. & rather more to
religious Exercises & Health. Omissions. Being asham'd of X$^{t.}$[328]

Sunday Evg. July 15$^{th.}$ 1792, King's Arms Yard

Alas! This week has gone on much like preceding ones in all Respects.
The same sins indulged, the same Carnal Mindedness, the same Coldness
& deadness to Spiritual Things. I have been today hearing 3 Excellent
Sermons, two from Scott on Acts 11:20,21st on the nature & Effects of
preaching the Lord Jesus &c.[329] the other on, There Remaineth a Rest
for y$^{e.}$ People of God,[330] & Cecil[331] on Heb 11, They wander'd abt. &c. of
whometh the world was not worthy &c.[332] I have been talking also with
Cecil & with excellent Grant as tho' I were a real Xtian, but God knows
the Heart. His promises & Invitation in X$^{t.}$ Jesus are held forth to all. I
see my misery, I see my guilt (O that I felt it more,) I humbly resolve to
forsake my evil ways, & I am sure I know that I can only do it thro' his
sustaining Grace. By his power even I may be recover'd. Let me <u>strive</u>
to enter in at the Straight Gate.[333] O how long have I been indolently &
hypocritically deceivg others & myself. Let me now in good Earnest turn
to God with my <u>whole heart</u>, laying aside every weight & the Sin that
does so easily beset me &c.[334] O God help me for X$^{t's}$ Sake. I will tomorrow

---

327. 1 Corinthians 10:31.
328. MS Wilberforce c. 40, fos. 36-38.
329. 2 Corinthians 4:5.
330. Hebrews 4:9.
331. Richard Cecil (1748–1810), popular evangelical Anglican minister, closely associated with the Clapham Circle, a close friend of Wilberforce, and co-founder with Newton of the evangelical Eclectic Society.
332. Hebrews 11:37-38.
333. Matthew 7:14.
334. Hebrews 12:1.

morning review my Life & daily Conversation by God's help & endeavor to form a Plan according to the advice of wise & experience'd Xtians.[335]

Sunday 29th. July 1792 Evg. Saml Thornton's Clapham

Alas! Alas! What Cause I have for Shame & Humiliation. How hard do I find it, how impossible to shake off my load of Lust, how Sin is work'd into my very frame. Yet the power of divine Grace is sufficiently powerful to quicken the dead in Trespasses, & it is promis'd to them that ask it. Rouze thyself then O my Soul, from this fatal Lethargy thou hast been too long indulging. Tis no petty Interest that is at Stake, tis thy Everlasting Condition. What a strange Creature I am. I seem to myself when I consider thoroughly resolv'd to devote myself to God, to throw myself at the foot of Jesus & take him for my Wisdom Rights. Sanctn & Redemption &c.[336] yet how soon do I find myself growing cold & dead & insensible & am so even whilst I am writing this very Lamentation.

O take away the Heart of Stone & give me an Heart of flesh.[337] I have for several Hours today been engag'd in religious reading, but heartlessly & languidly, even at Church both morng & aftn I fell asleep. But this I hope partly bodily - This week I had some very serious talking with Mr. Pearson abt. Solitude. He strongly press'd it both from Reason & Scripture & his own personal Experience. I believe he is right & mean to consider the point. O may God enable me for Xt's Sake yet to turn to him, no longer to waver between two opinions, but to make a complete Surrender. His promises are immutable. They that wait on the Lord shall renew their Strength &c. &c.[338]

Friday 24th. August 1792 – Bath -

O with what Shame do I take up my Pen. I have been looking over (but too coldly) the principal Events of my past Life, & what abundant Cause do I find for the deepest Contrition, & for admiring the Long Suffering of God, That he did not cast me off whilst in the full Career of Wickedness & Sin, when enjoying every advantage & opportunity I have been puttg them to so little Purpose. I can only hide my face in the Dust & say God be merciful to me a Sinner.[339] My present State is Truly deplorable. Much the same as for some time back, occasional Convictions & Resolutions, the latter with Prayer quiet the former. Being easy I forget God, I really place my Heart on the Gratifications of the World & the flesh, whilst I call on the name of God. I deceive even myself, & much more, others by having Religion in my mouth,

---

335. MS Wilberforce c. 40, fos. 39-40.

336. 1 Corinthians 1:30.

337. Ezekiel 36:26.

338. Isaiah 40:31; MS Wilberforce c. 40, fos. 40-41. *Life,* i. p. 359 has, 'I have today been for several hours engaged in religious reading but too languidly I have had this week some very serious talk with Mr. Pearson He strongly pressed solitude from reason Scripture and his own personal experience I believe he is right and mean to seek more quiet and solitude than I have done to consider the point and draw up my thoughts upon it.'

339. Luke 18:13.

whilst my Heart is far from it.[340] I go to the utmost Bounds, & often exceed them, in such sensual Indulgences as are not scandalous, & tho' I spend much time in Reading &c. &c. yet to little purpose for the Power of vigorous attention seems to have left me, & my memory to have decayed extremely, either from giving way to wandering Thoughts, or from some bodily Cause.

I am now entering my 34th year, about the Half of my Life is spent & I have not yet begun to live. I should despair of doing better & sink into utter languor or sensuality but that God holds forth in X[t] to all on this side the Grave Assurances of Grace & Strength if they are applied for heartily & perseveringly, & this Sincerity & Perseverance He will also grant to our petitions. Relying then on his Help & using all the means which my own Reflection & Experience of others suggest, I will press forward, first to secure my Eternal Salvation, & next to qualify myself for the Discharge of the Duties of Life with ability, "Give an account of thy Stewardship, for thou mayest be &c."[341] O may I never forget this aweful address which will one Day be made to me. How thankful ought I to be that notwithstanding the past shameful misapplication both of my Intellectual & Bodily Powers, they are still left me.

O spare me yet thou God of mercy, if it may please thee & render me yet an Ornament to my Xtian Profession, but here make me altogether resign'd to thy will, give me only the Love of thee & a Victory over my Corruptions & a mind renewed after thy Image. I had designed to spend this day entirely in Religious Exercises, & had set down certain Heads of occupation but I know not how, it has gone off with[t.] this, too much in my usual way. It has been chiefly spent however in Reading Relig[s.] Writings & meditation & the Remainder of this Evg will be devoted to the same. For Self-examination I may consult 37, 38 of this Book & perhaps I shall draw up Heads in another. But my Eyes being indiff[t.] hinder my writing, I must desist.[342]

Sunday, August 26[th.] 1792

Accompanied the Miss Mores to Shipham, Hounswick,[343] Axbridge,[344] and Cheddar. God seems indeed to prosper their work, both amongst

---

340. Matthew 15:8.

341. Luke 16:2.

342. MS Wilberforce c.40, fos. 41-44. *Life*, i. p. 367 has, 'Spent this day chiefly in religious exercises and had much serious thought but found my heart often earthly and wasting time in what was rather general staring than distinct self-examination I have been looking over the principal events of my past life and what cause do I find for contrition and for admiring the long suffering of God that he did not cut me off whilst in the full career of thoughtlessness or since when enjoying every advantage I have put them to so little purpose I am now entering my thirty fourth year above the half of my life is spent Oh spare me yet Thou God of mercy and render me yet an ornament to my Christian profession yet in this make me altogether resigned to Thy will give me only the love of Thee and a victory over my corruptions.'

343. Wilberforce was a supporter of the schools the More sisters established, one of which was in Hounswick.

344. Axbridge, simply meaning a bridge over the River Axe and dating from the 9th century, is a small town in Somerset, adjacent to Cheddar. King John had a Royal Hunting Lodge there

young and old are those who are turning to him. Near a thousand children in all. One mere child had Brought all his father's household to family prayers. On the 27th, returned to Bath.[345]

Sunday Evg. 2^d Sept^r - Bath

Alas! Alas! How strongly are my Corruptions rooted in my Nature, how they are incorporated into the very frame of my Soul! I have gone on I think little or no better than before often failing where I had most resolv'd ag^st. it, forgetting all my Spiritual determin^n. & objects. I cannot write, my Eyes smart. I go to pray to God for X^t's Sake yet to have mercy on me & to enable me to turn from my Iniquities & live to his Glory. Even at Miss. More's, even today when tete-a-tete with Eliot, I have been indulging my sensual disposition, & how has this Sabbath pass'd by with^t. Enjoyment or Improvement. Is this the Blessedness I tho't of, this the Spiritual Retirement I had promis'd myself at Bath? O what shall I do when I go to places where there is no fear of God & I am engag'd in the Company of the wicked. O Hide thy face in the Dust, O my Soul, be cover'd with Shame & Confusion. Yet return unto the Lord & he will have mercy on thee, & He will put his Law in thy Heart & write it in my mind.[346] How do the poor people of Cheddar disgrace me. O what if Death should surprize me! I have no Resource but in God's Mercy in X^t. I go to pray that he may be made unto me Wisdom & R' & Sanc^tn. & Red.[347] & that Satan may be bruised under my feet.[348]

Sunday, September 9th. 1792, Hamels

Alas! This last Week has gone on worse than preceding ones, my frame less spiritual, & more sensual, my Resolutions sadly broken, & my Heart so cold & stupid as scarcely even now to feel its wants, yet my Understanding clearly condemns me. Let me fly to the Throne of Grace, & pray for Strength & Grace & Power from above. It seems providential that _____[349] sho'd not be here (being call'd away) that I may have more time to myself. O quicken those things that are ready to die.[350] Pray I strive after a single Eye.[351] They that wait on the Lord shall renew their Strength.[352]

---

which still survives, and a Mint was also located there. As an ancient borough it returned M.P.s in the reigns of Edward I and Edward III. The population in 1801 was approximately 810. Wilberforce was a supporter of the schools the More sisters established, one of which was in Axbridge.

345. *Life*, i. pp. 367-368.
346. Hebrews 8:10.
347. 1 Corinthians 1:30.
348. Romans 16:20. MS Wilberforce c. 40, fo. 45.
349. Wilberforce didn't name anyone here, but simply put a brief line.
350. Revelation 3:2.
351. Matthew 6:22.
352. Isaiah 40:31. MS Wilberforce c. 40, fo. 46.

Battersea Rise[353] Sunday 16[th.] Sept[r.] 1792

My Eyes are too indiff[t.] to allow me to write, but I must just note down that all goes ill with me. Sensual, Earthly minded, cold & dead. O for a new Heart, or even for a sincere Desire after one. At present my Understandg convinces me of my folly & danger, but O how little do my feelings fall in with my Knowledge. O take away the Stony Heart out of my flesh &c. &c. &c.[354]

Walmer Castle[355] Oct[r.] 4[th.] Thursday Evg - 1792

I have been going on everyway ill, & the Effects of this bad frame have appear'd in my almost constant Mens: Excedgs as usual both in ferms & otherwise, wherein I find also, I cannot bear the same irregularities as formerly - O may God help me to amend, & <u>that</u> thoroughly. I came here hoping that I might really find an opportunity of talking seriously with Pitt what a wretch am I to do so with anyone - O X[t.] help me.[356]

Yoxall Lodge Nov[r.] 4[th.] Sunday 1792

My eyes have been indiff[t.] ever since I was at Walmer which has prevented my writing. I don't perceive that I at all yet forward, on the contrary I fear I grow more callous. O God take away the Heart of Stone & give me a Heart of flesh,[357] may I lothe & abhor myself. The same besetting Sins as before,[358] Indolence, Sensuality, Forgetfulness of God, of X[t's] Love, of the Hope of Glory, of thy own Corruption & Weakness, of the Temptations of Satan & the constant Help of the Spirit promis'd to our Infirmities - I am I fear less earnest for the Souls of others & am less diligent even in my Secular Affairs and more trifling in conversation. O with what Shame must I contemplate myself in this nearly beginning of the 8[th.] year since I began to make a more serious Profession. Awake thou that Sleepest & arise from the Dead & X[t.] shall give thee Light.[359]

---

353. Battersea Rise, a Queen Anne house on the west side of Clapham Common, had an oval library, which may well have been personally designed by William Pitt the Younger. Henry Thornton purchased the house and enlarged it substantially by adding two wings, resulting in its having 34 bedrooms. From a period beginning in 1792, Wilberforce resided there whilst unmarried. Thornton also had two smaller properties built on the estate, Broomfield Lodge (later, Broomwood House), and Glenelg, which was purchased by Charles Grant, M.P. Battersea Rise was destroyed in 1907.

354. Ezekiel 36:26. MS Wilberforce c. 40, fo. 47.

355. Walmer Castle is a pocket-castle on the Kent coast, built by Henry VIII in 1539. Since 1708, it has been home to the Lord Warden of the Cinque Ports, who included the Duke of Wellington, who died in his armchair there in 1852. His simple, low-ceilinged bedroom has been retained as it was, alongside the camp-bed he slept on.

356. MS Wilberforce c. 40, fo. 48. *Life*, i. p. 369 has, 'At night alone with Pitt but talked politics only did not find myself equal to better talk I came here hoping that I might really find an opportunity of talking seriously with Pitt. What am I to do so with any one. O Christ help me.'

357. Ezekiel 36:26.

358. In left margin he wrote, 'Besetting Sins'.

359. Ephesians 5:14; MS Wilberforce c. 40, fos. 48-49. *Life*, i. 372 has, 'I have been employing most of this morning, in reading St. Paul's Epistles to the Romans and the Galatians. Though utterly unworthy, I thank God for having enabled me to pray with earnestness. Oh that this may not be as the morning cloud and as the early dew! By his grace I will persevere with more earnestness than ever, laboring to work out my own salvation in an entire and habitual dependence upon him. I have been praying earnestly to God for his Spirit through Christ to renew my corrupt nature and make me spiritually-minded, what folly is all else! Let me take courage, relying on the sure promises of

Sunday Evg 4[th.] Nov[r.]

Alas! this very Evg in spite of my midday tho'ts & Purposes I have to record my own Intemperance once more. Regl broke, Spiritual Relish Disregarded. Help me O God to reform thoroughly, make the Tree good &c. &c.[360]

Monday Evg 5[th.] Nov[r.] Y'll Lodge

This day I have gone on but very poorly in Spite of all my Repentance of yesterday, part[y.] at mens. I must prescribe positives to these tho'ts & prevent thoughtless failures.[361]

Sunday Noon, November 11[th.] 1792, Y'll Lodge

Alas! this week I have been going on too much as usual, violating all my Resolutions, if such they were, forgetting God, Mens: Regls, breakg &c. &c. yet now & then I hope more warmth in Prayer tho last night unconquerably cold, distracted - May I more remember practically that all my Strength must be from God thro' X[t] by the Spirit & live more in continual Dependence on him, & with universal Reference - I am call'd away & my Eyes being bad, I may not be able to take up the Pen today again. May God for Xt's sake, renew & sanctify me.[362]

Sunday Noon Nov[r.] 18[th.] Y'll Lodge

I have gone on full as ill during the past week I fear, as before or at least nearly so, & offended in the same Ways. My Eyes are bad, therefore I may not write but I recommend myself to God's Mercy thro X[t.] & pray for his Holy Spirit to take away my Ht of Stone,[363] & fill me with all holy affections. By God's Grace still I will persevere, with more Earnestness than ever, laborg to work out my own Salvation,[364] in an entire & habitual Reliance on him, & striving to adorn the Gospel of our heavenly Father in all things.[365] In particular this ensuing Week, let me attend to those particulars of daily occurrence which so often are the occasions of drawing me into Evil, & aim however at the Root of the matter - Make the Tree good &c.[366] I go to Prayer. Lord help me tho utterly unworthy. I thank God for havg enabled me to pray with some Earnestness. O that they may not be as the mg cloud & early dew.[367]

Thursday Midday Nov[r.] 22[d.] 1792 Y'll Lodge

Most pleasing State. I have been employing most of this morning in reading St. Paul to the Romans & Galatians, & have since been praying

---

God in Christ and the powerful operations of the Spirit of grace. Though I am weak he is strong. I must more cherish this heavenly inhabitant.'

360. Matthew 12:33; MS Wilberforce c. 40, fo. 49.
361. MS Wilberforce c. 40, fo. 50.
362. Ibid.
363. Ezekiel 36:26.
364. Philippians 2:12.
365. Titus 2:10.
366. Matthew 12:33.
367. Hosea 13:3. MS Wilberforce c. 40, fos. 50-51.

earnestly to God for his Spirit thro' X^t to renew my corrupt nature and make me spiritually minded - O what folly is all else! Let me take Courage relying on the sure Promises of God in X^t & the powerful operations of the Spirit of Grace - Tho' I am weak he is strong. I must more cherish this heavenly Inhabitant, "to be carnally minded &c. but to be spiritually minded &c. &c."[368] It is also said "Work out your own Salvation[369] & "for God worketh in you &c. &c."[370] & "Follow Holiness."[371] My[372] Eyes are bad, I can't write, but I humbly Resolve to amend my ways & turn to the Lord with my whole Heart.[373]

Friday 30th Novr. Wilford

Alas! I have been going on no better, sadly sensualized, breakg mens: & other Regl. Eyes are bad so can't write. I have prayed to God with Earnestness & must humbly begin again.[374]

Sunday Decr 16th 1792 Palyd[375]

Alas! Alas! How sadly have I been going on. My Heart engross'd by the things of this World, & yet even they ill selected & ill attended to, & my Devotions curtail'd, sometimes omitted. O let me not forget the one thing needful.[376] Awake thou that sleepest & arise from the Dead & Christ shall give thee Life.[377] O may I awake, & call on X^t for Help. I should despair but for the Hope of his promis'd Grace. Let me examine & try my Ways & turn again unto the Lord. My faults much the same as always formerly (with less Diligence in Business), all bottoming in an Aversation to God & Holiness & the Spirit^l Life, & a carnal mind, & the minding of the Things of the flesh.[378]

Tuesday 25th Decr. - Hamels

My Eyes are very indifferent & therefore must spare them, but I take up my Pen for a moment to note down that I am now endeavoring to quicken those things which are ready to die.[379] I have been reading Owen on Temptation[380] & am much struck with it, but O how little am I really impress'd with heavenly things. How transient are my serious Thoughts. There is something in my natural languid temper of mind, but may it never appear so mark'd as in what regards my

---

368. Romans 8:6.

369. Philippians 2:12.

370. Philippians 2:13.

371. Hebrews 12:14.

372. In left margin is written, 'Vide Page 37 Reso.'

373. MS Wilberforce c. 40, fo. 52.

374. MS Wilberforce c. 40, fo. 53.

375. In left margin is written, 'After being occupied by Parlt^y Bus^s & kept up late 3 nights successively'.

376. Luke 10:42.

377. Ephesians 5:14.

378. MS Wilberforce c. 40, fo. 53.

379. Revelation 3:2.

380. Wilberforce here refers to John Owen's *Of Temptation* (London, 1658).

Soul's Concerns. Awake thou that sleepest & arise from the dead & X^t·
shall give thee Light.[381]

I am perpetually givg myself a false & premature peace. A general
negligent frame comes on then I fall into Breaches of Mens: Regls. &c.
falls from which Worldly Principles are sufficient to secure men of the
world. I want chiefly a deeper Sense of the guilt & danger of Sin. This
would keep me humble & watchful & lookg to X^t· for Help. Let me pray
to God for this Sense & use the means suggested by Scripture & Reason.
O take away the Stony Heart & give me a Heart of flesh.[382] O let me be
indeed what I profess myself & no longer disgrace my Xtian profession.
I yesterday exceeded Mens: Regl. & have been all along sensual in Heart
if not in act. O that I were indeed pure & holy in Spirit. This & all other
graces are to be obtain'd from the fulness that is in Jesus.[383]

---

381. Ephesians 5:14.
382. Ezekiel 36:26.
383. Ephesians 4:13. MS Wilberforce c. 40, fo. 54.

The Spiritual Reflections
of
William Wilberforce

1793–1800

William Wilberforce 1793–1800

This period of Wilberforce's life saw him initiating Bills for Abolition in 1793, 1795, 1796, 1797, 1798 and 1799, but all are defeated by the very strong opposition he faced in Parliament. He also introduced a Bill in May 1793 to amend the Charter of the powerful East India Company, to break their prohibition of mission and chaplaincy work in their foreign areas of control. He faced incredibly strong opposition from the Company to that too, with that Bill also being defeated. It will take him twenty years to see success with such amendment, after he mounted a very well organized campaign.

This period in Wilberforce's life was very charged period politically, with Louis XVI of France being executed in January 1793, and Revolutionary France declaring War on Britain just the following month. These events led to the fight for Abolition becoming less of a priority for debate, as Britain moved from simply having feared French aggression to now facing it in reality. Any affection for France in the days leading up to War had been viewed with increasing suspicion, and again the Abolition movement had suffered as a result, as anything that tended toward a lack of British patriotism could easily be misconstrued as revolutionary tendencies.

Though Wilberforce did not see any real success in his parliamentary campaign in this period, he did have a number of things to be very thankful for. On 12 April, 1797, he saw the publication of his *A Practical View*. Wilberforce had agonized and prayed a great deal over its writing, that God would bless and use it to challenge the spiritual apathy of the higher classes in Britain. It was a project that had taken him several years, for it was on Saturday 3 August, 1793 that he wrote in his Journal, 'I laid the first timbers of my tract.' He wrote the book for several reasons: to explain his Great Change, to confront his own upper-class generation with an evangelical gospel, and to do for the wealthy what the evangelical revival of his day had done for the lower classes. Very few could even have dared to imagine, how well-received, influential and blessed that volume would become. In fact, such was the opposite pre-publication view, that even Thomas Cadell the book's publisher was of the opinion that it would have so little appeal that 'he was dubious as to whether Wilberforce would want to affix his name to it ... Cadell was convinced that he would be fortunate to sell 500 copies. Several of his friends tried to discourage him from writing the book at all, stating that such works never sold well.'[1] In reality, however, the book became such a best seller that by 1826, fifteen editions had been printed in Britain and twenty-five in America, with translations into Dutch, French, German. Italian and Spanish.[2] 'In time, it came to be regarded as the manifesto of the evangelical movement.' Wilberforce's sons even add the wonderful testimony, that, 'Not a year passed throughout his after-life, in which he did not receive fresh testimonies to the blessed effects which it pleased God to produce through his publication.'[3]

The following month he had further cause for rejoicing, by his marriage to Barbara Spooner, his 'Dearest B' as he came to lovingly refer to her. Wilberforce recorded a number of times, how interested he had so quickly become in several potential marriage-partners. He also recorded how he longed to be married, possessing as he felt he did strong physical impulses. Two years before his wedding for example, he wrote of an experience that wasn't unique for him as he recorded them in honest reflection,

> This last week has been rather idled away, at least little or no solid Study has been redeem'd out of it - Yesterday I din'd at Will Smith's, a mix'd Party, Ladies & Gentlemen & I sadly loose in imagination. Many Ladies came in at night & I too nearly approaching or rather quite to committing adultery in the Heart - Eat up too with Vanity - God forgot, his Spirit griev'd. My mind remarkably distracted. Something of loose Imagination has been suffer'd much to grow on me of late. Last Sunday got in carriage, lascivious, Oimoi. O may I be pure as God is pure. My Heart has been today in some degree solemnized, but my Conscience is defil'd & I dare scarce look to God with Hope, whilst I so disgrace his Gospel. What a thing is it for one who is writing such a Book as I am to behave as I did last night.[4]

Wilberforce was introduced Barbara Spooner by his good friend Thomas Babington, meeting her for the first time on April 15, 1797. Wilberforce proposed just eight days after that introduction, and they were married on May 30th. They spent their honeymoon touring the schools close to Bath that Hannah More has established with Wilberforce's support. So began in Wilberforce's own words, 'thirty-five years of undiluted happiness.' Within ten years they had four sons and two daughters, and he was devoted to all seven of them. William Jr., their first child,

---

1. William Wilberforce, *A Practical View of Christianity*, ed. Kevin Belmonte (Peabody, MA: Hendrickson, 1996), p. xxv.

2. Ibid., pp. xxv-xxvi.

3. *Life*, ii. p. 207.

4. Journal entry Sunday evening.

was born just over a year after they were married. 'What a blessing,' Wilberforce would say later to a houseguest when all one could hear were his children shouting and playing, '… to have these dear children! Only think what a relief, amidst other hurries, to hear their voices and know they are well.'

Wilberforce deliberately made time for his family, even in the midst of all the busyness that was his life, actively joining in many of their games. Guests would be amazed as his children treated him as one of them. Robert Southey, the British Poet Laureate, recorded one such a scene when visiting Wilberforce at home. He described, '… the pell-mell, topsy-turvy and chaotic confusion' he witnessed, and there in the midst of it was Wilberforce, who 'frisks about as if every vein in his body were filled with quicksilver.'[5]

Wilberforce's main concern for his family above anything else though, was their spiritual state. He wrote letters to his children regularly, reminding them of his and their heavenly Father's unconditional love, always encouraging them to walk closely with Christ. So touching and unique were those letters, especially written at that time and by one in such a position as he, that one should not be surprised to discover that they were recently published as *Amazing Dad: Letters from Wilberforce to his Children*. As a major part of that spiritual concern, he also determined as often as he could make possible, that his household – family, servants and any houseguests – would have regular times together of worship. He would expound on some passage of Scripture, and they would sing and pray. Wonderfully, we have one such devotional time recorded in humorous detail by Marianne Thornton,

> The scene at prayers is a most curious one. There is a bell which rings when Mr. W begins to dress; another when he finishes dressing; upon which Mr. Barningham begins to play a hymn upon the organ and to sing a solo, and by degrees the family come down to the entrance hall where the psalmody goes on; first one joins in and then another; Lizzy calling out 'Don't go near dear Mama, she sings so dreadfully out of tune, dear,' and William 'Don't look at Papa, he does make such dreadful faces.' So he does, waving his arms about, and occasionally pulling the leaves off the geraniums and smelling them, singing out louder and louder in a tone of hilarity: 'Trust Him, praise Him, trust Him, praise Him ever more'.[6]

Wilberforce also faced tragedy, though, in connection with his much-loved children, as he will lose two of the six before his own death, and William Jr. caused him much concern and personal financial loss and sacrifice. The newly married couple settled in Clapham, which was then a village, close to but outside of London proper. This led inevitably to

5. *The Life and Correspondence of the late Robert Southey*, ed. Charles C. Southey, 6 vols. (London: Longman, Brown, Green and Longmans, 1849–50), vol. iv, p. 317.

6. E. M. Forster, *Marianne Thornton: A Domestic Biography* (London: Edward Arnold, 1956), pp. 137-8.

Wilberforce becoming a prominent member of what became known as the Clapham Circle or Sect.

During this period he had no relief from physical pain and affliction, writing for example, 'I have been confin'd to my House for a week by the Piles (no pain) but require reclining & abstinence from motion.'[7] Later he was worried by the certainty of imminent pain from his bad teeth. Yet even in the midst of this great anxiety, he was able to turn it to become more of a spiritual challenge to himself and an occasion of thankfulness,

> How cowardly am I with regard to my apprehensions of bodily pain - I am afraid of going out of the neighborhood of London on account of 2 or 3 bad teeth, which perhaps cannot be drawn in the country. Think what X^t suffer'd - what his people have suffer'd - what Strength he can give - & support in pain - Pearson's story - & learn to trust him & to be less anxious & regardful of this short & uncertain State - Expect Evils & pain here - How little have I had of them. How much more almost everyone I know.[8]

Two years later he suffered very badly from severe intestinal issues, a disease that flared up very badly at times, as here when he believed it might have been a fatal episode,

> It has pleased God of his great mercy to raise me up again when on Mon 7, I was attacked with a Bowel Complaint which threatened much - I then tho't Death probably near. O that I might now better employ the time it has pleased God to allow me. May I be enlighten'd & purified & quicken'd, & havg sadly wasted my precious faculties ever since my thinkg more seriously, may I now more constantly act as an accountable creat^e who may be suddenly call'd away to his Reckoning. God for $X^{t's}$ Sake Sanctify me by his Spirit, & may they dwell in me.[9]

Today his condition would probably be diagnosed as Ulcerative Colitis, a very painful Irritable Bowel Disease (IBD) that causes inflammation and ulcers in the digestive tract. The only real relief in Wilberforce's day was the Laudanum prescribed by his physician. Laudanum is a tincture of opium that contains almost all the opium alkaloids including even morphine. It did indeed therefore help Wilberforce with the pain, but its side effects were brutal. He became addicted, experiencing hallucinations, nightmares and a severe inability to do his work as a result.

He also recorded two entries in this period that describe Barbara going into labor with the first two of their children. He is reminded thereby of God's goodness and power, of his complete powerlessness in such situations, the uncertainty of life, and also of the challenge and example to him of Barbara's piety and hope. With the near arrival of William his first child, he wrote,

---

7. Journal entry, Sunday, 3 March, 1795.
8. Journal entry, Tuesday, 30 June, 1795.
9. Journal entry, Sunday, 8 January, 1797.

My dearest B. is now in labour - How dependent does this make me feel on the power & Goodness of God. What a humbling Impression have I of my own Inability & of all my Happiness & all else that belongs to me, being at the disposal of the Supreme Being - So it ought always to be. This it is, to <u>walk softly</u>, - my dearest love, how compos'dly waiting the coming on of her pains - With what pious lowliness & Resignation shew'd with Xtian Hope. O may I learn from her, and may I be more grateful than I have been. I see already much to be thankful & as usual the kind Hand of a gracious God disposing little Incidents with a favouring kindness. Underwood was going out today at one to Shooting Hill. It was a special mercy the labor came on before he was gone. We did not think it so near. She might have been taken at the Aucklands. Mrs. Bab told me just now, my Love was <u>so patient</u>. O God, support & comfort her & enable me whatever may be thy will, to submit with humble acquiescing Confidence. Began to be sufferg ab[t.] 4 & now ¾ past 4. Entire intermissions. If God should now see fit to release her from this World of Sin & Sorrow, <u>doubtless</u> She would go to Glory & perhaps be spared many a Suffering which I foresee not. O may the Language of my inmost <u>Heart</u> be "Thy will be done."

In a similar vein concerning the uncertainty of life, he also wrote of the diseases contracted by his children, which today, in the developed world especially, have generally become no real threat. It was very different in Wilberforce's day, and just as when Barbara had been in labor, so now he is again brought to reflect seriously on the fragility of life,

Our Childn have had the Measles, & now have the Hoopg Cough. How uncertain is life. O may I feel my depend[ce.] & my obligat[ns.] Amen. Yet however vile & worthless, prompted by a Sense of misery & helplessness I come to thee O X[t.] because thou art able to save to the Uttermost them that come to God thro' thee, I come, imploring Mercy & Grace to help in time of need.[10]

The last thing to be drawn out from his Journals of this period, are entries that once again detail Wilberforce's critical reviews of his life. This is a constant in his reflections, that his life and behavior fall far short of what might well be expected by one with all the privileges and blessings he had received. So for example in September 1796, before the publication of his book and his wedding, he reflected on what he referred to as 'Notables in my life,' they included the following,

What a mercy to have been born a human creature with a fortune, talents &c. &c. an Englishman in the 18[th.] Centy of decently relig[s.] parents &c. &c. &c. … My being providently engag'd in the Sl: Trade Business, thro' what we call accident, I remember well how it was. What an honorable Service. Deliv[ce.] from Sickness in 1788 & 1796. How much the Circumstance of Milner's going abroad with me depended on contingencies. His comg to Hull with his Brother. Being known to my Grandfather, distinguishg himself &c. &c.

---

10. Journal entry, Sunday, 27 April, 1800.

As he rejoiced in God's sovereignty and Providence in these matters, he was well aware that these and the many other 'Notables' he described, should only produce an overwhelming sense of gratitude, accompanied by a desire to live to please the One who so ordered these events. He has to admit to himself in his Journal, that his life has been filled with everything but that kind of fruit,

> What Selfishness do I discover in myself everywhere & how little real disinterestedness. Alas, for the latter years of my being at School I was irreligious, practisg one Sin in partic^{r.} which I believed hateful to God - Then at College totally idle & wicked in every way - O had I been then cut off, but the mercy of God spared me - Then for the first 5 years of my being in Parl^{t.} from 1780 to Novr. 1785 - sadly wicked - living with^{t.} God in the World - no Desire to please him & only kept from total Idleness by Vanity & Ambition - Since that time when awaken'd - not striving as I ought to grow in Grace - but livg carelessly & satisfied too much with name & Credit of being religious & taking others opinions of me which knew to be false ag^{t.} my own judgement. Yet I hope all along – I have at Intervals humbly cast myself on the free mercy X^{t.} & that I now throw myself only on his infinite Compassion & rely only on his effectual Grace. I am in myself most weak & vile.

It is of God's unmerited goodness that I am selected as the agent of usefulness. I see his overruling power. I go to adore his wisdom and goodness, to humble myself before him, and to implore his forgiveness for Christ's sake.

William Wilberforce, 1793

1793

Sunday March 10[th.] 1793

The bad State of my Eyes has with other Causes operated to prevent my writing in this Book. I have put down a few Hints elsewhere. I have much the same Confessions to make as heretofore, yet I hope on the whole, I have of late read Scripture with rather more attention & preserv'd in my Mind rather a more constant Sense of the divine presence, yet sadly failing in all the old ways. I cannot now write, but I go to the throne of Grace desiring to beg in all anew, & to be enabled to receive the powerful Help from on high which may change me indeed. Self-examin[n.] little practiced. Mens: Regl & Compy Regl bad. Vanity great - Self-denial little. Little tho't for 6 Hours spiritual good &c. &c. &c. a sad distracted Heart. O may God for X[ts] Sake renew me by his Spirit.[1]

Easter Sunday March 31[st.] 1793 Batta Rise

My eyes too indiff[t] to allow me to write. Else I must record my own shame & Dishonor - O how carnal Sensual to Excess, partic[y] in ferms, how indolent, how vain, selfish, lukewarm, ab[t.] others' good, peevish, &c. &c. & how have all these had their Root from Forgetfulness of God, Contracted & distracted Devotions - Self-examin[n] neglected - Scripture little thought of & above all, Inattention to that Prime Injunction, To live by Faith on the Son of God,[2] & Look to the things that are unseen.[3] Awake O my Soul to a true Sense of thy Situation. Ask thyself where art thou, & where wouldst thou be if God were now to summon thee away, & he is pleas'd still to spare thee rouze thyself, & strive to enter in at the Strait Gate.[4] Fight the good fight of faith.[5]

Above all: Prayer & Self Examin[n.] Scripture Studying & Xt. thoughts. Self-denial throughout. Sensual[y] &c. &c. Mortify. Humility. Secret Duties. Redeem y[e.] Time. Compy. & Relax[n.] Regls. Volatility & Indolence care. Procrastination avoid. Watch for Souls of others. Religion thy Solace. God's Eye, & Satan watchful. Doddridge's Directions. Aspirations frequent.

To try to renew my Time account & Self Examin[n.] settg down main faults in this Book. Try less wine. I have often lately eat & drank if not so as to disorder my Reason yet nearly so, how little does this accord with, "be Sober, be vigilant because &c."[6] I know that my Constitution requires good living but I have exceeded alike to the Injury of Body & Mind. Much assuredly a capitol Sermon of Scott's on Good Friday on "It is finished."[7] Venn good today on He shall see of the travail of his

---

1. MS Wilberforce c. 40, fos. 54-55.
2. Galatians 2:20.
3. 2 Corinthians 4:18.
4. Matthew 7:13
5. 1 Timothy 6:12.
6. 1 Peter 4:7.
7. John 19:30.

Soul &c. &c.[8] My grand faults seem to be those which include in them all others: Vanity & Pride & Sensuality - Mortify these daily - Even my religion is practic'd with a view to the praise of men - How much more am I concern'd to show my Infirmities before Grant, H. Th[n.] &c. &c. than before God - O sanctify me thou Spirit of Life, I <u>must</u> lay down my pen on acct of my Eyes. I go to prayer - Evil Speaking. Care. House Attention & Parl[ty.] Duties.[9]

Tuesday Evening, April 2, 1793, Batt[a] Rise

Cecil has been with me yesterday a truly spiritual man. O that I were like him, today Scott too & impeded by Burgh. Alas! How cold is my Heart & indispos'd to religious Duties - How void of a lively Sense of Gratitude to God whose mercies I am continually experiencing - Chief faults: My chief faults today amidst innumerable others - Not self-denying at mens. &c. Want of that humble lowly watchful spirit becomg a Xtian. Satan not tho't of - Good to others Souls forgot. Too little <u>real Respect</u> for the excellent of the Earth - Aspirations too few. Impatient & unkind on W[m's] provocations - Not kind enough to Arnot. I set down these faults with little Sense alas, of that Sorrow & Humiliation which on such a Review ought to fill my mind.[10]

Monday 15[th.] April

I am little if at all minding. Today the same Sensuality, the same frittering away of time &c. &c. Yesterday I exceeded. O that it might it please God to enable me to reform thoroughly. I still must persist. My night devotions always lost, or shorten'd.[11]

Friday 16[th.] April[12]

Alas! What a hurrying Life I lead. Little or no time for serious Reflection - All this must be that "<u>overcharging</u>" which Scripture forbids,[13] & must be in some Way or other just an End so. I have people all afternoon long coming in to me as into a Tavern. The Expense, the Waste of time, the Plague &c. & perhaps the solid Injury to my health, cannot be estimated. May God direct me aright in it. Certainly I find more quiet better for me, both[14] Body & Soul, & all this falls in with my natural Infirmities of volatility &c. &c. &c. & I think lately the Tumult attending of my House have increas'd, & that I have attended less than I ought to have done to my Parl[ty.] Business, on acc[t.] of the clashing of my Dinner, hereby giving occasion to the Enemies of Religion to

---

8. Rev. John Venn, Rector of Clapham from 1792. Isaiah 53:11.

9. MS Wilberforce c. 40, fos. 55-57.

10. MS Wilberforce c. 40, fo. 58.

11. MS Wilberforce c. 40, fo. 60.

12. 16 April, 1793, was not a Friday but a Tuesday.

13. Luke 21:34.

14. Here in left margin is written, 'Seriously with prayer for Direction & a regular Investigation'.

calumniate it. Hatsell told me, 'my private Business was neglected.' O let me pray for wisdom. I go to consider this matter.[15]

Batta R[e.] Sunday May 5[th.]

I have so bad a Cold in my Head & Eyes that I cannot write, at large, yet, if it please God for my future Benefit, let me note down my own Shame & Dishonor. Alas! There seems scarce any more in me than a general Sense of the Truth of divine things, & an adherence to the Externals of Religion, more perhaps from Constancy - Motives &c. than from the power of Grace in my Heart. The same Sins & Infirmities which I have before noted, continue, But above all, what is the Root of this Bitterness, a Heart little or not at all habitually conscious of the Guilt of Sin & of the Excellency of the Knowledge of X[t.] Jesus the Lord.

Let me by humble Prayer implore him to give me the Heart of flesh,[16] that I may be truly humbled & contrite, & that I may be thereby led to the Cross of X[t.] the only Cure of all our maladies. May X[t.] Jesus be made unto me Wisdom & Right[s.] &c.[17] May I behold the Lamb of God[18] & learn daily to love him more & devote myself more absolutely & unreservedly & diligently to his Service - My Time,[19] fortune, Talents, opportunities, Connections &c. &c. O let me not be asham'd of him, but plead his Cause, & magnify his saving Grace in the midst of an unbelieving Generation.[20]

PalYd May 19[th.]

My time is contracted & my Eyes bad, yet must I first record my own Shame, for O how much Cause of Humiliation do I see, & above all the Grace & Goodness of God in enabling me to be the Instrument of carrying thro' the E. Ind[n.] Clauses - never was his over-ruling providence more conspicuous than in the Whole of this Business. O let me remember that Judas was us'd as an Instrument with the rest of the 12 disciples, & that many will say, "Have we not prophesied &c. - & he will say Depart from me, ye Workers of Iniquity."[21] This affair gives me fresh occasion to discover the pride & vanity of my own Heart & O how much more is Grant &c. properly affected - Yet Let me take Courage. It is of God's unmerited Grace & Goodness that I am selected as the agent of Usefulness. I see his overruling power - I go to adore his Wisdom & Goodness, to humble myself before him & to implore his forgiveness for X[ts] Sake - Amen.[22]

---

15. MS Wilberforce c. 40, fo. 59. *Life*, ii. p. 23 has, 'Alas! What a hurrying life I lead, with little time for serious reflection! – Some serious thought this morning, and found the benefit of early rising, but it sadly wears my frame.'

16. Ezekiel 36:26.

17. 1 Corinthians 1:30.

18. John 1:29.

19. From 'Time' to the end of this entry, a large cross in different ink has been placed over the words.

20. MS Wilberforce c. 40, fos. 60-61.

21. Matthew 7:22.

22. MS Wilberforce c. 40, fos. 61-62. *Life*, ii. p. 25 has, 'Scott morning. Cecil afternoon. Called at Grant's – Miss More there. The hand of providence was never more visible than in this East Indian

Sunday Aft[n.] 26[th.] May Pal Y[d.]

How mysterious are God's Dispensations. The Clauses thrown out on the 3[d] Reading by a little Tumult in the Court of Proprietors.[23] O may not this have been because one so unworthy as myself undertook this hallowed Cause & carried it on so carnally, with so little of true Humility & faith & Self Abasement & Confidence in God thro' X[t.] Yet where can I go but to thee, blessed Jesus, Thou hast the Words of Eternal Life.[24] I am no more worthy to be called thy Son,[25] yet receive me, & deliver me from all my Enemies & Hindrances, & by the powerful Efficacy of thy renewing Grace, render me meet to be a partaker of the Inheritance of the Saints in Light.[26] I <u>know</u> my Lord's Will but how little have I the real mind of X[t.] - It is from him only I can receive it, & I go to seek it in humble prayer.[27]

June 2[d.] Sunday Aft[n.] Clapham

Alas! I have gone on much the same - Little Sense of divine Things on my mind, little habitual thought of Jesus! O may I yet turn to him. My devotions still curtal'd &c. nimis ferms - yet X[t's] promise is sure. God's arm is not shorten'd nor his Ear heavy![28]

Clapham Sunday 9[th.] June Aftn

Eyes bad therefore must not write. This week no better - in some things worse - late Hours &c. O how merciful God is to me. I have this day commemorated his redeeming Love - O may it be to me the Beginning of a new Era.[29]

---

affair. What cause have I for gratitude, and trust, and humiliation! ... My time is contracted and my eyes bad, yet I must record the grace and goodness of God in enabling me to be the instrument of carrying through the East Indian clauses. Never was his overruling providence more conspicuous than in the whole of this business. Oh let me remember that Judas was used as an instrument with the rest of the twelve disciples, and that many will say, 'Have we not prophesied in Thy name,' to whom he will answer, 'Depart from me, ye workers of iniquity.' This affair gives me fresh occasion to discover the pride of my own heart. How properly is Grant affected! Yet let me take courage. It is of God's unmerited goodness that I am selected as the agent of usefulness. I see his overruling power. I go to adore his wisdom and goodness, to humble myself before him, and to implore his forgiveness for Christ's sake. Amen.'

23. The East India Trading Company was a joint-stock company formed for pursuing trade with the East Indies and Caribbean, and granted a Royal Charter by Elizabeth I in 1600. The government owned no shares and had only indirect control. The Company came to rule large areas of India with its own private armies, and assumed massive administrative functions. The company was led by 1 governor and 24 directors, and they in turn reported to the Court of Proprietors (the body of shareholders) which appointed them.

24. John 6:68.

25. Luke 15:19.

26. Colossians 1:12.

27. MS Wilberforce c. 40, fos. 62-63. *Life*, ii. p. 27 has, 'How mysterious, how humbling, are the dispensations of God's providence! I see that I closed with speaking of the East India clauses being carried, of which I have now to record the defeat; thrown out on the third reading by a little tumult in the court of proprietors. Oh may not this have been because one so unworthy as I undertook this hallowed cause, (Uzzah and the ark) and carried it on with so little true humility, faith, self-abasement and confidence in God through Christ? Yet where can I go but to the blessed Jesus, Thou hast the words of eternal life – I am no more worthy to be called Thy son; yet receive me, and deliver me from all my hindrances, and by the power of thy renewing grace, render me meet to be a partaker of the inheritance of the saints in light.'

28. MS Wilberforce c. 40, fo. 63.

29. MS Wilberforce c. 40, fo. 64. *Life*, ii. p. 30 has, 'I have this day been commemorating the redeeming love of Christ. May this be to me the beginning of a new era.'

Clapham Sunday Evg 16th. June

I may refer to Page 60 & re-write what I wrote on the 5th. of May - The carnal mind - O how hard is it to trust in X^t for all - This is that simple faith that humble child-like principle which proves its divine origin by its nature, & produces Love & Peace & Joy - O let me fly to Xt for Help & seek it diligently today whilst it is called today.[30]

Clapham Sunday Evg 23d. June 1793

My Eyes poorly from dust, therefore I cannot write. Alas! How little have I of the mind of X^t. How much malice do I discover in my Heart, glad I fear to catch Serv^ts in fault, & to see others Vices & Infirmities. Envious also of their merits. O how different this base Selfishness from the enlarged Philanthropy & purified affection this consists in the Love of Holiness as such & the detestation of Sin as such, in ourselves or others which are the Characteristics of the real Xtian. I have been mixing a little with worldly people & their Pursuits & Cares & Joys &c. do indeed seem most contemptible but it is not enough to see this one should also be filled with the Love of God & X^t. & of all mankind for his Sake, with a fix'd Desire to please him & do all to his Glory &c. O may I then hunger & thirst after Righteousness.[31] Create in me a clean Heart, O God &c. for X^t's Sake.[32]

Sunday Evg. Perry Mead July 21st. 1793

Alas! Alas! What proofs have I been receiving for this fortnight past, of the Hardness & Coldness & Deadness of my Heart, of its averseness to God, of its Sensuality & Selfishness & Indolence & Want of Spirituality. I have had Venn with me near a fortnight. He is heavenly minded & bent on his Master's work, affectionate to all around him, & to X^ts people above all as much. What a wretch am I. O let me labor with undoubted Diligence to enter in at the Strait Gate.[33] An indolent soothing sensual Religion will never support the Soul in the Hour of Death, then nothing will bring us up but the Testimony of our Conscience that we have fought the good fight.

Help me L. Jesus & by thy Spirit cleanse me from my Pollutions. Give me chiefly a deeper abhorrence of Sin & a more confirm'd Conviction of my own Vileness. Still let me press forward. Ho! Everyone &c.[34] & a thousand gracious appearances stand forth in his Gospel. I will endeavor to discover what those Sins are which done chiefly let & hinder me in

---

30. MS Wilberforce c. 40, fo. 64. *Life*, ii. p. 30 has, 'How hard do I find it to trust Christ for all! Yet this is that simple faith, that humble, child-like principle, which produces love, and peace and joy. Oh let me seek it diligently whilst it is called today.'

31. Matthew 5:6.

32. Psalm 51:10. MS Wilberforce c. 40, fo. 65. *Life*, ii. p. 30 has, 'How much do I yet want of the enlarged philanthropy and purified affection (this consists in the love of holiness as such, and the hatred of sin as such in ourselves and others) of the real Christian. I have been mixing a little with worldly people: and their pursuits and cares and joys do indeed seem most contemptible; but it is not enough to see this, I should be filled also with the love of God and Christ, and of all mankind for his sake, with a fixed desire to please him and do all for his glory.'

33. Matthew 7:13.

34. Isaiah 55:1.

running the Race set before me.[35] O enlighten me to see & strengthen me to subdue them. I would humbly pray to be enabled to attend more to my Secret Devotions & praying over Scripture. I have been very careless here.

July 28th rather mended. Aug[t] 4th D[o.] Interlacing Thoughts of God & X[t.] Sadly negligent here. 28 rather mended. Aug[t] 4th D[o.] Holy Spirit's Help forgot & Satan sadly. 28th very midl, Aug[t] 4th D[o.] Less Volatile. Aug[t] 4th a few weak Efforts ag[t] it. More humble more Cause than Success. More bold for X[t.] afraid to speak to Mr. Ansty ab[t] family prayers. O how Scandalous. Hypocrisy, O how much more careful to appear well before men than God - More fearful of Venn than God. X[t's] Sufferings have been little tho't of. In short I fear I have gone on worse than usual, no Love or Warmth this day. My Eyes bad, I must stop. Help me O God for X[t's] Sake, by thy Spirit.[36]

Sunday Evg July 28[th.] Perry Mead

Alas! Alas! How little am I what might well be expected from me, considering all the opportunities I have enjoyed, the Knowledge I possess, the Strivings of God's Spirit. This last Week has abounded with sensuality & Indolence & if I have had more Thought of God, yet how coldly have I felt toward him. How little dispos'd to find my Happiness in the Enjoyment of his Presence. How monstrous is this Hardness of Heart. O God, for Jesus Christ's Sake, wash away my Sins, & sanctify me by thy Spirit - I have felt afraid to speak to Mr. Ansty about having prayers - & if ever I give away money, or perform any external act of Religion, O what a Self-righteous Spirit breaks forth. Nothing is left but to pray earnestly to God to take away the Stony Heart & give me a Heart of flesh.[37] His Grace is sufficient.[38] To thee therefore I fly for Succour, thou Life-giving Saviour.[39]

Saturday, August 3[rd.] 1793

I laid the first timbers of my tract.[40]

Sunday Evg August 4[th.] 1793 Perry Mead

Every Day brings me fresh Proofs of my deplorable Corruption, & my perpetual Acts of Disobedience to the divine Law, yet sensible as I am

---

35. Hebrews 12:1.

36. MS Wilberforce c. 40, fo. 67. *Life*, ii. p. 32 has, 'I have had Venn with me near a fortnight; he is heavenly-minded, and bent on his Master's work, affectionate to all around him, and above all to Christ's people, as such: how low are my attainments! Oh let me labor with redoubled diligence, to enter in at the strait gate. An indolent soothing religion will never support the soul in the hour of death; then nothing will buoy us up but the testimony of our conscience that we have fought the good fight. Help me, O Jesus, and by thy Spirit cleanse me from my pollutions; give me a deeper abhorrence of sin; let me press forward. A thousand gracious assurances stand forth in Christ's gospel. I humbly pray to be enabled to attend more to my secret devotions; to pray over scripture, to interlace thoughts of God and Christ, to be less volatile, more humble, and more bold for Christ.'

37. Ezekiel 36:26.

38. 2 Corinthians 12:9.

39. MS Wilberforce c. 40, fo. 68.

40. *Life*, ii. p. 33.

of this when I look into myself, how cold am I, how callous, how little mov'd at the Sight, & even how unmov'd at y[e] Table of the Lord. Mens: Regl. broke repeatedly. Time idled away. Vanity given way to, & Sloth. This afternoon Lustful Thoughts even in y[e] House of God, yet I hope on the whole this last week has gone on rather better than some preceding, that I have been more conversant with spiritual Subjects, been more earnest in Prayer. O may God of his Infinite Mercy in X[t] enable me by his Spirit to <u>give him my Heart</u>, to devote myself unfeignedly & unreservedly to his Service, that I may discern in myself the Evidences of a saving Change & may <u>assume</u> to myself the Promises his Gospel holds forth to penitent Believers.

The same particular Sins & the same Graces continue to claim my peculiar attention & particularly: Seriousness of Mind contra Volatility. Aspirations frequent. Spirit of God & Xt the Sanctifier. X[t's] Death & Intercession. Temperance. Love to God & Man contra Selfishness. Vanity check & Envy & Evil Speaking. Diligence. Venn preached this morning at the Abbey Church, where I had asked for the pulpit from Dr. Phillott.[41] I more interested for his credit, alas! than his usefulness.[42]

Tuesday Night Aug[t] 6th

The above particulars have been alas but little at least far too little kept in View, & today Dr. Harington[43] & his Son & Mr. Whitwell dining with Venn & me several indecent things were said, I express'd I hope by my cold Looks some disapprobation, but I did not face them as I ought, & how should I, for I was transgressing the Bounds of temp[ce] in Wine. O remember the Expression, wherein is Excess,[44] & let it be your Care to be filled with the Spirit & never to be unfit for communion with God. Gratitude at meals more. Company & Convers[n] Regls.[45]

Wed[y] Evg Aug[t] 7th

This has been a bad day little Business done - Mens Regl. Broke, & little sense of God's presence preserved - & Vanity felt – Oimoi - I will by God's Help strive to be more temperate tis monstrous thus offending almost with[t] nay altogether with[t] motive except my own depravity, no Gratitude mens.[46]

---

41. Rev. Dr. James Phillott (1750–1815), Rector and Archdeacon of Bath, 1798–1815. Educated at Oxford, he married in 1808 Lady Frances St. Lawrence, daughter of Thomas St. Lawrence, 1st Earl of Howth, and Isabella King.

42. *Life*, ii. p. 32.

43. Henry Harington (1727–1816), composer, alderman, mayor and magistrate in Bath, and physician in Wells, descended from Sir John Harington, Henry VIII's army treasurer. He wrote popular music, glees, poetry and sacred music. He also published *The Geometrical Analogy of the Doctrine of the Trinity Consonant to Human Reason and Comprehension* (1806).

44. Ephesians 5:18.

45. MS Wilberforce c. 40, fo. 70.

46. MS Wilberforce c. 40, fo. 71.

August 18th. Sundy. Evg Batta. Rise

Alas! With how much Shame may I look back on the last 6 weeks which have elapsed since I left this Place. How little have I preserv'd a cordial Love of heavenly Things & a true Relish of their Enjoyment & practical Sense of their Value. Exceedg Mens: Regl & ferms.[47] Volatility & Vanity & Indolence have been sadly given into. What Proofs do I receive from my Promptitude to enter into the Pleasures of dissipation & Sensuality, when at such a House as Ld. B's, where it does not shock by the broad Stamp of gross vice.

O may I thro' God's Grace learn to be spiritually minded, minding (i.e. regarding <u>relishing</u> the Things of ye. Spirit). May I from this day begin anew, living to the praise of God's Glory, a diligent Self-denying Life so far as a Regard to my weakly frame & social duties (Mother & Sister) will allow, & endeavorg by God's help thro' the Spirit, for Xt's Sake to live in all things no longer to myself but to him that died for us & rose again.[48] The ladies all good natured but alas I made nothing of it. Some talk with Y but he not serious and I perhaps too timid. I think Lady Y has a feeling of religion. Music at night. How relaxing all this is to the mind.[49]

Saturday Augt 24th. 1793 - Batta Re

Referring to my Entry of this Day last year I find too much Reason to adopt the whole of it. My Eyes are too bad to allow of my writing, but what a Spectacle <u>does</u> my Life exhibit to <u>me</u>. I will, unless I rouze now at length from my Lethargy & lay hold effectually on the Grace of God in Xt. How many, how great, how almost unequall'd have been my Mercies, how many, how great my Sins & follies. The Good things I enjoy of God's providing, the Evils I labor under of my own, I mean with God's blessing, & relying on his Spirit to enter henceforth on a new Course. O let me not deceive myself, Remember always 1st to seek the Kingdom of God,[50] & next to glorify him with all the faculties & opportunities he has afforded thee. My Eyes smart, I must desist. I believe I shall begin a practice Book.[51]

Sunday Aftn 25th. Augt. B Re

O how deceitful is the human Heart.[52] How sluggish is my soul this Day & how little am I alive to the Realities of my Situation! May God quicken me by his Spirit for Xt's Sake. Let me press forward with all Diligence.

---

47. Wilberforce appears to use this abbreviation 'ferms' when referring to fermented drinks.

48. Galatians 2:20.

49. *Life*, ii. p. 34.

50. Matthew 6:33.

51. MS Wilberforce c. 40, fo. 73. *Life*, ii. p. 36 has, 'How many, how great, how almost unequalled have been my mercies! How many and how great my sins! The good things I enjoy, of God's providing; the evils I labor under, of my own. Let me press forward with all diligence, and may God for Christ's sake quicken me by his Spirit. I hope I have been more under the habitual fear of God, and yet how little do I live worthy of my high calling! My time has been wasted; let me labor to improve the talents God has given me, and to use them for his glory.'

52. Jeremiah 17:9.

Though my Eyes are so bad that I <u>must</u> spare them, I propose to draw up some Hints & Observations for my Conduct &c. & a Statement of some of the most remarkable particulars of my Life &c. in order to help Self-examination, & enable me to avoid the Temptations & obtain the advantages of my peculiar Situation.

Chief Mercies of my Life: D⁰. Events & Turns of D⁰ & Providences. Chief Goods of my Condition: Evils & Sufferings of D⁰. –

My chief Defects -

My general Duties - G. Oth. Inf.

My peculiar Duties: G. O. M. D⁰ Temptations.

Chief Sins of my Life.

My Chief Proper Objects of Endeavor both in Spiritually & intellectually.

Friends list &c.

Hints for Conduct, throughout.

Diffᵗ. Employments for diffᵗ States of Mind.

Understanding Improvemᵗ. Hints & Plan forming.

Observations, both Religˢ & Moral & Political.

Examine yourself what Studies Books &c. &c. you have in fact found more useful, both in Religion & other Pursuits.

O how my Time, & all my faculties & Powers have been wasted. Let me now begin in earnest to press towards the Mark of my High Calling, & to endeavor to improve my faculties to the Glory of my God & the advancement of his Cause in yᵉ World. A List of Subjects of Meditation &c. as God, Xt. &c. Examine how I may glorify God more by my Talents, <u>Fortune</u>, Connections, &c. &c. Love of Xᵗ how to improve in it. How to cultivate a Taste for Heaven & its enjoyᵗˢ.[53]

Battᵃ Rise Sunday Evg Septr 1ˢᵗ 1793

I hope I may have been rather more under the habitual fear of God, but O how little am I living in a manner worthy of my high Calling, how cold am I in spiritual things, how earthly & sensual. Fill me with the Love of thee, thou merciful Redeemer by thy Grace & relying on thee for all, may grow more & more conformed to thy Image. My Time has been sadly wasted. My Indolence indulged. Let me now labor to improve the Talents God has given me & to use them for his Glory. I am dubious whether or not I ought to go to Windsor[54] tomorrow Under the Cover of visiting Cookson[55] to take the Chance of getting into conversation with some of the Royal Family. Lady Elgin[56] may afford me the opportunity,

---

53. MS Wilberforce c. 40, fo. 75.

54. Windsor in Berkshire began as a Saxon village, but was taken by William the Conqueror as his own, and he built a royal castle there. It was extended by Henry II and Henry III in 12ᵗʰ and 13ᵗʰ centuries. In 1801, the population of Windsor was numbered at 3,361. The Castle is still a royal residence, and is the oldest and largest occupied castle in the world.

55. Rev. Dr William Cookson (1754–1820), Anglican Rector of Forncett, Norfolk (1788–1804) and Canon of Windsor (1792–1820).

56. Mary Nisbet (1778–1855), the only child of William Nisbet of Dirleton, was from a Scottish landowning family, and was heir to a fortune. She married Thomas Bruce (1766–1841), 7ᵗʰ Earl of

also I may perhaps do good to Mrs. Nugent & Mrs. Harcourt & yet I distrust myself.

I fear my Eye is not Supremely & chiefly set on God's Glory in this scheme. I am sure other Ends suggest themselves. It is rather too much in my slightly abused way, yet perhaps I should do better to attend to my proper Business, & this is Satan's artifice to draw me off, yet on the other hand, If any good done, it is great & hardly any Body else perhaps approaches them who is able to instruct them, & yet the Chance again of even gaining an opportunity of opening is so small. I will pray to God, to direct me.[57]

Sunday Evg Batt[a] Rise Sepr 8[th.]
Eyes bad, & have been so all this Week. I have been today in a sad stupid frame wanderg in Devotions. This week (for want of W[m.] partly) uncommonly indolent. O how little done, how cold my Heart! How useless my Life! May I thro' God's Grace reform thoroughly. I go to prayer.[58]

Bat[s] Rise Sepr. 15th Sunday Evg 1793
Eyes very poorly so can't write. In some particulars I hope more heavenly minded today but sleepy this afternoon at Church. But indiff[t.] in Health. I resolve thro' God's Blessing to lead a new Life, walking in his holy ways with a perfect Heart & willing mind.[59]

B. Rise Sep[r.] 22[d.] Sunday Evg
Eyes but poorly! This last week has been worse on the whole than preceding ones, less done, more interrupted by Company, being in Town twice, & receiving woeful proofs of the alienation of my Heart from God. O what a Wretch am I considering my many opportunities & how does it become me with deep Shame for y[e.] past & humble purpose of universal Self-amendment to implore the Saviour of Sinners to have mercy on me, & bring me back to his fold. O that by any means I might learn to maintain a humble watchful self-denying loving frame. Living above this World, looking forward to a better, & having here fellowship with the Father & with his Son Jesus X[t.] thro' the Spirit.[60] I go to pray humbly & earnestly, & by God's Grace,

---

Elgin, on 11 March, 1799, shortly before he headed to Constantinople. They would have two sons and three daughters, but would be divorced in 1807 in England. Lord Elgin is remembered especially for the removal of the Elgin Marbles from the Parthenon in Greece.

57. MS Wilberforce c. 40, fos. 76-77. *Life*, ii. p. 35 has, 'Doubtful whether or not I ought to go to Windsor tomorrow to take the chance of getting into conversation with some of the royal family. Lady E. may afford me the opportunity. Also I may do good to N. and H. Yet I distrust myself; I fear my eye is not simple, nor supremely set on God's glory in this scheme. Perhaps I should do better to attend to my proper business, and this is Satan's artifice to draw me off. Yet on the other hand, if any good is done it is great. I will pray to God to direct me. Thought over the Windsor scheme and resolved against it.'

58. MS Wilberforce c. 40, fo. 77.
59. MS Wilberforce c. 40, fo. 78.
60. 1 John 1:3.

I will labor after that glorious Prize which is set before us.[61] My chief hindrances seem -

Sensuality in which I may comprise Selfishness Indolence, &c. too little care of Souls, Vanity, which produces & cherishes Volatility, Envy (from Competition) Malice (from wounded Pride) Evil Speaking & other Tongue faults. Volatility as oppos'd to Soberness of Mind. Selfishness in all ways, not Golden Rule enough both in greater & smaller Matters &c. Of all these & of all my Corruptions the grand Root is <u>Carnal Mindedness & Want of y^e. Love of God</u>. O that I might attain to this & how should I purify myself even as he is pure.[62] I go to pray. O take away y^e. H^t of Stone &c.[63]

Sunday Afternoon Octr. 6th. B Rise

My eyes are bad so I can't write, alas! I could only note down as usual my Defects, yet I hope I have gone on rather better, & that now my Humiliation is deeper, my Seriousness more abiding, & that thro' God's Grace my purposes of Amendment will be more permanent. May God strengthen me for X^t's Sake. What Cause of Shame do I see in the Progress the Montagues have made, compar'd with mine, yet I trust that thro' X^t's Help I may press on to the Heights of Holiness, & yet again I dare scarce think so.[64]

Monday Night - 7th. Oct^r.

This has been a sad idled day, partly owing to my being indiff^t. Venn only with us, but I in no degree in a good frame, nor can I become now interested really in heavenly things.[65]

Tuesday Night, October 8th. 1793

Day sadly trifled away & my mind in a sad cold frame. O may it please God to revive me.[66]

Sunday Night Octr. 20th. B. Rise

My Eyes indiff^t so can't write - Heard Scott preach two excellent Sermons today on, I would thou wert cold or hot,[67] & Go & preach the Gospel to every Creature.[68] Much affected in Morng - O may it be for Good. O may I turn from my Evil ways & labor after a more decided State. Never

---

61. Philippians 3:14.

62. 1 John 3:3.

63. Ezekiel 36:26. MS Wilberforce c. 40, fos. 78-79. *Life*, ii. p. 45-46 has, 'I am more seriously-minded I hope than formerly. I hope I have gone on rather better, that my humiliation is now deeper, my seriousness more abiding, and that through God's grace my purposes of amendment will be more permanent. May God strengthen me for Christ's sake. Oh that by any means I might learn to maintain a humble, watchful, self-denying, loving frame of mind; living above this world, looking forward to a better, and having here fellowship with the Father, and with his Son Jesus Christ.'

64. MS Wilberforce c. 40, fo. 80.

65. Ibid.

66. Ibid.

67. Revelation 3:15-16.

68. Mark 16:15.

surely was there more of a Laodicean[69] than me if I even deserve that name. I find dining just after the Sermon puts it out of my Head & unfits me for aftern ~~Work~~ Sermon & obliges me to eat at night, when often I exceed - I will not dine between the Services in Town, but only snack & dine aftds. I go to meditate & pray - Lord help me![70]

Yoxall Lodge Sunday Nov[r.] 10[th.] 1793

Alas! How little, if indeed any at all, of the true Xtian spirit belongs to me! How sensual, selfish, proud, indolent am I. How little, if at all, is God really my delight & his ways pleasant to me - I daily am drawn in by the temptations under which I have a thousand & a thousand times fallen. Yet I bless God that doubtless for X[t's] sake, & thro' the help of his Grace, I am not even worse than I am - I feel a deep conviction (mix'd sometimes with vague doubts of X[ty] altogether not solidly form'd objections & I fly from them) that one thing is needful, & I humbly resolve to aim high. His strength is perfected in weakness.[71] O tarry thou the Lord's leisure & labor & strive earnestly. How unreasonable wo'd it be for me to expect after havg liv'd so long a lukewarm life even since I profess'd some Religion, to experience at once its power & energy. This hardly ever happens, tho' sometimes open profligates are suddenly reclaim'd. But God's promises in X[t.] are yea & amen.[72] They that wait on the Lord shall renew their strength.[73]

My eyes are too indiff[t] to allow me to write much, but I will note down my chief faults, which are to be specially guarded against: Vanity & Volatility of mind, making me soon forget heavenly things, & lose the sense of them even when it has been in my mind. Stony ground hearers it causes. Trifling talk &c. God & X[t.] forgetting &c. & heavenly things & Living Temple & Satan.

Hence aspirations forgot &c. Selfishness, to which belong Vanity, Pride, Self-Talking, unfair measure in expectations of others' conduct to me. Sensuality & Indolence: This produces intemperance &c. &c. Idleness & lack of <u>strenuous application</u>. Aversation to heavenly things: Vide Owen. No relish for family prayer. No real disappointment for sake of things themselves when religious opportunities lost. Want of love: Hence proceeds thoughts of unkindness to inferiors, &c. & not embracing possible opportunities of doing them good. Envy & even malice at times: Apt to be pleased when a preacher I dislike preaches ill, vice versa. Rather glad when such do wrong. Oimoi. Evil-speaking: Lying. Not careful enough here. Want of humility: Idle talkg & shewing off.

By God's mercy in X[t.] & by the help of his Spirit, I would resolutely & humbly strive most vigorously against my manifold corruptions, endeavorg so far as my health will allow, to mortify my prevailing

---

69. Revelation 3:14-17.
70. MS Wilberforce c. 40, fo. 81.
71. 2 Corinthians 12:9.
72. 2 Corinthians 1:20.
73. Isaiah 40:31.

corruptions & to lead a self-denying spiritual, diligent useful life to his glory. I am nothing, very weakness & guilt, but X^t is able to save to the uttermost.[74]

Sunday Novr 24th Yoxall Lodge

Last Sunday I did not take the pen because my eyes bad, as they are today. So I hasten to lay it down. O how diff^t is it to talk or write of Religion from feeling its power. I have been engaged on my heart, but how little spiritually minded & in all respects except I hope mens: Regls. not better than before - May Divine Grace quicken me - I have the same Lord, rich in mercy to all that call on him. O that I may look more to him & less to myself - With^t me ye can do nothing.[75]

Sunday Decr 1st Yoxall Lodge

Not well of my cold in my head, so not at Church. Eyes but moderate. I have been praying with seriousness, & considering that the Promises of free grace, & repentance, & a new heart, & strength, & peace, & joy in believing, are made to all that wait on God thro' Christ & will be performed thro' the powerful operations of the Spirit in spite of Satan's hindrances. O may I become the Temple of the Holy Ghost, & be enabled to look continually to the Cross of X^t & to the goodness of God in sending him to die for us.

Hereby may I be constrain'd to all holiness, & even ascribe to his undeserved mercy, & blessed agency, all the ability & hope I may have, in securing him. With what shame do I discover my hollow heart, more desiring of gaining worldly credit by my Tract, than of really glorifying God & X^t & benefitting my fellow creatures. Record mens: Regls. I have been rather well lately & more diligent, but sadly carnal & dull in spirituality. O quicken me by thy Grace. I go to read the Word by God, may it be blessed to me. I have found this morning the advantages of a little <u>religious solitude</u> (I have prayed ¾ of an hour for myself, family, friends, &c). Let me seize proper occasions for it, & not make my Sundays days of hurry. Solitude seems to give one over as it were, from worldly to spiritual things, & to realize the latter.[76]

---

74. Hebrews 7:25. MS Wilberforce c. 41, fo. 5. *Life*, ii. p. 46 has, 'I feel a deep conviction (mixed sometimes with vague doubts of Christianity altogether, not solidly formed objections; and I fly from them) that one thing is needful, and I humbly resolve to aim high. His strength is perfected in weakness. Oh tarry thou the Lord's leisure, etc. labor and strive earnestly. How unreasonable would it be for me to expect, after having lived so long a lukewarm life, to experience at once the power and energy of religion. This scarcely ever happens. But God's promises in Christ are yea and amen. They that wait on the Lord shall renew their strength.'

75. John 15:5. MS Wilberforce c. 41, fo. 4.

76. MS Wilberforce c. 41, fo. 5. *Life*, ii. pp. 46-47 has, 'I have been praying with seriousness, and considering that the promises of grace, and repentance, and a new heart, and strength, and peace, and joy in believing, are made to all that wait on God through Christ, and will be performed in spite of Satan's hindrances. Oh that I may be the temple of the Holy Ghost. With what shame do I discover my worldly heart desirous of gaining credit by my tract! I have been more diligent and self-denying lately: I have found this morning the advantages of a little religious solitude; (I have prayed three quarters of an hour, for myself, my country, and friends, etc.) let me seize proper occasions for it, and not make my Sundays days of hurry: solitude seems to give me over as it were from worldly to spiritual things.'

Sunday Decr. 8th. Y'll Lodge

O how diff^t a thing is it to have Religion really in the heart, from merely talking & writing ab^{t.} it, & having it in the understanding. Though I have been mainly & really with diligence employed on my Tract this week, yet how little spiritual have I been in my affections. Sadly otherwise - O blessed Lord, help me to love thee more, & may I be enabled more to realize my knowledge.[77]

1794

Wedy. Jany. 8th. 1794 - B. Rise -

Alas - I fear I have at best not got forward lately, tho' having every advantage of example &c. may God enable me.[78]

Sunday Jany 19th. 1794 Bata Rise

I fear I don't get on. I dare not believe I am spiritually minded when by so many marks, I may discern that I am mainly minding earthly things. O, let me not acquiesce in this sad state but resolve to press forward towards the prize of my high calling.[79] I am now about to enter on a troublous stage, & these are times which admonish us to examine all our foundation & see that it be secure. O may I believe in Xt. & love him & desire to serve him & to devote all I have & am by him, thro' the Spirit to the Glory of God.

... troubling stage upon which I am now entering, I proceed to frame a kind of plan for a Journal of my interior and exterior conduct, on which I propose almost daily to examine myself with a view to progress in holiness, tenderness of conscience, and that watchfulness which my situation in life, so abundant in snares, particularly requires. This scheme is to be drawn up with a view to my most besetting sins and temptations.[80]

At S. all day – extremely good tempered, pleasant people. This kind of society indisposes me sadly for religious communion; I either had not, or seized not, opportunities of religious conversation; no good done therefore by this visit, except in general, showing that I have no tail, which to them well known already. Dined at Hampstead to meet Jay, the American envoy,[81] his son, etc. – quite Americans – sensible. I fear there is little spirit of religion in America; something of French,

---

77. MS Wilberforce c. 41, fo. 6.

78. Ibid.

79. Philippians 3:14.

80. *Life*, ii. p. 48 here adds, 'these times of self-examination are regularly recorded in a plan which extends through this and the five succeeding years; with such persevering diligence did he watch over his heart, and so strictly pains-taking and practical was his personal religion.'

81. John Jay (1745–1829), American Founding Father, lawyer, President of the Continental Congress 1778–1779), signatory of the Treaty of Paris, Secretary of State for Foreign Affairs (1784–1789), Governor of New York State (1795–1801), and Chief Justice of the Supreme Court (1789–1795). Jay was also an ardent opponent of slavery and secured the emancipation of all slaves in New York.

tinctured with more than English simplicity of manners; very pleasing, well informed men. American Abolition of Foreign Slave Trade.[82]

Sundy Evg

I proceed to frame a kind of plan for a Journal of my interior & exterior conduct, in which I propose almost daily to examine myself, with a view to progress in Holiness, Tenderness of Conscience, & that watchfulness which my situation in life so abundant in snares, particularly requires. This scheme is to be drawn with a view to my most besetting sins & temptations, vide Book * Page 9 & 10.[83]

Sunday Night ½ past 11 oClock

After the above & some religious reading, & some earnest private prayer I attended Venn in the family with less distraction than usual, & was not faint after it, yet have been too free in meat & wine so as to carnalize my mind rather, & to unfit me for cool Bed &c. instead of striving for an opportunity of denying self. May God help me in future. Amen.[84]

Sunday Night Jany 26th. Pal. Yd.

My eyes are too indifferent to allow me to write by candlelight. This last week has gone off but ill. Paying many (necessary) visits, (as I am abt. to take in the ensuing weeks) seeing many new faces hurried. O how little heavenly minded. May God's Grace support me, & lead me into the right way. This is a truly aweful time when it becomes us to examine our foundations & be ready to die. With many doubts I this day received the Sacrament.[85]

Sunday Feby 2d. Pal Yd.

Alas! Alas! My time has been of late fritter'd away, my mind has gone to decay. Oimoi. My eyes are bad, I cannot write but let me humbly resolve by God's help now to amend & bring forth fruits meet for repentance.[86]

Monday 10th. Feby - Pal Yd.

I have too much cause to make the same complaint for the interim since my last writg. I am now hurried (unwell too) & cannot write - May God for Xt's sake, renew me by his Spirit.[87]

Sunday Aftn Feby 17th. Pal Yd.

My mind has been today more seriously impress'd than usual with divine things. O may this not be a transient but an abiding impression. I have gone on but very poorly during the last week, but by God's help

---

82. *Life*, ii. p. 57.
83. MS Wilberforce c. 41, fo. 7.
84. Ibid.
85. MS Wilberforce c. 41, fo. 8.
86. Ibid.
87. Ibid.

thro' Xt. I will press forward, & his promise of the Spirit standeth sure. Amen.[88]

Sunday Aft[n.] Feb[y] 23[d.] PalY[d.]

I have gone on worst last week than before, & perhaps the foundation of all my other defects has been that my prayers have been sadly hurried over, or sometimes almost wholly omitted or distracted. Mens: exceedg have been frequent - Spiritual thoughts few - Withal, little Business done, time being fritter'd away; & from late hours &c. &c. (which chiefly unavoidable) my health also has suffered. I have today heard from Scott an excellent Sermon on Preparation for y[e.] Fast. May I be really prepar'd. O let me rouze from these vain dreams, & be that which hitherto I have only profess'd myself. I go to prayer.[89]

Sunday Aftn March 2[d.] Batt[a] R[e]

Friday last was the Fast Day. I made but bad[ish] work of it, for tho' justly bef[e] Lock, Scott instructing my family a little &c. yet whittled away time in rest of day, by coming to B Rise & havg Venn & Parry who came callg & eatg per mod[y.] at ½ past 2. I was hungry at night & <u>rather</u> exceeded so that on y[e.] whole had but little time today for private meditation & prayer. Mens: more than 3 are hardly ever a religious really an edifying society. I mean at meal times to one so frail as I am, mem: avoid broken days plans, &c. except perhaps when I come to B. Rise alone.

My heart alas! is little set on divine things, if indeed at all. My judgment approves but my relish is for sensual & worldly ones, the praise of men, carnal fleshly gratifications. But I humbly resolve to strive to enter in at the Strait Gate.[90] I propose this Evg. to begin my Evg devotions frequently with imploring the divine help & against Satan's distractions. Then self-examination long. Looking back on all my last & recent & present sins & humbling myself, imploring God's mercy thro' Xt. & an interest in him, & for all Xtian Graces for all my schemes & Poor Slaves. East Ind[n.] miss[ns.] Home reform &c. Intercession for Sts. &c. & for help to be useful to them & here set down hints &c.

Recount (& set down, if eyes &c.) my chief particular causes for gratitude to God. Then solemn surrender &c. & prayer for help & strength (autea) Prayer for my Country &c. &c. at this critical time &c. For grace to discharge all my duties &c. Self examin[n] into my ways of going on throughout; Time, Money, Opportunities of Usefulness &c. &c. I have prayed at large &c. for 1 & ½ hours but with but little contrition, yet wait O my soul, on the Lord, in time he will come, wait I say on the Lord![91]

The same night 10 mins past 12

Being kept late for supper (10) & havg dined at 2, eat too much & oblig'd to sit up: wasted time, injur'd health, lost morning hours & purity of soul.

---

88. MS Wilberforce c. 41, fos. 8-9.

89. MS Wilberforce c. 41, fo. 9.

90. Matthew 7:14.

91. Psalm 27:14. MS Wilberforce c. 41, fos. 9-11.

It all has been the result of not checking a foolish disposition to continue eating, when no pleasure from it, & when conscience forbids. I must have a general Regl. but from experience I fear I should not observe it.[92]

Sunday Night March 9[th.] Pal Y[d.]

This last has been a very hurrying week, with Business & Company. Many sad Mens: exceedgs, & my heart in general in a very carnal frame. Today I have been seriously impress'd with divine things & I find it better when health allows, to eat a sandwich before Churches & dine afterds. This gives thinkg. time after morg service, & prevents eatg much & late sittg at night. But then it prevents Evg being so lively & profitable. I now go to prayer seriously to renew my prayers for divine grace thro' X[t.] & I only hope in him.[93]

Sunday Aft[n.] 16[th.] March – 94 - B. Rise

This last has been a more hurrying week from Business than any preceding one. The House & sometimes my own imprudence has kept me up late. My private devotions at night have been hurried over if not entirely omitted. This morning up so late, that no time for private devotions befe Church. I seem to have felt the effects of this all day. Wandering & distracted at Church, & sleepy, all which perhaps partly owing to my being very poorly, a sad, unspiritual frame all day, & even now, a sense of extreme stupidity & carnality with scarce a desire of amendment. God & X[t.] have been quite forgotten.

O how little am I looking for y[e.] coming of our Ld. Jesus X[t.] I have also been peevish with my Servts, in the House tow[ds] Ld. Sheffd.[94] O how vain am I & proud - May God help me to amend - I go to pray for the Grace of X[t.] NB - To try to have more time to myself this week for evening devotions. Earlier hours & morning devotions. Labor after heavenly mindedness & passing thro' this world as a stranger - Last night lying awake in bed, how much more naturally my thoughts rest on sensual than spiritual things - Surely I have no love for the Lord Jesus Christ. If I could be sure to escape Hell I fear I should care for heaven & its joys very little. Oimoi. Oimoi. Let me lay aside every weight &c.[95] They that wait on the Lord shall renew their strength.[96]

Sunday Aftn March 23[d.] 1794 B. Rise

The last week has been extremely hurrying in business & trying for my body. I have gone on but very poorly. Oimoi. Yet I hope rather better in

---

92. MS Wilberforce c. 41, fo. 12.

93. Ibid.

94. John Baker Holroyd (1735–1821), 1st Earl of Sheffield, M.P., President of the Board of Agriculture, Fellow of the Royal Society and close friend and literary executor of the writer and historian, Edward Gibbon, Sheffield would oppose Wilberforce's 1791 motion for the Abolition of the Slave Trade, on the ground that the West Indian Assemblies alone could deal with the question fairly in all its bearings.

95. Hebrews 12:1.

96. Isaiah 40:31. MS Wilberforce c. 41, fos. 13-14.

devotions than preceding week. But let me press forward & strive after the heavenly prize with more decided endeavoring this week.[97] Evening devotions mending &c. &c.[98]

Sunday Aftn March 30th B. Rise

This last has been a busy week, sad mens: excesses with temptation. Prayers I hope, more lively. The rising matters of Dawson & Kimber[99] look to be foul. O that I were truly right with God & then I would not care for ought. My Eyes bad.[100]

Sundy Aft[n] 6th Ap[l] B. Rise

I firstly thought I would stay in Town today & make it a Day of peculiar devotion, receiving the Sacrament &c. but I hastily changed at H. Thornton's motion & came to Battersea Rise. Is it on this account that I have been & am today particularly dead & cold in my frame. No sense of divine things. Lord help me! I have gone on but poorly this last week. May the ensuing holidays be to me a season of solemn recollection & issue me in a renewed state.[101]

Sundy Aft[n] 13th April B Rise

Sunday before Easter. Late hours & have sadly curtailed my devotions this week & Mr. Ashley's Read less Scripture. Cetera fer moderate.[102] As the solemn season approaching may I quicken what is ready to die or dead.[103]

Easter Sunday 20th Apl 1794 B Rise

How hard & unspiritual is my Heart. I gave myself much up to readg Scripture & meditation yesterday morning, & was much impress'd, yet in the afternoon I grew dull & all today I have been sadly dull & carnal

---

97. Philippians 3:14.

98. MS Wilberforce c. 41, fo. 14.

99. John Dawson, one of the largest slave-traders in the world, with a fleet of nineteen ships. John Kimber from Bristol, was captain of a British slaving ship, ironically called 'Recovery', whom Wilberforce named in a speech on 2 April, 1792, for brutally assaulting and flogging to death a 15 year old pregnant black girl. Kimber placed adverts in newspapers proclaiming his innocence, but his trial for murder went ahead in June that same year. It was reported, however, that throughout the trial, the Admiralty judge Sir James Marriot seemed very heavily positive towards the defense. Kimber ended up being acquitted with Marriot committing two prosecution witnesses for perjury. Kimber wrote to Wilberforce demanding a public apology, £5000, and a comfortable post in government. For the next two years, he would harry and menace Wilberforce, often waiting outside of Wilberforce's house and even intercepting him in the street. Wilberforce admitted that Kimber's acquittal and subsequent behavior caused him real distress. Lord Sheffield intervened and warned Kimber to stop harassing Wilberforce, who had taken to traveling with a bodyguard. See *The trial of Captain John Kimber, for the murder of two female Negro slaves, on board the Recovery, African slave ship: tried at the Admiralty Sessions, held at the Old Baily, the 7th of June, 1792* by John Kimber (London, 1792).

100. MS Wilberforce c. 41, fo. 15. *Life*, ii. p. 51 has, 'The rising matters of Dawson and Kimber look foul. Parliament meets again and this awkward business of Kimber's is coming on in which my life perhaps is at stake.'

101. MS Wilberforce c. 41, fo. 15.

102. Latin: tolerate all the rest in moderation.

103. Revelation 3:2. MS Wilberforce c. 41, fo. 15.

& unmov'd even at the Lord's Table. How good God is to me in allowing me Leisure, Peace, kind & religious friends. O that his Grace might enlighten me & warm my frozen heart. Nothg else, nothg else, will do - O Lord, take away the heart of stone.[104] Meanwhile let me resolve to aim high & to strive after universal holiness. In Spite of all my Experience of the Inefficacy of my own Efforts & of my repeated Relaxations of them I fear I trust too little to God's Grace & am too readily acquiescing in the Sufficiency of my own Efforts - Look to Jesus.[105]

Easter Tuesday Evg 22d Apl. Bata Rise -
Read this morng Scott on Repentance & Baxter[106] & meditated with much serious Thought - Too little (O how very hard is my heart) affected, but humbly resolved by God's Grace to press forward. How sadly defective am I living & how opposite of the Xtian Character.[107]

Sunday April 28th. 1794 B. Rise
My Eyes bad therefore I can't write - How strong a proof has this week afforded of my Deadness in Spritualy - Tho' here in Quiet, not broken in upon by Business, & little by Visitors, giving myself much to religious Thought, readg (as much as Eyes allowed, Ackley ill) &c. yet I have been almost uniformly quite dead & cold never more so & incapable of being otherwise. May the Grace of God quicken me - Awake thou that sleepest &c & Xt shall give thee light.[108] Meanwhile Parlt meets again, & this awkward Business of _____[109] is coming on, in which my life perhaps is at stake. O may I be prepar'd for the coming of Xt that havg obtain'd an Interest in him, I may be found of him in peace witt. Spot & blameless.[110]

Sunday 4th. May B. Rise
Alas! Alas! I don't find that I have gone on better this last week. Today Sensual & sleepy at Church morng & aftn, tho' had previously tho'ts of fasting – Oimoi. O may I awake to Righteousness.[111] I have been this week as usual sensual, exceedg mens & ferms indolent &c.[112]

Sunday Evg B. Rise May 11th. 1794
Bad work of it this week. Much in the old way. Today sad self-debatings abt. comg here. At Beaufoy's[113] yesterday how much overcome by many

---

104. Ezekiel 36:26.

105. Hebrews 12:2. MS Wilberforce c. 41, fo. 16.

106. Richard Baxter (1615–1691), Puritan theologian and prolific writer, remembered especially for his *Reformed Pastor* (1656) and *The Saint's Everlasting Rest* (1654). In Wilberforce's personal library, now held at the Wilberforce House Museum in Hull, there is a copy of Baxter's *A Call to the Unconverted* (1823).

107. MS Wilberforce c. 41, fo. 16.

108. Ephesians 5:14.

109. Uncertain word.

110. 2 Peter 3:14. MS Wilberforce c. 41, fo. 17.

111. 1 Corinthians 15:34.

112. MS Wilberforce c. 41, fo. 17.

113. Henry Beaufoy (1750–1795), M.P., Dissenter, and founder of Hackney College. He was son of a Quaker and educated at Hoxton and Warrington academies, then at Edinburgh University.

of my besetting Sins. O that I might awake to Righteousness.[114] Indolent this last week.[115]

Sunday Evg B. Rise May 18[th.] 1794

Alas! I have gone on but poorly all the last week, much the same as before, strongly impress'd at the Lock this morng but I fear I cannot but charge myself with supremely minding earthly things instead of heavenly ones. Let me labor to work out my salvation &c.[116]

Sunday Evg PalY[d.] May 25[th.]

Though sometimes in the last week strongly impress'd with a Sense of the Importance of Eternal Things, how little does my Heart abide under the power of them; may God by his Grace revive & warm my dead & frozen Soul, filling me with peace & Love & Joy in believing i.e. all bottom'd in & operating from a strong Principle of living faith. What a world of Misery & Vanity is this! and Eternity fast approaches. Be wise O my Soul, ere it be too late - The promises of God in Christ are still extended to thee. Therefore let me pray earnestly that I may be enabled to believe in the Lord Jesus X[t] unto Etern Life.[117]

B. Rise Sunday Afternoon - June 1[st.] 1794

This last week has been trifled away sadly, & from Disuse I seem incapable of application. How much Ill-Nature might I discover in myself respecting Rothn's foolish Breakfast. How sensual at Ld. Camn's. How selfish passim - How discompos'd ab[t.] R[n]. How little am I walking by faith instead of sight. May God for X[t's] Sake change my heart & enable me to love him supremely, to despise earthly things, to devote all I have & am to his Glory. My Evg. Devotions have been sadly curtail'd. Henceforth, earlier in Evg when can, & short prayer in middle of day. Vanity prevails in me. I thank God for these Seasons of Recollection. I have been today seriously impress'd with divine things. O may it be for good: Private & famy devotions. Self-denial in mens. &c. &c. Sensuality & passions. Fighting ag[t] Vain Glory &c. Sobermindedness ag[t]. Volatility, God, X[t], Satan Sp[t.] &c. &c. &c. &c.[118]

Bat[a.] Rise - Sunday Aft[n.] June 8[th.] 1794

But little change for the better in the last Week. Exceedgs Mens: frequent & self-denials forgot, even today after Sacram[t] so that asleep in y[e.] prayers this afternoon, & my heart how hard & dull. Let me now awake & quicken those things which are ready to die.[119] I have had serious conversations today, but this last week fritter'd away.[120]

---

114. 1 Corinthians 15:34.

115. MS Wilberforce c. 41, fo. 18.

116. Philippians 2:12. MS Wilberforce c. 41, fo. 18.

117. MS Wilberforce c. 41, fo. 18.

118. MS Wilberforce c. 41, fo. 19.

119. Revelation 3:2.

120. MS Wilberforce c. 41, fo. 19.

Bat^{a.} Rise June 15th. Sunday Evg

Alas! Alas! All is wrong with me - I have not the Spirit of X^{t.} & therefore am none of his, yet I bless God I am much affected with a Sense of my own wretchedness & danger & I go to seek in Prayer for true Repentance & living faith.[121]

B. R^e Sundy Evg June 22^d

No better - This week whittled away sadly, & mind in a sad distracted State – Today - much Self-debating. This foolish Portsmouth Scheme! O for more Love! firmer faith &c.[122]

B. Rise Sundy Evg July 6th. 1794

This last has been a hurrying fortnight! My Heart not right with God, I can't find any real Interest in divine Things. O for more Faith, more Love, more Humiliation. My many Acquaintances &c. &c. particularly injurious to such a scatterbrain'd fellow as I am, but I am heart Sick. O for a new Heart! May God for X^{t's} Sake hear my prayer.[123]

B Rise Sunday July 13th. 94

This last week gone much like the rest & nothing done in it. This is sad work. I am got into an idle unprofitable Course to which also being too much dispos'd this situation bad for me, Oimoi. Should I not have had more time if 3 Weeks ago I had dash'd off into Cumb^{d.}[124] now to seal'd 22.[125]

Xmas Day Night 94 - Bat. Rise

I have gone on ill. No maintenance of a Sense of God's presence. Cold & stupid on this day. Sleepy this Evg in famy Devotions. Too sensual at other Times. My time whittled away sadly, little done, all this, when the Judgements of God admonish to Righteousness. O let me awake to Righteousness.[126] I go to prayer.[127]

Batt^{a.} Rise Sunday Evg Decr. 28th. 1794

My time has gone away in political Conversations rather too babbling & vain, in which came to no point, yet honestly meant to make up my mind, But how unspiritual have I been! How little have I felt that Hope which is full of Immortality & which renders all earthly Things less interesting. Parl^{t.} much on Tuesday. I am going to Lond^{n.} tom^{w.} & I am little fortified for that Scene of Distraction & Dissipation into which I am about to enter. Perhaps my differg from Pitt, lessening my Popularity, & shewing me my co-comparative insignificance, may not

---

121. MS Wilberforce c. 41, fo. 20.

122. Ibid.

123. Ibid.

124. Cumberland was a historic county in north-west England, but from 1974 it became part of Cumbria. Muncaster, a favorite haunt of Wilberforce, is located there.

125. MS Wilberforce c. 41, fo. 21.

126. 1 Corinthians 15:34.

127. MS Wilberforce c. 41, fo. 21.

be bad for me in spiritual.[y] I would now humbly resolve to enter on a more strict Course as becomes me on entering a Scene of increas'd Temptations: Sensuality, Self-denial, Vanity, Envy, Malice, Indolence, House Attention, Love to all, & Good for Evil. In particular to bear with Kindness the Slights & Sarcasm I must expect from political Causes. O may God enable me to walk more by Faith & less by Sight, to see the Things that are unseen. O may he fill my Heart with true Contrition, abiding Humility, firm Resolution in Holiness, & Love to him & to my fellow Creatures. I go to pray to him, as I have often done to direct me right in politics, & above all to give me a new Heart.

Vanity & Ambition detected.[128] It is a proof to me of extreme vanity, that tho' I foresee I shall suffer much in my feelings (passim) from differg from Pitt, & might & <u>do</u> foresee how indiff.[t] a Figure I shall most likely make, yet the Idea of taking a Line for myself is gratifying to me, & flatters my consequential Selfishness. Motives of Ambition to insinuate themselves, Give me O Lord a true Sense of the Comparative Value of earthly & of heavenly Things. This will render me soberminded, & fix my affections on Things above.[129]

1795

Sunday Evg Jany 11[th.] 1795 -

The last ten or twelve Days have gone on sadly. One almost unvaried Course of Distraction, Vanity, & Worldly Cares, and now my Heart is in a sad Condition - carnally not spiritually minded - I have been fritterg my time away (more than I need have done tho' in a great Degree tis almost unavoidable in London except my system quite chang'd) in fruitless Talkg, discussions, civilities, careless of my friends Spiritual State, & with no serious Sense of invisible Things weighing on my own Heart - Also sadly too free mens: & ferms, careless of all Regls - Vain &c. &c. Oimoi. Remember O my Soul! "If any man have not the Spirit of X[t.] he is none of his,"[130] & "Take heed lest at any time &c. &c."[131] My

---

128. In the left margin, next to the main text, 'Decr. 28th Continued Vanity & Ambition detected'.

129. MS Wilberforce c. 41, fo. 22. *Life*, ii. p. 60 has, 'Parliament meets on Tuesday. I am going to London tomorrow, and I am too little fortified for that scene of distraction and dissipation, into which I am about to enter; perhaps my differing from Pitt, by lessening my popularity and showing me my comparative insignificance, may not be bad for me in spiritual things. I would now humbly resolve to begin a stricter course, as becomes me on entering a scene of increased temptations, self-denial, attention, love to all, and good for evil - in particular to bear with kindness the slights and sarcasms I must expect from political causes. Oh may God enable me to walk more by faith, and less by sight, to see the things that are unseen. Oh may he fill my heart with true contrition, abiding humility, firm resolution in holiness, and love to him, as I have often done, to direct me right in politics, and above all to renew my heart. It is a proof to me of my secret ambition, that though I foresee how much I shall suffer in my feelings throughout from differing from Pitt, and how indifferent a figure I shall most likely make, yet that motives of ambition will insinuate themselves. Give me, O Lord, a true sense of the comparative value of earthly and heavenly things; this will render me sober-minded, and fix my affections on things above.'

130. Romans 8:9.

131. Luke 21:34.

path is indeed difficult & dangerous, but if I wait on God humbly & diligently, he will support me - To try for:

More Temp[ce.] & Mens. Regl Talk &c. Evg Devotions less curtail'd &c. More cont[l] Sense of God's presence & universal Reform - vide supra.[132]

I was so much hurried last Sunday by Sir C. Mid[n.] here (being up late & no prayer before Church) din[g] after Church & talkg with him - Then Venn & Grant suppg till late, &c. on that I foreboded this last week wo'd go on ill - I have this day had more opportunity for Readg & Reflection - O may they be bless'd to me.[133]

Wedy Evg Bat[a.] Rise Jany 14[th.] 1795

Tho' I have been interrupted by Eliot's comg having designed to devote this Evg chiefly to serious Readg & Exercises, (my own fault still that I have not) yet this is Solitude compar'd with London, & how serious a thing is it to look into one's own Heart - to think of Heaven & Hell & Eternity - How cold & callous am I, who can think even of these Subjects with little Emotion. But incite in me O God more lively Sensations, & enable me to awake to Righteousness.[134] These two days have been spent with[t.] the Sense of God's presence, & much, too much as before, yet I would humbly hope for good, that God has not quite forsaken me, from the Seriousness of Spirit I now feel - It seems favor'd by this Solitude, & I will try the Effect of often retiring from the world, to commune here with my own Heart - I go to prayer.[135]

Sunday Evg Bat[a] R[e] Jany 18[th.] 1795

I have since liv'd in a Crowd & much as usual. Today I have been sleepy at Church both times, (extremely cold) & little Spirituality, now dull & cold. O may I be renewed in the Spirit of my mind![136]

Sunday Evg Bat[a.] Rise Jany 25[th.]

This has been a very hurrying week, seeing many People at Home, &c. Milner & Bob Smith with me; today much affected. Morng I received the Sacrament, but fasted till late & so overcome by Dinner that invincibly cold & sleepy this Evg (NB found afterwards that ill at this time). I have sadly exceeded Mens & ferms this Week. I have been sensual selfish, self-denial forgot. Evg Devotions extremely curtail'd, sometimes almost quite omitted. Scripture little read. Oimoi – Oimoi - I humbly resolve on Reform, universal - yesterday exceeded Mens, disagreed with me & very poorly today - O how am I asininal by Excess when so many are starving from cold & want.[137]

---

132. Latin: See above.
133. MS Wilberforce c. 41, fo. 29.
134. 1 Corinthians 15:34.
135. MS Wilberforce c. 41, fo. 30.
136. Ibid.
137. MS Wilberforce c. 41, fo. 31.

Sunday 3 oClock Palyd Feby 1st 1795

Alas! Alas! This week has been a sad one. My Evg Devotions & often even my Morng ones, sadly curtail'd or (almost) wholly omitted - No Scripture readg - How much more interested abt my Body than my Soul. Some of this week's faults partly owing to bodily Infirmities, yet O how little are these really an Excuse. Today at <u>Church</u>, never more wanderg & distracted in Prayer. My Heart felt hard & stupid. Morng devotions quite omitted for want of time, & not affected at all durg whole Service. Since I have been trifling time away, alas! This is not the Life of one who is working out his Salvation with fear & Trembling,[138] and then this has been a sad idle week, nothg really done in it. How little like the Life of one who is really livg under the Influence of that 'faith which worketh by Love'.[139] Soften my Heart O God! Thy grace only can effect this. I will endeavor humbly to wait on the Lord, that I may find him gracious to my Soul.[140]

Feby 1st Sunday Aftn 6 oClock Palyd

I am quite unfit for the discharge of the Duties of the Station to which the Providence of God has call'd me thro' Idleness, Inattention &c - &c - I might otherwise have excell'd in pubc speakg &c. I must now labor with more Diligence to recover my lost Time, as Health, Engagements &c. will allow me, praying to God for Humility - Even now, how prone am I to Vanity - to set down how adhere to Plan.[141]

Feby 16th Tuesday night ¼ past 11 PalYd

I was prevented partly by ye complaint in my eyes (which are now very indifferent) partly by other causes, from writing on ye Sundays. I have gone on but very poorly, tho' on both Sundays, strongly impress'd. Today how has it been wasted. I had people (on Business) to Breakfast. That & other things kept me till 1, then out & but little done before 3 ¼, when din'd <u>alone</u>, meang to employ Evg in preparg for Slave Discussion &c. &c. But how has it ended difft friends came in & discuss'd & at last a long Talk with Will Smith on Religion (& tho' not havg lost my Reason at all) yet certainly to <u>my own feelings</u> fluster'd with Rum & Water, havg been so also at Dinner), which I fear has done no good. A little prudence might have foreseen, anticipated & prevented <u>all this</u>. Oimoi – Oimoi - what a waste of Time! O that I felt more its Value - But I must lay down the Pen. Cleanse me O God from my manifold Corruptions & enable me to love thee & serve thee better & to believe from the Heart in the Lord Jesus Xt & to walk worthy of him that hath called us to his Kingdom & Glory.[142] Yesterday (I hope it was in some Degree bodily Infirmity) I was excessively sleepy, if not quite asleep both at morng & Evg Service - These things ought to humble me, & to infuse the most serious Doubts & apprehensions.[143]

---

138. Philippians 2:12.
139. Galatians 5:6.
140. MS Wilberforce c. 41, fos. 31-32.
141. MS Wilberforce c. 41, fo. 32.
142. Ephesians 4:1.
143. MS Wilberforce c. 41, fo. 32.

Sunday March 8[th.] 95 - 3 oClock Palyd

I have been confin'd to my House for a Week by the Piles[144] (no Pain) but require recling & abstinence from motion. My Time has been extremely fritter'd away up at 8 or after, just time to dress before fam[y] prayers, then hurried & distracted, & often interrupted & forc'd to postpone private Dev[ns.] which at last, ill-perform'd - Oimoi - Oimoi. I have been lookg into myself today, & I see I have abundant Reason to fear that I am going on a Plan of what may be term'd, "Religious Sensuality," Self-Gratification by avoidg pain, administering to Vanity &c. &c. is my main Object & to perceive Self Complacency & freedom from Pain of Mind it requires to abstain from gross disquieting Sins, & perform moderately, religious offices, but this is not to have the Conversation in Heaven,[145] to be spiritually minded,[146] to be constrain'd by the Love of Xt.,[147] to have the Spirit of Xt.[148] Can I say from the <u>Heart</u>, not in my Judgement merely, "whom have I &c." Psalm 73.[149] Alas! Alas! My mind is still unrenewed. But as God of his infinite Long Sufferg has not blinded me to my true condition, let me strive earnestly to emerge from it, more quiet - more Devotion & Meditation (for this earlier Hours). God waits to be gracious & they that wait on him shall renew their Strength.[150] I will trust in his promises & labor diligently, in the Strength of X[t.-] Help me O God by the Hy Sp[t.] for X[t's] sake.[151]

Sunday – March 15[th.] 95 - Bat[a] Rise Evg

This has been an unprofitable Sunday, & the last Week tho' <u>rather</u> better than preceding in point of morng Devotions but little Scripture Readg has gone on but very poorly on the whole. I have been hurried today & no secret Readg or prayer, of the latter I will try for some. Wasted Time in singing with little Spirituality & much Vanity at Grant's, alas! how hard is it to live & walk by faith havg the Conversation in Heav'n. Oimoi, may God help me. I will try in the ensuing Week for earlier Hours & more quiet Scripture readg more Self-denial &c.[152]

Sunday March 22[d.] Bat[a] R[e] ¼ bef[e] 3 oClock

The last week has been a very unprofitable one, & today my Heart is callous & dull - Frequent Exceedgs ferms &c. - I <u>must</u> amend here. Better resolve on avoidg appearances of Evil - I <u>must</u> more Scrip[e] readg better. Evg devotions sadly curtail'd - Little or nothg of spirituality in compy tho' some in other parts of day, perhaps this God's Blessing on morng

---

144. Hemorrhoids.
145. Philippians 3:20.
146. Romans 8:6.
147. 2 Corinthians 5:14.
148. Romans 8:9.
149. Psalm 73:25.
150. Isaiah 40:31.
151. MS Wilberforce c. 41, fos. 34-35.
152. MS Wilberforce c. 41, fo. 35.

Scripture Readg. My Heart is not supremely & habitually fix'd on God's favor & on pleasg X[t.] O may I now amend. How deep a Hypocrite I seem to myself. How little do I deserve the sola quietem.[153] Miss. More gave of me to Ly Waldegrave,[154] that I live (xlling) up to my Convictions. But by God's grace in X[t.] I hope to be renewed in the Spirit of my mind.[155] Try this week more Self-denial in mens. & ferms. Earlier Hours. More Bus[s.] discuss clear comp org. &c more Truth. Today live well, but in moderation.[156]

Sunday Afternoon ½ past 6, March 29, 1795, Palyd

This last week has been a sad one Extremely hurried. Hours as late as before. Evg devotions as curtail'd if not quite omitted, from being so late. Much Compy. Heart little set on God or heavenly Things, Oimoi, Oimoi. I hope now to amend.[157]

Good Friday Ap[l.] 3[d.] B[a.] Rise ½ past 6

I came down here yesterday meang to be quiet, & to endeavor to excite the alm[t] dead principles of devot[n] in me, but findg the Balfours were to be here I went to Town this morg & have heard Scott twice, good both times; how does he reproach me! How little have I, if I have anything of the Xtian character! May this little Recess from the Hurry of Life enable me seriously to look into my Heart & Plan of Life & whole Conduct, & to turn to the Lord with my whole Soul. O what can be too much for him who bo't us so dearly, & how dreadful must be that Punishment from which he died to rescue us! I go to Prayer.[158]

Easter Sunday B. R[e.] Ap[l] 5[th.] ¾ past 2

What a blessing it is to be permitted to retire from the Bustle of the world & to be furnish'd with so many Helps for realizing to oneself unseen Things. I seem to myself to be in some small degree today under the power of real Xtianity. Conscious, deeply conscious of radical Corruption, indulged habitual vices of the Heart & Life & great Unprofitableness, yet to such an one repenting & confessing his Sins, & looking to the Cross of Xt. is Pardon & Reconciliation held forth & the Promises of the Holy Spirit, to renew the Mind in the Image of God & to enable him to conquer his spiritual Enemies, & get the better of his manifold Corruptions. Be not cast down O my Soul.[159] But with Humility & penitence owning thy Sins, & lamenting thy great Unworthiness plead the atoning Blood of Jesus, & importunately & perseveringly ask for Grace from the fulness which is in Jesus. "He is made unto us says the apostle <u>Wisdom & Righteousness & Sanctification</u>[160]

---

153. Wilberforce here may mean the Latin: the only rest.

154. Lady Elizabeth Laura Waldegrave (1760–1816), wife of George, 4th Earl Waldegrave.

155. Ephesians 4:23.

156. MS Wilberforce c. 41, fos. 35–36.

157. MS Wilberforce c. 41, fo. 36.

158. MS Wilberforce c. 41, fos. 36–37.

159. Psalm 42:5.

160. 1 Corinthians 1:30.

as well as Redemption. He came not to call the Right[s] but <u>Sinners</u>.[161] He was the friend of <u>Sinners</u>. Look therefore unto him & plead his promises, & firmly resolve thro' the Strength deriv'd from him to struggle with thy lusts, with <u>all</u> of them, allowing <u>none</u> of them in any <u>degree</u>.

Apply also for Wisdom & Spiritual Understanding, that thou mayest walk worthy of the Lord unto all pleasing,[162] yielding thy members Instruments of Righteousness,[163] & endeavorg to devote all thy faculties (hitherto alas how wasted) to his Glory. My Frame of Mind at this time seems to me Compounded of Humiliation & Hope, a kind of sober determination to throw myself on the promises of the Gospel as my only Confidence, & a Composure of Mind (but not unmixed with fears that I am judging too favorably of myself), resulting from a Reliance on the mercy & Truth of God. I have also this Comfort that I feel Love tow[ds.] my fellow Creatures - This however would naturally follow from being in good Humour with myself. I still feel at this moment, vanity &c. working - But X[t] is made unto us Sanctification,[164] & our heavenly father will give his Holy Spirit to them that ask him.[165] Wait therefore on the Lord![166] Wait, watch & pray & wait.[167]

Monday Night, April 6, 1795, B Re

Meditated this morng seriously, & prayed, yet today exceeded ferms rather sadly unspiritualized in frame. Mr. & Mrs. Gordon din'd, when I asked them I meant serious Talk, but I quite unfit for doing them good. God forgive me, & suffer me not to relapse into my old sad way of going on. Body and mind, Oimoi. I rather tho't that I exceeded last night ferms, with Venn discussing.[168]

Tuesday 9 oClock Evg - BR[e.]

This has been a sad day. The morning roll'd away whilst I heard the debates with[t.] attention. They have scarce left a print, & at Dinner most absurdly (let me rather say wickedly) & unaccountably, without temptation, or any assignable Cause, I have exceeded so in mens, guarantg as greatly to disorder myself, when havg a Cold I had meant to be moderate, & havg Buxton[169] here design'd to talk with him seriously. But I made myself quite unspiritual. I stand amazed at my own

---

161. Luke 5:32.

162. Colossians 1:10.

163. Romans 6:13.

164. 1 Corinthians 1:30.

165. Luke 11:13.

166. Psalm 27:14.

167. MS Wilberforce c. 41, fos. 37-39.

168. MS Wilberforce c. 41, fo. 39.

169. Sir Thomas Fowell Buxton (1786–1845), M.P. and leader of the cause for abolition in Parliament after Wilberforce stepped down. After meeting Joseph John Gurney (1788-1847), a Quaker prison reformer, Buxton later married his sister Hannah in 1807. He also became involved in the prison reform campaign of another of Joseph's sisters, Elizabeth Fry. In 1823, Buxton formed the Society for the Extinction of the Slave Trade, and in 1838 published, *The African Slave Trade and its Remedy*. He was made a Baron in 1840.

monstrous stupidity. O Lord give me not over to the power of indulg bad Habits - Last night & tonight read Scripture with[t.] the smallest feeling. O that I could be free.[170]

Wedy 10 oClock Night Pal Y[d.] 8[th.] Ap[l]

This morng has been but indifft[ly.] bestowed & my frame all Day indiff[t.] Vain & affected & forgetful of God & still more of X[t.] O may he be not forgetful of me - Poor Buxton & Mrs. B[n171] should make me ashamed of myself. This Visit like that of Gord[n's] day before yesterday, does not seem to have done any good thro' my unpreparedness. Rather better in spirit today than some days.[172]

Sunday Midday - B Rise 12[th.] April

This last week has witness'd frequent Excedgs &c a general unspiritual frame. Time unprofitably us'd, last night & night before I put off serious readg on that account. I have meditated in morng generally & from it have had rather a more serious frame of Spirit durg the Day, but how little duly so. O may the Grace of X[t.] renew me in his Image, that I may live soberly righteously & godly, lookg for that blessed Hope & the glorious appearing of our Lord Jesus X[t.173] I mean God willing to try after a more temperate Course, such however as agrees with my Health. But may my Heart be holy humble penitent Self-denying - Help me O God, for X[t's] Sake.[174]

Sunday Evg B Rise Ap[l.] 19th

This last week has been rather idled away, at least little or no solid Study has been redeem'd out of it - Yesterday I din'd at Will Smith's, a mix'd Party, Ladies & Gentlemen & I sadly loose in imagination. Many Ladies came in at night & I too nearly approaching or rather quite to committing adultery in the Heart - Eat up too with Vanity - God forgot, his Spirit griev'd. My mind remarkably distracted. Something of loose Imagination has been suffer'd much to grow on me of late. Last Sunday got in carriage, lascivious, Oimoi. O may I be pure as God is pure. My Heart has been today in some degree solemnized, but my Conscience is defil'd & I dare scarce look to God with Hope, whilst I so disgrace his Gospel. What a thing is it for one who is writing such a Book as I am to behave as I did last night. How little was I mov'd as I ought to have been on the Loss of the Sunday Bill - Today I have rather exceeded Mens, & this week tho' more tempta yet have forgot self-denial. May God enable me to crucify the flesh with the affections & Lusts - & to be spiritually minded. Poor old Mr. Momaine.[175]

---

170. MS Wilberforce c. 41, fo. 39.

171. Hannah Buxton nee Gurney (1783–1872), daughter of John Gurney and Catherine Barclay Bell, wife of Thomas Fowell Buxton Bt. MP, and sister of Elizabeth (Gurney) Fry.

172. MS Wilberforce c. 41, fo. 39.

173. Titus 2:13.

174. MS Wilberforce c. 41, fo. 40.

175. MS Wilberforce c. 41, fos. 40-41.

Sunday Night ½ past 9 – Ap[l.] 26[th.] 95 B Rise

I had meant to be quiet today & had hop'd to be able to employ myself in devotional Exercises. How are our Plans broken! After church, where I was much distracted. Pitt came with Eliot, (from E's out of kindness), so I could not but stay with him & walk back with him. Then Bob Smith, which kept me till 3, then Rennell[176] came knowg of Dr. Coulthurst[177] & could not well leave him. I so far exceeded as to be unspiritualized - and wander'd at Service this Aftn, & am now cold & stupid. My Eyes are bad I can't write. Help me, O God! Rennell has a great Respect for Piety & Goodness & talents to make him eminently useful - O may God support me in this hurrying Week on which I am entering.[178]

May 3[d.] Sunday 2 oClock

This last has been a hurrying Week & mind has been little attended to. Mens Excedgs, no Xtian Hope cultivated, & bad in all my old ways. Time fritter'd away. Health but indiff[t.] O may I now reform & turn to God with my whole Soul. I go to prayer. It is not right for me entirely to abstract myself from the World, yet what a gay dream was yesterday, Oimoi, Oimoi. O God, do thou for X[t's] Sake fill my Soul with the Love of thee, & all other things shall grow insipid. I find on Reflection that my Evg. devotions during this last week have been so curtail'd, as to be almost next to quite omitted. A few serious Ejaculations after got to Bed, often talkg late to Milner. O how can I expect to amend when I thus neglect the grand Means of Grace. I yesterday reprimanded about beginning dinner before grace said, rather jocularly than seriously, not so as if I thought it wrong but informal. O how differently if I were seriously fill'd with the Love of God. How jealous should I then be of his Honor. Also, I have lately once or twice been givg a half indecent allusion. O how wrong.[179]

May, 1795, Battersea Rise

Old Newton breakfasted with me. He talked in the highest terms of Whitefield, as by far the greatest preacher he had ever known.[180]

May 10[th.] Sundy B Rise - ½ past 2

Alas! How little am I livg like a Xtian I must reform throughout - I do so little good to others but perhaps much Harm by going to g[t.] dinners,

---

176. Thomas Rennell (1754–1840), Dean of Winchester Cathedral and Master of the Temple.

177. Rev. Dr Henry William Coulthurst (1753–1817), J.P., and evangelical Anglican minister in Halifax, Yorkshire, who because of his gifts, was selected to be the opponent of Isaac Milner in a disputation when he kept 'The Splendid Divinity Act.'

178. MS Wilberforce c. 41, fo. 41. *Life*, ii. p. 86 has, 'Venn morning. I had meant to be quiet today, and had hoped to be able to employ myself in devotional exercises, when after Church Pitt came with Eliot; and considering he did it out of kindness, I could not but walk back with him. He talked openly, etc. After my return home, R. Smith came to see me, and afterwards Rennel came, self-invited, to dinner, and staid, talked all the afternoon, very clever, much good in him, great courage, scarcely serious enough, but much respect for good, and zeal against vice – talents to make him eminently useful. Oh my God support me in this hurrying week upon which I am entering.'

179. MS Wilberforce c. 41, fo. 41.

180. *Life*, ii. p. 93.

& suffer so much myself both in Mind & Body that I am very <u>doubtful</u> if I ought not to give them up, yet I don't think this right neither. "<u>No, not to eat</u>" implies this is the least Intercourse if any kept up. But let me earnestly pray for more Grace & then - O how little have I now - Lord Jesus help me![181]

Sunday Night May 10th

I have been conscious this Evening of a mind of rising ag[t.] Religion whilst Henry reading, of a sort of hatred to it, something of y[e.] same Kind at Church,[182] & rejoicing in Iniquity. Glad when they come too late to Church & hop[g] in Spite of my judgement that they may do so. Besides much Hardness of Heart & insensibility & wandering distracted Tho'ts. Help me, O God - Even when I would do Good, Evil is present with me.[183] But thou hast laid up in Jesus a rich Supply of every Grace - O may I partake of his fulness. Create in me a clean Heart O God, & renew a right Spirit within me.[184]

Monday Evg 11th. May

Alas! I feel sadly unspiritual. How soon all my thoughts & lively feelings of the invisible world vanish when the Hurry of worldly things assails me. I <u>must</u> live more Quiet, if I cannot gain more Strength - I thought it distracted my mind this morng to be thinking of dinner Invitations before my devotions &c. Bankes tells me that Pitt is furious about our meaning to resist the Prince's additional £25,000.[185]

Sunday Aft[n.] B. R[e.] May 17[th.] 95

This last week has been a bad one, no Scripture read but a little in Leighton on Peter[186] (excellent). Prayers Evg. curtail'd. Little done, much Mens. Excedg, vanity & insincerity at D[k] of Glosters.[187] I fear no Good done, & I quite forgot how to turn it to good use. Tho' all the while uneasy from consciousness that going on ill. Heard a most excellent & searching Sermon from Scott on "Be ye doers of y[e.] Word & not hearers only &c."[188] O much does it apply to me. Instruct me O God, & teach me my wants & enable me to live by faith in X[t.189]

---

181. MS Wilberforce c. 41, fo. 42.

182. In the left margin at this point is written, 'Secret Corruptions'.

183. Romans 7:21.

184. Psalm 51:10. MS Wilberforce c. 41, fos. 42-43.

185. *Life*, ii. p. 88. On 14 May 1795, Wilberforce angered Pitt by opposing the government's decision to increase the Prince of Wales's grant to £125,000 per year, excluding the revenues which came to him from the Duchy of Cornwall. On 8 April, the Prince had married Caroline of Brunswick, and claimed the raise would be needed for his new household. Wilberforce objected on the grounds that George had already run up huge debts at a time of national financial difficulties, when the poor were suffering from high inflation.

186. Robert Leighton (1611-1684), saintly scholar, Archbishop of Glasgow, Principal of the University of Edinburgh, and a signer of the 'Solemn League and Covenant' (1643). He had a personal library of 1,400 volumes. His work on 1 Peter was published posthumously in two volumes in 1693 and 1694, as *A Practical Commentary upon the First Epistle of St. Peter; and other Expository Works: by the Most reverend Father in God, Robert Leighton, D.D.*

187. Prince William Henry (1743-1805), Duke of Gloucester and Edinburgh, grandson of King George II and brother of George III.

188. James 1:22.

189. MS Wilberforce c. 41, fo. 43.

Sunday May 24th 95 – B. Rise Whitsunday[190]

Alas! This last week also has been ill spent, I have not felt the power of Religion. What advantages do I possess & how little do I correspond with them - A companion to pious & sensible is a treasure. But alas! my Heart is full of the fear of man & of the Love of his favor, & little impress'd with the Love & fear of God. But the grace of X^{t.} is promised to all that seek for it; Ho! Every one that thirsteth.[191] Therefore I will pray for that power to turn to the Lord which he alone can give - My Devotions in the Evg have been almost & generally curtail'd into a few Ejaculations this week, & Scripture Readg, except a little Leighton, omitted - Let me try to gain more time for religious offices this ensuing week - O how much more am I interested ab^{t.} my bodily health & comfort, than abt. my Spiritual State. It is by the increase in my Sense of the Value & Importance of Heavenly things, that the former will shrink to their true Dimensions - Assist me O Lord in this work. I go to prayer.[192]

Monday Evg B. Rise May 25th 95

Yesterday evening sadly sleepy at Church & cold afterwards … O how much more in earnest is Robt. Athenon.[193] I have little or scarce at all felt the presence of God today, or been in a watchful frame. I am vain & light. How much better am I thought of than I deserve.[194]

Wedy 3 oClock June 3 '95 Pal y^{d.}

Last Sunday was a very unprofitable one, very much from my own misconduct, & ever since my mind has been in an unspiritual State. Rouze O my Soul to a Sense of heavenly things, which are no less real than if they were objects of bodily Sight. I am but a nominal Xtian. How much more is my excellent friend H. Thornton livg by faith in the Son of God[195] & in the diligent Use of the means of Grace. How much more, Miss. H. More,[196] Miss Bird & all of them! How little they know me. Turn me O God of thy Mercy in X^{t.} Jesus.[197]

Sunday June 7th. B. Rise ½ past 2

Alas! how little am I pursuing heavenly things with my whole Heart, with its decided Reference &c. - O may I no longer have a name to live

---

190. Whitsunday is the Anglican term for Pentecost, the 7th Sunday after Easter. The name is a contraction of 'White Sunday' from the *Old English Homilies*.

191. Isaiah 55:1.

192. MS Wilberforce c. 41, fo. 44.

193. This could very well be a reference to Robert Thornton, of whom Wilberforce had previously been writing. 'Athenon' is Greek for 'without strength' and so he could well be using this as a descriptor rather than as a surname. Corroborating evidence for this comes from the Public Record Office who do not list any surnames 'Athenon' in their wills for this period.

194. MS Wilberforce c. 41, fo. 44.

195. Galatians 2:20.

196. Hannah More (1745–1833), poet, philanthropist and Christian activist, close friend of both John Newton, who acted as her spiritual guide, and William Wilberforce, whom she described as her guide, philosopher and friend. Wilberforce used her home, Cowslip Green, as his honeymoon home.

197. MS Wilberforce c. 41, fo. 45.

whilst I am in fact dead,[198] but may I thro' the Influence of the Holy Spirit be fill'd with the Love & fear of God & X[t.] & growing more indiff[t.] to any earthly things may I set my affections on things above & press diligently forward towards the Prize of my high Calling.[199]

Sunday Night -

I have been very unspiritual today - wandering in famy devotions & sleepy at Evg. Church - Spouting passages with Rennell, vain &c. – Oimoi – Oimoi - My Imagination has been running on marrying - O how hard is it to maintain a heavenly-minded composure. Fill me O Lord, with Love.[200]

Sunday 2 oClock 14[th.] June B. Rise

I have today felt more than lately the Corruption of my own exceeding Sinfulness & Unprofitableness, yet O how little compar'd with what I ought - What Mercies have I receiv'd, & am I daily receivg, & how little do I live under a Sense of the Goodness of God - Yesterday, I was vain, unprofitable, no Sense of God's & X[t's] presence, no Seriousness of mind - Excedg. too rather in mens, tho' from God's Kindness, Medicine rescues my Body. O awaken my Soul to a true Sense of My Condition - May I turn to the Lord with my whole Soul. I have this day receiv'd the Sacrament - May I present myself a livg Sacrifice.[201] O give me thy Grace, for I am all Weakness & Corruption - No Scripture read all last Week, tho' some serious readg - Evg Devot[ns] broken & curtail'd.[202]

Tuesday 16[th.] June Palyd

I exceded yesterday & Health suffers today, Oimoi. Yet I thank God that not blind to my Condition. O may I be enabled to press forward towards the prize of my high Callg.[203]

Saty June 20[th.] B. Rise

Alas! Tho' I hope I feel something of a Desire of Amendment, yet how cold & dead am I, & how little able to practise Self-denial, or any other Xtian Grace. Help me O Lord, by thy Power & work in me both to will & do accordg to thy promise.[204]

Saty Night - BRise -

At Mr. Astell's - Tho' not perhaps so distracted as usual, yet exceded ferms & deed - Self-denial bad, tho' observ'd in part, Oimoi - unspiritual

---

198. Revelation 3:1.
199. Philippians 3:14. MS Wilberforce c. 41, fo. 45.
200. MS Wilberforce c. 41, fo. 45.
201. Romans 12:1.
202. MS Wilberforce c. 41, fo. 46.
203. Ibid.
204. Ibid.

- & unfit when went upstairs for any serious & useful talk. O let me still resist, yea, even unto Blood.[205]

Sunday Aft[n.] B Rise June 21[st.] 1795

I was waken'd in the middle of the night by being ill in my Bowels & Heartburn from Dessert disagreeg with me - Medicine thro' Mercy has made me better than I expected (O how much better than I deserved), & I have been more serious today than of some time before. O may it be the Grace of God. I have felt settled Shame & Demerit, yet Hope in the Mercy of God in X[t.] & O may I henceforth live more to his Glory & be a real (tho' alas a weak), & not merely a nominal Xtian. I have too little tho't of Self-denial. I would endeavor it, trying its passion, & strivg to get the better of that Sensuality & indulgent Habit of Excess which does so easily beset me. I will try henceforth. Mod[tn.] Satiety – Ferms - not more than 1W or 2 & W. & Water except by prev[s.] Res[n.] No Dest. of any kind - & O may I in all my Rules Strive to improve.[206]

Monday Midday June 22[d.] - B R[e]

Half asleep at Evg. Church prayers - partly I hope Bodily Indispos[n.] But unspiritual at famy Dev[ns.] & all Evg aft[ds.] - & this Morng at Bkft a sort of pleasure resultg from thought that now Sunday over, no need to talk Relign. How diff[t.] this from the frame of the true follower of God, Psalm 145. I waste much time at Bkft & to amend & to keep at least when all day at B R[e] or one place a time account.[207]

B Rise Tuesdy Midday 23[d.] June -

Alas! I am sadly unspiritual, cold & dull as to heavenly things, Oimoi, yet let me persevere in using the Means of Grace, watching ag[t.] all known Sin &c.[208]

B R[e.] Midday Wedy 24[th.] June

Alas: yesterday broke my dinner Res[ns.] as to des[t] & rather as to wine, which to relax (so as not to be very particular) in moderation, when company with us. How vain I & unspiritual. I am now feelg the effects of it – Oimoi - Oimoi.[209]

B. R[e] Friday - Midday

Alas, Every day I find fresh proofs of my great Corruption & want of Spirituality. How impatient yesterday for dinner because a little Grumbling. How hard yesterday & day before, to keep to Des[t.] Rule, yet I thank God I prevail'd. Too careless of truth with Henster &c. too vain & unsolicitous & watchful to do good – Oimoi – Oimoi - I go to

---

205. Hebrews 12:4. MS Wilberforce c. 41, fo. 47.
206. Ibid.
207. Ibid.
208. MS Wilberforce c. 41, fo. 48.
209. Ibid.

prayer. Cleanse me O Jesus, by Thy Grace - Poor Lavater[210] (I am now readg his Diary), how simple & desirous of lovg & serving God. O had he possess'd my Relig[s.] Knowledge, & other advantages.

Resol[n.] To read a verse or two, not more every Morng when say my prayers (more wo'd then extremely hurt my Eyes), & keep one passage in the mind as the day thought, accordg to Doddridge's direction & Lavater's practice. Reminded by Lavater.

Resol[n.] To meditate or rather aspirate a little before & after meals, suitably & as seriously as I can. I have been us'd to say Grace with my Lips, but O how <u>little</u> with my Heart. This suggested by Lavater.[211]

B Re Sunday Midday June 28[th.] 95

I thank God I have been enabled to adhere to my Temp[ce.] Regls pretty well – O how many by drive of mere common prudence without Religion, without effort, find it easy without Strength to get the better of this low temptation which I find it so hard to master – Forgot much my Mens – Gratitude Res[n.] & Conversat[n.] Reg[ls] – Gave into Evil Speaking at R[t.] Thornton's a[bt.] West[d.] – & O how many deviations from the strictness of Truth – How much is Vanity ruling within me – Help me O God for Xt's Sake & that the power of his Spirit to become more truly a Xtian – I am quite unspiritual today, wanderg & inattentive at Church – Oimoi –
This week – Try –

Reslns. Mens: Gratitude – Convers[n.] – Sense of God's Presence - & Previous & Subsequent Gratitude – Moderate Self Denial – Truth – How commended to us in Y[e.] Psalms Humility –

How many Instances of the Covert Vanity do I discover in myself – I was vex'd not to find my name in the American's Rep[t.] Of Sierra Leone.
Resn. Avoid Evil Speaking.[212]

Monday 29[th.] June -

Sadly wanderg yesterday Evg at Church & in family - Forgot Mens, aspir[ns] &c. yesterday at dinner. Talk'd with too much complacency tho' in language of Condemnation, of my conduct at & after College. Wasted Time idly at night rather - This morng, dull in spirtualy.[213]

Tuesday 30[th.] June Midday. B. Rise

Yesterday went off unprofitably. I broke my mens, Regl. Des[t.] & forgot my previous dinner aspiration. No attempt to serve Ch. Grigby. Vanity rather than affection made me play with the Children, "the propriety of my assumed Character." O how hollow is my Heart. Cleanse me O Lord,

---

210. Johann Kaspar Lavater (1741–1801), a Swiss poet, philosopher, Zwinglian pastor, mystical writer, but remembered especially for his work as a physiognomist, specifically for introducing the idea that physiognomy related to the specific character traits of individuals, rather than general types. See *Secret Journal of A Self-Observer; or, Confessions and Familiar Letters of the Rev. J. C. Lavater* 2 vols. (1770). In Wilberforce's personal library, now held at the Wilberforce House Museum in Hull, there is a copy of *Essays on Physiognomy* by Johan Kaspar Lavater (n.d.).

211. MS Wilberforce c. 41, fo. 48.

212. MS Wilberforce c. 41, fo. 49.

213. Ibid.

by thy Grace - Eliot affected me today when he took leave. He seems apprehensive ab[t.] want of provisions. I have been readg the 22[d] Psalm, O what did Christ suffer for me, & yet how forgetful of him am I. Let me go & meditate of & pray to him, & for Grace to conduct myself better in the worldly Company into which I am now going -

How cowardly am I with regard to my apprehensions of bodily pain - I am afraid of going out of the neighborhood of London on account of 2 or 3 bad teeth, which perhaps cannot be drawn in the country. Think what X[t.] suffer'd - what his people have suffer'd - what Strength he can give - & support in pain - Pearson's story - & learn to trust him & to be less anxious & regardful of this short & uncertain State - Expect Evils & pain here - How little have I had of them. How much more almost everyone I know.[214]

Tuesday July 1[st.] 1795 B R[e.] Midday

I hope I yesterday did rather better in Company than sometimes, yet how much was then to blame. How much Vanity Insincerity & Sensuality - want of Spirituality. Evg. devotions neglected - to have these before family prayers when can, otherwise I get sleepy.[215]

Sunday Evg B. Rise 5[th.] July -

This last has been a hurrying Week - & I have gone on little as one lookg into himself, after the Tempestuous Service of the Session & preparg for my Yorkshire Encounter - Today I was under serious Impressions of eternal Things, but came to dinner & forgot previous & subsequent serious Tho't - Self-denial - Exceded rather, & my Stomach being out of order it prov'd much quite unspiritualized - O Lord - enable me to live soberly righteously & godly purifying myself even as thou art pure.[216] The Bell Rings - I must go to prayer.[217]

Thursday, July 9, 1795, B. Rise

To town about Sheffield corn business.[218] Privy Council.[219] Hawkesbury,[220] Portland[221] etc. Honest looking baker. Busy all day writing letters about

---

214. MS Wilberforce c. 41, fo. 50.

215. Ibid.

216. 1 John 3:3.

217. MS Wilberforce c. 41, fo. 51. *Life*, ii. p. 98 has, 'This last has been a hurrying week, and I have gone on too little as one looking into himself, after the tumultuous service of the session, and preparing for my Yorkshire encounter. Gisborne presses me much to this expedition. My judgment has been extremely puzzled whether to visit it, or go on with my work.'

218. John Baker Holroyd (1735–1821), 1st Earl of Sheffield, M.P., and President of the Board of Agriculture, published his *Observations on the Corn Bill now depending in Parliament* in 1791, with the Corn Regulation Bill being introduced early that year.

219. His Majesty's Most Honourable Privy Council, usually referred to simply as the Privy Council (with 'privy' being related to 'private'), is a formal body of counsellors and advisors to the reigning monarch. Council membership is usually composed of senior politicians, present or former members of either House in Parliament, the Church of England, and the Judiciary. The sovereign may appoint anyone to the Council, and there is no statutory limit to its membership.

220. Robert Banks Jenkinson (1770–1828), Lord Hawkesbury and 2nd Earl of Liverpool. Prime Minister of the UK from 1812 to 1827.

221. William Cavendish-Bentinck (1738–1809), 3rd Duke of Portland, and Prime Minister of the UK from 1807 to 1809.

scarcity. This now much dreaded. Meeting of merchants and bankers. Privy Council agreement.[222] Alas I fear my Visit to the Speaker's must have done Harm & not good & I have much to reproach myself with tow^ds. Him - How insincere my apparent cordiality, compared with his. How little watchful to do good - My Views seem to lower when with worldly people. Oimoi. O may God enable me for Xt's Sake to repent from y^e. Heart & to quicken those things which are ready to die.[223] I have today exceded Des^t at first forgetfulness, but then persisted &c. Oimoi - Oimoi.[224]

Monday July 13th. Night - B. Rise

Eyes bad so can't write so late. Exceded sadly mens & bad unprofitable in Compy, forgettg God. O what madness – Oimoi - I was serious yesterday but sleepy at Church both Morng & Evg. O Lord, pardon my great iniquities. What else can I do but fly to thee, & implore of thee Mercy & Grace to help in this time of need - The meanest temptation overcomes me with^t. Thee.[225]

Tuesday Night 11 oClock B Rise -

Alas! Today also I have sadly offended, mens. Excedg greatly - Lost Sense of God's presence. No good Convers^n. attempted, no seriousness of mind, alas! Yet this morning, serious. O how hard is it to perceive anything of a heavenly frame of mind. Pardon me O Lord & help me for X^t's Sake. Day rolls away after Day - little done & no mental Improvement - My Tract not even in its outworkg resum'd - My time quite fritter'd.[226]

Wednesday July 15th. 1795 B Rise. 2 oClock

It seems something providential, that wanting to devote this day mainly to secret Religious Exercises, fasting in fact as my Health allows, (Self-Examination, Humiliation, Supplication for self & others), & not knowing whether I could manage it. I should be left alone, T. Unwin going which I did not know - & Henry not comg back tonight - I have rather trifled away a part of the morng, but have been lookg into myself, & confessing my multiplied & great sins with a feeling of my sad condition & imploring the mercy of God for Xt's Sake, & Strength for the future. Tho' my Judgement dictates that lesson is supremely to be learn'd. I dare not say, that I should not be content to enjoy worldly prosperity for ever on Earth, instead of going to Heavn. This proves low Sense of Heavenly things, Low Ideas of God X^t. &c. want of Spiritual Affections -

---

222. *Life*, ii. p. 94.
223. Revelation 3:2.
224. MS Wilberforce c. 41, fo. 51.
225. MS Wilberforce c. 41, fos. 51-52.
226. MS Wilberforce c. 41, fo. 52.

My deliberate Plans arc form'd in the fear of God & with Reference to his Will, viz. How I shall spend my Time, select acquaintances - choose Residence, yet when I go into Company (on which I resolve as pleasg to God), I forget him, my Seriousness flies away in fumo[227] - The temptations of the moment to Sensuality Vanity Volatility, tho' small, get the better of me. Often also sad Intemp[ce.] both in Eating & drinking flustered to my own sensuality tho' others I believe perceive it not.[228] If I have any secret misgivg[s.] at the time, they are a sullen low grumbling of Conscience which is disregarded. All this makes my Life a Course of sinning & repenting, not defective in external Duties to God, or grossly so towards in opera operanda my fellow Creatures, (but rather the contrary, tho' here no man but myself knows how much Blame I deserve), but aboundg in Acts of Intemperance - constant Vanity - & sad forgetfulness of God & X[t.] - I seem therefore to want especially a larger Measure of that True faith, which realizes unseen Things & produces Seriousness - of that Vigour of the religious affections which by makg Communion with God & X[t.] thro' the Spirit, more fervent & habitual, might render apt & alert to Spiritual Things.

I dare not say I find Pleasure in Religious offices, distinct from the Complacency which attends the performance of an act we know to be right - This argues want of religious affections, which would render me warm & intense, & also dispose me really to love God's ordinances &c. (David's Psalms everywhere) - This argues Want of the Holy Spirit - This might not be to be inferr'd so positively in every Case because diff[t.] Mental Constitutions are diff[ty.] affected. Mine I take to be such as incapable of a high Relish of Religion. I ought to be thankful for this. I am responsible for it - It will be a Blessing & a Help well us'd, & if neglected, it will increase my Condemnation - Therefore: Res[n.] Cultivate y[e.] Relig[s.] Affections. Vide Edwards[229] for these. Watts on love of God & Use of Pass[ns.] in Relg[n.][230] Baxter &c.

I think it was better with me formerly, particularly when I first began to amend my life, e.g. in the Beginning & middle of the year 1786 - at least I then felt much more of Spiritual Sensibility - This was in part natural, but O let me quicken those Things which are ready to die.[231] I have now a name to live, whilst in fact I am dead.[232] Letters have met my Eye which of so pressg a nature that it would have been wrong not

---

227. Latin: in smoke.

228. At this point in left margin, he wrote 'Often also sad Intemp[ce.] both in Eating & drinking flustered to my own sensuality tho' others I believe perceive it not.'

229. *A Treatise Concerning Religious Affections* (1746) by Jonathan Edwards (1703–1758), is a volume in which Edwards describes his thinking about the process of conversion. The volume is based on observations of his Northampton congregation during the First Great Awakening of the mid-18th century.

230. Isaac Watts *Discourses of the Love of God and The use and Abuse of the Passions in Religion, with a Devout Meditation suited to each Discourse. To which is prefix'd, A plain and particular Account of the Natural Passions, with Rules for the Government of them* (London, 1729).

231. Revelation 3:2.

232. Revelation 3:1.

to answer them. I must go on in the Evg, dining very modest[y.] & readg some Life, or similar afterds.[233]

Wedy Evg

My Eyes are very indiff[t.] (the least of Tears always makes them so, & this obliges me to check myself in any religious offices). I cannot write much, but I will try a little. Perhaps I ought to try more strict Rules, tho' I have never found myself able to keep these. Let me endeavor however, not conceivg that anything but the Grace of God in X[t.] thro' the Spirit can enable me to keep them.

Humbly praying then for more Strength, I would resolve on:

1. Mens: Mod - & no Dis: ferms two or 3 mainly besides Wine & W[r.] & as little more sippings as can help (except when Health really requires more)

2. Compy & Conv[n.] Regls -

3. More seriousness of mind -

4. Daily Text & center'd in & past Tho'ts

5. Check Falsehood, Envy, Peevishness, Vanity, & encourage Love, Truth, Meekness, Humility, (Servants &c.)

6. Evg Devotions better, & Scripture much -

7. Friends' spirit[l.] good -

8. Self-denial & evident trouble for others, to win on them

9. Courage & fortitude as to pain &c (I am sadly cowardly & soft)

10. Boldness in X[t's] Cause - I am asham'd of him

11. Sense of God's Presence & frequent Thoughts of & Love of (mix'd with Reverence) God & the Redeemer & Holy Spirit's Help look'd to & Satan dreaded -

12. Trust in God reconcil'd by X[t.]

13. Cherish a Catholic Spirit.[234]

---

233. MS Wilberforce c. 41, fos. 54-55. *Life*, ii. 96 has, 'Spent the day in more than ordinary devotional exercises and fasting and found comfort and hope some benefit. It seems something providential that wanting to devote the day mainly to secret religious exercises fasting self-examination, humiliation and supplication for myself and others I should be left unexpectedly alone. The result of examination shows me that though my deliberate plans are formed in the fear of God and with reference to His will yet that when I go into company on which I resolve as pleasing to God I am apt to forget Him my seriousness flies away the temptations of the moment to vanity and volatility get the better of me. If I have any misgivings at the time they are a sullen low grumbling of conscience which is disregarded. Although therefore I am not defective in external duties to God or grossly towards my fellow creatures but rather the contrary though here no man but myself knows how much blame I deserve yet I seem to want a larger measure 1st of that true faith which realizes unseen things and produces seriousness and 2nd of that vigor of the religious affections which by making communion with God and Christ through the Spirit more fervent and habitual might render me apt and alert to spiritual things. My finding no more distinct pleasure in religious offices vide David's Psalms everywhere argues a want of the Holy Spirit. This might not be inferred so positively every case because different mental constitutions differently affected. Mine I take to be such as capable of a high relish of religion. I ought to be thankful for this I am responsible for it. It will be blessing and help well used and if neglected it increase my condemnation. Therefore let me cultivate the religious affections. I think it was with me in this respect formerly at least I felt more religious sensibility. This was in part natural. Yet let me quicken those things which are ready to die.'

234. MS Wilberforce c. 41, fo. 56.

Sunday 19th. July 1795 B Rise 2 oClock

This last has been a sad hurrying week on the whole, my Time fritter'd away insensibly, my Regls. & Resolutns. but little attended to. No.2 & 4 sadly forgot, tho' better than sometimes. - I think I receiv'd Benefit from Wedy last, tho' so crippled in the Day's Business by my own foolish Management, being taken off in the Evg by Venn's Comg, which hardly repaid me - Wanderg also in prayers & today my Heart feels hard & cold. Yet O Lord, thou encouragest Sinners to come to thee - Thou art the Fountain of Light & Life - O quicken, & instruct me, & strengthen me to serve thee diligently with my whole Heart, accordg to the Gospel of thy Son - My Heart & judgement have been, & are extremely puzzled what to do abt. visiting Yorkshire, going on with my Tract &c. &c. Direct me aright O God, for Xt's Sake.[235]

Monday Night – B. Rise – 20th. July. 11 oClock

This has been a most useless & misspent day. Ross here - Vaght &c. Vain - Sensual - &c. Time wasted - Conversatn. not improv'd &c. &c. - O how little am I qualified to write on religious Topics - Pardon me O God, & have Mercy on me for Xt's Sake - Henry possesses himself far more than me.[236]

Sunday Evg – 26th. July 1795 Sleaford[237]

This Sunday has been rather wasted, yet in the Morng I felt the comfort of religs. Self Convn. But true Xty. lies not in frames & feelings, but in diligently doing the Will of God - My Eyes are but poorly & I cannot write - I am now abt. to enter on a very trying Scene - O that God may give me Grace, that I may not disgrace but adorn his Cause, that I may watch & pray more earnestly & seriously. I am weak, but God has declar'd that they who wait on him shall renew their Strength.[238] I would fly to him pleadg the Merits of the Redeemer - How much in earnest poor Clarke[239] seems.[240]

Sunday Augt. 2d. 1795 Scarbro'[241]

This has been but a bad Sunday, & my general going on here has been very indiff.t indeed - Far too little interest'd about the Happiness of my fellow Creatures. Little interested for the Glory of God & the travail of

---

235. Ibid.

236. MS Wilberforce c. 41, fo. 57.

237. Sleaford is a market town and parish in in Lincolnshire, 17 miles south of Lincoln, settled as early as the Iron Age. In the 12th century, Sleaford Castle was built for the Bishops of Lincoln. In 1801 the population of Old Sleaford was approximately 120.

238. Isaiah 40:31.

239. Adam Clarke (1760/2–1832), a Methodist theologian and Biblical scholar.

240. MS Wilberforce c. 41, fo. 57. Life, ii. 97 has, 'Sunday. This morning I felt the comfort of sober, religious self-conversation. Yet true Christianity lies not in frames and feelings, but in diligently doing the work of God. I am now am about to enter upon a trying scene. Oh that God may give me grace, that I may not dishonor but adorn his cause; that I may watch and pray more earnestly and seriously.'

241. Scarborough is a north-eastern coastal, spa town, about 40 miles from Hull, probably founded by the Danes in the 10th century. In 1801, its population was numbered at about 6,000, but for the rest of the century it would grow rapidly, to be over 30,000 in 1901. Wilberforce spent the summer at Scarborough in 1784, and it would be at Scarborough that he met Isaac Milner, and there invited him to be his companion on what transpired to be his very significant European tour.

X^{ts} Soul - Too light, trifling & unprofitable. Help me O God for X^{ts} Sake - Devotions neglected - Ferms too free & scarce kind to Mr. Clarke - Scarce kind & dutiful enough to my Mother - O may I feel more of the power of divine Grace.[242]

Sunday Augt 9th 3 oClock Marton

This rambling life amongst worldly people, abounds with Temptations to Vanity, Falsehood, Forgetfulness of divine Things, wanderg prayer, want of Boldness in asserting X^{ts} Cause, & I too sadly yield to them - I am & have been for several days more than commonly dead to religious feelings - Short & confus'd devotions &c. &c. My Health is not equal to this vagarious kind of life, & at the same Time preservg & redeemg time for serious Things - O how much ought I to quicken the things which are ready to die.[243] My Plan was undertaken from a Conviction of its being right, but it sadly distracts & disorders me mentally - Keep me O Lord God for X^{ts} Sake.[244]

Thursday Morng Augt 13th Welton

Alas! This hurrying Company Life does not agree with my Soul's. How much do I forget God! How little Courage I have in professing the Gospel of X^t Help me O Lord, to be indeed a Xtian. I embrace no opportunities of serving the spiritual Interests of my friends.[245]

Sunday Af^{tn} Hull Augst 16th

Eyes bad so cannot write - I am but in a very indiff^t State, unspiritual & cold. O how far more lively is old Henry who is now going on his Tour.[246]

Sunday Evg August 30th Halifax[247]

This hurrying Life sadly unspiritualizes me, yet as it more plainly discovers me to myself it may be of Service - How much Insincerity am

---

242. MS Wilberforce c. 41, fo. 57.

243. Revelation 3:2.

244. MS Wilberforce c. 41, fo. 58. *Life*, ii. 104-105 has, 'This rambling life amongst various people abounds with temptations to vanity, forgetfulness of divine things, and want of boldness in Christ's cause; and I too readily yield to them. My health is not equal to this vagarious kind of life, and at the same time preserving and redeeming time for serious things. Oh how much ought I to quicken the things which are ready to die! This plan was undertaken from a conviction of its being right, but it sadly disorders and distracts me mentally.'

245. MS Wilberforce c. 41, fo. 58. *Life*, ii. 105 has, 'This hurrying company does not agree with my soul. How little courage have I in professing the Gospel of Christ! How little do I embrace opportunities of serving the spiritual interests of my friends! How much insincerity am I led into! How much acquiescence in unchristian sentiments! I wish I had written my tract, that my mind might be clear; yet as all this more plainly discovers me to myself, it may be of service. If my heart were in a more universally holy frame. I should not be liable for these temptations. Remember they show your weakness, which when they are away, you are apt to mistake for strength. Entire occasional solitude seems eminently useful to me. Finding myself without support, I become more sensible of my own wretchedness, and of the necessity of flying to God in Christ, for wisdom and righteousness, and all I want here and hereafter.'

246. MS Wilberforce c. 41, fo. 58.

247. Halifax is a Minster town in West Yorkshire, named in 1091 as Halyfax, was a center of woolen manufacture since the 15th century. In Wilberforce's time, cotton, wool and the carpet industry dominated the town's manufacturing industries. In 1800, Halifax's population was numbered at almost 9,000, and had several elegant Georgian mansions including Clare Hall, Hope Hall and Somerset House.

I led into? How much acquiescence in Sentiments unXtian &c. - I wish I had written my Tract,[248] that my mind might be clear.[249]

Sunday 2 oClock, September 6, 1795, Cannon Hall

My Life is not spent with sufficient diligence, & a thousand vain Imaginations distract me about Miss M$^{t.}$ &c. yet Hope I do some good by my Conversation, & I thank God I this day enjoy a more heavenly minded frame than common. Alas! Alas! How ignorant are people of X$^{ty.}$ How grateful ought I to be for the numberless Blessings I enjoy. May the Want of some temporal Comforts lead me to set my affections on things above.[250]

Sunday 12 oClock, Sep$^{tr.}$ 13$^{th.}$ 95. Muncaster[251]

How many Scenes have I gone thro' & to how many dangers have I been expos'd since I was last here in 1788. I ought to be very grateful - My Heart however is cold & dull - My habitual frame very unspiritual. How diff$^{t.}$ from excellent Macaulay[252] & T. Babington - They are all Life & Vigor & T.B. (the other probably also but I don't know him), all Humility too - I have a name to live, but I am in fact dead.[253] Alas! Alas! Let me labor by Prayer & Supplication to quicken those things which are ready to die.[254] O that I may grow in Grace & in the Knowledge & Love of X$^{t.}$ & in a Disposition to be ever abounding in the Work of the Lord.[255] What Reason have I to devote all my powers to the Service of God, who has preserved me from innumerable Evils, & still holds out to me the Hope of mercy. I am vex'd, that I gave no serious Book & had no serious talk with Miss Waterhouse, yet I scarce had any opportunity.[256]

---

248. 'Pamphlet' was written but then crossed out.

249. MS Wilberforce c. 41, fo. 58.

250. Colossians 3:2. MS Wilberforce c. 41, fo. 59. *Life*, ii. 107 has, 'A quiet Sunday is a blessed thing; how much better than when passed in a large circle! My life is not spent with sufficient diligence, yet I hope I do some good by my conversation; and I thank God I this day enjoy a more heavenly-minded frame than common. Alas! How ignorant are people of Christianity!'

251. Muncaster Castle at Ravenglass in Cumbria, described as a craggy fortress, has been in the Pennington family since 1208. However, much of what is now seen was designed in 1862 by Anthony Salvin.

252. Zachary Macaulay (1768–1838), prior to his activity amongst the Clapham Circle, he had been an estate manager in Jamaica. He married Selina Mills who he was introduced to by Hannah More, and the couple settled in Clapham. Known for his incredible memory and research ability, Macaulay was not only a leading figure in the abolition movement, the first major editor of the very influential *Christian Observer*, on the governing committees of nine religious and philanthropic organizations, a founder of London University, but also Governor of Sierra Leone for six years. There is a memorial to him in Westminster Abbey.

253. Revelation 3:1.

254. Revelation 3:2.

255. 1 Corinthians 15:58.

256. MS Wilberforce c. 41, fo. 59. *Life*, ii. 108-109 has, 'How many scenes have I gone through, to how many dangers have I been exposed, since I was last here in 1788! I ought to be very grateful. What reason have I to devote all my powers to the service of God, who has preserved me from innumerable evils, and still holds out to me the hope of mercy! I am vexed not to have had any serious talk with M, yet I scarce had any opportunity. Muncaster, to whom I have told my feelings about E. thinks him irreligious, and that he would not bear to be spoken to.'

Sunday Night 13th. Septr. Muncaster

This has been a sad unprofitable Sunday - In the Society part of it no religious talk - also mens: excedg most foolishly – Oimoi - Alas! Alas! Yet rather more affected than common with divine things this morning.[257]

Sunday 27th. Septr. Muncaster - Morng

I have been going on whilst here but very indifferently - too sensual - too forgetful of God & Xt. - too little watchful for doing spiritual good - Alas! Alas! How little am I of a real Xtian - Forgive me O God for Xt's Sake & enable me to serve thee better - I have been but Idle here. My mind & Imagn. has been continually infected with lascivious Images from meditating marriage. Alas! Alas! How should this shame me, rememberg what poor Abel Smith[258] told me that he never thought of Miss Appleton when just going to be married to her, in that way, tho' he suppos'd his natural desires would rise when occasion naturally call'd them forth - O let me labor after more purity & Heavenly mindedness, 1 John 3:3.[259]

Sundy Evg -

How excellent is Macaulay. I felt him a Sort of Restraint on me, & certainly wish'd him gone, tho' I yet lik'd his Company, & greatly respected him. Does not this show that I don't really love the Brethren - I have been too sensual today.[260]

---

257. MS Wilberforce c. 41, fo. 60.

258. Abel Smith (1717–1788), M.P., and the founder of the Nottingham Smith's Bank. In 1745 he married Mary Bird (1724–1780), whose younger sister Elizabeth Bird would become the mother of William Wilberforce. Abel and Mary had eight children, five of the sons following their father into Parliament, including Abel Smith (1748–1779) and Samuel Smith (1754–1834). Samuel had eleven children, one of whom, Abel Smith (1788–1859), also became a banker and M.P., as did many members of the family. He was also a correspondent with William Wilberforce and their two families were intertwined for over 100 years, according to research by Sue Castle-Henry. For further background see, https://www.ucl.ac.uk/lbs/person/view/43657. Abel Smith's grandfather, Abel Smith (1717–1788) was apprenticed at 15 (c. 1732) to Wilberforce's grandfather, William Wilberforce (1690–1776). Wilberforce's mother, Elizabeth Bird (1730–1798), was the daughter of Thomas Bird, and Mary Bird's sister. Abel Smith was, therefore, a 1st cousin once removed of Wilberforce. Thomas Bird's son, John Bird, married Judith Wilberforce, daughter of William Wilberforce (1690–1776). Their son was William Wilberforce Bird (1758–1836) M.P. Wilberforce's sons, Samuel Wilberforce (1805–1873) and Henry William Wilberforce (1807–1873), married respectively Emily Sargent (1807–1841) and her sister, Mary Sargent (1810–1871). Abel Smith was the 2nd cousin of Samuel and Henry. He was also 1st cousin once removed of Emily and Mary Sargent who were great-granddaughters of Abel Smith (1717–1788) and Mary Bird, being granddaughters of Abel Smith (1748–1779) who was the brother of Samuel Smith (1754–1834) who was father of Abel Smith (1788–1859). Samuel and Henry Wilberforce were 2nd cousins once removed of Emily and Mary Sargent. Harriet Smith (d. 1856), of whose marriage settlement to Lt Col John F Crewe (1788–1840) Abel Smith (1788–1859) as a trustee was awarded the compensation for Raymond's estate in Vere, Jamaica, was the daughter of Robert Smith 1st Baron Carrington (1752–1838), who was the 3rd son of Abel Smith (1717–1788) and Mary Bird. Harriet was thus also a 1st cousin once removed of William Wilberforce. See https://www.ucl.ac.uk/lbs/person/view/43657.

259. MS Wilberforce c. 41, fo. 60.

260. Ibid.

Tuesday Evg Askrigg[261] Sep[tr.] 29[th.]

Alas! Alas! How ought I to weep & lament for my wretched State - In spite of all my previous Resolutions, Recollection &c. &c. I almost deliberately set myself to tempt, & if she had been as bad as me, should have been as foolish as before. O what Cause for suspecting that I am yet in the Bond of Iniquity. I purpose in all Sincerity & Seriousness to endeavor to repair the Effects of my wicked light & foolish Conduct, telling her how I reproached myself &c. I now go to earnest prayer, havg felt much today - We are promis'd that to them who seek, & knock, it shall be open'd.[262] O let these proofs of entire weakness, stimulate me to strive more earnestly for the Grace of X[t.] that I may be turn'd from all my Evil ways & be renewed in the Spirit of my mind.[263] Marriage I observe in this frame appears less desirable. O of what trivial moment is all but the securg an Interest in X[t.] If my Heart were in a more universally holy frame, I should not be liable to these temptations. Remember they <u>shew</u> your weakness, which when they are away you are apt to mistake for Strength -

Entire occasional Solitude (as tonight) seems eminently useful to me - Findg myself without Support I become more sensible of my own Wretchedness; & of the necessity of flying to God in X[t.] for Wisdom & Righteousness & all I can want here or hereafter. I have been praying fervently & O may my being sensible of my vileness be a Sign that I am not forsaken by the Grace of God.[264]

I have been much too sensual at Munc[r.] & often given in to Evil Speaking & Carelessness ab[t.] friends' Spirit[l.] Concerns, & lately Breakg of Strict Truth – Oimoi – Oimoi - no Sense of God's presence at meals &c. &c.[265]

Friday Night Cosgrove[266] Oct[r.] 2[d.]

Alas, how sadly I lost my good temper towds. Ma[ted] day bef[e] yesterday - much humbled for it, & felt force of our havg master in Heav'n - Today I have been foolishly exceedg in dessert tho' very indiff[t.] to begin with. Alas! Alas! what folly, or rather guilt. I will humbly endeavor now to mend in this Respect. Surely my bodily Health will be the Victim of my Intempce.[267]

Sunday Night Cosgrove Oct[r.] 4[th.]

Alas! This has been a sad Sunday - how little Love I felt any of the power of Religion. Sensual – indolent - earthly minded - havg a Name

---

261. Askrigg, a small town which was in the North Riding of Yorkshire, now North Yorkshire. It was an ancient town, known especially for its clock makers, and for being the town where the house stood, that was used as the fictional vet James Herriot's home.

262. Matthew 7:7-8.

263. Ephesians 4:23.

264. At this point in left margin he wrote 'Faults'.

265. MS Wilberforce c. 41, fos. 61-62.

266. Cosgrove is a village in Northamptonshire, about 12 miles south of Northampton. Cosgrove Hall was built for the Furtho family in the 18th century, but was gutted by fire to just its shell in October 2016. At the time of Wilberforce's entry, the Hall was owned by George Biggin (d. 1803). The population of Cosgrove in 1801 was 505.

267. MS Wilberforce c. 41, fo. 62.

to live, but being dead.[268] This being with irreligious people very mischievous, I convey no proper Idea of my Character. How much more in earnest is Mrs. Regnal. Poor Burgh seems going on sadly in aidg & comforting.[269]

Monday Evg Cosgrove 5[th.] Oct[r.]

I have been rather excedg today dest &c. I would resolve no Dis &c. How sadly Time is wasted here. How little do I feel of the power of divine Things! Devotions Evg curtail'd. When came up last night, incapable of Prayer to my own Conceptions & sat stupidly musing - Alas! Alas! O for more Life.[270]

Sunday Evg 18[th.] Oct[r.] 1795 Yoxall Lodge

I have been going on here but idly - I hope I feel some Degree of Xtian Humiliation for it, but too faint a Determin[n.] of amendment. I hope today I have enjoyed some spiritual Satisfaction, tho' alas! I ought to deplore my Sensuality & Hardness of Heart - How much does Henry everyway go beyond me - I have been rather light today. May I improve & learn to live like one bought with the price of the Blood of X[t.] havg my frame made up of adoration Gratitude Desire & Trust. Witherspoon's Sermon on Heavenly State.[271] I have been sadly indolent Henry properly reprov'd me.[272]

Sunday Night Oct[r.] 25[th.] Pal Y[d.]

A quiet Sunday is a blessed thing. How much better than when spent in a Large Circle - I have heard an excellent Sermon today from Scott & have felt I would humbly hope, some Comfort in Religion, but O, how much alloyed & debased by wanderg sensual vain thoughts. I am now about to enter once more on a London Winter. Let me look before me & solemnly implore the aid of the Grace of God to guide & direct, to support, to quicken, to preserve me - I am all corruption & weakness, but X[t.] is able & willing to support them that wait on him for Succour - Let me consider what in former years have proved to me chiefly Occasions of falling, & endeavor to provide against them.

No.

1. Intemperance both in eatg & drinkg -
2. Falsehood -
3. Anger & Malice, Fretfulness, & procrasta -
4. Shame of God & X[t.] -
5. Fear of temporal Evils, Pain, &c. -

---

268. Revelation 3:1.
269. MS Wilberforce c. 41, fo. 62.
270. Ibid.
271. 'Witherspoon's Sermon on Heavenly State' inserted here above the line.
272. MS Wilberforce c. 41, fo. 62.

6. Secret Devotions & Med[n.] & Scrip[e.] Evg where can conveniently -

7. Check Vanity & contra Humility - "He that exalteth hims &c."[273] 10 times repeated

8. Compy. & Convers[n.] Regls; Relax[n.] Occup[n.] &c.

9. Time redeem where can. Diligence in all Business - fervent in Spirit &c. &c.[274] -

10. Friends spirit[l.] good -

11. Mens: Gratitude & fug[t.] Occas[l.] aspir[ns.]

12 Self Denial passim & Trouble &c for others -

13. Endeavor to soar above the Turmoil of this tempestuous World & to experience Joy & peace in believg -

14. Conscious of Satan 1 Peter 1[275]

15. Remember God's Presence -

16. Let Love of X[t.] constrain who died to save us from Misery & is now at God's right hand making Intercession for us[276]

17. Xtians peculiar Character

18. Gravity in House

19. Cheerfulness & kindness & placability, but Secret guard & hidden seriousness & sober mindedness everywhere

20. Preserve Sense of Vanity of earthly greatness, Honors, &c. &c. &c.[277]

Sunday Nov[r.] 1[st.] 1795 - B. Rise

This last has been but a bad week considering that I have been in no Hurry of any kind. Today I have been too sensual rather, tho' I felt at Dinnertime rather the want of food wine warmth &c. But it has made me Sleepy & unspiritual this afternoon - This week I have fail'd particularly in N[o.] 15, 16, - 6 (devotions at Church today distracted, sadly). 3 rather with Scott. 7 little tho't of - 8 too much forgotten, indeed scarce tho't of - 11 Greatly forgot - 10 But middg. 13 - very bad - 14 Forgot much. 17 much forgot – 19 - D[o.] - 20 - Hardly enough - I have been all today remarkably cold & unspiritual. O for more Life, & for more Desire of it.[278]

---

273. Luke 14:11.

274. Romans 12:11.

275. 1 Peter 5:8.

276. Romans 8:34.

277. Points 17-20 were written lengthways in the left margin of the page. MS Wilberforce c. 41, fos. 62-63. *Life*, ii. p. 115 has, "Let me look before me and solemnly implore the aid of God, to guide, quicken, and preserve me. Let me endeavor to soar above the turmoil of this tempestuous world, and to experience joy and peace in believing. Let me consider what in former years have proved my chief occasions of falling and provide against them. Let me remember the peculiar character of a Christian gravity in the House cheerfulness kindness and placability with a secret guard and hidden seriousness. Let me preserve a sense of the vanity of earthly greatness and honor."

278. MS Wilberforce c. 41, fo. 64.

Sunday Nov[r.] 8[th.] Evg - Pal Y[d.]

This has been but an indifft. week in No 6 today at Church particularly 7, 8, 9. Time has been fritter'd away. I hope I have maintain'd rather more than sometimes a Sense of God's presence & a Desire of his favour, but today I have been remarkably dull & unspiritual & I have not improv'd my opportunity of religious Conference with Eliot &c. I will humbly pray that God would bless me with the Light of his Countenance, & enable me to preserve a Sense of the superior worth of heavenly things whilst yet I am diligent in my worldly Calling. What a mercy, to be assured that God will hear the Prayers offer'd in his Son's Name.[279]

Tuesday Nov[r.] 10[th.] 95 Pal Y[d.] Night

Alas! what a tumultuous State of mind have I experienced & am I now experiencing? Made up of Vanity of Concern ab[t.] worldly Reputation - Now havg rather exceeded ferms (wholly with[t.] temptation & after it, havg only Macaulay, H. Thornton, & Ld. Grant). My mind is pleas'd with the Idea of having done well, anxious from fear of not havg done so well as I wish, I am unquiet & tumultuated Alas! Alas! O God give me thy Peace! Pardon My Iniquity for it is great - forgive my great offcules - Enable me to be grateful for thy Mercies, & to pour out my Soul before thee in deep Humiliation & entire Reliance on the Blood of the Redeemer.[280]

Saturday Night Nov[r.] 15[th.][281] Palyd

I have been ding out & afd[s.] an assemblg, at the Chief Baron's.[282] - Alas! Alas! How little like a Company of Christians - Surely I have no Business at such Places. What dost thou here Elijah?[283] Vanity is excited, or one's Pride is mortified, a Sort of hollow cheerfulness in every Countenance. I grew out of Spirits - thinkg partly I hope of better Things, but also mainly influenc'd also by findg myself unfit for such Society.[284]

Sunday Noon 16[th.] Nov[r.] B. Rise

I had not been at Pains last night to fit myself for Compy, by a Store of Conversation Topics, Launchers &c. &c. I felt some Sense of the divine Presence & breathings after God whilst at dinner, but unless one can much mend these things I can scarce approve of them - tho' this was just what I wanted to establish. 1 Card table only. I hope this last Week I have felt rather more abidg Sense than sometimes of divine Things, yet

---

279. Ibid. John 14:13-14.

280. MS Wilberforce c. 41, fos. 64-65.

281. The Saturday in November here was actually the 14th not the 15th as Wilberforce here records it. Similarly with Sunday's date as he recorded it, as Sunday was the 15th and not the 16th as he wrote it.

282. The Chief Baron of the Exchequer was the first baron or judge of the English Exchequer of Pleas. He would preside in the Equity Court and speak for the Court in the absence of the First Lord of the Treasury and the Chancellor. The Chief Baron at the time of Wilberforce's entry was Sir Archibald Macdonald (1747–1826), 1st Baronet, M.P. and Lord Chief Baron (1790–1813).

283. 1 Kings 19:13.

284. MS Wilberforce c. 41, fo. 65. The entry is listed as Saturday night, but November 15 was a Sunday. *Life*, ii. pp. 104 has, 'I have been dining out and was then at an assembly at the Chief Baron's. Alas! How little like a company of Christians! A sort of hollow cheerfulness on every countenance. I grew out of spirits. I had not been at pains before I went to fit myself for company, by a store of conversation topics, *launchers*, etc.'

O how much too little; Today I have I hope felt something of a Christian frame. But O my Soul, learn to grow in Grace - Watch & Pray & strive, in Reliance on the operat[n.] of the Spirit thro' the Intercession & for the Sake of X[t.] from the faithfulness of God. I have this week sadly found my want of Launchers & Friends paper. Let me now provide myself with them.[285]

Sunday Night

Alas! How distracted & sleepy was I at Church this Eveng, & in our Evg Service which just over - How much more intent ab[t.] the danger of tomorrow, from the Tumult &c than ab[t.] my Duty to God & Communion with him. Pardon O Lord my Sins, for X[t's] Sake. Pity & Succour my great weakness, & enable me to get the better of my Infirmities.[286]

Thursday Night 19[th.] Nov[r.] Pal Y[d.]

I have gone on but mod[tly.] these few Days - Alas! Alas! What Cause have I for Humiliation. O How many Blessings am I daily receivg at the Hands of God, & how diligently ought I to devote myself to his Service.[287]

Sunday Aftn. 22[nd.] Nov[r.] Kg's Arms Y[d.]

This week has been but ill improv'd, & this day tho' partly feeling the Influences of divine Grace as I wo'd humbly hope, at times, inciting desires of amendment, yet at other times how cold & carnal - How little have I felt as I ought considerg the prest tumultuous & dangerous State of Things - I am now an Object of popular odium - O how fleeting is popular favor - I greatly fear some civil War or Embroilment & my Cowardly Heart shrinks from the Dangers & difficulties to which from my weak Health & my peculiar Infirmities. But put thy Trust in God O my Soul! If thou prayest earnestly to him, confessing thy Sins imploring pardon for X[t's] Sake, & laborg for Amendment, thou wilt be accepted, & then, all things shall work together for thy Good.[288]

God protected me from Norris,[289] Kimber, Williams - & innumerable other dangers - He is still able & willing if it be for thy good! O then seek his face seriously & diligently. I staid in Town today breakg Light with Eliot to go to Ly Waldegrave[290] & Euston,[291] chiefly the latter. May it be for good! May I be enabled to do them Service & receive Benefit - O

---

285. MS Wilberforce c. 41, fo. 66.

286. Ibid.

287. Ibid.

288. Romans 8:28.

289. Probably Robert Norris, slave-trader, who was questioned by a Committee of the House of Commons in 1788.

290. William Waldegrave (1753–1825), 1st Baron Radstock. He held several positions including Admiral, Governor and Commander-in-Chief of Newfoundland. He married Cornelia Jacoba Van Lennep (1763–1839), daughter of the chief of the Dutch factory, on 28 December, 1785 in the Anglican Church in Smyrna, Izmir, Turkey, the city where she was born.

291. George Henry FitzRoy (1760–1844), Earl of Euston, M.P., and Lord-Lieutenant of Suffolk. As early as 1791, he voted for abolition of the slave trade, and was a staunch supporter of the cause in 1806. He was also an assistant mourner at Pitt's funeral. On 16 November, 1784 he married Lady Charlotte Maria Waldegrave (1761–1808), daughter of James Waldegrave, 2nd Earl Waldegrave; they would have eleven children.

how vain now appears all Successful Ambition - Poor Pitt! Alas! Alas! O if he knew the way of Life.[292] Resol. Pr. To have a Text daily as poor Lavater, whose most interesting Diary I have been hearg rather too long & too carelessly.[293]

Sunday Night ½ past 11, November 22, 1795

I sat near 2 hours with Ladies Waldeg[ve.] & Euston. I wish it may have been to advantage. My imagination roving &c Since I am come home I discover an <u>unodorous</u> spirit had stolen on me. My Heart feels like a Stone almost, this is perhaps partly bodily fatigue, but O Lord do thou soften & warm me. I go very shortly to Prayer & then to rest. My devotions have not been at all full today, no af[tn.] or Evg Intercession. Let me try tom[w.] morng.[294]

Sunday 2 oClock, December 6, 1795, B. Rise

My Heart is today very hard & cold & my Thoughts wanderg at Church. O what multiplied Causes for Thankfulness have I had durg the last week. I have gone out & return'd home in Safety. My Health has not suffer'd from fatigue &c. &c. & favor & a kind Reception have attended me. Alas! How little do I lay these things to Heart. Last night ding at Ryder's, wasted opportunities & forgot God's presence & Xtian Profession. This morng when I heard that yellow & putrid fevers were rife, my Heart misgave me that I was not prepar'd to die. Yet I have in some Respects I hope a little gone on better. The Day thought I have generally retain'd, & I find the practice fixes it deeply in my mind. O may the Grace of God enable me to live to his Glory & really to desire it, for its own Sake.

Faults Chief: I have been harsh & unkind to Ashley & rather so to other Serv[ts.] Puff'd up with Praise at York & with Regls. in Lond[n] & Envy also quite alive if had been call'd out. Breaches of y[e.] Strictness of Truth. Scarce honest in askg on Friday night ab[t.] army Extraordin[y.] Not thoughtful suffg ab[t.] f[ds.] Spiritl. good. How little have I that Xtian Grace, "Rejoiceth not in Iniquity."[295] I seem glad to catch friends, Serv[ts.] &c. in faults. O how this argues want of Love & presence of a Satanic Spirit. How little do I think enough of my pecul[r.] Character.[296]

---

292. There is then a horizontal line drawn across the page, with 'Resol.' And 'Pr.' is written in the left margin at the continuation of the entry. *Life*, ii. p. 115 has, 'How vain now appears all successful ambition. Poor Pitt! I too am much an object of popular odium. Riot is expected from the Westminster meeting. The people I hear are much exasperated against me. The printers are all angry at the Sedition Bills. How fleeting is public favor. I greatly fear some civil war or embroilment and with my weak health and bodily infirmities my heart shrinks from its difficulties and dangers. Put thy trust in God, O my soul. If thou prayest earnestly to Him, confessing thy sins, imploring pardon, and laboring for amendment, thou wilt be accepted, and then all things shall work together for thy good. God protected me from Norris, Kimber and innumerable other dangers. He is still able to protect me and will if it be for my good.'

293. MS Wilberforce c. 41, fos. 66-67.

294. MS Wilberforce c. 41, fos. 67.

295. 1 Corinthians 13:6.

296. MS Wilberforce c. 41, fo. 68.

Sunday 2 oClock, December 13, 1795, B. Rise

This last week has been but a baddish one, much hurried by Business &c Yesterday (at Hatsell's)[297] went on sadly, mens: excedg &c. & frame quite unspiritualiz'd. O how little careful ab[t.] my own or others Souls. How forgetful of God's Presence. How utterly so of X[t.] How little inward feeling, & how light my Expression of Concern &c. when Hatsell mention'd that most people now seem'd to disbelieve X[ty.] Today I have been hearg an excellent Sermon from Venn, on Rev. 1:7, "Even so Lord Jesus," & receivg the Sacrament. My thoughts have been partly wandering, yet on the whole my frame has been more serious & sensitive than in general & my Desire has been to improve, & be freed from the Bondage of my Corruptions. O Lord Jesus pity & deliver me.

I have been still not kind to Servts & Ashley, tho' to the latter I hope rather better. Scarcely adherg to Truth. Often vain & envious, not careful of opportunities with Pitt. O my God, cleanse me from my Sins, instruct my Ignorance & pity Strengthen my Weakness in that difficult Path wherein I have to walk, & enable me to live more as a real Xtian, habitually srvg thee in my Generation, & at length fallg asleep in thy peace, & awakeng with Joy in the gen[l.] Resur[n.] I cannot but think that I suffer from the Want of more Prayer Meditatn. & Scripture Readg & from keepg too much worldly Company, yet tis hard to know how to act considerg the whole of my Situation. Let me however pray for divine Direction, & use diligently the Opportunities I really have, strivg to live & act in the faith of unseen things, & havg my Conversation in Heaven.[298] I have found the Day Thought useful.[299]

Sunday Night, December 13[th.] 1795

I could not help dropping asleep at Church this Evening at Prayers & was drowsy at family Devotions. Stupid also & cold at & since dinner. Alas! Alas![300]

Wednesday Night ½ past 11, December 16, 1795, Old Pal Y[d.]

Alas! Let him that thinketh he standeth take Heed lest he fall.[301] I set out well today in Scripture Reading & prayer & felt all day, as I hop'd, a remarkable Sense of God's Presence. I lifted up my Soul, tho' not fervently (going alone with that Intent), to God, on my way to St. James's Place,[302] yet I have been strangely excedg in mens: & that most foolishly

---

297. John Hatsell (1733–1820), clerk of the House of Commons from 1768, remembered especially for his *Precedents of Proceedings in the House of Commons* (4 vols. 1776–1796), which was Thomas Jefferson's most important source when researching rules of conduct and political process for his own work.

298. Philippians 3:20.

299. MS Wilberforce c. 41, fo. 69.

300. Ibid.

301. 1 Corinthians 10:12.

302. St. James's Place is a street in the St. James's district of London, first developed c. 1694. It was here in the house then owned by his uncle William and aunt Hannah, that Wilberforce came to live as a boy, and which he would later inherit. Banastre Tarleton (1754–1833), Wilberforce's particular opponent in Parliament, interestingly also lived in St. James's Place.

& with$^{t.}$ temptation. I suppose my Body must be disorder'd, with which mind also will sympathize. I am without Grace & can only cry, God, be merciful to me a Sinner.[303] Poor Smith from Newfoundland[304] who has been livg for some while on dried fish & Biscuits & water. O pardon me, & enable me to do better in future. This makes ag$^{t.}$ my dings out.[305]

Sunday 2 oClock, December 20, 1795, B Rise

I have been going on I hope, rather better than worse, yet O how forgetful of God how vain & earthly minded, how little Tho't of Xt. I have been but vain & am but poorly, & low today, distracted at Church & very sleepy durg Sermon. This I hope, Bodily Infirmity, but I should be deeply humbled for it.[306]

Sunday Night, December 20$^{th.}$ 1795

Too sensual, <u>rather</u> at dinner & could not help sleepg & being distracted durg Ch$^{ch.}$ Prayers this Evg. But I hope, Bodily Weakness.[307]

1796

Sunday night ½ past 8, January 3, 1796, B. Rise

I have this week suffer'd from livg at Speaker's,[308] tho' a batter man than the common run, yet nothg of the conversation in Heaven,[309] & I alas too little watchful to improve opportunities of Intercourse even for his Benefit. Last Sunday my affections were very lively, & my love overflowg. Macaulay & Henry with me here. Quite overset, when I found Miss H. not at Speaker's. Alas! even Juvenal[310] would correct my inordinate willfulness. On Friday last exceded sadly, the New Year's Day & up early, for Prayer. Today I have been very cold & dull in heavenly things, & not feeling humbled as I ought in tellg Henry the Incidents of my past life. Yet this morning also up earlier for prayer & read Leighton. But let me wait on God, in the name of X$^{t.}$ supplicatg for the Spirit that I may improve in all Holiness. His promise is sure. Tis only our Unbelief & Indolence that keep us back.

---

303. Luke 18:13.

304. Wilberforce could well here be referring to Rev. George Smith, a Methodist missionary, who sailed from Poole, England, arriving in the harsh conditions of Newfoundland in 1794, and who helped to spread Methodism into Bonavista Bay.

305. MS Wilberforce c. 41, fo. 70.

306. Ibid.

307. Ibid.

308. The Speaker of the House of Commons in 1796 was Henry Addington (1757–1844), 1st Viscount Sidmouth. He was a Tory statesman, holding the offices of Prime Minister and Chancellor of the Exchequer 1801–1804; Home Secretary 1812–1822; and Speaker of the House of Commons 1789–1801.

309. Philippians 3:20.

310. Juvenal (Decimus Junius Juvenalis), was a Roman poet of the 1st and early 2nd century A.D., remembered especially for his *Satires*, a series of at least 16 poems covering a vast range of topics across the Roman Empire.

I will humbly endeavor this week to live a more Xtian life. Last week sadly forgot God's Presence & Xt. & the Spirit & Satan & my Day Text, & Mens Regls & self-denial & Talk, & gave into much Evil Speaking & worldly mindedness. O may I now improve, humbly praying & striving to advance in all Holiness.

I have had little Time to look back on y$^{e.}$ Events of the year, but I will tomorrow, or when opporty serves, humbly pray for pardon for its many offences & for a Blessing on the year on which I am entering. I now go to Prayer. Excellent Henry! How careful for his Servts. May I learn to imitate his Example. Makg a Sermon himself for George[311] before he goes tomorrow. I have been sadly wanderg & distracted today in public & family Devotions, Alas! How I trust thro' faculties, weakness, but bro't on by bad tho'ts all I hear passes thro' me.[312]

Monday Evening, January 4, 1796, B Rise

Tho' ding alone today but came on when just din'd, toothache & with no manner of Temptation, with my mind cool &c. yet I exceeded in Quantity, & have much disorder'd my Stomach, & disabled myself for strenuous application. O how does this shew my weakness, & how ought it to make me more earnest & watchful, that I may no longer live that indulging Life I have been doing, but a more self-denying, sober one. I refus'd to go to Grant's today that I might be quiet, but how little have I done staying at Home, & even this morng not strenuously applying. Oimoi. Oimoi. Pardon me O Lord, & quicken me by thy Grace.[313]

Wednesday Evening, January 6, 1796, B. Rise

What weaknesses of mind am I conscious of, & how do I catch myself lusting after the objects the world pursues so eagerly. Alas! Alas! Yet it is a gracious Promise that God will give his Holy Spirit to them that ask it. Today I have forgot self-denial. Yesterday the Vaughans din'd & staid all night; a tedious Evg, & I fear no good, at least directly done.[314]

---

311. In his Spiritual Journals, Wilberforce mentions three of his household servants, George, as here in 1796, and John and Walter in 1799. Robert Southey, who visited Wilberforce on a number of occasions, writes that due to Barbara's poor management and William's tenderness of heart, it could be quite a chaotic household. The cause of such stemming from the fact that though the Wilberforces had the usual number of servants for a house their size, about thirteen or fourteen, it seems that several of them were long-serving and incompetent. For example, Southey records that their coach driver who admitted driving like a madman was allowed to keep his position. See J. Warter *Life and Correspondence of Southey*, vol. 4 (London, 1849), pp. 316-317.

312. MS Wilberforce c. 41, fo. 70.

313. MS Wilberforce c. 41, fo. 71.

314. Ibid.

Sunday Evening, January 10, 1796, Haverlock[315]

This has been a sad, unprofitable Sunday, wherein little has been done. I have felt little of the Power of Religion in my Soul, no warmth of Heart. Too sensual. Little Sense of God's presence. Conceited. O how terribly vain when Singth was readg my tract the other night, how anxious for applause, how callous almost to every other Emotion. Oimoi. Oimoi. I fear it has not been well done to come here on Sunday. The Ly Waldegrave is deeply in earnest & how much farther does she go in fact, than I do. I forgot to put down, sad wandergs today, both in public & private prayer. Alas! Alas![316]

Friday Noon, January 15, 1796, B. Rise

I had resolv'd to set apart this Day not entirely because I have some Bus[s] which won't bear any delay, ab[t.] y[e.] poor![317] chiefly to religious Exercises, fasting in my way i.e. being moderate in food, which only does with me, & less wine, or scarce any. My Eyes are very poorly, so that I cannot write as fully as I wish, but shortly. My chief vices are Reasons for this Exercise.

Chief Reasons for Day of secret Prayer & Exercises:

1st. all is wrong with me vide Bennet Ovg 2[d]. 124. I have a name to live, but I am dead.[318] No Love to God or X[t.] Seeking my Happiness in the Lusts of the flesh, & in dreams of earthly pleasure & Honor, rather than in converse with God, & rejoicing in X[t.] Therefore Self-examination Humiliation, earnest prayer for pardon, for renewing Grace, for Wisdom, for strength, are necessary.

2[dy.] I have been habitually givg into many sins, to which naturally prone (Vide, page 63) particularly 1, 2, 3 (to Ashley Servts &c.) 5, 7, 8, 9, 11, 12, 13, 14, 15, 16 (St. Paul's anathema[319]) 19, 20.

3[dy.] I have been sadly, in particular sufferg my Time to pass away in indolent application, not being fervent in Spirit, as servg the Lord. I have neglected my Parl[ty] Duty &c.

4[thly.] I want direction with Regard to my changing my Condition, being ab[t.] (somewhat too hastily, & too self-willedly) to be introduced to Miss H.

5 The State of public affairs is highly critical & calls for earnest deprecation of y[e.] Divine displeasure.

6. I have been graciously supported in difficult situations of a public nature. My health has been preserv'd notwithstanding my Intemperance & I would humbly Hope that what I am now doing is a proof that God has not yet withdrawn his Holy Spirit from me, tho' so

---

315. This reference to Haverlock by Wilberforce has not been identified with certainty.

316. MS Wilberforce c. 41, fo. 72. *Life*, ii. p. 138 has, 'Sunday. Walked long after church with Lady Waldegrave. Her deep interest for Lord Cornwallis and Thurlow. Thurlow's kindness and generosity to her. Lord Cornwallis says he is an unhappy mortified man but Lady Waldegrave does not think him so. Lady Waldegrave told me that when a girl she was conscious of the unprotected and dangerous state of herself and her sisters, and prayed to be kept from evil.'

317. Then at this point in left margin of new page he wrote, 'not entirely because I have some Buss which won't bear any delay, ab[t.] y[e.] poor!'

318. Revelation 3:1.

319. 1 Corinthians 16:22.

grievously provoked. I am cover'd with mercies. Return then unto thy Rest, O my Soul, for the Lord hath dealt bountifully with thee.[320]

7. My Station in Life is a very difficult one, wherein I am at a Loss to know how to go on. Direction therefore should be specially sought from time to time.

8. I had no good opportunity for lookg back on the past year, on New Year's Day last, being at Woodly.[321] God despiseth not the Sighing of a contrite Heart, nor the Desires of such as be sorrowful. I am indeed infinitely criminal & what must I appear to the pure Eyes of God, which see all my past Life, as clearly and <u>as near</u>, as when it was actually going on. The scenes of distant Riot, Lasciviousness, Uncleanness &c. &c. are now forgot by me, or appear but faintly in general Recollection but to God they are all particularly present in unabated Strength & Size. O may the blood of X[t.] cleanse me. To him I fly, my only Hope & Refuge, for pardon of the past, & Grace for the future. I will pray for forgiveness, for a new Heart, for Love to God & X[t.] for holy seriousness & fear, for Humility, for Heavenly Mindedness, for temperance & Self-Denial, for an active useful affectionate Spirit full of meekness & fervor, for wisdom & power, & for the Grace of God in all, that X[t.] as alone able to keep me from falling.

Retrospect: My youth from the business of the Last year I was at School till 1785, was a Scene of continual Idleness (at least <u>very little</u> done or studied) Vanity, Intemperance (when Ill Health did not absolutely forbid) Lust & all evil Tempers & works of the flesh, & I fear that tho from y[e.] Winter of 1785, 6 I have mended, & for some time liv'd really in the fear of God, yet that I have for some time been livg a Life of religious Sensuality, a Course something altogether diff[t.] from the self-denying, humble, pious, Heavenly-Minded frame of the Gospel. But the Lord's Arm is not shorten'd that he cannot save, nor his ear heavy that he cannot hear.[322] <u>Pray therefore, for pardon & Help in the name & for y[e.] sake only of X[t.]</u> NB. Tis strange today that I have felt peculiarly prone to fretfulness, & a sort of secret aversation & ill will (a grudging of the day &c.) tow[ds.] Religion. This is surely the working of the Evil one, but X[t.] is able to save to the Uttermost.[323]

---

320. Psalm 116:7.

321. Woodly is a town and parish in Berkshire, now a suburb of the city of Reading. Woodley Lodge (Bulmershe Court), built in 1777, was purchased by Henry Addington when he was Speaker of the House of Commons, and who later became Prime Minister. Addington lived there when not in London, and would there entertain such notables as Pitt and possibly even George III. The house was demolished in the 1960s.

322. Isaiah 59:1.

323. Hebrews 7:25. MS Wilberforce c. 41, fo. 75. *Life*, ii. p. 138 has, 'Resolved to set apart chiefly for religious exercises, fasting in my way, i.e. being very moderate in food, which only does with me. I cannot employ it so entirely, because I have some business about the poor which will not bear any delay. My chief reasons for a day of secret prayer are,

1[st.] That the state of public affairs is very critical, and calls for earnest deprecation of the Divine displeasure.

2ndly. My station in life is a very difficult one, wherein I am at a loss to know how to act. Direction therefore should be specially sought from time to time.

3rdly. I have been graciously supported in difficult situations of a public nature. I have gone out and returned home in safety: my health has not suffered from fatigue: and favor a kind reception

Saturday Evening 8 ½ oClock, January 16, 1796, B. Rise

Yesterday, tho' I rather trifled away my Time, yet on the whole, I prayed with earnestness, & was under serious impression the whole Day & this morng also. Yet strange to say, tho' only the Gambiers[324] & Parry &c. Unwin with us. I have rather exceded, at least offendg Dis: (tho' havg still an impression of seriousness,) & rather, in ferms too, yet some little Self-Denial I did practice <u>at</u> Dinner. Oimoi. Oimoi. How does this discover my very great weakness & what cause have I for deep Humiliation & Penitence. The Consciousness of Sin incapacitates me for going to God with the humble freedom & filial Confidence we ought to feel & might feel. My Iniquities separate bet[n.] me & my God. I will go & humbly pray for mercy & forgiveness & more Strength for y[e.] Time to come.[325]

Sunday Evening, January 17, 1796, B. Rise

I this morng have felt more of a spiritual frame than usual, but it was clouded & dulled by Dinner, tho' moderate. I read this morng & much struck by Dr. More's Life.[326] Evg, indispos'd to worship at Church & sleepy in Prayers. Alas! Alas! How weak am I & how much ought I to watch unto prayer, for the Spirit of Grace to renew my Soul in the Image of God, & strengthen me in all Holiness. What a Scene of Temptation & Turmoil am I to be expos'd to tomorrow & how little am I fit for it. I observe that when, as today, my Heart is more set on heavenly things,[327] I think less of marriage & my imagination less wanderg out after Miss H.[328] whom I am to see tom[w.329]

---

have attended me. I would humbly hope too, that what I am now doing is a proof that God has not withdrawn his Holy Spirit from me. I am covered with mercies. Return then unto thy rest, O my soul, for the Lord hath dealt bountifully with thee.'

324. James Gambier (1756–1833), 1st Baron Gambier, Admiral of the Fleet, and evangelical Anglican activist. His aunt, who brought him up, was Lady Middleton, the wife of Sir Charles Middleton (later Lord Barham). Gambier was the 1st President of the Church Missionary Society, and was active in many Christian and philanthropic causes, including the Naval and Military Bible Society and the Episcopal Floating Church Society. He was also a founding benefactor of Kenyon College in America, and the town that was founded with it. Gambier, OH is also named after him, as is Mount Gambier in Australia, and Gambier Island in British Columbia.

325. MS Wilberforce c. 41, fo. 76. *Life*, ii. p. 138 has, '16th. Morning felt the fragrant impression of yesterday.'

326. Dr Henry More (1614–1687), philosopher, prolific writer of verse and prose, and Fellow of Christ's College, Cambridge. See *The Life of The Learned and Pious Dr. Henry More, Late Fellow of Christ's College in Cambridge, To which are annex'd Divers of his Useful and Excellent Letters* by Richard Ward (London, 1710).

327. Colossians 3:2.

328. Miss Mary Ann Hammond was the daughter and co-heiress of Leonard Hammond of Cheam, Surrey. She was suggested to Wilberforce as a possible wife by Speaker Henry Addington, when Wilberforce breakfasted with him on 7 July, 1795. Miss Hammond was Addington's sister-in-law. Wilberforce probably knew of Mr. Hammond from his also being a Subscriber to Thornton's Marine Society. After he had met her for the first time on 18 January, 1796, he wrote that she seemed very affectionate. Addington arranged a second meeting on 1 February, and afterwards wrote that he was exceedingly pleased with her. But he would soon cool in his affection toward her, based partly on her not sharing his evangelical views, she being a moderate Anglican, and partly on advice from close friends, especially Cecil and Isaac Milner.

329. MS Wilberforce c. 41, fo. 76.

Tuesday Morning, January 19, 1796, B Rise

Oimoi, Oimoi. How much am I the sport of my own Impatience, & too lively imagination. I could not sleep last night for think̄g of Miss H., whom I saw & did not see last night. How much more alas, does this shew me that I am interested ab̄ᵗ· earthly, than ab̄ᵗ· heavenly things. My prayers are disturb'd &c. Guide me O Lord into the Right, & make me more interested ab̄ᵗ· heavenly & less ab̄ᵗ· earthly things.[330]

Sunday, January 24, 1796, B. Rise

This has been an unprofitable Week. Little done, & liv̄g much with worldly people & with̄ᵗ· sufficient Guard, my Heart little impress'd with divine Things & today cold & heavy in Spiritualy. O for that settled & deep practical feeling of unseen things which may make me act always as in the presence of God. I have discover'd Pride in myself ab̄ᵗ· not being will̄g to own my leav̄g glass door open, which broke by wind. And Sensuality at Pitt's & Pride & falsehood in pretend̄g to understand Latin which read to me more than I did, & keep̄g back that I knew Ld Wellesley's (Morn̄ⁿ'ˢ) Verses[331] – his. O for a Heart more simple, more indiff̄ᵗ· to the favor of man, & more humbled before God & hunger̄g & thirst̄g after Righteousness.[332]

Friday Night, January 29, 1796, Pal Yᵈ·

I have been much hurried for some days & in yᵉ· mornings have been prevented from my Devotions, & in Evgs by foolish sitt̄g up with Milner. Today I have been exced̄g sadly in mens Regls. Oimoi, & have been quite void of presence of God. O how ought I to be humbled in yᵉ· dust. O how weak am I. I now feel no real sorrow tho' am much stricken with my tiredness & folly. Alas! Alas! Shall I ever be free?[333]

Sunday Evening, February 7, 1796, B. Rise

I have been going on in many Respects very indifferently. For Information's sake I have been talk̄g with Milner ab̄ᵗ· Intercourse with women & that has led to Bosh & Indecency & Late Hours & Waste of Time. Unkindness to & of Greathed.[334] How inconstant is my Mind. At the beginn̄g of the week I was all on fire ab̄ᵗ· Miss H. I could not sleep for thinking of her. My Bowels have been out of order. This has relaxed me & (Truly, therefore) I now feel easy & calm ab̄ᵗ· it. I also want too much to carve for myself & too little to yield to God's Guidance & holy Injunctions. How much more in earnest is Henry, in his approaching

---

330. MS Wilberforce c. 41, fo. 77.

331. Richard Colley Wesley (1760–1842), 1ˢᵗ Marquess Wellesley, styled Viscount Wellesley (1760–1781), and Earl of Mornington (1781–1799), an Irish and British politician and colonial administrator: Governor-General of the Presidency of Fort William (1798–1805), Secretary of State for Foreign Affairs (1809–1812), and Lord Lieutenant of Ireland (1821–1828).

332. MS Wilberforce c. 41, fo. 77.

333. Ibid.

334. Wilberforce may here be referring to his nephew Edward Greathed.

Union. How little have I been improving my time, how little thinkg of God & Xt. Evg Devotions sadly curtail'd & today sleepy at Church & not heavenly-minded, yet I will labor & strive to improve in all these particulars in the ensuing week & pray for the Guidance of God.[335]

Tuesday Night, February 9, 1796, Pal Y[d.]

My spirits were yesterday low all Day, & so they have been today, yet not suffering. I was much hurt last night by only seeing in general Miss H. for a short time & getting no convers[n.] Still relaxed in one particular way & strange as it seems like a Visitation. I have been half inclined to think it so. M[rs.] A. last night talk'd of the operas, Plays, &c. which she was to go to this winter, before Miss H. & I could say nothg. I am clear that at present she is not a woman I ought to marry, & perhaps God is graciously preventing it. With so many Blessings, ought I to pine after one, (like Jonah's Gourd)[336] which is denied me. What if Miss H. were as much tinged with Disloyalty as she is with worldliness? How clear would my friends then be?

My Heart I hope has today, been more than usually turn'd to God, & so I find it when internal comforts fail. Shorten me then O God in internal things, only lift thou up the Light of thy Countenance upon me.[337] Then I may be sure that all things shall finally work together for my Good,[338] & I may with[t.] anxiety, leave all to the Disposal of my heavenly Father. My time & Health have both been fritter'd by dinner Engagem[ts.] which destroy my Evgs. I think after this week, generally to decline dinners, except payg Debts, & to be more diligent.[339]

Sunday, February 14[th.] 1796

This has been a baddish week & a bad Sunday. Chatting too unprofitably all y[e.] aftn with Henry ab[t.] Miss S & Miss H[d.] Oimoi. Oimoi. A trying week is comg & I am not prepar'd for it. This Evg quite sleepy at prayers. Excedg most unprov'd badly today in soft puddg, a trifle it may seem but it disorders me, unspiritualizes me & so is no trifle in its Effects. I go to prayer, wretched & miserable & poor & blind & naked.[340] Havg a name to live but in fact dead.[341] O quicken me thou Saviour & Friend of Sinners.[342]

Sunday, February 21[st.] 1796

This last has been a bad week & today, tho' in y[e.] morng I have felt some sort of holy comfort from Idea of makg Sacrifice of Miss H. if right, yet now cool'd again, which looks too much like mere animal spirits.

---

335. MS Wilberforce c.41, fo.78.
336. Jonah 4:6.
337. Psalm 4:6.
338. Romans 8:28.
339. MS Wilberforce c.41, fo.78.
340. Revelation 3:17.
341. Revelation 3:1.
342. MS Wilberforce c.41, fo.78.

I go to pray earnestly, may God direct me in this diff[t.] affair & enable me to seek his favor, & the one thing needful[343] with <u>all diligence thou Redeemer and Sanctifier.</u>[344]

Monday Night, February 29, 1796, Pal Y[d.]

I had no Scripture Reading all last week & I fear I felt the Effect of it in being remarkably dull in spiritualy & forgetful of God & heavenly things. O how asham'd ought I to be of myself, & how much more am I in talk than in fact, havg a name to live, whilst I am dead.[345] O spare me & help me God of all Grace and Mercy for X[t's] sake.[346]

Sunday, March 13, 1796, B Rise

Tho' I hope I have felt & thought more religiously than sometimes for some few days past, I have been & am very cold & dead today, tho' receivg the Sacrament, no life in my spirits. Alas! O that my will was more fixedly set on God's favor thro' X[t.] by the Spirit, then all the rest were nothing. I grow easier ab[t.] Miss Ham[d.] & begin to think I have been forcing on the affair too much, & that my path is more that of single Life. Whatever it be, may God's Grace conduct me remind[g.] me the time is short. I had yesterday a very narrow Escape from a broken limb at least by a kick from a horse. Be thankful O my Soul. I was musing repeating at the time on Psalm 90[th.][347]

Tuesday, March 15[th.] 1796

Dined before House. Slave Bill thrown out by 74 to 70, ten or twelve of those who had supported me absent in the country, or on pleasure. Enough at the Opera to have carried it. Very much vexed and incensed at our opponents. I am permanently hurt about the Slave Trade.[348]

Sunday ½ past 1, March 20, 1796, BRise

Alas! this week has roll'd away but unprofitably. My Evg Devotions curtail'd. My Heart unspiritual & dead. Today also the same till just now, when I begin to feel a little how sadly I am going on & how little I have of the divine Life, the Love of God & X[t.] How mistaken an Impression do I convey of myself, yesterday exceeded at din[r.] This no trifle, considerg it affects Health, therefore usefulness, & my members ought to be Instruments of Righteousness.[349] O that I might grow in Grace & love God & X[t.] &c. &c.[350]

Wednesday Night, March 23, 1796 Pal Y[d.]

This is Passion Week, on which account chiefly I refus'd to go to Duchess of Gloster's private Concert. Yet at dinner today, havg Company I

---

343. Luke 10:42.
344. MS Wilberforce c. 41, fo. 78.
345. Revelation 3:1.
346. MS Wilberforce c. 41, fo. 79.
347. Ibid.
348. *Life*, ii. pp. 141–142.
349. Romans 6:13.
350. MS Wilberforce c. 41, fo. 79.

have sadly exceeded so as to be unfit for anything spiritual (Oimoi, Oimoi) & even anything of rational application. O what Weakness & Wickedness is this. I surely shall never escape from this most beastly of all Subjections, Oimoi, Oimoi. Everyone is more temperate than me. O Lord, create in me a real Horror of this my Sin, & a sincere strenuous Desire to forsake it.[351]

Good Friday Afternoon, March 25, 1796, Pal Y^d.

My Eyes are so indiff^t. from wind & dust & too much readg that I can't write. I have been going on in some particulars rather better vide Table, yet but very ill alas. Today I hope I have felt & do feel somewhat of the Reality of invisible Things. O what a Blessing to have a Saviour & Sanctifier held forth to us.[352]

Easter Sunday ¼ befe 3, March 27, 1796, B Rise

Today I am little <u>impress'd</u> by Eternal Things, & find little Resource in them, yet let me look to God for Comfort thro' X^t. & by the Spirit, & for Sanctification & cvg Grace. Eyes indiff^t. & time curtail'd. At Church today Thot's wanderg & sleepy. O pardon & help me.[353]

Easter Monday Night 10, March 28, 1796, B. Rise

Today has been sadly idled away: doing nothg in a Commee Room morng. Impatient for Dinner, when exceeded (Sam's) no seriousness, no Sense of God's Goodness or presence, Oimoi. Oimoi. O may I amend Tues aftn.[354]

Wednesday Night 10 oClock, March 30, 1796, Old Pal Y^d.

Both last night & tonight, I have been exceedg ferms at Dinner, accordg to the Scripturl Criterion, "Wherein is Excess."[355] Pitt & I din'd tete-a-tete today, & how little have I been really enough on my Guard to do him Service. How little duly conscious of the presence of God, Oimoi. Oimoi. I go to prayer in humble Self Condemnation & Shame. O that I might still be enabled to repent & turn to God with my whole Soul, truly lovg & servg him with Diligence & lowliness & cheerful Spiritual-Mindedness.[356]

Sunday ¾ past 1, April 3, 1796, B. Rise

Alas! I have been going on but ill, Mens: Excedgs, Forgetfulness of God & X^t. &c. my time not well improv'd. O let me pray earnestly for the Grace of X^t. & humbly resolve ag^t. any Excess, that I may use all the Gifts of God to his Glory. How great has his Mercy been to me, & how little have I been living conformably.[357]

---

351. MS Wilberforce c. 41, fo. 80.
352. Ibid.
353. Ibid.
354. MS Wilberforce c. 41, fo. 81.
355. Ephesians 5:18.
356. MS Wilberforce c. 41, fo. 81.
357. Ibid.

Monday Night, April 4, 1796, Pal Y[d.]

Tho' much impress'd yesterday & Impressions not worn off I hope today, yet how indifferently going on, all things considered. Self-denial little or not at all kept in mind, nor God's presence, yet let me struggle & strive lookg to the promis'd Grace of X[t.] as my only Stay & sure ground of Reliance. H. More ask'd me how I did to preserve a heavenly spiritual frame, alas, I don't preserve it, yet I would humbly aspire after at it, all else is folly & Vanity & Vexation of Spirit.[358]

Sunday Evening ¼ past 7[359] April 17, 1796, Pal Y[d.]

My Eyes are very indifferent, so I cannot write much. I have been indispos'd for 10 days & have had my Head a good deal weaken'd. My mind has I thank God been in an easy tranquil State repos[g.] on the Promises with a Consciousness of deep Demerit, yet trusting in God's Mercy thro' X[t.] I fear sometimes, that I have been crying to myself peace too easily, yet I hope I have felt a Desire after Holiness & an entire Renunciation of every other plea than that of X[t's] atong Blood. I have lately felt & now feel a Sort of Terror on reenterg the World, lest I should fall into old Sins, lose Sense of God, & prostitute my Faculties & Powers. But let me earnestly pray for y[e.] Grace of X[t.] that the divine work may go on in my Heart & that I may daily grow more & more meet to be a partaker of the Inheritance of the Saints in Light.[360] I pray for Light & Strength & Holiness & Love & all Goodness.[361]

Thursday Evening, April 21, 1796, Pal Y[d.]

I have tho't more than often ab[t.] Spiritual Things & I hope have felt some proper frame of mind, yet too little animation & real Hatred of Sin, a Sort of settled lookg up but I fear not, I am sure not, enough of the Hunger & Thirst after Righteousness.[362]

Sunday Evening, April 24, 1796, B. Rise

This morng & chiefly thro' the day, I hope I have had a tolerably Xtian frame of mind, but sleepy at Church this Evg. Alas! Alas! How little am I suitably affected with Heavenly things. Stay musing in Comfort, not being able to go to Church. Let me pray earnestly. God can & for X[t's] Sake he will by his Spirit renew us, & make us Meet to be Partakers of the Inheritance of y[e.] Saints in Light.[363] I hope in gen[l.] I have lately done rather better than usual, yet not enough considerg God's late Call of Illness. Nor am

---

358. Ecclesiastes 1:14. MS Wilberforce c. 41, fo. 82.

359. '6' was written but then '7' was written on top of the 6.

360. Colossians 1:12.

361. MS Wilberforce c. 41, fos. 82-83. *Life*, ii. p. 144 has, 'I have been indisposed for ten days, and have had my head a good deal weakened. My mind has, I thank God, been in an easy, tranquil state, reposing on the promises with a consciousness of deep demerit, yet trusting in God's mercy through Christ. I trust he will not spurn such a one from him. I have lately felt and now feel a sort of terror on reentering the world.'

362. Matthew 5:6. MS Wilberforce c. 41, fo. 83.

363. Colossians 1:12.

I now desirous enough of Health & Strength that I may be more active but rather secretly glad that I have a privilege to be idle & indulge my sensual temper. This is base. What should I think of it in anyone else? In anyone who should be glad that a not painful Lameness compell'd him to live quiet & indulging at Home, instead of going about in the Service of some great Benefactor. How little could I bear for the World to see me as God does, to whom all is naked & open.[364] Cleanse my Heart O God &c.[365] I feel a Self-Complacency in my Discernment whilst I live out the secret workings of my Heart tho' they discover my Baseness, Alas! Alas![366]

Tuesday Night, April 26, 1796, Pal Y[d.]

Tonight (in y[e.] House) I discern'd in myself, manifest Workings of Envy & Pride & Anger, & more fear & Solicitude from Apprehension of havg got into a Scrape by offendg. 2 the possible consequential Loss of Credit &c. &c. than ab[t.] the favor of God, Oimoi. O how corrupt is my Heart. What need O Lord of thy heavenly Grace.[367]

Sunday Night 9 oClock, May 1, 1796, BRise

Today & yesterday, tho' no temptation exceeded Din[r] ferms, rather & very sleepy as last Sunday also I think at Church in Evg., alas, alas! How little is this mortifying the flesh with its affections & Lusts,[368] also too delicate & fastidious today. How many would have been glad of what I despis'd. Last night wastg Time talkg of Dinners, eating &c. &c. This last week in general pretty diligent but O may I still amend throughout & turn from every evil way, & live soberly righteously & godly in this present World, lookg for that blessed Hope.[369]

Sunday 8[th.] May - 3 oClock BRise - 1796 - After Sact

Alas - Mine is an unprofitable Life. My time is fritter'd sadly away. My Powers unimprov'd & applied to little purpose - My Health indeed disables me, yet I might do more - O how ought I to pray for Grace that the fruits of the Spirit may more & more abound in me - Envy & Malice today in Spite of myself ab[t.] friends comg too late to Church. Strange mental workings ab[t.] Duncombe's[370] dealing - contradictory &c. &c. Muncaster seems half doubt my exertg myself. O Lord - set

---

364. Hebrews 4:13.

365. Psalm 51:10.

366. MS Wilberforce c. 41, fos. 83-84. *Life*, ii. p. 145 has, 'I have not enough considered God's late call of illness, nor am I now desirous enough of health and strength that I may be more active, but rather secretly glad that I have a privilege to be idle. This is base. What should I think of it in any one else who should be glad that he was compelled to live quiet and indulge at home, instead of going about in the service of some great benefactor.'

367. MS Wilberforce c. 41, fo. 84.

368. Galatians 5:24.

369. Titus 2:13. MS Wilberforce c. 41, fo. 84.

370. Henry Duncombe (1728–1818), M.P. for Yorkshire (1780–1796). In the General Election of 1784, both he and Wilberforce stood as Pittite candidates, and were returned unopposed, their opponents withdrawing after a poll showed the two had an overwhelming majority.

my Affections on things above[371] & fill me with thy Grace, that I may adorn the Doctrine of G my S[r.] in all things. [372]

Sunday Night 9 oClock 8[th.] May -

I eat & drank to the full today, perhaps exceded ferms - tho' certainly good just now for Health - I became sensual & stupid, unfit for Enjoyment of spiritual things, half asleep at least, all Sermon & part of prayer time and now cold & formal – Alas - Alas! O when shall I be set above these ordiny Temptations & be ever wary & watchful, walkg circumspectly.[373]

Wedy Night May 13[th.] 1796[374] – Palyd 10 oClock

I fear I have been exceedg ferms &c. sadly for several Days & that I generally do - Alas. This is not crucifying the flesh with the affections & Lusts mortifying the Deeds of the Body.[375] Help me, O God - to recover from this Depth of Sin into which I am fallen & let me no longer be satisfied with havg a Name to live whilst I am dead.[376]

Sunday Night 9 oClock BRise May 15[th.]

My days have lately been sadly whittled away - This morng & last night at Prayer time, sadly self-debating mys more ab[t.] fds to Din[r] &c. &c. & no spirit[l] frame. At Lock some attention - at & after Dinner no Care to improve Conversation or cultivate Spirit[l] mind. So afternoon stole away unimprov'd - & this a Sunday, especially when going into a perturbed Scene where much Grace requir'd - This Week I have felt occasionally much anger & Malice & Revenge ab[t.] Sl: Carg Bill, & scandalous neglect of its friends. I fear at y[e.] momt I co'd have done them any mischief, much Selfishness & some Duplicity in the Yorkshire Business - O may the Grace of God support me & enable me to improve in all Holiness & adorn the Doctrine of God our Saviour in all things.[377]

Sunday May 22[d.] 1796 – Brigg ½ past 1 oClock

I was in Hopes of a Day of religious Retirement before my Bustle, but God has order'd it otherwise. I fear I have been too ready to enter into Bustle ab[t.] Election Matters, yet I feel the Emptiness of Worldly things & am I trust this day in some Degree thirsting after the Water of Life - How vile am I not to be more penetrated with the Goodness & Mercy of God to unworthy Sinners - Let me pray earnestly for Grace, to stand firm within amidst all the Turmoil into which I am ab[t.] to enter - How much of vanity have I felt in myself from a Sense of the Situation in which I stand in the County. It

---

371. Colossians 3:2.

372. Titus 2:10. MS Wilberforce c. 41, fo. 85.

373. MS Wilberforce c. 41, fo. 85.

374. Wilberforce wrote Wednesday May 13[th.] 1796, but May 13th 1796 was a Friday. MS Wilberforce c. 41, fos. 85-86.

375. Romans 8:13.

376. Revelation 3:1.

377. Titus 2:10. MS Wilberforce c. 41, fo. 86. *Life*, ii. p. 145 has, 'This week I have occasionally felt a sinful anger about the Slave-Carrying Bill, and the scandalous neglect of its friends.'

is all the unmerited Goodness of God - Can I be vain, Wretch that I am. I go to earnest prayer & would endeavour after self-dedication to God in X[t.] thro' the Spirit - I have been readg Mr. Babington. What a purified Heart is his, that of one meet to be partaker of the Inheritance of the Saints &c.[378] Why is not mine like his. Let me pray &c. &c. X[t.] is faithful.[379]

Sunday May 29th Yorke 2 oClock

This last has been a very hurrying week with these Elections. Little Time for Devotions & Scripture neglected for which I ought to have found Time. But I thank God that I hope I have desir'd & wish'd for a quiet opportunity of communing with him & my own Heart, & today I adore with some Degree of Gratitude, that gracious Providence, which has led me all my Days in ways that I knew not, & has given me so much favor with Men. It is his work. His be the Glory. I hope I really feel how entirely it is his doing, that I have nothg of which I can boast or be proud, that it is what I could never have effected by my own Counsels or Might, & O may I be enabled to be grateful (duly I cannot be) & to devote myself first to God's Glory & then diligently to the Service of those Constituents who are so kind to me. Let me remember the Temptations to which my Situation is expos'd. Poor Sam[l.] Th[n380] who wo'd have been torn to pieces at Hull, if people had dared to do it, deserv'd much better of them than I do of my Constituents. Praise the Lord, O my Soul.[381]

Sunday Evg 8 oClock - June 5[th.] Hull

This last week like the last hurrying, careless also ab[t.] mens. & ferms, & have suffer'd from it - Little Devotions or Scripture Readg, & but little thot ab[t.] fds spir[l.] good. Much Vanity also - Today rather trifled away necessarily with Isaac & Jos[h.] Milner - yet felt serious compensation & I hope Resolut[n.] thro' Grace to amend - O might I do it radically - Let me pray earnestly - I am not intoxicated with my Situation - My temptations more base order.[382]

---

378. Colossians 1:12.

379. MS Wilberforce c. 41, fo. 86. *Life*, ii. pp. 148-149 has, 'At Brigg no service on the Sunday morning, and the people sadly lounging about. Stanhope filling my head with election matters. I was in hopes of a day of religious retirement before my bustle, but God has ordered it otherwise. I fear I have been too ready to enter in to election matters; yet I feel the emptiness of worldly things, and am, I trust, this day in some degree thirsting after the water of Life. Let me pray earnestly for grace to stand firm within, amidst all the turmoil into which I am about to enter. How much vanity have I felt in myself from the situation in which I stand in the County? It is all the unmerited mercy of God, can I be vain? I go to earnest prayer, and would endeavor after dedication of myself to God in Christ through the Holy Spirit.'

380. 'Was being' is crossed out and 'who wo'd' is inserted above the words.

381. MS Wilberforce c. 41, fo. 87. *Life*, ii. p. 149 has, 'This last has been a very hurrying week, little time for devotion and Scripture neglected, for which I ought to have found time. But I thank God, that I hope I have desired and wished for a quiet opportunity of communing with him and my own heart, and today I adore with some degree of gratitude, that gracious Providence, which has led me all my days in ways that I knew not, and has given me so much favor with men. It is his work. His be the Glory. I hope I really feel how entirely it is his doing; that I have nothing of which I can boast or be proud; that it is what I could never have effected by my own counsels or might. Oh may I be enabled to be grateful, (duly I cannot be,) and to devote myself first to God's Glory and then diligently to the service of those constituents who are so kind to me.'

382. MS Wilberforce c. 41, fo. 87.

Sunday 12th June 1796 Hull 8 oClock Evg

I have but a moment - This has been a sad unsabbatiz'd Sunday, Oimoi, Oimoi, & at Constable's[383] & with other friends. How little have I been strivg to do good & serve the Cause of Relig[n] Sad Excedgs mens. & ferms - O what can I do but fly to the Throne of Grace & plead the Blood of Jesus & pray for Strength to amend - He can enable me, I am most vile.[384]

Wedy Night 11 ¼ oClock June 15th Wakefield – Taylors

All this dining publickly &c, & incessant Company is sad Work - How sadly I am going on yet in mens & ferms better than sometimes, but in Dis – bad - I scarce dare resolve on no dis, yet I do. But O that I might really feel deeply a Desire of something better than all this & hunger & thirst after Righteousness.[385] I don't know that I could well have avoided all this after the kind Conduct of my friends towd[s] me, yet I wish I had, & almost think I would if it were now to do over again - I seem to be gaining in Credit on false pretences, Alas! Alas! O Lord quicken me by thy heavenly Grace, & have mercy on me I most humbly beseech thee.[386]

Sunday ½ past 12 Halifax June 19th

Alas! I am going on sadly - I judg'd it right, but surely I might did I but pray more earnestly, possessg more of divine Help to fortify me ag[t] these many temptations to which expos'd - I have done less good this time than usual in the way of relig[s] Conversat[n] & givg Books, & I fear am less set on it - Here, I don't attempt it I will try, but it is really hard. I go to prayer. Help me O God, for X[ts] Sake. I am all weakness. I fear I am exactly to say the best of me, in the Laodicean State, neither cold not hot.[387]

Sunday ¼ past 7 Evg June 26th Buxton

Alas. I have been going on loosely, & today I have not been duly careful to seize a Day of Leisure for religious offices commending my Soul to God, & imploring his pardon for the past & Help for the future. Alas. Alas! How justly may it be said of me that whilst I have a name to live I am in fact dead.[388] Yet I will vigorously press forward, earnestly intreating Grace from above, & Wisdom & Strength & beginning anew, & devoting myself afresh to the Service of God - Let me watch over myself, & endeavor to amend & abound not partially, but in all Holiness.[389]

---

383. John Constable (1776–1837), English Romantic painter and member of the Royal Academy, remembered especially for his landscapes of the area of his Dedham Vale home.

384. MS Wilberforce c. 41, fo. 88. *Life*, ii. pp. 156-157 has, 'Milner preached, very practical and good. Joseph Milner dined with us, simple and pleasant. At night my mother affected at parting, and whispered "Remember me in your prayers". Milner thinks her weaker.'

385. Matthew 5:6.

386. MS Wilberforce c. 41, fo. 88.

387. Revelation 3:15, 16. MS Wilberforce c. 41, fo. 88. *Life*, ii. p. 157 has, 'I have done less good than usual this time in the way of religious conversation and giving books. Yet to do so is really hard.'

388. Revelation 3:1.

389. MS Wilberforce c. 41, fo. 88.

Friday July 8th 1796 Buxton ½ past 6 Evg

I have this week read Scripture (the Acts) constantly & seriously, & have had much new Light thrown on them. I have felt at other Times, walkg &c. a Sense of the presence of God, but in Company have been vain & gay, & I fear not duly attentive to Edificat[n] of friends. O that I might be enabled to purify myself even as God is pure,[390] & to be useful as God has bless'd me with Light - O what cause have I for Thankfulness, lest havg a Name to live I am in Truth dead.[391] This af[tn] after dinner, I am heavy & stupid in my affections & unspiritual, Oimoi.[392]

Friday Night 10 ¼ oClock July 8th Buxton -

Alas! This week little has been done. I have from Vanity & folly been wastg my time rather - too much thought ab[t] Miss Dawes,[393] - who cert[y] not fit for me - Mens. Regl. breakg consty. Quoad Dis & Self den. Today - dis: Excedgs have much disorder'd Stomach & unfitted me for work, Alas, Alas - what a wretch am I, so to trifle with & abuse the Bounty of God to me - I am very unfeeling too, ab[t] my dear Mother, ab[t] Milner &c. O how diff[t] am I, from what I write to others to be & how much like the lukewarm Xtians I am condemning. How little Love of God do I feel when Col. Ormsly swears, Alas. Alas. Resol[n] I will endeavor to observe mens. Regl. & no Dis. Regl. - O may God enable me.[394]

Sunday aftn ½ past 5 July 10th Buxton

Alas! On lookg into myself I see many grievous faults, but I hope I may safely throw myself on the Mercies of God in X[t] They are my only Hope & Confidence - O that I may be enabled more to adorn the Doctrine of God my Saviour,[395] to cleanse myself from all filthiness of y[e] flesh & Spirit, perfecting Holiness in the fear of God,[396] Sensuality, Vanity, particularly the latter in a sad Degree, are my chief Sins - O that I might be more filled with Love, & that I would starve every other Vice & foible. Perhaps tis more Vanity than ought else, that I am now a little uneasy

---

390. 1 John 3:3.

391. Revelation 3:1.

392. MS Wilberforce c. 41, fo. 89. *Life*, ii. p. 160 has, 'I have this week read Scripture (the Acts) constantly and seriously, and have had much new light thrown on them. I have felt at times, when walking, etc., a sense of the presence of God, but in company have been vain and gay and I fear not duly attentive to the edification of friends. O how different am I from what I advise others to be, and how much like the lukewarm Christians I am condemning!'

393. Wilberforce spent most of July and August 1796 in Buxton taking the waters. He met a Miss Dawes who was there with her brother, William (1762–1836), just returned from Sierra Leone where he had been acting Governor. William went on the First Fleet to New South Wales in 1788, as did Richard Johnson, for whom Wilberforce and Pitt gained Royal Warrant to travel as Chaplain. Johnson was the first to take the Gospel to Australia. William and his sister were the children of Benjamin Dawes, clerk of works in the Ordnance Office at Portsmouth, England. In his diary Wilberforce wrote 'Quere, will she turn out well – but 18! Poor Lass!' (c. 34, 120). When the siblings left Buxton on 10 July, Wilberforce again records in his diary, 'I half fond of Miss D & sorry to part with her.' (c. 34, 120). Here in the Spiritual Journal, Wilberforce similarly records his feelings here on 8 July, and then too on 10 July.

394. MS Wilberforce c. 41, fo. 89.

395. Titus 2:10.

396. 2 Corinthians 7:1.

on partg with Miss Dawes, & even have some Tho'ts ab[t.] her. Sursum Corda.[397] - I hope I have today enjoyed & am now in a small Degree enjoying the peace of God.[398]

Sunday ~~Morning~~ 1 oClock, Buxton July 17[th.] 96 -

Today - remarkably heavy - wanderg in prayer & unspiritual. Oimoi - My desires flat also. In gen[l.] I have been but indiff[t.] in Body, & have got on but poorly in Business, & universally. How much more thoroughly Xtians are Henry & Mrs. Hy. now with me - yet let me press forward.[399]

Tuesday Night July 19[th.] Buxton

I have sadly exceded ferms at dinner of late & if not fluster'd yet quite unfitted for serious Work, & still more for Spiritual Exercises - Today also & the other day – dessert - My Stomach has suffer'd - May I now repent & turn from all folly - Help me O God, I have no Hope but in thee - How much better Henry & Mrs. are. It does not hurt me as it ought to hear Col. Ormsly swear.[400]

Sunday - 20 mins bef[e] 5, July 24[th.] Buxton

Praise the Lord O my Soul! Let me praise the name of the Lord - I am less than the very least of all his mercies, but he is ever gracious & kind - Alas! I have been going on but poorly not feelg as I ought ab[t.] Orms[y's] Swearg - Mens: Exceedings ferms & dis. &c. yet I would humbly resolve to amend & pray earnestly for divine Grace to aid my weak Endeavors - I feel today a Peace the world cannot give,[401] lookg to the mercy of God in X[t.] for Pardon - What infinite Blessings do I enjoy. How does my Cup over flow, & yet how cold am I commonly. But to our earnest prayers, God has promis'd his Grace, & that can make us to abound in wisdom & spirit[l.] understanding & Holiness - When I see so many careless & thoughtless around me, what a mercy sho'd I deem it, to be bro't to a Sense of my Condition & of the Way to pres[t.] peace & future Glory - O may I be humble & diligent & grateful & self-denying, strivg continually to love God more, serve him more entirely & adorn the doctrine of God my Saviour in all things.[402] - My Heart has been much soften'd & affected by some of the excess Reforg Tracts Ashley has been readg me since dinner. My eyes smart - I will go to prayer.[403]

Monday Night ½ past 10 – 25[th.] July Buxton

Alas! So soon - so very soon after - to have to record my own disgrace - Exceeded Dis[t.] today which has quite disorder'd my Stomach, defil'd my conscience &c. I scarce dare resolve, because I have so often fail'd that I fear I cannot keep my Resolution tho' in so little a thing, yet I

---

397. Latin: Lift up your hearts.
398. MS Wilberforce c. 41, fo. 89.
399. MS Wilberforce c. 41, fo. 90.
400. Ibid.
401. John 14:27.
402. Titus 2:10.
403. MS Wilberforce c. 41, fo. 90.

would humbly pray to be strengthen'd. Tis not little as a Sin, seeing it so disorders me, & impairs that Health which is the great Engine of one's Usefulness & which God did not give to be wasted in my beastly appetites - It was of Temperance that Paul argued before Felix.[404] - What a Pig & how contemptible should I think anyone who sho'd offend as I do to the injury of Health, ag.[t] Resolutions &c. - Help me yet O God, for the Redeemer's Sake - I wo'd humbly resolve, generally, on Temperance & observing mens: Regl. Gratitude &c.[405]

Sunday Evg July 31[st.] Hull 7 oClock

It is mention'd by Paul as one of the <u>judicial</u> Crimes of the ancient World, that they were with.[t] natural affection.[406] Certainly, I am sadly so. I feel little ab.[t] my mother or anything but myself - Therefore the rather I would not neglect her & I came to Hull I hope, meaning to please God, & sorry to quit my Tract, which wish'd to finish this Recess - This has been a hurrying unspiritual Sunday so far - Sleepy at Church in aftn. May I yet get a little time for prayer - I would set wholly on the Grace of God in X.[t] I have been wastg my time with Milner rather.[407]

Hull Aug[t.] 7[th.] Night 8 oClock, August 7, 1796

My Eyes are very poorly so I must not write. I fear I have fritter'd away my time more than need have done, partly with Milner. When ill I lose the power of praying distinctly & fully & earnestly, but God is faithful & just to forgive his Sins to the vilest Sinner who humbly confessg them looks to him for free pardon in X.[t] I go humbly to intreat him to quicken me, to enable me to love him & fear him and X.[t] more, to serve him more diligently & that I may employ the powers my own Intemperance & vices have left me, in henceforth Glorifying my heavenly Father, & turning many to Righteousness.[408]

Buxton Sunday Night ½ past 8, August 14[th.] 1796

This has been a heavy Day with me upon the whole. I fear I have felt little of the power of Religion. Alas. Alas! how many would rejoice to have my advantages, which are so sadly wasted on me. I fear I am low very low indeed, let me estimate myself by what standard I will. Help me O God, to improve in all Holiness, to be renewed in the Spirit of my Mind,[409] & to adorn the Doctrine &c. <u>in all things</u>.[410] - I go to pray.[411]

---

404. Acts 24:10-21.

405. MS Wilberforce c. 41, fo. 91.

406. 2 Timothy 3:3.

407. MS Wilberforce c. 41, fo. 91. *Life*, ii. pp. 164-165 has, 'Sorry to quit my Tract, which I wished to finish this recess.'

408. Daniel 12:3. MS Wilberforce c. 41, fo. 92.

409. Ephesians 4:23.

410. Titus 2:10.

411. MS Wilberforce c. 41, fo. 92.

Buxton 8 oClock – Sunday Evg Augt. 21st. 96

Alas - This last week has gone on but ill I have done little, but trifling over my Tract rather wastg time with Milner instead of turng to profitable Discourse, for which he always fit. Testy & hot in disputing with Milner, & alas often on religious points - Vain, Sensual. O Lord! Quicken me by thy Grace. Today I have prayed with some Degree of Earnestness - I return to prayer.[412]

Buxton 7 oClock Sunday Evg Augt. 28th. 1796

I hope I have had today some feelings which indicate in a little Degree the Grace of God - a day for X^t's Honor - a Desire after Communion with him, a Disposition to repose all my Hope on him, and a Sense of the Vanity of earthly things - Yet O how low am I in all these & other things - What a Sermon today, Alas! Alas! O may I labor to enter in at the Strait Gate,[413] & not deceive myself. How little do I correspond with the Mercies I have receiv'd. Having no time on the 24th. Birth day, as I had intended, I now put down a few memorables for the last year - affair with Miss Seward. The more I think of it, the more I ought to be most thankful that it went off, & yet my precipitancy would have forc'd it on, but for the Mercy of God overruling &c.

Notables in my Life: How strikg Mrs. H's Death. Then my disappointm^t. in not meetg her[414] at Woodly at Xmas. All these preach'd that not to be. My Illness in the Spring which might have been fatal, well recover'd from. In former times how often protected from Evil danger &c. & things turng out creditable &c. Kept from Norris' hand & Kimber for 2 while I going together. Rollestone[415] Furious w. Indians. My Election over with little Trouble & Expense. Sad mens. Excedgs &c. Dis. &c. to reproach myself with. Sad Behav^r. at Culgarth.[416] O how ought I to humble myself in the dust & implore the undeserved mercy of X^t. I go to prayer & Thanksgiving & Grace to help & renew & quicken. My Eyes are weakish & tis alm^t. dark.[417]

---

412. MS Wilberforce c. 41, fo. 93.

413. Matthew 7:13.

414. 'Miss' inserted here above 'her'.

415. Rolleston was a slave trading captain who challenged Wilberforce to a duel, which Wilberforce was opposed to on Christian principles, and so refused the challenge, deeming that a 'proper and easy explanation of my determination and views in respect to dueling, might be in all respects [an] eligible [response].' Nothing further is known of the issue. In the Wilberforce manuscripts there is an unpublished paper by Wilberforce entitled, 'Essay on Duelling', written in 1828.

416. Culgarth (Calgarth) near Windermere is in Westmoreland, and Calgarth Hall was home of Richard Watson, the Bishop of Llandaff. Wilberforce visited there a number of times, including here and in September 1795. The sad behaviour he refers to, may well have to do with Watson's daughter, who Wilberforce had become much taken with on that previous visit. He records that 'she seem'd all alive in passions', with the result that 'I could not sleep at night from lewd Ideas – alas, alas!' (MS Wilberforce c. 43, fo. 85).

417. MS Wilberforce c. 41, fo. 93. *Life*, ii. p. 164 has, 'Miss Seward went on Friday. Erskine, Milner, and I too much with her, flattering her, etc. I called once to get serious talk, but in vain. She commended the preacher at the rooms. I said I like sermons better which made people uneasy.'

Sunday Sep[t.] 4[th.] 1796 ½ past 1 One - Buxton

Alas, I have too much a name to live whilst I am dead.[418] I have just seen at Church many around me much affected, but I am, was not - but cold &c. O may I humbly prostrate myself before God, pleadg the mercy of X[t.] relying only on his Intercession & on the Help of his Spirit, solemnly recommending myself into his Hands as at the first, & imploring him to enlighten me & fill me with Love & humility & a sense of the powers of the World to come -

Notables in my Life for which I sho'd return Thanks or be humbled or be suitably affected:[419] The singular accident as it seemed to me of askg Milner to go abroad with me in 1784, havg first asked Burgh who refused, which first bro't me acquainted with the Truth as it is in Jesus. If M[nr.] had been as ill as afterw[ds.] if I had known his char[r.] probably certainly we should not have gone together. My being prevented from marrying Miss W[n.] in[420] 1777 or thereab[ts.] which must have terminated in misery to me -

Notables in my Life: My Deliverance from Norris & Kimber. D[o.] from Kimber. Challenge peace clear'd up. Mr. Rollestone, Kimber & my comg away from Bath so providentially & unknowingly probably many others.

My being raised to my pres[t.] Situat[n.] just <u>before</u> my becomg acquainted with Truth & a year & ½ before in any Degree experienced its power. This humanly speakg could not have taken place afterwards. My going into Yorkshire last year 1795, & wanted _____dication.[421]

Doddridge's *Rise & Progress*[422] havg so providentially fallen in my Way whilst abroad, given by Unwin to Mrs. Smith, thence comg to Bessy & when taken abroad.

What a mercy to have been born a human creature with a fortune, talents &c. &c. an Englishman in the 18[th.] Centy of decently relig[s.] parents &c. &c. &c. Even Gibbon[423] felt grateful for this, & shall thou not praise y[e.] Lord O my Soul.

My being providently engag'd in the Sl: Trade Business, thro' what we call accident, I remember well how it was. What an honorable Service. Deliv[ce.] from Sickness in 1788 & 1796.

---

418. Revelation 3:1.

419. 'Notably in my Life for which I sho'd return thanks or be humbled or be suitably affected' written here in the left margin.

420. MS Wilberforce c. 41, fo. 94. He continues from previous page, by writing 'Notables in my Life' in the upper left margin of the page.

421. Word illegible.

422. Philip Doddridge, *The Rise and Progress of Religion in the Soul; illustrated in a course of Serious and Practical Addresses, suited to persons of every character and circumstance; with a devout Meditation or Prayer added to each chapter* (London, 1745). It would be this volume that would be instrumental in the conversion of William Wilberforce, whilst on his European tour with Isaac Milner.

423. Edward Gibbon (1737–1794), historian, writer, and M.P. In the same year as Wilberforce's entry here, Gibbon's friend Lord Sheffield compiled and published an account of his friend's life from six fragmentary autobiographical works, which appeared as *Memoirs of My Life and Writings* (1796). It is likely that the comment Wilberforce makes about Gibbon's view was taken from these memoirs.

How much the Circumstance of Milner's going abroad with me depended on contingencies. His comg to Hull with his Brother. Being known to my Grandfather, distinguishg himself &c. &c.

My chief sins now:

How much more solicitous ab[t] Bodily Health than Spirit[l] - how much more promptly alive & wakeful to Loss of Character for parts, or of credit in any way, than to Decline in Grace - This argues Affections cold & torpid - Cure - Humble Confess[n] to God in X[t] & imploring his Spirit - More serious Prayer Scripture Readg &c. - I was certainly more in earnest the first Winter of my seriousness, more watchful over myself, more awake for my friends. Not suff[y] impress'd contin[y] with a Sense of the pres[ce] of God X[t] Sp[t] & of all which these Ideas sho'd suggest to my Soul - The heavenly world or Satan &c. - Too sensual, even when I don't indulge it in act. (very difficultly placed here, because my Health requires Indulgence).

Faults: Too Contentious, not meek enough disputing with Milner. This is Vanity & Want of Humility - O that I were lowly as I ought to be, but here much more ashamed sho'd I be to be known to be what I am than to find myself such as I am –

More interested now to gain Credit by writg my Tract than to benefit Souls of Men – Oimoi. Not enough shewg myself to be a despised Xtian. Ashamed of X[t] - <u>where</u> Credit really to be lost, by supporting his Cause, countenancing his people &c.[424]

Not enough careful for Souls of others.

Not 1000th part desirous enough of Growth in Grace.

O how little real Love either of God or fellow Creatures - I have a strange rejoicg in Iniquity.

Prayers often cold & formal.

Glad[425] to find Excuses for not defendg them or profess mys to be of the Set in their being faulty anyhow, tho' right probably in y[e] main.

Not enough attentive & active in doing Good, how careless here compar'd with H.T., my Sister &c.

A Sort of Contempt for Persons inferior in Knowledge of X[ty] How inconsistent with true Xtian Humility.

Often little Deviations from Truth –

What Selfishness do I discover in myself everywhere & how little real disinterestedness.

Alas - for the latter years of my being at School[426] I was irreligious, practisg one Sin in partic[r] which I believed hateful to God - Then at College totally idle & wicked in every way - O had I been then cut off, but the mercy of God spared me - Then for the first 5[427] years of my being in Parl[t] from 1780 to Nov[r] 1785 - sadly wicked - living with[t] God in the World - no Desire to please him & only kept from total Idleness by

---

424. A symbol resembling a large 'H' inserted here, denoting insertion here of section which appears later.

425. Here he wrote the symbol 'H' as noted above.

426. '& College' is here crossed through.

427. 5 is written over a different number.

Vanity & Ambition - Since that time when awaken'd - not striving as I ought to grow in Grace - but livg carelessly & satisfied too much with name & Credit of being religious & taking others opinions of me which knew to be false ag[t.] my own judgement. Yet I hope all along – I have at Intervals humbly cast myself on the free mercy X[t.] & that I now throw myself only on his infinite Compassion & rely only on his effectual Grace. I am in myself most weak & vile.

But do not I owe all my know[ge.] of X[t.] little as it is & my not havg been given up to gross Vice, to the Goodness of God. Here I must be a Calvinist. It is thou O Lord that hast given the very small Increase there has been & that must give all if there be any more. I have not been enough desirous of worshippg God, by going twice to Church &c. since here. Today Mr. Swiney had a charge. What a reproach to me, when Rain y[e.] Cause of my not going this af[tn.] if not too late now (½ past 3 almost) how dine by ourselves & do it.[428]

Sunday Night 10 oClock Sept[r.] 4[th.] 96 Buxton

Today as too often on Sundays, render'd quite unspiritual by what eat & drank at Dinner. Was it a punishment for my ding in y[e.] Room – Alas - tis too common with me - Evg tonight I have been excessively cold & flagging in prayer - quite lifeless - Alas! - Alas! Must I not be wrong in so far eatg & drinkg as quite to unspiritualize myself - much depends on place - Compy, Convers[n.] &c. &c. Surely none now so cold as I - Yet I am not grieved at my Hardness of Heart as poor Mrs. Balfour was - alas.[429]

Sunday Evg ½ past 8 – Hope – Sept[r.] 11[th.] 1796

I scarce think I acted wisely in coming here to spend Sunday. I might have foreseen it wo'd not be well spent. Today I have been quite unspiritual & little read, much time wasted in frivolous conversation, tho dinner more rational & suited to y[e.] day than usual. O let the Grace of God quicken me. I go to pray.[430]

Sunday Evening ½ past 8, September 18, 1796, Bat[a.] Rise

This has been an unprofitable Sunday tho' so much to render it otherwise. However I ill, or very poorly. Sleepy this Evg at Church to a sad degree. O may I now earnestly pray to God to proportion my Strength to my trials & to enable me to grow continually in his faith & fear & Love. I felt spiritually minded this Morng. rather, but my time not well improved, & on the whole my judgement not enough deeply fix'd on God. I am plunging into a depth of trials - O help me.[431]

---

428. MS Wilberforce c. 41, fo. 94.
429. Ibid.
430. MS Wilberforce c. 41, fo. 95.
431. MS Wilberforce c. 41, fo. 96. *Life*, ii. p. 169 has, 'Sunday. Oh may I pray earnestly to God to proportion my strength to my trials, and to enable me to grow continually in his faith, and fear, and love. I am plunging into a depth of trials, O help me.'

Friday Night Septr. 23^{d.} Paly^d 96

Alas![432] Alas! How unquiet & self debatg have I been today ab^{t.} little things as GG (chiefly) ding at Home or with Pitt & my day has been trifled away in this self-debatg, & then foolish Intemperance rather carelessly than ought else - But how foolish to be anxious ab^{t.} anything of this Sort - O my weak vain foolish Heart - How little really set on heavenly things.[433] - Raise O God, my low Desires & warm my Cold Heart.[434]

Sunday 25th. Septr. B. Rise 2 oClock

What Cause for Humiliation do I find within me, but stupid & cold & unspiritual, yet the declarations of the Gospel stand sure. Ask and ye shall receive &c. - Be ye reconciled &c.[435] Therefore I will calmly repose myself on them & throw myself on the Mercy of God in X^{t.} beseechg him by his Spirit to enlighten pardon & purify me. My Health seems breakg. & alas! I fear I shall be of little more Use in the world - What a Cumberer of the Ground have I been - fruges consumere[436] - & what Cause have I had of late years for Exertion. But whether able to be active or not, let me still look to God & resolve to be entirely his & struggle to drive out of my Heart all other competitors.[437]

Wednesday Night ¼ before 10 Paly^{d.} Septr. 28th. 96

I was rather beguil'd into partaking of a grand dinner at Pitt's today & how unprofitable a Day has it been, & alas! I have exceded so as both to have unspiritualized myself & to have injured Health. I would humbly resolve if it might be never to exceed to observe strict tempce. with full Livg. Today I thought not of God. He might well leave me to myself. I was not at all on my guard, I will amend.[438]

Sunday Octr. 2^{d.} 2 oClock B. Rise 96

Alas! how unprofitably do my Days slide away. My constitut^{n.} is broken. Complaints multiply on me. These & the world closg the avenues to its pleasures & lookg forward & pain & weakness of which I am afraid, my cowardly nature shrinking back from suffering. I am driven to take Refuge in God, alas! alas! That I sho'd not more in the little vigor of my Life have sought earnestly & served diligently the Saviour & Redeemer of Sinners, who so dearly bought a title to their Gratitude. But O thou merciful Redeemer, thou pitiest us in our misery & art always ready to recover us. I prostrate myself before thee, with tears & Supplication, renouncg every other plea than that of unqualified Depend^{ce.} on thine unmerited mercy - O pardon me - Send me thy Grace to fill me with the real Love of thee, & if any power of Usefulness

---

432. 'Time' written in left margin.
433. Colossians 3:2.
434. MS Wilberforce c. 41, fo. 96.
435. Matthew 7:7 and 2 Corinthians 5:20.
436. This is a Latin quote from Horace, 'We are but numbers, born to consume'.
437. MS Wilberforce c. 41, fo. 96.
438. MS Wilberforce c. 41, fo. 97.

be still left me, O may it be diligently used to thy Glory. Let me covet it for thy Service. Enlighten my darkness that I may discover the means whereby I may serve thee, & warm my cold & languid Affections - Let me be a monument of thy pardong Grace.

How long how long have I trifled with thee & had a Name to live, when in truth dead.[439] But may I henceforth experience the power of Godliness & live in the near & constant View of heav[ly.] things, my Heart fill'd & overflowg with y[e.] Love of God & Man & deeply tinged with Humility.

How[440] sadly was my time wasted yesterday in foolish S[f.] deb[gs.] ab[t.] as triflg a thing as arrang[g.] Dinner parties for next week - Indeed since I have been living near London now a fortnight, nothg has been done. Let me pray to God for direction & form a plan & to try to adhere to it, as much as my very poor Health will allow. Why[441] was I not the poor blacks those espy. on whom I feel myself lookg down with disdain when my notion of Equality presents itself.[442]

Sunday Night 8 ½ oClock

I have enjoyed a good deal of Comfort today, but have been sadly sleepy at Church tonight -The subject If any man love not y[e.] L[d.] Jesus let him &c.[443] alas, do I love X[t.] O let me watch unto prayer, God will not refuse an importunate Suitor.[444]

Sunday Night ½ past 8 Oct[r.] 9[th.] BRise

The last week has roll'd over with but little done. A good deal in Compy, & this tho' for y[e.] most part rational, yet unspiritualizes. Time fritter'd away in Lond[n.] Today I receiv'd the Sacrament & felt much this morng, but this af[tn.] at & after dinner got into a worldlyish Talk with Eliot & quite unspiritualized, & sadly sleepy in spite of every Effort this Evg at Church. Alas. Alas. O may I now awake to Righteousness,[445] - redeem the Time & strive to use all my faculties to God's Glory. Tho' not very intempte, I have not been as temp[te.] as I ought & as many are from merely bodily views, may God enable me, & then with less mischf. I shall mix in Compy.[446]

Monday Night ¼ past 11 Paly[d.] Oct[r.] 10[th.]

Today I have been excedg both mens, & dis - alas, alas, what folly - Thus disabling myself - O Pardon me I beseech thee - I will determine

---

439. Revelation 3:1.

440. Here in left margin he wrote, 'Pr Time'.

441. In left margin here he wrote, 'Pride'.

442. MS Wilberforce c.41, fo.97. *Life*, ii. p.179 has, 'I was asked to dine at Lord Hood's, how much more pleasant is a day of Christian solitude! On Thursday, M. at dinner. His loose religious notions. Thought all sects equally acceptable to God, that error was innocent, sincerity all, etc. Alas!'

443. 1 Corinthians 16:22.

444. MS Wilberforce c.41, fo.97.

445. 1 Corinthians 15:34.

446. MS Wilberforce c.41, fo.97.

henceforth to be more mod[te.] to eat plainly & no dis – Oimoi – Oimoi - O fool! fool![447]

Tuesday Night 10 oClock – Paly[d.] 11[th.] Oct[r.]

Today I have given a Dinner & tho' less flagrantly, I have broke my Resolution – alas - alas! I prayed earnestly this morning to be strengthen'd, But I was carried off by Vanity & Volatility, alas. Yet I would humbly resolve, & earnestly strive to amend - It has this Evg been Dis &c. which has been contra & much undue Solicitude for all going off well.[448]

Friday Night ¼ before 10 Paly[d.] Oct[r.] 14[th.]

Yesterday I again foolishly exceeded. Today <u>rather</u> better. But O what madness is this & how deeply humbled ought I to be under a Sense of my deep Guilt & Folly - Why Condemn M[nr.] or anyone for disobeyg in one Instance than myself in another - I wo'd humbly resolve to amend.[449]

Sunday Night ¾ past 8 oClock B Rise – Oct[r.] 16

This has been a very hurrying week, out or Compy at Home every Day but one, & Stayg out in Evg - Evg Devotions exceedgly curtail'd & Scripture Readg almost entirely neglected - No wonder that today I feel flat & unspiritual & that sleepy at Church this Evg - Little also done in y[e.] Way of Business or Study - My time fritter'd away insensibly I know not how, alas! Alas! I would humbly resolve by God's Help durg the ensuing Week - more strict & large in Evg Devotions. - Daily Scripture Readg the first vact. morning time - Yesterday large Party at Speakers, very irrational - Let me strive also to do more. O that I might yet serve God in my Generation & them that honor him, he will honor.[450] Sadly sleepy at Church tonight in spite of utmost Efforts I hope bodily chiefly.[451]

Sunday ½ past 2, October 23, 1796, Pal Y[d.]

This last has been a very hurrying Week. Every day either Company at Home, or visitg. as forc'd to it. Exceeded mens, Oimoi. My mind too - by all this unspiritualized - Surely too much Worldly Communications & too little habitual Thought of God - I staid in Town today - on purpose to have the day to myself, in quietness & Self-Exam[n.] But how little on lookg into myself do I see cause for Self-Satisfaction. O Lord - pardon my sins for they are very great - Guide me in thy ways & teach me - Instruct me in the right way. I go to confession & prayer - Fasting really disagrees with me, but let me be moderate today & humbly seek the mercy of God. O what a mercy it is that we have a Throne of Grace to

---

447. MS Wilberforce c. 41, fo. 98.
448. Ibid.
449. Ibid.
450. 1 Samuel 2:30.
451. MS Wilberforce c. 41, fo. 98.

go to. Today ask'd to dine at Lord Hood's. How much more pleasant is a Day of Xtian Solitude, Self-Humiliation, but humble Confidence in X[t.] & dependence on his promise of pardon & final peace & joy.[452]

Sunday Night ¼ before 9 -

I took before dinner a walk wherein enjoyed much inward Peace, but I fear lest it sho'd have been false peace. However it was Self Renunciation & humble depend[ce.] on God's mercy in X[t.] Tonight I have been at Davis's Church. Sleepy & unspiritual. But let me not go by frames & feelings, but by the fruits of the Spirit by the Graces of the Xtian temper & the Life of Faith. My time has been sadly fritter'd away, I know not how. Little done, yet never very idle. But let me strive to be a more profitable Servant. O what a mercy it is to have a God who declares himself willg to receive the returng penitent - I go to Confession & Petition. Have mercy on me O X[t.453]

Sunday Night 9 oClock – BRise Oct[r.] 30[th.]

This last has been a bustling week & this but an unprofitable Sunday - Unspiritual in mind & affections - Scripture more read in y[e.] week, but time fritter'd away - There is a Talk of Invasion.[454] O Let me prepare for the worst, that I may then either find death Gain or Life, Christ - O purify & strengthen me, Saviour.[455]

Sunday ~~Morn~~ 2 oClock BRise Nov[r.] 6[th.] 1796

The last week has rolld away insensibly - I have been very busy yet little done. I get up late but I really believe that this necessy to my Health. But O how unprofitable a Serv[t.] am I. How much more useful is Mr. Pitt, & how ought I to pray & to strive that I may glorify God - I fear I discover some lurkg Envy & malignity in my Mind, perhaps rather pride in my Tempers towds. Ad[v.] & alas - what Vanity & Solicitude ab[t.] hum[n.] approbat[n.] & aftd[s.] base fear in y[e.] House the other night - O for a Heart more set on divine Things. Today I go deep earlier & have prayed & in some degree felt in earnest. But it being cold & I indiff[t.] I have suffer'd f[m.] early risg - O may I be more in earnest - I much struck the other day with the thought how little able to stand y[e.] fiery trial, to which many Serv[ts.] of X[t.] have been call'd.[456] O let me strive to grow in Grace[457] & bring forth much fruit.[458]

---

452. MS Wilberforce c. 41, fo. 99.

453. Ibid.

454. The Greatest influence on British naval strategy and the large scale fortification of the southeast England at the end of the 18th and start of the 19th century, was the very real threat of a French invasion. Plans for the invasion of the first French *Army of England* in 1798 were called off finally in 1802. Once war broke out in 1803, preparations for invasion were once again started, but in 1805 these too were called off.

455. MS Wilberforce c. 41, fo. 99.

456. 1 Peter 4:12.

457. 2 Peter 3:18.

458. John 15:8. MS Wilberforce c. 41, fo. 99.

Monday B. Rise ½ past 2 oClock Nov[r.] 14[th.]

The last week was spent more in Company than any time since my being in Town - & little or no Bus[s.] done[459] & yet this was unavoidable, I being in Town. Had company twice. Both times Bus[s.] vent, din'd at Guildhall Bankers on Bus[s.] & Chancellors. Yesterday but a bad Sunday of it. Much polit[l.] & financial talk in the week. Alas, Alas. I wish I had done my Tract. I would humbly pray to God to guide & direct me. My time has been exceedingly fritter'd & expended in gen[l.] talk, which yet right, but my Tract not done, nor in a way to be so - My bad Health really renders it requisite for me to have much sleep, but I sho'd & with God's Help, I will strive to lessen useless discuss[n.] time & thus redeem what Hours I can for solid work. Little Scripture read last week. Devotions curtail'd.[460]

Friday May 1 ½ oClock – Buckden Nov[r.] 18[th.] 96

My Life alas is sadly unprofitable. And tho' I really doubt in y[e.] sight of God whether the longtime I sleep be not requisite, it sadly curtails my day. O how active have other Serv[ts.] of God been. May X[t.] strengthen me, quicken & purify me, fill me with the Love of him & the desire far before Health & Ease & all else to use my faculties diligently in his Service. I trust I mainly am subject to him, but I am too apt to be drawn off into deviations particularly by fleshly Indulgences - which needful for my bodily weakness - May God in X[t.] who is as loving as he is powerful (what an Idea this), enable me to be more positively unreservedly & actively his.[461]

Sunday Night 8 ¾ oClock Buckden Nov[r.] 20[th.] 96

Alas! this has been a sad Sunday - My affections have been perfectly dead today. My prayers wanderg. This Evg I have not been able to pray. Alas! Alas! This is not the Life of Religion. How heavy a Service is it! How cold my Love today both to God & man - O let me be humbled in the Dust, & own that Christ only by his Grace can quicken me. Ld Westmd by his intrusion this aft[n.] has ruin'd our Day! Yet it is somethg even to sigh after spiritual things, & to deplore their absence. I have today been too exceeding rather, yet not much so but nothg to warm my affections or raise them & all the Talk ab[t.] worldly things. O how much better off at B. Rise, & what a State that I be in if married to a worldly Wife.[462]

Thursday Night Stevenage 9 oClock Nov[r.] 24[th.] 96

My visit has been a less profitable one I fear than it ought to have been, yet not useless in many Respects. It has certainly produc'd a more favorable impression than before of y[e.] Bp. Mrs. G[n.] &c. Whilst at y[e.] same time it has shewn me the faults of their Religion as well as its

459. In left margin here he wrote, 'Time'.
460. MS Wilberforce c.41, fo.99.
461. MS Wilberforce c.41, fo.100.
462. Ibid.

Good - I wo'd humbly resolve to improve - & also to set as vigorously as possible on my Tract & try to get it out this winter. I hope I may.[463]

Sunday B Rise ½ past 2 Nov[r.] 27[th.] 96

<u>Alas</u>! I am a poor Xtian indeed! How loudly do I talk to men, but how low & weak in the Sight of God. Scripture not read much last week. _____[464] mercy to be honor'd by God in _____[465] truly permitted by him to put in at York Mr. Graham[466] but I fear I have done too much all 3 livings. I am too vain ab[t.] my Tract & too little humble. May the Grace of God touch me more deeply & fill me with deep Remorse, & through enlightn'd spirit of practical Holiness. I am going to resume my Town life - O may I be <u>more</u> careful of time than I have been, more watchful over my ways &c. - I trust I shall get my tract ready for the press by the End of the Xmas Recess, if God spares my Health.[467]

B Rise Sunday 2 oClock Dec[r.] 4[th.] 96

The last week has gone on ill - Two days heard more Indecency in conversat[n.] with less manifested displeasure than I ought, & unkind before & today to Bab[n.] he all Love. The cold pinches me, & I yield to it & am cross instead of thinkg at such a Season what uncommon Bounties I enjoy - Little also has been done this week. What wonder then, if today I find in my Heart no lively Sense of Devotion or of Love either to God or man - Alas! Alas! How little am I livg the life of growg in the Graces of a Xtian, but as I see my State let me fall down before the Throne of X[t.] pleadg his atong Blood & implorg his Spirit to enlighten & purify & warm me. This week - God's Eye & X[t.] & the Spirit & Satan - Love to all. Diligence, particy at Tract. Kindness & meekness & Temperance - I have exceeded here more than once, & my Health has suffer'd – Oimoi – O Lord, enable me really to bring forth abundantly the fruits of Righteousness to the praise & Glory of thy Name. Short Evg Devotions past week.[468]

B Rise Sunday Dec[r.] 11[th.] ½ past 2 – 96 -

This week has discover'd to me much Vanity & jealousy of Worldly Estimation. In House &c. Unkindness & Concert in Haldane's Case.[469] -

---

463. Ibid.

464. Word illegible.

465. Word illegible.

466. Sense here uncertain.

467. MS Wilberforce c. 41, fo. 100.

468. MS Wilberforce c. 41, fo. 101.

469. Haldane is an aristocratic Scottish family dating back to at least the 13th century. Robert Haldane (1764–1842), a naval captain who after his evangelical conversion and, with his brother Robert, established almost 100 free churches in Scotland and Ireland. From 1816 onwards, he was also used to spread revival throughout Europe. He visited Wilberforce in October 1796 to share with him his vision for a mission in Bengal. Wilberforce's sons, however, record the following entry in their biography, supposedly by Wilberforce, dated 4 October, 1796, 'I am sorry to find that all perfect democrats, believing that a new order of things is dawning, &c. Haldane very open. I told him I thought that he, by imprudence, had injured the cause with Dundas.' Alexander Haldane in his biography of Robert and J. A. Haldane stated that if accurately copied, this entry is glaringly unjust. (*Memoirs of the Lives of Robert Haldane of Airthrey, and of his brother, James Alexander Haldane*

How unlike the Xtian Spirit today cold & unspiritual, nil mirror.[470] O may I turn to God & give up all for him & walk with him humbly, relying on his Grace & strivg after all Holiness &c.[471]

B Rise Sunday Dec[r.] 25[th.] Xmas day

I am a poor Xtian; yet I would humbly throw myself at the footstool of God & beseech him for X[t's] Sake, to forgive & cleanse me. Sad proofs lately from House occurrence (Lafayette),[472] of Vanity, most in the Love of World's Esteem &c., also of being too sensual, anxious ab[t.] Health & suffg more than duty. May X[t.] sanctify me by the Spirit & may I strive to grow in Grace & in the Knowledge & Love of God & X[t.] watchful & fearful of falling.[473]

1797

Palace Yard Sunday Jan[y] 1[st.] 1797 - ¾ past 5 oClock

Din'd alone today & staid in Town for relig[s.] Retirement, & I have felt much Comfort & some Humiliation – alas - What cause have I for it on[474] this day failing, with what Shame ought I to be fill'd - My life alas, has been a sad unprofitable one, when my opportunities are consider'd - How much sad mens. Excedg[s.] forgettgs of God, X[t.] Spirit, Satan - How much wanderg in Prayer. Little or no mens, Gratitude, or Self-denial thought, or Compy or Conversat[n.] Regl. or Recollection of pcl[r.] Character - How much Vanity – Pride - Falsehood - Fleshly Lust - How often fretful & selfish - Wasting time & powers - Seldom Self-Exam[n.] I would humbly now resolve to amend in all these particulars, & thro' God's Grace, to live soberly righteously humbly & godly -

This year I have been preserv'd from many Evils - What a black aspect do public affairs present, & what a Lesson to us to make here of a better Inheritance - How seldom have I prayed for my Country, yet

by Alexander Haldane: London, 1852), 101. Robert Haldane's own account of the meeting is rather different. The fact is that Haldane had been in London for four months before seeing Wilberforce. He had met with many leading Church figures and government officials concerning his mission plans, including the Archbishop of London, the Bishop of London, the Lord Chancellor, as well as several conversations with Dundas. Haldane also records that when he met Wilberforce, Wilberforce was suffering so badly from gout with his feet wrapped in cloth, that he could not rise to greet his visitor. But Haldane said he had not been speaking long concerning his vision of mission in India, before Wilberforce forgot everything else and was walking around the room. Haldane's plan was for a vast mission to Bengal which he would fully fund from the sale of his estate. As it turned out, the British East India Company refused to sanction the scheme, which then was abandoned.

470. The Latin, 'nil miror' is translated as, 'No wonder.'

471. MS Wilberforce c. 41, fo. 101.

472. Marie Joseph Paul Yves Roche Gilbert du Motier, Marquis de Lafayette (1757–1834), often referred to simply as Lafayette, as Wilberforce himself does, was a French aristocrat and General, who was a key figure in the French Revolution and the War for American Independence. Wilberforce had initially met him in 1783, when Pitt, Eliot and Wilberforce were touring together in France. The three friends dined at Lafayette's, with Benjamin Franklin and his grandson also being there. Wilberforce wrote that Lafayette was a 'pleasing enthusiastic man and his wife a sweet woman.'

473. MS Wilberforce c. 41, fo. 101.

474. Written in top left margin of the page is '102 1796 Pr past & Resolutions' with a bracket covering first ten lines of the page.

I humbly trust I am not cast away & I will press forward, laying aside every Weight & trustg entirely to the Grace & Strength of X^t· - The Recess for 6 Weeks is commencing. I once meant to try to finish my Tract, but I now rather think that this time being (that part of it at least which co'd so employ), too little for so very serious a Work. I shall devote great part if not all of it to preparat^n· for H. of Coms. after Recess - Improvem^t· in Speakg which sadly neglected, & in Knowledge &c. &c. - May God preserve me the while from Vanity, & enable me to continue humble, & to devote all my Faculties Powers & Studies to his Service.[475]

Sunday Jan^y· 8th· 1797 BRise ½ past 2 oClock
It has pleased God of his great mercy to raise me up again when on Mon 7, I was attacked with a Bowel Complaint which threatened much - I then tho't Death probably near. O that I might now better employ the time it has pleased God to allow me. May I be enlighten'd & purified & quicken'd, & havg sadly wasted my precious faculties ever since my thinkg more seriously, may I now more constantly act as an accountable creat^e· who may be suddenly call'd away to his Reckoning. God for X^t's Sake Sanctify me by his Spirit, & may they dwell in me.[476]

Sunday Jan^y· 15th· 3 oClock Bath
May I be enabled to engage in this busy Scene with Benefit to others & with^t· Harm to myself. O that I may feel the Power of divine Grace in my Heart to fill me with Love of God & X^t· & thy fellow creatures. O how much do I want. What unnumbered blessings do I receive at the Hands of God, & how unequal is my Return, yet let me remember he has encourag'd us to apply to him for his Holy Spirit, & "let him that is athirst, come."[477] Create then in me this sacred Thirst & satisfy it with that peace of God which thou only canst supply.[478]

Sunday 3 ¼ oClock Bath 22^d· Jan^y·
I have this week been ding every day with irreligious people. Today to which I look'd forward as a relig^s· Season with Hope & Pleasure, my Heart is little warm I fear tho' my judgement is fix'd, yet let me earnestly pray to God to give me his heav^y Grace, to guide me, to preserve me, to render me useful here & in the End, a partaker of his Glory.[479] I did not feel just as I ought at Palmer's, swearing yesterday, alas! Alas! How much more anxious for our worldly Credit or friends than for our best friend. O increase my Love of thee, thou God of all Grace & Consolation.[480]

475. MS Wilberforce c. 41, fo. 102.
476. Ibid.
477. Revelation 22:17.
478. MS Wilberforce c. 41, fo. 102.
479. 1 Peter 4:13.
480. 1 Peter 5:10. MS Wilberforce c. 41, fo. 103. *Life*, ii. p. 189 has, 'I have this week been dining out every day. Today, to which I looked forward as a religious season with hope and pleasure, my heart is little warm I fear, though my judgment is fixed. Yet let me earnestly pray to God to give

Sunday Evg 8¼ oClock Jany. 29[th.] 1797 - Bath -

I find little time here for Study, not above 2 or 3 Hours in a morng hitherto, at Tract. Calls of which I make ab[t.] 60 & receive as many. Water drinkg, Dings out with people, who expect one to stay. Many Letters to write. All this leaves me tho' hurrying much & I hope not idling, yet with very little Time. I have kept late Hours at night & conseqly Morns. Let me try to gain an Hour here tho', I must not abridge my Sleep, my Health will suffer & perhaps even ding so long after I get up. But let me try. Also, I have been & am still livg with irreligious People. This is bad work. My Affections cool & I fear my desires languish. However, I ought not to forswear Society & tis difficult to engage in at all & not too much. May God for Xt's Sake bless me with Wisdom & fill me with Love & every Xtian Grace- Poor Gordon. He in a truly Xtian frame. She less so, but resign'd on y[e.] whole- yet what a blessed thing Relign is, which can thus cheer in Sorrow.[481]

Sunday Feb[y.] 5[th.] Bath - 97 - 3½ oClock -

My Evg devotions have been sadly curtail'd this week & livg constantly in Compy is[482] unfavorable to pious frame of mind, yet right for me so to do I trust. O let me however, yield myself more heartily to God & more & more desire to serve him with all my Faculties & powers. I have been receivg the Sac[t.] God knoweth I am not what I ought to be, yet Blessed be God for his Goodness in offerg me free Pardon & Grace to help in time of need for X[t's] Sake. My Heart is but cold today, but I trust I may humbly look to God as reconcil'd by X[t.] & that he will enable me yet to live more & more to his Glory.[483]

Sunday Feb[y.] 26[th.] Palyard 1797 - ½ past 2 oClock

The last fortnight in London has been most hurrying. Little & interrupted Prayer. Little or no Scripture Readg &c. but little thought of God - alas! Alas! I cannot wonder that today sadly unspiritual. O what need of deep Humiliatn & of livg by faith. I have felt much Vanity & self Confid[ce.] &c. &c. I wo'd now resolve - Earlier Hours, that I may have more time for prayer & Reflection, & more of these & Script[e.] Readg. Health but poorly & requirg much Indulgence but then I may go to Bed earlier - Let me pray to God in X[t.] & he will hear me. I am correcting my Book & the press full of polit[l] tho'ts also. O that I might put my whole Trust in God & not fear what man can do ag[t.] me.[484]

---

me his grace, to guide me, to preserve me, to render me useful here, and in the end a partaker of his glory.'

481. MS Wilberforce c. 41, fo. 103. *Life*, ii. p. 190 has, 'I find little time here for study, not above two or three hours in a morning hitherto, at Tract. Calls, of which I make about sixty, and receive as many, water-drinking, dinings out with people, who expect me to stay; many letters to write; all this leaves me, though hurrying much, and I hope not idling, very little time.'

482. 'Is' is written on top of another word.

483. MS Wilberforce c. 41, fo. 103. *Life*, ii. p. 190 has, 'Randolph's. Sacrament, which received. Afterwards serious talk with Acklom. Heard at Pump-room of Austrian defeats. Poor Burke came down quite emaciated.'

484. MS Wilberforce c. 41, fo. 104.

Sunday March 5th. – 97- ¼ past 3 oClock Pal Y^{d.}

Alas! This last has been a sad hurrying week & God & Eternal things little thought of, tho' so much call to seek for true Rest in them, much vanity &c. &c. Today ill fr^{m.} (probably), foolishly not self-denying Des^{t.} Oimoi. O that my Heart were right with God. This last week, Prayer alm^t omitted in Evg & short & hurried in Morng, Oimoi. Let me try to mend here - O may the mercy of God yet spare me for future usefulness.[485]

Wed^{y.} March 8th. 97 Fast-Day 3 oClock

My frame has been for some time sadly unspiritual. I now feel very hard & cold. O how little as I ought. How great have been my mercies & how little is my Gratitude, & how apt am I to regard anythg I do for God's Glory, not enough as the Effect of his operatg Grace. O may I turn to him with my whole Heart. I would humbly resolve, to redeem time more, to keep God more in view & X^{t.} & all he has suffer'd for us, & the unseen World where X^{t.} is now sittg at the R^t Hand of God interceding for his people.[486] I would grow in Love & tender Solicitude for my fellow Creatures' Happiness. In Preparing for any Events which may befall me in this uncertain State. I may be called to sharp trials, but Christ is able to strengthen me for the Event, be it what it may. O may I then live a life of faith walking by Love, & bring forth abundantly all the fruits of ye. Spirit.[487] I doubt if it would not be right in these times to be more open in acknowledgements of the Providence of God & Recognition of his Chastisements.[488]

Sunday 2 ½ oClock, March 12, 1797, Pal Yard

Alas! I have been sadly unspiritual. Devot^{ns.} particy much curtail'd & no Scripture Readg or meditation from late Hours at both night & morng. I must try for earlier Hours at night. My shatter'd frame not being able to go on witht 8 ½ or 9 Hours Bed. How much more anxious have I been & am I ab^{t.} this affair of Sir G C, &c. &c. than ab^{t.} my soul's Interest - fearg disgrace &c. - fear I have not quite adhered to truth, yet I did not mean to deceive, certainly I trust I can say so, & all the parties now go from their words. I will pray to God to carry me thro' this scrape with^{t.} great discredit, & commit myself to him. How angry today at organist. Oimoi. Oimoi. Try for ½ an Hour or even an Hour's meditatn & Scrip^{e.} Readg evg morng & labor in earnest to get to Bed at night - Evil Speakg this week, poor _____[489] & less hurt by displeasg God in it than last. L^{d.}

---

485. Ibid.

486. Romans 8:34.

487. Galatians 5:6 and 22.

488. MS Wilberforce c. 41, fo. 104. *Life*, ii. p. 196 has, '(The resolutions with which he had begun this busy season, were,) "to redeem time more; to keep God more in view, and Christ, and all He has suffered for us, and the unseen world, where Christ is now sitting at the right hand of God interceding for his people. I would grow in love and tender solicitude for my fellow-creatures' happiness, in preparedness for any events which may befall me in this uncertain state. I may be called to sharp trials, but Christ is able to strengthen me for the event, be it what it may".'

489. Word illegible.

Auckld[s490] connect[n] should make it awkward. Not trust, when Lassater said that rather & d of Norfolk[491] drunk &c. O let these things shew me my Heart - May I have more the mind of X[t.] & Strive to love him more & be more entirely his.[492]

Sunday March 19[th.] 1797 Pal Yard ½ past 2

Alas. I've been hearg. Scott preach excellently today on Relig[s.] Hypocrisy, its Symptoms &c. &c. I have some of the Symps. I fear in particular I had diff[t.] indifft. Companies, to men & to God, but yet I hope I allow myself in no Sin that I am Strivg. agt it & in some degree praying & watchg agt it. But O Lord Jesus, by thy Grace quicken me, enable me to mortify my pride Vanity Sensuality, Volatility Solicitude ab[t.] Worldly Estimatn., & fill with me more real Love of God, & fear, & of X[t.] & more earnest hungerg & thirstg after righteousness. Evil Speakg faulty & not strict in Observance of Truth this week, Oimoi, Oimoi.[493]

Sunday March 26[th.] Pal y[d.] ½ past 2 oClock - 97

This week has flown away like one morng. How soon will Death be here at this rate. I have a proof how far too much I am interested ab[t.] Worldly favor, in my being much mov'd by the falsehood cast in me in the Cambridge paper.[494] But I hope I am endeavorg to fight against the bad Tempers of Revenge & Pride &c. &c. which it is generating &c. & endeavorg to combat them by thinking of all our Saviour suffer'd in the way of calumny. X[t.] accused & Stephen also of Blasphemy. Paul &c. &c. all falsely accused. Let me humbly watch myself, so far as this false charge may present to me method of Amendment, & also I ought to be very thankful that with the many faults of which I am conscious, some of them likely to be discover'd (Culgarth &c.), yet it has pleased God that I have never been charged justly, or where I could not vindicate myself - O Lord, enable me to turn to thee with my whole Heart, to repent of every evil way & forsake it & to devote myself with every faculty of Mind & Body to thy Service.

---

490. George Eden, 1st Earl of Auckland (1784–1849). MP, three times First Lord of the Admiralty, and Governor General of India, 1836–1842.

491. Charles Howard (1746–1815), 11th Duke of Norfolk, Earl Marshal of England, and M.P. He spoke against the Anglo-American War but in favor of Parliamentary reform. As Wilberforce notes here, it is recorded that Norfolk's servants would have to wash him in his drunken stupors, as he detested soap and water when sober. See Gordon Goodwin, 'Howard, Charles, eleventh duke of Norfolk (1746–1815)', Rev. S. J. Skedd, *ODNB*, Oxford University Press, 2004 (http://www.oxforddnb.com/view/article/13890, accessed 3 Nov 2016).

492. MS Wilberforce c. 41, fo. 105.

493. Ibid.

494. Wilberforce was attacked in the newspaper, the *Cambridge Intelligencer*, in which he was seemingly charged with always having a prayer-book with him in the Bath Pump-Room and also saying his prayers there. Isaac Milner advised Wilberforce that this was simply a matter of outright persecution, and that he should simply ignore it and not enter into some kind of debate with the paper. The *Cambridge Intelligencer* was called the most vigorous and outspoken liberal periodical of its day, and was published between 1793 to 1803. Its editor was Benjamin Flower who was imprisoned for contempt of the House of Lords, for remarks made in the newspaper against Richard Watson, Bishop of Llandaff.

The foolish Cambridge Charge kept me distracted in Prayer today. Also, perceiv'd Symptoms of great Pride yesterday, in secret feelgs tow^{ds.} Sir R. Hill & sensual imaginat^{ns.} How good is God, this Bus^{s.} of Sir G.C's[495] going off well. I left it more to him than I have often done in such Cases - Be this remember'd for future Practice - The real Truth is that at Bath, I carried sometimes New Test^{t.} & Horace & Shakespeare in my pocket, & generally the first, got by Heart or occupied in walkg or staying in the Pump Room.[496] I had bo't a testament which had not the common Dress of one, on purpose. I cannot recollect havg had any secret movements of Vanity or Spiritual Pride on this Ground, but resolve I tho't it a profitable way, & got 2 or 3 St. Paul's Epistles by Heart, when otherwise quite idle, & had rather resolv'd to get by Heart much of Scripture in this way, rememberg old Venn's Comfort from it. Thou Lord, here knowest I trust my integrity & it will finally appear, meanwhile let my Usefulness not be prevented by this Report or that essay Book be thus acted - What a blessed Institution is the Sunday.[497]

Sunday April 2^{d.} 1797 ½ past 2 oClock Pal yard

Alas! How flat I feel - This is partly bodily indeed, but it is also a good deal from the low State of Relign in my mind. I fear I live too much with worldly people & not enough either with serious ones, or what is far more important, of Prayer & Meditat^{n.} & Scripture Readg - For some 2 or 3 days, I have suffer'd from the old folly or rather wickedness. Dessert nibbling, Alas, Alas. What folly. No dis. & mens. Mod. Try when really can with Propriety, for earlier Hours at night & then d^{o.} morng & prayer & Scrip^{e.} Readg.

---

495. Cook, Sir G.

496. The Grand Pump Room in the Abbey Church Yard, Bath, and though not finished, was opened on 28 December 1795. It was described in a contemporary guide book this way, 'This noble room was built in 1797 under the direction of Mr Baldwin, architect. It is 60 feet long by 46 wide, and 31 feet high. The inside is set round with three quarter columns of the Corinthian order, crowned with an entablature, and a covering of five feet ... In the Centre of the South-side is a marble vase from which issue the waters, with a fire-place on each side.' (John Feltham, *Guide to all the Watering and Sea-Bathing Places, for 1813.*' The Wilberforces would, beginning from the very first week of their relationship, visit Bath and the Pump-Room many times.

497. MS Wilberforce c.41, fo. 105. *Life*, ii. pp. 197-198 has, 'My being moved by this falsehood is a proof that I am too much interested about worldly favor. Yet I endeavor I hope to fight against the bad tempers of revenge and pride which it is generating, by thinking of all our Savior suffered in the way of calumny. St. Stephen also and St. Paul were falsely accused. Let me humbly watch myself, so far as this false charge may suggest matter of amendment, and also I ought to be very thankful that with the many faults of which I am conscious, it has pleased God that I have never been charged justly, or where I could not vindicate myself. How good is God! The business of C. off so well, I left it more to Him than I have often done in such cases. Be this remembered for future practice. The real truth is that at Bath I carried sometimes a New Testament, a Horace, or a Shakespeare in my pocket, and got by heart or recapitulated in walking or staying by myself in the Pump-room. I had got a Testament which had not the common dress of one on purpose. I cannot recollect having had any movement of spiritual pride on this ground, but remember I thought it a profitable way. I got two or three of St. Paul's epistles by heart when otherwise quite idle, and had resolved to learn much Scripture in this way, remembering Venn's comfort from it. Thou, Lord, knowest my integrity, and it will finally appear, meanwhile let my usefulness not be prevented by this report, or that of my book thwarted. What a blessed institution is the Sunday!'

On looking back to my past Life, I see many Instances, some greater, some smaller of God's Providential Care over me, & kindness to me. These infuse into me a humble Hope that the public affairs wear a most gloomy aspect, yet I shall be rescued from future Evils & shall be a Specimen of his undeserved Grace & Kindness to those that humbly look up to him. It would to some superstitious to note, how good God has been to me in a Variety of little Instances, preservg me from Evil, from Shame &c. &c. I was quite unprepar'd on Thursday for Ellis's motion,[498] when quite unexpectedly it was put off. Later Sir G. Cook's,[499] & in more important cases &c.[500]

Sunday[501] ¾ After 3 Paly[d.] April 9[th.] 1797

This last has been a very hurrying week, & yesterday many bad passions indulged, particy Vanity, & shewg off in compy, & too light minded on Thursday in the House & much malignity & anger with opponents. The wrath of man worketh not the Righteousness of God.[502] Little Scrip[e] Readg this Week, Oimoi. And today, sadly wanderg in prayer at Church. O how can I expect the Blessg of God on my Book, or, how much more careful ought I to be than I am, that I may not disgust by the inconsistency bet[n.] the picture of a Xtian which I draw & which I exhibit. May the Grace of God revive & quicken me. I've been readg Witherspoon on the world crucified by Cross.[503] How little do I correspond.[504]

Good Friday April 14[th.] Bath 3 oClock 1797

I thank God that I <u>now</u> do feel in some degree as I ought on this day. I hope I feel true Humiliation of Soul from a Sense of my own extreme unworthiness, a humble Hope in the favor of God in X[t.] Some Emotion from the Contemplation of him, who at this very moment was hanging on the Cross. Some Shame of the multiplied mercies I enjoy, some Desire to devote myself to him who has so dearly bought me. Some degree of that universal Love & Good-will which the sight of X[t.] crucified is calculated to inspire. O if the Contemplat[n.] <u>here</u> can produce these Effects in my hard Heart, what will the Vision of X[t.] in

498. Charles Ellis (1771–1845), 1st Baron Seaford, M.P., who as Wilberforce here records, introduced into the Commons a proposal for 'the Amelioration of the Condition of the Negroes in the West Indies'. It involved calling for Improvements in living conditions, and the start of slave education, with a view toward eventual abolition. Wilberforce opposed it, saying 'from the present plan it was impossible to the slave trade should ever be put an end to', since the Jamaican legislature had never yet looked upon the trade as an evil, and that Ellis's motion put the responsibility for action in the hand of the colonial legislatures. Speech given by Wilberforce on 6 April, 1797.

499. Wilberforce may here be referring to Sir George Cooke (1768–1837), General who lost his arm at Waterloo, and who later became Lieutenant-Governor of Portsmouth.

500. MS Wilberforce c.41, fo.105.

501. MS Wilberforce c.41, fo.106.

502. James 1:20.

503. See The Works of John Witherspoon, as detailed in footnote 196.

504. MS Wilberforce c.41, fo.106; Life, ii. p.204 has, 'How careful ought I to be that I may not disgust men by an inconsistency between the picture of a Christian which I draw, and which I exhibit! How else can I expect the blessing of God on my book? May his grace quicken me.'

Glory produce hereafter. I feel somewhat too of Pity for a thoughtless
world – And O what Gratitude is justly due from me (the vilest of
Sinners when compared with the mercies I have receiv'd), who have
been brought from darkness into Light, & I trust from the pursuit of
earthly[505] things, to the prime Love of things above. O purify my Heart
still more by thy Grace, Quicken my dead Soul, & purify me by thy
Spirit, that I may be changed from Glory to Glory, & be made even
here in some degree to resemble my heavenly Father.[506]

I would now in prayer, which I set down for my own memory,[507]
Good Friday Employment. Lament my Sins both the chief all my Life,
& my habitual ones, & carefully Self examine with penitence. Look
back also on the mercies of God thro' Life. O how numerous & how
freely, & gratuitously bestowed. Pray for Success of my Book, just
come out. For pardon, Acceptance, Holiness, peace, Holy Spirit &c.,
Courage, Humility & all what I chiefly want. Wisdom, Love, Heavenly
Mindedness. Try Quintilian[508] - Phantasi - as to X^t's Crucifixion.
Think over Enemies with forgiveness & Love & pray. &c. D^o. over
friends & acquaintances & pray. Pray for political Wisdom. Pray for
Country, both Spiritually & temporally. Make Launchers in Evg &
think how may do Good to acquaintances, friends & in general & pray
for Wisdom here. To be guided aright respectg Miss Spooner[509] whom
have not yet seen tis somethg remarkable her name Barbara. For poor
Slaves. For Abolitn. For Sierra Leone. For Mission. Success. Form Plan
of Study Readg &c.[510]

---

505. 'Power of the' has been written and then crossed out, and 'pursuit of earthly' has been
inserted here above the line.

506. 2 Corinthians 3:18.

507. In left margin beginning here he wrote, 'Good Friday Employment'.

508. Marcus Fabius Quintilianus (c. A.D. 35–c. A.D. 100), was a Roman rhetorician from
Hispania, widely acknowledged and used in medieval schools of rhetoric and in Renaissance writing.
His writings are also sometimes included in modern anthologies of literary criticism, in the history
of education, in discussions of professional writing, and the nature of figurative language.

509. Barbara Ann Spooner (1777–1847).

510. MS Wilberforce c. 41, fo. 106. *Life*, i. pp. 6-7 has, 'How eventful a life has mine been, and
how visibly I can trace the hand of God leading me by ways which I knew not! I think I have never
before remarked, that my mother's taking me from my uncle's when about twelve or thirteen and
then completely a Methodist, has probably been the means of my being connected with political
men and becoming useful in life. If I had staid with my uncle I should probably have been a bigoted,
despised Methodist; yet to come to what I am, through so many years of folly as those which elapsed
between my last year at school and 1785, is wonderful. Oh the depths of the counsels of God! What
cause have I for gratitude and humiliation!
Three o'clock, Good Friday. I thank God that I now do feel in some degree as I ought this day. I
trust that I feel true humiliation of soul from a sense of my own extreme unworthiness; a humble
hope in the favor of God in Christ; some emotion from the contemplation of him who at this very
moment was hanging on the cross; some shame at the multiplied mercies I enjoy; some desire to
devote myself to him who has so dearly bought me; some degree of that universal love and goodwill,
which the sight of Christ crucified is calculated to inspire. Oh if the contemplation here can produce
these effects on my hard heart, what will the vision of Christ in glory produce hereafter! I feel
something of pity too for a thoughtless world; and oh what gratitude is justly due from me (the vilest
of sinners, when compared with the mercies I have received) who have been brought from darkness
into light, and I trust from the pursuit of earthly things to the prime love of things above! Oh purify
my heart still more by Thy grace. Quicken my dead soul, and purify me by Thy Spirit, that I may be
changed from glory to glory, and be made even here in some degree to resemble my heavenly Father.

Friday Evg 6 oClock[511]
How eventful a Life has mine been, & how visibly I can trace the Hand of God, guiding & leading me by Ways which I knew not. I don't think I ever before remarked, that probably my Mother's Taking me from my Uncle's when ab[t.] 12 or 13, & then completely a Methodist, probably has been the Means of my becomg useful in Life, connected with political men &c. If I had staid with my Uncle, I sho'd probably have been a bigotted, despised Methodist: yet to come to what I am thro' so many years of Vice & folly as those which elapsed bet[n.] my last year at Pocklington,[512] & 1785, 6, is wonderful - O the depth of the Counsels of God. What Cause have I for Gratitude & Humiliation.[513]

Easter Day April 16[th.] **1797 Bath 3 ¾ oClock**
I humbly bless God, that I have enjoyed part of this morning a very large degree of internal Comfort & that my Heart has been tender; but I fear it has been too much animal transport & Emotion, partly from ideal forms of Conjugal Happiness to which Miss Sp[r.] Introduction to, has led me. But what a solid Satisfaction is it to reflect that our ascended Lord views us with a pitying & Sympathetic Eye. That he knows what it is to have a feeling of our Infirmities, that he promises & that he is Truth as well as Love, that they who wait on him shall renew their Strength.[514] Praise the Lord O my Soul.[515]

Sunday Night near 9 oClock
What a blessed Sunday have I been permitted to spend, how happy at dinner &c in Love. Excellt. Babn. & Mrs. B[n.] O may I be duly thankful for the manifold mercies of God.[516]

I would now in prayer (which I set down for my own memory) lament the chief sins of all my life, and carefully examine myself with penitence. Good Friday employment: Look back on the mercies of God through life. Oh how numerous, and how freely bestowed! Try Quintilian's plan (Phantasia) as to Christ's crucifixion. Pray for pardon, acceptance, holiness, peace; for courage, humility, and all that I chiefly want; for love and heavenly-mindedness. Pray to be guided aright respecting my domestic choice, etc. Pray for my country both in temporal and spiritual things. Pray for political wisdom; for the success of my book just come out; for the poor slaves; for the Abolition; for Sierra Leone; for the success of missions. Think over my enemies with forgiveness and love, over my friends and acquaintances, and pray for both. In the evening make launchers, and think how I may do good to my acquaintances and friends, and pray for wisdom here.'

511. In left margin here he wrote 'Past Life'.

512. Pocklington School near York was founded in 1514 by John Dolman (d. 1526), a lawyer and clergyman. The school, which still operates though out of later buildings, had Wilberforce as a student from 1771 until 1776. His fees were high even for the day, £300-£400 per year, indicating that not only did he have his own room, but additional perks unlike the other twenty-eight pupils, such as lodging and dining with, and being taught by, the Headmaster. It was the same school that Wilberforce's grandfather had attended. A statue of both a freed slave and Wilberforce as a boy are to be found on the school's grounds.

513. MS Wilberforce c. 41, fos. 106-107.

514. Isaiah 40:31.

515. MS Wilberforce c. 41, fo. 107. *Life*, ii. p. 210 has, 'I humbly bless God that I have enjoyed this morning a very large degree of internal comfort, and that my heart has been tender, but I fear animal transport and emotion. But what a solid satisfaction is it to reflect that our ascended Lord views us with a pitying and sympathetic eye; that he knows what it is to have a feeling of our infirmities, that he promises as well as truth as well as love, that they who wait on him shall renew their strength! What a blessed Sunday have I been permitted to spend!'

516. MS Wilberforce c. 41, fo. 107.

Sunday[517] April 23[d.] 1797 - 8 ¾ oClock Bath

This last week seems a month - Alas - I fear I have been too eager ab[t.] earthly things. It seems as if I had been in a fever. I have constantly however prayed to God for his Direction & read his Word. I yesterday had resolv'd to wait before I determin'd ab[t.] Miss Sp[r.] but She quite captivated me last night by her Behaviour to her parents, the Lillingstons[518] & myself & the Babing[ns.] Such frankness & native Dignity, such cheerful waggish Innocence from a good Conscience, such mutual confidence & affection tow[ds] her parents & her. Then her Brothers, being awkward & not comfortable, her modesty & propriety. I could not sleep for think[g] of her, & being much agitated this morn[g] at & after Church, I wrote a long, rambling Letter to her, which She has just return'd with favorable answer - Iacta est alea.[519] I believe indeed, She is admirably suited to me & there are many Circumstances which seem to advise the Step. I trust God will bless me - I go to pray to him - I feel sadly too absorbed in the Love of her &c. but I trust this will go off by use, & that I shall find Miss Sp[r.] what I believe her, a real Xtian - Affectionate, Sensible, rational in Habits, moderate in Desires & pursuits, & capable of bear[g] Prosperity with[t.] Intoxicat[n.] & adversity with[t.] Repining - I doubt I have been too precipitate - If so, forgive me O God. But if as I trust we both shall love & fear & serve thee, thou wilt bless us, accord[g] to thy sure Word of promise.[520]

Sunday May 7[th.] Paly[d.] 1797 - ½ past 12 oClock

Alas! What cause for deep Humiliation do I find in myself, on look[g] back on the last fortnight. At Bath, sadly too sensual ab[t.] B. Hard & unkind I fear to Dr. C, too selfish, in not enough denying myself for his Sake - Proud, a little in manner.[521] But[522] alas, how much more so in mind tow[ds.] Excellent Bab[n.] (a man whom I must declare before God ten times farther than me advanced in the Xtian life), & to honest Clarkson, not enough pitying the latter's weaknesses. How much kinder Milner to him than I was. Then not kind enough to little Tom, rather disgusted

---

517. The entry published in The Life, incorrectly gives April 23rd. as a Tuesday, and not the Sunday as given in the Journal itself.

518. Abraham Spooner Lillingston (1770–1834), son of Isaac and Barbara Spooner, and brother of Barbara who married William Wilberforce. Abraham married Elizabeth Lillingston, the only child of Luke Lillingston, whose family home was Elmdon, near Warwick. Abraham assumed Elizabeth's family name.

519. 'The die is cast,' is a Latin phrase attributed by Suetonius to Julius Caesar on January 10, 49 B.C. as he led his army across the River Rubicon in Northern Italy. With this step, he entered Italy at the head of his army in defiance of the Senate and began his long civil war against Pompey and the Optimates.

520. MS Wilberforce c. 41, fo. 107. *Life*, ii. pp. 214-215 has, 'Jacta est alea. I believe indeed she is admirably suited to me, and there are many circumstances which seem to advise the step. I trust God will bless me, I go to pray to him. I believe her to be a real Christian, affectionate, sensible, rational in habits, moderate in desires and pursuits; capable of bearing prosperity without intoxication, and adversity without repining. If I have been precipitate, forgive me, O God! But if as I trust we shall both love and fear and serve Thee, Thou wilt bless us according to Thy sure word of promise.'

521. MS Wilberforce c. 41, fo. 107.

522. Ibid., fo. 108.

by his appearance than pitying it (his lips), not so where love really strong in the Heart, as S G when B. ill. Too sure of happiness with B.[523]

Submit to his Chastisement & endeavor to learn from it the Lessons it was intended to teach me: Humility - Sense of my own Weaknesses, Infirmities, Wants &c. What a poor Creature I am - Feeling for others, in Sickness Languor &c. & anxiety. Thankfulness to God, (I felt too little of this in this connexion) for Exemption from Evils I see others undergoing. Purity & raising my mind to higher Gratific[ns.] than the flesh affords. Sense of Dependence, on God for all I possess or hope for. He has destroyed my little Strength to teach me, that all is in his power, & to feel practically & habitually, that I must look up to him for daily Bread & constant Support. Moderation in Views. (I was sadly too sanguine in ideas of certain Happiness with B) I am now grown more chastised. Conscious how precarious are all human prospects & that we are ever to bear in mind "the fashions of this world passeth away."[524] "It remaineth that they who have wives, be as tho' they had not &c."[525]

I still fear I may have been too precipitate, not so much in offerg to Barbara, as in resolving to marry at all. I remember well on this day fortnight, I durst not resolve fairly to weigh the argum[ts.] on both Sides & then determine honestly. It is now too late to retract if wrong - O Lord God, do thou forgive me if I have yielded too hastily to the force of affection or the impulse of appetite - I will humbly & perseveringly pray to thee for pardon, & for renderg this Step conducive to thy Glory, to my own & my B.'s Improvement & Usefulness. She I really trust, is a dear Child of God, & I derive very great Comfort from that Reflection. May the Father of our Lord Jesus X[t.] hear & have mercy on me, thro' the Intercession of the Redeemer. Meanwhile I humbly resolve to amend my Ways with renewed Diligence, to cleanse myself from all filthiness of the flesh & spirit, perfecting Holiness in the fear of God.[526]

Sunday May 28[th.] 1797 Maidenhead Bridge[527]

Alas! Alas! On lookg back upon my Conduct for some little time past, as well as further back - I see abundant Cause for the deepest Humiliation - I have been consuming my time in writing to B. & readg her Letters, when it ought to have been used diligently & my mind vigorously applied to Politics whereas I have scarce not been able to think of them. Yet the consequence of this, I do not alas feel the pain I ought on the discovery, and I am more dispos'd also to be insensibly derivg complacency from formg Resolutions of Amendment, than for flying to the Cross of X[t.] O how justly might God now punish me by renderg my approaching Union

---

523. Where the next two lines of text were, the ink has almost completely faded away.

524. 1 Corinthians 7:31.

525. 1 Corinthians 7:29.

526. 2 Corinthians 7:1. MS Wilberforce c. 41, fo. 108.

527. Maidenhead Bridge today carries the A4 over the River Thames at Maidenhead in Berkshire. The first bridge at that point dates from 1280. The bridge Wilberforce refers to was a toll-bridge, opened in 1777, at a cost today of over £2.3 million.

with <u>B</u>. a Curse, rather than a Blessing. I scarcely dare think that it is not in some degree to punish as well as humble me, that it has pleased God that I have never got well since my illness, & I now am shatter'd &c. If I had not promised to go down unless hinder'd by Parlty Bus[s.] surely hardly right now, yet I can't be easy from B. again - When I consider that she has been hungerg & thirstg after Righteousness, & is verily as I believe a Child of God, & that tho' most weakly & unsteadily, I have been in some degree strivg to attain somethg like y[e.] Xtian State, my Hopes revive & still more, when I reflect that our God hears the prayers of them that call on him – Doubtless - in all this affair I have been too precipitate - yet my judgement never varies - If it be right for me to marry <u>at all; & in the Sight of God, I can't say that it is not, then B. is above all Women who ever liv'd I believe, qualified to suit me, & I hope, I in some degree to suit her.</u>

I go humbly to pray for pardon of my manifold Sins. Last Sunday & Sunday before, sadly spent. Writg all Interval to Barb[a.] then discuss all aft[n.] with H. More. For the last week, Scripture Readg omitted. Prayer sadly Curtail'd, particty Evg. Few, very few Thoughts of God durg day. Barb[a.] always in possession, tho' Sometimes in a relig[s.] connexion - Alas! Alas! then sadly sensual & unspiritual - <u>dearest Barb</u>[a.] findg comfort from Script[e.] Readg in Evg & social & relig[s.] talk. I alas! no such thing. Also - I sadly unthankful & thoughtless about Book, not callg down divine Blessing on it, not carg enough to adorn havg written it, or thankful for its Reception. Also, sadly indifferent ab[t.] State of Country & not <u>really</u> enough lookg to Providence for Help. Also, not <u>really</u> kind enough to Greathed tho' much fuss ab[t.] it & too much out of Humour at his unreasonableness.

Also - Impatient of Heat, of Indisposition, &c. &c. St. Barthol[w's] Hosp[l.] Bus[s.] put off.[528] I fear I listen'd too readily to Eliot suggest that Sunday Bill could not be got on this year - Pearson & Bean's affair. Cum muttis allies of political kind.[529] But above all polit[l.] Bus[s.] neglected. Oimoi. Oimoi. Perhaps new minority might have been form'd. I go to a throne of Grace to ask for Mercy, to confess my Sins & pray for the Hy Spirit to guide me into the right way.[530]

Bat[a.] Rise Sunday June 11[th.] 1797 - 3½ oClock

Last Sunday, when with Mores & therefore unable to write, I had to look back with infinite Grief & Shame on a Week (first after marriage)[531] wasted

---

528. St. Bartholomew's Hospital was founded in 1123, with the Priory of St. Bartholomew, by Rahere, a courtier of Henry I. A vision of St. Bartholomew whilst Rahere was sick on a pilgrimage, inspired him to found the priory and hospital at Smithfield in London. In the beginning, the sick were cared for by the monks and sisters in the Priory, but by 1420 the hospital had become entirely independent. The first regular physician, however, would not be appointed until 1567, and yet only forty years later, it would employ William Harvey, who discovered the circulation of the blood.

529. Latin: with mutterings, political allies.

530. MS Wilberforce c. 41, fo. 109. *Life*, ii. pp. 205-206 has, 'My book is universally well received, especially by the Archbishop of Canterbury, and the Bishops of London, Durham, Rochester, and Llandaff, the Duchess of Gloucester, Sir J. Scott. Much pleased by a letter from Lord St. Helen's, most highly commending it as adapted to the good of worldly men.'

531. William married Barbara Ann, daughter of Isaac Spooner in Walcot Church, Bath. Her parents had a house in Royal Crescent, Bath, and William would later stay there in the winter of 1798.

lost in sensuality & ad temps & folly, little of the due fear of God or Love or Gratitude to him & this tho' B. rather resistg, callg me to Religious office & seriousness &c. Hymns at night & morng in Bed &c. &c. I trust I felt deep Remorse most justly & made earnest work of amendment. God might justly have withdrawn himself from me forever and have punish'd me most severely. But his long suffering bore with me. This last week better but still not well, not duly diligent, or devotional, testy & scarce grateful to cous. Henry & I was much too carnal also. O may I amend in all wherein I require amendment & endeavor to redeem the time.[532]

O[533] let me now commence a new era, guarding cautiously against all Infirmities to which personally or from circumstances liable, & endeavorg to cultivate all the opportunities - Help me, O God - May I bring forth the fruit of the Spirit, to the Praise of thy Glory. Sadly sleepy this Evg at Church, & Heart coldish all day today – Oimoi - Too much vex'd at Henry ab[t.] little thing. Settg clock for Church in morng.[534]

Sunday 2 oClock June 25[th.] 1797 Broomfield[535]

Alas! On looking back upon the time since my Marriage I find the utmost Cause for the deepest Humiliation. In how many Ways have I been culpable, I who bound & stimulated by so many Motives. Time how sadly wasted. Health injur'd by mens. exceedg. Hours too late. Private prayer curtail'd & hurried & often omitted. Very Little Scripture Readg. Sadly sensual, minding earthly things & not affections set on things above.[536] How much more so than Mont[u.] from what he told me, & how peculiarly wrong & foolish this in me. And my dearest B., all the while not drawg me into Evil but contra. Heart not soften'd or warm'd with Love or Gratitude to God or X[t.] No Sense of Humiliation in my Heart tho' my Head cannot but recognize such abundant Cause for the most poignant feelings of it. No sense of peculiar Cause for calling down the divine Grace since my Marriage & my publishing my Book. Then how little Business done. No plan form'd.

---

532. MS Wilberforce c. 41, fo. 109.

533. MS Wilberforce c. 41, fo. 110.

534. MS Wilberforce c. 41, fo. 110. *Life*, ii. pp. 221-222 has, 'Let me now commence a new era, guarding cautiously against all infirmities to which I am personally, or from circumstances, liable; and endeavoring to cultivate all opportunities. I go to prayer; may the grace of God give me repentance. Fix, O Lord, my natural volatility; let not Satan destroy or impair these impressions. I fall down before the cross of Christ, and would there implore pardon and find grace to help in this time of need. Let me use diligently and prudently to Thy glory all the powers and faculties Thou hast given me. Let me exhibit a bright specimen of the Christian character, and adorn the doctrine of God my Savior in all things. Let me go forth remembering the vows of God which are upon me; remembering that all eyes will be surveying me from my book, my marriage, etc., that my political station is most important, my means of doing good numerous and great; my cup full of blessings, spiritual above all. The times how critical! Death perhaps at hand. May God be with me for Christ's sake.'

535. Broomfield Lodge, later Broomwood House, was only 4 miles from Westminster Bridge. Henry Thornton had the house built, but it was then bought by Edward Eliot. After Eliot's death, Wilberforce lived in the lodge from 1797–1808. The house, demolished in 1904, is commemorated at the site by a square brown plaque which reads, 'On the site behind this house stood until 1904 Broomwood House (formerly Broomfield) where William Wilberforce resided during the CAMPAIGN against SLAVERY which he successfully conducted in Parliament.'

536. Colossians 3:2.

No plans for B's usefulness. Then how little <u>B</u>. enjoyed as God's Gift, or Endearments with her accepted & closed as Recreations sho'd be to refresh & restore to Business (with Gratitude to God), but rather sought mainly for the Sake of the pleasure found in them & I fear, I regret my being unwell, less on account of its incapacitating me for the rigorous discharge of the Duties of my Station, than because it lessens my pleasures with her. Then, How much Vanity in Company. Secretly indulging it. How little the feelings which ought to possess my Bosom of Prostration before God, considering what I am & what I might have been, & how humble sho'd I be, & how despised, if men could see in me, all which God sees. My Heart seems today with[t.] feeling. Whilst I see my Guilt & Danger, I do not <u>really</u> feel it, or suffer from the Sight - O Lord, take away the Heart of Stone & give me a Heart of Flesh.[537] I go to prayer - May the Grace of God give me Repentance - O smite the Rock that the Waters may flow.[538] O create in me a true Sorrow for my Sins, & a firm Resolution to forsake them. O enlighten my Understandg - Create in me a Hunger & thirst after Righteousness, & teach me thy Statutes. Warm me with the Love of the Redeemer, with Gratitude for all thy mercies. I will open myself to B. O may I be enabled to forward instead of retarding her advancement in the Road to Glory - Fix my natural Volatility - let not Satan destroy or impair these Impressions - I fall down before the Cross of X[t.] & would there implore pardon & find Grace to help in this time of need - Let me use diligently & prudently to thy Glory, all the powers & faculties thou hast given me - Let me exhibit a bright Specimen of the Xtian Character & adorn the Doctrine of God my Saviour <u>in all</u> things.[539] Let me go forth, in remembering the Vows of God which are upon me, rememberg that all Eyes will be surveying me from my Book, my Marriage &c. &c. that my polit[l.] Station is most important, my means of doing Good numerous & great. <u>My Cup Full of Blessings</u>, above all spiritual ones, the times how critical, Death perhaps at Hand. My Country not prayed for heartily & little political thought. May God be with me for X[t's] Sake thro' the Spirit - Amen.[540]

After prayer: What a Blessing is the Sunday. In which if we preserve even the form of Godliness, we are led to retire from the Crowd, & are thus put in the way of becoming impress'd with a Sense of our true Condition. I trust I do in some degree <u>feel</u> the Humiliat[n.] I ought, & do come to X[t.] for a Cure. I am weakness itself, but he is all powerful & we are assur'd that they who seek shall find, & of his fulness his people receive & Grace for Grace. They are changed from Glory to Glory by the Spirit of the Lord. Quicken me then & sanctify me. Stablish, Strengthen, settle me.[541] - Amen & Amen.[542]

---

537. Ezekiel 36:26.

538. Exodus 17:6.

539. Titus 2:10.

540. MS Wilberforce c. 41, fo. 110.

541. 1 Peter 5:10.

542. MS Wilberforce c. 41, fo. 111.

Sunday ¼ before 3, Broomfield - July 2[d.] 1797

I have little or no time to write in, & there is the less need, from my copious writing last Sunday. I have last week gone on rather better I hope, but very indifferently, partly I hope from bodily Indisposition, bad nights from fleas &c. &c. Scripture more read & private prayer more attended to, but alas time fritter'd & slidg away insensibly. Several bad tempers too apparent tow[ds.] Pitt &c. Why am I more angry, when his Breaches of Golden Rule directed ag[t.] myself - O may I attend to what written last Sunday, & strive earnestly after the Grace of X[t.] all else is Dross. But havg secur'd an Interest in him, let me be careful to maintain Good works, & improvg in all wisdom & Spiritual Understanding, may I walk in Wisdom tow[ds.] them that are with[t.] redeemg the time,[543] being fruitful in every good Word & Work.[544]

Sunday 3 ½ Broomfield July 9[th.] 1797

Alas! I fear part of the Humiliation I feel is to be ascribed to the bodily languor. But I trust not wholly, & that while I smite on my Breast & cry God be merciful &c.[545] I can also look to God thro' X[t.] in humble Hope, as a reconciled Father who will give his Holy Spirit. Let me then diligently seek it & wisely & vigorously cultivate it. God will not be wanting to us. Let me not be to myself. What cause have I for Gratitude, that I have a wife to whom I can open my Soul & who helps me forw[d.] instead of retardg my progress. O may I henceforth turn to the Lord with more confirm'd purpose of Soul, & be wholly his & Xt's, Servg, Lovg & diligy obeying. I have been this week, sadly idle, carnal, Selfish, & Sensual in mind, curtailg & sleepy over Evg prayers, forgettg God & that I too adorn the Gospel.[546] O quicken me by thy Grace, & change me from Glory to Glory. Self-denial forgot. Impatient under little Griev[ces.] Servts. Stealg &c. B. here much here & free from Imitation. Self-Examin[n.] forgotten sadly &c. O may I now turn to God & be made in X[t.] a new Creature.[547]

Sunday July 16[th.] 2 oClock Battersea Rise Middle of day

Alas! This last week has gone on almost less profitably & spiritually in some things, than before. Time sadly fritter'd with little object &c. House very late, sleepy ill partly Cause of it. Readg with Barb[a.] little or none, yet no Readg or thought of other kind. How is it? Evg prayer curtail'd. I sit therefore God frowns on me. Help me O God, by X[t.] Fill me with the Sense of being more useful with the Resolution of servg thee with all my Body & Soul, formg a rational plan of Usefulness & adhering to it. My frame today is very stupid & flat, but thank God, that I decide my stayg or going not by Criterion of pleasures, but by that of pleasg God. I go to pray for my excellent B. How ready for every good

---

543. Colossians 4:5.
544. 2 Thessalonians 2:17. MS Wilberforce c. 41, fo. 111.
545. Luke 18:13.
546. Titus 2:10.
547. MS Wilberforce c. 41, fo. 111.

Word & Work,[548] but liable to be drawn away by those whom loves & confides in. Time has been undesignedly wasted, much occupied in calls &c. I fear it may have been partly own fault.[549]

Sunday 2 ½ oClock July 23[d.] Broomfield

Alas! Alas! This last week has gone off with little Business Improvement or Spirituality. Constantly in Company, & unavoidably, if one would not be wanting in the common decencies of Society - Hours late, little Prayer or readg with B. Too sensual in Ve: Oim. Today angry &c. with B. mentally for havg been led as it were to be more idle from Connexion with her, yet this most unjust, for she ready to every good Word & Work.[550] Simeon with us - How on fire for X[t.] How[551] full of Love & of desire to promote the Spiritual Benefit of others. O that I might copy him as he X[t.] My path is indeed difficult & full of Snares, but God in X[t.] can & will Strengthen & uphold us if looking to him. I was today also mentally & spiritually stupid & well I may, for I have not been trying to maintain a Spiritual frame of Spirity. But O Lord of thy mercy quicken me, let the dead be revived to sing thy praises. Let me try this week earlier Hours, more redeeming time, moderatn in Sensuals, &c. Spiritual mindedness, & Love, & diligence. May the Love of X[t.] fill my Heart & dispose me to all Righteousness.[552]

Sunday Evg Aug[t.] 20[th.] 6 oClock Hull 1797

Tho' I thank God that living with those who have y[e.] fear of God & more regular devotional Exercises & Scripture Readg has kept my mind in rather a better frame than sometimes, yet alas how little worthy of its advantages. Who has so many, & my dearest B., ready for every good Word & Work.[553] I am not kind enough or feeling enough for my poor Mother. I am sadly selfish. I feel little for others - O do thou O Lord, warm my Heart with more Love - I hope for 2 or 3 days I have felt more desire of spiritual Progress. O let me press forward - How much does Dr. C.'s death - C. Staniforth's, & a thousand other Events, warn me to watch & make preparation for Eternity - O may X[t.] by his Grace, draw me & fill me with love & fear of God, & desire to be active & incessant in his Service - Amen.[554]

Monday, August 21[st.] 1797

Late morning hours and early dining, many calls, a vast many letters, and attention to my mother, prevent my getting anything done. Reading the Bible with my wife. I wish I could have a recluse, devotional,

---

548. 2 Thessalonians 2:17.
549. MS Wilberforce c. 41, fo. 111.
550. 2 Thessalonians 2:17.
551. 'Sun' is inserted here in left margin.
552. MS Wilberforce c. 41, fos. 111–112.
553. 2 Thessalonians 2:17.
554. MS Wilberforce c. 41, fo. 112.

thinking birthday, but that is impossible. On its return I have the utmost cause for self-humiliation, for gratitude, for grateful confidence, for earnest breathings after usefulness. I have no time to write, but let me use the few minutes I have in praying to God in Christ, the Author of my mercies, beseeching him to hear me, to fill me with spiritual blessings, and enable me to live to his glory. My marriage and the publication of my book are the great events of the past year. In both I see much to humble me, and to fill my mouth with praises. Let me resign myself to God, who has hitherto led me by ways that I knew not, and implore him yet to bless me.[555]

Hull Aug[t.] 24[th.] 1797 Thursday 1 ½ oClock

On[556] the Return of this day I have the utmost Cause for Self-Humiliation, for Gratitude & for grateful Confidence, for earnest Breathings after usefulness. I have no time to write but let me use the few minutes I have in praying to God & X[t.] the author of all my mercies, beseechg him to hear me to fill me with Spiritual Blessings & enable me to live to his Glory. My Marriage & the publication of my Book are the great Events of the past year. In both I see much to humble me & to fill my mouth with Praises. Let me resign myself to God, who has hitherto led me by ways which I knew not & implore him yet to bless me.[557]

Temple Sept[r.] 3[d.] 97 - 7 oClock Evg -

Alas. Alas. My Heart is sadly more alive to earthly than to heavenly things. O how little am I what I ought to be. How much more so is my dearest B! How little Gratitude do I feel for the Goodness of God - so great to me, that Milner not thinkg it possible for anyone to continue so happy - O may I be renewed by thy Grace, Saviour of Sinners. May I yield myself O God to thee, Body & Soul. May I learn to live above this world, submitting myself to thy pleasure with <u>perfect</u> cheerfulness, & loving thee with my whole Heart.[558]

Bath Sept[r.] 17[th.] 1797 - 2 ¾ o'clock

Alas. How much cause do I see in myself for Humiliation, still living too much on the opinions & estimates of others & with all knowledge, too little sadly too little, setting my affections on things above,[559] yet my dearest B. helps & incites me. O may I learn to be more thine, Saviour of Sinners. Be thou made to me Wisdom, Righteousness, Sanctification & Redemption.[560] May I learn to overlook this life, except for thy Glory & fellow Creatures good & fix eyes in X[t's] Coming - Meanwhile may I be grateful, full of love of God & men, fervent in spirit, meekness, patient,

---

555. *Life*, ii. p. 232.
556. A large 'X' is inserted here in the left margin.
557. MS Wilberforce c. 41, fo. 112.
558. Ibid.
559. Colossians 3:2.
560. 1 Corinthians 1:30.

humble, self-denying, not envious or false in any degree, ever abounding in the work of the Lord.[561] Thus change <u>me from Glory to Glory</u>[562] <u>& may I be a new creature</u>[563] <u>and B. also, renewed after thy Image.</u>[564]

Bath Oct[r.] 8[th.] Sunday 2 ¾ oClock

Alas! I am very heartless and cold, and today feeling little of that Xtian feeling of penitent sorrow mix'd with melting gratitude and hope, as I have sometimes felt. O may God take away the heart of stone and give me a heart of flesh;[565] enable me to love him predominantly in and thro Xt, to serve him diligently and be ever looking to unseen things, as one who is here a pilgrim and stranger.[566] Only dearest B. continues ready for every good work.[567]

Pal Yard Nov[r.] 5[th.] Sunday Evg 9 oClock - 97 -

For some time past my religious affections very languid & dead - Alas! Alas! I talk of Religion but I don't feel it - My time has been sadly fritter'd away, little Business done - No Scripture read since being in Town. Today wanderg in prayer at Church - 2 last Sundays at Glendon[568] sad ones & the week there a very idle one - O may God warm my Heart, with the love of him & dispose me yet to serve him with Zeal, Gratitude & severing alacrity, Self-denial, Humility & Benevolence. O may God for Xt's sake by the Spirit, warm my Heart & quicken it. I go to prayer. O may I be accepted for sinners' sake -

This ensuing week I humbly resolve on increasg diligence Earlier Hours, Scripture readg & private prayer, which this last week sadly hurried over, ½ an Hour at least daily comp for discuss - O may I grow in <u>love, & every Grace & bring forth the fruits of y[e.] Spirit – Great</u> vanity during last week in H of Coms & otherwise. I think some Breaches of truth, still selfish also - O <u>that</u> I were what I know I ought to be - Pride, being ready to laugh at Bern[d.] ab[t.] Chimney Sweeper tho' approv'd of him, Oimoi.[569]

Sunday Night Nov[r.] 12[th.] 9 ½ oClock Pal Y[d.]

This last week mended in some Respects. <u>My dearest B.</u> a help to me. Being hurt at late, gettg up, & prayer & meditatn curtail. She made a

---

561. 1 Corinthians 15:58.

562. 2 Corinthians 3:18.

563. 2 Corinthians 5:17.

564. Colossians 3:10. MS Wilberforce c. 41, fo. 112.

565. Ezekiel 36:26.

566. 1 Peter 2:11.

567. MS Wilberforce c. 41, fo. 112.

568. Glendon village in Northamptonshire, mentioned in the *Domesday Book*, was finally enclosed in 1514, with the buildings being demolished. Glendon Hall, built c. 1514, and extended in the following centuries, probably incorporated the parish church of St. Helen's which had been in the village. The population of Glendon in 1801 was based solely on one house, Glendon Hall, which was recorded as having 48 in residence. It was the seat of the Booth family, and at the time of Wilberforce's entry the heir was Richard Booth (1756–1807).

569. MS Wilberforce c. 41, fos. 112-113.

Spring, & got up earlier. I follow slowly - She read Leighton to me 3 or 4 morngs with advantage. Excell[t.] Girl. Always heavly-minded. Today her face lighten'd up with joy & comfort from y[e.] Sermon. Scott excellt & I felt it on they that whole need not Physic[n.] but they that sick.[570] B rather thinks that she maybe preg[t.] If so, O may God rule it for good. No time really for ½ Hours intended discuss last week, not once. Letters unanswer'd many. Calls unmade - Nothg seems done, yet time fritter'd & gone - How is it. I Rece'd Sact. today & devoted self to God. O may I now resolve to be his, & Body & soul to his Glory.[571]

Sunday Aft[n.] Nov[r.] 26[th.] 6 oClock Old Pal Yard -

This last week little has been done. Much in Company, which however necessary, unless were to change System - But alas, No Scripture Readg. Prayers hurried over. Heart sadly unspiritual all y[e.] week, no wonder therefore that so today - felt in Self Motions of pride, & Envy, & an undue Solicitude ab[t.] human Estimatn. Half Hours never but one day since resolv'd to try 3 Weeks ago. Little Gratitude for B.'s Situat[n.] tho' it seems an answer to prayer, not catchg myself at prayer for Dilner's Success - or mov'd at poor Joseph Milner's[572] death & for Isaac - How exquisitely he feels. I yesterday asked Mrs. Greathed, I hope greatly induc'd by desire of doing Good to her. O may God render my B. useful to her. Dearest B. is patient, & all tenderness. Hardly diligent enough perhaps, but this rather my fault & that of her State.[573] Next week more Prayer, Scrip[e.] Readg, Heavenly-mindedness, Humility. Try for ½ Hours &c. - Sect. Evg after Prayers. My dearest B. urges me to good.[574]

Sunday 2 ¾ oClock Pal Yard Dec[r.] 3[d.] 97

The last week, I hope rather better, but yet very middling. Some little Scrip[e] most days. Hours better, indeed as much I believe as health will allow. Still much in Comp'y & not spiritually minded. Today, excellt Sermon of Scott's on Martha, Martha, &c., and since I've been visitg to Speaker & Pitt, conferring one & urging the other to Relinquish most of propos[l.] writg of Income durg. War if they wo'd not wait till tomow. My Spirits have been weak from Health today but poorly, & sure found much Comfort just now in prayer. I look up for pardon to the sure Mercies of X[t.] I feel I am an unworthy Sinner, but Reconciliation is held out to such. May my Hatred of Sin only be increas'd & may I live more holily, diligently usefully self-denyingly circumspectly. Help me O God,

---

570. Mark 2:17.

571. MS Wilberforce c. 41, fo. 113.

572. Joseph Milner (1744–1797), evangelical divine, born in Leeds, Yorkshire, and brother of Isaac, who had an influential role in the conversion of Wilberforce. He was appointed Headmaster of Hull Grammar School, as well as being given the living of Holy Trinity Church in the center of Hull, close to the school and Wilberforce's High Street home. It is argued that it was due to his ministry that Hull became a thriving center of evangelicalism. He also secured a place for Isaac at the school as an usher, leading to the beginning of his relationship with Wilberforce, who would attend there as a pupil.

573. 'Res[ns]' is inserted here in the left margin.

574. MS Wilberforce c. 41, fo. 113.

for Xt's Sake by the Spirit, & may I walk by faith, Seekg X[t.] for Wisd[m] Right[s] Sanctif[n] & Red[n.] My dearest B. all tenderness.[575]

Sunday[576] Night 11 oClock Pal Yard Dec[r.] 10[th.]

Tir'd tonight, & too late tonight to write. This last week much Company, but hope gone off better than some, yet sadly unmindful of God X[t.] & the Spirit. Today, I have enjoyed my Sunday much. May this evening W Wm.[577] be spent to God's Glory.[578] Try more constant Scripture Readg often, assured of it last week by.[579]

Sunday[580] Pal Yard Night Dec[r.] 17[th.] 97

Last week I fear God has been little habitually present to my mind, either in H. of Coms or in gen[l.] Today, I have felt I hope a disposition to resign all to God, my dear B. in a critical Situatn - But much of this I fear natural indifference. Yet I thank God for it. O how little have I of the power of Godliness, but God in Xt. is the friend of them that seek him & I will press forw[d.] - But little Scripture this week, yet some - Not kind to Greathed or remg. Golden Rule in his Instance. But I hope strivg with some Success. God's providence in Mrs. H.T.s seeing & warng my wife on Thursday Evg.[581]

Tuesday[582] Dec[r.] 18[th.] Pal Yard 2 ¼ oClock Thanksgivg Day -

Tho' I have been at the Lock, not in the Cavalcade, how little has my Heart join'd in the praises of the day from the Heart. How wandering in prayer - How little really impress'd as I ought with sense of heavy things, yet I hope laboring after them, strivg to raise mind - go to prayer to bless God for his mercies, & will enumerate several, for public &c. political Blessings, for his personal Kindnesses, & will pray to him for my Country & for Wisdom myself how to act &c. O may the Love of Xt warm me - may the Resolut[n.] to live to his Glory, be uppermost in my Soul, & may I learn a holy Resignation to his will, endeavorg to work while it is Day,[583] in Love & peace & yet to be easy & cheerful & composed & disinterested & happy, enjoying the peace of God.[584]

---

575. Ibid.

576. In the left margin covering the length of the whole entry is written, '_____ till too late. Oimoi'.

577. William, his son.

578. In left margin he has written, 'Still sit till too late oimoi'.

579. MS Wilberforce c. 41, fo. 113.

580. Ibid., fo. 114.

581. Ibid.

582. Wilberforce here wrote 'Tuesday', but December 18[th.] 1787 was a Monday.

583. John 9:4.

584. MS Wilberforce c. 41, fo. 114. *Life* ii. pp. 252-253 has, 'Though I have been quietly at church and not in the cavalcade, yet how little has my heart joined in the prayers of the day! How little am I impressed as I ought to be with a sense of heavenly things! and yet I hope I am laboring after them, and striving to raise my mind. I go to prayer, to bless God for his mercies; and I will enumerate several: Public and political blessings; his kindnesses to myself personally. I will pray to him for my country, and for wisdom for myself, to teach me how to act. Oh may the resolution to live for his glory be uppermost in my soul, and may I learn a holy resignation to his will; endeavoring to work whilst it is day, and yet to be easy, cheerful, disinterested, composed, and happy, enjoying the peace of God.'

Xmas day, 8 ¾ oClock Evg Palace Yard

My prayers have been wanderg today - & my Heart cold and not tender I think as used - O let me take Care that this not consequence of being married. Little conscious I fear, of light of God's presence. Little lookg to him for Support & Help in these dangerous times, nor grateful for the many mercies I enjoy - O let me watch & pray, & strive to enter in at Strait Gate,[585] and bless God for honorg me as an Instrument in any Case. Rather busy of late. Vain rather than grateful from probable Success of my financial Endeavors. I feel alas, little of God's presence - O may the Spirit of Xt. dwell in me. I go to pray, for personal, spiritual & tempers.[586]

Sunday 31st. Decr. 2 ¾ Palace Yard – 97 -

Alas! Alas! With what Shame ought I to look at myself. Yesterday how much put out of my Way by Dinner Disappointment, and then in House of Coms. what a Storm of conflicting Passions. Mortified pride, anger, malice, fear of Loss of Reputn. Resentment from Ingratitude in P. tho' I ought not expect Gratd. from him & can well bear with his faults to God. All working with anger at myself from Consciousness that not what a Christian sho'd be - O what a troubled State, when I got home, I hope I prayed to God, looked to him in some Degree for Help thro' Xt & have in some measure found my Heart restored to peace, to Love, to Reconciliatn (which in House but Hollow appearance I fear), & to desire of returning good for Evil & of being above the little Slights & Rufflements of this Life, Looking upwards & forwards - But even still, I find my Heart disposed to harbor resentful & angry thoughts &c. I have found golden Rule recd. useful in quietg my mind, puttg myself in Pitt's place, &c. O may this teach me to know myself, to walk more humbly, more watchfully, to seek more earnestly for Strength & Help & peace & Love & the meekness & Gentleness of Xt. O may God guide me.

I may be indispensably occupied tomorrow, so here let me look back on ye past year & bless God for its many mercies - O how wonderful his ways are, and an Eventful year with me. My Book, Marriage, more Scripture reading when Health restor'd in Sickness. How ungrateful have I been & how often tempting God to withdraw from me. But his mercy endureth forever, and the vilest, prostrating himself before him with Penitence & faith in the Blood of Jesus, may obtain Remission of Sin & the Spirit of renewing Grace. This is my Hope. Here I rest my foot. Friends died this year: Eliot, Dr. Clarke, Milner Jos., my poor Mother still spar'd. Public events, Mutiny terminated, Dutch Victory. I will go to prayer, humble myself before God. Beseech him to accept me thro' Xt & to change my hard carnal proud Heart, & soften it by his Grace, & set my affections on things above, not on things on ye. Earth.[587]

---

585. Matthew 7:13.

586. MS Wilberforce c. 41, fo. 114.

587. Colossians 3:2. *Life*, ii. pp. 253-254 has, 'I may be indispensably occupied tomorrow, so let me now look back on the past year, and bless God for its many mercies. Oh how wonderful are His ways! An eventful year with me – my Book – my marriage – health restored in sickness. How

The Lessons I have learn'd of my defects &c teach me to strive earnestly against Pride & Inordinate Love of the favor of Men. Every feeling of Malice & Revenge, Selfishness in not judging fairly between others & myself, above all, Earthly mindedness, not havg my mind rais'd above the Region of Storms &c. May I learn Wisdom & Watchfulness from past falls, & grow in Grace. Last week, my prayers have been much hasty in Eveng. hurried curtail'd & Scripture Readg quite (I fear), omitted. Let me walk in fear & Love of God always, & be continually lookg for his Spirit thro' X[t.] & conscious of my own Corruptions & the Temptat[ns.] & wiles & constant Hostility of Satan - O what a blessed thing is the Sunday for givg us opportunity of serious Self-Examin[n.] & Retrospect, & of drawg water from Wells of Salvn.[588] What is it but divine Grace which has made me in any degree what I am. My passions naturally violated &c. O let me praise him for his mercy & say I will praise thee for all that is past &c.[589]

1798

Sunday Jan[y.] 14[th.] 1798 – Bath ¼ past 3

Entire Solitude I find a diff[t] thing from even being with my wife only. It seems to give me over more entirely to the power, & throw me more absolutely on the mercy of God. O what Cause have I for Gratitude. But my Heart has been cold & my tho'ts unspiritual, yet I hope, I desired today to have my Heart softened, & in some degree have found it grow more tender. My Eyes are very indiff[t.] & must spare them. I mean today solemnly to implore the pardon of God in X[t.] & his Grace to guide, renew & quicken me. My dearest B is indeed I trust a Child of God. How sadly disturb'd was I at Fox's[590] imputing great Rudeness & Acrimony to me. More alas, I found on scrutinising, from fear of losg Credit with all immoderate opportunists &c. &c. - But I think I can appeal to God that his Charge was false, & that I feel even Good-Will to him - O may I learn to distrust & keep my Heart with all diligence.

---

ungrateful have I been, and how often tempting God to withdraw from me! But His mercy endureth for me; and the vilest, prostrating himself before Him with penitence and faith in the blood of Jesus, may obtain remission of his sins, and the Spirit of renewing grace. This is my hope – here I rest my foot. Friends died this year – Eliot – Dr. Clarke – Joseph Milner. I still spared. How strongly do these events teach us that the time is short! Oh! May I learn and be wise. Public events – mutiny terminated – Dutch victory. I will go to pray, and humble myself before God.'

588. Isaiah 12:3.

589. MS Wilberforce c. 41, fos. 114-115. *Life*, ii. p. 254 has, 'I will go to pray, and humble myself before God. The lessons I have learned of my defects teach me to strive earnestly against pride; inordinate love of the favour of man; every feeling of malice; selfishness in not judging fairly between others and myself; above all, earthly-mindedness, not having my mind raised above the region of storms. May I learn wisdom and watchfulness from past falls, and so grow in grace. Oh what a blessed thing is the Sunday for giving us an opportunity of serious self-examination, retrospect, and drawing water out of the wells of salvation.'

590. Charles James Fox (1749–1806), Britain's first Foreign Secretary (1782, 1783, and 1806), known for his heavy drinking and gambling, with two resultant bankruptcies. With Wilberforce, it was Fox who championed the abolition of the slave trade in the House of Commons, and it was he who proposed the Bill that became law in 1807, as the Slave Trade Act.

It is overgrown with weeds. May God enable me at this crowded place to live to his Glory.[591]

Sunday Jan[y.] 21[st.] ½ past 8 Evg. 1798 - Bath

My Eyes being bad I must be short, it is besides the time for meeting my Barbara in prayers. This last has been a sad hurrying Week from bad nights (fleas) & Eyes bad, little done. Time fritter'd in Calls &c. & ding out every day – alas - alas! This is sadly unfavorable to the Life of God in the Soul - How murmuring & repining was I at the little Grievance of a sleepless night or two. This Week, little Sense of God & X[t] on my Heart – Oimoi - O may I be enabled to preserve a more heavenly-minded frame. Let me try more time for Meditatn & Scripture. Barely a Chapter hastily each day - I go to prayer, to Humiliation & commendation to God in X[t] beseeching his Spirit. Jay excellent tonight. Evil-Speakg. Offended. Dining out every day has a bad Effect on the mind - I will try to dine at Home at least once, & if well can twice evy week, or if not so, with truly serious, where spirit[l.] Convers[n.] Alas! I have had my Heart little conversant with heavy Objects. I did not feel as I ought at Eacle's most indecent & brutal Stories the other night. My distress arose more I fear from its being contrary to assum'd Character & consciousness that observ'd by looking more I fear if once but Earle and I not much mov'd. O the Depravity of the heart, which when the judgment is thoroughly informed, can be more impress'd by any fellow Creature than the invisible God & the Saviour & the angels & all the Cloud of Witnesses - O may I learn to be more humble & full of Love and lookg to Jesus for continual Supplies of Grace & Strength.[592]

Sunday Night 9 oClock Jan[y.] 28[th.] 1798 -

This morng I felt I thought some of the power of the World to come, when I went to Church. Randolph not evangelical, tho' meaning to be so on, I am Way, Truth & Life,[593] then Greenwood broke in upon my Walk intended for Meditation. When came in, only time to write to Barb[a] then Sir R. Hill to dinner Jay's this Evg. Since walkg & H. More's - Now nearly time to meet Barb[a] in prayers. O What Cause have I to pray to God thro' X[t] for his continual Grace - I've found this Week the Benefit of Reading Scripture almost daily - Much impress'd with Jerem. 17:6 & 8, Cursed &c. blessed &c. who trusteth &c. O may I love God & X[t] more & obtain Wisdom & Holiness & Love & Peace. Sadly wanderg in Jay's prayer tonight, partly because eaten poor, partly I hope Complaint in Stomach.[594]

---

591. MS Wilberforce c. 41, fo. 115. *Life*, ii. p. 254 has, 'Entire solitude I find a different thing from even being with my wife only; it seems to give me over more entirely to the power, and throw me more absolutely upon the mercy, of God. Oh what cause have I for gratitude; but my heart has been cold – it is overgrown with weeds; may God enable me at this crowded place to live to His glory.'

592. MS Wilberforce c. 41, fos. 115-116.

593. John 14:6.

594. MS Wilberforce c. 41, fo. 116. *Life*, ii. p. 255 has, 'This morning I thought I felt some of the powers of the world to come when I went to church. G. broke in upon my walk intended for meditation. I have found this week the benefit of reading Scripture almost daily.'

Sunday Night – Feby 18th 1798. Palyd 9 ¾ oClock

My time since my Return to town & in particr last week, which fresher in my memory, sadly fritter'd away. I scarce know how little or nothg done, yet I always am hurried, not even Letters got thro' - Hours too late, but this partly necesy to my weakly frame. Much fritter'd away in Compy. & then sadly inattentive to Improvemt & forgetful of Regls, Oimoi. Also Truth I fear, often broken in upon - God's Presence forgotten. Xt & Spirit and Evil Spt little tho't of. Evg prayers sadly curtail'd (Try havg them in Evg when can). I am much distress'd & disturbed betn Sense of necesy of not givg up the World & the Evil Effects from my prest great Intercourse with it both to Heart understandg & Buss O may I try to begin anew, to live a Life of faith workg by Love, walking in the fear & Love of God Xt & fellow Creatures. Endeavorg to improve in all Holiness. Sadly defective in Duties of MP - O may I be able to do better, & above all to put on Xt - havg him for Wisdom, Rights Sanctn & Redn.[595] Let me try to renew all my Regls. for Compy &c. Relaxn &c. &c. Sad tendency to Evil Speakg & malicious foolish talk abt the Rabbit proves to me in my Reception of it, my own Unkindness, & I have perceiv'd a strange alienation of mind towds havg Pride towds poor Martin, & sometimes even secret unkindness to my dearest B. Alas, Alas! how deceitful & corrupt is my Heart![596]

Sunday Feby 25th 1798 Palyd - 1 ¾ oClock

This last hurrying Week has kept & now leaves my Soul in a sad, unspiritual frame - How little does my Heart seem to have its affections above. I doubt much abt givg up much of this raffled hurrying System. May God for Xt's Sake guide & support me. My dearest B. all Kindness & Concessn Wishg for quiet. Milner rather adores breakg off the System. Let me consider it well, & aim even before I change my plan success to obtain more calm Retirement & meditn Certainly on lookg back, my Time has been wasted too much in Compy. I had better far adhere except in very rare Cases to my 3 oClock dinner Rule. How much bad passions duplicity do I observe in myself by my Sensuality &c. on the Voly Contribn Oimoi, Oimoi! Milner also tells me plainly that I take too little part in Public Buss Parlty. speak too seldom on great Questions & this from sufferg frivolous hospy to interfere with H. of Coms If I co'd but keep to 3 & _____[597] I might do.

Last week, very angry from pride at Pitt & Speaker from triflg Cause, also vain in 10,000 Instances is my prayers in famy &c. O that my heart were fill'd with Love. This wo'd unclear all other means & more selfish passions. How little trust in God also, vide tere.[598] What risings of vanity

595. 1 Corinthians 1:30.
596. MS Wilberforce c. 41, fo. 116. *Life*, ii. p. 274 has, 'I am much disturbed between a sense of the necessity of not giving up the world, and the evil effects from my present great intercourse with it both to my heart and understanding. Many doubts about company, whether I ought not in great measure to give it up.'
597. Word illegible.
598. Latin: see grind.

did I feel ab^t poor Ricks whereas what did I more than others, and now I feel vang from perspicacity in discovg my own secret defects. O for a more pure & simple Heart, & for a Sincere desire to possess it & wish for it. Vain in regard to Belsham Letter & to Will Smith yesterday at din^r sadly sensual – Oimoi - O what a multitude of mercies have I to be thankful for! Comparg my lot with Rick's.[599]

Sunday March 4$^{th.}$ 1798 Pal Y$^{d.}$ 2 oClock

Today I am but dull & cold, partly I hope from bodily Infirmity. But not altogether. Last Week has roll'd away insensibly, little improved I fear & for want of acc$^t.$ I scarce know how. Let me try to keep acc$^t.$ that I may better discover how time really goes. I am very little I fear livg the Life I now live &c. by the faith of the Son of God.[600] - I have failed partly in Want of habit^l spirit^l minded$^s.$ O may God for X$^{t's}$ Sake convert my Soul, & fill me with all Joy & peace & Love & holy reliance & humble Determin$^{n.}$ to devote Body & Soul to the diligent Service of God. Also, Rem$^{r.}$ to trust in God & not Man - with strict Vanity checks. This ensuing Week, bear much in mind Ezek. 9:4, & try to abound in that Duty of truly lamentg my own & others Sins, & also Jere. 17:5,7, Cursed & Blessed man who trusteth in man & in God respectively. How little true Love of God have I & jealousy for X^t O soften my hard Heart & warm it. Private prayer in Evg sadly curtail'd last week, try amend.[601]

Tuesday March 7$^{th.}$ Fast-Day 3 oClock – 98 Pal Y$^{d.}$

On lookg back to page 104, March 8th last fast day, I see reason to record all I there wrote. O may it be laid home to my heart and may I also attend particularly to Ezek. 9:4 and Jere. 17: 5,7 - as in last Sunday's writing. I feel a firm confidence that if thro' God's Grace, I am enabled to keep close to him in Love fear trust & obedience in the true & large Sense includg all my Duties & Sensat$^{ns.}$ &c tow$^{ds.}$ X$^t.$ the Sp^t &c. I shall go on well, most likely even in this Life - being perhaps remarkably preserv'd from Evil. But at all Events I shall be supported under whatever may be imposed on me. These are days when one should especially strive to grow in preparedness for changing worlds, and for whatever sharp trials one here may be called to - Oh what humiliation becomes me when I think of my innumerable mercies, especy my last & greatest, my B next to spiritual blesgs - O may the grace of X^t quicken me with warm & growg & dev'd thankfulness.[602]

---

599. MS Wilberforce c. 41, fos. 116-117. *Life*, ii. p. 274 has, 'This last hurrying week has kept and now leaves my soul in a sad state. How little does my heart seem to have its affections above! I doubt about giving up much of this raffled hurrying system. May God for Christ's sake guide and support me. Last week, angry from pride at Pitt and the Speaker, vain in regard to Belsham's letter. Oh what a multitude of mercies have I to be thankful for! Compare my lot with K.'s.'

600. Galatians 2:20.

601. MS Wilberforce c. 41, fo. 117. *Life*, ii. p. 273 has, 'This last week rolled away like a day, and little done I fear, always out, or people to dinner, too little time or reading. I will try an account to check and discover how it is. Last week: Letters, Lord Clare's Speech, Bible almost daily.'

602. MS Wilberforce c. 41, fo. 117.

Sunday March 11th. 98 2½ oClock Pal Yd.

Tho' my - general plan of life be form'd with deliberate approbatn in reference to God's Word, yet how prone am I in the Course of it to forget the divine presence, Xt. the Spt. Satan & in short, how prone am I to walk by Sight rather than by faith[603] - But yet I resolve humbly, to persist in praying & strivg for a Heart more truly renewed after the Image of God, that Xt being made to me <u>Wisdom & Righteousness & Sanctifn & Redempt</u>n[604]. I may grow more & more meet to be a partaker of the Inheritce of the Saints in Light,[605] fill'd here with Love & Gratitude & holy fear & humble Self-abasement, mix'd with joyful Hope & firm Confidence.

O may I & my dearest B., be both growg daily in Grace & adorn the Doctrine of God our Saviour in all things.[606] Conv. & Compy Regls sadly neglected, laugh'd impropy at somethg rather profane Pitt said (printers devils), much struck today with _____ or fear, or _____[607] I have very much forgot Self-Examn. O how sadly defective am I in Humility. When I look into myself, I find myself wretched & poor indeed compared with my highly favor'd State, but how little do I feel this <u>Habitually</u>, tho' when I examine myself, I <u>see</u> it clearly. How fond am I of distinction of notice &c. &c. This wo'd not be if <u>truly</u> humble <u>within, at the Core</u>. Here meditatn daily might do much, or as frequent as might be. Let me try for it. Vanity is my constitl. vice & O how little is its power weaken'd.[608]

Sunday March 18th. 98 Pal Yard 2¾ oClock -

This last Week has gone on but ill. How little have I duly observ'd my Resolves, in Ht. tho'tless proud vain carnal. With what delight sho'd I view my B. set on thgs above, & what a Call to us is Ld. C's death, to remr. the fashion of this world passeth away.[609] How conscious Miss H. O may I henceforth improve more from all my unequall'd advantages.

---

603. 2 Corinthians 5:7
604. 1 Corinthians 1:30.
605. Colossians 1:12.
606. Titus 2:10.
607. Illegible words here.
608. MS Wilberforce c. 41, fos. 117-118. *Life*, ii. pp. 274-275 has, 'This last week, in which I hoped so much to be done, has gone by, and how little got through! And though my affections this day are a good deal called forth, how little have I of late been under the influence of real Christian tempers! How sadly defective am I in humility! When I look into myself I find myself poor indeed compared with my highly-favored state; but how little do I feel this habitually! How fond am I of distinction (my constitutional vice)! This would not be, if I was truly humble within, at the core. Here meditation daily, or as frequent as might be, would do much. Let me try for it. Oh may this day be of lasting service to me! and at this time, when probably war and tumult are at hand, may I serve God and fear nothing. May I boldly walk in the might of the Lord, and sigh and cry for the abominations done in the land. May I grow in humility, peace, and love, in meekness, holy courage, self-denial, active exertion, and discreet zeal. I feel a firm confidence, that if through God's grace I am enabled to keep close to him in love, fear, trust, and obedience, I shall go on well; most likely even in this life, being perhaps remarkably preserved from evil; but at all events I shall be supported under whatever may be laid upon me. These are days in which I should especially strive to grow in preparedness for changing worlds, and for whatever sharp trials I may be called to. Oh what humiliation becomes me when I think of my innumerable mercies!'
609. 1 Corinthians 7:31.

Beware lest a castaway after preaching to others.[610] May I grow in Love fear Holiness Humility Spirit[l] Mindedness.[611]

Sunday Ap[l.] 1[st.] 1798 Palyard 9 oClock Night

This last week I have gone on ill, in all the old Respects. Much hurried. Bad tempers discover'd ab[t.] Speaker's[612] non-Compliance & fiery attack on me – Oimoi - Evg Devotns sadly hurried, & little excuse for it. Frame unspiritual commonly. Ill temper'd to Ashley, seriously unkind & proud tow[ds.] Thorn, even unfriendly to Henry. O what a fount of wickedness is there within me. But may it be purged. Yesterday mens. Excedgs Des[t.] O how foolish, rather how guilty for a crime it indeed is, to trifle with that Health which ought to be devoted to God. O forgive me, & may I amend. Much medicine today, (how thankful sho'd I be for it), has just set me up again.[613]

Good Friday Ap[l.] 6[th.] 1798 Paly[d.] 5¾ oClock -

This last has been a hurrying Week from necessy Bus[s.] O what Cause for thankfulness, that my <u>B</u>. & I are together desirous of strivg to enter in at Strait Gate.[614] I am full of Sin, but I wo'd humbly resolve to grow in Grace prosecution where most fail, let me labour most. I have had today a rather lively Sense of invisible things.[615]

Sunday April 15[th.] 98 Pal y[d.] 9¼ oClock

This last week of the Session which I hoped so much to be done, has gone off & how little got thro' And tho' my affections this day a good deal call'd forth, how little have I of late been under the Influence of real Xtian Tempers. Tow[ds.] poor Martin & W. Dickson, how tyrannical in Heart. Also how little time this Week of Recess did I receive for Scripture Readg or prayer. Evg prayers curtail'd, broke for B's <u>Sake</u> - O may this day be of lastg Service to me and at this time when probably war & Tumult are at Hand, may I serve God & fear nothg, may I boldly walk in y[e.] might of y[e.] Lord & sigh & cry for the abom[ns.] done in the Land, & not trust in Man or an arm of flesh - May I learn to <u>be</u> a Xtian, growing in Humility & peace & Love & meekness & holy courage & Self-denial & active caution & discreet Zeal. My B. who has suffer'd so much lately, uniform in humble patient gratitude & I weakness - full of Love & piety - What Cause have I for Gratitude. Resol[ne.] To try to bed by 11 & before, & up by 7 & before & to have Hour for serious Medit[n.] & prayer & Script[e] & prepar[n.] for these dangerous times in which live, & also more time for unbroken tho't ½ or ¾ of an Hour on Parlt[y.] Topics.[616]

---

610. 1 Corinthians 9:27.

611. MS Wilberforce c. 41, fo. 118.

612. The Speaker of the House of Commons in 1798 was Henry Addington (1757–1844).

613. MS Wilberforce c. 41, fo. 118.

614. Matthew 7:13.

615. MS Wilberforce c. 41, fo. 118.

616. MS Wilberforce c. 41, fo. 118. *Life*, ii. pp. 275-276 has, 'I resolve to be up in time to have an hour before breakfast for serious meditation, prayer, and Scripture preparation for these

Sunday 22^d. Ap^l. 98 2¾ oClock Pal Y^d.

This last week I have got up earlier & had a little time in morng for serious readg & Reflectn. But not duly improv'd the opportun^y & in the Evg^s of which 3 in Compy & ding late, unframed for Relig^n & prayer curtail'd &c., Alas, Alas! I have been walkg a musing walk & alas what cause do I find for Humiliation & Sorrow. How little have I got forw^d in the Xtian Life. But pardon & peace are proclaim'd, Ho ev'y one that thirsteth.[617] I fear I have not coasted on God, but I will humbly press forward & our God & Saviour are the same yesterday today & forever,[618] ready to receive, & even meet ½ way the returng prodigal to take him in again & strengthen & wash & comfort & keep & defend him.[619] Amen, so be it. This ensuing week if Milner be with us, as is likely, I shall be subject to sev^l. temptatns, as heretofore. Let me now resolve, to keep to earlier Bedgoing, & not curtail Evg prayer. Turn the Convers^n to profitable & rational Topics always. Be meek & gentle & humble & kind. How much I owe him! How kind he is to me![620]

Sunday May 6th. 98 Clapham 2¼ oClock

This last fortnight has gone on but ill, the concludg last Resol^ns. not kept, Oimoi. Too short & broken devotions partcy. In Evg & today my Heart hard & dead, tho' I hope this partly bodily, being very middg & shabby. My Eyes bad, so I durst not write. May God for X^t's Sake & thro' union with him grant me a new Heart, more humble, holy, tender & spiritual-minded. Scripture less read last week. Wickedly angry with Will. Smith & I fear not void of ostentation in my making up again. How extremely kind is Milner to me & how little do I return his affection & how little duly thankful for it to God. How little careful also to improve in knowledge from Intercourse with him. Not proper feelings in Matthew's Case & others, Martin &c.[621]

Sunday May 13th. Clapham 2:50 -

This last week, I have not mended in the particulars before wrong. Hours have been latish. Evg devotions curtail'd & even morng. No abiding Sense of God's presence, Scripture little read. Today I can't wonder that I am hard & cold & stupid. Let me try earnestly for more time for serious tho't readg & prayer partcy in morng. I have I fear trifled away much of my time also & not been fervent in Spirit, tho my Health may I hope be

---

dangerous times; also more time for unbroken thought; half or three-quarters of an hour on parliamentary topics.'

617. Isaiah 55:1.

618. Hebrews 13:8.

619. Luke 15:22.

620. MS Wilberforce c. 41, fos. 118-119. *Life*, ii. 276 has, 'This week I have got more morning time for serious reading and reflection. I have now been taking a musing walk, and, alas, what cause do I find for humiliation! During the ensuing week if M. be with us, as it is likely, I shall be subject to several temptations as heretofore. Let me now resolve to keep earlier hours; not curtail evening prayer; turn the conversation to profitable and rational topics; be meek, and gentle, and humble, and kind. How much I owe him!'

621. MS Wilberforce c. 41, fo. 119.

in part to blame. O may God thro' X^t & the Spirit quicken & renew me, & give me a Heart full of Love Joy peace & heavly-mindedness, living & striving by faith in X^{t.} & receivg largely of his fulness. If I wait on him diligently, doubtless it will be so His promise is sure. O may I be deeply humbled for the past, & walk softly & humbly,[622] as becomes one who has so offended & so long trifled with the divine forbearance. I have been & am specially wanting in Solicitude ab^{t.} the Souls of others. Thus all Graces die when Communion with God &c. flag. O renew me.[623]

Sunday May 20th. 98 - 5½ oClock, Broomfield
I feel the Comfort of the Sunday very sensibly today, perhaps I allow myself to take too much Comfort from it. Eyes bad so can't write. I mean D.V. to be more diligent, more fervent in Spirit, serving ye. Lord, more heavenly-minded. Today on first comg here too Castle buildg. O check these follies. Is it not enough. X^{t.} says, Come &c. &c. &c.[624]

Sunday May 27th. 98 – Broomfield - 10½ oClock
This Sunday has gone off without much Improvement, tho' I hope I have walk'd in it a good deal by <u>faith</u>, <u>spiritually</u> minded. O what Cause for Humiliation in the tempers betrayed in the House on Friday Evg, when Pitt mortified my pride by interveng betn me, & Lush^{n.} & puttg off Slave Car^{g.} Bill to Thursday. Alas. Love how cold in me. I felt not cordially for ye. Slaves, but for my being lower'd before Bystanders. I was near resenting it on the Spot. I now am thankful I did not. O God, how full of mercies hast thou been to me - O may thy Spirit cleanse & quicken & renew me - My Eyes smart, so no more. How little did I think that Pitt's selfish^{s.} which poor fellow made him mortify me wo'd draw him as it did into the Scrape which produc'd his duel, which took place today at 3 oClock - How thankful for X^{ty.} to sooth my angry Spirit & with what pleasure I looked back on my conduct soon after on that Sunday tis now June 17th. on that same day, makg it up with him, with^{t.} the Shew.[625]

June 17th. Sunday Broomf^{d.} 2¼ oClock
Alas - I am little or not at all Spiritually minded in the frame & temper of my Soul - I pass the day little thoughtful of God & X^{t.} Tho' I say my prayers & read the Scripture - This is not livg in the faith of ye. Son of

622. Isaiah 38:15.

623. MS Wilberforce c. 41, fo. 119.

624. MS Wilberforce c. 41, fo. 119. *Life*, ii. p. 274 has, 'I feel the comfort of Sunday very sensibly today.'

625. MS Wilberforce c. 41, fo. 119. *Life*, ii. p. 280 has, 'Whitsunday. Pleasant day, spent as Sundays should be.' *Life*, ii pp. 286-287 has, 'What cause have I for humiliation in my temper in the House of Commons on Friday evening, when Pitt greatly provoked me, by intervening between me and Lushington, and putting off the Slave Carrying Bill. Alas, love how cold in me! I was near resenting it upon the spot. I now am thankful that I did not. God, how full of mercies hast Thou been to me! How little did I think that Pitt's conduct, which, poor fellow, made him mortify me, would draw him, as it did, into the scrape which produced his duel, which took place on the very day (of my former entry) at three o'clock. How thankful for Christianity to soothe my angry spirit!'

God.[626] O may I try (now that I shall be less hurried), to acquire a more habitual & abidg Sense of Heav[y] things & a warmer Love & Gratitude, & a more constant practice of my Rules. Oimoi, What cause I have for thankfulness. In what a State is Ireland. On lookg back, I find for the last month or more, my life a sad Blank. My situat[n] here tho' so comfortable, will require much watchfulness & plan & circumspection, or my time will be fritter'd away, my Usefulness abridged & my Soul unspiritualized - I will think it over well, how to turn it to most account & form my plan deliberately with prayer for Wisdom & for Strength to keep Resolves. Mrs. W's Health assur'dly requires a Villa. D[o] Soul. She all Kindness & sweet dispos[n] & compliance. Let me go to prayer. I have great Cause for Hum[n] I fear I did not act simple & faith[y] Thurs[dy] night, fear stepp'd in & on Frid[y] fear <u>rather</u> nimes ferms. Evg - O let me watch ag[t] Sin & Strive to be renewed daily to amend in all & <u>grow</u> & 100 fold &c. A plan of Study also & of Time arrangement to be form'd, & the Recess's Bus[s] to be chalk'd out - O what cause for Shame, comparg Self with advantages, mercies, &c. &c.[627]

Sunday ½ past 2 oClock Broomfield June 24th 98

My poor dear B., ill from pain in face, by which kept awake almt all night. Tho' fond of her, & concern'd, yet I see in myself Selfishness & Impatience ready to rise - Surely God is punishg me for a feeling of Exultation from her being so well. "I said in my Prosperity, I shall never be moved. Thou Lord of Thy Goodness hast made my Hill so strong, thou didst turn thy face & I was troubled" &c.[628] How uncertain are all human things. I hope I feel some Xtian Resignat[n] & holy Reliance on the Mercy & Goodness of God & the Saviour. This last week a hurrying one, & this, ab[t] to have much Compy with us, if B. well enough. I hope however to be instructed by divine wisdom & to be enabled to live to God's Glory, in & thro' X[t] O how rich in Mercy is God to me! & how little am I what I sho'd be! May I learn more to him a Life of Heavenly Mindedness, of diligence, of Zealous Xtian Service. I go to prayer. After my debt if Bus[s] clear'd, I will form a plan with deliberate objects & settled means of pursuit. Alas! on lookg back, What Shame of X[t] did I feel when Speaker here! How monstrous! In Heart asham'd of famy prayers, & what a Relief to me when he went just before reading in morng. O how weak is my Love & fear of God & X[t] indicated hereby, Alas! Alas! Then so selfish. I fear I am secretly pleas'd that the Pain B. suffers is not mine.[629] O the Uncleanness of this defil'd Heart. <u>Renew</u> it O God. Then Vanity is

---

626. Galatians 2:20.

627. MS Wilberforce c. 41, fos. 119-120. This entry was actually recorded by Wilberforce on May 27. *Life*, ii. pp. 286-287 has, 'How little did I think that Pitt's conduct, which, poor fellow, made him mortify me, would draw him, as it did, into the scrape which produced his duel, which took place on the very day (of my former entry) at three o'clock. How thankful for Christianity to soothe my angry spirit!'

628. Psalm 30:6-7.

629. In left margin here he wrote, 'Recess Resolves'.

comprising, & Desirg of applause of men in talkg with Arthur Young & Wm Spooner.

At Bp London's yesty too sensual, too little watchful & Spiritly minded. To try this Recess on which I am enterg, at near 6 Hours betn Bkfast & dinner if Health will allow, & 2 Hours before Bkfast for tho't & Real Bus[s.] tryg Bed before 11 & up by 7, at latest 7½. There is a proud confessg of X[t.] when Credit is to be got by contendg for the faith. There is Self-Complacency. But alas this author, feelg how diff[t.] from true Xt[n.] Release from being asham'd of X[t.] when really humbled for the moment before the World, by Respect for or Obedience to him. Asham'd of family prayers!!! How sottish. How monstrous! As well as basely ungrateful! Such Instances teach me how little I am advanc'd, & cause me to press forw[d.] with renewed Diligence - X[t.] offers his Grace. Less ferms. din[r.] & in order that time may not be wasted and I sooner fit for Work. All my Regl[s], Conv[n.] Compy &c. mens: &c. diligently & Self-Exam[n.] frequent. Times allotted to distance Bus[s.] Preparat[n.] of Topics, both for thought & convers[n.] &c.[630]

Sunday Night July 1[st.] 98 - 10¾ oClock

This has been a sad day & I cold & unspiritual; from a large party, not quite sympathetic. My past days, trifled too much away – Oimoi - My devotions hurried of late, both Morng & Evg - . I hope to amend.[631]

Sunday Afternoon July 8[th.] ½ past 5 oClock - Stamford

I have felt this day I hope in some degree dispos'd as a Xtian sho'd be, but O let me not confound occasional feelings with being a true Xtian, and yet, O Lord, I wo'd resolutely endeavour to walk worthy of my high & holy Calling. O enlighten my Ignorance & purify my Corruptions & warm my Coldness & fix my Volatility - O may my Mother's death impress me. I don't seem to have felt enough on this Event. O God renew me for X[t's] Sake in thine image & may I henceforth live no longer to myself, but to him who died for me & rose again.[632] - May I crucify the flesh - O what manifold mercies have I received - God has remarkably prospered me on my way, he seems to give me present encouragement for obeying him. My poor B. unwilling to part, but gives her time & the desire to please God carries it. This seems a sad careless place – Oimoi - Oimoi.[633]

---

630. MS Wilberforce c. 41, fo. 120. *Life*, ii. p. 294 has, 'Surely God is punishing me for a feeling of exultation. "I said in my prosperity, I shall never be moved. Thou, Lord, of Thy goodness hast made my hill so strong. Thou didst turn away Thy face, and I was troubled." How uncertain are all human things! I hope I feel some Christian resignation, and holy reliance on the mercy and goodness of God and my Savior.'

631. MS Wilberforce c. 41, fo. 120.

632. 2 Corinthians 5:15.

633. MS Wilberforce c. 41, fo. 120. *Life*, ii. pp. 295-296 has, 'My dear mother did not suffer in death, and I trust she is happy. The change gradually produced in her during the last eight years was highly gratifying to all who loved her, and looked forward. It was a solemn and an affecting scene to me, yesterday evening, to be in my mother's room, and see the bed where I was born, and where my father and my mother died, and where she then lay in her coffin. I was alone, and I need not say

Sunday Evg 9 oClock - July 15[th.] Broomfield

This but a bad Sunday from company in the House - and this last week too little done - O may God direct me right in all my Ways & enable me to live diligently improving faculties, but for God's Glory - livg above y[e.] World. This Evg I was sleepy at Church, Oimoi. I fear I am livg much below my Xtian privileges. Too little love of X[t.] & fear of Sin. Love of holiness &c. &c.[634]

Broomfield[635] Saty. July 21[st.] 1798 35 mins. past 11 Morng -

My dearest B. is now in labour - How dependent does this make me feel on the power & Goodness of God. What a humbling Impression have I of my own Inability & of all my Happiness & all else that belongs to me, being at the disposal of the Supreme Being - So it ought always to be. This it is, to <u>walk softly</u>,[636] - my dearest love, how compos'dly waiting the coming on of her pains - With what pious lowliness & Resignation shew'd with Xtian Hope. O may I learn from her, and may I be more grateful than I have been. I see already much to be thankful & as usual the kind Hand of a gracious God disposing little Incidents with a favouring[637] kindness. Underwood was going out today at one to Shooting Hill. It was a special mercy the labor came on before he was gone. We did not think it so near. She might have been taken at the Aucklands.[638] Mrs. Bab told me just now, my Love was <u>so patient</u>. O God, support & comfort her & enable me whatever may be thy will, to submit with humble acquiescing Confidence. Began to be sufferg ab[t.] 4 & now ¾ past 4. Entire intermissions. If God should now see fit to release her from this World of Sin & Sorrow, <u>doubtless</u> She would go to Glory & perhaps be spared many a Suffering which I foresee not. O may the Language of my inmost <u>Heart</u> be "Thy will be done."[639]

How merciful She was not taken ill, or alarm'd while I on my Yorkshire journey lately. I have been far too little careful to improve the opportunities of Usefulness afforded by my Situation in married life. I have liv'd too Self-indulgent & slothful & careless & likely God might

---

to you, or seek to conceal from you, I put up my prayers that the scene might work its due effect. It is late, and I must retire. Had a delightful contemplative evening walk in Burleigh Park. I have felt this day, I hope, in some degree rightly disposed; but oh let me not confound occasional feelings with being a true Christian. And yet, O Lord, I would resolutely endeavor to walk worthy of my high and holy calling. O enlighten my ignorance, purify my corruptions, warm my coldness, and fix my volatility. Oh may my mother's death impress me! May I crucify the flesh. What manifold mercies have I received. God has remarkably prospered me on my way, he seems to give me present encouragement for obeying him. This seems a sad careless place, alas! I talked to several common people. Found the butchers' shops open. At church, miserable work. Remnant of Sunday school only eight children, and no more in the place. I have seldom seen a more apparently irreligious place. A shopkeeper said, none of the clergy active, or went amongst the poor. One Presbyterian meeting.'

634. MS Wilberforce c. 41, fo. 120.

635. Ibid., fo. 121.

636. Isaiah 38:15.

637. 'Favouring' is here written over a word that has been crossed out.

638. George Eden, 1st Earl of Auckland (1784–1849). MP, three times First Lord of the Admiralty, and Governor General of India, 1836–1842.

639. Matthew 6:10.

justly punish me. I have not been duly careful to polish that Jewel I reced so very bright, <u>scarce a flaw</u>, & to improve from the Contemplation of it. O may I practically remember how I now wish I had liv'd, & may I be enabled to do better in the time to come, & if God should give me an offspring, may I bring it up in His faith & fear & love, as a Xtian sho'd be & educated to go thro' such a World as this.[640]

Sunday July 29[th.] 98 Broomfield 2 oClock
O what abundant Cause have I for gratitude! How well all has gone on, both with Mother & child, & how sweet a frame does my Love preserve. Except being a little low in y[e.] morng. All well, but her pain in face day. My Head is middg & Eyes too but I will take a musing praying walk, of Gratitude & Intercession. O may I be a Child of God. May I look into my self, my Situa[n.] &c. & see how I can but improve it.[641]

Sunday Aug[t.] 5[th.] 98 2 oClock Broomfield
Alas - when I look into myself seriously & impartially how little do I find myself correspondg with the Character of a Child of God. I feel my wretchedness & misery more this day than common. O blessed be God that Hope is held forth to Sinners in y[e.] Gospel, yet let me not deceive myself, but strive, labour, grow in Grace - How defective in Habitl Spiritual Mindedness, Love, meekness, talkg &c. at Random Regls Forgot, Vanity, Pride, Self-Exam[n] forgot, & peculiar Character. How little tho't of doing Good. I should despair but for the promise of y[e.] Grace of X[t.] Help Lord, I pray. I am wretched & miserable & poor & blind and naked.[642] <u>When</u> Tom Bab[n] so kindly told me of my speakg harshly to Servts tho' took it well outwardly, how anger'd did I feel inwardly. Alas. Alas! and how testy & tyrannical have I felt tow[ds]. him, towar[ds] d_____[643], towar[ds.] Sally & Ashley & others & Martin. O create in me a new heart O God & renew a right Spirit within me.[644] How full of mercies is God to me, & how dead I am, & void of Gratitude. How sensual also, often offend ferms & at least wasting time. How little desirous of diffusing y[e.] Happiness so freely given to me.

O may I feel still more the weight of my Brethren, charging it on myself & pressing it home. Placg of myself in X[t's] sight in angels in Spirits of just men made perfect[645] & arguing on all the Grounds of aggravation. O what if world knew me as really am? How vain towards Stephen - O Lord renew me - Let this Corruption put on Incorruption,[646] even here in

---

640. MS Wilberforce c. 41, fo. 121.

641. MS Wilberforce c. 41, fo. 121. *Life*, ii. p. 307 has, 'Venn on "rich and poor meet together", good. People about to build a new chapel because he "does not preach the gospel." He much disturbed. Much talk with Milner about his preaching, and the growing faults of the young clergy. He conceives them getting into a rational way of preaching.'

642. Revelation 3:17.

643. Word illegible.

644. Psalm 51:10.

645. Hebrews 12:23.

646. 1 Corinthians 15:54.

Heart & bring forth the Graces of the Spirit. Xt says y[e.] Apostle is made to us Wisdom, Righteous[ns] &c.[647] Let us lay aside evy weight & y[e.] Sin &c. [648] lookg unto Jesus.[649] O Lord, help me. The Blood of X[t.] cleanseth from all Sin[650] & his Spirit will give us y[e.] Victory - Help Lord once again, against World flesh Devil. Again I fear I have been living a sensual sort of life, trifling away my Time, & tho' they may in part be requir'd for my Body yet I fear time too much fritter'd away for want of plan. O may I amend throughout. Tree good & fruit good.[651] How little Tenderness & Sympathy have I felt for Henry, have a secret Enmity ag[t.] Bab[n.] for his Goodness. Alas. Alas. Harsh to Servts, unkind in Tempers tow[ds.] Pearson. O let me think of the terrors of y[e.] Lord & of X[t's] mercies & Invitat[ns.] & be constrain'd by Love & urg'd by fear & maintain a more habitual Impression of Spirit[l] things, morng or Evg med[n.] & if can, both, & prayer. Plan, Time passes, Self-Exam more frequent, kindness to B. Gratitude &c. - Remember.[652]

Sunday[653] Night near 10 -

O the Selfishness of this hard Heart. It seems insensible ab[t.] all but itself. I put it down that if God gives me more Love & tenderness I may hereafter bless Him, yet People think me feeling, alas. What deceits we put on each other - I dare not say I have any Love of X[t.] yet what says St. Paul of those who are destitute of this - yet do I take the means have prescrib'd in my Book? How justly might the words be address'd to me, out of thy own mouth &c.[654] Thou wicked &c.[655] O save me![656]

Sunday 12[th.] Aug[t.] ½ past 2 Broomfield

Tho' I felt so keenly on Sunday last, I began to cool in aftn & Evg. Cooler on Monday & yet part of the week have been very dead, alas, alas! To what can it be owing? Perhaps that not care paid to use of means. Evg partly Devotions neglected,[657] Scripture Readg too little. Too much contending in own Strength, yet rather better than sometimes I hope. How much more pleasg to God poor Sally's nervous apprehensions - O may I this week amend. Shun procrastinat[n.] Redeem time. Labour as my Health will allow. But above all Seek God's favour & X[t's] Love & Spirit's Help. Forgettg him seems chief Crime. Found dear B. last night praying for our little Boy. I have receiv'd the Sact. this day. O may it be to me a true Renewal of Grace.[658]

---

647. 1 Corinthians 1:30.

648. Hebrews 12:1.

649. Hebrews 12:2.

650. 1 John 1:7.

651. Matthew 12:33.

652. MS Wilberforce c. 41, fo. 121.

653. Ibid., fo. 122.

654. Luke 19:22.

655. Matthew 25:26.

656. MS Wilberforce c. 41, fo. 122.

657. Here he wrote '2' over 'Evg' and '1' over 'partly'.

658. MS Wilberforce c. 41, fo. 122.

Sunday Aug[t.] 19[th.] 98 Bfield 2 oClock

The last week spent at home but time rather fritter'd away, tho' I hope rather mended, yet how much less than ought & my Heart cold, my affections dull. For these 2 or 3 morngs I have got a little more time, but how weak am I in prayer & faith. Alas. Alas. O may God renew me in his Image. May I grow more like X[t.] My life seems to run to waste a good deal. O may I be wholly God's thro' X[t.659]

Sunday 26[th.] Aug[t.] 98 - 2 oClock Broomfd

I tried hard to keep Friday my Birth day quiet for relig[s.] uses but in vain, & that day & yesterday partly from being indiff[t.] less Prayer & Readg than usual. Today thoughts & mind very wanderg in prayer Sermon & Spiritual Affections cold & dead - The last year has carried off Eliot 17[th.] Sept[r.] 1797 - Joseph Milner ab[t.] Novr 20 97 - & my Mother[660] Bet[n.] 1[st.] & 2[d.] of July 97 - How strongly these Events teach us that the time is short! O may I learn & be wise. I am sadly defective at present. But may I cleave to God & give myself wholly to him. I go to prayer. O what mercies have I been lately receivg. No man's child ever less gave solicitude on Ground of Health. B.'s excell[t.] Recovery. Her desire to do her duty. O how little have I done for God this year. How much my time fritter'd away with little use. How much sho'd I strive to be useful. How earnestly pray for spirit[l.] direction Ability & Success. How little am I duly grateful for the multiplied mercies I enjoy. Let me be thankful that my own Health on the whole better than correspondg months of last year.[661]

Sunday Sept[r.] 2[d.] 98 Broomfield 2 oClock

How excell[t] a Sermon has Venn been preachg on Luke 14[th.] 28, countg y[e.] Cost if we profess to be Xtians. It affected my Heart, it humbled me in the dust. How little have I preserv'd the Xtian's peculiar Character. How little been livg in X[t.] & X[t.] in me. O may I do it more. My dearest B. delighted with y[e.] Sermon & greatly affected with whole Service. O may I be more a Xtian experience more of the power of Religion. My Days pass away in Hurry & my time is thereby fritter'd away. Alas. Alas! Yet I don't think it right to go on the retir'd plan. O may I wait on God diligently. He will then level Hills & fill up plains before me Isa. 40:4. O what unXtian tempers have I found in myself this week. Not kind & not considerate enough tow[ds.] Sally poor thing. Last night lookg at stars more devoutly than for sometime.[662]

---

659. Ibid.

660. A word is crossed out here.

661. MS Wilberforce c.41, fo.122.

662. MS Wilberforce c.41, to.122. *Life*, ii. p. 307 has, 'How excellent a sermon has Venn been preaching upon Luke xiv. 28, counting the cost if we profess to be Christians. It affected my heart, it humbled me in the dust. My days pass away in hurry, yet I do not think it right to go upon the retired plan. Oh may I wait on God diligently! He will then level hills and fill up plains before me.'

Sunday 1 oClock Elmdon[663] Sept[r] 23[d] 98

This last fortnight or 3 weeks has gone on too much like others. No gross times, but O how far too little of the power of X[ty] How low in Love. How full of marks of Want of due habitual Regard to God - Once it was better with me. Rem[r] from whence art fallen & Repent.[664] I have been sometimes affected much walkg in fields here - & for the last day or two from reading Rev. 2 & 3, Ephesus, Sardis, Laodicea - O may I pray more earnestly, prayer has been sadly neglected & Scripture too little read here, never of late but a little with B & Anne & Eliza & Mrs. Gough & sometimes Mrs. Spooner & Will[m] Also prayer too hurried & curtail'd. How little also do I feel habitual Gratitude & Humiliation. Today at Mr. Dilke's sad Sermon, my Emotions more of anger at him than Sorrow for him & flock, & gratitude for Self. How Anne & Eliza shame me & Dear W[m] I must try for more Solitude - My Hours for meditation & Prayer are so curtail'd by the quantity of my Bus[s] & the multitude of my acquaint[ces] that I lose naturally Spiritual Mindedness for Want of aliment, & <u>watching unto prayer</u>. But O X[t] quicken me by thy Spirit & as thou hast graciously given me to know the truth with my understandg, may I experience its renewg power on my Heart & whole nature. May Paul's Prayer for y[e] Ephes[ns] be fulfill'd in me that he wo'd grant unto &c. &c. to be strengthen'd &c. that X[t] may dwell &c.[665] Even so Come Lord Jesus.[666]

My poor dear B. has been too solicitous I fear ab[t] our dear little Boy, but tis hard to observe the exact limit, where to go far is even a duty. Dear Soul, She has been aiming at Usefulness, settg up Schools &c. How much more interested ab[t] this than me - How little have I observed my peculiar Character. How vain glorious in truth. How little Solicitous for friends' Spirit[l] Good. How secretly malicious, Oimoi, not strict as to Truth. Sadly wanderg in famy prayer. But may the promise be fulfill'd in me 1 Cor 1:30. I wo'd not be Superstitious but havg felt last night ab[t] Bedtime, a Sort of glorying, rather, & then a flea in Bed convincing me of Weakness, & prayg to God that by catchg it my night might be no longer disturb'd & I be unfitted for Service of this day. I caught it almost immedy. A similar Instance happen'd lately. Rem[r] Locusts, Grasshoppers, Flies &c. made God's Instruments, & whatever really lowest convinces of weakness, &c drives to him & see more 1 Cor. 1:30.[667]

---

663. Elmdon Manor near Birmingham, England was built in 1547 by John Boteler, but was sold three years later to the Mayne family. In 1760 it was sold again to the Industrialist Abraham Spooner (c.1690–1788), together with an estate of 2,000 acres. He demolished the house and began building its replacement, Elmdon Hall, but did not live to see its completion, that being accomplished in 1795 by his son Isaac Jr. (1736–1817). After Isaac Jr.'s death, the house and grounds were then inherited by his son, Abraham Spooner Lillingston (1770–1834). Isaac Spooner Jr. was the father of Barbara Spooner, who married William Wilberforce in 1797, and the couple lived in the Hall for some time afterwards.

664. Revelation 2:5.

665. Ephesians 3:17.

666. Revelation 22:20.

667. MS Wilberforce c. 41, fos. 122-123.

Sunday Sep^{t.} 30th. 98 Elmdon H^{e.} near 8 oClock Evg -

I felt I hope somethg of the Comfort of Religion this morng. But alas since dinner how cold have I been & how little under the lively influence of Spiritual things. My time is short havg since Church been at Lillington's School. O tis a blessed thing to have the Sunday devoted to God, & his promises are sure. May I amend & be renewed in the Spirit of my mind,[668] by Grace, from the fulness of X^{t.} I suspect ferms excedg night once or twice Oimoi, but I hope shall keep resol^{n.} ag^{t.} Repetit^{n.[669]}

Sunday Octr. 14th. Bath 2¾ oClock

I have not been enough availg myself of ye. opportun^{s.} this place affords me of spirit'l Improvement, yet I hope I feel not unwarrantably some Good Hope spring from the assur'd truth of Gospel promises. O let me watch & pray & strive more. Meditate more & live ye. life I now live in ye. flesh by &c.[670] X^{t.} is all - O what Causes of Gratitude does this place enforce on me.[671]

Sunday Octr. 28th. Bath 2¼ oClock 98

I am not livg that humbly, grateful, fearful, watchful Life which becometh one who has to work out his Salv^{n.} with fear & trembling,[672] who may look up a reconcil'd father in X^{t.} & to a lovg Redeemer & Intercessor - My Soul is starv'd by ye. Want of Meditation, &c. My prayers are too curtail'd I fear & broken. O let me press forw^{d.} lest havg taught others, &c. a Castaway.[673] How scanty my Love. How improper my feelgs on Randolph's Sermon, & tow^{ds.} him & others - O God, take away ye. H^{t.} of Stone & give me a H^{t.} of flesh.[674] - Fill me with Peace Love Joy holy Fear & grateful Resignat^{n.} May I labor to appropriate the Blessings & Riches of X^{t.} desirg from him as the Branch from ye. Vine, the Supply of all Graces. Amen. I go to prayer. Above all things, how much more Solicitous & thoughtful, in my Heart tho' not in my judgment, concerng the Estimat^{n.} of man, than concerng ye. present favour of God. How constantly do I find myself unable to banish from my mind in secret the complacency arisg from what wo'd be the Praise or Approb^{n.} of a Bystander.

   O Lord, give me a single Heart, pure warm humble & penitent Love - the temper of a redeem'd Sinner become a Child of God, & a Member of X^{t's} Body, who is changing from Glory to Glory,[675] yet is pressg forw^{d.} not as tho' already attain'd.[676] Perhaps my being for so great a proportion of my time engag'd on worldly Bus^{s.} & worldly Compy. & not med^{n.}

---

668. Ephesians 4:23.

669. MS Wilberforce c. 41, fo. 123. *Life*, ii. p. 274 has, 'Oh it is a blessed thing to have the Sunday devoted to God.'

670. Galatians 2:20.

671. MS Wilberforce c. 41, fo. 123.

672. Philippians 2:12.

673. 1 Corinthians 9:27.

674. Ezekiel 36:26.

675. 2 Corinthians 3:18.

676. Philippians 3:12.

enough, may keep me so low in faith & Love - O let me strive for more progress, by usg the means with humble Prayer - X[t.] is characterized as He who is faithful, & Isa. 40 last.[677]

Nov[r.] 18[th.] 98 Sunday 3 oClock Bat[a.] Rise

O what Cause for Gratitude does every week afford. Our dear Boy arriv'd safe back to us, & we all well assembled here. Alas, how little am I as I ought to be. But I will by God's Grace labour, yet O let me not now desire Complacency from Resolutions, which not true Xtian Humility & Trust in X[t.] but from the Promises in the Gospel of pardong mercy & strengthening Grace - I would pray to be enabled to have a little time for prayer & medit[n.] in town evg morng early - Bed early of course, for Health requires 8 ½ Hours sleep. My B. How truly Xtian in main, tho' poor Soul, so fond & solicitous ab[t.] child, that I fear his being taken away, again She is increasg. O what Cause have I for thankfulness. May I improve in all Holiness. O what a blessed Instit[n.] is Sabbath. I have squander'd today ½ an Hour, unawares that so long on Journal. O that my frame may be more humble grateful watchful fearful full of the Love of X[t.] & of holy Indifference to Earthly things, except as connected with Eternal. What kind friends I have. Poor Delay'd! I might have been like him! How few so favour'd as me - How few M.P.'s have been led to any knowledge & desire of X[t.] Rem[r.] O my Soul my Responsib[y.] so much greater. O may I press forw[d.] Lookg unto Jesus &c.[678] Amen.[679]

Sunday Nov[r.] 25[th.] 98 Palace Yard - 7¼ oClock Evg -

My feeling when so ill on Wedny morng was, that I had not been active enough in the Cause of God. O let me now employ with greater activity the faculties he has restored. O that I may be more truly humble, diligent, heavenly minded; lookg for X[t.] Heb. & livg in the faith of unseen things - God has promised that they who wait on him shall renew their Strength.[680] - Let me then wait & watch & pray & humbly yet confidently hope for the mercies of God in X[t.] & for Grace to lighten, direct, conform & further me - Amen. How little Gratitude do I feel for my Recovery. How little for y[e.] signal mercies I enjoy. How full is my Cup. How little am I livg by faith. O quicken me by thy Grace. X[t.] thou Supplier of all spiritual Wants.[681]

Thursday 3¼ oClock, November 29, 1798, Palace Yard

Alas I feel little Gratitude today[682] or rather none, tho' my Judgement tells me I should be grateful, alas, alas! I've no time to write now.

---

677. MS Wilberforce c. 41, fo. 123.

678. Hebrews 12:2.

679. MS Wilberforce c. 41, fo. 123.

680. Isaiah 40:31.

681. MS Wilberforce c. 41, fos. 123-124. *Life*, ii. p. 319 has, 'My feeling, when so ill on Wednesday morning, was, that I had not been active enough in the cause of God: oh let me now employ with greater diligence the powers which he has restored.'

682. 'Thanksgiving day' is inserted here above the line.

Perhaps I may resume my pen. But scarcely any man has such Cause for Gratitude. Last thanksgivg day Dec[r.] 18[th.] 1797.[683]

Sunday Dec[r.] 9[th.] ¼ past 8 in the Morning Pal Y[d.]

The last 10 days have gone on sadly indeed, & particy my Bus[s.] has not been done or my Letters answer'd, owing to my time being fritter'd away. Up late near 9 people call while at Bfst & thence till I go out. Perhaps then I walk a good deal; & when I return tis dinner time. Then havg din'd too late ½ past 3 or near 4, the H of Com[s.] has been neglected and tho' there has been no urgent Business, yet I have neglected much which belongs to my Station, & still more have not let my light Shine as a good County Member. I am this morng up earlier and I hope to continue earlier night & morng, and by eatg a very <u>moderate</u> dinner early (with less Wine) to be in the House when Bus[s.] begins; to get thro' my Letters, the Accumul[n.] & then be punctual. Alas. Alas! what Cause have I for Humiliat[n.] I am indiff[t.] my Head is hurt by writg & I must stop.[684]

Sunday Dec[r.] 16[th.] 1798 Pal Y[d.] 9¾ oClock Evg

The last Week has stolen away rapidly. I hope going on rather better than at sometimes yet but poorly. Hours no better, & but ill fitted for House on enterg. Not spiritual enough, not love enough tow[ds.] Bab[n.] Martin.[685]

Sunday Night Dec[r.] 23[rd.] 98 near 10 oClock

O what Cause for Humiliation do I find in the last 2 or 3 days. What Vanity. What Solicitude ab[t.] Worldly Estimat[n.] (which perhaps y[e.] root of all y[e.] Rest), what undue anger at Turney & at myth for woundg pride - O God forgive me & may the Spirit of X[t.] rule in me. I humbly hope I have been schooling myself, but O how much do I want of that unruffled & irresistible Love which sho'd reign in the Heart of the true Xtian. This need not, I think nor should it, prevent his actively & perhaps even warmly engaging in debate, reprovg Vice, &c. &c. But there sho'd be Love within, & where that is, it will shew itself in marks outwardly. I hope I now feel no Ill Will to any of these, & I pray & strive ag[t.] It. O what are the little Reproaches & assaults I encounter compar'd with those under which Stephen co'd say L[d.] Lay not this Sin to th[r.] charge[686] & Father forgive them &c.[687] Let me try to grow in Humility in Dis Esteem & Dis. Relish of Worldly Estimat[n.] & in Love. O How full, overflowg with Vanity, in what a fermentation of Spirits was I on the night of answerg Courtenay. How jealous of Character & greedy of applause. Alas. Alas. Create in me a clean Heart O God & renew a right Spirit within me.[688]

---

683. MS Wilberforce c. 41, fo. 124.
684. Ibid.
685. Ibid.
686. Acts 7:60.
687. Luke 23:34.
688. Psalm 51:10.

Then also how vain of what after all Babbington's Discovery respectg Income Tax Bill – Oimoi - Oimoi.[689]

1799

Pal Yard Jan[y.] 1[st.] 1799 - 10 oClock Tuesday Night
I <u>meant</u> today to be devoted to religious offices, but the House's meeting - My bad last night & other Hindrances I fear from Self, hinder'd me, & except the Lock & Sact this morng & a little Scripture tonight, nothg done in this way - nor any private prayer to which however now going – Alas - What Cause have I for Humiliation do I find in myself? How little am I living by faith & not by Sight. How little the new Creature, with whom all things will become new & all things are of God - O Lord, renew me by thy quickening Grace. Give me faith & love & Hope & Joy & peace in believing,[690] and all the Graces of the Spirit, Meekness, Heavenly-Mindedness, Sadly defective here.

I mean thro' God's Help, to try at earlier Hours night & morng, not curtailing my Sleep which my Health will not bear, but try at 11 & ½ or ¾ past 7. Then ½ or ¾ of an Hour of Scripture Readg prayer & med[n.] evy morng, whereas all have been sadly shorten'd. And in Evg try at ½ or ¾ or an Hour Scrip[e.] & med[n.] & prayer. May I also keep <u>my</u> <u>Heart with all diligence</u> & watch unto prayer. What sad marks have I lately found in myself of defective Love, of Envy, of Excessive Desire of Worldly Estimation. O cleanse me & I shall be clean.[691] - Also I have been unkind to my Sister, harsh to Servts. O may I here improve. Really vain of givg away, tho' affectg contrary. O let me watch & pray. Thrown off my guard by little things. Ashley's Enor on Sunday. Asnor's little dispute Saty night. All this from temper not habitually school'd. O may I walk & live by faith & in the Spirit, followg the Example of X[t.] & fill'd with his & his Apostle's tempers - O what Room for Improvement! How asham'd sho'd I be of backg others myself so wantg real Progress. Help me O X[t.692]

---

689. MS Wilberforce c. 41, fo. 124. *Life*, ii. pp. 322-323 has, 'Found causes of humiliation in these last few days. What solicitude about human estimation! (which is perhaps the cause of all the rest.) I humbly hope that I have been schooling myself; but oh how much do I want of that unruffled love which should reign in the heart of the true Christian! This need not, nor I think should it, prevent his actively, and perhaps even warmly, engaging in debate, and reproving vice. But there should be love within, and where that is, it will show itself in outward marks. I hope I feel no ill-will to any, and I pray and strive against it. Oh what are the little reproaches and assaults I encounter, compared with those under which Stephen could say, 'Lord, lay not this sin to their charge', and, 'Father, forgive them!' Let me strive to grow in humility, in disesteem and disrelish of worldly estimation, and in love. In what a fermentation of spirits was I on the night of answering Courtenay! How jealous of character and greedy of applause! Alas! Alas! Create in me a clean heart, O God, and renew a right spirit within me.'

690. Romans 15:13.

691. Psalm 51:7.

692. MS Wilberforce c. 41, fo. 124. *Life*, ii. p. 324 has, 'I meant today to be devoted to religious offices, but the House's meeting prevented more than receiving the sacrament this morning, and a little reading tonight. I am now going to private prayer. What cause have I for humiliation, what room for improvement!'

Sunday Night 9 oClock, January 6, 1799, Pal Y[d.]

O Lord if thou wert extreme to markg what I have done & daily do amiss, I could not stand[693] in thy presence, but I throw myself on thy mercies in X[t.] & look to his Cross for pardon peace & Hope. O may I by thy Grace be conform'd in my purposes of amendment & enabled to carry them into Effect. Too little Scripture readg of late. Too much Worldly mindedness, alas, alas, & pride & Vanity & love of human Estimation. But O cleanse me by thy Grace & fill me with the Graces of y[e.] Spirit.[694]

Sunday Evening 6 oClock, January 20, 1799, Broomfield

Alas. Alas! What unholy angry tempers have fermented with me of late, tow[s.] Servts today to John[695] & also tow[ds.] Sister debatg ab[t.] whether more women or men among first Xtians. Alas! Alas! O may God forgive me, & may the Spirit of X[t.] more live & Rule within me. My Eyes are weak & I must leave off. O what pride. What unmortified Impatience of Contradiction in the least things! How little true Love! How unfit for Heav'n. O Lord soften & calm me, & give me to partake of y[e.] Meekness & Gentleness of X[t.] How strongly do I see the want of these amiable tempers in others, in Mrs. & Mr. Dixon,[696] my conscience tells me now. I've been unkind to Mailing often & to my affecting defenceless Sister. Even a little to B. who is all tenderness. O take away y[e.] Ht. of Stone[697] & give me a more kindly compounded nature, a new Heart, of Love.[698]

Friday, January 25[th.] 1799

My life has been too much spent at Random of late, at least too loosely. Not care enough of time, not plan enough as to readg, even Relax[n.] Hours, Comp[y] Conv[n.] Bus[s.] &c. Hours too late mg & night. Evg devot[ns] curtail'd & sadly Conducted. Ferms also at night & either that as to plan! At din[r.] far indisposed too long to any attentiv[e.] mod[tn.] from it. What envy the other day caused by Canng, let me practice my Rules ab[t.] him. Let me humbly resolve to try to get up ab[t.] 7 & Bed or a very little after 11, or rather sooner if anythg in Aim. Try for 5 ½ Hours bet[n.] Bkft & din[r.] & waste no time Bfst. Then Bus[s.] & time plan, pursue more modera[te.] mens. Conv[n.] Compy Topics, friends Spir[l.] Good. Evg Retire at 9 or rather sooner in aim or ½ an Hour bef[e.] famy prayers when people with us, & pray meditate & read, famy Prayers early, &c. Evg Self Exam[n.] & ½ or ¾ of an Hour morng also.

How unkind to poor Sally have I been. O let me more cultivate meekness & Love. My poor B. not lovg with[t.] dissim[n.] I fear even tow[ds.]

---

693. Psalm 130:3.

694. MS Wilberforce c. 41, fo. 124.

695. In his Spiritual Journals, Wilberforce mentions three of his household servants, George in 1796, and John and Walter here in 1799.

696. In later references, Wilberforce identifies a certain Mr. and Mrs. Dixon as being amongst his household servants.

697. Ezekiel 36:26.

698. MS Wilberforce c. 41, fo. 125.

her. O God, inspire me with thy fear & Love & for X[ts.] Sake put thy Spirit within me, to renew my Heart, and Thou O Saviour, Be thou made unto me Wisdom & Righteousness & Sanctificat[n.] & Red[n.699] May I be directed right in worldly matters. May I walk by Faith & not by Sight,[700] endeavorg to use my faculties & talents <u>all of these</u> with a reverent & prudent, diligent humble, dependent Grateful, & confiding Devotedness of Intention & Strenuousness of active exertion to thy Glory. Amen.[701]

Sunday Evening 7 ½, February 10, 1799, Pal Y[d.]

Alas! How diff[t.] is Knowledge from practice, tho' I so well know what is right, how little do I practice it. O may I amend throughout. <u>Renew me O God</u>. Let the Change be entire. O may I look more to thy favour & less to all else. My Weak Shatter'd frame requires much Indulgence, but O may I be spiritually minded & better Hours, more Love, Meekness, Humility, Gratitude, fear &c. Looking unto Jesus;[702] & walkg by Faith not by Sight.[703]

Sunday Night 10 ¾ oClock, February 10, 1799

I found it so late after writg the above that I had no time to pray before readg to fam[y.] So I tho't we wo'd read directly & I'd pray aftds when Famy Service over, but stopp'd ¼ of an Hour or more by Mrs. Dixon's being wasted to make Whey for poor old Mrs. W[ms.] Then after Fam Prayer staid talkg, felt hungry, supp'd,[704] chatted & tis now Bedtime & I tir'd, with[t.] prayer to call it much this whole day, Alas. Alas. O God forgive me. O may I more improve my time & strive to turn it to account.[705]

Sunday Evening 7 ½ oClock, February 17, 1799, Pal Y[d.]

Alas. Alas. This last week has I fear been trifled away. How little do I execute, how little am I conductg myself well even estimated by the low standard of this Life. But still more how unspiritual. How little am I livg this Life I now live in y[e.] flesh in the faith &c.[706] active fervent grateful humble as a redeem'd Sinner ought to be. O may I strive more to grow in Grace. For the next week Earlier Hours. Evg prayer less hurried. Contin[n.] of Scrip[e.] Readg. & more meditatn on it.[707]

Sunday 2 ½ oClock, February 24, 1799, Pal Yard

This last week has been rather more diligently spent, also Scripture almost daily after Bkft with B. but Evg evening prayers curtail'd &

---

699. 1 Corinthians 1:30.

700. 2 Corinthians 5:7.

701. MS Wilberforce c. 41, fo. 125.

702. Hebrews 12:2.

703. 2 Corinthians 5:7. MS Wilberforce c. 41, fo. 125.

704. In the left margin at this point he wrote 'Sunday'.

705. MS Wilberforce c. 41, fo. 125.

706. Galatians 2:20.

707. MS Wilberforce c. 41, fo. 125.

hurried from being at Bedtime & therefore perhaps mind in bad frame. Oimoi. Little tho't of God X$^{t.}$ &c. habitual & new sickness & stupified Bowels middlg languid &c. unfit for prayer & all Spiritual Exercises. Alas. Alas. O may I strive more to purify myself, to be fill'd with peace & joy in believg &c.[708] O what Cause for Gratitude have I, that honor'd by being allowed to get Best ordain'd, & also by being the Instrument of good to poor persecuted Jersey Methodists.[709] On lookg into myself, I find the greatest Reason for Shame & Remorse, in that time so wasted & Parl^{ty} Duty so little perform'd. Amici fures temporis[710] <u>never</u> more true than with me. I humbly purpose amendm$^{t.}$ & livg more usefully, actively, Independently than being a Slave to customs of World more mod. mens. & ferms. Again, what pride have I found & still is in me, manifest tow$^{ds.}$ Martyn.[711] Tyrs Ledhytt Dent. Speaker[712] &c. Oimoi. Oimoi. Also, alm$^{t.}$ daily heated & flush'd with ferms at _____ at first, tho' partly _____ & too _____[713] O that I may walk by faith[714] & "in the Spirit".[715] If any man not X$^{t's}$ Spirit, none of his.[716] Again what infinite Cause for Gratitude have I, that such a wife I never saw that woman near so suitable, Praise y$^{e.}$ Lord. O let me not lower the Spiritual Mindedness of my.[717]

Wednesday Fast-Day 8:20, February 27, 1799, Pal Y$^{d.}$

Alas how cold & dead my Heart feels. My judgement condemning me but my sensibility dormant, and alas I feel myself lookg forward thro' the day as a long & tedious prospect if all to be spent in Offices of Religion. I have been meditatg & praying & bless God I am not so dead as I was. O what cause have I for Humiliation! What vanity, or compound of it I am, in doing good I cannot banish Love of praise from being powerful. But I will resume pen Evg when Eyes better & more Leisure. Resolve mens. mod. & ferms. that may not waste time, or opportun$^{s.}$ of doing & gettg Good, but be fervent in Spirit serving the Lord. O what mercies have we to be thankful for, yet how little are we conscious & affectingly & habitually sensible of them. Was for six or 7 years, yet what have I

---

708. Romans 15:13.

709. MS Wilberforce c. 41, fo. 125. Methodism came to Jersey and Guernsey some time after 1780, and persecution occurred within months of its appearance. In 1786 for example, Rev. Adam Clarke author of *Clarke's Commentaries*, was appointed to the islands, and experienced severe persecution. The house in which he preached was frequently surrounded by mobs, nearly destroyed and his life threatened. See for example, Josiah H. Barr, *Early Methodists under Persecution* (New York, Methodist Book Concern, 1916).

710. 'Amici fures temporis' is Latin: Friends the thieves of time.

711. Wilberforce may well be referring here to Henry Martyn (1781–1812), the Anglican chaplain to the East India Company, and missionary to India and Persia, whom he would meet again.

712. The Speaker of the House of Commons in 1799 was Henry Addington (1757–1844).

713. Several words here are illegible.

714. 2 Corinthians 5:7.

715. Galatians 5:16.

716. Romans 8:9.

717. MS Wilberforce c. 41, fo. 125, entry seems incomplete but entry ends with a horizontal line across the page.

suffered? O may I desire to praise God & X[t] & present Body & Soul a reasonable service of sacrifice.[718]

Sunday ¾ past 2, March 10, 1799, Pal Yard

The last 10 days I fear, but very poorly. Today I feel more spiritual than sometimes, but let me not be gov'd by frames & feelings but cherish a resolute determination for God & desire to serve him. O may I be able recover more time both for mental and physical Improvement. O what causes have I for Gratitude. Must stop. I may perhaps resume my pen.[719]

Sunday Night 10 oClock, March 10, 1799

I've been at Rowland Hill's[720] but have been dull & unspiritual. Poor Fernot, how in earnest. O how he shames me. Enable me, O God, for Christ's sake, to turn to thee. How little do I find in myself the glowg Spirit of a lively Xtian, faith working by love. O may I be renewed, warm'd, purified & fill'd with Love, peace & joy in the Holy Ghost. May I be active & unwearied in doing good[721] & improving my time &c. Amen. Live by faith above all. My dearest B loves Row Hill.[722]

Sunday 12 oClock, March 17, 1799, Pal Yard

Alas. My Heart seems little improv'd & hinder'd with Spiritual feelings & objects. My judgement apprehends but have no Sense, no practical feeling of divine things lively & habitually. What unXtian tempers have I felt this week. Anger about H. of Commons slights over Slave Bus[s] How little grateful for better Light. How little thankful for the great mercy of being raised up again from sickness for the Easements I then had, the Blessg. of a kind friend & a most tender Wife. O the mercies of God. O how secretly vain & self-complacent ab[t] being charitable. Tho' no necessary self-denial even when Mrs. Bow[r] wrong, she ag[t] it however. I hope & wo'd strive to grow in grace. How much more friendly Bankes to Auckland ab[t] Miss Eden & Wallace I wrong in Evil-Speakg. too loosely. O with what Shame do I look on my situatn, opportunities & faculties &c. think how little good I've done. Surely God wo'd bless me & my labouring more if I was earnest in waiting on him & livg by faith on X[t] & his Grace & Spirit. Oimoi. O enable me more to be a burng. & shing. light & let this Wish be less

---

718. Romans 12:1. MS Wilberforce c. 41, fo. 126.

719. MS Wilberforce c. 41, fo. 126.

720. Rowland Hill (1744–1833), powerful and popular evangelical preacher, a leading financial support of the London Missionary Society, a founder of the Religious Tract Society, and brother of Sir Richard Hill (1733–1808), and a friend of Wilberforce. Except for his disagreement with the Countess of Huntingdon it is thought that he might have become Whitefield's successor. An itinerant preacher for several years, he would attract crowds of up to 20,000 on his Scottish tours. He would divide much of his time between Gloucestershire and Surrey Chapel, the 3,000 seat center of Hill's ministry. It had thirteen Sunday schools with over 3,000 children; a Dorcas Society, helping poor married women; a clinic, at which he personally vaccinated thousands of children; and several other ministries.

721. Galatians 6:9.

722. MS Wilberforce c. 41, fo. 126.

alloyed with vanity & be more sincerely grateful & pious & humble
& love resulting.[723]

Good Friday Near 12 noon, March 22, 1799, Pal Yard
Not being well enough to go to Church safely, my dearest B.'s last night
commendg the old strict way of keepg Passion Week has bro't me to
serious Sense of y^e. Evil of so wastg precious opportunities & trifling with
the Bounty of God & X^t. alas. Just recover'd from dangerous Sickness
that evy motive, yet my askg Comp^y. yest^y was the real Result of my
wanting a deep practical Sense of the important & affectg Considerat^ns.
& feelings which this season sho'd inspire. Alas! Alas! I am indeed a
wretched Sinner & I sho'd not dare to look up for mercy but that X^t.
has died & that God invites us to be reconciled. O may the Spirit of
Grace & Truth then convince me more & more deeply of Sin, that I may
with the more unreserved & cordial faith embrace the Saviour in all his
Characters. Renew in me a clean Heart O God & a right Spirit.[724] Raise
my affections.[725] May I henceforth live under a more habitually lively
Sense of the mercies of X^t. & of my own Unworthiness of the Goodness
of God of the Joys of Heaven & of the pains of Hell, above all, may the
Love of X^t. constrain me[726] to live no longer to myself, but to him who
died & rose again. O may I be able to say, for me! May I present my Body
& Soul a livg Sacrifice, holy, acceptable to God, my most reasonable
Service.[727] May I also be most thankful for my dearest B., who has been
made the Instrument I hope of awakeng me from Sleep & revivg the
faintg principle of Grace. O may my Heart be fill'd with Love Joy peace
&c. &c.[728] & may the World be crucified to me & I to the World.[729] Vide
Withersp^n. 1st. Sermon.

Not duly tender to Bab^n. to Mrs. Dixon and other servants. Vain of
giving money. Not looking forward to this day and Easter Sunday as
I ought, but rather thinking of quitting Scripture Reading yesterday
because about to have so much of it. Also how little have I been
governed habitually by any higher practicals principle aputhena[730]
restrain, sense made up partly of religion but still more I fear of what
belonging to a proud character. How ashamed should I be if my heart
and its warmings could be known to others. How little have I been
prompted by a lively principle of love & fear & filial fear & love of God
& X^t. O may this contemplation impress me more deeply with a sense
of the corruptions which belong to me. May I walk softly,[731] work out

---

723. Ibid.
724. Psalm 51:10.
725. Colossians 3:2.
726. 2 Corinthians 5:14.
727. Romans 12:1.
728. Romans 15:13.
729. Galatians 6:14.
730. Word here uncertain.
731. Isaiah 38:15.

my salvation with fear & trembling,[732] relying on him who worketh in us &c.[733] I will try earnestly as far as health allows for earlier hours, 11 & 7 or 7 ½, & ½ or ¾ of an hour prayer & meditation, both morning & evening with Barbara & boys.[734]

Easter Sunday 9 ½ Evening, March 24, 1799

Alas! How extinguished did all my spirituality & even kindly affections seem yesterday. How cold & carnal & moiled, & today both at Church & elsewhere, little sense of divine things & yet I see that no other way. Help Lord, I perish.[735] I renew my Resolves & still I have more earnestly.[736]

Sunday 2 oClock, March 31, 1799, Broomfield

I hope this week's quiet has had some good effect on my Heart, enabling me a little to realize unseen things & live more in the fear of God. I feel today more of spirituality & of disposit[n.] to repose only on God for Security. But alas, on lookg back even durg this week, what Cause do I find for Humiliat[n.] & for callg for increase of Grace. How little love! How little Meekness Humility &c. How much Pride, anger, Roughness, tyranny &c. &c. even when not breakg forth, what way within. Bab[n.] was kind to me, in tellg me my faults. When shall I feel tow[ds.] him as I ought to do, & tow[ds.] Excell[t.] D[r.] T[n.] & tow[ds.] Serv[ts.] Alas! O cleanse me & I shall be clean. Renew my Heart O X[t.] at least. I bless thee that I am not blind to these remaining polluting corrupt[ns.] that I see & in some degree deplore them & strive ag[t.] them. O teach me to long more for the glorious Liby of the Child[n.] of God.[737] May X[t.] be & live & work in me.[738]

Sunday Evening 7 ½ oClock, March 31, 1799

Bab[n.] & Gisborne came soon after 3 & have sadly broken in upon us & have render'd day unprofitable. Oimoi. O my unspiritual Heart. Yet O God cleanse, raise, purify me.[739]

Sunday 2 ¾ oClock, April 14, 1799, Broomfield

Alas! My heart is cold and unspiritual today. How little disposed to do good or enjoy spiritual communion. This I hope partly bodily but not I fear, chiefly so.[740]

---

732. Philippians 2:12.
733. Ephesians 3:20.
734. MS Wilberforce c. 41, fo. 126.
735. Matthew 14:30.
736. MS Wilberforce c. 41, fo. 126.
737. Romans 8:21.
738. MS Wilberforce c. 41, fo. 127.
739. Ibid.
740. Ibid.

Sunday Evening 7 oClock, April 14, 1799

We have Lady Waldegrave & Stephen with us which checks spirituality. But alas! Allowing for this, how cold & stupid am I. How little under any due impression of the reality of unseen things. Alas! What pain I got on Tuesday night when that Explan[n.] with John & her giving me warning. May I fear wounded pride than concern for him or even sorrow for having been too fretful. But I humbly resolved by God's grace to amend my ways & trust I have amended. O may God through X[t.] & by the Spirit enable me now to live in faith & by love.[741]

Sunday 8 ¼ oClock, April 21, 1799, Broomfield

I hope I have been enabled to bridle my passions this week & be more meek & gentle & full of love, but alas! how little duly impressed with a sense of deep repentance & gratitude to God. How little endeavoring to live by faith on an unseen Saviour. O may I more & more grow in all Christian graces: love, fear, humility, meekness, diligence, heavenly-mindedness. Amen.[742]

Sunday 2 ¼ oClock, April 28, 1799, Broomfield

Alas! I am not what I ought to be, yet I humbly hope I look up with faith as the only way of obtaining all spiritual blessings, renouncing any other plea but Christ's merits & the Scripture promises. My evening prayers & exercises have been too hurried & abridged. O forgive, renew, warm, purify & fill me with joy & peace & love & humility & heavenly-mindedness.[743]

Saturday ¼ past 12, May 4, 1799, Broomfield

I have with some difficulty & management kept this day clear, to be a day set apart for humiliation & devotion. But alas! My body & mind & little famy. businesses intervene. Yet now after hearing & reading Bp. Atherston's last days & reading with B. since Bkft. for abstinence from food my body won't bear. I am about to fall to self-examination, & confession, & humiliation, looking into myself & condemning myself before God, & imploring forgiveness for Xt's sake. O what a terrible array of sins do I behold when I look back! Early renunciation off God, perhaps much hypocrisy in pretendg. when at Bay, more Relign. than I felt, but here is something against. I know not certainly but have a confused recollection of something of y[e.] kind. Then many years entirely sinful in the lusts of the flesh, both bodily & mental. Then, since the good providence of God drew me forth from this depth of iniquity & stopped me in my mad career in 1785 Autumn, thro' Milner's instrumentality, how little have I improved and grown in grace & therefore probably God has not more used & blessed me & enabled me to glorify him. Let me

---

741. Ibid.

742. MS Wilberforce c. 41, fo. 127. *Life,* ii. p. 333 has, 'I have been more able to bridle my passions, and be more meek and gentle, and really full of love.'

743. MS Wilberforce c. 41, fo. 127.

now humble myself, chiefly for forgetfulness of God, & Xt. & the Holy Spirit, & invisible things; for ingratitude to God, though loaded with mercies, recalled by sicknesses; a thousand gracious providences, and my marriage. such a happy one. And my Boy!!!!!!!!!

Then how defective in <u>love to God & man</u> & towards servants, my sister, even to B., Milner, H. Thornton, H. More & all my kind friends, Babington, &c. of whom never man had so many!!! Angry & fretful passions towards Serph[s.] & dependents, Sally &c. even to B.[744] Alas! Alas! Not improving opportunities of doing good in my particular situation by my influence, bodily & mental faculties, &c. &c. If I had waited on God continually & lived on him & Xt. by faith I should have brought forth more fruit 10 times 1000 times over. Yet how vain, secretly often of a little good done!!! Not attentive enough but sadly otherwise to spiritual good of servants, friends, &c!!! Often tho' I thank God less of late than formerly; sensual in eating & drinking & foolish exceedings which hurtful to health & ergo important. How little grateful to God for his multitudinous mercies!!!!! How often offending against strict truth, Alas! in pretending love & kindness which I have not really felt, enlarging in conversation, &c! Procrastination sadly given way to.

How much better probably would my servants have been, how many friends might I have been the means of rescuing or improving if I had duly watched & prayed & labored for their souls. How full of vanity, of valuing world's esteem, of pride, how vain of almsgiving. I go to prayer, humbly throwing myself on the promised mercies of God in Christ, Is. 61.1, 2, 3. Matthew 11 End. I will arise & go to my father.[745] I will also pray for all which I specially want vide supra[746] & praise God for his abundant mercies. Then resolve in prayer. What a blessed privilege to have a villa as a retreat.

O remember,[747] O my soul that except as thy sins blotted out by X[t.] God sees them all as fresh, as particular, as large, as black as ever, my early uncleanness. Even in 1796, Bishop Landaff, Babington & Sister unkind.[748] Falsehood in promising constituents both practical & general, more diligent attention, punctual &c. than I have been. Not counting opinions of doing good pointed out by providence, following Samuel Halyburton &c. &c. &c. &c. O if I could see into the heart & life through as I do my own, how dubious at the least sho'd I be of such an one's state except that I hope. I humbly despair of self & fly to thee O Xt.

Perhaps many of my servants might have been turning to God, some gone from me, some dead. Poor Walter.[749] Friends too much grave. Poor

---

744. Wilberforce wrote, 'Serph[s.] dependents, Sally &c. even to B.' in Greek letters.

745. Luke 15:18.

746. Latin: see above.

747. 'Hum[n.] & Resol[n.] to amend metanoia', is written here in the left margin. Wilberforce wrote 'metanoia' in Greek letters.

748. Wilberforce wrote, 'Bishop Landaff, Babington & Sister' in Greek letters.

749. In his Spiritual Journals, Wilberforce mentions three of his household servants, George in 1796, and Walter and John here in 1799.

mother twas as not duly careful ab[t.] I fear by anger & fretfulness I have produced a prejudice in servants' minds against religion & a neglect at least, tending to undervalue holy tempers &c. How little have I lived a life of prayer & watchfulness & diligent self-examination & humble devoting of myself to & drawing support from Xt. in the winter of 1785, 6 & this was my course.[750]

Sunday Night 9 oClock, May 5, 1799, 9 oClock, Broomfield[751]

Today I have been but in a middling state of mind. Sadly sleepy at church this evening, bodily I hurt in pain. O may God thro' Xt. enable me to amend my ways, to live a life of faith & prayer. <u>Humble, devout</u>, full of meekness & love, intent on friends' spiritual good, earlier hours, morning & thereby prayer & meditation time. Kind to servants,[752] sister[753] &c. Looking unto Jesus.[754] Striving against vanity. Strict truth. Cultivating heavenly-mindedness & living & walking in the Spirit. Amen. Forgetfulness of God, Doddridge (Vide) *Life* 266 (L 8 Sect 8).[755]

Sunday Night, 9 oClock, May 12, 1799, Broomfield

Alas! I find my heart cold & dead & flat. Today I received Sacrament but how cold & dead was I. I have Mr. Ford on Halyburton with me but I get nothing good to him. O God, do thou by Xt. enlighten me & quicken me. O may I attain what is real in Christian experience, without running into a sect, or party set of opinions. O may I feel my heart renewed & assimilated to Xt. by grace.[756]

Sunday Night ¾ past 9, May 19, 1799

My heart has been moved by the society of my old friends at Pitt's. Alas! Alas! how sad to see them thoughtless of their immortal souls; so wise, so acute! I hope I felt in some degree properly on the occasion &

---

750. MS Wilberforce c. 41, fo. 127. *Life*, ii. pp. 333-334 has, 'Saturday at Broomfield all day. I meant it to be a day devoted to God. The morning serious, by myself, though not so completely as I had wished. I had refused several friends, but Carlyle came suddenly with offer about Lord Elgin, and compelled to see him. I have with some difficulty and management kept this day clear, to be set apart for humiliation and devotion, and such abstinence as my body will bear. I am now about to fall to self-examination, and confession, and humiliation; looking into myself; condemning myself before God, and imploring forgiveness for Christ's sake. Oh what a terrible array of sins do I behold when I look back! Early renunciation of God; then, many years entirely sinful; then, since the good providence of God drew me forth from this depth of iniquity in the autumn of 1785, how little have I improved and grown in grace! Let me now humble myself, chiefly for forgetfulness of God, and Christ, and the Holy Spirit, and invisible things; for ingratitude to God, though loaded with mercies, recalled by sicknesses; … a thousand gracious providences! I go to prayer, humbly throwing myself on the promised mercies of God in Christ.'

751. MS Wilberforce c. 41, fos. 127-128.

752. Written in Greek letters.

753. Written in Greek letters.

754. Hebrews 12:2.

755. Then line at end of entry hard to decipher but includes, 'To realize God's and Christ's presence.'

756. MS Wilberforce c. 41, fo. 128. *Life*, ii. p. 334 has, 'Though, I thank God, I am less sensual than I was, yet I find my heart cold and flat. Today I received the sacrament, but how dead was I! O God, do Thou enlighten me. May I attain what is real in Christian experience, without running into a sect, or party set of opinions.'

afterwards. O that I might feel more, & act more, & be more useful. O God bless me through X[757]

Sunday 7 oClock, May 26, 1799, Broomfield

I must not be long but shortly. I have much cause for humiliation on many grounds. Alas! Alas! how little love & fear of God do I feel. How little true zeal last night. I continued reading Booth instead of going to Scripture & God punished me deservedly but in mercy. Also this week much in company, time frittered away, little effectual done. Heals? Activity shames me, I am a poor creature. O may God give me wisdom, zeal, love of God & man. More gratitude for unequalled mercies. How forcibly does Mrs. Parry's danger impress on me the uncertainty of human life & prepares my soul for whatever may happen. Alas! I dare not flatter myself that I feel that spiritual taste which makes other things flat & insipid compared with the excellency of knowledge of X[t.] I fear I could be content to live always here, if in bodily ease & circumstances of comfort as now. I dare not say I groan under my corruptions feeling the burthen of them. O Lord, do thou soften my heart & fill me with a trembling conviction of my own ungrateful sloth & ineptitude and aversation in spiritual things.[758]

Sunday 10 ¼ oClock, June 2, 1799, Broomfield

Alas! Alas! I am but a nominal Xtian. Little better having only a name to live.[759] Oimoi. How little am I living a self-denying, watchful, humble, penitent & spiritual life. How little finding my chief delight in communion with my Saviour & living under an habitual sunset of his grace & love. O may I now henceforth devote myself more gratefully to God in X[t.760]

Sunday 2 ¼ oClock, June 2, 1799

Alas! I am sadly unspiritual yet I throw myself at the feet of God & thro' & by a loving Saviour, desiring I hope to be delivered from the bondage as well as punishment of sin. O how penitent & contrite I should be. I will humbly resolve thro' grace & pray to be enabled to keep my resolution to lead a new life in the fear & love of God & by the faith of unseen things. O Saviour of sinners who art now making intercession, pity & deliver me.[761]

Sunday Night 9 oClock, June 2, 1799

Strange to say this very day, rising from prayer & going to dinner, exceeded dessert, self-denial forsook. Stomach disordered. Oimoi. O may God strengthen me. To thee I fly.[762]

---

757. MS Wilberforce c. 41, fo. 128. *Life*, ii. p. 334 has, 'My heart has been moved by the society of my old friends at Pitt's. Alas! Alas! how sad to see them thoughtless of their immortal souls; so wise, so acute! I hope I felt in some degree properly on the occasion and afterwards; oh that I might feel more, and act more, and be more useful, may God bless me through Christ.'

758. MS Wilberforce c. 41, fo. 128.

759. Revelation 3:1.

760. MS Wilberforce c. 41, fo. 128.

761. Ibid.

762. Ibid.

Sunday 3 oClock, June 9, 1799, Broomfield

Alas! Alas! this week has gone on too much like former ones & having been a little imprudent in dessert yesterday. I am very indifferent from it, more than I could have conceived. Alas! yesterday. Wrangham[763] &c. with me. How full of vanity. How little exhibiting the natural character of a humble, circumspect Xtian. Long should such an one as I appear to object to him or not prefer him. O may I be enabled to lead a new life by faith, watching unto prayer, improving in knowledge & love of God & X[t.] & sighing & crying for the prevalent abominations. O may I be a real Xtian constrained by love of him who died for me.[764] Hear me, O Lord, visit me with thy effectual grace.[765]

Monday, June 17[th.] 1799

Better, but still kept unwillingly from London. Little done, but today serious thoughts on loving God and Christ, and prayer, Leighton, &c.[766]

Sunday Evening 9 ¼ oClock, June 23, 1799, Broomfield

I can't write largely from y[e.] want of time, but let me briefly note my today's frame of mind which I bless God, better than for some time past but since Tuesday last. May I hope that the Leisure & Season & Space for Recollection afforded by my late indispositn has been the blessed means of revivg what was dead of Xtian Hope & faith. Yet O how languid are they still with me. What cause have I for earnest prayer & diligent Readg of Scripture, & constant Watchfulness & Self-Examination. O Lord God, have mercy upon me, & for the Redeemer's Sake receive me & supply me out of the fulness which is in Xt. that I may go on from Grace to Grace & Strength to Strength. I bless God I enjoyed the 2 Hours Interval bet[n.] Church & Dinner more than for many a day past with B, walkg, reading musing, part alone, in prayer & meditn. in arundinia. Then this af[tn.] I hope very edifying talk with S[pr.] Lillingston,[767] who seems truly in earnest. O God, how little do I deserve all y[e.] Honour thou puttest upon me, but may I be more active in thy Service & live more by faith, doing all to the Glory of God, & in the name of the Lord Jesus, givg thanks to the Father thro' him.[768]

---

763. The Venerable Francis Wrangham (1769–1842), Anglican Archdeacon of the East Riding of Yorkshire, was also a prolific author, translator and an ardent supporter of abolition, whose daughter, Agnes, would marry William Wilberforce's son Robert Isaac. He also advocated for the education of women, charity schools and hospitals, and Christian missions. Several of his poems won various prizes. He also attended Hull Grammar School, as did William Wilberforce.

764. 2 Corinthians 5:14.

765. MS Wilberforce c. 41, fo. 128.

766. Ibid.

767. Abraham Spooner Lillingston (1770–1834), son of Isaac and Barbara Spooner, and brother of Barbara who married William Wilberforce. Abraham married Elizabeth Lillingston, the only child of Luke Lillingston, whose family home was Elmdon, near Warwick. Abraham assumed Elizabeth's family name.

768. Colossians 3:17. MS Wilberforce c. 41, fo. 129. *Life*, ii. p. 339 has, 'My frame of mind better, I bless God, than for some time past. I hope that the leisure, and season, and space for recollection afforded by my late indisposition, has been the blessed means of reviving what was

Sunday Night ½ past 9 oClock, July 14, 1799

Alas, how cold have I been all day, Alas! Alas! Tho' my judgement decidedly for God, yet my Heart hard & torpid. O God! quicken me by thy Grace, & O Merciful Saviour enable me to walk more worthily of thee. I am now commencing a long Vacat[n] O may I employ it to the Glory of God, using well my time, talents, Influence &c. Today alas at dinner too full & excdg ferms for serious Tho't & spiritual-mindedness, Oimoi, Oimoi, & sleepy at Church. O may I be more spiritual & watch unto prayer.[769]

Sunday, July 21[st.] 1799

Praise the Lord, O my soul for all his goodness. My life is overflowing with mercies, yet alas! I am too little corresponding to the great goodness of my God! But I humbly resolve to press forward to the prize of my high calling[770] and O might I bear in mind that glorious promise, Let him that is athirst come and let him that will take of the Water of Life freely.[771] My dearest B. is at this moment in labor here, little do I seem to feel. Poor dear girl, I trust God & her Saviour support and comfort her. I can't truly say that should it please God to take her hence, I should entertain no doubt of her safety, of her being taken to Glory. O that I were as sure of myself, but may I lay aside every weight[772] & press onwards.

The recess is beginning. Oh may I spend it well, & try more & more to devote my understanding, & heart, & all my faculties & powers, to the glory of God & X[t.] being more & more weaned from vanity, & the love of this world's praise, yet more & more active, useful, indefatigable, adorning the doctrine of &c.[773] O for more gratitude & love. Heard today of a clergyman in the Isle of Wight,[774] to whom my book was blessed, by Samuel Thornton. Oh praise, praise![775]

---

dead of Christian hope and faith. Yet, oh how languid are they still! What cause have I for earnest prayer, and diligent reading of Scripture, and constant watchfulness and self-examination!'

769. MS Wilberforce c. 41, fo. 129.

770. Philippians 3:14.

771. Revelation 22:17.

772. Hebrews 12:1.

773. Titus 2:10.

774. Rev. Legh Richmond (1772–1827), evangelical Anglican minister and writer. He attributed his conversion to evangelical beliefs to his reading of Wilberforce's *Practical Christianity*, even naming one of his sons Wilberforce. Richmond is especially remembered for his three famous tales of village life *The Annals of the Poor* (1814). In 1805, he became briefly assistant chaplain to the London Lock Hospital, the chapel of which institution Wilberforce would often worship. He was a member of many societies, including the British and Foreign Bible Society, the Church Missionary Society, and the London Society for Promoting Christianity amongst the Jews.

775. MS Wilberforce c. 41, fo. 129. *Life*, ii. p. 341 has, 'The recess is beginning. Oh may I spend it well, and try more and more to devote my understanding, and heart, and all my faculties and powers, to the glory of God and Christ, being more and more weaned from vanity, and the love of this world's praise, yet more and more active, useful, indefatigable, adorning the doctrine of God our Savior. Oh for more gratitude and love. Heard today of a clergyman in the Isle of Wight, [Rev. Legh Richmond] to whom my book was blessed. Oh praise, praise!'

Sunday ½ past 2 oClock, July 28, 1799, Broomfield

My heart is not what it ought to be. Alas! what room for improvement, yet O Lord God, thou art represented as giving to all liberally &c., to thee therefore I look up thro' X$^{t.}$ with hope, humbly imploring through X$^{t.}$ thy renewing grace, that I may be filled with the real Xtian love which may long train me to live the longer &c. I go to prayer. O what cause have I for gratitude, my dearest B. died not. She & little girl well. Poor Stephen too ardent but how kind & generous & in many respects right-minded. O guide us & direct us & teach us to remember practically that the time is short. Guide me also to usefulness, O Lord. I'm ashamed being so unprofitable a servant. O may I amend here. Alas! Alas! O Christ, help me by thy Spirit.[776]

Sunday 2 oClock, August 25, 1799, Broomfield

O the grace and mercy of Christ which are still ready for me, a poor, persevering sinner, who have so long trifled with the concerns of my soul's salvation. I could not be quiet yesterday, & even today I have less time than I could wish for looking back thro' the year & awaken pious gratitude for the multiplied mercies of God. How often have I been sick & restored! How few if any days of pain & suffering either bodily or mental! My wife & my child W$^{m.}$[777] going on well, & Barbara[778] born & doing well! Instances repeatedly heard of, of my Book doing good! How gracious is God in X$^{t.}$ so to fill my Cup with Blessings yet not to lessen or commute in what still more important. But I dare not say I have attain'd. Alas! Alas! I know not what to think of myself I can only resolve by the Grace of X$^{t.}$ to press forwd, assured that all who wait on him shall renew thr Strength, & that whosoever is really athirst shall have the Water of Life to drink freely.[779] I go to prayer being straiten'd in time.[780]

Sunday Night 9 ¾ oClock, August 25, 1799

I was soon interrupted alas by Ld. Elgin who going next morng to _____[781] I could have refus'd to see him but vex'd. Milner has now been readg Baxter's sermon on self examinat$^{n.}$ to us, a truly humbling one to me. O Lord God give me peace & pardon thro' X$^{t.}$ Change me. Renew me. O X$^{t.}$ hear me. I go to prayer.[782]

---

776. MS Wilberforce c. 41, fo. 129.

777. William Wilberforce, Jr. (1798–1879).

778. Barbara Wilberforce (1799–1821).

779. Revelation 22:17.

780. MS Wilberforce c. 41, fo. 129. *Life*, ii. p. 344 has, 'I could not be quiet yesterday though I got a contemplative walk, and even today I have less time than I could wish for looking back through the year, and awakening pious gratitude for the multiplied mercies of God. How often have I been sick and restored! How few, if any, days of suffering, either bodily or mental! My wife and child going on well, and a daughter born (July 21st) and doing well. Instances repeatedly heard of my book doing good. How gracious is God "through Christ, to fill my cup with blessings, yet not to lessen or commute in what is still more important!" Milner preached his Buxton Sermon on Christianity's corruptions. All serious persons much struck with it. Afternoon, Milner and I talked about Carlyle's affair. Much difficulty about his money. Then disputed with Milner about final perseverance.'

781. Word illegible.

782. MS Wilberforce c. 41, fo. 129.

Sunday Evening ½ past 7, September 15, 1799, Marlbro

Alas! Alas! I have too little cause to look on myself with any complacency. How little do I seem to love God & X[t.] I am now 40 years of age & more, yet how little advanced do I seem in the Xtian life. Alas, how much more earnest & anxious ab[t.] appearg myself in the sight of man than of God. How uneasy ab[t.] the Speaker &c. O it is such incidents as these which shew me the Hollowness of my Heart, again at Teston. How little warm Love of God, or of man. How little zealous desire & Endeavour to do Good to others who with us. I have now a long period before me, & I hope I may be enabled to make it a Season of more Quiet. O may I spend my time profitably, & above all, may I grow in Grace, in Love and be made more meet to be a partaker of y[e.] Inheritance of the Saints in Light.[783]

Sunday ½ past 2, September 22, 1799

Alas. I am a poor Creature. How flat do I feel today. How little real Earnestness & Longing for spiritual food. O what Cause have I to pray and Strive for Improvement & Growth in Grace, for I find myself low & weak in Love, either of God or X[t.] or fellow Creatures. How much more spiritual poor B.[784]

Thursday, October 3[rd.] 1799

For some days I have resolv'd to endeavour to allot this day to God, to spiritual Exercises, especially in the Way of Humiliatn. I got up at my usual time & have been hearg Doddridge's & readg way of managing these seasons. Fasting disqualifies me, <u>God knoweth</u> for relig[s.] Communion by disorderg my Body, so all I can do here is to be <u>very temperate</u> especy in ferms. I have <u>rather</u> wasted time this morng from want of a plan & of a Book ready to hear & read. I now am <u>in fact</u> beginning the day. Let me make it in part a Substitute for my Birthday in which sadly hurried & interrupted. I am now likewise about as it seems, but let me remember how uncertain are all earthly prospects, to spend near 4 months <u>quietly</u> compared with my past Life, wherein I shall be able to attend to my Health, which next to my Soul's prosperity, it seems right to make my chief Object, & at the same time to study a good deal & cultivate faculties my neglect of which I number among my very criminal omissions. My objects therefore in this day of solemn supplic[n.] & in my measure fasting &c., to beg God's Guidance & Blessing on my Endeavours to spend the ensuing Interval bet[n.] this day & Parl[ts.] Meetg piously, usefully, wisely, holily. First however humbly imploring pardon for all my past manifold Offences which to be particy noted, & earnestly supplicatg for Grace to deliver me from y[e.] Bondage of my Corruptions. After Humiliation & Supplicat[n.] should surely come praise & Thanksgiving for the multiplied & prodigious Mercies & Blessings of God.[785] Then lastly Intercession.

---

783. Colossians 1:12. MS Wilberforce c. 41, fo. 129.

784. MS Wilberforce c. 41, fo. 130.

785. Here he inserted an 'H' sign, to indicate an insertion of text from below.

To prepare me for Humiliat[n.] & indeed all y[c.] rest, let me open by earnestly prayg to God thro' Xt. by y[e.] Spirit to bless me in my present attempt, to chase away from me all Evil Spirits, all Wanderg thoughts, all worldly Interruptions & to soften & enlighten & warm & enlarge & sustain my Heart & my Spirits. Also, that I may not weary in the work, but delight in it, & rejoice in the privilege of spendg a day in Communion with my God & Saviour. H.[786] Then Resignation & Self-Dedicat[n.] to God, desiring to submit myself to him, to do & suffer his Will. Confession, for which Self-Exam[n.] vide page 127, 8 for Sins of Boyish years, youth & Even Manhood & since 1785, 1786. Even of late I have too much Cause to bewail my Sins tow[ds.] God, Neighbor, Self. What reproaches do I find on lookg at my other Book Pa 9,10,11 for Table of Duties. Forgetfulness of & Coldness tow[d.] God,[787] Xt. & the Spirit. Private Devotions curtail'd, Scripture carelessly read & wandering & cold particy of late & in Evg. Public Dev[ns.] Also wanderg. Evil Spirit forgotten & holy Angels, mens. Gratitude very little. Company & conv[n.] Regls. sad & friends spirit[l.] Good sadly neglected. Fretfulness pride & unkindness old sin to my mother, to Sally, Stephen, Servants & Even B. & poor little W[m.]

Affecting Superiority instead of Golden Rule. Evil Speakg sadly offendg, alas ab[t.] manifd the other day. How little genuine Love, enlarging & warmg my Heart. Then as to Self. How often Truth violated. Envy felt & a Sort of longing for worldly Enjoyment, and dignities. Above all, Vanity & Emulation & Love of human praise. It is my master passion. Humility little cultivat'd.

How little my own peculiar Character consider'd & the obligat[ns.] it brings on me. How little Heavenly-Mindedness. What secret grudging God a day often. Even as to this very day. Self-Denial forgot. How much disposition to Self-Indulgence. How little hardening of my mind ag[t.] Pain or Shame or Whatever God may call me to. Alas! What Ingratitude to God & X[t.] Ingratitude to, Unmindfulness of a Crucified <u>Saviour</u>. Then to go back to Duties to others again. Parliamenty Duties & Obligatns, as to studies, diligence &c. sadly neglected. Intercess[n.] forgotten. I seem to feel no Love for others, to have so selfish a Heart, that I care not for my Country or Even for my nearest & dearest friends! How strange this. Here interrupted by my poor B.'s being sadly worried & flurried which has overcome her tender weak spirits & I have been cherishing & comforting her.[788]

Thursday 12:10, October 3, 1799

Now I resume my Self Exam[n.] & Humil[n.] & desire in conjunction with my Sins to consider the peculiar mercies of God to me, & above all the miracles of mercy in X[t's] Death & Sufferings. When these things are well

---

786. Then here is the 'H' sign and the following paragraph which he has circled around.
787. Here in left margin he wrote 'fault'.
788. MS Wilberforce c. 41, fo. 132.

contemplated, how astonishg how monstrous is Ingratitude. Revenge also & anger, too perceptible, tho I hope striven against.[789] Too little candor in judging (Danberry, Pitt, Sugar Bus[s]). Vanity as to givg away Money in Charity, often detected in myself, & in almost all I do, say or think. Alas! Alas!

Continued in prayer till ab[t] 1. _____[790] fermented & contemplated my Sins & a little my Obligations to God & X[t] & prayed for various Blessings and Imprimes for Reconciliat[n] & a new Heart. Soon after 1 went to Pump Room, where kept a little by people, read Letters &c. B.'s dinner & W[m] a little hinder'd me. I scarcely seem'd kind enough to sister but did not mean to be otherwise, but my mind grieved. O I should strive ag[t] peevishness more on days when my mind thus tender'd & humbled & I am grieved & vexed at Interruptions from abt. 1¾ readg Witherspoon's Sermon on View of God humbling,[791] & aft[ds] more prayer for Grace which till now.[792]

Thursday 2:50, October 3, 1799

O how sadly my Heart is under the power of Sin, but I look with humble Hope to the promises of Scripture, Ho Evyone that thirsteth &c.[793] Let him that is athirst come &c.[794] Ask, Seek, Knock &c.[795] & <u>as I live</u> saith the Lord, I have no pleasure in the death of a Sinner,[796] & If any man lacks Wisdom &c.[797] whoever willeth let him take of the Water of the foun[tn] of <u>Life freely</u>.[798] I pray to be enabled to observe a due medium between undue[799] conformity with the world & excessive separation & peculiarity. How much does keeping Love in exercise keep all y[e] rest Right & produce a sweet demeanour which will palliate & excuse many failings & Instances of reproachg _____[800] shews a difference from worldly people or neglect them.

It is now ab[t] 9 in the Evg. I have been to Jay's, but alas I was so drowsy great part of the time, that I lost what pass'd. O God forgive me. X[t] forgive me. Let me now go to prayer, in particular Intercession & Thanksgiving.[801]

---

789. In left margin at this point he wrote, 'Faults'.
790. Word illegible.
791. See *The Works of John Witherspoon*, as detailed in footnote 196.
792. MS Wilberforce c. 41, fo. 132.
793. Isaiah 55:1.
794. Revelation 22:17.
795. Matthew 7:7.
796. Ezekiel 33:11.
797. James 1:5.
798. Revelation 22:17.
799. A word has been crossed out here and 'undue' is inserted above it.
800. Word illegible.
801. MS Wilberforce c. 41, fo. 133. *Life*, ii. p. 351 has, 'For some time I have resolved to allot this day to God; to spiritual exercises, especially in the way of humiliation. Fasting disqualifies me, God knoweth, for religious communion by disordering my body, so all I can do here is to be very temperate. I am now about, as it seems, ... but let me remember how uncertain are all earthly prospects, ... to spend near four months quietly, compared with my past life; wherein I shall be able

Sunday Night near 9, October 6, 1799, Gay Street Bath

I bless God the occupat[n.] of Thursday[802] last has not been wholly in vain. My Heart has felt more of the power of Religion; yet alas how little & jestg rather offended ferms, when dg Bridges & Stephen with me. Unfit for Ejaculat[n.] unprofitable visit to Duchess of Leeds,[803] perhaps from that very Cause. Today my Heart has been but in bad State, but this Evg at Jay's I have rather enjoyed the Sermon & was able to attend better than usual. O how ought I to strive to live to God's Glory, having been hitherto so unprofitable a Servant. O may my time, my fortune, my Understanding, & all my Talents be more diligently improved, but may the one thing needful[804] be the Grand Concern with me, & let not my Heart be overcharged with Lusts of other things. Love of Estimation, of Praise, of Knowledge &c. But may I grow in Love, Humility & Heavy Mindedness. Amen. Amen. Even so O L[d.] Jesus, by thy Spirit.[805]

Sunday Night 8 ¾, October 13, 1799, Gay Street

This last week better than sometimes, yet very poorly. Alas! O how little spiritual mindedness. Sadly worried by people, not a due degree of Xtian Love. My Eyes bad. I go to prayer. O that I were as solicitous to grow in Grace as in Knowledge & power of doing good. There is much probable Self-deception in the latter. Help me O God to desire to do or suffer thy Will. Jay has been excellent on the mercies of X[t.] to the penitent Thief. My dearest B. is thoroughly in earnest. O let me press forw[d.] with renewed vigour, laying aside every weight, &c.[806] & growg in Heavenly mindedness & Love & Joy & Evy Xtian Grace.[807]

Sunday[808] 2 ¾ oClock, October 27, 1799, Gay Street

Alas! Alas! I am indeed a poor unfruitful unthriving Christian. How yesterday discover'd the Hardness pride & deceit of my Heart tow[ds.] even my poor B. who all Humility & tenderness tho' from serious weakness culpable. Thus thro' this week, how little real Love of X[t.] or real spiritual mindedness! I must change my Course & obtain it by Violence, more

---

to attend to my health, which, next to my soul's prosperity, it seems right to make my chief object; and at the same time to study a good deal, and cultivate faculties, my neglect of which I number among my very criminal omissions. My objects therefore in this day of solemn supplication and (in my measure) fasting, are to beg God's guidance and blessing on my endeavors to spend the ensuing interval between this time and the meeting of parliament, piously, usefully, wisely, holily; first, however, humbly imploring pardon for all my past manifold offences, which to be particularly noted, and earnestly supplicating for grace to deliver me from the bondage of my corruptions. Then should come praise and thanksgiving, for the multiplied and prodigious mercies and blessings of God. Then resignation and self-dedication to God, desiring to submit myself to him to do and suffer his will. Lastly, intercession.'

802. Some word has been partly written over by 'Thurs' with the rest of 'day' still being used.

803. Catherine Anguish married Francis Osborne, the 5th Duke of Leeds, in 1788. The Duke died in January 1799, and the dowager Duchess of Leeds died 1837.

804. Luke 10:42.

805. MS Wilberforce c. 41, fo. 133.

806. Hebrews 12:1.

807. MS Wilberforce c. 41, fo. 133.

808. Inserted in left margin here, he wrote, '2¾ oClock'.

Quiet. Bless me O God. Gordon is in Bath I must see him. O may I be a real vital Xtian & then such visits will even be profitable & edifying.[809]

Sunday[810] Night, October 27, 1799

What a Lesson of Humility has my dearest B exhibited to me & of tenderness, on account of her little grievg of me yesterday. How again & again did she beg my pardon & never be enough vex'd at herself & humbled. O that I may be duly thankful for such a treasure. Tonight how sad a Sermon on Habb$^{k.}$ 3:17 Tho' y$^{e.}$ fig tree &c. all on the virtue & vice plan. X$^{t.}$ forgotten. The 2$^{d.}$ Lesson, Galatians 6$^{th.}$ at the Free Church. Alas! Alas! O how wanderg was I in the prayers. How cold am I now but I go to prayer & will still pray with hope & reliance on the promises of Scripture.[811]

Sunday Night near 11 oClock, November 3, 1799, Lambridge

This day, tho' to my Grief & Shame, I found myself ready to say, at least inwardly saying, what shall I do, when will it be over has run away insensibly & I have had little prayer or readg. Tis now late. Eyes bad. So I will lay down pen. I have felt I hope some Humiliatn today partic'y at Sact & desire to amend & devote myself to God. O may I be enabled to live more a life of faith & diligent & active Devotedness to God's Service. Heavy minded humble full of Love peace & Joy in the Holy Ghost. Amen.[812]

Sunday Night 8 oClock, November 10, 1799, Lambridge

I have been sadly unspiritual in Heart today. Little or no apparent Love of God or Joy in him & X$^{t.}$ in the Hope of a Xtian. Alas! Alas! How cold my affections, yet I have been spendg this week diligently, too much however I fear in a worldly Spirit. Too little Scripture readg, too little habitual Livg by faith, Prayer, Meditat$^{n.}$ O may I have my Conversation in Heaven[813] & my affections set on things above,[814] looking for the coming of our Lord Jesus Xt.[815]

Sunday Evening 7½ oClock, November 17, 1799, Lambridge

I have been but cold today & unspiritual & flat, except in prayer in morng. Sleepy in Church this aft$^{n.}$ I hope this bodily for both in dan$^{r.}$ & ferms careful. This week has been diligently spent. I hope I am livg with a view to God's favour tho' alas how weak is my faith. How <u>much</u> do I need to make me a thrivg flourishg Xtian. If God was thinkg of it, should see fit to try me with sharp afflictions like Mr. Babn especially with bodily pain; I fear I sho'd find myself sadly put to it. But let me live by faith & pray to God to animate my hope & to raise my desires &

809. MS Wilberforce c. 41, fo. 133.
810. Inserted in left margin here, he wrote, '2¾ oClock'.
811. MS Wilberforce c. 41, fo. 133.
812. MS Wilberforce c. 41, fo. 134.
813. Philippians 3:20.
814. Colossians 3:2.
815. 2 Peter 3:12. MS Wilberforce c. 41, fo. 134.

views to Heavy things that I may devote myself here to God in X[t.] thro' the Spirit & at length dwell with him forever. I go to prayer.[816]

Sunday Evening 8 oClock, December 15, 1799, Lambridge

This day has hurried away & Barker's Intercession has preoccupied the time I had destined to Self Conversatn. I must be very short. The last month has hurried away insensibly. I have lived quietly; but this almt incessant going to Bath, which places me in Compy at Relaxn Hours, cuts off that relig[s.] Relaxn. always so beneficial to me. I have been reading hard for me: But not thinkg enough, or composing. I get little done. Evgs close in fast & prayer is too often abridged & Scripture prevented in part or even in whole. My Heart is little turned to God, alas. I am sadly defective in Love in Zeal, in Spiritual Mindedness. O quicken me by thy Grace & guide me to right objects, & enable me to prosecute them with purity of Interest with Wisdom diligence & persevering Zeal. And may I grow in Love & Humility & Meekness & Benev[ce.] & Evry Xtian Grace.[817]

Sunday 11½ oClock, December 22, 1799

My Bowels being[818] out of order I thought it dangerous to go out into the Cold with motion also immediately after O, when serious threatenings, so I stay from church. My dearest B. tenderness in all, she sadly agreed to go without me, unwilling but submitting to me. Alas! Alas! How little is my Heart right before God. How low am I in Love of God or Man, of X[t.] the[819] Saviour.[820]

For some time, priv[e.] devot[ns.] in Evg sadly rushed over & even in Morng bad from being tir'd at night & takg them last thing. Script[e.] Readg neglected, & alas! How is the Result what might be expected. Tho' my judgement be right, how little are my affections so. Tow[ds.] God, how little habitual Reverence Gratitude, Desire, Admiration, Trust &c. Towds. X[t.] alas! the Spirit! Then in myself, vide supra,[821] & my neighbour. How little Regl. for Spir[l.] Good! O my God, I go to prayer. I am dead, quicken thou me by thy Grace, thro' the Spirit, for X[t's] Sake. Make me a new Creature, renewed in Knowledge & Love & beholdg the Glory & chang'd into the Image of our Lord. I have been praying to God thro' X[t.] & I will humbly trust to his promises, Ho! Every one that thirsteth.[822] Let him that is athirst &c.[823] Come unto me all that Labour & are heavy laden &c.[824]

O may I be strengthen'd with might by the Spirit in the Inner man, that X[t.] may dwell in my Heart by faith &c.[825] O may I grow in Grace

---

816. MS Wilberforce c. 41, fo. 134.

817. Ibid.

818. The word 'daily' has been crossed out here.

819. MS Wilberforce c. 41, fo. 134.

820. MS Wilberforce c. 41, fo. 135.

821. Latin: see above.

822. Isaiah 55:1.

823. Revelation 22:17.

824. Matthew 11:28.

825. Ephesians 3:17.

& be filled with all the fulness of God. Amen. Amen. Keep me humble circumspect watchful. I humbly hope to endeavour. I scarcely dare resolve so often, have I been foil'd <u>to read Scripture more Seriously</u> (Evg & a <u>little</u> medit[n.] Morng.) <u>Think much of God X[t.] Holy Spirit Evil Spirit, Of Heav'n & Hell Angels &c.</u> 3 To cultivate <u>Humility Love Meekness. 1. Prayer less distraction & more serious & Earlier Evening, Malachi. 2.</u> Truth Peace Joy, Self-denial & Spiritual-Mindedness, <u>Vanity</u> Candour, Kindness, Evil Speakg, Care & Envy & Anger & Revenge & <u>Vanity</u> Diligence, Improvg time, Relax[n.] &c. doing all to Glory of God.[826] Love, Desire, Gratitude, Trust, Venerat[n.] Humiliation. Compy & Conv[n.] Regls. What good. Rational &c. Friends' Spir[l.] Good. Alas! How little the right feelings ab[t.] flattery &c. Vanity &c. Let me strive to increase my <u>Sense of the Evil of Sin</u>. Here my great defect as indeed the general one. O may I strive to improve here, vide Scott on Repentance.[827]

Wednesday Xmas Day 7½ oClock, December 25, 1799, Lambridge[828]

Alas! Both Monday & yesterday Evg. (the latter with more reason) did not retire for Devot[ns.] before Supper & little Scripture Readg & little if at all better in other things than before. I was much struck today with the Text, God hath <u>chosen</u> the foolish things of y[e.] world[829] &c. & with the argument thence afforded for particular Redemption tho' not for irresistible Grace. O God & Saviour, Bless & sanctify me & enable me to be an active & thriving Believer, doing all to Glory of God.[830]

1800

Sunday Evening, January 5, 1800, Lambridge

I could not well obtain Quiet on Jany. 1[st.] Last year has been mark'd with mercies to me. B. bringing forth her child B who well, ag[t.] probability. Spooner Lillingston I hope in earnest. Alas! I dare not say I have gain'd ground. My Head rather aches therefore I must not write. I humbly confess my Sins before thee O God, the same as before particy Readg of Scripture & Devot[ns.] Curtail'd & former often omitted Love of God & Xt. Cold. I humbly devote myself to God in Xt. & beseech him by his Spirit to bless me & renew me & enable me to live to his Glory.

After prayer this morning I had some Religious Sensib[y.] But this Evg tho' very careful & moderate ab[t.] dinner yet how dull & unfeeling. My understandg tells me I ought to be affect'd, but alas I am not so. How testy & angry often to Sister. How selfish discover'd in Respect of B. Alas! When I look[831] back[832] on the time spent here

---

826. In left margin here he wrote, 'God Triune'.
827. MS Wilberforce c. 41, fo. 135.
828. MS Wilberforce c. 41, fo. 135.
829. 1 Corinthians 1:27.
830. Ibid.
831. Ibid.
832. MS Wilberforce c. 41, fo. 136.

it seems but a week or two, instead of since the 28th of Oct[r] & when I look forward to London Life, now so near I seem to recoil from it. I have wasted my time alas! O may I make a better use of it & from purer motives. Being more intent on glorifying God, & benefitg mankind, less on worldly Reputation. O Lord enlighten & guide & sanctify & bless me.[833]

Sunday Evening near 8 oClock, January 12, 1800, Lambridge

I have scarcely any time & must therefore only put down that I have been this last week cold & stupid & earthly minded. Little Scripture reading & tho' rather better in Evg devot[ns] yet but very poorly. Oimoi! I mean D.V. to allot tomorrow chiefly to relig[s] Exercises, so I will go to prayer tho' alas I have no Heart for it.[834]

Monday 12 oClock, January 13, 1800, Lambridge[835]

After rather frittering & losg insensibly too much morng, I am now beginning to spend the day more especially as serious. O God discover me to myself & humble me. O what Cause have I for humiliat[n] Early backslidings,[836] many years wickedness & systematic profligacy, even beyond passions, above all even when y[e] mercy of God restrain'd me in 1797[837] my vanity, my wasted time, my often intemperate formerly, my forgetfulness of God, Ingratitude for domestic Happiness, unkindness to Sister even to B.[838]

Selfishness in Milner's Case & passim. Lately, Bible readg & meditat[n] neglected, & Devotions hurried particy Eveng, but in morng, also injur'd from Pump Room before prayers. How little spiritual mindedness thro' the day have I felt. How little diligence in doing good. How little due Interest in Happiness of friends or relatives, Oimoi. Oimoi. Vide 132,3. Last similar day. But much more when I consider God's mercies with my Sins & Ingratitude, my Baseness will appear. I seem a monster to myself & I can only fly for Refuge to X[t] for Wisdom Righteousness Sanctifc[n].[839] Let me humble myself in prayer & Confession before I supplicate for mercies.[840]

---

833. MS Wilberforce c. 41, fos. 135-136. *Life*, ii. pp. 352-353 has, 'Last year has been marked with mercies to me ... When I look back upon the time spent here, it seems but a week or two, instead of since the 28th of October; and when I look forward to London life, how do I recoil from it! I humbly hope that I am resolutely determined for Christ, and not solicitous about worldly greatness, wealth, reputation. And now that I am on the point of returning to London, I would humbly pray for a large measure of grace to enable me to stand against the world, the flesh, and the devil. I would humbly resolve through the Spirit to live by faith, and to go on diligently, devoutly, humbly, endeavoring to glorify God and benefit my fellow-creatures.'

834. MS Wilberforce c. 41, fo. 136.

835. In the left margin here he wrote, 'Vide 132,3 Last Sunday'.

836. In left margin he wrote, '1. Humiln. & Confessn.'

837. There then follows the word, 'Bissop's', transliterated into Greek letters.

838. In left margin he wrote, 'Talsehood Vanity [double underlined] & Evil Speakg Indolence Pride Selfishness Envy Indolence.'

839. 1 Corinthians 1:30.

840. MS Wilberforce c. 41, fo. 136.

Monday 1 oClock,[841] January 13, 1800

How hard it is to feel oneself really alone with God. I seem to be as it were 2 selves, a double person, but I hope I humbly feel the depth of my own Sinfulness, with which I have been striving to affect my Heart. Alas! Alas! yet I humbly look up to God in X^t I will go out & walk (after doing one necessy Job) partly to be free from interrup[tn] partly to muse this fine day, carrying Doddridge &c. My plan will be to pray for (after a <u>moderate</u> dinner & edifying talk <u>with</u> B. & perhaps a little readg) for Business.[842] Pray for Wisdom, Parliamenty & <u>genl</u> for Guidance thro' the Maze of opinions in Relig[n] & for a more complete conversion, for Grace & evy Grace separately, especy ag[t] besettg Sins & for opposite Graces (vide supra 132,3 – 114, 106 xxx 52,3,4 – 37, 94,5 – 73,4, 60) for usefulness.[843]

Life & direction to right schemes & blessing on performance & effect of them on Hearts of others, for influence & on my Book; on Plans, various, (sadly neglected), Intercession, Country, friends, &c. &c. &c. Praise & thanksgiving for public & private & personal Blessings. Devoting[844] Self to God & X^t by Spirit.[845] Form a plan for Bus[s] &c. & at dinner today put down objects, Convers[n] topics good doing to friends, Launchers &c.[846]

Monday About 7 in the Evening, January 13, 1800

Not dining till 4 I was rather in want & tired after it. Little done, Papers playg Children, Letters & still now Journal lookg &c. till ½ past 7, vide 2, 3 & other Book 9, 10, & this 10. I hope humbly that I am resolvedly determin'd for Christ, & not solicitous about Worldly Greatness Wealth, Reputat[n] &c. but alas I am sadly unspiritual in my common feelings, and by long Habit of inattention, sadly careless in study or hearg or readg. SS.[847]

Monday ½ past 9, January 13, 1800

I hope I have been lookg to God humbly thro' X^t tho' alas but coldly. Yet they who wait shall renew Strength. I will press forward. Let him that is athirst come. Whoever will, let[848] him[849] take of the Water of Life <u>freely</u>.[850] Even so Lord Jesus. Amen.[851]

Sunday 3 oClock, January 19, 1800, Lambridge

This last week notwithstandg Monday has gone on very ill. Is it that neglected my Resolut[ns] ab[t] Evg Devotions & too hurried in Morng & not

---

841. '1 oClock' was written here in the left margin.

842. In the left margin here, he wrote, '2 Supplic'.

843. In the left margin here, he wrote, '3 Intercession & 4 Praise'.

844. Over 'Devoting' here he wrote '4' but look as if he changed it to '5'.

845. In the left margin here, he wrote, '5 Self Devotion'.

846. MS Wilberforce c. 41, fo. 136.

847. Ibid.

848. Ibid.

849. MS Wilberforce c. 41, fo. 137.

850. Revelation 22:17.

851. MS Wilberforce c. 41, fos. 136-137.

enough Scripture reading. With[l.] Watering &c. no crop to be expected. Help me O God, enable me to turn to thee with my whole Heart & to serve thee in newness of nature in X[t.] I renew my Resolutns to improve in all the particulars already noted down on my pocket paper especy devot[ns.] & Scripture, & I go to prayer to be enabled to fulfil my, but for grace, fruitless Resolut[ns.][852]

Sunday 2 ½ oClock, January 26, 1800, Batt[a.] Rise

Alas, but little Use made of this last week in any way, and how little especially has God been in my tho'ts. I fear this is a punishment of my not havg read Scripture duly or attended duly to private devot[ns.] especy Eveng ones. Now that I am on the point of returning to London, I would humbly pray for a larger measure of Grace, to enable me to stand ag[t.] the World the flesh & the Devil. I would humbly resolve, thro' the Spirit, to live by faith & to go on diligently, devoutly, humbly, endeavorg to glorify God & benefit my fellow Creatures. I go now to prayer.[853]

Sunday Night 9 ¾ oClock, February 9, 1800, Old Pal Yard

Alas, the last fortnight has rol'd rapidly away. Little <u>almost</u> nothg appears to have been done in it tho' always busy or rather hurried. My time chiefly spent in business for correspond[ce.] del[e] subject yet never less prepared. Oimoi. I fear more solicitous ab[t.] my Credit than ab[t.] truth. Then I seldom have been so unspiritual & forgetful of God as for y[e.] last fortnight. Perhaps this may be in part owing to my having been so hurried & curtail'd in priv[e.] devot[ns.] & Script[e.] readg & no meditat[n.] My Health requires much Sleep, 9 hours or thereab[ts.] & being up late, I am broke in upon before I have had anytime to myself, my Servants likewise uninstructed. Alas. How greatly do I need a thorough Change. How cold & dead is my heart. I wish I may have been thoughtful enough in my political decision; yet I humbly trust I meant to be right. My Eyes bad, it is late. O may the Grace of God enable me to live a less unprofitable life, using my faculties more to God's Glory & walking by faith & bring[g.] forth fruit abundantly.[854]

Sunday Evening 7 oClock, February 23, 1800, Old Palace Yard

Alas. Alas. How little have I been going on at all satisfactorily, & how little under a Sense of God's presence of X[t's] Grace. Private prayer being abridged & hurried over too often from being up late & broken in upon. No Scripture reading with family or very little, or meditat[n.] or Script.[855] reading[856] for self. Hence perhaps all ill. Here the source. God does not bless me. They who wait on y[e.] Lord shall renew th[r.] Strength.[857] I dare

---

852. MS Wilberforce c. 41, fo. 137.
853. Ibid.
854. Ibid.
855. Ibid.
856. MS Wilberforce c. 41, fo. 138.
857. Isaiah 40:31.

not say I have waited, or watch'd unto prayer. But I would humbly try, & then I may use the means, earlier Hours night & morng. I cannot do with[t.] full complement of Sleep. I have much before me & nothg yet done of all I had design'd this Spring. O that God would enable me & move the Hearts of others, doubtless I might better hope it, if I were duly earnest in prayer. Alas. Alas. I was never so cold as this time in spiritual[y] in Town.

O may I be deeply humbled & feel how weak & corrupt I am. May my Vanity lessen, my hurry abate. How much do I find of both of them workg secretly or rather too plainly. May Love grow, & may I become a new Creature, constrain'd by <u>Love of God & X[L.] to live wholly to his Glory</u>. How much have I been under the Workings of Envy of others who excelling me in the House, of pride (when foil'd in attempts especy in public) of unkindness to Sally[858] & Indifference ab[t.] friends Spiritual Good. Then some duplicity, above all a strange aversation from God & X[t.] & heavenly things, & a lively Sensibility ab[t.] Earthly Things, especy Worldly Estimation. How much more display than solidity in my Parliamentary Conduct. O Lord, do thou enable me to be less of an Unprofitable Servant. How I am shamed by Abbot[859] & a number of others. O may I more be enabled to bring forth fruit & livg under the power of divine Grace, walkg by faith to live to God's & X[t's] Glory.[860]

Sunday Evening 7½ oClock, March 16, 1800, Pal Y[d.]

Alas. Alas. I find abundant Cause to renew all that I wrote last. My Eyes are bad & I cannot write more. I have of late begun readg to famy morng & kept rather earlier Hours, & Bible & prayers, but in Evg short hurried prayers & no meditat[n.] Now when God seems about to try his people, what Cause have I to pray & gird up the Loins of my mind.[861] O may I grow in Grace[862] & become more a Child of God, more meet to be a partaker of the Inheritance of y[e.] Saints in Light.[863] How amiable the Simple Childlike Spirit of Ly Cath[e.864] O may I grow in the fear & Love of God & Xt. & may I be an habitation of God thro' the Spirit, 1 Cor. 6:1.[865]

---

858. 'Friends' crossed out here and 'Sally' is inserted above the line.

859. Charles Abbot (1757–1829), 1st Baron of Colchester.

860. MS Wilberforce c. 41, fos. 137-138.

861. 1 Peter 1:13.

862. 2 Peter 3:18.

863. Colossians 1:12.

864. Lady Catherine Graham (1765–1836), née Stewart, married to Sir James Graham (1761–1824), M.P. for Ripon, Yorkshire.

865. MS Wilberforce c. 41, fo. 138. *Life*, ii. pp. 359-360 has, 'We know not what times are coming on, but if God be for us, who can be against us? Oh may I therefore lay up treasure in heaven, and wait upon the Lord. Now that he seems about to try his people, what cause have I to pray, and gird up the loins of my mind! May I grow in grace, and become more "meet for the inheritance of the saints in light." How amiable is the simple, childlike spirit of Lady Catherine Graham! I have much before me, oh that God would enable me, and move the hearts of others: doubtless I might better hope it, if I were deeply earnest in prayer.'

Sunday Evening ½ past 8, March 23, 1800, Pal Y^d 866

Alas. Alas. This last week no better than before tho' moderate Illness sho'd have call'd me to God. Alas! Alas! But O, may I turn to God yet with my whole Heart & devote myself to him Body & Soul & live the life I now live in y^e. flesh &c.[867]

Sunday Night ½ past 10, March 30, 1800, Pal Y^d.

Alas! This last week has gone on much as before. O may I turn to the Lord with my whole Heart. I hope I trust not to my Resolutns but only to the Scripturl Character of God & X^t. as full <u>rich</u> in mercy & long suffering & to the promises, Ask &c.[868] I will give to him that is athirst &c.[869] & Ho Evyone &c.[870] & alas! what anger, pride, worldly mindedness, some falsehood, Sensibility ab^t. Reputat^n. Lukewarmness to God's Cause & X^t's want of love of fellow Creatures, malignity, Envy. O may I obtain from the fulness that is in X^t. & Grace for Grace. I hope to keep earlier Hours as means whereby I may obtain more time for prayer & Scripturl meditat^n. & also to try Doddridge's Practice & bearg in mind God Xt. Spirit Soul Spt. &c.[871]

Sunday[872] Evening Easter Sunday ¾ past 8, April 13, 1800, Pal Y^d.

Alas. I have been of late going on sadly. The good seed has been choked by y^e. Thorns.[873] Alas. I have neglected Scripture Readg, my private prayers have been hurried & rambling, no meditat^n. Late up much hurried, yet little Business got thro' with little Love or none alas of God, or Man, and within & without, full of Corruption. May Good Friday & this day be blessed unto me & I was much affected by Scott's Sermon this morning. I humbly trust I have humbled myself before God & come to him thro' X^t. & tho' my Heart be so hard & cold & inconstant yet I will humbly trust that his mercy will be extended, even to me. X^t. is able to save even to the Uttermost.[874] He will give to him that is athirst of the fountain of y^e. Water of Life freely.[875] Wait on him therefore O my Soul, with penitence & godly Sorrow, with hunger & thirst after Righteousness;[876] with faith in his power & Willingness to save. I would use the Means of Grace more carefully, prizing them higher & constantly readg prayg & meditatg. Try for this earlier Hours &c. Let me pray for Wisdom. We know not what times are coming on. But if God be for us, who can be against us![877] O may I therefore lay up treasure in Heaven[878]

---

866. MS Wilberforce c. 41, fo. 138.
867. Galatians 2:20. MS Wilberforce c. 41, fo. 138.
868. Matthew 7:7.
869. Revelation 21:6.
870. Isaiah 55:1.
871. MS Wilberforce c. 41, fo. 138.
872. MS Wilberforce c. 41, fo. 139.
873. Matthew 13:7.
874. Hebrews 7:25.
875. Revelation 22:17.
876. Matthew 5:6.
877. Romans 8:31.
878. Matthew 6:19.

& wait on the Lord & receive continual Supplies of his Spirit, rendering me more & more meet to be a partaker of the Inheritance of the Saints in Light.[879] Amen.[880]

Sunday 2¼ oClock, April 27, 1800, Pal Y[d.]

Alas! I have been sadly neglectful of the Means of Grace of late (especially morng & Evg devot[ns.] from being up late & continuing too long at Bus[s.] at night, neglectg Scripture reading & medit[n.] almost entirely.) I find the bad Effects in a cold hard dull Heart, insensible to the Value of the Ordinances of God, & going & wining in them from form rather than from y[e.] heart. No Gratitude! No Love, little Self-abasement. Wandering in Evg prayers &c. O may God by his Grace quicken me & deliver me from this Bondage. I have rece'd the Sact as on Easter Sundy. May I be enabled to turn to y[e.] Lord with my whole Heart, & be fill'd with <u>Love</u> Joy peace Humility Meekness Gratitude &c. I humbly resolve to try earlier hours at night by 11 or sooner to Bed, as preparatory to earlier in Morng 7½ or earlier if possible; but God knoweth only, whether tis bodily weakness or not that I feel a great & permanent languor all day, unless I have <u>full</u> 9 Hours Sleep & more, (I geny sleep well). Scripture morng & a little Evg. O may I thus receive the good Seed <u>& God give a large</u> Increase.[881] Amen. Amen.

Our Childn have had the Measles, & now have the Hoopg Cough. How uncertain is life. O may I feel my depend[ce.] & my obligat[ns.] Amen. Yet <u>however</u> vile & worthless, prompted by a Sense of misery & helplessness I come to thee O X[t.] because thou art able to save to the Uttermost them that come to God thro' thee,[882] I come, imploring Mercy & Grace to help in time of need.[883] I humbly plead thy gracious declarat[n.] whosoever will let him take of the Water of Life freely.[884] O may I experience its quickeng cleansg renewing power, producing a Copious Growth of all the fruits of y[e.] Spirit. He who searcheth the heart, knoweth that in spite of all my bustling, I have been a most unprofitable Servt, both in motive & execution, but may I henceforth be more fervent in Spirit, & may God give me wisdom to know & ability to do his will & to glorify him upon Earth, & exert all my faculties strenuously humbly & successfully to his Glory.

God has not bless'd me in my work because I have not labour'd in his faith & fear but vaingloriously. O may I henceforth be more actuated by Love & Gratitude & holy filial fear, & dutiful submission & humble zeal with Love of God & Man burning strongly within me. Satan has triumph'd over me, but may he now be put down under my feet.[885]

---

879. Colossians 1:12.
880. MS Wilberforce c. 41, fo. 139.
881. Matthew 13:8.
882. Hebrews 7:25.
883. Hebrews 4:16.
884. Revelation 22:17.
885. Romans 16:20. MS Wilberforce c. 41, fo. 139.

Sunday Evening Arrived Yesterday, August[886] 24, 1800, Bognor Rocks[887]

I this day complete my 41$^{st.}$ & enter into my 42$^{d.}$ year. Alas, the Review of the past may well fill me with Shame & Sorrow. How little have I done for God since I devoted myself to him. I fly for pardon to the mercy of God in X$^{t.}$ I betake myself to a Saviour, my only Hope & Refuge. But I would not make X$^{t.}$ the Minister of Sin. I would grow in Grace, & labour to live a Life more honourable to God & more useful to man. O Lord purify my Soul[888] from all its Stains. Warm my Heart with the Love of thee, animate my Sluggish nature & fix my Inconstancy & Volatility, that I may not be weary in Well doing,[889] That I may bear ab$^{t.}$ with me a Sense of thy presence & live the Life that I now live in the flesh in the faith of the Son of God,[890] as one who is here a Pilgrim & a Stranger,[891] who is waiting for the coming of our Lord Jesus X$^{t.}$ & who having the Hope of seeing his Lord face to face, is purifying himself even as he is pure.[892] To thee therefore O God, I humbly devote myself thro' X$^{t.}$ by the Spirit, to be wholly thine, in Truth & Love, and O Strengthen my weakness. Bear with my Infirmities, draw me & I will run after thee.[893] Enable me to work while it is yet day,[894] stimulated by the humiliating Sense of my past Unprofitableness.

Teach me however, to desire that thy Will may be done, whether by my doing or Suffering, & may I be full of Love & Peace, & if it please thee of the[895] Joy in believing.[896] Guide me by thy Counsel & at length receive me to thy Glory.[897] I go to prayer & the above shall be the Substance of my Supplication. I am conscious from Experience of the danger of being drawn by Study from God, yet it seems to be my Duty, striving continually to retain in my mind a lively Sense that the Glory of God is to be my fix'd Aim & the Love of X$^{t.}$ my habitual Motive, to qualify myself better for discharging the Duties of the elevated Station in which it has pleased God to place me. I have sadly neglected the Cultivation of my natural talents. Let me now attend to it, imploring the divine Blessing. I will form a plan of Study & Exercise, havg a special Reference to the

---

886. MS Wilberforce c. 4, fo. 1.

887. At the top of the sheet Wilberforce wrote, 'Not having my Book I must write on loose sheets.' Bognor (Regis) is a seaside town in West Sussex, and was simply referred to as Bognor until the 18th century, when through the influence of Sir Richard Hotham it became a fashionable resort. Its population in 1801 was 700, growing rapidly from then throughout the 19th century.

888. 'Soul' is written over another unidentifiable word.

889. Galatians 6:9.

890. Galatians 2:20.

891. 1 Peter 2:11.

892. 1 John 3:3.

893. Song of Solomon 1:4.

894. John 9:4.

895. 'Of the' is inserted here above one or two words that have been crossed out.

896. Romans 15:13.

897. Psalm 73:24.

faults of my Intellect, whether natural or superinduced. Let me however ever bear in mind the one thing needful[898] & leave y[e.] rest to God.[899]

Sunday 2 oClock, September 7, 1800, Bognor

Alas! Alas! I am strangely cold & torpid in all Spiritual things, tho' I am persuaded of the reality of them, how little am I suitably affected. I have just been receiving the Sacram[t.] yet even in that solemn Ordinance little mov'd or not at all. O what mercies have I received & how little am I duly grateful for them. I dare not say that I <u>love</u> God & X[t.] it must be some great fault in me which keeps me back. But may I by thy Grace be led on from Strength to Strength. O X[t.] to thee I fly for help. On thee alone I would rely. O make my Heart right before thee. Give me a single Eye[900] & a simple Heart, Humble, pure, full of reverential fear of thee, of enlighten'd & steady Love & Gratitude. May I labour to qualify myself for the discharge of the Duties of Life not with an Eye to worldly Estimat[n.] or advancement, but with a deliberate & earnest & single View to thy Glory & to the Good of my fellow Creatures. I go to prayer for these things.[901]

Sunday Night ½ past 10, September 14, 1800, Bognor

Alas! Alas! How rapidly the Week has flown away. I have been readg a good deal, but got to little profit I fear. It seems right for me thus to acquire Knowledge, yet I fear I am doing too little Good, and alas how cold & stupid is my Heart. O how little am I truly servg God with the warmth I ought to feel. How little[902] lovg[903] X[t.] as I ought. O may I grow in fear & Love in desire to change Worlds, in Devotedness to X[t.] & his Service.[904]

Sunday Evening, October 19, 1800, Bognor

Thro' what Scenes have I pass'd since I last wrote; O how have I experienc'd the lovingkindness of the Lord, yet I am grown cold again & unfeeling. Alas! Alas! I can only humble myself before God, & implore his Grace thro' X[t.] I have not time to write fully, but I hope before I return to Bus[s.] again, to set apart a few Hours for solemn Humiliation & prayer & thanksgivg. O may I press forward with renewed diligence & strive more earnestly to make[905] a progress in the way that leadeth unto Life Eternal, Amen. Amen.[906]

Saturday, October 25, 1800, Bognor

Knowg that the Dean would leave us yesterday, & reflecting that this was no fast day, I had resolved to devote it to God, as a fast day meo more[907]

---

898. Luke 10:42.
899. MS Wilberforce c. 4, fo. 2.
900. Matthew 6:22.
901. MS Wilberforce c.4, fo. 2.
902. Ibid.
903. Ibid.
904. MS Wilberforce c.4, fos. 2-3.
905. 'Make' is written over an unidentified word.
906. MS Wilberforce c. 4, fo. 3.
907. Latin: in my own style.

(i.e. not fasting which disorders me both at the time & afterwards, but eating moderately, & drinkg less wine than common, as little as is quite necessary to my Health). As a Lesson of:

1st. Self-Examin[n.] especy of State & Life prior to Barbara's late illness & Humiliation before God for my past Sins, especly for those which drew on his late Chastisement & for misconduct during y[e.] course of d[o.]

2[dly.] Also consider & note down what Lessons probably meant to be enforced on me by it, & to what I sho'd try to make it &c.

3[dly.] Praise for her recovery. Here consider & enumerate all the particular mercies most observable in my late Visitation.

4[thly] Gen[l.] Humiliation for the Sins of my Life &c. O how many.

5[thly.] Prayer & Supplicat[n.] for pardon & renewed pleadg of the Blood of X[t.] & Devoting of myself to him in Covenant & solemn Surrender of myself to him with all I am & have.

6[thy.] Supplicat[ns.] for Myself, for Wisdom & Spiritual Understanding, in readg Scripture &c. for Growth in Grace, especy ag[t.] besetting Sins & for graces most wanted. After serious Self Examin[n.] to discover them, also Holy resolutions in God's & X[t's] Strength thro' the Spirit.

7[y.] - for Wisdom & prudence to enable me ably & usefully to discharge my Parliamenty & other public Duties, a Blessing on my Studies, Pursuits, &c. Also my Civil, family, domestic, social & all other Duties. To guide me to useful plans prayer for success on some of them &c. &c. To fit me for all future Scenes & make me a Blessing to many, espECY a Blessing on my approaching Winter's Labors & pursuits.

8[y.] Copious Thanksgivings for the multiplied mercies I have receiv'd & am receivg at the Hands of God particulars of them. "There is no End of his Goodness." O how well may I adopt this Expression of the Psalmist.

9 Intercession, for Wife & Child[n.] near Relatives & friends, particularizing &c. for my domestics (especy for a Blessing on our famy devotions), for all who kind to B. in her late Illness or active in serving her. For her Physicians, espECY. Milner &c. for my Old Acquaintances nomination. For My Country, Our King, Rulers, Bishops, Clergy &c. to the extent little _____[908] being particular, depreating chastisements of Consumption &c &c &c - for France & Frenchmen, for all my fellow-Creatures lying in darkness & Vice, espECY Africa - for Success of Abolition Efforts.

Consider[909] in what public duties you have been most defective & how may best improve in future, & what especially lies before you now. Resolutions &c. plans & pursuits for future Service. Prayers for Strength in going to Town, enterg into political turbulence &c. &c. &c.

My time has not been duly improv'd & redeem'd today, not being very well, I co'd not get up till ab[t.] ½ past 8. I expounded to fam'y &

---

908. He has inserted words into the line, making it difficult to decipher with certainty here.

909. Then at this point on page is a symbol resembling a large 'H' which denotes insertion higher on the page, where the mark also appears for insertion, before 'Infra'.

after bkft perhaps a little trifled with B. tho' her being indiff^t. tryg y^e. Cause & other unavoidable little hindrances. Then at 12, I had more trouble & difficulty than almost ever in my life with indurated feaces,[910] & when hoped in a few minutes to get to my work, kept about an Hour from it. Then I sat down to write this as preparation, being hinder'd however by my late troublesome operation, which still requires constant attention to y^e. parts to prevent mischief, partly as a Guide to my devotions, & partly that I may look at it hereafter to help me.[911]

---

910. 'Indurated feaces' written here in Greek letters.
911. MS Wilberforce c. 4, fos. 3-4.

The Spiritual Reflections
of
William Wilberforce

1801–1815

William Wilberforce 1801–1815

Socially and politically this was a fast-moving and important period in the history of Britain. 1801 began with the Act of Union between Great Britain and Ireland coming into effect, thereby creating the United Kingdom of Great Britain and Ireland. Within weeks of that happening Britain had its first Census with the population numbered at 8,892,536. All was looking good for Britain, especially with the Treaty of Amiens that occurred the following year that brought about peace with France. However it was a short-lived peace, with War recommencing one year after that. In 1805 Britain celebrated the incredible victory over the French at the Battle of Trafalgar, but it was a celebration tempered with the bitter blow of the loss of Admiral Lord Nelson. Wilberforce himself experienced his own very personal loss in 1806, with the premature passing of his great friend William Pitt the Younger, who thereby did not get to share in Wilberforce's soon to happen rejoicing at the passing of the Abolition Act just the following year,

> Attended Pitt's funeral, an affecting ceremony. What thoughts occurred to me when I saw the coffin letting down, and just before! I thought of our appearance before God in heaven. May the impression be durable. Oh what cause do I find for humiliation and gratitude, looking back to my own and Pitt's public life![1]

In 1812 Britain entered into War with the United States, while in that same year Wilberforce was elected member of Parliament for the Bramber constituency. Britain had further cause to celebrate though, when in 1815 the Duke of Wellington defeated Napoleon at the Battle of Waterloo. As for Wilberforce personally, he enjoyed several wonderful events during this period. With three years still to go before Wilberforce could rejoice in the ending of the Slave Trade, John Newton wrote to Wilberforce with a confidence that what they have dreamed of, prayed for and worked so diligently for, would indeed soon come to

---

1. Journal entry, Saturday, 22 February, 1806.

pass. Wilberforce replied with thanks for Newton's kind words, that it did look possible that such a wonderful events may just happen in God's providence, but that it was not yet assured, for there was still real opposition, especially within the confines of the House of Lords. In Newton's letter we read,

> Though I can scarcely see the paper before me, must attempt to express my thankfulness to the Lord, and to offer my congratulations to you for the success which he has so far been pleased to give to your unwearied endeavours for the abolition of the slave trade, which I have considered as a millstone, sufficient, of itself sufficient, to sink such an enlightened and highly favoured nation as ours to the bottom of the sea ... Whether I who am within two months of entering my eightieth year shall live to see the accomplishment of the work, is only known to Him, in whose hands are all our times and ways, but the hopeful prospect of its accomplishment will, I trust, give me daily satisfaction so long as my declining faculties are preserved.[2]

To Newton's letter Wilberforce sent this reply,

> I steal one moment from business and bustle to thank you most cordially for your kind congratulations. I really scarcely deserve them ... Pray for us, my dear Sir, that we also may be enabled to hold on your way, and at last to join with you in the shout of victory. I fear the House of Lords! But it seems as if He, who has the hearts of all men in His power, was beginning to look with pity on the sufferings of those poor oppressed fellow-creatures whose cause I assert. I shall ever reckon it the greatest of all my temporal favours, that I have been providentially led to take the conduct of this business.

They did see the miracle of the passing of the Abolition Act in 1807, something that in a way has been immortalized in an incredible quote highlighting one aspect of that time. The Act received Royal Assent on March 25, but we are told of the events a month earlier in Parliament, when on February 24, 1807 at 4.00am, the House of Commons, by an overwhelming majority of 283-16 voted to abolish the Slave Trade. 'They rose to their feet, turned to fellow legislator William Wilberforce and began to cheer while Wilberforce bowed his head and wept.' In this same time period, Wilberforce also rejoiced in the births of his final four children, Elizabeth (1801), Robert (1802), Samuel (1805) and Henry (1807). So in one year 1807, he experienced the successful passing of the Act of Abolition, the birth of his son Henry, and the publication of his Letter on Abolition.

Wilberforce received vast amounts of correspondence every week, and he often made notes in his Journals about the burden they were, and he frequently mentioned too, that he was either reading them, or carrying bundles of them with him as he traveled, intending to personally reply to as many as he was able when he had a few moments. He felt a need to reply himself out of a sense of 'Christian courtesy,' and

---

2. Letter of John Newton to Wilberforce, June 5, 1804.

it was that character trait amongst others, that made Wilberforce so winsome. Of course the time taken in simply replying did not even take into account the time involved in all the correspondence he initiated. In one entry he gave a detailed account of the course of a typical day in his life, including comments about how important his family was to him, and even how he listened to his children read for an extended time. But even here, the letters were never far from his mind,

> I get up about seven; then serious time and devotions for an hour; then dressing and hearing one of the children read to me for three-quarters of an hour. After breakfast, letters, and writing; dictating; etc. We dine together early, and then some of the children read till we walk out, from about six till eight; then coming in I have an hour serious. Then family prayers, supper, and bed about eleven. I must try to see more of the children, and to obtain more time for study; hitherto I have done little but write letters.[3]

In an entry from 1811 he revealed the motive behind his replying to letters, as well as how important he viewed some of the letters. He also included an intriguing reference to the second book he was contemplating writing, a volume he envisaged in an entry elsewhere to be a political/theological volume and would, he believed, be even more important than *A Practical View*. Unfortunately he was never able to bring the vision to completion. In this particular entry here, though, he also included a note about some of those he was corresponding with including the ex-President Thomas Jefferson,

> Almost entirely consumed by letters, yet it appears the part of Christian courtesy to answer correspondents; and so much suffering would in each case be produced by my not answering, compared with the trouble it costs, that I know not how to abstain. I have written lately an immense number, several on important objects, today one on missions. Having heard of the Duke of York's being designed for commander of the army, I resolved, however invidious, to state objections strongly, and wrote to Perceval. I am now writing to Jefferson in America, to obtain some agreement between the two nations, for giving effect to Abolition, by allowing each country to take the other's slave ships. I long to write my projected religious work, but have first several jobs to do, not one of which however is yet begun. My letters still almost engross me. True, they are important letters, keeping up connection with constituents in absence from the county; also some religious letters, and some letters of friendship.[4]

Wilberforce's reasons to celebrate included another major victory in 1813, with his successful amending of the East India Company's Charter, requiring that they permit missionary work and chaplaincy to be conducted in areas they had authority over, especially in India,

---

3. Undated entry, 1813.
4. Undated entry, 1811.

The East India Bill passed, and the missionary, or rather the Christian, cause fought through, without division, to the last. We were often alarmed. Lord Castlereagh has managed it admirably, coolly and quietly. The petitions, of which a greater number than were ever known, have carried our question instrumentally, the good providence of God really.[5]

As was said earlier, this took Wilberforce twenty years to achieve, having failed in his 1793 attempt. This time his campaign was much better organized, and was far more ready to respond to the expected opposition of the Company. In connection with this work he has entries in this section that record his meetings with Andrew Fuller as Secretary of the Baptist Mission Society, and with the Baptist leader, Joseph Ivimey. Wilberforce recorded too some wonderful words about William Carey, who became the British Baptists' first foreign missionary, and had personally experienced negative treatment at the hands of the East India Company in India. Wilberforce had personally persuaded Carey to take a non-British ship to the mission field of India, so that the Company would not be aware of his mission there,

I do not know a finer instance of the moral sublime, than that a poor cobbler working in his stall should conceive the idea of converting the Hindoos to Christianity; yet such was Dr. Carey. Why Milton's planning his Paradise Lost in his old age and blindness was nothing to it. And then when he had gone to India, and was appointed by Lord Wellesley to a lucrative and honorable station in the college of Fort William, with equal nobleness of mind he made over all his salary (between £1000 and £1500 per annum) to the general objects of the mission.

Wilberforce makes many entries, as he did in 1813 too, on the theme of his enjoying the beauty of God's creation that he observed all around him. His entries included his happiness at the opportunities he had for times of solitariness, including walking, praying, reading and reciting memorized Scripture by himself – especially the Psalms,

I am reading the Psalms just now, comparing the two versions, and reading Horne's commentary. What wonderful compositions! What a decisive proof of the Divine origin of the religion to which they belong! There is in the world nothing else like them.[6]

As for his love of nature, he would lay on the grass, simply observing the stars overhead and marveling in all he saw. The following are a small sample of such entries,

Last night lookg at stars more devoutly than for sometime.[7]
A charming day. Walked about an hour with Cowper's Poems. Delightful – park – deer – water – wood.[8]

---

5. Journal entry, Monday, 12 July, 1813.
6. Undated entry, 1803.
7. Entry dated September, 1798.
8. Entry, Friday, 5 August, 1803.

> A delightful morning. Walked out and saw the most abundant
> dew-drops sparkling in the sunbeams on the gazon. How it calls forth
> the devotional feelings in the morning when the mind is vacant from
> worldly business, to see all nature pour forth, as it were, its song of
> praise to the great Creator and Preserver of all things! I love to repeat
> Psalms civ. ciii. cxlv. etc. at such a season.[9]
>
> Meditating more on God as the Creator and Governor of the
> universe. Eighty millions of fixed stars, each as large at least as our
> sun. Combine the considerations hence arising with the madness and
> guilt of sin as setting up our will against that of God. Combine with
> it Christ's unspeakable mercy and love, and that of God in Christ.[10]

He reflected again too on the events of his conversion, and marveled at
how clearly God so ordered the details. Yet he is also ashamed as often
he was, of how little progress spiritually he has made since those years,
and uses his 44th birthday to reflect along the very same lines, especially
as he enumerates the many blessings he had received,

> My birthday was worse kept this year than I have long known it, from
> its being my last day at a friend's house. This therefore to be a sort of
> birthday review. I am come here into the arbor by the river side, and am
> quite secure from interruption. How greatly are my sins aggravated by
> the extreme goodness to me of my God and Savior! I am encumbered
> with blessings, my cup is so full of them as to overflow. During life all
> has gone well with me, so far as God has ordered matters, and all the
> evil has been the result of my own follies.[11]

In an attempt to keep himself constantly aware of the importance
and imminence of spiritual things and of his need to live accordingly,
he devised a novel method to keep such thoughts at the forefront of
his mind,

> Let me try to keep myself reminded of invisible things by something
> which will call attention, though not produce pain, and by varying the
> expedients; when I grow familiar with one, I may use another. I did
> try a little pebble in my shoe. Why should such secondary means be
> despised? Oh that they were unnecessary, and so they may become by
> degrees! Oh may I learn to live above this world, and set my affections
> on things above![12]

The entries that follow in this period 1801 to 1815 were recorded by
Wilberforce in his manuscripts referred to as MS Wilberforce c. 42 and
e. 24, the latter volume bearing the handwritten note by Wilberforce
on its cover that reads,

> Private Religious. [which has been crossed out]
> Dec. 1815. Resumd Oct. 7th 1826 (after many years).

---

9. Journal entry, October 23, 1827.
10. Undated entry, 1831.
11. Journal entry, Friday, 9 September, 1803.
12. Journal entry, Sunday, 10 February, 1811.

For dearest Bs perusal only WW – 1826.

Then on the inside of the front cover in pencil is written, 'Dec. 7th 1815 – Oct. 7 1816. Religious.'

How wonderful that a private man should have such an influence on the temporal and eternal happiness of millions; literally, millions on millions yet unborn! O God, make me more earnest for Thy glory; and may I act more from real love and gratitude to my redeeming Lord.

William Wilberforce, 1813

1801

Sunday, December 20ᵗʰ· 1801

I have of late perceived on looking inwards, the workings of ambition, of love of this world, its honors, riches, estimation, and even of worldly desires for my family, of which before I do not recollect that I was conscious. The settled judgment of my mind I would humbly hope is right. I trust that I am comparatively indifferent in my cool estimate of things to the goods of this life: but, alas! I become soiled and worldly-minded.

That our feelings do not correspond with our judgments, is one of the strongest proofs of our depravity and of the double man within us. I believe that retired, domestic life is by far the most happy for me, blessed as I am with affluence, etc. Yet when I see those who were my equals or inferiors, rising above me into stations of wealth, rank, &c. I find myself tempted to desire their stations, which yet I know would not increase my happiness, or even be more truly honorable. I speak not of the desire of an increased power of usefulness. That is another and a right feeling. Mine, against which however in its risings I struggle, and which I strive to suppress, is a sadly depraved appetite, rooted in an inordinate love of this world. Oh may the compunction I now feel be the blessed operation of the Holy Spirit.

I suspect I have been allotting habitually too little time to religious exercises, as private devotion, religious meditation, Scripture reading, etc. Hence I am lean, and cold, and hard. God, perhaps, would prosper me more in spiritual things if I were to be more diligent in using the means of grace. And though in the main I have thought myself pursuing the course chalked out for me by Providence, and with a diligence prompted and enjoined by the injunctions of Scripture, yet I suspect that I had better allot more time, say two hours or an hour and a half, to religious exercises daily, (besides Sundays,) and try whether by so doing I cannot preserve a frame of spirit more habitually devotional, a more lively sense of unseen things, a warmer love of God, and a greater degree of hunger and thirst after righteousness, a heart less prone to be soiled with worldly cares, designs, passions, and apprehensions, and a real, undissembled longing for heaven, its pleasures, and its purity.

I know that all external means are nothing without the quickening Spirit, but the Scripture enjoins constant prayer, and the writings and example of all good men suggest and enforce the necessity of a considerable proportion of meditation and other religious exercises, for maintaining the spiritual life vigorous and flourishing. Let me therefore make the effort in humble reliance on Divine grace. God, if he will, can turn the hearts of men, and give me favorable opportunities, and enable me to use them, and more than compensate for all the hours taken from study, business, or civility, and devoted to him. O God, give me a single heart and a single eye,[1] fixed on Thy favors, and resolutely determined to

---

1. Matthew 6:22.

live to Thy glory, careless whether I succeed or not in worldly concerns, leaving all my human interests and objects to Thee, and beseeching Thee to enable me to set my affections on things above;[2] and walking by faith,[3] to wait on Christ, and live on him day by day here, till at length, through his infinite and wholly unmerited mercy, I am taken to dwell with him hereafter in everlasting happiness and glory.[4]

1802

Undated, 1802

Reflections in the reed house,[5] put down on paper, that they might not be the fugitive thoughts of the moment, but the deliberate conclusions of his judgment recorded for my own use; or possibly, that my dear wife, for the benefit of my children, may know the considerations by which I am guided in the direction of my labors and the employment of my time.

When I look into my own mind, I find it a perfect chaos, wherein the little knowledge which I do possess is but confusedly and darkly visible; and where, from the want of classification and recapitulation, and from having satisfied myself with a superficial acquaintance with things, and having propositions brought into and left in my mind, without settling the result, discriminating the true from the false, the certain from the uncertain, I am in truth shamefully ignorant of many subjects which I seem to know, and should be thoroughly acquainted with. What has brought me into this state is a treacherous memory, and my having from nature a quick perception and lively imagination, with an understanding (either naturally or from bad habits) defective in the power of steadily contemplating many objects without confusion. This is really weakness of intellect, but it might have been lessened by early and habitual efforts. The mathematics and algebra would here have been eminently useful to me, method too might have been highly beneficial in keeping me from a habit of half attention. Alas, these remedies were neglected, and from 17 to 21, when I ought to have been under that strict and wholesome regimen which the peculiar diseases of my intellectual powers seemed to require, I was strengthening these natural maladies: and this till aet. 26. And though since that time I have been endeavoring to employ my talents, in the largest sense, to the glory of God, and the good of man, yet, alas, how ineffectually! and my peculiar situation, and the great variety of things and persons with which it renders me conversant, has kept me sadly back.

I am tempted to think that it is now too late to mend my plan practically, with any effect, yet as it has pleased God to call me again to Parliament, and as the greater my natural infirmities the more every aid is wanted, I

---

2. Colossians 3:2.

3. 2 Corinthians 5:7.

4. *Life*, iii. pp. 21-23.

5. 'Reed house' was a favourite arbor of Wilberforce in his garden. Wilberforce here records, quite unusually, that he hopes that his Journal entries, as here, might be of value not just for his own spiritual recollecting, but for his wife and children to some similar purpose too.

am resolved to enter on a course of more systematic retention of the little I know or can acquire, and I mean to note down roughly the scheme of study it will be best for me to pursue. I would not overrate knowledge, or proficiency in any human pursuits or acquirements; but inasmuch as God works by human means, it seems to be our duty to labor diligently in the pursuit of those qualifications, which appear to be the instruments of usefulness for our particular station and occupation in life.

Eloquence in its right sense is of great effect in every free community, and as it has pleased God to endow me with a certain natural turn for public-speaking, and by his providence to place me in a situation in which there is room for the use of that talent, it seems to be my duty to improve that natural faculty, and cultivate that true eloquence which alone is suitable to the character of a follower of the Savior, who was full of love, truth, and lowliness. Besides, the very basis of eloquence, in the sense in which I use it, is wisdom and knowledge, a thorough acquaintance with one's subject, the sure possession of it, and power of promptly calling up and using it. But let me ever remember here what cause there is for continual watchfulness and godly jealousy, lest the pursuit should lead to an inordinate love of worldly estimation, to vanity, and pride; and if to them, in its consequence to the malignant passions.[6]

Tuesday, August 17th. 1802

I have been thinking seriously and praying to God for direction as to the right employment of my time and direction of my studies: and I put down such propositions as are pretty clear. All this suggests that I should misapply my few remaining years, by devoting my whole or even my chief time and efforts to oratory. This may justly occupy some degree of them, especially so far as concerns, first, the invigorating the powers of my mind, and fixing my attention, and exerting at once attention, memory, and invention; and, secondly, the fixing, securing, and retaining necessary knowledge of different kinds, and bringing it forth for use.

I resolve to make the cultivation of these powers my secondary object, having as my main object, the promotion of my moral and religious usefulness. Besides whatever dreams of ambition I may have indulged, it now seems clear, that my part is to give the example of an independent member of Parliament, and a man of religion, discharging with activity and fidelity the duties of his trust, and not seeking to render his parliamentary station a ladder by which to rise to a higher eminence. What has passed of late years, (the number of country gentlemen made peers, etc.) renders it particularly necessary to give this lesson; and from whom can it be required, if not from him who professes to have set his affections on things above,[7] and to consider himself as a stranger and a pilgrim on the earth?[8] If it should ever please God to call me to any

---

6. *Life*, iii. pp. 57-59.
7. Colossians 3:2.
8. 1 Peter 2:11.

situation of power, or to any higher eminence, which I do not expect, he would furnish me with the talents necessary for the discharge of its duties. But as this is highly improbable, I should do wrong to sacrifice an opportunity of usefulness which is within my reach, in order to qualify myself for a station I am not likely ever to fill.[9]

Tuesday, August 24th, 1802

I find books alienate my heart from God as much as anything. I have been framing a plan of study for myself, but let me remember that one thing is needful, that if my heart cannot be kept in a spiritual state without so much prayer, meditation, Scripture reading, etc. as are incompatible with study and business, I must seek first the righteousness of God.[10] Yet, O Lord, when I think how little I have done, I am ashamed and confounded, and I would fain honor God more than I have yet done. Oh let me record his signal mercies during the past year. My health has been uniformly good till lately; and now I suffer no pain. Many instances of mortality around me of younger and stronger men, and I am spared. My children, who were all ill last winter, have enjoyed remarkably good health. And can it be aught but the mercy of God which overruled the hearts of my friends in Yorkshire, and rendered them all so kind and zealous towards me, though I had never been there since the former election. All went off well.

Indeed, who is there that has so many blessings? Let me record some of them: Affluence, without the highest rank. A good understanding and a happy temper. Kind friends, and a greater number than almost any one. Domestic happiness beyond what could have been conceived possible. A situation in life most honorable; and above all, a most favorable situation for eternity. The means of grace in abundance, and repeated motions of conscience, the effect, I believe, of the Holy Spirit. Which way soever I turn, I see marks of the goodness and long-suffering of God. Oh that I may be more filled with gratitude!

How merciful that I was not early brought into office, in 1782–3–4! This would probably have prevented my going abroad, with all that through the providence of God followed. Then my having such kind friends, my book, etc. All has succeeded with me, and God has by his preventing grace kept me from publicly disgracing the Christian profession. O my soul, praise the Lord, and forget not all his mercies.[11] God is love, and his promises are sure. What though I have been sadly wanting to myself, yet we are assured that those that come unto him he will in no wise cast out.[12] I therefore look to him with humble hope, I disclaim every other plea than that of the publican, offered up through the Redeemer; but I would animate my hopes, trusting in him that he will perfect, stablish, strengthen, settle me.[13]

---

9. *Life*, iii. pp. 59-60.

10. Matthew 6:33.

11. Psalm 103:2.

12. John 6:13.

13. 1 Peter 5:10. *Life*, iii. p. 61-62.

1803

Sunday, January 2nd. 1803

I will press forward and labor to know God better, and love him more, assuredly I may, because God will give his Holy Spirit to them that ask him,[14] and the Holy Ghost will shed abroad the love of God in the heart.[15] Oh then pray, pray, be earnest, press forward and follow on to know the Lord. Without watchfulness, humiliation, and prayer, the sense of Divine things must languish, as much as the grass withers for want of refreshing rains and dews. The word of God and the lives of good men give us reason to believe, that without these there can be no lively exercise of Christian graces. Trifle not then, O my soul, with thy immortal interests. Heaven is not to be won without labor. Oh then press forward: whatever else is neglected, let this one thing needful[16] be attended to, then will God bless thee. I will try to retire at nine or half-past, and every evening give half an hour, or an hour, to secret exercises, endeavoring to raise my mind more, and that it may be more warmed with heavenly fire.

Help me, O Lord, without Thee I can do nothing.[17] Let me strive to maintain a uniform frame of gratitude, veneration, love, and humility, not unelevated with holy confidence, and trembling hope in the mercies of that God, whose ways are not as our ways, nor his thoughts as our thoughts.[18] I should almost despair of myself, but for his promises. Strive, O my soul, to maintain and keep alive impressions, first, of the constant presence of a holy, omniscient, omnipotent, but infinitely merciful and gracious God, of Christ our Almighty Shepherd, of the Holy Spirit, of the evil one, and the invisible world in general. Secondly, of the real nature and malignity of sin, as a holy curb on my inclinations, which will check me and keep me from evil. Thirdly, of my own vileness and unprofitableness. And to these let me add a fourth, a sense of the multiplied blessings of my situation. Surely never cup was so full. Oh that I were more thankful I My ingratitude should humble me in the dust.[19]

Sunday, May 15th. 1803

I have been at prayer, and I hope with some fervency of desire for the blessings for which I prayed; but alas, my worldly mind! Surely it is the temptation of the evil spirit. Having called for the first time at Grant's on the way from church, and having talked quite at random of my probably taking a house near him with a back door

---

14. Luke 11:13.
15. Romans 5:5.
16. Luke 10:42.
17. John 15:5.
18. Isaiah 55:8.
19. *Life*, iii. pp. 79-81.

to Museum Gardens,[20] my mind keeps running on it, it absolutely haunts me, and will recur do all I can. Oh may Christ by his Spirit give me that self-possession and sobriety of mind, that low estimate of temporal things, that strong impression of their uncertainty and transitoriness, that I may not be thus at the mercy, the mere sport of my imagination. In these times especially (yesterday the news of Lord Whitworth's[21] leaving Paris, and consequent expectation of war) I should be weaned from this world, and be as one who is here a stranger and a pilgrim.[22]

Friday, August 5th. 1803

A charming day. Walked about an hour with Cowper's Poems.[23] Delightful - park - deer - water - wood. Delightful walk in the evening, a most romantic scene for a gentleman's park. They have family prayers night and morning. What a lesson to try to do good by speaking to others! I remember when at Wilford, many years ago, I mentioned to my cousin about family prayers, and he adopted the custom the very next night.[24]

Friday, September 9th. 1803

Half-past eleven. Destined this day for fast-day, meo more, with that degree of abstinence which may best qualify my weak body to go through the day without molesting the soul. My chief objects in this act of humiliation are, to deplore the sins of our country, and still more my own grievous share of them; my manifold provocations of the righteous displeasure of my God and Savior. To deprecate the wrath of God from our land, and draw down His blessings on us. I would also beg a blessing on our residence at this place, that my time here may tend to my religious advancement, that it may be productive also of benefit to my children and family, and to others with whom the providence of God connects me. For instances of the language of good men in acts of humiliation, vid. Dan. ix. 3-21. A fast-day, Neh. ix. 1; Jonah iii. 5.

---

20. William Wilberforce lived in Gore House, Kensington, from 1808 to 1821, and in a letter from there to John Jay in 1810, he wrote, '... about a year and three quarters ago I changed my residence, and found myself in the habitation which my family now occupies, and which we find more salubrious than Clapham Common. We are just one mile from the turnpike gate at Hyde Park corner, which I think you will not have forgotten yet, having about three acres of pleasure ground around my house, or rather behind it, and several old trees, walnut and mulberry, of thick foliage. I can sit and read under their shade, which I delight in doing with as much admiration of the beauties of nature (remembering at the same time the words of my favourite poet: "Nature is but a name for an effect, whose cause is God,") as if I were two hundred miles from the great city.' *The Correspondence of William Wilberforce* edited by R. I. and S. Wilberforce (London, 1840), vol 2, p. 177.

21. Charles Whitworth (1752–1825), 1st Earl Whitworth, Lord Whitworth (1800–1813), Viscount Whitworth (1813–1815), Lord Lieutenant of Ireland (1813–1817), British diplomat and politician.

22. 1 Peter 2:11. *Life*, iii. p. 98.

23. William Cowper (1731–1800), as detailed previously, composed both poems and hymns, and also saw many letters published. Compilations of his poems began appearing in print from 1782 onwards.

24. *Life*, iii. p. 112.

Half-past twelve.

Let me go now to confession and humiliation, in direct prayer, for my time wears away. Let me deplore my past sins, many years in which I lived without God in the world; then my sins since my having in some degree become acquainted with him in 1785–6. My actual state, my not having duly improved my talents, my chief besetting sins.

My birthday was worse kept this year than I have long known it, from its being my last day at a friend's house. This therefore to be a sort of birthday review. I am come here into the arbor by the river side, and am quite secure from interruption. How greatly are my sins aggravated by the extreme goodness to me of my God and Savior! I am encumbered with blessings, my cup is so full of them as to overflow. During life all has gone well with me, so far as God has ordered matters, and all the evil has been the result of my own follies. All that I enjoy has been from God, all I suffer from myself. My temporal blessings are superior to those of almost any human being who ever existed. But then my spiritual! Born in the happiest country, at a season of the greatest enjoyment, for hitherto I have suffered nothing from the storms which have raged around me. In a condition of life perhaps the happiest of all, except that possibly a little lower might be both safer and happier, (because I can live less to myself, less in the privacy and quiet I am now enjoying,) but mine is surely one of the very happiest. Then as to what is personal, good natural talents, though not duly improved, and injured by early neglect; a cheerful and naturally sweet temper (a great blessing); the want of that proud self-confidence, though this has grown in me to the fault of too great diffidence, which is unfavorable to the reception of religion; a most enjoyable constitution, though not a strong one; an ample fortune, and a generous disposition in money matters. I speak of this as mere natural temper, not as having in it the smallest merit, for I hope, at this moment, I can feel that it is no more than any other natural instinct, except as referred to the will and power of God. To these blessings have been added most affectionate friends, and near relatives.

My being honored with the Abolition cause is a great blessing. But far more my spiritual blessings. How few are there in Parliament on whom the mercy of God has been so bounteously vouchsafed! On none of the early acquaintances with whom I entered life. Praise the Lord, O my soul, and forget not all his benefits.[25] Above all, let me adore God's unspeakable kindness and long-suffering, in not being prevented from calling me to his fold, by the foreknowledge which he had of my hardness of heart and ingratitude. Then the preventing grace of God. What else has prevented me from bringing a scandal on my profession and Thy cause? Let the impression of these incidents ever remain with me, to humble me, to keep me mindful how weak I am in myself, how constantly I need the grace of God, how carefully I should avoid all temptation but such as occurs in the path of duty.

---

25. Psalm 103:2.

After having lamented my sins before God, that I may feel them the more, and the contrition which they should produce, let me meditate awhile on the guilt of sin, on the majesty and holiness of God, on the base ingratitude and sottish stupidity of man. I will read (meditating-way) Witherspoon's excellent sermon, 'A View of the Glory of God, humbling to the Soul.'[26] O Lord, let Thy Spirit accompany me, let it make me see and feel towards sin as Thou dost, and long to be delivered from every remainder of my corruptions, and to be holy as Thou art holy. I am reminded, by thinking I hear somebody coming, to pray ejaculatorily to God, to keep me from peevishness if I am interrupted. I have taken the best precautions against it, let me desire this day particularly to be full of love, meekness, and self-denial.[27]

Friday, near half-past 2, September 9, 1803

I have been hitherto quite free from interruption, and even the fear of it. Let me now go to prayer, after a short meditation on the promises of God. I have been large, though how imperfect, in confession. It remains for me to supplicate for the pardon of my sins, and for growth in grace, for a blessing on this place and its employments, for a blessing on my intercourse with others. (Constant previous ejaculatory prayer.) Intercession for country and mankind, slaves, enemies, then for servants, friends, enumeration of different classes, and wife and children. Then thanksgiving enumeration. O Lord, give me Thy Spirit to help me to pray, and praise Thee acceptably, to worship in spirit and in truth. Amen.

As I am likely D.V. to continue here three months, and to enjoy more leisure than usual, I proceed to fix the objects of my attention, and will be as diligent as a due care for the recovery of my health will admit. I will adhere to my plan as closely as I well can, having employments suited to different states of understanding, so that without fatigue I may yet be always employed. In the morning I will try to get two or three hours for composition - drawing up, and storing topics, etc. (After having read Brougham on Colonial Policy,[28] and Adam Smith.[29]) I will have in reading a book for minor attention, (into which class may come any novels, plays, or other works of imagination,) for seasons when unfit for much mental application. I mean to read the Greek Testament for at least half an hour daily, and to meditate over parts before read with my morning prayers. Walking out, to learn passages by heart, and keep them up. In conversation to adhere to plan, to have topics ready. I must

---

26. See *The Works of John Witherspoon*.

27. *Life*, iii. pp. 122-125.

28. Henry Peter Brougham (1778–1868), 1st Baron Brougham and Vaux, Lord Chancellor, and one of the pall-bearers at the funeral of Wilberforce at Westminster Abbey.

29. Adam Smith (1723–1790), Scottish moral philosopher, pioneer of political economy, and a leading figure in the Scottish Enlightenment. Remembered especially for his *Theory of Moral Sentiments* (1759), and his *Inquiry into the Nature and Causes of the Wealth of Nations* (1776).

keep a time account, beginning it tomorrow, and try to redeem time on Sundays for serious, as on common days for general purposes; except that a walk, meditating and solitary, to be a part, when fine, of Sunday's occupations, for I never find my mind more lifted up to God than when thus meditating sub Deo. May the Lord bless my plan, and enable me to redeem the time in future, and to live by rule, (yet never peevish when broken in upon,) and whether I eat or drink, or whatever I do, to do all to the glory of God.[30]

Wednesday Public Fast-Day[31] October 19, 1803

It becomes me on this day to humble myself before the Lord; first, for national sins, those especially wherein I have any share. And alas, I may too justly be said to be chargeable with a measure of that guilt, which I have not sufficiently tried to prevent. Have I then used my utmost endeavors to amend the public, or my own particular circle, or even my own family? Who knows but that if I had been sufficiently on the watch, and had duly improved all the opportunities of doing good, and preventing evil, which have been afforded me, many who are now strangers and enemies to God might have become known and reconciled to him? Many grievous sins, which greatly swell the sum of our national account, might never have existed. What openings for usefulness have I enjoyed as an M.P. both in and out of the House of Commons; as an author, actual and possible; as a friend, an acquaintance, a master, etc. Alas, which way soever I look, I see abundant cause for deep humiliation. How much guilt might I have kept out of existence, and consequently how much misery: East Indian idolatries; internal profaneness; even Slave Trade. And especially, have I sufficiently supplicated God, and done my utmost in this most effectual way, by calling in his aid?

Secondly, for my own manifold transgressions. These I have down on another paper; they are present with me, and I humbly hope I lament them before God. We know not what scenes we may be called on to witness. My own death may be at hand. O then, while it is day,[32] work out, O my soul, thy own salvation.[33] Pray to God for thyself, that thou mayest be accepted in the Beloved;[34] that thou mayest be supported under whatever trials it may please God to expose thee to; and if it be his holy will, but not otherwise, that thou mayest be continued with thy wife and children in the enjoyment of domestic peace and happiness.

---

30. 1 Corinthians 10:31. *Life*, iii. pp. 126-127.

31. See for example, *A Form of Prayer to be used in all Churches and Chapels throughout England, Ireland, Wales, and the Town of Berwick upon Tweed, upon Wednesday the Nineteenth of October 1803, being the Day appointed by Proclamation for a General Fast and Humiliation before Almighty God, to be observed in the most Devout and Solemn Manner, by sending up our Prayers and Supplications to the Divine Majesty: For obtaining Pardon of our Sins, and for averting those heavy Judgements which our manifold Provocations have most justly deserved; and imploring His Blessing and Assistance on the Arms of His Majesty by Sea and Land, and for restoring and perpetuating Peace, Safety, and Prosperity to Himself, and to His Kingdom* (London, 1803).

32. John 9:4.

33. Philippians 2:12.

34. Ephesians 1:6.

For thy country, that God would have mercy on us, and deliver us from the power of our enemies; that he would also bless to us our difficulties and dangers, and cause them to be the means of our turning to him with repentance and holy obedience; that he would restore to us the blessing of peace, and sanctify to us our enjoyments. For our rulers, the King and his ministers, and all the public functionaries. For my friends, acquaintances, and connexions, particularly for those whom I habitually remember in my prayers.

Another class. These are relics of old times. I would especially implore the Divine mercy for Pitt, who is peculiarly exposed. Let me pray fervently and sincerely for our enemies, that God would have pity on them, that he would turn their hearts, etc. Let me pray for all my fellow-creatures, for all that are in pagan ignorance, particularly for the poor negroes, both in Africa and the West Indies. O Lord, do Thou at length visit them with spiritual blessings and a termination of their temporal sufferings. Amen.

And to all my supplications and intercessions, let me add abundant and warm thanksgivings; for, O Lord, Thou hast been to us, and above all to me, abundant in loving-kindness. For our unequalled national blessings, both temporal and spiritual. Run them over in detail, whether as exemption from evils, or possession of goods, etc. For my own blessings. So peculiarly full a cup amidst so liberal a banquet. All around me are feasting, but mine is Benjamin's mess.[35] Consider, O my soul, thy country, the period of the world wherein thy lot is cast; thy station in life; thy personal circumstances as to body and mind; thy externals - rank, fortune, favor with men, and especially numerous, kind, and useful friends; the events of thy life; thy having been kept out of office, and too intimate connexion with political companions; thy being kept from utter falling, etc.[36]

Tuesday, October 25th. 1803

Walked with pencil and book, and wrote. A charming day. I was sitting by the river-side, with my back to the water, on a portable seat, when suddenly it struck me that it was not quite safe. Writing, I might be absent, and suddenly slip off, etc. I moved therefore a few yards, and placed my stool on the grass, when in four or five minutes it suddenly broke, and I fell flat on my back, as if shot. Had it happened five minutes sooner, as I cannot swim, I must, a thousand to one, have been drowned, for I sat so that I must have fallen backwards into the river. I had not the smallest fear or idea of the seat's breaking with me, and it is very remarkable, that I had rather moved about while by the river, which would have been more likely to break it, whereas I sat quite still when on the grass. A most providential escape. Let me praise God for it.[37]

---

35. Genesis 43:34.

36. *Life*, iii. pp. 127-130.

37. Ibid., p. 132.

Undated, 1803

A servant here is dangerously ill. I know they have no objection to my talking to him, yet I feel a sad lukewarmness, and even averseness to it. Did Christ feel the same towards me and other poor sinners? Whatever be the cause of my disinclination, shyness, pride, what it may, let me not search out for reasons to justify the abstaining from what I wish to avoid, but obey the plain primary dictates of conscience. Praying with the sick servant. I saw the poor man for twenty minutes, and prayed with him.[38] Nothing could exceed the kindness with which our friends received us. Alas, it grieves me to see a family, in all respects so amiable, fooled at all by the world. Their wealth is their bane. It connects them with fashionable, thoughtless neighbors, connects their children with frequenters of scenes of dissipation. Oh may God bless them! How hard is it for them that have riches to enter into, and keep in, the narrow road! Beware, O my soul.[39]

I have allowed so little time for evening devotions, that my prayers have been too often hurried over. Tis my old fault; my profane studies, or my letters, engross me. Yet if we be alienated from God at all, it matters not by what it is, whether our hearts be overcharged with surfeiting, drunkenness, or cares of this life; whether with literature, or pleasure, or ambition. I have often on a Saturday evening found in myself, though I hope not allowed, this kind of sentiment – 'Oh I shall have time enough for religious occupations tomorrow, and how shall I find sufficient employment for the Sunday?' O Lord, this indicates a sad want of love. How different David's feelings, Psalm lxxxiv. Oh quicken me in Thy righteousness. Give me all holy affections in their just measure of vigor and force.[40]

I fear I am not improving time to the utmost, in reading and hearing so much. I am seduced by the pleasantness of it. I will try to compose more, and to write something that may be useful. Composing will at least be beneficial to myself, and politics as my trade, and remarks drawn from history, must be useful. Also I will in the evening read for half an hour at least the Old Testament, with which I am not well acquainted. When can I do it, if not now, when I have my time so much at my own command?[41]

I am reading the Psalms just now, comparing the two versions, and reading Horne's commentary.[42] What wonderful compositions! What a decisive proof of the Divine origin of the religion to which they belong! There is in the world nothing else like them, and that this proof should

---

38. Ibid., p. 133.

39. Ibid.

40. Ibid., pp. 133-134.

41. Ibid., p. 134.

42. George Horne (1730–1792), Bishop of Norwich from 1790 to 1792, author of the volume Wilberforce notes here, *A Commentary on the Book of Psalms, in which their Literal or Historical sense, as they relate to King David, and the People of Israel, is illustrated; and their application to Messiah, to the Church, and to individuals, as members thereof, is pointed out: with a view to render the use of the Psalter, pleasing and profitable to all orders and degrees of Christians* 3rd ed. 1794).

exist where there are so many others of the same kind, and of other kinds. If the Psalms, suppose, and some other parts of Scripture, belonged to different systems … as the 3rd chapter of St. Matthew; 5th, 6th, 14th, 15th, 16th, 17th, of St. John; St. Paul's Epistles; Isaiah, etc. … we might, were this internal evidence the only proof afforded, be divided and puzzled. But how wonderful, how unaccountable, except on the true hypothesis, that each should in itself be so excellent, and should belong to, and be connected with, the others, and have the same confessed source and origin![43]

Let me beware, lest I make Christ the minister of sin, by comforting myself too easily when any temptation has prevailed over me, with the reflection, that I have a remedy at hand; it is only to humble myself and implore pardon, and, the promises being sure, to obtain forgiveness. There is in truth no other way; but beware, O my soul, lest thou provoke God to withdraw his Spirit and leave thee to thy natural weakness. Not I hope that I sin in the view of this willingness of God to forgive, but I fear, after having discovered the workings of corruption, that I too easily take comfort. Let me rather, when I have thus detected in myself the humiliating marks of my imperfect state, go softly for some time. Let me think of that God and Savior with whom I have trifled; of my base ingratitude; of the aggravating circumstances of my sins; of the multitude of the mercies which have been poured out on me; of the signal advantages and privileges with which I have been favored. These reflections, through the goodness of God and the working of his Spirit, may produce a more settled lowliness and watchfulness of mind.[44]

Sunday, December 18th. 1803 and Sunday, December 25th. 1803

My heart is in a sad state. O heal my backslidings. Bring me back to Thee. Take away the heart of stone, and give me a heart of flesh.[45] Blessed be God that I am not now about to plunge immediately into the bustle and hurry of London and parliamentary business, but that a recess is before me, in which I may have the means of some privacy, and opportunities of meditation and devotional abstraction. O Lord, do Thou vouchsafe me Thy quickening Spirit; without Thee I can do nothing.[46] Mortify in me all ambition, vanity, vain-glory, worldliness, pride, selfishness, and aversation from God, and fill me with love, peace, and all the fruits of the Spirit.

This is a dull day with me; my mind is sadly heavy. I see with my judgment the great truths which this day commemorates; that he who enjoyed the glory of the Father before the world was, came down, emptied himself, and became a wailing infant for our sakes. I see that it was unutterable love, but I seem incapable of feeling anything.

I have got up early this last week, and have had some three quarters, or an hour, for private devotion in a morning. I hoped to have perceived on this day the blessed effects of it, but I believe I have

---

43. *Life*, iii. pp. 134-135.
44. Ibid., pp. 135-136.
45. Ezekiel 36:26.
46. John 15:5.

too much reckoned on it as a settled thing, as any effect follows its cause. Res delicata est Spiritus Dei.[47] Perhaps this dull, spiritless frame is designed as a punishment to me for this thought. But this same course, with more constant humility and watchfulness, must be right. O Lord, enable me to press on. How wonderful is this callousness! a sort of mental paralysis. It may not however be without its uses; it may make me feel more how absolutely helpless I am in myself; may keep me more simply dependent on the grace arid Spirit of God. O Lord, I know not what I am, but to Thee I flee for refuge! I would surrender myself to Thee, trusting Thy precious promises, and against hope believing in hope. Thou art the same yesterday, today, and forever;[48] and therefore however cold and dull I am, yet, waiting on the Lord, I trust I shall at length renew my strength. Even now my heart seems to grow warmer; oh let me fall again to prayer and praise, and implore fresh supplies of strength and grace.[49]

Saturday, December 31st. 1803

I have read too little of the Bible this week. In course, I am in Deuteronomy, but to rouse my sluggish heart I have been occasionally dipping into the Prophecies and Epistles. Give me, Lord, spiritual understanding; let me drink of the water of life.[50] To Thee, O Lord, I fly for succor; Thy promises are sure; and Thou wilt cast out none that come to Thee.[51] There is my stay; otherwise Thou mightest well cast me out; but by commanding us to 'have grace,' 'to grow in grace,' Thou showest that we may. Oh let me then rouse myself, lest, having preached to others, I myself should be a cast-away.[52] I have found my heart much affected by looking at past entries in my Journal; and at the idea that, to the eye of God, all my various crimes, vanities, and follies, are present, in their full, unabated, unsoftened size and character, as they at the time appeared to me. O Lord, enable me to purify myself as Thou art pure.[53]

I humbly hope I feel deeply humbled at the footstool of God's throne, and prostrate I plead the atoning blood of Christ, and humbly trust in his promises of pardon and of grace. When I look forward to the scene before me, and think how ill I have gone on, I shrink back with dread. But, O Lord, I cast my care on Thee,[54] I flee to Thee for succor. Savior of sinners, save me. Help, Lord, help, watch over me, and guide and guard me. Amen. Amen.[55]

---

47. Latin: A sensitive thing is the Spirit of God.
48. Hebrews 13:8.
49. *Life*, iii. p. 144.
50. Revelation 22:17.
51. John 6:37.
52. 1 Corinthians 9:27.
53. 1 John 3:3.
54. 1 Peter 5:7.
55. *Life*, iii. p. 144.

1804

Sunday, April 22nd. 1804

I am distressed just now by the state of political parties. My distress arises partly I hope from real doubts how I ought to act, yet I fear there is also a mixture of worldly fear, and also a weakness of nature, which though not unamiable, ought not to be suffered to influence conduct, or even to discompose me. O Lord, to Thee I will pray, to enlighten my understanding and direct my judgment, and then to strengthen me to take the path of duty with a firm and composed though feeling mind. Poor Addington! with all his faults, I feel for him. But what a lesson does he read me! Had he really acted up to his principles, he might probably have been above his present difficulties. O Lord, Thou rulest, Thy will be done. And keep me from being absorbed by, or too solicitous about, worldly things, remembering that a Christian is to regard and feel himself a stranger and a pilgrim,[56] and to have his portion, his conversation, his treasure, his country in heaven. Be these my habitual feelings, through Thy grace, O Lord.[57]

Wednesday, May 30th. 1804

Morning, breakfast, friends about sending the gospel to the Indians. Mr. Norton's Mohawk's dance. Venn, Dealtry,[58] Cookson, John Thornton, much discussion. We are all extremely struck with Mr. Norton, the Mohawk chief (ugent);[59] his blended modesty and self-possession; his good sense and apparent simple propriety of demeanor. May it be a providential incident thrown in my way to send the gospel to those ill-used people. He again danced his war dance more moderately.[60]

---

56. 1 Peter 2:11.

57. *Life*, iii. pp. 153-154.

58. William Dealtry (1775–1847), evangelical Anglican minister who attended the same Grammar School in Hull (1790–1792) as William Wilberforce, and was a student under the same evangelical headmaster, Joseph Milner. He was an active supporter of the Church Missionary Society, the British and Foreign Bible Society, the Society for the Promotion of Christian Knowledge, and the Society for the Propagation of the Gospel. He contributed several pieces to the evangelical 'Christian Observer,' and was active in the cause of abolition. In 1813, he took over in Clapham after the death of John Venn. In 1847, he was chosen by Lord John Russell to deliver the sermon to both houses of Parliament on 24 March, the day of national penitence and fasting in response to the Scottish and Irish famines.

59. John Norton, called Teyoninhokarawen (1770–1831?), was leader of the Mohawk Indians. His father is thought to have been a Cherokee from North Carolina that a soldier adopted in 1760, who was then taken to Scotland. He became a printer and married a Scottish woman, Christian Anderson. After both he and his father enlisted in the British Army, they were posted to Canada, along with Norton's mother, who worked as a servant. Father and son deserted, with young Norton adopting the complete lifestyle of a native American. He was adopted as the nephew of Mohawk leader Joseph Brant, and given the chiefly name as above. When Brant died in 1807, Norton succeeded him. He met Wilberforce as here in 1804, after returning to London to seek a military commission and to represent Indian interests. As an evangelical Anglican himself, Norton was befriended by several prominent Quakers and evangelical Anglicans. Norton even translated John's Gospel into Mohawk for the British and Foreign Bible Society. See Carl Benn, 'Norton, John (1770–1831?)', *Oxford Dictionary of National Biography*, Oxford University Press, 2004. (http://www.oxforddnb.com/view/article/68142, accessed 3 Nov 2016).

60. *Life*, iii. p. 188.

1805

Sunday, January 6th. 1805

If it were not best to acquiesce cheerfully and entirely in the will of God, I should grieve at being so poorly today, because it is probably my last Sunday before I go to London to engage in the hurly-burly scene I there dwell in. I feel like one who is about to launch into a stormy sea, and who knows from fatal experience how little his own powers are equal to its buffetings. O Lord, do Thou fit me for it. Enable me to seek Thy glory, and not my own; to watch unto prayer; to wait diligently on God; to love him and my Redeemer from the heart; and to be constrained by this love to live actively and faithfully devoting all my faculties and powers to his service, and the benefit of my fellow-creatures. Especially let me discharge with fidelity and humility the duties of my proper station, as unto the Lord, and not unto men; submitting patiently to the will of God, if it be his will that we should be defeated in our effort to deliver our country from the load of guilt and shame which now hangs round her neck, and is, perhaps, like a gangrene, eating out her vital strength, and preparing, though gradually, the consummation of her ruin. O Lord, do Thou lead and guide me.

On looking back, what sad proofs have I had lately of the inward workings of ambition, on seeing others, once my equals, or even my inferiors, rise to situations of high worldly rank, station, power, and splendor! I bless God, I do not acquiesce in these vicious tempers, but strive against them, and not, I hope, in vain. Remember, O my soul, no man can serve two masters.[61] Have I not a better portion than this world can bestow? Would not a still higher situation place both me and my children in less favorable circumstances for making our calling and election sure?[62] Covet not then, O my soul, these objects of worldly anxiety. Let God be thy portion, and seek the true riches, the glory and honor which are connected with immortality. Yet turn not from those who have these honors with cynical or envious malignity, but rejoice in their temporal comfort and gratification, while you pray for them, and strive to do them good by preventing them from being injured by their exaltation.[63]

Sunday, January 13th. 1805

Through God's good providence we are all returned in peace and safety; and now, before I plunge into the stormy sea I am about to enter, I would pray to God through Christ, by the Holy Spirit, to strengthen me with might in the inner man;[64] to enable me to walk by faith,[65] to let my light shine before men,[66] and to become meet to be a partaker of the inheritance

---

61. Matthew 6:24.
62. 2 Peter 1:10.
63. *Life*, iii. pp. 208-210.
64. Ephesians 3:16.
65. 2 Corinthians 5:7.
66. Matthew 5:16.

of the saints in light.[67] O my soul, remember thy portion is not here. Mind not high things. Be not conformed to this world.[68] Commit thy way unto the Lord, and delight thyself in God.[69] Let the men of this world pass by thee in the race of honors, but thine be the honor which cometh of God, thine the glory which is connected with immortality.[70]

Sunday, March 3rd. 1805

I bless God that I feel more than of late I have done, that humble, peaceful, confiding hope in the mercy of God, reconciled in Christ Jesus, which tranquillizes the mind, and creates a desire after that blessed state, where we shall be completely delivered from the bondage of our corruptions, as well as from all our bodily pains and sicknesses, and all our mental anxieties and griefs; where the injustice, oppression, and cruelty, the wickedness, the falsehood, the selfishness, the malignity, of this bad world shall be no more; but peace, and truth, and love, and holiness, shall prevail forever.

O Lord, purify my heart, and make me meet for that blessed society. Alas, how sadly do I still find myself beset by my constitutional corruptions! I trust the grief I felt on the defeat of my Bill on Thursday last, proceeded from sympathy with the wretched victims, whose sufferings are before my mind's eye, yet I fear in part also less pure affections mixed and heightened the smart - regret that I had not made a greater and better fight in the way of speaking; vexation at the shame of the defeat. O Lord, purify me. I do not, God be merciful to me,[71] deserve the signal honor of being the instrument of putting an end to this atrocious and unparalleled wickedness. But, O Lord, let me earnestly pray Thee to pity these children of affliction, and to terminate their unequalled wrongs; and O direct and guide me in this important conjuncture, that I may act so as may be most agreeable to Thy will. Amen.[72]

1806

Saturday, February 22nd. 1806

Attended Pitt's funeral, an affecting ceremony.[73] What thoughts occurred to me when I saw the coffin letting down, and just before!

---

67. Colossians 1:12.

68. Romans 12:2.

69. Psalm 37:4.

70. *Life*, iii. p. 210.

71. Luke 18:13.

72. *Life*, iii. pp. 213-214.

73. William Pitt the Younger died on 23 January, 1806 at the age of forty-six, and was serving as both First Lord of the Treasury and Chancellor of the Exchequer simultaneously. He had been ill for some time before his death. The House of Commons voted that he be given a public funeral. His body lay in state in the Painted Chamber in the Palace of Westminster on Thursday 20 and Friday 21 February, and was visited by many people. The public funeral was held on Saturday 22 February, with the procession beginning at 10am. The Chief Mourner was Pitt's brother, the Earl of Chatham. William's body was described as being covered with a black velvet Pall, adorned with Eight Escutcheons of the Arms of the Deceased. Four supporters of the Pall were the Archbishop of

I thought of our appearance before God in heaven. May the impression be durable. Oh what cause do I find for humiliation and gratitude, looking back to my own and Pitt's public life![74]

Saturday, April 5th. 1806

How wonderful are the ways of Providence! The Foreign Slave Bill is going quietly on. How God can turn the hearts of men! Lords Grenville and Henry Petty[75] wish my general Abolition Bill not to come on, till the Attorney-General's Bill carried through. I believe they are right, and at all events must give way to their wish. Perceval sentit idem.[76]

Thursday, April 10th. 1806

We carried our resolutions 100 and odd to 14, and my address without a division. If it please God to spare the health of Fox, and to keep him and Grenville together, I hope we shall next year see the termination of all our labors.[77]

Friday, April 18th. 1806

We have carried the Foreign Slave Bill, and we are now deliberating whether we shall push the main question. O Lord, do Thou guide us right, and enable me to maintain a spiritual mind amid all my hurry of worldly business, having my conversation in heaven.[78]

Friday, May 25th. 1806

After meeting Fox at Lord Grenville's, and holding some anxious consultations with them, and also with my own friends about the expediency of proposing the general question this year; when it was almost decided to try, I most reluctantly gave up the idea on Lord Grenville's sure opinion, that no chance this session in the House of Lords; the bishops going out of town, etc. But we are to have a general resolution for Abolition both in Commons and Lords. How wonderful are the ways of God, and how are we taught to trust not in man but in him! Though intimate with Pitt for all my life since earliest manhood, and he most warm for Abolition, and really honest, yet now my whole human dependence is placed on Fox, to whom this life opposed, and on Grenville, to whom always rather hostile till of late years, when I heard he was more religious. O Lord, Thou hast all

---

Canterbury, and Dukes of Beaufort, Rutland, and Montrose. The funeral was held at Westminster Abbey and was attended by many nobility and many from both Houses of Parliament.

74. *Life*, iii. p. 254.

75. Henry Petty-Fitzmaurice (1780–1863), 3rd Marquess of Lansdowne, known as Lord Henry Petty (1784–1809). He was the son of Prime Minister William Petty, 1st Marquess of Lansdowne, and became an M.P. himself, holding among other positions, that of Home Secretary, and Lord President of the Council. At the time of Wilberforce's entry, Petty was Chancellor of the Exchequer (1806–1807).

76. *Life*, iii. p. 260. 'Sentit idem' is Latin: feels the same.

77. Ibid., p. 263.

78. Ibid., p. 261.

hearts in Thy disposal, oh that it may be Thy will to put an end to this abhorred system.[79]

Thursday, June 28[th.] 1806

The Abolition looked more promising than for many years.[80]

Sunday[81] Evg 8 ¾ oClock Lyme[82] Aug[st] 17[th.] 1806

We arrived here yesterday ab[t.] ½ past 3 or near 4 oClock & I grieve to say I wasted the Eveng sadly, in looking over ye books in the Lib[y.] so that what with that & with talkg to Will[m] & John, my Evg was all gone & it was full Bedtime with[t] my havg had any private devot[l] Exercises which wo'd have been highly proper, both as being Sat[y] & as it was my first arrival - The fault arose from my not <u>watching unto</u> prayer i.e. carefully lookg out for all proper opportunities of worshippg God & of cultivat[g] a spiritual Taste & a lively Impress[n.] of his Goodness & of all his Excellencies & perfections. I must stop & resume aftd[s] lest I sho'd be interrupted by family Prayers.[83]

9 ¼ after fam Prayers

We are likely I hope to spend 6 or 7 quiet Weeks in this place. O that God may shine on them with his Blessing. I have brought a vast pile of unanswered Letters w. me & my accounts. I have a Slave Abolit[n] Pamphlet to write & to attend to my Health. But amid all my other Cares, may I chiefly care for ye one thg needful & endeav[r.] to grow in Grace. I have been but in a very stupid frame today considerg ye highly favourable circumstce[s.] This quiet & sweet place in a heavenly day; But surely God has been more gracious to me y[n.] I deserv'd for it is only they who wait on him that must expect to enjoy ye Light of his Countenance. It surely cannot be wrong for me to spend an Hour at night & y[e] same in y[e] morng in Spirit[l.] Exercises. O Lord, Help me to act accordg to my plan & to really to grow in Grace. I grieve to think that it is now near 20 years since I first began to seek God, yet how little is ye advancemt I have hitherto made. O Lord quicken soften fix warm me & fill me w[th.] Love peace Joy & evy Xtian Temperament.[84]

Sunday 24th Aug[t] 10 oClock Lyme

I was going to write, but I had better reflect first & try by holy meditat[n] on y[e] past & by S. Exam[n] to obtain a more distinct case of y[e] mercies of God, of my own Sins & I may excite Humiliat[n.] Devotion Gratitude & Love. O Lord, do thou quicken me & enable me to improve these blessed Seasons of sacred Rest from Oly[85] Business. O how inexpressibly

---

79. Ibid., pp. 261-262.

80. Ibid., p. 271.

81. MS Wilberforce c. 42, fo. 3.

82. Lyme, or Lyme Regis, is a coastal town in West Dorset. It lies in Lyme Bay and is noted for the many fossils discovered in the cliffs, part of the Jurassic Coast. In the 18th and 19th centuries, it became fashionable for the wealthy to spend extended time in places such as Lyme Regis or Bath, as did Wilberforce. Jane Austen (1775–1817) also visited in 1803 and 1804, and in her *Persuasion* (1816) she describes the town in detail. Population in 1801 was numbered at 1,451.

83. MS Wilberforce c. 42, fo. 3.

84. Ibid.

85. This is a symbol Wilberforce uses for the world.

valuable they are. How little duly estimat'd or improv'd. Lord give me a larger Measure of thy Grace. Amen. Amen.[86]

Sunday Evg 7:35

I have not had quite time enough for Reflection & Retrospection today (8 oClock havg been interrupted) & now ye time is so far spent that I must be brief. On lookg back I see much Cause for thankfulness. How little did I once think I sho'd survive poor Pitt. What a Subject for Gratitude is our havg carried thus far the Abolit[n] of ye Sla. Trade. My dear B. & our dear little ones preserv'd to me & I to them. On lookg into myself, I see ye strongest Reason to blame myself for having neglected prayer & SS readg. O how Criminal is this in me. It is against my Clear Knowledge of the Commands of God, against the Experience & Example of all good men, ag[t.] my own repeated Resolutn[s] &c. Even tho' it might be scarcely possible to secure adequate time free from Interruption when Parl[t] is sitting, & not easy at Bfield, yet here, where we have our time so much at our own Command. I am deeply & inexcusably criminal for havg failed so to[87] cultivate[88] the Spirit of Relig[n.] which all agree gradually dies without suffic[t] prayer & what that sufficiency is must be determin'd so by one's situat[n]. Here another morng & d[o] Evg is not at all too much. I fear my Heart is but in a low State & I have long intended as soon as my arrear of Letters shall have been finished, to devote day to setting myself to seek God. I hoped my Letters wo'd have been done 'ere now, but they are not finished & they still not yet. O may I wait on God more diligently & Endeavor to maintain a more lively Sense of y[e] Reality of Spiritual things. Lord without thee I can do nothg,[89] with thee all things.[90] O quicken me, cleanse me warm me & please fill me with all peace & Joy in believg,[91] Amen, Amen.[92]

Tuesday Morng Aug[t] 26[th.] 7:42

Alas I seem to have lost all my relig[s.] feelings, & espec[y] from a bad habit. I doubt not havg been establish'd by use, in readg y[e] Bible at night particy I read it with interest & tho' my judgment reminds me tis y[e] Word of God, my feelings will not correspond, O Lord quicken me, this surely is Hardness of Heart. O do thou take it away & give me a new a tender Heart. Yet O Lord I will wait on thee, thou only art the fountain of living Waters & as thou hast said, Whosoever[93] will, let him take the Water of Life freely.[94] I will humbly trust that in thy

---

86. MS Wilberforce c. 42, fo. 3.
87. Ibid.
88. MS Wilberforce c. 42, fo. 4.
89. John 15:5.
90. Philippians 4:13.
91. Romans 15:13.
92. MS Wilberforce c. 42, fos. 1-2.
93. 'So' is inserted here above 'whoever'.
94. Revelation 22:17.

good time thou wilt give me spiritual feelings. Can I expect that after indulging a careless irreverent lukewarm plan for a long time, that at once, on calling, I should find all just as if I had been diligently watching unto prayer, keeping my Heart w. all diligence &c no surely. But He is faithful who hath promis'd & therefore I will go on asking, in due time I shall receive, tho' the promise tarry I will wait for it,[95] it will surely come. Help me O Lord thus to walk by faith[96] & in love givg up myself to thee in all things. Amen.[97]

Wedn^y Augt 27th.

Alas I still am cold & heavy & I wander sadly in prayer & I am sadly apt to feel no suitable Emotn^s in family Readg & prayer. O Lord quicken me for I seem dead & torpid. But I will wait, I will try to renew a practice I once had & foolishly left off, of setting myself to call on God more deliberately for a minute or two a little befe dinner. Even in my busiest times I might lift up an Ejaculatn. Let me renew the practice. O Lord, shed abroad thy Love in my Heart[98] & warm & sanctify me. How excellently Babn's son seems going on. It is ye reward of all his prayer & labour. I have been sadly defective here as elsewhere. O Lord enable me to discharge well my Parental duties.[99]

Saturday Augt 30 7:40

I regret my havg had a bad night bec^e it will make me less strong & clear today, & I had destin'd this day for a day of <u>setting myself to seek God specially</u>. But as I have prepar'd for it & knew not what may intervene to prevent me anytime, I will persist please God in my intention. My objects will be Self-Examination, Humiliation, Devoting myself to God, Humble implorg of pardon & pleadg ye Blood of X^t. implorg ye Holy Spirit, Studying ye Xtian Duties & tempers a little w. reference to myself. Considerg my own Special Duties, arising out of all my various Relations of life, as M.P. Man of fortune Influence. How my various Talents employed & improv'd show maybe &c. Husb'd father Brother friend acquaintc^e Companion &c Ex^n. how far I have grown in Grace. Then Beg a solemn Blessing on Abolit^n labours espec^y my intended publication ab^t. to be commenc'd. Then thanksgivg. O how abund^t sho'd it be & particular. Intercession, particular all my Relations & friends.[100]

12 oClock

I have been in private for ab^t an hour review in some measure my life for Humiliation. O what Cause have I to cry God be merciful.[101]

---

95. Habakkuk 2:3.
96. 2 Corinthians 5:7.
97. MS Wilberforce c. 42, fo. 2.
98. Romans 5:5.
99. MS Wilberforce c. 42, fo. 2.
100. Ibid.
101. Luke 18:13.

If I look to my first declension & for[102] ab[t103] 12 years spent in Sin & folly (true madness) from ab[t.] 1771 or 1772 to ab[t] y[e] close of 1785. O how enormous my wickedness how aggravated How inexcusable. No palliation from strong nat[l] Appetites at one time. Evg Sensuality.[104] God mercifully kept me from open Shame in some instances even then. But O should thou have reced ag[n] into favour one who had behav'd so to thee. Surely O Lord thy Ways are not as our Ways.[105] To think that God not only hears us when at last we cry for mercy, but that He moves[106] us to cry, & arranges & disposes Events so as to move us & bears with & overcomes with infinite longsuffering, our Hardness & Backwardness & natr[l] Circumstances by his Providence to our peculiar Case & Circumstances. In my Case Milner &c. O Lord, how wonderful are thy Ways. Surely God is Love. O may I be in some little proport[n] grateful adequately & earnestly.[107]

At a former Envy Vanity Evy wicked & malignant passion & what a considerat[n] is it throughout that God sees all as fresh as at first, except so far as blotted out by X[t's] Blood. But still more, my Professg State, & some grievs Instances of Sin in which one espec[y] if God had left me to myself I should have disgrac'd my Xtian profess[n] & have ruin'd my Character forever. O let me learn my own Weakness, or rather ever let me feel it for surely I have learn'd it. Ag[n] one standg & continuing Instc[e] of God's mercy preventg Evil in a Way which might have been inconceivably distressg shockg & disgraceful, were I not so much in fault, tho' I know not (thou God knowest) in what degree I may have been faulty. But surely I can never enough praise God for his Goodness. But my not havg made greater progress is a most just Cause of Humiliation. It is humiliating to compare my Zeal Humility Sorrow for Sin Love of God, Solicitude for friends Spiritual Welfare, Readg & Spirit[l] Mindedness, Sense of Xtian's peculiar Char[r] & desire to adorn y[e.] Gospel[108] & do Credit to y[e.] Xtian Char[r], in 1786 Summer when first sent down to Scarbro' to Mother & Mrs. Sykes[109] &c. & aftd[s] & y[e.] followg year I think to Wilford.

---

102. MS Wilberforce c. 42, fo. 2.

103. MS Wilberforce c. 42, fo. 3.

104. 'Doubtless #' then inserted above line, with the following paragraph to be inserted here, denoted by the sign '#' later on the page.

105. Isaiah 55:8.

106. 'Moves' here was inserted over word he had crossed out, looks like 'desires'.

107. This is the end of the inserted paragraph.

108. Titus 2:10.

109. The Sykes family was originally from Sykes Dyke, Cumberland, who then settled in Leeds as clothier merchants. Joseph Sykes (1723–1803) made his fortune from being a mine-owner, trader and shipper, and moved to West Ella Hall near Hull, which he purchased in 1750. He had married Dorothy Twigge and with their seven children, became one of Hull's wealthiest, owning several opulent houses. Joseph was chamberlain (1751), Sheriff (1754), Mayor of Hull (1761, 1777), and Deputy-Lieutenant of the East Riding of Yorkshire (1769). The family beautified the village of West Ella so much so, that much of the area is now under a conservation order. When Wilberforce was brought back from London by his mother, he developed a strong bond with the Sykes children, spending many holidays with the family and coming to think of them as almost his own siblings. He grew up especially close to their daughter Marianne (1765–1815), who when she grew up, married Wilberforce's close friend and cousin, Henry Thornton, and had nine children. The Wilberforce

O let me try "to quicken ye things that are ready to die"[110] to "be zealous & repent"[111] to "do ye first Works."[112] "O Lord I can only come to thee to draw from the fountain of living Waters, a renewed Supply of those quickening Streams."[113] It is from Xt. that the Restorat^n & Invigorat^n of all my Xtian Graces must proceed & O merciful Saviour I cast myself before thee & I humbly implore thee to quicken renew stablish make me perfect strengthen settle me, Amen.[114] I purpose to wait daily at ye Throne of Grace & never to cease my Importunity, (endeavorg all ye while not to grieve or quench but to stir up ye Spirit), till I find myself really created anew in X^t Jesus[115] & made meet to be a partaker of ye Inheritance of ye Saints in Light.[116] Yet while I continue in ye Body, I shall never be perfect. But O what room is there for growth in Grace, what Space for advancemt yet let me now mix humble praises for any little desire of those spirit^l Blessings, that God has not given me over to a reprobate Mind[117] & allowed me to be so harden'd by ye Deceitfulness of Sin[118] as to lose all Spiritual Sensibility.

I have deep Cause for Humiliation for my defects & Sins as an M.P. as a Master, a Father a Friend a Companion. How little have I duly (sympathized with X^t)[119] for the State of Sinners. How little kept my Conv^n & Compy Regls. How little adequately endeav'd to adorn & do Credit to the Gospel.[120] How Self-indulgently have I often gone on. How Sensually seduc'd by ye really necessary Indulgences my weak Body requires. But here ag^n I see numerous Instances of ye astonishg Goodness & Long Sufferg of God not sufferg my own folly & Imprudence[121] to[122] produce their full Effects. God's forbearance & Long Sufferg Goodness to me is utterly astonishg. O Lord thy Ways are not as our ways.[123] I have partic^r Instances here also in my mind which I hope never to forget. All that has happen'd creditably or beneficially for me, has been

---

and Sykes families became closely connected. Dorothy Sykes took a very sympathetic interest in Wilberforce's conversion that he gave her a minor but significant part in his narrative. When rumors reached Hull that he had gone mad, he records that she said to his mother that if he had become so deranged, she hoped it might be all their experience. In the following year, 1787, Joseph Sykes and his 24 year old son, John, were admitted partners in Wilberforce and Smith in a deal that made them the largest shareholders in the company.

110. Revelation 3:2.
111. Revelation 3:19.
112. Revelation 2:5.
113. John 7:38.
114. 1 Peter 5:10.
115. 2 Corinthians 5:17.
116. Colossians 1:12.
117. Romans 1:28.
118. Hebrews 3:13.
119. Above 'sympathized' is the word 'felt' and above 'with' is the word 'for'.
120. Titus 2:10.
121. MS Wilberforce c. 42, fo. 3.
122. MS Wilberforce c. 42, fo. 4.
123. Isaiah 55:8.

clearly referable to God. All that has been tendg to Shame or Evil has been my own doing. And I doubt not I should have utterly ruin'd myself but for the preventing Grace & Goodness of my God. But my present State is justly a Ground of y^e. deepest Self Abasemt. Alas, how low are my Graces compar'd with those of almt all the Xtians I see around me in the Sight of God who searches y^e. Heart. My dearest B. shames me. How Bab^n and Gisbe shame me & Wm Spooner & Lill^n & young Bab^n. O may I be stir'd up to greater diligence & zeal & not suffer myself to be deceived by y^e. opinion entertain'd of me by those who do not see the Heart. How faint my Love my Zeal my longings for Communion w God. My actual delight in him Compar'd w what they ought to be Conseqy my Joy in him. How weak my Sense & Hatred of sin compar'd w. X^t's & w. what it ought to be. O Lord, I humbly flee to thee here also. O supply me out of thy fulness. Be thou made unto me Wisdom & Righteousness & Sanctificatn & complete Redemption.[124] Redemption from the power as well as punish't & Guilt of Sin & give me an abundant Increase in ev^y Virtue. Above all shed abroad the Love of God in my Heart[125] & strengthen & enliven my faith & Hope & Joy in God in X^t. again.[126]

2:25 Augt 30

I was carrying in my Bible & meang to read Owen when passg by ye Windows saw Mr. & Mrs. Babbs in y^e. Parlour whom I'd been afraid of all morng, it was Evidently the Provid^ce of God & I rem^bd Doddridge's bear^g of these Interruptions with^t Impatience & I thank God was able to be unruffled. But alas I did not as I have since recollected, endeav^r enough if at all to practice my Conv^n Regls my Ejacns to God to Enable me to do & get good. O let me try more to live thus by faith continually. They staid till 1¾ when I walked out w. Owen on sp^l mindedness & Newton on Comm^n w God[127] & read walk^g & now I'm come in to pray a little bef^e dinner to supplicate Blessg^s shortly & for short gen^l thanksgiv^g. I go to prayer. O what an unspeakable Blessing is it to have such blessed Means of Grace. Retirem^t & excell^t Books & whatever can help y^e. languid mind & excite y^e. torpid affectn^s, yet remember O my soul, it is the Spirit alone that helpeth our Infirmities.[128] It is X^t. that maketh intercession for us,[129] & the Love of God is to be shed abroad in our Hearts by the Holy Ghost given unto us.[130] O may this be more & more my blessed Experience. Amen, Amen.[131]

---

124. 1 Corinthians 1:30.

125. Romans 5:5.

126. MS Wilberforce c. 42, fo. 4.

127. Wilberforce is here referring to Omicron's Letter 24: On Communion with God, first published as *Twenty-Six Letters* by Omicron (London, 1774). Available in *The Select Works of the Rev. John Newton; to which are prefixed Memoirs of his Life, &c.* by Rev. R. Cecil (Edinburgh, 1831).

128. Romans 8:26.

129. Romans 8:34.

130. Romans 5:5.

131. MS Wilberforce c. 42, fo. 4.

Sat^y Aftn 5:10

I eat today moderately but my stomach being Empty before & very
uncomfortable for Want of food, tho' I drank not above 2 Glasses of Wine
if so much pure & about as much with Water, yet I have felt manifestly
affected by it not in the least intoxicated, but flurried, unspiritualized,
& unfit for Spiritual Exercises.[132]

6:35

I walked partly out of doors partly indoors with B. & played a little w.
C. I now resume the pen and now I feel less unspiritual. I am reminded
of the Contrast, be not filled w. Wine but be &c.[133]

Sunday Evg 8¼ oClock Novr. 2^{d.} Pye Nest[134] near Halifax

How truly may I say that Goodness & Mercy follow me all the days of
my life.[135] It is really astonishing. The Continued attachment to me of
all these people both Merchnts & Squires, with so little of ye. eadem
velle[136] & noble, with their usual prejudices ag^t Religion, without my
cultivatg their good will by solid Services or personal attentions nay
refusg their Requests & not visiting them, their shewg such wonderful
publick spirit & justness of Principle & Conduct, is quite astonishg, &
is only to be ascribed to ye. overruling Providence of God, who turneth
the Hearts of men at Will. O what a lesson is this to put our trust in
God & I humbly hope I have been enabled to see him in all these Events
- I have also been preserv'd from all accidents. One narrow Escape,
night before last, from a Waggon heavy loaded & going oppos^t way to
my Chaise L & in ye. dark, & grazed very hard. Also to be so popular
among all ye. common people, Clothiers & all. O tis ye. Goodness of y^{e.}
Almighty & may I be more & more thankful for his infinite Bounty. I
must lay down my pen, alas this has been a sad Sunday. I longed to be
quiet at ye. Vicarage, but Edw^{ds} wo'd not be denied & He is so kind &
Hospitable that I could not bear to give him pain. I am quite at a loss
how to behave on a Sunday w. irreligious people. If I sulk, it wo'd be
misunderstood, yet to be cheerful & talk as on other days scarce seems
right. I have tried to put in a word or two serious now & then, but alas,
alas. O Lord give me a warmer Love of my fellow Creatures & dispose
& enable me to be more essentially useful to them in ye. best things.
O Lord, give me more Grace. Quicken, warm, soften me, & make me
more & more meet to be a Partaker of ye. Inheritance of ye. Saints in

---

132. Ibid.

133. Ibid. Ephesians 5:18.

134. Pye Nest, two miles from Halifax, Yorkshire, was purchased by John Edwards (1737–1823)
from Japhet Lister. It was inherited by his son Henry Lees Edwards (1775–1848). Pye Nest was
adjacent to Crow Wood estate, also owned by Edwards and which included Crow Wood Mansion.
It then passed to his son Sir Henry Edwards (1812–1886), 1st Baronet, M.P., Deputy Lieutenant of
the West Riding of Yorkshire, and one of the major landowners around Halifax.

135. Psalm 23:6.

136. Latin: the same will.

Light.[137] With[t] thee I can do noth,[138] Amen, Amen. I bless God I have felt some Gratitude this Evening.[139]

1807

Sunday, February 15th. 1807

What an awful moment is this! The decision of the great question approaches. May it please God, who has the hearts of all in his hands, to turn them as in the House of Lords; and enable me to have a single eye,[140] and a simple heart, desiring to please God, to do good to my fellow-creatures, and to testify my gratitude to my adorable Redeemer.[141]

Sunday, February 22nd. 1807

Never surely had I more cause for gratitude than now, when carrying the great object of my life, to which a gracious Providence directed my thoughts twenty-six or twenty-seven years ago, and led my endeavors in 1787 or 1788. O Lord, let me praise Thee with my whole heart: for never surely was there any one so deeply indebted as myself; which way soever I look I am crowded with blessings. Oh may my gratitude be in some degree proportionate.[142]

Tuesday, April 28, 1807

… a narrow escape from breaking my leg just when setting out, Deo gratias, how are we always in his hands![143]

Undated, 1807

Surely it calls for deep humiliation, and warm acknowledgment, that God has given me favor with men, that after guiding me by his providence to that great cause, he crowned my efforts with success, and obtained for me so much goodwill and credit. Alas, Thou knowest, Lord, all my failings, errors, infirmities, and negligences in relation to this great cause; but Thou art all goodness and forbearance towards me. If I do not feel grateful to Thee, oh how guilty must I be brought in by my own judgment! But, O Lord, I have found too fatally my own stupidity; do Thou take charge of me, and tune my heart to sing Thy praises, and make me wholly Thine.

When I look back on my parliamentary life, and see how little, all taken together, I have duly adorned the doctrine of God my Savior.[144] I am ashamed and humbled in the dust; may any time which remains, Lord, be better employed. Meanwhile I come to the cross with all my

---

137. Colossians 1:12.

138. John 15:5.

139. MS Wilberforce c. 42, fo. 5.

140. Matthew 6:22.

141. *Life*, iii. p. 295.

142. Ibid., pp. 295-296.

143. Wilberforce's sons state here that it was on leaving London that Wilberforce had the accident here noted, *Life*, iii. p. 316.

144. Titus 2:10.

sins, negligences, and ignorances, and cast myself on the free mercy of God in Christ as my only hope and refuge. Lord, receive and pardon me, and give me Thy renewing grace. Oh how inexpressibly valuable are the promises of Holy Scripture! Thy ways, O Lord, are not as our ways;[145] Thou art infinite in love, as in wisdom, and in power. O may I never forsake Thee; guide me, guard me, purify me, strengthen me, keep me from falling, and at length present me faultless before the presence of Thy glory with exceeding joy.[146]

There is something so stupendously great in the salvation of God, that when we are enabled to have some realizing sense of it, one is ready to cry out, 'Not unto me, O Lord, not unto me',[147] surely I am utterly unworthy of all Thy goodness and love. So thou art, but Christ is worthy; and he shall see of the travail of his soul, and shall be satisfied.[148] And all the company of the redeemed, with the holy angels, and surely with myriads of myriads of beings, according to their several ranks, and orders, and faculties, and powers, shall join in adoring the infinite love of the Redeemer, and shall make up the chorus of that heavenly song, 'Worthy is the Lamb that was slain, to receive honor, and glory, and blessing,' etc.[149] Oh may I bear a part in that bright and glad assemblage! Who will, who among them all can, have more cause than myself for gratitude and love? Meanwhile may I prove my gratitude on earth, by giving up myself to Thy service, and living universally to Thy glory. O Lord, enable me to be thus wholly Thine.

O Lord, I humbly hope that it is Thou who knockest at the door of my heart, who callest forth these more than usually lively emotions of contrition, desire, faith, trust, and gratitude. Oh may I hear his voice, and open the door and let him in,[150] and be admitted to intercourse and fellowship; may I be really a thriving Christian, bringing forth abundantly the fruits of the Spirit to the glory of God. O Lord, I am lost in astonishment at Thy mercy and love. That Thou shouldst not only quit the glory and happiness of heaven to be made man, and bear the most excruciating torments and bitter degradation for our deliverance and salvation; but that Thou still bearest with us, though we, knowing all Thy goodness, are still cold and insensible to it. That Thou strivest with our perverseness, conquerest our opposition, and still waitest to be gracious; and that it was in the foreknowledge of this our base ingratitude and stupid perverseness, that Thou didst perform these miracles of mercy. That Thou knewest me, and my hardness, and coldness, and unworthy return for all Thy goodness, when Thou calledst me from the giddy throng, and shone into my heart with the light of the glory of God, in the face of Jesus Christ. O well may we exclaim, 'Thy ways are not as our ways, nor Thy thoughts as our thoughts; but as the heavens are higher than the

---

145. Isaiah 55:8.
146. Jude 24.
147. Psalm 115:1.
148. Isaiah 53:11.
149. Revelation 5:12.
150. Revelation 3:20.

earth, so are Thy ways higher than our ways, and Thy thoughts than our thoughts.'[151] O Lord, I cast myself before Thee, O spurn me not from Thee; unworthy, though I am, of all Thy wonderful goodness. O grant me more and more of humility, and love, and faith, and hope, and longing for a complete renewal into Thine image. Lord, help me and hear me. I come to Thee as my only Savior. O be Thou my help, my strength, my peace, and joy, and consolation, my Alpha and Omega; my all in all. Amen.

I have far too little thought of the dangers of great wealth, or rather of such affluence and rank in life as mine. O my soul, bethink thee of it; and at the same time bless God who has given thee some little knowledge of the way of salvation. How little also have I borne in mind that we are to be pilgrims and strangers on the earth![152] This impression can be kept up in those who are in such a state of prosperity and comfort as myself, by much prayer and meditation, and by striving habitually to walk by faith and to have my conversation in heaven. O Lord, direct me to some new line of usefulness, for Thy glory, and the good of my fellow-creatures. I have been thinking of lessening the number of oaths.[153]

1808

Saturday, January 16, 1808

Day set apart for prayer and meditation, and other religious exercises, with moderation in food. Praying above all for the love of God and my Redeemer, that this blessed principle may be like the mainspring of the machine, prompting all the movements, and diffusing its practical influence through every disposition, action, plan, and design. And (if it be consistent with the Divine will) for a more assured hope of the favor of God and Christ. May the God of hope fill me with all joy and peace in believing.[154] O Lord, do Thou break, soften, quicken, warm my cold heart; and teach me to feel an overflowing love and gratitude, or rather a deep and grateful sense of obligation, not as a transient effusion, but as the settled temper and disposition, the practical habit of my soul: that so I may here begin the song of praise, to be sung with more purified and warmed affections in heaven, Worthy is the Lamb; and blessing, honor, glory, and power, etc.[155]

1809

Undated, 1809

Reading much, correcting the Practical View for a new edition, and much with family. Oh what a blessing it is to be living thus in peace!

---

151. Isaiah 55:8-9.
152. 1 Peter 2:11.
153. *Life*, iii. pp. 338-339.
154. Romans 15:13.
155. Revelation 5:12. *Life*, iii. p. 356.

Surely no one has so much reason to say, that goodness and mercy have followed me all the days of my life.[156] Never was any one so exempted from suffering, so favored with comforts. Oh that I were more grateful![157] O Lord direct and guide me, so as to make my residence here a blessing to me. Laying out plans so as to secure time for evening devotions, emptying my mind of business and literature; examining myself whether my mind had wandered whilst reading the responses or the psalms in church, or during the singing of praises to God; and reminding myself, that if here I find not my mind ungovernable, yet that this is a most favorable situation: all about me favorable to holiness, except that I commonly find literature more seductive than anything. I should then be striving for the habit of heavenly-mindedness, that I may maintain it in more worldly scenes and societies.

O blessed days these, which call us from the bustle of life, and warrant us in giving up our studies and our business, and cultivating communion with God.[158] Lord, increase my love to others for ambition, or rather worldliness, but ill cured, often bubbling up and breaking out, though my judgment I trust does not allow them, and though I am ashamed of them. Alas! can I say that I find more pleasure in religious meditation than in literature, which always presents itself to my mind as an object of gratification!

How does this review, in which my own mind fixes on specific objects, shame me! How should I be ashamed if others could see me just as I really am! I often think I am one grand imposture. My heart is heavy; oh, there is nothing that can speak peace to the wounded spirit but the gospel promises, and the promise is sure. God is love; and is able to save to the uttermost,[159] and he will cast out none who come to him.[160] He it is I trust who has excited in me a disposition to come, and I will therefore press forward, humbly indeed, but trusting to his mercy who has promised so many blessings to them that seek him. O Lord, yet strengthen me, and, if it please Thee, fill me with all peace and joy in the Holy Ghost. Amen.[161]

I humbly hope that I have felt this day, and still feel, somewhat of the powers of the world to come. I feel indeed the deepest sense of my own sinfulness; but blessed be God for his gracious promises. To Thee, O Lord, I humbly devote myself; O confirm me to the end. Make me perfect, stablish, strengthen, settle me.[162] O praeclarum illum diem. What cause have I for thankfulness! Which way soever I look I am heaped up with blessings, mercies of all sorts and sizes. I wish not to spend time in writing, but, oh let me record the lovingkindness of the Lord.[163]

---

156. Psalm 23:6.
157. *Life*, iii. p. 422.
158. His comments about Sundays.
159. Hebrews 7:25.
160. John 6:37.
161. Romans 15:13.
162. 1 Peter 5:10.
163. *Life*, iii. pp. 424-425.

Sunday, December 24th. 1809

After giving a dinner to Lord N. and I. H. who chatted till late; Lord N. a strange twist; I fear the evening was sadly misspent. No efforts to improve the opportunity and impress them aright. When in my closet, as now, I feel a sincere desire to do good to others, and to embrace occasions for it; but, alas! when in society I am too apt to lose the sense of God's presence, or possess it feebly and faintly, and I do not try to turn the conversation, and practice the company regulations which I have made. Lord, quicken me.

I have a vast multiplicity of objects soliciting my attention, and I seem to myself to be failing in the discharge of the duties of my several relations, as Member of Parliament, as father, and as master. To Thee, O God, I fly, through the Savior; enable me to live more worthy of my holy calling; to be more useful and efficient, that my time may not be frittered away unprofitably to myself and others, but that I really may be of use in my generation, and adorn the doctrine of God my Savior.[164] I long to carry the plan through for lessening the number of oaths, for reviving the Proclamation Society; but I am a poor, helpless creature, Lord, strengthen me.[165]

1810

Sunday, January 7th. 1810

Alas! How little time have I for private devotions, or Scripture reading and meditation. I must either give up having so much company and so many friends in the house, or I must leave them, so as to render hospitality and their society compatible with the measure of spiritual exercises which my constitution of soul requires. The last alternative surely is right; but if on trial I find it needful, I must give up society as the right hand or eye, which it is my peculiar duty to cut off or pluck out. But, O Lord, quicken me. I have been hearing an excellent sermon from Simeon, on Aaron's death, pressing towards the close on torpid believers; Alas! Alas! to me that name belongs, but blessed be God it need not belong always! Thou hast declared that Thou wilt be found of them that seek Thee.[166] To Thee, O Lord, I fly; O forgive and receive Thy unworthy wanderer! O come and dwell within me! Alas, how forgetful am I of the presence of God; and thence of my company and conversation regulations! Yesterday evening I fell into the vice of evil speaking.

O Lord, fill me with love, with brotherly kindness, and grateful humility. How thankful should I be for my signal privileges, and how candid and tender in speaking, or judging, or thinking of those who have been destitute of the advantages I have enjoyed! If they had

---

164. Titus 2:10.
165. *Life*, iii. pp. 435-436.
166. Isaiah 55:6.

possessed my advantages they would most likely be far superior to me. How shocking is it to think that now for twenty-four years I have been seeking after God, and that my progress has been so little! Yet, O Lord, I would humbly hope that though I am weakly and feeble, yet that Christ is knocking at the door of my Laodicean heart, and that I shall open the door and admit my heavenly visitant.[167] O Lord, rouse me effectually, and make me an active, zealous, fruitful Christian; let me beware of getting into the way so forcibly described by Owen, as a trade of sinning and repenting. Oh most blessed promise, I will give to him that is athirst of the water of life freely![168] The main spring having thus been set flowing, may it water every distant branch, and may I fulfill the duties of all my various relations, as M.P., master, acquaintance, etc. now so ill performed. Oh how little have I adorned Thy doctrine;[169] and yet how much better do people think of me than they would if they knew me as I really am! Lord, do Thou completely sanctify me. Amen.[170]

1811

Sunday, February 10th. 1811
Lying awake long in the night my thoughts were not naturally so serious as usual, and my mind more disturbed by the rushing in of a great variety of topics. Alas! How much of my life is fumed away in trifles which leave no mark behind, and no fruit! O Lord, enable me to redeem the time better in future; to live more on plan, though really this has been in some degree my object, and to be more devoted in heart and life to Thy glory, and to the good of my fellow-creatures.

Let me try to keep myself reminded of invisible things by something which will call attention, though not produce pain, and by varying the expedients; when I grow familiar with one, I may use another. I did try a little pebble in my shoe. Why should such secondary means be despised? Oh that they were unnecessary, and so they may become by degrees! Oh may I learn to live above this world, and set my affections on things above![171]

Saturday, April 27th. 1811
Spent nearly an hour in private devotions. At breakfast had a number of people, Mr. Guinness,[172] of Dublin, about Irish brewery. Colonel Morison,[173] from Trinidad, Smith's friend, very acute and pleasing,

---

167. Revelation 3:20.

168. Revelation 22:17.

169. Titus 2:10.

170. *Life*, iii. pp. 436-437.

171. Colossians 3:2. *Life*, iii. p. 437.

172. Arthur Guinness II (1768–1855), brewer, banker, M.P., philanthropist and supporter of Catholic Emancipation.

173. Joseph Wanton Morrison (1783–1826), born in New York, Morrison would ultimately attain the rank of Brigadier General in the British Army. He is especially remembered for his command of British troops at the Battle of Crysler's Farm in the War of 1812.

wishing for instruction of Black corps, shocking account of Trinidad. William Hoare,[174] about Scilly missionaries. Had each alone, besides general breakfast. Lord Teignmouth too called. Then to town, letters, lodgings. To Exhibition dinner, looked at the pictures, blamed myself for looking at a Scriptural subject without emotion, as at a common fabulous picture. Dined, sat near Sir T. Bernard, Rose, and Bankes. Set down Rose at his house, he quite sure that he shall show the Bullion Report to be the most blundering ever laid before Parliament. Surely the opposite opinions of men, able, honest, and experienced in the business, should teach diffidence in holding your own opinions, and candor in judging others. Lord Carrington, Perceval, and Vansittart,[175] all dissevered by party; and Rose, Samuel Thornton,[176] and Thomas Thompson against committee, whilst Henry Thornton, John Smith, and Bankes, most decidedly for the Report. Wasted twenty or twenty-five most precious morning minutes today; for time misapplied is wasted.[177]

Herstmonceaux[178] Place[179] July 21st. 1811 - 2 ¾ Sunday

Hav[g] left my 4to Book in town, I must use this paper for recording now & then the State of my Heart & Affections, & any particulars also of Conduct which it may be useful to note down. But alas, poor dear Eliz has engrossed so much of my time this morng since Church, that having had scarce 5 minutes for relig[s] Exercises before Bkft, I must husband what remains before dinner & may y[e.] Hour or 2 which I hope to have at my disposal, be blessed to my Soul. Alas! let me strive to impress on my Heart, from y[e.] odious appearance of her bad tempers, how hateful my own, tho' differing in kind, yet no less contrary to God's & X[t's] holy nature, how far more hateful they must appear to God & my Redeemer. What base Ingratitude! What provoking neglect of y[e.] Means of Grace! What Unprofitableness. What Vanity & inordinate love of human Estimation. What Coldness & deadness! What deficiencies in pursuit of love & Solicitude & active Exertions for my fellow Creatures, are imputable to me.

I must stop. But O my Soul, fall down before y[e.] Lord in speechless Confusion of face, or beat thy Breast & say God be Merciful to me a

---

174. Possibly refers to William Henry Hoare (1776–1819).

175. Nicholas Vansittart (1786–1851), 1st Baron Bexley, lawyer, M.P. for Old Sarum at the time of Wilberforce's entry, Chancellor of the Exchequer, and cousin of Henry Addington.

176. Samuel Thornton (1754–1838), M.P. for Hull along with William Wilberforce, a member of the Clapham Circle, and one of the sons of John Thornton. Director and Governor of the Bank of England.

177. *Life*, iii. p. 513.

178. MS Wilberforce c. 42, fo. 6.

179. Herstmonceux is a village and parish in East Sussex, which includes Herstmonceux Castle and Place. The name comes from a combination of 'Hyrst', Anglo-Saxon for 'wooded hill', and Monceux, which was the family name of the 12th century lords of the manor in this area. The castle dates from the 15th century, and the impressive Herstmonceux Place is located in the north-west corner of the park.

Sinner.[180] O Blessed be God! That I may do more than this! That we are assured that if we confess our Sins, He is faithful & just to forgive us our Sins & to cleanse us from all unrighteousness.[181] To thee then O Sav[r] of Sinrs I flee for refuge.[182] I come to thee O Lord on y[e] Throne of Grace by that new & livg way thou hast[183] provided[184] to find Mercy & Grace to help in this my time of need.[185] O Lord quicken soften, cleanse warm sanctify me, & make me meet to be a partaker of y[e] Inheritance of the Saints in Light,[186] full of Humility & peace & Love & Hope & Joy. Amen. Amen.

O when from surveying myself in y[e] gen[l] in relation to God, I examine in detail my past demerits in all my various Relations, of M P., Father, Master, Friend, Companion, I am overwhelm'd with y[e] number & magnitude of my Sins; so many, so persever'd in, under such Means of Grace & Mercies, so little truly struggled ag[t]. But yet O Lord I humbly trust it is thy Grace which disposes me to examine myself, which opens my Eyes to my real Character & Conduct & which draws me to fly for Refuge to the Cross, there to be wash'd from my Sins in X[t's] own Blood & to obtain not peace only but Wisdom & Righteousness, Sanctification & Redemption[187] & Grace for Grace out of y[e] fulness which is in X[t] Jesus. Lord help me, for y[e] Redeemer's Sake. Amen. Amen.[188]

Sunday 1:40, August 4, 1811, Herstmonceaux

I have but little time at Command as I am going to Church in ab[t] an Hour. Let me however note down a little of my Goings on & State. Alas I have been going on sadly in some partic[s] since I came here, Espec[y] as to my Evg devotns, y[e] Old fault. I hope it partly & indeed chiefly arises from Bodily Weakness, that often in writg Letters even in a morn[g] I am so sleepy, I can scarcely keep awake, & still more at Night, that I can not help sleeping both in pri. dev. bet[n] 9 & 10, & aftds at 10, Mr. Kemp's fam[y] prayers. This is sad work & in part at least, I am much in fault for I do not enough secure time in y[e] Evg for pri. dev. Let me rem[r] Owen, on giv[g] God y[e] best of our time. Let us rem[r] God's own Reasong on this very subject Malachi.

Again, I am sadly wastg my time here, not enough strivg to improve y[e] opportuny of Leisure I enjoy. Then, Childrn I fear neglected yet here I feel so incompetent. O Lord help me. Then not maintaing enough of a spirit[l] mind, not being enough watchful to improve Conversat[n] for good. O let me humble myself deeply before

---

180. Luke 18:13.
181. 1 John 1:9.
182. Hebrews 6:18.
183. 'Hast' is written here over a previous word.
184. Hebrews 10:20.
185. Hebrews 4:16.
186. Colossians 1:12.
187. 1 Corinthians 1:30.
188. MS Wilberforce c. 42, fos. 6-7.

God, & strive by meditat[n] & prayer to call down a measure of y[e.] flame of divine Love into my Heart. O what Blessgs what privileges have I enjoyed. How little proportionable to them has been my progress in Relig[n.] yet Lord, fulfil in me all the good pleas[e] of thy Goodness & y[e.] Work of faith w. power. Lord to thee I fly. Vouchsafe me thy quickening Grace. Strengthen my Humility faith love Hope & make me a Xtian in deed & in truth, walkg & livg by faith & love[189] Right[s] Peace Joy in HG. Amen. Amen.[190]

Sunday 2 ½ oClock Aug[t] 11[th.] Herstmonceaux

I have been employed rightly I Trust, in a short Letter of Charity, & a longer (just finished) ab[t.] y[e.] Injuries of y[e.] poor Missionaries & Slaves in Trinidad, & as it is now time to go to Aft[n] Church I determine to stay at home & employ the remaining 2 hours bef[e] dinner better y[n] if I were there. Alas. What sad work this morng. I have been employed this week alm[t] entirely in Letter writg, on Roberts's Letter (alm[t] 40 pages), & on Letters ab[t] y[e.] methods & false Report & my Retiring fm Yorke. I scarcely ever write more in y[e.] morng. I bless God I feel today I hope, some measure of Xtian [191]Humiliation[192] combin'd w. faith & Hope.

I go to Confession & prayer & Intercession after deeply bewailing my Sins, that God will for X[t's] Sake, accept & bless me w. all Spirit[l] Blessings in Xt Jesus, that He will strengthen me w. might &c. &c. & make me meet to be a partaker of y[e.] Inherit[ce] of y[e.] Saints in Light.[193] Also, that He will guide me right in this to me most important Instance, whether to retire from Yorkshire[194] or not, on y[e.] grounds of takg y[e.] Intimation from y[e.] first tendencies of which I am conscious to both bodily & mental faculties declining, & of my growing family & y[e.] attention they call for, W[m] especy, now 13. Also that He may bless my dear Child[n] & especy Wm.

O Lord, Let thy Spirit help my Infirmities & enable me to pray to thee as I ought. Alas, I have not for y[e.] last week been duly attentive to my proposd reform, either in the Case of earlier Hours, or Evg devotions less hurried, at least if some amendment, by no means enough. But O let me not acquiesce in my present state or make X[t.] y[e.] minister of Sin, but let me press forwd, forgettg y[e.] things t are

---

189. 'Love' is inserted here from previous insertion.

190. MS Wilberforce c. 42, fo. 7.

191. Ibid.

192. MS Wilberforce c. 42, fo. 8.

193. Colossians 1:12.

194. Wilberforce was elected to Parliament from Hull in 1780, and from the more important seat of Yorkshire in 1784. In the 1807 Yorkshire election, for example, which held the record as the most expensive election before the Reform Act of 1832 and which was Yorkshire's first contested election since 1741, there were three candidates competing for the two seats: the two sitting MPs, Wilberforce and the Hon. Henry Lascelles, and a challenger, Charles Fitzwilliam, Lord Milton. Lascelles was the son of the Earl of Harewood, whose incredible wealth was based on his Caribbean plantations. It was a very close election, with Wilberforce winning first place with 11,808 votes, narrowly defeating Milton's 11,177, with Lascelles in third place with 10,990 votes.

behind[195] & hungering & thirstg after Righteousness,[196] strivg to purify myself even as God is pure[197] & to perfect Holiness in the <u>fear</u> of God.[198] O deliver me from my besetting Sin the inordinate Love of Human Estimation. How difficult, how impossible I find it to be as indifferent as I ought to be to this, except in y^e. Relations & measures, allowed in Scripture. I feel much more worldly also I am persuaded than I ought to be, & how much do my feelings ab^t this unjust Charge concerng y^e. Methodists condemn me.

O let me learn Sursum Corda, more & more. Strict truth also I fear violated. And how little duly on y^e. Watch to be useful. O if I examine myself by page 83 of my 4to Book, what Sins of Omission & Commission do I discover. O Lord I come to y^e. fountain open'd for Sin &c. Lord deliver me from the Bondage of my Corruptions & bring me into the full Enjoyment of y^e. glorious liberty of y^e. Child^n of God.[199] O fill me with Humility faith love Hope & Joy. Amen. Amen. I am utterly unworthy of all these Blessg^s. But O y^e. Blessed assurance my ways are not as y^r Ways, nor my thoughts &c. &c.[200] Lord, O supply me out of thy fulness & make me wholly thine. Amen. Amen.[201]

Augt 24th. Sat^y 12 ½ Herstmonceaux

I've been writing in Journal Book so much that all to be said here, is that I am going to pri. dev^n. for Humiliatn, gen^l Unprofitableness, & also Barrenness as to Xtian Graces & practice, espy Love & faith & Joy in y^e. H G^t. Faults of y^e. Tongue. Here Ld. Sidmth's affair certy furnishes Cause, tho' so much Exagg^n addit^n & malignant falsehood in y^e. Story which is circulated. Divine direction as to resigng Yorks & also as to retiring altogether or not. Prayg for Childn & that I may be enabled to discharge my parental duties better. I feel my own Incompetence here, but assuredly God will strengthen me if I put my trust in him & strive to prepare my Heart for seekg his blessed aid, & cut off y^e. Rt. Hand, which wo'd prove y^e. prevential to my performg a father's duties. Praying geny for Growth in Grace, that I may be render'd more meet to be a partaker of y^e. Inheritance of y^e. Saints in Light,[202] Amen. Amen.

But O let me not omit the duty of praise & thanksgivg. Who was ever so loudly calld on to perform it? Who has been so highly favord as myself? Surely when I look over in detail & for y^e. last 40 years the Course of my Heart & life, when I call to mind what I have been & what God has done for me, & by me. When I sum up all together & recollect

---

195. Philippians 3:13.
196. Matthew 5:6.
197. 1 John 3:3.
198. 2 Corinthians 7:1.
199. Romans 8:21.
200. Isaiah 55:8.
201. MS Wilberforce c. 42, fos. 8-9.
202. Colossians 1:12.

that never to be forgotten Considerat^n that all y$^{e.}$ past present & to come are under y$^{e.}$ View of God, in fresh & lively Colours, I am lost in astonishm^t & can only exclaim, thy ways are not as our ways, nor thy thoughts as our thoughts.[203] I will try to look back thro' my past life & to affect my Heart as it ought to be, by y$^{e.}$ review, w. Humiliat^n Gratitude Love & humble Confidence, mix'd with reverential fear, & O, I must adopt y$^{e.}$ verse Ezek 16.63, that thou mayest remember & be confounded & never open thy mouth because of thy shame <u>when I am pacified</u>[204] to thee (poor old Newton's Story), for all that thou hast done saith y$^{e.}$ Lord God. Amen. Amen.[205]

---

203. Isaiah 55:8.

204. 'Reconcil'd' is crossed out here and 'pacified' is inserted above the line, and '<u>when I am pacified</u>' is underlined twice.

205. MS Wilberforce c. 42, fo. 9. *Life*, iii. pp. 533-534 has, 'My birthday again, born in 1759, so fifty-two complete. I had wished to spend it in religious exercises, but I cannot. I have some very urgent African and other business; but I am going to spend an hour or two in religious exercises, self-examination, humiliation, etc. And oh let me not omit the duty of praise and thanksgiving! Who was ever so loudly called on to perform it! Who has been so highly favored! Surely when I look over in detail for the last forty years (Deut. viii. 2) the course of my heart and life; when I call to mind what I have been, and what God has done for me, and by me; when I sum up all together, and recollect that consideration which should never be forgotten, that all the past, present, and to come, are under the view of God in lively colors, I am lost in astonishment, and can only exclaim, "Thy ways are not as our ways, nor Thy thoughts as our thoughts." I will try to look back through my past life, and to affect my heart, as by the review it ought to be, with humiliation, gratitude, love, and confidence, mixed with reverential fear; and oh I must adopt the words of Ezek. xvi. 63, "That thou mayest remember, and be confounded, and never open thy mouth anymore because of thy shame, when I am pacified toward thee" (poor old Newton's story) "for all that thou hast done, saith the Lord God." I wished to devote today specially to the important purpose of seeking God's direction on the question, whether or not I should resign Yorkshire and if so, whether to come in for a small borough. I have not time now to record the arguments in full particularity. Babington and Stephen are clearly for my giving up the county, on the ground that neither my body nor mind are equal to the pressure which it must bring upon me. The reasons for retiring from Yorkshire are chiefly,

1. The state of my family. My eldest son just turned thirteen, and three other boys, and two girls. Now though I should commit the learning of my boys to others, yet the moral part of education should be greatly carried on by myself. They claim a father's heart, eye, and voice, and friendly intercourse. Now so long as I am M.P. for Yorkshire, it will, I fear, be impossible for me to give my heart and time to the work as I ought, unless I become a negligent M.P. such as does not become our great county. I even doubt whether I ought not to quit public life altogether, on the ground that if I remain in the House even for Bramber, which Lord Calthorpe kindly offers, I shall still be so much of a political man, that the work of education will not be set to heartily. This consideration of education is, in great measure, the turning point with me; but,

2. The state of my body and mind, especially the latter, intimate to me the solve senescentem, particularly my memory, of the failure of which I find decisive proofs continually. At present I can retire incolumi fama, and that is much. (See Johnson's last Rambler but one.) But there are some other considerations. I do not believe there would be any serious contest, and am not prompted to retire by the fear of being turned out, so that I may leave out altogether this class of considerations. But if there should be any contest, the Sidmouth and Methodist story would be circulated with all the scandalous exaggerations and calumnies which the evil spirit could stir up, and people hostile to religion, and suspecting all religious persons of hypocrisy, would believe it; and the credit of true religion might with my own be tarnished. It weighs with me too that the services to religion, both in the House and out of it, which I might render if I were to stay in parliament, might perhaps be rendered by persons not laboring under the stigma of Methodism. My most faithful friend William Smith (oh how I wish he were even as we in the most important particulars!) could do what was needful, and so could others. I must go to devotional exercises, but I will just add that when I look into my own heart, and realize the scene before me, I cannot deny that I feel very deeply the loss of my high situation, and being out of the dramatis personae whilst all my friends are acting their parts; but so far as this is vain-glory it is to be resisted to the very utmost. To serve God is the true honor of those who are not their own, but are bought with

Private Religious[206]

Sunday Sep[tr.] 1[st.] Herstmonceaux 1:50

Some time has been spent on Letters necessarily since return'd fm Mr. Wilson's[207] excell[t] Sermon, & but ¾ of an hour remains bef[r] Church, therefore I must only for a minute or 2, record my State of mind. Tho' conscious alas of so many & great deficiencies, & such sad Unprofitableness, yet casting myself on the promis'd mercy of God thro' y[e.] Redeemer, I humbly hope for mercy & also for sanctifying Grace. Mrs. Bab[n] has discern'd much of my Interior I suspect. It is true, I feel sadly the sinking fm my high Situat[n] & y[e.] loss of Worldly Conseq[ce] & being out of y[e.] dramatis personae[208] when all my friends are acting th[r] parts & I am engag'd in y[e] humble office of Educat[n]. But surely if it be right for me to retire & when my own leanings towd[s] that conclus[n] are confirm'd by y[e.] judgm[t] of dear Bab[n] Stephen, Will Sn[r] & Ld Calth[e], all as far as Yorks concern'd & Bab[n] still farther.

Have I not Cause to think it is right tho' I give up such a field of service, if it be right to retire, I trust God will strengthen my mind & smooth my path, & even vouchsafe to prosper my labours & endeav[s] with my Child[n.] When I look forw[d] & think of them carrg on irreligiously, it quite shocks me & should I not then, set to Work w[th.] my whole force, & except perhaps being in y[e.] House for one Session (for a new Reign's outset), & unless some alter'd or new circumstances, no more, give up Parlt entirely, lest if I remain I should be givg my mind still chiefly to politics & not my Heart & time & thoughts & Efforts to y[e.] work of Educat[n.] O Lord guide & direct me, thou hast been my Succour. O guide me w. thy Counsel & at length receive me to thy Glory.[209] I go to prayer, sorry not to have more time. Hence to 4to Book - on returng to K. Gore, Sept 6[th.] 1811.[210]

Private Religious[211]

Sunday Oc[tr.] 6[th.] 1811 – Elmdon 1:20

Alas. I am going on ill here, where I have every advantage almt that I can desire, & except too much time necessy spent at & after dinner (Mr. and Mrs. Sprs age, demands Submission in lesser & lawful matters). I may

---

a price; and the point is, to learn what his will is. It is unspeakably comfortable to me to have Babington, Stephen, and other friends, confirming my own view as far as relinquishing Yorkshire goes. Then I may humbly hope to be enabled by God to discharge my parental duties better, if I strive to prepare my heart for fulfilling them, seeking his blessed aid, and "cutting off the right hand" which would prevent my performing a father's duties. I trust God will strengthen my mind, and smooth my path, and vouchsafe to prosper my labors and endeavors with my children. If my line of duty be a humble one, shall I not gladly pursue it, if I see reason to believe it is the path to which the Almighty directs me?'

206. MS Wilberforce c. 42 the fo. is numbered top right, with both an 8 in pencil and a 5 in ink.

207. Daniel Wilson (1778–1858), evangelical bishop of Calcutta from 1832 to 1858. At the time of Wilberforce's entry, Wilson was the assistant Curate at St. John's Chapel, Bedford Row, Bloomsbury, where Richard Cecil had earlier been incumbent. He was associated with the Clapham Circle and helped found the Lord's Day Observance Society.

208. Latin: persons of the drama.

209. Psalm 73:24.

210. MS Wilberforce c. 42 the fo. has both an 8 in pencil and a 5 in ink. Manuscript page ends with the completion of the entry.

211. MS Wilberforce c. 42, fo. 10.

spend my time as I please. I think not so much of my Sleepiness just now at Church, tho' I (deeply, I hope,) regret[212] it. But how cold are my Affections in general. How little do I duly keep my Heart, i.e. watch over its thoughts & feelings &c. How little strive duly to amend the Conversat[n] in Comp[y.] tho' I hope I do try in some degree. My Evg devot[ns] how hurried & short, & no SS. I must secure for pri. dev[ns] &c y[e.] time fm 8 to 9, while here, & O let me endeavour to maintain a Spirit of Gratitude, Love, Reverence Humility Hope, & desire. Also, a more habitual Solicitude for y[e.] Souls of others. Rem[r] O my Soul, Xt's address to the Church of Ephesus "bec[e] thou hast lost thy first Love,"[213] & then mark the threatening, & the Injunction closing w. do thy first Works.[214] I can remember how earnest I then was in prayer, how deeply contrite for Sin, how watchful over my Heart, my Words, espec[y] my Comp[y] Regls, or how hurt if they were neglected. How solicitous & active for y[e.] Souls of others, O how much I am fallen off here. Rem[r] therefore Whence thou art fallen & repent & do thy first Works else, O aweful declarat[n] I will take away thy Candlestick.[215]

O Lord quicken, soften, warm, strengthen me, & fill me w. Right[s] & peace & Joy in y[e.] H. Ghost,[216] that I may be made more & more meet to be a partaker of the Inheritance of y[e.] Saints in light.[217] I am very stupid & Cold, but I will go to prayer & try to gain somewhat of Spirit[l] Warmth, yet let me remember, that the promises of God are sure, & his Dispositions to fulfil his Word vary not according to my varying frames & feelings. O Lord Hear me, I come to Thee wretched & miserable &c. O supply me fully &c. &c. &c. Amen. Amen.[218]

Elmdon[219] Tuesday Mg Oct[r.] 8[th.] near 12 -

Havg been late up & not havg read SS[220] before Bkft, I am doing it now and O let me seriously take myself to task for havg sadly exceded yesty at dinner, tho' scarcely if at all aware of it at y[e.] time. We are so long at table, that unless is one is much on one's guard, a person of a weak Stomach like me, & who is advis'd to live well, is apt to be intemperate Unawares. But a Xtian ought to be much on his guard. I have been for some time living too freely I fear, & must strive to be more moderate both in eatg & ferms that I may be fitter for Bus[s] soon, & t. I may not be so unspiritualized as (alas) I am render'd. Yesty Evg tho' had done dinner ab[t] 5, I had no Heart for prayer at 8. O let me strive to amend here. I know so well my own Weakness, that I can only hope to do it by looking to thee O X[t] for Spirit[l] Strength. How much more spirit[ly] minded do I feel in a morng, now for instance, y[n] in y[e.] Aft[n] or Evg.

212. 'Deeply, I hope, regret' have superscripts '3' above deeply, '2' above 'hope' and '1' above 'regret'.
213. Revelation 2:4.
214. Revelation 2:5.
215. Revelation 2:5.
216. Romans 14:17.
217. Colossians 1:12.
218. MS Wilberforce c. 42, fos. 10-11.
219. MS Wilberforce c. 42 the fo. is numbered 2 but it is not the second page in the MS.
220. Wilberforce's shorthand symbol for Scriptures.

O Lord, let me see myself as I truly am. How sadly weak I am not to have y^e· Clear Command of myself in such a trifle as this. Let me think how I should account any one else, who overcome by such a temptation. Really, tis unaccountable, like y^e· temptat^n of Satan, for I do not indulge any luxurious habits as to food. O let me beware of grievg y^e· Spirit.[221] If my Body should even suffer a little, were it not well, for y^e· Sake of y^e· inner man, but a moderate Satiety, not a spare diet, might be full as good & better than my overdoing it as I often do, by not being enough on my Guard. O Lord soften warm quicken me & shed abroad y^e· love of X^t· in my Soul, that I may call thee father O God, & feel to thee always with the Reverence Humility yet Desire Gratitude O & affiance. Amen. Amen. (NB also less Brandy & water at night).[222]

Sunday 1:50 – Oct^r· 20th· 1811 Elmdon -

I must not employ[223] much of y^e· precious time bet^n Church, my few hrs in aft^n· (y^e· best by far) that I have, in writing, yet let me record y^e· blessed Effects of these invaluable days, on which I humbly hope God Christ vouchsafes graciously to knock at y^e· door of my Heart[224] & to shed abroad in some small measure the love of God in my Soul.[225] Yet O how faintly how inadequately do I love, & feel grateful for the unspeakable Bounty of God to me. I have felt tod. in some degree, the Contrition & Humiliation justly to be excited by y^e· Rememb^ce of my Sins. O when I review my past life & recall them & consider that God sees[226] in unfading freshness of Colourg & Completeness of parts, I am lost in y^e· Sense of my own Vileness & abhor myself & I adore the astonishg Mercy & Love of God, who gave up his Son to die for us, that thro' faith in his Blood God might be just & the Justifier of him who is of y^e· faith of Jesus.[227] I have not secured time as I ought for my Evg devotn^s but I have been more temperate of late. I must amend here, or I shall grieve the Spirit. Already I find myself less impress'd than I was with the Sense of my Sinfulness in so curtailing & losg my Evg devotn^s· O this is a dangerous & should be an alarming sign. Remember O my Soul, the Evidence of all Good Men as to priv^e prayer, Dodd^e espec^y. O what cause have I to bless these blessed Seasons of Abstraction from the Bustle of life. We have had a Sacramt, but no Sermon this Mg.

Alas. Alas! How Vanity, & Vain Glory & y^e· inordinate Love of Human Estimation still retain possession of my Soul. How incessantly do I find my Soul suggesting the Ideas of others Comments on my thoughts or affectns which at all of a pleasing kind. Yet I humbly hope I discourage these, yet I can derive fuel to my Vanity f^m this very discourag^g & so on again & again.

---

221. Ephesians 4:30.
222. MS Wilberforce c. 42, fo. 11.
223. 'any' is here at this point.
224. Revelation 3:20.
225. Romans 5:5.
226. MS Wilberforce c. 42, fo. 10.
227. Romans 3:26.

O let me think what should I think or say if anyone who was thus ye prey of incessant Vain Glory. O let the Consciousness of it humble me in ye dust & make me long to be purified more f^m this vile passion & to be more entirely possessed with ye grateful Love of my God & Saviour. O make me more meet to be a Partaker of ye Inheritance of ye Saints in Light.[228] Amen. Amen.[229]

Sunday 3 ½ Novr 3rd 1811 Yoxall Lodge

Alas, How dull & stupid I am, & tho' it may partly proceed f^m my being poorly, f^m 2 or 3 indiff^t nights all together, yet I fear it is also in some degree the hiding of God's face, as a punishm^t for my neglectg my Evg devotn^s even more instead of less y^n my last Entry. I dare not resolve, but I would humbly pray to be enabled to amend here, & also to be enabled to read the SS in an Eveng with more seriousness & profit. O let me try to maintain a Consciousness of my own Weakness here, & to look up to Christ for Grace & Strength. O I am wretched & miserable & poor &[230] blind & naked.[231] The only encouraging Circumstance is that I know & feel that this is ye Case with me. O Lord supply me out of thy fulness,[232] shed abroad thy Love in my Heart by ye H Spt[233] & give me a Spirit of Humility & Faith & Love & Trust & Hope & Gratitude, & if it please thee even of Peace & Joy. Amen. Amen.[234]

Thursday, November 7th 1811[235]

I am too like her in one particular, that, I mean, of the proportion of my time spent on writing letters. But not I trust from the same motives. Mine are really necessary. She seems to have cultivated the acquaintance of all persons of any note, literary, social, or of any other kind; when separated from them a correspondence sprung up; hence her 144 quarto volumes of letters between 1784 and 1810; the first, the very year I became M. P. for Yorkshire. She really had talents and reading; but how much more usefully and honorably would she have been employed, had she, like Hannah More, been teaching the poor, or still more in writing such books as Hannah More![236]

Sunday Novr 17th 1811 - Yoxall Lodge 3:20 -

I have been trifling away some of my time foolishly nay rather wickedly perhaps 20 or 30 min. in readg inattentively Life of Fenelon[237] &c. i.e. what

---

228. Colossians 1:12.

229. MS Wilberforce c. 42, fo. 11.

230. Ibid.

231. Revelation 3:17.

232. Philippians 4:19.

233. Romans 5:5.

234. MS Wilberforce c. 42, fos. 11-12.

235. He recorded this entry after reading Miss Seward's letters. Anna Seward (1747–1809), known as the 'Swan of Lichfield'.

236. *Life*, iii. pp. 373-374.

237. François de Salignac de la Mothe-Fénelon, usually simply referred to as François Fénelon (1651–1715), was a French Catholic Archbishop, theologian and writer, remembered especially for his *The Adventures of Telemachus* (1699). The work Wilberforce here mentions is a two-volume publication by M.L.F. De Bausset, *The Life of Fenelon, Archbishop of Cambrai; compiled, from original manuscripts* (London, 1810).

not my Business at y[e.] time & I've no time for writg. Let me then to my knees & humbly implore mercy thro' y[e.] Redeemer confessg[238] my Sins. I have not been going on well, not makg progress. I see my excellt friend Gisbe improv'd. O let this be a lesson a Warning to me. Let me strive in good earnest to press forward & really to grow in Grace. Assuredly I may, or y[e.] Command wo'd not be given. O then Press Forward & may I find my Soul more spiritual, my whole Self more conform'd to y[e.] Image of God & y[e.] likeness of Xt, that I may become more & more a Pilgrim here, whose life is hid w. Xt in God.[239] O make me meet to be a partaker &c.[240] Amen. Amen. I go to confession & prayer.[241]

Undated, 1811

Almost entirely consumed by letters, yet it appears the part of Christian courtesy to answer correspondents; and so much suffering would in each case be produced by my not answering, compared with the trouble it costs, that I know not how to abstain. I have written lately an immense number, several on important objects, today one on missions. Having heard of the Duke of York's being designed for commander of the army, I resolved, however invidious, to state objections strongly, and wrote to Perceval. I am now writing to Jefferson in America, to obtain some agreement between the two nations, for giving effect to Abolition, by allowing each country to take the other's slave ships.

I long to write my projected religious work, but have first several jobs to do, not one of which however is yet begun. My letters still almost engross me. True, they are important letters, keeping up connection with constituents in absence from the county; also some religious letters, and some letters of friendship.[242]

Sunday Nov[r.] 24[th.] 1811 Yox[ll] Lodge 3:5

Havg been walkg &c yet I hope not wasting time, tho' not shewg suffic[y] to make y[e.] most of it, I must not expend in writing y[e.] little T remains before dinner, yet I am so sleepy that I can scarcely keep away & at Church this morning sadly sleepy. Bodily I trust. My Evg devot[ns] have been but ill manag'd. The post comes in ab[t.] 8 or 8 ½ & some require answer & thus my time is insensibly whittled away. Then I owe friendly Civility to my Connections & when I come up again I am sadly sleepy. The time also before prayers & Bkft too short often, but I read y[e.] SS then afterw[ds.] O Lord, do thou soften quicken warm my hard dead Cold Heart. I go to prayer. I am indeed wretched & miserable &c.[243] Lord to thee I fly for refuge. O supply me out of thy fulness, Even Grace for Grace.[244]

---

238. 'Confessg' here is written over another word.

239. Colossians 3:3.

240. Colossians 1:12.

241. MS Wilberforce c. 42, fo. 12.

242. *Life* iii. pp. 374-375.

243. Revelation 3:17.

244. John 1:16. MS Wilberforce c. 42, fo. 12.

Sunday Decr. 1st. 2¼ Kensⁿ Gore[245]

Return'd Friday Evg last. I have been spendg too much time just now in writg my Journal & therefore I will go directly to prayer, havg only till 3 & this being my best time. Alas, I wasted my time last night most wickedly. I might have secured a good Hour or Hour ½ in preparing for this day. Surely tis for this God made me. (Most unusually) have as bad a night almt as thro' his exceeding goodness, without pain or Irritation, it could be scarcely Conscious of sleeping all night long, yet pretty well today I suspect opium & nourishment & X^{t.} enabled me to doze a little tho' unperceived. I go to prayer he'll pardon Sins &c. &c.[246]

1812

Wednesday, January 1st. 1812

Oh what mercies have I to acknowledge during the past year! Surely it is a solemn season, but I go to prayer, only let me put down my gratitude and humiliation. I must especially try to husband time more. O Lord, enable me to redeem it! I must try to keep an account of time and work, to take security against trifling.[247]

Monday, February 3rd. 1812

Bankes thinks with me that there is no chance of the Prince's changing the ministry, or consequently of a speedy dissolution, but we both fear an American war. I am wanting my voice much, that I may plead the cause of Christianity in India, and soften the asperity of hostile tempers between Great Britain and America.[248]

Sunday, March 15th. 1812

I love human estimation too well, though I trust I strive against it; and I have no temptation to seek dishonorable gain. Now how ready am I to condemn those who addict themselves to the latter! Yet am not I as criminal in loving the former, for it is the not loving God that is the vice? O Lord, purify me, and make me meet to be partaker of the inheritance of the saints in light.[249]

---

245. Kensington Gore or Gore House was a mansion built in the mid-eighteenth century, and decorated by the renowned architect, Robert Adam. Wilberforce, who lived there from 1808 to 1821, had the house enlarged to consist of a dining-room, drawing-room, a library, two studies, a long gallery and ten bed and dressing-rooms. After being purchased to serve as a restaurant for the Great Exhibition of 1851, the house was demolished to make way for The Royal Albert Hall, built in 1871, whose main entrance today stands almost exactly where the entrance to Gore House was.

246. MS Wilberforce c. 42, fo. 12.

247. *Life*, iv. p. 1.

248. Ibid., p. 5.

249. Colossians 1:12. *Life*, iv. p. 341.

Friday, April 24th 1812

Attended the general meeting of the Church Missionary Society for Africa and the East.[250] A grand assemblage, I spoke with acceptance. It went off well.[251]

Wednesday, May 6th 1812

British and Foreign Bible Society, annual meeting, all went off admirably. Immense meeting, I spoke with acceptance, several bishops present.[252]

Undated, 1812

O Lord, purify me, make me meet for the inheritance of the saints in light.[253] I trust that I have grown in self-abhorrence, and in longing for deliverance from the burden of sin. O Lord, quicken, cleanse, soften me. How differently, even to a man who is used to religious views, do all things show when we are on a sick-bed! How little one can think at all in earnest in such circumstances! Oh what a business must it be to those who are on a sick-bed to have their attention first called to the subject, or their views corrected! Oh may I strive to tread in the apostle's steps, and forgetting the things that are behind, to press forward.[254] O Lord, supply all my need out of Thy riches.[255] Alas, in my feelings and sudden impulses, if not in my settled temper, I am too solicitous about the praise of men. I abhor myself for this vileness; though at the very time when I hope I abhor myself, it is as if there were two men, two principles struggling within me.

O Lord, to Thee I fly for refuge; O cleanse, soften, quicken, and glorify me. I have been much affected by hearing old Scott of the Lock for the first time these many years. The beginning of his sermon, 'I have been young, and now am old', that twenty-seven years ago he preached for the first time in that chapel, was remarkably applicable to me, for then first heard him at the beginning of my Christian course. Oh how truly may I say, that goodness and mercy follow me![256] And may I not hope that my being thus humiliated is a sign that the Savior is knocking at the door of my heart, and that I am ready to let Him in?[257] Mr. Sargent[258] preached, and pleased us all greatly, simple seriousness, and consequent pathos, the character of his preaching.

---

250. The Society for Missions to Africa and the East, then the Church Missionary Society, and now the Church Mission Society (CMS) in Britain, was founded in 1799 and has sent out more than 9,000 missionaries. The original proposal was sent to Wilberforce and Charles Simeon in 1787 by Charles Grant and George Uday of the East India Company, and Rev. David Brown of Calcutta. It was officially founded at the 12 April, 1799 meeting of the Eclectic Society, supported by members of the Clapham Circle. Wilberforce declined the approach to be the Society's first President, becoming instead a Vice President. Henry Thornton became treasurer and Thomas Scott the founding Secretary.

251. *Life*, iv. p. 21.

252. Ibid.

253. Colossians 1:12.

254. Philippians 3:13.

255. Philippians 4:19

256. Psalm 23:6.

257. Revelation 3:20.

258. Rev. John Sargent (1780–1833).

What a blessing is a cheerful temper! I felt most keenly _____'s[259] behavior about Bowdler, and his not coming to me; but for his sake, and I hope from Christian principles, I resolved to struggle against bad temper about it, and now all is over.[260] Heard of the death of _____ [261] She died about 3 o'clock today. All the lower parts had been dead some time, but she would not believe she should die, (that way madness lies,) and reproved her daughters during her illness for looking as if they were going to a funeral. I heard that she was very irritable, and had no idea that she would see me; however I did call on Wednesday, and again yesterday, when she must have been dying.[262]

I was much affected last night after seeing poor S. in an agony of pain, with thinking what hell must be, pain without hope. With all my defects and unprofitableness, I humbly hope that it is my main desire to please Thee. Oh may I walk softly, deeply feeling my own unworthiness, repenting in dust and ashes; guarding against self-deception, lest I lose the precious opportunities of communion with God.[263]

Sunday, October 25th. 1812

After having prayed with _____,[264] and had a tete-a-tete with Mrs. _____,[265] I set off for Leicester.[266] Poor dear Hoy, he was much affected at parting with me, turning round and bursting into tears, first quietly, and afterwards with sobs. I was near crying too as I said to Mrs. _____,[267] 'I must get off, or else', but she I trust will watch over him with Christian care.

I am much grieved at having yesterday passed by, without stopping, a man in a ditch by the roadside between Barnet[268] and London, whom two or three gentlemen were attending to. The Leeds coach with the back seats empty was just behind, and multitudes of passengers, so that

---

259. He does not identify this person.

260. *Life*, iv. pp. 43-44.

261. He does not identify this person. Wilberforce's sons add that Wilberforce, 'had known intimately in the prodigal enjoyment of youth, and rank, and wealth, and beauty.' *Life*, iv. p. 44.

262. *Life*, iv. p. 45.

263. Ibid.

264. He does not identify this person.

265. He does not identify this person.

266. Leicester probably started as a Celtic settlement, but which was captured by the Romans who built a fort there in A.D. 48. By the time of Wilberforce's entry, Leicester had been transformed by the industrial revolution, with a population in 1801 of 17,005, but by 1841 it was already 40,000.

267. He does not identify this person.

268. Barnet is today a suburban borough in North London, and is the second largest by population. It was created in 1965 by the amalgamation of several areas. But Barnet was recorded as early as 1070 as 'Barneto', and is a name derived from Old English meaning 'burning', and in the Middle Ages its fields were cultivated in grass for hay. Its strategic location on the main road between St. Albans and London, made it a center for inns and markets. With the coming of railways in the mid-19th century, population rose sharply. In 1801, the civil parishes that make up the modern borough of Barnet numbered 6,404, though that would be somewhat larger than Barnet proper, as it was.

help could not be wanted; yet it was wrong in all respects to pass by. It is an adjudged case since the good Samaritan parable, at which I should have been instinctively prompt. It was not hardness of heart I believe either. I was busy hearing Bowdler's paper upon Dugald Stewart,[269] and I was flurried by the Leeds coach, on the outside of which were people who I thought knew me; yet if so it was worse, not glorifying God, etc. Lord, forgive me, forgive me! I felt (and now condemn it) more, that today is the anniversary (Oct. 25th) of my escape from drowning in the Avon,[270] by a most providential suggestion.[271]

Undated, 1812

When not unavoidably prevented by company or House of Commons, to take an hour, or at least half an hour, for private devotions, including Scripture reading and meditation, immediately before family prayers. Besides other benefits, one will be to send me back into society with a more spiritual mind, and to help me to preserve it through the evening, and to make the conversation more edifying and instructive. How can I expect a blessing otherwise? Oh let me reform here, it has been my standing sin of late: I must therefore remember that I shall find it difficult to adhere to the reformed system. The best hope will arise from my bearing about with me a deep impression of the difficulty, and of my own weakness, and of the urgent need of Divine help. Also aim at universal holiness, guard against self-indulgence, and love of human estimation. Oh how that vile passion will creep in! Even now it is at work fold within fold. Lord, Thou knowest me, I cast myself on Thy pardoning mercy and sanctifying grace.[272]

I have had serious doubts, whether or not it is right to do so when I have so many important subjects to consider, and so much to do; yet the examples as well as writings of good men, and above all, the Holy Scriptures, taking the precepts which directly treat of fasting and comparing them with others, warrant it. N.B. Christ's words about the demons, which expelled only by fasting and prayer.[273] Then as to my being now extremely occupied, Owen's remark in some degree applies, (inference from Malachi,) that we should give God if needful our best time. O Lord, Thy blessing can render far more than a day's time as nothing even in my worldly business, and if the main-spring's force be strengthened, and its working improved, (cleansed from dust and foulness,) surely the machine will go better. Lord, what I do I trust is pleasing to Thee - accept and bless my service.

---

269. John Bowdler the younger (1783–1815), detailed earlier, wrote several pieces whilst suffering from tuberculosis, including his *Select Pieces in Prose and Verse*, (published posthumously in 2 vols., 1816), which contained, as Wilberforce records here, Bowdler's exposition of Dugald Stewart's (1753–1828) philosophical theories and religious essays and poems.

270. The River Avon is the name given to several rivers in England, though the main river of that name is to be found in the south west of England, and as such is often referred to as the Bristol Avon. It rises near Chipping Sodbury, and empties into the Severn Estuary.

271. *Life*, iv. p. 73.

272. Ibid., pp. 81-82.

273. Matthew 17:21.

I put these things down, that I may fix, and ascertain, and reconsider my own corruptions and the deceitful working of my mind and passions. There are two souls within me; Lord, help me to expel the fleshly occupant. Of thankfulness, of prayer. That I may plan my system of life wisely, and execute it properly in the new circumstances in which I am placed. Of intercession, for my dear children, now main and special objects with me; for private friends, and especially my god-children.

As to my plan of life, I conceive that my chief objects should be, First; My children. Secondly; Parliament. Thirdly; When I can spare time, my pen to be employed in religious writing. Hints and thoughts for my intended book. Oh with what humiliation and thankfulness should my Practical View fill me! As I have certainly begun to find my faculties, especially my memory, (perhaps my imagination, but it may be only my memory,) decline, I should strive to make up for the declension by more pains; and now that I shall not be a constant attendant, and shall not have Yorkshire business, I must prepare more. I conceive it to be my duty to attend to this object; yet, O Lord, enable me to do it from first to last with a simple eye to Thy favor and Thy glory, and with less love of human estimation.

Let me look over my 'grounds for humiliation,' my 'company regulations.' How sadly apt am I to lose all recollection of these, and of keeping my heart when I am in society! Lord, strengthen me with might. Let Christ dwell, not merely occasionally visit, but dwell in my heart by faith. Let me cultivate more an habitual love of God. Butler and Barrow, habitual gratitude. Let me try some memorandum analogous to the phylactery. See Numb, xv. 38, 40.[274]

Tuesday, December 8th. 1812

Fuller of Kettering[275] breakfasted, and talked much about East Indian Gospel Communication plan. Then town, Manufacturers'

---

274. *Life*, iv. p. 82.

275. Rev. Andrew Fuller (1754–1815), was the Baptist minister in Kettering from 1782 to 1815. He is remembered especially for his *The Gospel Worthy of All Acceptation* (1801), and for his work in the creation of what became the Baptist Missionary Society. Wilberforce met Fuller on at least two occasions, as here, and shared Fuller's concern for the freedom of missionary activity in India. On one such visit, Wilberforce moved to introduce Fuller to one of his sons after his arrival had been announced. 'You know Andrew Fuller?' he asked him. 'No, I never heard his name,' was the reply. 'Oh then you must know him,' Wilberforce said, 'he is an extraordinary man, whose talents have raised him from a very low condition.' When Fuller came in, Wilberforce later recorded that Fuller was, 'a man of considerable powers of mind,' but bearing 'very plainly the vestigia ruris,' for he looked 'the very picture of a blacksmith.' Wilberforce was accurate as such in his description, and surely intended no disparagement in his words, but his phraseology is very representative of how the Anglican establishment viewed the writings of such Dissenters. With no access to a University education until the late 19th century, the writings of Dissenting ministers would be viewed as somewhat rustic in style, form and wording. Nevertheless, Wilberforce considered Fuller's 1800, anti-Deistic work, *The Gospel Its Own Witness*, as the most important of all of Fuller's writings. Kettering in Northamptonshire, was first mentioned in A.D. 956. In 1801, the town of Kettering had a population of more than 3,000. Its main industries at the time of Wilberforce's entry were wool, and the manufacture of boots and shoes. Fuller is remembered in Kettering in the Fuller Memorial Church and Fuller Street. Victorian Kettering was a center of religious non-conformity, with William Carey, William Knibb and Fuller.

Committee. Duke of Kent[276] in the chair, and very civil. Then Hatchard's, letters, home to dinner. Stephen, Simeon, the Dean, and others, the House engaged on Lord Stanhope's Bullion Bill,[277] a most intricate question. We are trying to stir up a spirit to relieve the poor.[278]

Undated, 1812

I must put down that I have had lately too little, time for private devotions. I must take at least an hour for them in the morning. I can sadly confirm Doddridge's remark, 'that when we go on ill in the closet, we commonly do so everywhere else.' I must mend here; I am afraid of getting into what Owen calls a trade of sinning and repenting. Yet where can I go else? Thou only, Lord, canst pardon and sanctify me. Oh what unspeakable comfort it is to cast oneself on the Savior as a guilty, weak sinner in myself, but as trusting in the gracious promises of God through the Redeemer! Let him that is athirst come.[279] Lord, I must flee to Thee, and cleave to Thee. Be Thou my All in All.

Unable to realize the presence of God. It was as if there had been a wall of separation that I could not penetrate or see over; and my heart - dead and cold. Surely it is not enthusiasm to notice these sensations, as David does. Lord, renew and quicken me.

I am just returned from a highly impressive sermon by Mr. Dunn. I hope that my sensibility is in some degree the effect of the Holy Spirit; the knocking of Christ at the door of my heart.[280] I must not spend any of my few minutes before dinner in writing; but let me just record my feelings of deep humiliation, yet of confiding, though humble faith, looking to the Savior as my only ground of hope. I cast myself at the foot of the cross, bewailing my exceeding sinfulness and unprofitableness, deeply, most deeply aggravated by the infinity of my mercies. I plead Thy precious promises, and earnestly pray to Thee to shed abroad in my heart more love, more humility, more faith, more hope, more peace, and joy; in short, to fill me with all the fullness of God, and make me more meet to be a partaker of the inheritance of the saints in light.[281] Then shall I also be better in all the relations of life in which I am now so defective, and my light will shine before men,[282] and I shall adorn the doctrine of God my Savior in all things.[283]

---

276. Prince Edward Augustus (1767–1820), Duke of Kent and Strathearn, fourth son and fifth child of King George III.

277. Lord Stanhope's Gold Coin & Bank Notes Bill passed the Commons on 24 July, 1812, and received the assent of the Prince Regent. It legislatively maintained the parity of value of paper money and gold. It became illegal to prefer gold to bank notes or to distinguish a difference of value between them. Charles Stanhope (1753–1816), 3rd Earl Stanhope was brother-in-law of William Pitt the Younger.

278. *Life*, iv. p. 88.

279. Revelation 22:17.

280. Revelation 3:20.

281. Colossians 1:12.

282. Matthew 5:16.

283. Titus 2:10. *Life*, iv. p. 93.

1813

Tuesday, March 16th. 1813

I sadly fear that we have been too negligent about the grand question of communicating Christianity to our Indian fellow-subjects. We have heard of excellent Martyn's death in Persia, on his way to the Mediterranean homewards.[284] It is a mysterious Providence. Alas, when the interior is opened, the missionary and religious party in India are not so much at one, nor so free from human infirmity, as I had supposed. Oh did the world see into the hearts of religious professors, how much would it triumph over them! Yet they are better as well as worse than the world suspects. It confirms old Baxter, 'Good men neither so good, nor bad men often so bad, as the world supposes.'[285]

Undated, 1813

Writing almost all morning about East India charter, examinations, sharp work, extreme ignorance and bigotry. We examine daily from half-past four to near eight before other business. Would not the appearance of bishops encourage a fear amongst the natives that force would ultimately be used to establish Christianity amongst them?[286] Would it be consistent with the security of the British Empire in India, that missionaries should preach publicly that Mahomet is an impostor, or speak in opprobrious terms of the Brahmins and their religious rites?[287]

Tuesday, April 13th. 1813

Early in the city, at the general meeting of the Church Missionary Society for Africa and the East. Made the report of our deputation, and agreed to a petition to both Houses, for introducing Christianity in India.[288]

Undated, 1813

Secured an hour for private devotions this morning and yesterday, and found the effects of it. This East Indian object is assuredly the greatest that ever interested the heart, or engaged the efforts of man. How wonderful that a private man should have such an influence on the temporal and eternal happiness of millions; literally, millions on millions yet unborn! O God, make me more earnest for Thy glory; and may I act more from real love and gratitude to my redeeming Lord.

---

284. Henry Martyn (1781–1812). After meeting Charles Simeon, Martyn became an Anglican chaplain to the East India Company, and a missionary to India and Persia, arriving in India in 1806. He preached and worked on Bible translation in Persian and Urdu. After having contracted fever, he made plans to head for a furlough in England via Constantinople. But being forced to stop in Tokat, which was experiencing an outbreak of plague, Martyn died there.

285. *Life*, iv. pp. 100-101.

286. Wilberforce's sons comment that the object of the enemies of missions may be seen in the general tenor of their questions, *Life*, iv. p. 107.

287. *Life*, iv. p. 107.

288. Ibid., p. 113.

Oh how does this little check of sickness impress on me the duty of working while it is day; the night cometh when no man can work![289] Let me not take my estimate of myself from others who do not know me, but from my own self-knowledge and conscience. Oh what cause have I for contrition! What misspent time, what wasted talents, what means of grace (no one so many and so great) with how little profit; what self-indulgent habits; what softness, instead of the hardness of a good soldier of Christ!

It may be shown in any improper want of self-denial. O Lord, may my faith and love be more active, bringing forth more the fruits of the Spirit. My mind is most deeply impressed with the importance of this East India subject. Lord, bless us; pardon our past lukewarmness and slothfulness, and make us more diligent for the time to come. I have not myself been duly attentive to this great subject.[290]

Tuesday, May 4[th.] 1813

Annual sermon, and meeting of Church Missionary Society for Africa and East. Dealtry. Excellent sermon. Meeting afterwards, and spoke. Late to Asiatic Society, where took the chair. Then House.[291]

Saturday, May 8[th.] 1813

Dean of Wells[292] breakfasted with me, and met Andrew Fuller and Mr. Ivimey.[293] Much talk of East India missionary affairs. Dined Lambeth,[294] public day, little company, all engaged at grand public dinner for celebrating Sir Joshua Reynolds's fame;[295] and the whole rooms of British Institution[296] filled with his pictures. Archbishop very civil, but talked with me about Roman Catholic Question, which coming on. I tried to get him on East India business. As I came back, called for an

---

289. John 9:4.

290. *Life*, iv. pp. 115-116.

291. Ibid., p. 128.

292. Henry Ryder (1777–1836), was the Dean of Wells at the time of Wilberforce's entry. Ryder is remembered especially for being the first evangelical to become an Anglican bishop, and was Dean of Wells (1812–1831). He was also canon of Windsor (1808–1815), Bishop of Gloucester ((1815–1824), and Bishop of Lichfield and Coventry (1824–1836).

293. Joseph Ivimey (1773–1834), Particular Baptist minister, prolific author and historian, remembered especially for his four-volume *History of the English Baptists* (1811–1830). First Secretary of the Baptist Society for Promoting the Gospel in Ireland, formed 1814.

294. Lambeth Palace, or as it was called, the Manor of Lambeth or Lambeth House, has been the London residence of the Archbishop of Canterbury for almost 800 years. The south bank of the River Thames is regarded as having been an attractive choice for the location of an Archbishop's palace, with its proximity to Westminster and the Royal Court. At the time of Wilberforce's entry, Charles Manners-Sutton was Archbishop (1805–1828).

295. Sir Joshua Reynolds (1723–1792), leading English portrait painter of the 18th century, theorist, friend of Dr Johnson, and in 1791, James Boswell dedicated his *Life of Samuel Johnson* to Reynolds. The 1st President of the Royal Academy in 1768, and knighted by George III the following year.

296. The British Institution for Promoting the Fine Arts in the United Kingdom (the British Institution), founded in 1805, disbanded in 1867, was a private 19th century society established at 52, Pall Mall, London, to exhibit the works of artists. It was also known as the Pall Mall Picture Galleries or the British Gallery, dominated by nobility and was a very popular society haunt, 'The Times' referring to it as the favourite lounge of the nobility and gentry.

hour at British Institution Rooms to see pictures. Fine assembly. Prince of Wales[297] came up to me and accosted me very handsomely, and spoke a minute or two. Poor Sheridan[298] took me up to his first wife's picture, and stood with me looking at it affectionately some time. All the lovers of the arts there.[299]

Sunday, May 16th. 1813

Having so little time I must not spend any in writing. Let me only record my own grief and shame; and all probably from private devotions having been contracted, and so God let me stumble. How much too strongly did I speak in the House of Commons, concerning Sir J. Hippisley![300] Alas, how little exhibiting the temper of the meek and lowly Jesus! Yet I humbly hope I have bewailed my sin with bitter contrition, and but for the weakness of my eyes could shed many tears. Lord, I flee to Thee for mercy, and do Thou guide and direct me. Yesterday's decision to have a committee of inquiry concerning the state and treatment in law and fact of the slaves and colored people in our West India islands, will bring on me an immense load, if I undertake it; greater I fear than I can bear. Yet, Lord, to Thee I look, for 'Thou delightest in mercy.'[301] O soften, quicken, warm, and sanctify me.[302]

Undated, 1813

I do not know a finer instance of the moral sublime, than that a poor cobbler working in his stall should conceive the idea of converting the Hindoos to Christianity; yet such was Dr. Carey.[303] Why Milton's planning

---

297. The Prince of Wales at the time of Wilberforce's entry was George Augustus Frederick (1762–1830), later King George IV (1820–1830).

298. Richard Brinsley Sheridan (1751–1816), M.P., under-secretary for the northern department (foreign affairs), author, playwright, theatre owner, a member of the Literary Club, where he met Burke, and Brooks's Club.

299. *Life*, iv. p. 114.

300. Sir John Coxe Hippisley (1746/8–1825), born John Cox Hipsley, was a lawyer, M.P., and diplomat. He held many positions in his lifetime, including service in the East India Company, but he was not popular, being called 'a great ass' in John Skinner's, *Journal of a Somerset Rector*. In 1810, Joseph Jekyll wrote that in one speech by Hippisley in Parliament, 'the house coughed him down five times in vain, and the catarrh lasted two hours.' Hippisley was active in the cause for Catholic Emancipation, and published several works on the issue. He was also concerned at the use of treadmills in prisons, and published an address to Robert Peel, then Home Secretary, on the matter in 1823.

301. Micah 7:18.

302. *Life*, iv. p. 128.

303. William Carey (1761–1834), linguist, professor, Baptist Pastor and lifelong Missionary to India, regarded by many as the 'Father of Modern Missions'. He was converted as a cobbler, and the first missionary sent by what became the Baptist Missionary Society (B.M.S.). Wilberforce not only openly supported Carey's illegal mission in India, but detailed the missionary's work to the House of Commons, which included accounts of the terrible poverty, degradation, disdain for relieving human suffering and human rights abuses of suttee (widow burning) and the consequences of the horrific caste system. Wilberforce told them, 'The remedy, sir, is Christianity ... Christianity assumes her true character ... when she takes under her protection those degraded beings on whom philosophy looks down with disdain or perhaps with contemptuous condescension ... Christianity delights to instruct the ignorant, to succour the needy, to comfort the sorrowful, to visit the forsaken.' He would soon be challenged that he was doing little more than "forcing his views" on the Indians, to which he responded, 'Compulsion and Christianity! Why the very terms are at variance – the ideas are incompatible ... Christianity is the law of liberty!' His argument was that since the East India Company had been granted a monopoly by Parliament, it was Parliament's responsibility to ensure that they practiced religious freedom in India. He also stated that, 'Next

his Paradise Lost in his old age and blindness was nothing to it.[304] And then when he had gone to India, and was appointed by Lord Wellesley to a lucrative and honorable station in the college of Fort William, with equal nobleness of mind he made over all his salary (between £1000 and £1500 per annum) to the general objects of the mission.

Dr. Carey had been especially attacked, and a few days afterwards the member who had made this charge came to me, and asked me in a manner which in a noted duelist could not be mistaken, 'Pray, Mr. Wilberforce, do you know a Mr. Andrew Fuller, who has written to desire me to retract the statement which I made with reference to Dr. Carey?' 'Yes,' I answered with a smile, 'I know him perfectly, but depend upon it you will make nothing of him in your way; he is a respectable Baptist minister at Kettering.' In due time there came from India an authoritative contradiction of the slander. It was sent to me, and for two whole years did I take it in my pocket to the House of Commons to read it to the House whenever the author of the accusation should be present, but during that whole time he never once dared show himself in the House.[305]

Monday, July 12th. 1813

The East India Bill passed, and the missionary, or rather the Christian, cause fought through, without division, to the last. We were often alarmed. Lord Castlereagh has managed it admirably, coolly and quietly. The petitions, of which a greater number than were ever known, have carried our question instrumentally, the good providence of God really.[306]

Summer, 1813

I get up about seven; then serious time and devotions for an hour; then dressing and hearing one of the children read to me for three-quarters of an hour. After breakfast, letters, and writing; dictating; etc. We dine together early, and then some of the children read till we walk out, from about six till eight; then coming in I have an hour serious. Then family prayers, supper, and bed about eleven. I must try to see more of the children, and to obtain more time for study; hitherto I have done little but write letters.[307]

---

to the slave trade, I have long thought our making no effort to introduce the blessings of religion and moral improvement among our subjects in the East, the greatest of our national crimes ... we have too many ... who seem to think our dominions safer under Brahma and Vishnu, than under that of the Almighty.' Wilberforce actively and successfully fought for an amended charter for the Company, that allowed missionary activity.

304. John Milton (1608–1674), poet, writer and civil servant under Cromwell's Commonwealth, referred to by some as England's greatest author, and is remembered especially for his *Paradise Lost* (1667). Milton became totally blind by 1654, the cause of which is debated, but from his descriptions of symptoms it is thought that retinal detachment or glaucoma were the most likely causes. He would go on to write several more volumes after becoming blind, including as Wilberforce notes here, *Paradise Lost.*

305. *Life*, iv. pp. 123-124.

306. Ibid., p. 125.

307. Ibid., pp. 140-141.

1814

Sunday, February 20th. 1814

Dined Duke of Gloucester's to meet Madame de Stael, at her desire. Madame, her son and daughter, Duke, two aides-du-camp, Vansittart, Lord Erskine,[308] poet Rogers,[309] and others. Madame de Stael quite like her hook, though less hopeful, complimenting me highly on Abolition, 'All Europe,' etc. But I must not spend time in writing this. She asked me, and I could not well refuse, to dine with her on Friday to meet Lord Harrowby and Mackintosh, and poet Rogers on Tuesday sennight. This would lead to an endless round of dinners, but it neither suits my mind or body; when I dine late, the previous hours are worth little, and the rest of the evening goes to society. I greatly doubt about the doing any good by dinings-out. By going out now and then in the evening, when I have dined early, and am fresher and brisker, I should be better fitted to adorn religion and seize occasions of doing good: now I am often sleepy, and not having duly cultivated the religious principle by private devotions, it is weak, and I grow worldly and useless. I may fairly assign weak health, and dine early, and so get more hours for business.

I must secure more time for private devotion, for self-examination, for meditation, for keeping the heart, and even doing the duties of life, or the most pressing claims will carry it, not the strongest. I have been living far too publicly for me, 'Notus magis omnibus.'[310] Oh may it not be 'ignotus moritur sibi.'[311] Lord, help me. The shortening of private devotions starves the soul, it grows lean and faint. This must not be. Oh how sad, that after trying to lead a Christian life for twenty-eight years, I should be at all staggered by worldly company, Madame de Stael, etc. I will not however, please God, enter and be drawn into that magic circle into which they would tempt me. See my Diary for a new plan.

Lord, forgive my past unprofitableness, and enable me to bring forth more fruit to Thy glory. It is reasonable that now, when I find a manifest decline in some of my faculties, I should require more study, and thus only it is to be secured, unless I adopt some such plan, my giving up part of my parliamentary attendance will only be to exchange it for social intercourse with the irreligious, which dissipates and injures the mind; not, as it ought to be, to barter it for family cares, and culture and more study and preparation for public business.[312]

---

308. Thomas Erskine (1750–1823), 1st Baron Erskine, lawyer, M.P., and Lord Chancellor (1806–1807).

309. Samuel Rogers (1763–1855), a celebrated poet and wealthy banker, who lived and died in the same street as Wilberforce lived, 22 St. James's Place, London. Acquainted with, and friends of several mentioned in other parts of Wilberforce's Journal, including Sir Walter Scott, Dr Robertson, William Wordsworth, Coleridge, Adam Smith, Charles Fox, Richard Sheridan, and Lafayette. Rogers is remembered especially for his *The Pleasures of Memory* (1792), a poem he originally published anonymously.

310. Latin: too much known to everyone.

311. Latin: dies to himself unknown.

312. *Life*, iv. p. 161.

Friday, March 18th 1814

Dined with Madame de Stael, her son and daughter, and two other foreigners, Lord Harrowby, Lord and Lady Lansdown, Sir James Mackintosh. Lord and Lady Granville Leveson[313] were to have dined, but Lady Spencer died that morning. She asked me to name the party. A cheerful, pleasant dinner. She talking of the final cause of creation, not utility but beauty, did not like Paley, wrote about Rousseau at fifteen, and thought differently at fifty. Evening, assembly, but I came away at half-past eleven. A brilliant assembly of rank and talent.[314]

Saturday, March 19th 1814

The whole scene was intoxicating even to me. The fever arising from it is not yet gone off, (half-past 8, A.M.) though opposed by the most serious motives and considerations both last night and this morning. How dangerous then must such scenes (literally of dissipation, dissipating the spirits, the mind, and for a time almost the judgment) be to young people in the hey-day of youth, and life, and spirits! How unfit for those who are to watch unto prayer, to walk soberly, to be sober-minded![315] Some-thing in my own case may be fairly ascribed to natural high spirits, and I fear, alas! much to vanity, and a good deal to my being unaccustomed to such scenes; yet after allowing for these weaknesses and peculiarities, must not the sobriety of my age, my principles, my guard, (prayer preceding my entering into the enchanted ground,) be fairly considered as abating the effect, so much as that I may be a fair average sample of the effect of such scenes on young people in general of agreeable manners, and at all popular ways and characters?

I am sure I durst not often venture into these scenes. Then the seasoning is so high that it would render all quiet domestic pleasures insipid. Even poor Paley used to say, (though I hope jokingly,) 'Who ever talks to his wife?' This showed even in him the danger of being fascinated by social gaiety. O Lord, enable me to view last night's scene in its true colors, and shapes, and essences. I have not time to trace out the draught. May I remember that they and I are accountable, dying creatures, soon to appear at the judgment-seat of Christ, and be asked whether we avoided temptation, and endeavored to preserve a frame of spirit suited to those who had to work out their salvation with fear and trembling.[316]

Sunday, March 13th 1814

I am now engaged to many parties, yet I must not go on thus. It unfits my mind for private devotions, and makes me too late, steals me from my children, and even from my business, which from my weak health I must

---

313. Granville Leveson-Gower (1773–1846), 1st Earl Granville, known as Lord Granville Leveson-Gower (1786–1815), Viscount Granville (1815–1833), and Earl Granville (1833–1846). M.P., British Ambassador to Russia (1804–1807), and France (1824–1828, 1830–1841).

314. *Life*, iv. p. 164.

315. 1 Peter 4:7.

316. Philippians 2:12. *Life*, iv. p. 165.

do by contrivance. O Lord, guide me; let me not do anything contrary to the liberal and social spirit of Thy religion, but let me have wisdom to see what is really required from me, and resolution to perform it. My own soul should doubtless be my first object, and combined with it, my children. How much better might I serve them if I cultivated a closer connection with God! my business, and doing good to others.

I am clear it is right for me to withdraw from the gay and irreligious, though brilliant, society of Madame de Stael and others. I am I hope thankful to God that I am not given up to these pleasures. O let me labor that I may not be merely gratifying an indolent spirit by staying away. Let me cultivate a spiritual mind, that if any be really in earnest I may then approximate and show them that I can feel; and oh may God touch their hearts also. How surely is everyone who is in earnest useful to others! Poor Lord G! Let me talk with him, and guard him against the deception of being satisfied with the world's religion. Indeed he knows too much for that. But O may I above all pray and strive for a larger measure of softening, warming, quickening grace. Amen.[317]

Sunday, April 17th. 1814

I stay at home today on account of my cold, and I am about, after a short prayer for the Divine blessing, to set to work on my letter to the Emperor. I do it as in God's sight. Surely this occupation is pleasing to him who says, Mercy is better than sacrifice.[318] I can truly say in the presence of the Searcher of hearts, that I do not engage in it from inclination, for the contrary is the truth, but because it is a business which presses greatly in time, and which tends eminently to the glory of God, and the present and eternal happiness of men.[319]

I will not quit the peculiar duties of the day for my Abolition labors. Though last Sunday I set about them with a real desire to please God, yet it did not answer; my mind felt a weight on it, a constraint which impeded the free and unfettered movements of the imagination or intellect; and I am sure that this last week I might have saved for that work four times as much time as I assigned to it on Sunday. Therefore though knowing that God prefers mercy to sacrifice, yet let me in faith give up this day to religious exercises, to strengthening the impression of invisible and divine things by the worship of God, meditation, and reading. I trust He will bless me during the week, and enable me to make up what might seem lost.[320]

Undated, 1814

O Lord, help me. I will try to assign at least an hour in the morning, and when circumstances will permit, the same in the evening, for Scripture reading, private devotion, and meditation. How little can I now realize the circle of angels and unseen spirits! Yet I hope I can truly say I allow

---

317. Ibid., pp. 166-167.
318. Matthew 9:13.
319. The background to the letter is to be found in the pages preceding this entry, *Life*, iv. p. 179.
320. *Life*, iv. p. 179.

not my corruptions. O Lord, strengthen my faith, send the Spirit of Thy Son into my heart, that I may call Thee Father, and set my affections upon things above.[321]

1815

Friday, March 10th. 1815

At my prayers this morning, I reflected seriously if it was not my duty to declare my opinions in favor of the Corn Bill, on the principle of providing things honest in the sight of all men,[322] and adorning the doctrine of God my Savior in all things.[323] I decided to do it. I see people wonder I do not speak one way or the other. It will be said, he professes to trust in God's protection, but he would not venture anything. Then I shall have religious questions and moral questions, to which my speaking will conciliate, and contra, my silence strongly indispose men. Besides, it is only fair to the government, when I really think them right, to say so, as an independent man not liable to the imputation of party bias, corrupt agreement with landed interest, etc. So I prepared this morning and spoke, and though I lost my notes, and forgot much I meant to say, I gave satisfaction.

I am sure that in coming forward, I performed a very painful act of duty, from a desire to please God, and to serve the interests of religion, and I humbly trust God will protect me and my house and family. If not, His will be done. Sir Joseph Bankes's house sadly treated; all his papers burnt, and his house nearly being so.[324]

Saturday, April 1st. 1815

Spurzheim the craniologist in London, and people talking about his system[325] L.[326] full of it. Ministers are disposed for war; saying the Allies will have 700,000 men, and he be unprepared; whereas if you wait he will be becoming stronger and better equipped, especially with the materiel of war, and you and the Allies less compacted: we however are so exhausted that we cannot afford to pay all the forces. Our foreign expedition last year cost above thirty millions sterling.

An affecting visit from Mrs. B. the wife of an attorney of respectable station and character, near thirty years in Leeds, convicted of forgery of stamps on deeds, (vitiating securities,) and to be hanged this day week. Poor thing! I gave her no hopes, and wrote to his friend at Leeds to tell him plainly that no hope of pardon; till that be clear they never will look eternity in the face. Alas, may not our bloody laws send many unprepared into another world from this very cause? I once saw a poor wretch whom nothing would

---

321. Colossians 3:2. *Life*, iv. pp. 200-201.

322. Romans 12:17.

323. Titus 2:10.

324. *Life*, iv. p. 245.

325. Johann Gaspar Spurzheim (1776–1832), a German physician and one of the chief proponents and popularizers of phrenology, traveling extensively throughout Europe and even to America, promoting his craniographic approach to the theory.

326. Probably London is again referred to here.

persuade he should not through his friends obtain a pardon, whereas I knew about ten at night that he was to be hanged early the next morning.[327]

Monday, April 10th. 1815
I humbly hope that I enjoyed yesterday more of a Christian feeling of faith, and hope, and love, than of late. But I have been to blame in point of hours. Lord, forgive my past unprofitableness, and enable me to mend in future. I really wished to give more time and pains to the Report than Macaulay has allowed me. This very morning I meant to have given to it, but he had taken it away with him; but I am conscious I grow incompetent, and if my infirmities, as is natural, increase, while my talents and powers decline, I must go off extremely in efficiency. Let me only, however, try to please God, and do my best, and he will, I doubt not, bless me as he has done hitherto in a marvelous degree.[328]

Sunday, April 23rd. 1815
I have been neglecting general politics, and am sadly behindhand in my ponderings on them, without having done adequate good elsewhere. O let me learn hence, 1. To guard against procrastination. 2. Whatever my hand findeth to do, to do it with vigor. 3. To humble myself deeply for my sad unprofitableness. How little do I deserve the character, which the good providence of God, and the uncommon kindness of uncommon friends, has preserved for me! I can only hide my face in the dust, and be speechless. Yet let me try to amend, and be active and efficient to the utmost of my remaining faculties. My judgment hesitates as to the political line I should adopt; but on this blessed day, let my motto ever be, and I bless God I am enabled pretty well to make my practice accord with it, (so far at least as public affairs and private business are concerned,) acquaint now thyself with God, and be at peace.[329]

Monday, May 29th. 1815
Wordsworth the poet[330] breakfasted with us, and walked garden, and it being the first time, staid long, much pleased with him.[331]

Friday, July 7th. 1815
Shocked to hear of Whitbread's death, having destroyed himself.[332] It must have been insanity, as the jury immediately found it. Oh how little

---

327. *Life*, iv. pp. 255-256.

328. Ibid., p. 256.

329. Ibid., pp. 257-258.

330. William Wordsworth (1770–1850), leading English Romantic poet, and Poet Laureate (1843–1850), especially remembered for *The Prelude* (posthumously published in 1850). His closest friends included Samuel Taylor Coleridge, Sir Walter Scott, Robert Southey, Charles Lamb, Sir George Beaumont, and Sir William Rowan Hamilton. In 1801, Wordsworth sent Wilberforce a copy of the 2nd edition of his and Coleridge's *Lyrical Ballads*. It was an interesting development in light of his general dislike of evangelicals, but Wilberforce was different, for he was actually admired by both authors.

331. *Life*, iv. p. 260.

332. Samuel Whitbread (1764–1815), M.P., detailed earlier in the entry for 7 December, 1812. In the last six years of his life, his health deteriorated significantly, including severe weight gain,

are we duly thankful for being kept from such catastrophes! Doubtless the devil's instigation.[333]

Thursday, August 24th. 1815

I hoped as well as wished to get much time for private devotions on this important and most humiliating day, but partly through my own fault, partly through dear W.'s keeping me in his room, I had very little. Yet I hope the season has not elapsed without serious reflection; and as iron sharpeneth iron,[334] oh may my spirit be incited by the good men here. W.'s little one, my godchild, received into the church. Dear W. all Christian fervor and love, but rather too fanciful; yet oh how far removed from the excesses of our dear _____'s![335] There it is self-conceit operating through the medium of religious doctrines. If even knowledge puffeth up,[336] how much more self-sufficiency! I am tempted to waste time in W.'s library - an immense variety, especially of old divinity.[337]

~~Private~~[338] ~~Religious~~
Dec.r 1815. Resumd Octr 7th. 1826 (after many years).
For dearest Bs perusal only WW - 1826
Dec. 7th 1815 – Oct 7 1826. Religious.[339]

Brighton Dec.r 7th. 1815 Thursday 2 ½

Havg receiv'd a very distressg account of _____[340] but subsequently a very penitent & most affectionate & therefore extremely consoling Letter from Himself, I had intended to make this day one of my devotional days, set apart to God, chiefly to beg convertg Grace for Him & also direction for myself, what Course best to pursue with him & where to place Him tho' rather frittering away my time I fear at first. I have been since Bkfast & partic. with 2 or 3 very little Interruptions, from family Calls, in writing a long Letter to Him, in reading Baxter's *Saints Rest* & Doddridge's *Life* a little & in Meditation & prayer for him - I must also pray for Light & direction generally respecting the destinatn of my Childn. being much at a Loss what to do with my 3 elder Boys just at present. Mr. Langston[341] being to leave me next June. I have been terrified _____[342] by witnessing

---

extreme fatigue, debilitating headaches and insomnia. He committed suicide at his house at 35, Dover Street, Piccadilly, by slashing his throat. In 1812, Wilberforce wrote that Whitbread, 'with all his coarseness, had an Anglicanism about him, that rendered him a valuable ingredient in a British House of Commons.' See 'The Saturday Review', 1872, p. 561.

333. *Life*, iv. p. 264.
334. Proverbs 27:17.
335. He does not identify this person.
336. 1 Corinthians 8:1.
337. Ibid., p. 268.
338. MS Wilberforce e. 24, fo. 1.
339. 'Dec. 7th 1815–Oct 7 1826. Religious' is written here in pencil on inside cover.
340. He does not identify this person.
341. Wilberforce may be here referring to Stephen S. Langston (1766–1816), a graduate of Christ Church College, Oxford, who for a period from 1812 acted as a home-tutor for Samuel Wilberforce.
342. Wilberforce deliberately does not identify this.

the deaths of good mens Child[n.] while yet young & I fear in a most alarming state, & the Child[n.] God knoweth, of better men than I am. O the Corruption of this deceitful Heart, suggesting Complacency which[343] it[344] knows at y[e.] same momt to be unjust, & then fresh Complacency for detecting & condemning its injustice & so on ad infinitum. There is no resource but that of coming with all one's duplicity all one's doubts & Complexities of mental feelings & risings, to the foot of the Cross, & exclaiming Lord Help my Unbelief.[345] I abhor myself. Pardon & deliver me from the Bondage of my Corruptions accordg to thy gracious promises in X[t] Jesus. Amen. Amen. I have nothg else to plead but that plea Blessed be thy Name shall never fail us. O may I urge it with more Earnestness & Humiliation & faith & Hope & Love. Amen. Amen.[346]

Sunday Morng 8:20 - I've no time - Dec[r] 31[st.] Sunday Night 7 oClock 1815

I have not time to write largely this Eveng but I must put down a few Words, Alas, Alas! How deeply do I feel my own wretched Incompetence as a Parent even more than in other particulars, tho this sad Course of doing no Business but Letter writg renders[347] me quite barren, & injures my powers of bringing forward arranging & enforcing[348] the[349] little Knowledge & few Ideas I do possess. I must try to mend here then in various other points of practice. I must try to S-Ex amend,[350] Procrastination, Frittering away of T., Punctuality want of, Trifling over my Business & over comparatively less important B., Method want of. Let me now go & pray for my Amendment in all y[e] above particulars, & let me strive to cultivate both in my Wife my Children & myself: S-Exn, Self-denial – Punctuality – Diligence - Time redeemg - Procrastinatn rooting out - But above all, let me strive to cultivate[351] more & more Every Xtian Grace, more particularly: Faith workg by Love, keepg God & Xt continually in my Eyes. Vanity & Worldly Estimatn inordinate Love of rooted out, & lookg for Gods & Xt's favour & the Applause of Holy Angels.

My Eveng devotions & SS readg to be more attended to I must go to prayer. Lord thou hast graciously promis'd to hear prayer & even the innumerable Injunctions to pray wo'd imply as much. Surely then I may humbly rely on thy calling my poor[352] Children[353] to the Knowledge & Love of Him, seeing I humbly & earnestly pray for them & make thr

---

343. MS Wilberforce e. 24, fo. 1.
344. MS Wilberforce e. 24, fo. 2.
345. Mark 9:24.
346. Ibid. MS Wilberforce e. 24, fo. 2.
347. At 'renders' he has written a large 'A' in the left margin.
348. MS Wilberforce e. 24, fo. 2.
349. MS Wilberforce e. 24, fo. 3.
350. To the left of 'amend' he has written, 'S Ex' in the left margin.
351. 'X' is crossed through at this point.
352. MS Wilberforce e. 24, fo. 3.
353. MS Wilberforce e. 24, fo. 4.

Spiritual Benefit my grand Object, before Learning Oly[354] Advancement or ought else. I humbly trust to thy mercy O Lord, for my poor Child[n.] & I will go on praying. I'm discourag'd by havg seen y[e.] Childn. of far better men than myself, (God knoweth I say this sincerely), die, I fear, unrepenting, yet Lord, I will still hope in thy Mercy & pray more & more. Lord Help me. Amen. Amen.[355]

Near 9 -

Lord - How shocked I am by thinkg how sadly the past year has been wasted. It presents to me no 12 in the Review but Letters. Durg y[e] Session, I frequently for a long time tog[r] receive Letters & Notes, 30 pr day & more. By y[e] End of Session a vast Arrear has accumulated & even now those of y[e] last Sessn remain unanswer'd. Alas, Alas. Meanwhile not only is no new Knowledge acquired but my old Stock is not kept up, for my memory declines fast & I fear my powers mental[356] in general. My imaginatn is duller, my feelings colder & more stiff & torpid, yet perhaps by active Regimen & mental discipline (such partly as Dugald Stewart), even _____ [357] of in y[e] case of y[e] memory. I might maintain my faculties apparently to others at y[e] same point, if I could exercise them,[358] give my time &c. & I must try to do this & be less wholly given up to Letters. O how I wish to do some things - The Register Bill - a gen[l] Bill for Negro Slaves Benefit, Personal & Relig[s] & Moral Oaths Lessening - Adultery Bill - O how little have I of late done Credit to y[e] Cause of X[t.] O may I try to redeem the time & To exercise, & improve my faculties & increase my Stores from Xtn Motives. (see Pa 3 Pr) But above all O Lord, Pour out on me abundantly thy sanctifying & renewg Grace. My Pri Dev[ns] SS readg & Meditatns being more fervent & devot[l] as in God's Sight, (more solemn & humiliated, rather than[359] passionate), may I this year live more in y[e] Spirit of a real Xtian Walkg by faith not Sight: Rememberg I am not my own, but Xt's Rom 14:7. Conscious with[t360] Xt I can do nothg but, Looking to Xt for Strength & evy Grace Rev. 3:18. Full of love to God & Man, more active in doing Good, & visiting Poor & <u>Sick personally</u>,[361] of Gratitude[362], of[363] Humility & Self Abhorrence, (See heads) for I have abund[t] Cause for Hum[n] & Self-Abhorrence yet of Hope, & O that it might be peace &

---

354. Wilberforce's symbol for 'world' is used here.

355. MS Wilberforce e.24, fos.2-4.

356. Over the word 'powers' he has a horizontal line over which he wrote '2', and over the word 'mental' another horizontal line, over which he had written '1'.

357. Illegible word.

358. Here in left margin he has a large 'A' with a vertical red line bracketing the next 7 lines, followed by a large 'B' bracketing the remainder of the page.

359. 'Rather than' is inserted here above a crossed out word.

360. A Cross symbol is inserted here, as if later words were to be inserted at this point.

361. 2 vertical lines with a single horizontal line symbol placed in left margin here with the words, 'sadly wanting love'.

362. MS Wilberforce e.24, fo.5.

363. MS Wilberforce e.24, fo.6.

joy in believing.[364] Thus practically feeling & living, that to me to Live
is Xt. & to die is Gain.[365] Strivg also to attend to all my Heads, conv^n
& comp^y &c. Not to faint or be weary in well doing[366] or of Self-denial,
& O Lord Help me, & enable me to live to thy Glory here & finally,
tho' most undeservg, to be made a Partaker of the Inheritance of y^e
Saints in Light.[367] Amen. Amen. Amen. NB To read over ye above Entry
occasionally.[368]

364. Romans 15:13.
365. Philippians 1:21.
366. Galatians 6:9.
367. Colossians 1:12.
368. MS Wilberforce c. 24, fos. 4-6. *Life*, iv. p. 281 has, 'Sunday Dec. 31st. Church morning. After church we and our six children together. I addressed them all collected and afterwards solemn prayer. How little likely on the 30th May, 1797, when I married, that we and all our six children, we never had another, should all be living and well. Praise the Lord, O my soul.'

The Spiritual Journals
of
William Wilberforce

1816–1830

William Wilberforce 1816–1830

During this fifteen-year period, Britain continued to experience a number of challenging events, just as it had in the previous period, including some that will be particularly serious. Eighteen people were killed and hundreds were injured in 1819, in what become known as the Peterloo Massacre. The tragedy happened when a number of Cavalrymen were ordered to charge a large demonstration in Peterloo, Manchester, where protestors were seeking reforms to the voting system. The following January, Britain lost its long-reigning monarch King George III, who died after a sixty-year reign. Ireland experienced a partial failure of the potato crop from 1821 to 1823, creating Britain's most serious period of food shortage in the early nineteenth century, with many deaths resulting from both starvation and typhus. The one highlight in the midst of all these challenges, especially to many Catholics in Britain, was their seeing the passing in April 1829 of the Roman Catholic Relief Act. This Law, sometimes referred to as the Catholic Emancipation Act, repealed all remaining Penal Laws against Catholics and allowed them to sit as members in the Parliament in London.

As for Wilberforce himself, he lost his sister Sally in 1816, and that loss may have been especially hard for Wilberforce, for in a number of his Journal entries he chastised himself that he was constantly unkind to her, not treating her as he should have,

> On arriving I heard that my sister had died yesterday at four o'clock. Poor Stephen much affected! Liable to strong paroxysms, at other times calm and pretty cheerful. I prayed by my dear sister's body, and with the face uncovered. Its fixedness very awful. I sat all the evening engaging Stephen, while the coffin was adjusting below. How affecting all these things; how little does the immortal spirit regard it! Looking at night, till near two o'clock this morning, over my dear sister's letters, many to and from myself, when she and I first in earnest in religion.[1]

---

1. Undated entry, 1816.

Along with the other Abolitionists, Wilberforce may have enjoyed the victory Abolition brought, but he continued to face strong opposition in his other campaigns, especially now of achieving full Emancipation. For that to be accomplished there was still a long and hard campaign ahead, and the opposition would be as fierce as ever,

> The stream runs most strongly against us. Marryatt's violent and rude publication, Matthison's more fair, and Hibbert's well-timed one, all come out to meet us at the first opening of Parliament. But how vast is the influence of government; it is of that only we are afraid! Yet our cause is good, and let us not fear; assuredly God will ultimately vindicate the side of justice and mercy. Marryatt's new pamphlet is extremely bitter against my religious profession, thinking that nail will drive. Poor fellow! I hope I can bear him no ill will, but allow for, and pity him.[2]

Wilberforce also had a number of other campaigns and causes he was involved with or even leading, many of which also took much of his time and energy. He was actively involved, for example, in seeking to bring about changes in the Penal Code, in sentencing and in reform of Prisons. On Tuesday, 17 February, 1818, he recorded too that he had not been able to sleep from 'thinking of the slaves' wretched sufferings, and partly the two poor women about to be hanged for forgery this day. Alas, how bloody are our laws!'[3] In that same vein, he wrote in the following month that he was much impressed with a book by Thomas Buxton, on British prisons and reform at the dreadful Newgate prison, a work initiated by Elizabeth Fry. 'What lessons are taught by Mrs. Fry's success,' he wrote, 'I am still warmed by the account. Were I young, I should instantly give notice of the business, if no one else did.'[4]

From the moment a campaign against animal cruelty first surfaced, championing such a cause also became a high priority for Wilberforce. Indeed he was present for and involved with every Parliamentary debate on the issue, even co-founding what became the Royal Society for the Prevention of Cruelty to Animals (R.S.P.C.A.). This was something which was all the more remarkable when one appreciates not just how unpopular such a cause was in his day, but was seen as something well below the dignity of a legislator to be involved in. Nevertheless both Wilberforce and Buxton co-sponsored Richard Martin's 1821 Bill against animal cruelty, and it received Royal Assent the following July. Martin died in 1834 and in the following year his original Act was enlarged, to then also ban the fighting and baiting of animals.

All of this work was quite apart from all the various committees and meetings Wilberforce needed to attend in the normal course of Parliamentary business. One even discovers from an entry in 1818 that he was sitting on a Secret Committee of the House of Commons. These

---

2. Journal entry, Wednesday, 14 February, 1816.
3. Journal entry, Tuesday, 17 February, 1818.
4. Journal entry, Tuesday, 31 March, 1818.

were committees usually set up by Prime Ministers for a particular purpose, as would have been the case here. Wilberforce gave us a glimpse into the demands of his life in an entry in May 1819, which is all the more shocking when one remembers this was not a usual business day for him, but actually a Saturday. 'British and Foreign School Society. Duke of Kent in the chair. Oh how glad I am that the tenth meeting is this day over! The consumption of time is really too great.'[5]

Wilberforce also had to somehow build time into his days for all the many people he was invited to meet with or be entertained by. In May 1817, for example, he breakfasted with the Scottish Evangelical Church leader Thomas Chalmers and recorded that he was, 'Much pleased with Chalmers' simplicity, walked and talked in garden.'[6] On May 25, Wilberforce went with several of his friends to the Scottish Presbyterian Church in London to hear Chalmers preach,

> Off early with Canning, Huskisson, and Lord Binning, to the Scotch Church, London Wall, to hear Dr. Chalmers. Vast crowds, Bobus Smith, Lord Elgin, Harrowby, etc. So pleased with him that I went again; getting in at a window with Lady D. over iron palisades on a bench. Chalmers most awful on carnal and spiritual man. Home tired, and satisfied that I had better not have gone for edification. I was surprised to see how greatly Canning was affected; at times he quite melted into tears. I should have thought he had been too much hardened in debate to show such signs of feeling.[7]

Wilberforce turned 60 in August 1820, the same year King George died, and Wilberforce's health, which had never been good, was obviously failing even more at that point, having been particularly badly affected as a result of his opiate addiction. Throughout his life he had been plagued with numerous chest infections, flare-ups from his ulcerative colitis, bouts of severe constipation, very painful hemorrhoids, and his eyesight, never the best, had by 1820 declined rapidly. The following year therefore it came as to no surprise to many, that Wilberforce handed over leadership of the campaign for the end of Slavery to Thomas Buxton. When he lost his daughter Barbara from tuberculosis at the end of 1821, his physician strenuously advised him to attend Parliament only 'very little' that coming Session. Wilberforce recorded the following about his beloved daughter's passing,

> I went and saw the coffin. How vain the plumes, etc. when the occasion is considered, and the real state of humiliation to which the body is reduced! I must elsewhere note down the mercies and loving-kindnesses of our God and Savior in this dispensation; above all, the exceeding goodness of giving us grounds for an assured persuasion that all is well with her; that she is gone to glory. When the hearse and our kind friends were gone, after a short time I came into my little room at the

---

5. Journal entry, Saturday, 15 May, 1819.
6. Journal entry, Friday, 16 May, 1817.
7. Journal entry, Sunday, 25 May, 1817.

top of the stairs where I am now writing and engaged awhile in prayer, blessing God for his astonishing goodness to me, and lamenting my extreme unworthiness.[8]

With his own health declining, the Wilberforces decided to sell their home in Kensington, London and instead leased a house away from the city, in Marden Park, Surrey. He was still hoping to write his second book, even at this stage of life and health, 'both a religious and a political work, which would not be without value,'[9] but the pressures of life, work and health would in the end make it impossible. He was reminiscing though in 1821, that now he had made it to the age of sixty-one years and a half, he remembered that 'though never a strong man,' he was in such a state of apparent weakness in 1788, that his physician, a certain 'Dr. Warren, of unrivalled sagacity', said confidentially (but it was soon told to my kind sympathizing friend Muncaster), that I had not stamina to last a fortnight. How wonderful is it that I continue unto this day![10] Wilberforce shared that same memory in 1828, though Dr. Warren's prognosis for Wilberforce's expected survival time had now been extended by an additional week. Wilberforce was obviously excited by all his family being present, as he recorded that all his descendants gathered together 'around the board – mine, of whom above forty years ago, when a bachelor in 1788, Dr. Warren declared that I had not stamina to last three weeks. Praise the Lord, O my soul.'[11] But survive he did and in 1823 he was able at that time, along with a number of others to be involved in forming the Anti-Slavery Society. Then for several weeks he worked feverishly on creating what would become its manifesto. It was published in the March as, *An Appeal to the Religion, Justice and Humanity of the Inhabitants of the British Empire, in behalf of the Negro Slaves in the West Indies.*

The following June he believed that all seemed especially good, for as he felt moved to write, 'to my surprise felt bowels alive and quite a loose motion.' This feeling was not to last, for very soon afterwards he became seriously ill. His physician again warned him that his Parliamentary work had become a very real danger to his life, and so after much thought and under clear pressure from Barbara, it was decided he would retire in February 1825.

I am not now much wanted in Parliament; our cause has powerful advocates, who have now taken their stations. The example of a man's retiring when he feels his bodily and mental powers beginning to fail him, might probably be useful. The public have been so long used to see persons turning a long-continued seat in Parliament to account for obtaining rank, etc., that the contrary example the more

---

8. Entry recorded after 30 December, 1821, the day of her death.

9. *Life*, v. pp. 106-7.

10. Journal entry, March 1821.

11. Journal entry, Tuesday, 10 June, 1828.

needed, and it ought to be exhibited by one who professes to act on Christian principles.[12]

In the May of 1825 they purchased a cottage at Highwood Hill, Hendon, north of London, which they moved into the following year. In 1827 he felt well enough to undertake a tour of Yorkshire, but by 1829 he was seriously thinking that he may well be in his final days. He reflected that however long he did have, his remaining time should be used for the best purposes,

> My future state should now be my grand, indeed-comparatively speaking, my sole concern. God's kind providence has granted to me a residue of life after its business is over. I know I must be near death, perhaps very near it. I believe that on the state in which death finds me, will depend my eternal condition; and even though my state may now be such as to produce a humble hope that I am safe, yet by a wise improvement of my time, I may augment my eternal happiness, besides enjoying delightful communion with God in the interval. Let me then make the improvement of my soul the first grand business of my life, attending also to the good of others, if possible both by my pen, and conversation, and social intercourse.[13]

By March 1830 Wilberforce almost totally blind, experienced serious family trouble when the dairy business which he had financially provided for his son William to operate, collapsed into severe financial trouble. Wilberforce made the conscious decision to financially rescue his son, though he had no legal responsibility to do so. The plan necessitated leaving and renting out their new home at Highwood, as well as selling outright the original family home of 25 High Street in Hull, as well as some nearby land they owned. It was a tragic end to this period of his life.

The Journal entries in this section were taken directly from the manuscript MS Wilberforce e. 24, with additional entries being drawn from the extracts published by Wilberforce's sons. The last written entry that we have from Wilberforce in his Spiritual Journals was made on October 7, 1826 at 1.25pm.

---

12. *Life*, v. pp. 233-9; Harford, *Recollections*, pp. 158-9; MS Wilberforce c.1 fo. 115.
13. Journal entry, Sunday, 5 February, 1829.

A delightful morning. Walked out and saw the most abundant dew-drops sparkling in the sunbeams on the gazon. How it calls forth the devotional feelings in the morning when the mind is vacant from worldly business, to see all nature pour forth, as it were, its song of praise to the Great Creator and Preserver of all things! I love to repeat Psalms 104, 103, 145, etc. at such a season.

William Wilberforce, 1827

1816

Sunday Night Jany 7[th.]

I've no time to write. Sad Procrastination I fear & late Hours both night & morng, & plan not kept to, partly I Hope from Pavilion invitations. yet much I fear chargeable on myself. This Evg my first serious talk w. Wm. for a short time. I must not expend in writg time better spent in prayer both for the poor Chn. & myself. Lord Help me. Bless me & these. To Thee I flee for Refuge, O merciful Savr. Thou hast promisd them to come &c. thou wilt in no wise cast out[1] & thou wilt grant what we ask. O what fairer or more Legitimate petit[ns] than for converting Grace for my Childrn., for W[m] especy. Lord to thee I flee, O Hear me, soften warm quicken sanctify me. Amen. Amen. Hence to my old 4to Book.[2]

Sunday, February 11[th.] 1816

From what cause soever it is, my heart is invincibly dull. I have again and again gone to prayer, read, meditated, yet all in vain. Oh, how little can we do anything without the quickening grace of God! I will go again to prayer and meditation. Blessed be God, his promises do not vary with our stupid insensibility to them. Surely God has always blessed me in all things, both great and small, in a degree almost unequalled, and never suffered me materially to fail when there has been an occasion for exertion.[3]

Wednesday, February 14[th.] 1816

The stream runs most strongly against us. Marryatt's violent and rude publication,[4] Matthison's more fair, and Hibbert's well-timed one,[5] all come out to meet us at the first opening of Parliament. But how vast is the influence of government; it is of that only we are afraid! Yet our cause is good, and let us not fear; assuredly God will ultimately vindicate the side of justice and mercy. Marryatt's new pamphlet is

---

1. John 6:37.

2. MS Wilberforce e. 24, fo. 6.

3. *Life*, iv. 337-338.

4. Joseph Marryatt (1757–1824), M.P., and chairman of Lloyd's (1811–1824). On 13 June, 1815 he opposed Wilberforce's proposed bill for a registry of slaves, arguing that it infringed the colonies' legislative rights; that with the slave trade abolished the planters had a vested interest in treating slaves humanely; that slavery would die a natural death, and that enforced abolition would ruin the West Indian colonies. He also condemned what he saw as the interference and propaganda of the African Institution, and in his 1816 pamphlet as Wilberforce here refers to, *Thoughts on the Abolition of the Slave Trade* he expanded these arguments and attacked the 'wild and dangerous political doctrines, that are now circulated under the guise of humanity' by 'a certain class of Methodists, a sect who profess superior sanctity'. He carried on his battle on this subject in subsequent pamphlets, *More Thoughts* (1816), and *More Thoughts Still* (1818), and in the House of Commons itself with both Wilberforce and Romilly, 22 April, 1818, 20 May 1818, and 3 June 1818.

5. George Hibbert (1757–1837), M.P., pro-slavery merchant, alderman of London, Director and chairman of the West India Dock Company. Though he lived in Clapham, he is remembered especially for his opposition to the abolition of the slave trade, as seen in his maiden speech in February 1807, and in his *Three Speeches on the Abolition of the Slave Trade* (London, 1807). He also gave a 40-minute address in the London Tavern, entitled 'The Slave Trade Indispensable …', in which he sought to demolish the arguments given in Wilberforce's speech. In 1824, Hibbert helped found what became the Royal National Lifeboat Institution.

extremely bitter against my religious profession, thinking that nail will drive. Poor fellow! I hope I can bear him no ill will, but allow for, and pity him.[6]

Friday, May 17th 1816

I stated honestly to Lord Liverpool, the pain it would cost him to oppose his government systematically on a question, which will I am clear, on the long run, (though now people are uninformed and therefore indifferent,) interest in our favor the bulk of the religious and moral part of the community; which will never sit quiet and leave 6 or 700,000 human beings in a state of studiously preserved darkness and degradation.[7]

Undated, 1816

On arriving I heard that my sister had died yesterday at four o'clock. Poor Stephen much affected! Liable to strong paroxysms, at other times calm and pretty cheerful. I prayed by my dear sister's body, and with the face uncovered. Its fixedness very awful. I sat all the evening engaging Stephen, while the coffin was adjusting below. How affecting all these things; how little does the immortal spirit regard it! Looking at night, till near two o'clock this morning, over my dear sister's letters, many to and from myself, when she and I first in earnest in religion.[8]

Sunday, July 7th 1816

What over-valuation of human estimation do I find within me! And then also what self-complacent risings of mind will force themselves upwards, though against my judgment, which at the very moment condemns them, and yet my heart then claims credit for this condemnation! Oh the corruption and deceitfulness of the heart![9]

Lowestofte[10] Septr 1st 1816 Sunday abt 6 oClock

On my first arrival at this place (came Evg before last), I sit down on return home from Pakefield Church[11] (over my Coffee), to record (alas!) a melancholy State. Alas! I may go to my Entry of Decr 31st 1815 Pa 2 & follg, for all that is there stated is now too true, & in some Respects I fear with aggravations, in respect of Want of punctuality, Alas, & in Procrastination, and with respect to my Children my difficulties & defects are even greater I fear. Yet O what Cause have I

---

6. *Life*, iv. pp. 282-283.

7. Ibid., p. 292.

8. Ibid., pp. 299-300.

9. Ibid., p. 341.

10. MS Wilberforce e. 24, fo. 7.

11. Pakefield is now a suburb of the town of Lowestoft in Suffolk, located about 2 miles south of the town center. Until 1934 though, Pakefield was a village and parish in its own right, mentioned in the *Domesday Book* as 'Pagefella'. It later developed as a fishing community. The former parish church of All Saints and St. Margaret's is located on the cliff top of what is Britain's most easterly town. Until the 18th century, they were actually two separate churches, as the name suggests, serving two separate parishes, until their merger in 1743.

for Gratitude here. Was it not quite a special Providence, that <u>such</u> a man as Mr. Rollestone, sho'd offer to come to live with us, Voluntarily & Gratuitously. But Alas, must I not confess that I Have not been pursuing yᵉ Course most likely to produce the Improvemt of all my Childn., in not growg in Grace more myself. How can I wonder at <u>their</u> faults, when my own (alas!) are so many & great. yet Hope forsakes me not. Yet I will fly to the Cross of Xt & thro' it to the throne of Grace, of that God who is[12] described[13] as, "<u>delighting in Mercy</u>."[14] I must especially be more regular &c. in Eveng Devotns. I should think an Hour in them & Serious Readg during Recess.

Strive for more walkg by faith & maintaining a stronger & more abiding Sense of Invisible things. And of Course, Strive for more abiding Humiliatn Gratitude Love & Watching unto prayer.[15] Then: Pray earnestly for Wisdom, to guide me in the Case of <u>all</u> my Children, (for I am sadly deficient in the Case of every One of them), & to strengthen me also & enable me to perform what is wisest & best. Strive also, for using my time better. See especially A & B, pages 3 & 5, & improvg my faculties & amassing Stores & <u>keepg Tools from decay</u>. Try to form a plan here. Also conversⁿ· Try to render it more profitable both when with Childⁿ· & with other Company, (see Watts's Rules), & practise more self-examination (I've been sadly defective here, Alas. Alas!). But O let all be done with a view to the favor of my God & my Redeemer. O let me learn more habitually to regard myself not as my own, but as bought with a price,[16] & that the Blood of yᵉ· Only Son of God & let me therefore live, think, feel, speak, & act, under the influence of yᵉ· great Governg principle of true Xtians, Rom. 14:7, "<u>none of us liveth to himself</u>".[17] O may I be enabled more & more thus to live. Of myself I can do nothg, but we can do all by thy Grace & Strength, O Lord. Even so Lord Jesus. Amen. Amen.[18]

8 ¼

I've been alone except 2 or 3 short & trifling Interruptions tho' one alas shewed me in Thos's Case that I was too little under Love's Influence, in being too forward to impute Evil.

Time: I will look over my Letters & separate those which Burnᵐ· can answer, from those I must ansʳ myself, to try to write them shortly. Those I <u>must</u> write & leave rest unansᵈ· Dear B. calls me down to yᵉ· Childn. & I must go, other[19] wise[20] I was going to begin Heads or rather

---

12. Page ends after word 'is', and next page begins with '8' top left and 'Micah concludg Verses' inserted above lines, with 'described' as first word on the line.

13. MS Wilberforce e. 24, fo. 7.

14. Micah 7:18.

15. 1 Peter 4:7.

16. 1 Corinthians 6:20.

17. Romans 14:7.

18. MS Wilberforce e. 24, fos. 7-9.

19. MS Wilberforce e. 24, fo. 9.

20. MS Wilberforce e. 24, fo. 10.

preamble of Gratitude for Heads, of my Life. But I believe I ought to yield to dear B.'s Call, not havg been with them today at dinner. O Lord, Bless & Keep me & Enable me more & more to love & serve thee. Amen. Amen.[21]

Monday 2ᵈ Septʳ 1816 Lowestofte 8 ½ -

I've been reading over the Above Entry, & O may I attend to all the Lessons it enforces & may I practically remember, Examining myself daily Evg if I can, alias Morng: Xtian's Grand Principle Rom 14:7. God's & Xt's Eye continʸ lookg up for Strength. Kindness universal, especy in reprovg Children, watch Reconciliatn moment (Sepʳ 3ᵈ). Conversatⁿ Reglˢ both Genˡ & Individˡ in Walkg (Sepʳ 3ᵈ). List of topics & for queries. Time redeeming: Procrastinⁿ Love. Punctuality, regular Hours as much as Health will allow (3ᵈ). Journal of timg. Self-Examination daily. Sepʳ 3ᵈ Mem Evil Spirits Influence, Eph 6:12, 1 Pet 5:8. Maintain continl Sense of my own Unworthiness & Weakness, for Humiliation & looking to Xt. for Wisdom & Strength.[22]

Wedy[23] Septʳ 4th. 1816 -

Yesty not fit to go to write or even any work until too long after dinner less care here, try less wine & water, & slow eating. Surely I might write very well an Hour ½ after conduct of dinner, but let me try honestly. Rememberg Dr. adding this Phrase, the Stomach the Body's Conscience, but let me act fᵐ a higher Conscience, & remʳ the infinite Importance of redeeming yᵉ time. O my Heart is quite sick abt Wm, & that while there are some good traits, there should be some such sad Qualities. O how much do I see yᵉ Effects of our own Self-Indulgence, Selfishness in one form or other his grand Vice. Lord, Help me to act wisely & O bless my Labours. I humbly trust thou wilt so do.[24]

Friday Novʳ 1st. 1816 Bath - 8 ½ -

From not being a Predestinarian I have not enough adverted to our being called, if at all, <u>by the Will of God</u>. O may I practically attend to this more in Gratitude, in prayer. It is enforc'd on me by readg 1 Cor 1:1 - see also Col 1:1 & 1 Cor 4:7 connected with it.[25]

Kensn Gore Novʳ 24th 2 ¾ - 1816 -

I've no time for writing, I have as yet had scarce any for pri. dev. still less for meditn, tho' for abt ¼ of an Hour preparg for it, by perusg Baxter. Alas. Alas. I have been going on sadly. Evg prayer & SS readg sadly neglected & slovenly perform'd. How can I wonder at all yᵉ rest going on so. In Conv. Regls. sadly too Self Indulgt at table &c. I've

---

21. Ibid.
22. MS Wilberforce e. 24, fo. 10.
23. MS Wilberforce e. 24, fo. 11.
24. Ibid.
25. Ibid.

no time, but O let me go to prayer and implore the pardong mercy &
sanctifying Grace of Xt my Sav^r. Lord, heal my backslidings. Renew
Sanctify and deliver me.[26]

1817

Friday, May 16th. 1817
Dr. Chalmers[27] breakfasted with me, Inglis,[28] old Symons and others.
Much pleased with Chalmers' simplicity, walked and talked in garden.
House late on Clergy Residence Bill, and slept in town.[29]

Monday, May 19th. 1817
Poor Sally More[30] died about a week ago, after long and extreme
suffering, yet never impatient, but perfectly submissive and resigned.
What a triumph of grace! All the world wild about Dr. Chalmers, he
seems truly pious, simple, and unassuming.[31]

Sunday, May 25th. 1817
Off early with Canning, Huskisson,[32] and Lord Binning,[33] to the
Scotch Church, London Wall,[34] to hear Dr. Chalmers. Vast crowds,
Bobus Smith,[35] Lord Elgin, Harrowby, etc. So pleased with him that
I went again; getting in at a window with Lady D. over iron palisades
on a bench. Chalmers most awful on carnal and spiritual man. Home

---

26. MS Wilberforce e. 24, fo. 11.

27. Thomas Chalmers (1780–1847), professor of theology and evangelical leader of both the
Church of Scotland and the breakaway, Free Church of Scotland at the Disruption.

28. Sir Robert Henry Inglis (1786–1855), 2nd Bart and MP for Dundalk 1824–1826, Ripon
1828–1829, and Oxford University 1829–1854.

29. *Life*, iv. p. 323.

30. Sarah (Sally) More (c.? 1743–d. 17 May, 1817).

31. *Life*, iv. p. 324.

32. Huskisson, William (1770–1830), M.P., Superintendent of the aliens office, chief clerk at
the War Office, close confidante of Pitt and Dundas, and involved in setting up Britain's modern
Intelligence Service. Unfortunately he also has the misfortune to be remembered as the first victim
of a fatal railway accident in Britain, which occurred on 15 September, 1830.

33. Thomas Hamilton (1780–1858), 9th Earl of Haddington, Lord Binning (until 1828), M.P.,
Commissioner for the Indian Board of Control (1809, 1814–1822), Lord Lieutenant of Ireland (1834–
1835), First Lord of the Admiralty (1841–1846), and Lord Privy Seal (1846).

34. The Scotch Church was established at Founders' Hall in the City of London, sometime
before 1665, moving to the London Wall in 1764. The Congregation became part of the Presbyterian
Church in 1843. Albion Chapel was opened in 1815, and stood on the site of the west wing of the
Bethlem Royal Hospital. Alexander Fletcher was minister at the time of Wilberforce's visit to hear
Thomas Chalmers. Fletcher was particularly interested in missions poverty, and was appointed
Director of the London Missionary Society. He was particularly popular with children and is
remembered for *The Children's Friend* and his quite unique gift of attracting vast audiences of
children.

35. Robert Percy 'Bobus' Smith (1770–1845) was relatively poor and a family friend procured
for him the office of Advocate-General of Bengal (1803–1811), and afterwards he returned to Britain
incredibly wealthy. He became an M.P. and in 1812 was appointed Lord of the Treasury by Lord
Wellesley. His maiden speech which Wilberforce described as having begun 'promisingly', was
viewed by many as very disappointing, if not a fiasco. He was anti-evangelical in his views, and in
the debates connected with the renewal of the East India Company's charter, he opposed allowing
Christian missions in India.

tired, and satisfied that I had better not have gone for edification. I was surprised to see how greatly Canning was affected; at times he quite melted into tears. I should have thought he had been too much hardened in debate to show such signs of feeling.[36]

Sunday, June 1st. 1817

Determined to keep an account, and watch in all ways to redeem the time. Having so many breakfasters sadly interrupts me. Often they have staid till nearly one o'clock. Thus everything falls into arrears. Let me strive to set the mainspring right, and then to mend the works also. God help and direct me; and though I deserve no such honor, enable me yet to do some good. I humbly hope that I have lost my deliberate vainglory; but for Christ's honor I should be sorry to sink, as I am now doing, into disrepute from my own mismanagement or indolence, added to a real decline of powers. May God purify my motives, while he prompts, quickens, and strengthens me for action. I have felt this day more comfort in religion than for some time past.[37]

Monday, July 21st. 1817

The birthday of my two eldest children. I regretted that I was so hurried; I had little time to give to them, or to prayer for them. A poor woman called immediately after breakfast, just when I had meant to spend a quiet hour in devotion; but I called to mind Christ's example, and looked up to him, hoping that I should please him more by giving up my own plan and pursuing his, writing for her.[38]

Monday, August 4th. 1817

Let me put down that I have had of late a greater degree of religious feeling than usual. Is it an omen, as has once or twice shot across my imagination, a hint that my time for being called away draws nigh? Surely were it not for my dearest wife I could not regret it, humbly hoping, deeply unworthy as I am, that there is a propitiation for our sins, and that the mercies of God through Christ would not fail me. But oh, let me check the emotions of indolence and of trying to have done with the turmoil of this vain world of perturbations, and give way to a more lively gratitude for the mercies of the Savior, and a more active determination and consequent course of holy obedience and usefulness. Alas, alas, considering my opportunities, I have been a sadly unprofitable servant.

Pardon me, O Lord, quicken, soften, warm, invigorate me, and enable me to rise from my torpor, and to imitate the example of holy Paul, doing this one thing, forgetting the things behind, and pressing forward towards the mark of our high calling of God in Christ Jesus.[39] Alas, I fear

---

36. *Life*, iv. p. 324.
37. Ibid., p. 325.
38. Ibid., pp. 331-332.
39. Philippians 3:14.

I sadly neglect my duties to my children, and also to the poor, for though I serve the latter more abundantly than by individual visitation, when with the motive of Christ's speech, (Matt. xxv. 40), I attend to whole classes and masses of them, yet individual visitation has its good also. O Lord, teach, guide, quicken me. Without Thee I can do nothing;[40] with Thee all things. Lord, help, bless, and keep me. Amen.[41]

Undated, 1817

Humiliation, means of, and topics for: Consider, all my motives and just causes for gratitude; constant, fervent, self-denying gratitude; and then with this contrast my actual state. All my means and motives also to improvement and greater advance in the Christian character. That if all that really passes within were visible, all the workings of evil positive and negative, especially if compared with my principles and lessons to others, all my selfishness of feeling, and coldness of affection, too often towards those even whom I love and ought to love most, all my want of self-denial, all my self-indulgence, what shame would cover me! Yet that comparatively I care not for its being known to God. And is this because of his and Christ's mercy? Oh what baseness! My incurable, at least uncured, love of human approbation, and my self-complacency or pain when much granted or withheld, even when my judgment makes me abhor myself for it. I trust I can say I do not allow this vicious feeling, but repress it with indignation and shame. Oh were all that passes within in this instance to be seen fully, what shame should I feel! Realize this. Look at various other Christians who have not enjoyed half my advantages or motives to growth in grace, yet how immeasurably they exceed me!

How little good have I done compared with what I might have done! What procrastination! Consider in detail how deficient in the duties of an M. P. father, master, friend, companion, brother. Resolutions broken. Intemperance often. How sinful this when taken in relation to motives to self-denial, from love to Christ and to self-extinction, for me a vile ungrateful sinner! Oh shame, shame!

Early advantages abused, and benefits often lost. What an almost hell of bad passions (despair absent), in my soul when a youth, from emulation, envy, hatred, jealousy, selfishness! Yet, alas! justice to myself requires my adding how ill-treated here. Time, talents, substance, etc. wasted, and shocking goings-on, Christianity considered, and after the revellings over, as egregious waste of faculties and means among the fellows, card-playing, etc. Consequent course of living almost without God in the world, till God's good providence checked and turned me, (oh miracle of mercy!) in 1785, through the Dean's instrumentality.

But, alas! since I professed and tried to live to God, sometimes only preserved from gross sin and shame by preventing grace. And, alas! even till now how little progress, how little of the Divine nature, how

---

40. John 15:5.
41. *Life*, iv. p. 341.

little spirituality either in heart or life, how little of a due adorning of the doctrine of God my Savior![42] How much vanity and undue solicitude about human estimation! (Oh if transparent here!) Procrastination, inefficiency, self-indulgence, living below principles and rules. Contrast all this with my almost unequalled mercies and blessings. And remember God and Christ foreknew all thy ingratitude. N. B. All thy sins, great and small, are open to God's eye as at first, entire, and fresh, and unfaded, except as blotted out by Christ's blood.

I find it one of the best means of gaining self-abhorrence, after such reflection as above delineated, to consider and press home what I should think and feel about another favored in all respects as myself, who should be such in all particulars as I am in point of sins, negligences, weaknesses, neglect and misuse of talents, etc.; and then contrast my sins with my mercies, my service with my motives, my obligations with my coldness, the gratitude due with the evil returned. Alas! Alas! God be merciful to me a sinner.[43]

Gratitude, motives to: Born in the eighteenth century, and in England, when the increased wealth and civilization have enabled me to enjoy so many accommodations necessary to my usefulness, much more to my comfort. NB Meditate under each head of its opposites, as first, not in Africa, or Hindustan, or China, or even in Italy, or France. And second, not when Britain sunk in barbarism and ignorance, or even when few of the conveniences by which bodily distinctions so greatly annulled, and mind elevated over body. Had I been born in any but civilized times, I could not have lived; much less have lived in comfort and action.

Born an Englishman; that I was born of parents religious according to the old school; and that I was made such as I am, both in body, mind, and circumstances. Blessed with acceptance, early and continued, both in public and private life. Raised to so very honorable a station as M. P. for Yorkshire, and enabled to retain it near thirty years, (elected five times, and no prospect of opposition when voluntarily resigned it,) though from considerations weighed in God's sight I neglected all the usual attentions to the county both generally and individually.

Providentially directed to such a pursuit as Abolition, and blessed by success. So many friends, and these so good in themselves, and so kind to me. Scarcely any one so richly provided with kind friends. This is a cause for continual gratitude. My domestic blessings. How few who marry so late in life have such affectionate wives! My children all kind and loving to me.

Above all, my spiritual blessings; having been called, I humbly trust, and drawn by the Holy Spirit, and enlightened, and softened, and in some degree sanctified. It is, I trust, my fixed resolution to desire to please God in all things, and to devote all I have and am to his glory,

---

42. Titus 2:10.
43. Luke 18:13.

through Christ and by the Holy Spirit; yet, alas, how little have I of late been living a life of communion with God, in faith, and hope, and love, and joy, and usefulness! God be merciful to me a sinner.[44]

More especially, the astonishing mercy, and long-suffering, and patience, and loving-kindness of my God and Savior: foreseeing all my unworthy returns, and yet merciful and gracious to me. The preventing grace of God in some notable instances, in which I was preserved from sin and shame by his unmerited goodness. So peculiarly favored by exemptions from failure, or with acceptance and success; never have I been suffered to fail egregiously on public occasions, and when once or twice brought into temporary ridicule, how soon over.[45]

Undated, 1817
Having so little time I must not write, my eyes too being indifferent, and this is always awkward when meditation brings tears into them, and which hurt them as much almost as anything. But what, alas! could I put down but what too often before. I have been extremely engrossed by business, made late at night, and so my private devotions have been contracted. Let me guard against procrastination; strive to be punctual and diligent; to grow in grace, living closer to God. Let me strive, though my children are with me, to prepare for the meeting of Parliament. Above all, let us live in Christ to God and all will be well. O God, I go to prayer.

Pardon, bless, sanctify me, and make me meet for a better world. My health is clearly not so good as it was, but I hope I regret it only as indicating my being called away before my work is done. Alas, alas! how much more might I have done, if I had been duly diligent and self-denying! But let me work at the eleventh hour.[46] Lord, work in and by me, Amen. Amidst all my weakness, I can look to God through Christ, with humble hope, and even peace and joy in believing.[47] Lord, what I know not teach Thou me. Wherein I am lacking, supply me with all needful supplies of grace and strength. I cast myself on Thy precious promises, and claim Thy offered salvation.[48]

1818

Wednesday, January 7th. 1818
Received an account of the dreadful murder of a poor slave, buried without a coroner's inquest, but dug up, and found all mangled, yet brought in by the jury, Died by the visitation of God. Then _____[49] tried to fasten the crime on his own driver, by the evidence of the poor slave to whom the

---

44. Luke 18:13.
45. *Life*, iv. pp. 343-347.
46. Matthew 20:6.
47. Romans 15:13.
48. *Life*, iv. p. 364.
49. He does not identify this person.

deceased was chained. But matter came out which led to his own trial, and he was sentenced to three months' imprisonment. Yet the governor seems merely to have sent word that a trial for murder, but that the jury only brought it in manslaughter. Alas! Alas! I must not write for the sake of my eyes; but my mind becomes so much affected by the sad state of those poor injured wretches that it keeps me awake at night. Oh may God enable us to possess the nation with a due sense of their wrongs, and that we may be the instrument of redressing them. But, alas! I grow sadly incapable, may I yet be strengthened to render this service.[50]

Tuesday, February 17th. 1818

Up late from having been awake thinking of the slaves' wretched sufferings, and partly the two poor women about to be hanged for forgery this day. Alas, how bloody are our laws! Secret Committee,[51] and House. Lord Folkstone's[52] motion for referring petitions to Committee. Spoke from being called up by Sir Francis Burdett.[53]

Sunday, March 8th. 1818

Lay awake several hours in the night, and very languid this morning. My mind is very uneasy, and greatly distracted about the course to be pursued in the West Indian matters. It is hard to decide, especially where so many counselors. This is clear, that in the Scriptures no national crime is condemned so frequently, and few so strongly, as oppression and cruelty, and the not using our best endeavors to deliver our fellow-creatures from them. Jer. vi. 6, 'This is a city to be visited; she is wholly oppression in the midst of her.' Ezek. xvi. 49, of Sodom's crimes: 'Neither did she strengthen the hands of the poor and needy.' Zeph. iii. 1; Amos iv. 1,8, etc. I must therefore set to work, and, O Lord, direct, and support, and bless me. If it please Thee not to let me be the instrument of good to these poor degraded people, may I still be found working, like dear Stephen, with vigor and simple obedience, remembering, 'It is well for thee that it was in thy heart.'[54]

Tuesday, March 31st. 1818

Much impressed by Mr. Buxton's book on our prisons, and the account of Newgate reform. What lessons are taught by Mrs. Fry's success! I am still warmed by the account. Were I young, I should instantly give notice of the business, if no one else did.[55]

---

50. *Life*, iv. p. 366.

51. Prime Ministers would sometimes establish Secret Committees of the House of Commons for a particular purpose, such as the one here that Wilberforce would sit on. Pitt, for example, set up such a Committee in 1794 to examine the confiscated papers of the London Corresponding Society, suspected of anti-Government actions.

52. William Pleydell-Bouverie (1779–1869), 3rd Earl of Radnor and styled Viscount Folkestone until 1828. M.P., Deputy-Lieutenant of Berkshire and Recorder of Salisbury.

53. *Life*, iv. p. 369.

54. 1 Kings 8:18. *Life*, iv. p. 374.

55. *Life*, iv. p. 376.

Wednesday, April 22nd. 1818

In Stephen's library for quiet, and preparing for discussion in the House on West Indian affairs. My motion for papers explaining about Registry Bill. Then Romilly's about Dominica cases of cruelty. I spoke long but not well—too much matter imperfectly explained, and without due method. But the mercenary feelings of some, and the prejudices of others, with the cry against me, make the reporters so inattentive to me that they do not affect to report what I say. May God only enable these poor injured creatures to find a deliverer: what men say of me is little, in some views it is even gratifying. I used to fear I was too popular, and I remember, 'Commit thy way unto the Lord; trust also in Him,'[56] etc. Only forgive me my own many defects, infirmities, and negligences.[57]

Sunday, May 17th. 1818

Trinity Sunday. Blessed be God, I felt today more sensibly than of late the power of divine things. Was it the present reward of not yielding to the impulse which I felt, but upon good grounds, to be longer in bed? I remembered Christ's rising long before day, and got up. Babington sent me a kind letter, warning me of H.'s excessive and vindictive rage, and intention to charge me with duplicity (I am sure I can say in the presence of God, none was intended) about the Bill for permitting the removal of gangs of slaves from the Bahamas to Guiana. Lord, undertake for me; let me not bring discredit on Thy holy faith. Thou hast the hearts of all under Thy power, O turn them favorably towards me. At least let me not discredit Thy cause.

I will not think on this business until tomorrow: but today I may say, 'Lord, be Thou my surety for good.'[58] How many are the passages in the Psalms which give comfort under the assaults of unreasonable and violent men! How strongly have I felt the double man within me today! I really despise and abhor myself for the rising of thoughts referring to human estimation; which nevertheless will rise even as to this very self-abhorrence, and so on ad infinitum. Oh what poor creatures we are! This should make us long for a purer heart and a better world.[59]

Kensn[60] Gore Sunday 3 ¼ July 5th 1818

I now resume this Book after an Interval of a year & 2/3. Alas! Alas! I have still to record my own Shame & even I fear a worse State than when I last used my pen. Yet O what mercies have I experience'd & now I trust my dear Lizzy[61] is really under the best Influence. I must go to

---

56. Psalm 37:5.
57. *Life*, iv. p. 378.
58. Psalm 119:122.
59. *Life*, iv. p. 379.
60. MS Wilberforce e. 24, fo. 12.
61. Elizabeth Wilberforce, later James (1801–1831), daughter of William Wilberforce, married Rev. John James.

her befr dinner & therefore lay down my pen - But O what a Blessing is this day of Sursum Corda. Lo I look to thee thro' Xt. Amen. Amen. Eyes but middling.[62]

Same Sunday Evg 9 ½

It is quite humiliating as well as aweful to think of, but I now can scarcely ever keep awake at Church either Morng. or Eveng. I Hope it is in some Measure the Effect of bodily Weakness, yet I dare not ascribe it all to that Cause. O Lord pardon me. Quicken my dull drowsy Soul, & enable me to be more spiritually-minded. I humbly trust my dear Elizth. is in earnest in Relig[n] & that Dear B. also has a serious Sense of divine things. O how unworthy am I of these favours. But God is Love, He delighteth in Mercy. I must stop. I have not been duly careful to get my family to bed rather earlier on Saturday Night. I must try to mend here that we may be earlier & have more time for priv[e] Dev[ns] on Sunday morng. O Lord enable me to attend to this.[63]

Thursday, December 24th. 1818

It is with a heavy heart that I look forward to the meeting; so many friends absent, and so many objects of pursuit, and I so unequal to them, yet had I duly used my powers I could do much. O Lord, do Thou quicken and guide me. I have resolved to dine out scarcely at all during this season. Health is a fair plea, and justly so at my period of constitution and life, and I shall get more time at command; my memory is certainly become very bad, but by expedients, (Feinagle's, etc.) I doubt not, I could in a great degree supply the deficiency. I must make sure of what is really important. But above all, may I grow in love, and serve and glorify more my God and Savior.[64]

1819

Tuesday, February 9th. 1819

Had a truly honest and Christian-like letter from Mr. Poynder[65] to which I replied I trust in the same strain, on my eulogium on Sir

---

62. MS Wilberforce e. 24, fo. 12.

63. Ibid.

64. *Life*, v. pp. 8-9.

65. John Poynder (1779/80–1849), lawyer, evangelical activist, clerk and solicitor to the royal hospitals of Bridewell and Bethlehem, under-sheriff of London, and one of the earliest members of the Church Missionary Society. He also served on the committees of the Reformation Society, the Lord's Day Observance Society, and the Protestant Association. As a proponent of Christian missions in India, he won several victories against the East India Company's practices, including being highly influential in the 1827 court of director's decision to outlaw suttee (widow immolation). A speech of his in this regard, was published as, *Speech of John Poynder, Esq. at a General Court of Proprietors of the East India Company, on the 21st December, 1836, upon a motion for carrying into effect The Letter of the Court of Directors of the 20th February, 1833, which ordered the withdrawal of British Patronage and Support from the worship and service of Idolatry, and the Extinction of all Taxation arising from the superstitions of Heathenism* (London: Hatchard, 1837). He is remembered, too, for his *Literary Extracts from English and Other Works, collected during Half a Century* 2 vols. (1844).

Samuel Romilly. Perhaps I went too far, though the newspaper made me say more than I did. But, alas, I well know how often I am led away into saying what I never meant! How can I but add the above when I am fresh from the House of Commons on Bennett's motion (for an enquiry into the condition of the country) in the debate on which most unaccountably, except from my not having at all meditated before-hand what I should say, I am told, and I fear justly notwithstanding some opposite assurances, that I was extremely harsh against Castlereagh. How strange this! I really have a personal regard for him, have always wished, and do now wish him well, and did not in the least mean to be severe, especially against *him*. He had no interest in preventing the inquiry. However, may God forgive me, and enable me to act in a way more agreeable to my Christian character of peace, and love, and meekness. I am truly and deeply hurt by the consciousness, though quite relieved by a few friendly words which passed between Castlereagh and me in going out of the House.[66]

Saturday, May 15th. 1819

British and Foreign School Society. Duke of Kent[67] in the chair. Oh how glad I am that the tenth meeting is this day over! The consumption of time is really too great.[68]

Sunday, December 12th. 1819

Walked from Hyde Park Corner, repeating the 119th Psalm, in great comfort.[69]

1820

Wednesday, April 26th. 1820

Went to Freemasons' Tavern Committee room,[70] and afterwards to the Hall on the Duke of Kent's Statue proposal. Duke of Bedford[71] in the chair. Lord Darnley[72] there, Breadalbane,[73] Clifford, etc. I seconded the first resolution, kept there latish. I am much pressed to attend the London

---

66. *Life*, v. p. 12.

67. Prince Edward Augustus (1767–1820), Duke of Kent and Strathearn, fourth son and fifth child of King George III.

68. *Life*, v. p. 21.

69. Wilberforce's sons comment that Wilberforce's learning this whole Psalm by heart in all his London bustle, is a striking instance of the care with which he studied the Bible. And in spite of his complaints, his memory could not have been materially injured, since he could, even with the help of a technical artifice which he frequently employed they say, 'acquire and retain perfectly this long and unconnected passage.' *Life*, v. p. 44.

70. Freemasons' Tavern was built in 1775 at 61-65 Great Queen Street, London, and acted as a meeting place for a variety of organizations until it was demolished in 1909.

71. Lord John Russell (1766–1839), 6th Duke of Bedford, Lord Lieutenant of Ireland (1806–1807), M.P., and father of John Russell (1792–1878), Prime Minister from 1865 to 1866.

72. John Bligh (1767–1831), 4th Earl of Darnley and remembered especially as a cricketer, appearing at least 27 times in first-class cricket matches (1789–1796).

73. John Campbell (1762–1834), 1st Marquess of Breadalbane, Earl of Breadalbane and Holland (1782–1831), Lieutenant-General and landowner, Fellow of the Royal Society.

Missionary Society, but I cannot do it. Last year I was at eight or nine of these public meetings in as many days, but I must not this year. But oh how humbled am I to find still in myself solicitude about human estimation! Yet I strive against it, and despise myself for it. O Lord, help me.[74]

1821

March, 1821

What cause have I for thankfulness, that even when ill I scarcely ever experience pain, or distress of body or mind! But then I learn, or rather I re-learn, from this attack, two important practical truths: when I become ever so little incapable of quiet continued reflection I can only gaze at known truths, and look up with aspirations of humble thankfulness to the will of my unwearied and long-suffering Benefactor. I should be ungrateful indeed, if I were insensible to the innumerable mercies which I have been receiving all my life long. But it is astonishing how little I feel the lapse of time. I forgot that I am now arrived at sixty-one years and a half, though never a strong man, and in 1788 in such a state of apparent weakness, that Dr. Warren, of unrivalled sagacity, said confidentially, (but it was soon told to my kind sympathizing friend Muncaster,) that I had not stamina to last a fortnight. How wonderful is it that I continue unto this day! But I shall probably have little warning: let me remember therefore Christ's admonition, 'Be y^e· also ready.'[75]

Again, how careful ought I to be not to let self-indulgence or inadvertence obstruct my usefulness. My powers of serving God (he best knows and ordains their effect) depend entirely on my health. Little things then, which in others are nothing, are in my instance important, since who has such motives for gratitude and active service as myself.[76]

June, 1821

My wife and daughter wish it, and I hope I shall secure more time for my family and myself when further from London; it will give my children country tastes and occupations, and they are virtuous pleasures. Treated with such kindness as I am, it would be strange if I were not to be happy anywhere. Oh these things are trifles, mere trifles, and so let us feel them. Here indeed my temper and principles coincide.[77]

Undated, 1821

How little does that child know how much it is loved! It is the same with us and our heavenly Father; we little believe how we are loved by him. I delight in little children, I could spend hours in watching them. How much there is in them that the Savior loved, when he took a little child

---

74. *Life*, v. pp. 52-53.
75. Matthew 24:44.
76. *Life*, v. p. 97.
77. This entry recorded after he had sold his house in Kensington. *Life*, v. p. 101.

and set him in the midst; their simplicity, their confidence in you, the fund of happiness with which their beneficent Creator has endued them; that when intelligence is less developed and so affords less enjoyment, the natural spirits are an inexhaustible fund of infantine pleasure.[78]

Day of daughter's funeral, 1821

I went and saw the coffin. How vain the plumes, etc. when the occasion is considered, and the real state of humiliation to which the body is reduced! I must elsewhere note down the mercies and loving-kindnesses of our God and Savior in this dispensation; above all, the exceeding goodness of giving us grounds for an assured persuasion that all is well with her; that she is gone to glory. When the hearse and our kind friends were gone, after a short time I came into my little room at the top of the stairs where I am now writing and engaged awhile in prayer, blessing God for his astonishing goodness to me, and lamenting my extreme unworthiness. And indeed when I do look back on my past life, and review it, comparing especially the numerous, almost innumerable, instances of God's kindness to me with my unworthy returns, I am overwhelmed, and can, with truth adopt the language of the Publican, God be merciful to me a sinner.[79]

Everyone knows, or may know, his own sins, the criminality of which varies according to his opportunities of improvement, obligations and motives to obedience, advantages and means of grace, favors and loving-kindnesses, pardons and mercies. It is the exceeding goodness of God to me, and the almost unequalled advantages I have enjoyed, which so fill me with humiliation and shame. My days appear few when I look back, but they have been anything but evil. My blessings have been of every kind, and of long continuance; general to me and to other Englishmen, but still more peculiar, from my having a kindly natural temper, a plentiful fortune; all the mercies of my public life; my coming so early into Parliament for Hull, then for Yorkshire, elected six times, and as will be known hereafter when I am dead, though now mistaken, my only ceasing to be M. P. for Yorkshire because I resigned the situation. Then my being made the instrument of bringing forward the Abolition; my helping powerfully the cause of Christianity in India; my never having been discredited, but being always supported on all public occasions. There would be no end of the enumeration, were I to put down all the mercies of God. My escape from drowning by a sudden suggestion of Providence. My never having been disgraced for refusing to fight a duel. Then all my domestic blessings. Marrying as late as 36, yet finding one of the most affectionate of wives, (Six) children, all of them attached to me beyond measure. And though we have lost dear Barbara, yet in the main, few men ever had such cause for thankfulness on account of the love of their children towards them.

---

78. *Life*, v. p. 104.
79. Luke 18:13.

Then my social blessings. No man ever had so many kind friends; they quite overwhelm me with their goodness, and show the wisdom there has been in my cultivating my friendships with men of my own rank, and remaining quietly in it, instead of trying to rise in life myself, or to make friends among men of rank; above all, the wisdom of selecting religious men for friends. The great and, noble now all treat me with respect, because they see I am independent of them, and some I believe feel real attachment to me. Then my having faculties sufficient to make me respectable, a natural faculty of public speaking, though the complaint in my eyes sadly hinders me in acquiring knowledge, and in writing.

Then, almost above all, my having been rendered the instrument of much spiritual good by my work on Christianity. How many, many have communicated to me that it was the means of their turning to God! Then all this continued so long, and in spite of all my provocations. These it would be wrong to put down, but my heart knows and feels them, and I trust ever will. And it is a great mercy that God has enabled me to maintain a fair, consistent, external course, so that I never have brought disgrace on my Christian profession. Praise the Lord, O my soul. And now, Lord, let me devote myself more solemnly and more resolutely to Thee, desiring more than I ever yet have done to dedicate my faculties to Thy glory and service.[80]

1822

Undated, 1822

Today I began the plan, to which by God's grace I mean to adhere, of having my evening private devotions before family prayers. For want of this they have too often been sadly hurried, and the reading of Scripture omitted, I have therefore resolved to allot an hour from half-past eight to half-past nine. It is a subtraction of the space to be allowed to business, but God seems to require it, and the grand, the only question is, what is God's will? The abridgement of my evening prayers has been a fault with me for years. May God help me to amend it, and give his blessing to a measure adopted with a view to please him. Amen. Began today to keep a journal of time.[81]

The Duke of _____[82] called on me, and sat for almost three hours. He and I came into life about the same time, though we have seldom met since. Oh what thanks do I owe to a gracious Providence which provided me with such parents, and guided me through such paths as I have trodden![83]

---

80. On the day of his daughter's funeral, Wilberforce was forced to stay at home, 'by the extreme coldness of the weather, and when the band of mourners had set out he went into his solitary chamber.' *Life*, v. pp. 111-114.

81. *Life*, v. p. 131.

82. He does not specifically identify this person.

83. *Life*, v. p. 143.

1823

Sunday, May 25th. 1823
Morning, Lock, and staid the Sacrament. Walked home with Lord Rocksavage,[84] S., and _____ [85], and being overdone staid at home evening. Read, enjoyed, and I hope profited, from a sermon of Dean Milner's on 'I have waited for thy salvation, O Lord.'[86] Private devotions, I hope, spiritual. Oh what blessings do I enjoy, what cause have I for gratitude![87]

Wednesday, July 2nd. 1823
Took possession of our new house at Brompton Grove.[88] May God bless our residence here.[89]

Sunday, November 23rd. 1823
John Bull[90] for three or four weeks past has been abusing me grossly. Blessed be God it is groundlessly. One of his paragraphs was sent me the other day, with only these three words, 'Thou vile hypocrite!' I should have been thirty or forty years in public life to little purpose, if this discomposed me.[91]

1824

March 1st. 1824
Went to the House for Martin's Bill on cruelty to animals.[92] It is opposed on the ground of the rich having their own amusements, and that it would be hard to rob the poor of theirs – a most fallacious argument, and one which has its root in a contempt for the poor. I love the idea of

---

84. George-James (1749–1827), 1st Marquis Cholmondeley, Earl of Rocksavage. He was appointed a Vice-Patron of the London Society for Promoting Christianity among the Jews, in 1826.

85. He does not identify this person.

86. Genesis 49:18.

87. *Life*, v. p. 180.

88. Grove House on Brompton Grove, now Brompton Road, was a 3-storey house in which Wilberforce lived from 1823–1825. It was the largest of the three houses built in 1763, and had previously been the residence of Sir John Fielding, the blind half-brother of the novelist Henry Fielding, and founder of the Bow Street Runners. He died in Grove House in 1780. The house was demolished in 1857.

89. *Life*, v. p. 187.

90. 'John Bull' was a Sunday newspaper established in 1820 by Theodore Hook, and printed in London. It ceased publication in July 1892.

91. *Life*, v. p. 204.

92. By 1821, the M.P. and animal and human rights activist Richard Martin (1754–1834), was regarded as the most committed promoter of anti-cruelty legislation in Parliament. His Bill, 'to prevent cruel and improper treatment of cattle', was introduced in the House of Commons, with Wilberforce and Buxton being amongst its sponsors. In the Bill's second introduction in 1822, the Bill easily cleared both houses, receiving Royal Assent on July 22, 1822. The published *Life* seems to have confused the date of the Bill with the date of the creation of the Society for the Prevention of Cruelty to Animals (SPCA), later the RSPCA, which was held in 16 June, 1824 in Old Slaughter's Coffee House, St. Martin's Lane, London. In the year following Martin's death, his Act was finally enlarged, to ban the fighting and baiting of animals.

having comfortable causeway walks for them along the public roads. This is most strictly congenial to the British constitution, which, in its political as well as its religious regulations, takes special care of the convenience of the poorer classes. The great distinction between our constitution and that of the ancient republics is, that with them the general advantage was the object, without particular regard to individual comfort. Whereas in England individual comfort has been the object, and the general advantage has been sought through it.[93]

May, 1824
Poor Smith the missionary died in prison at Demerara! The day of reckoning will come.[94] Preparing for Smith the missionary's business. I was at the House the first time for eight weeks or more.[95] Brougham made a capital speech, by Mackintosh well termed impregnable. I doubt not he will be great in reply. Mackintosh's own, was most beautiful, his mind teemed with ideas. I very much wish, if my voice should be strong enough, to bear my testimony against the scandalous injustice exercised upon poor Smith.[96]

The case proved against him is greatly short of what I thought it might have been. I myself once saw a missionary's journal, and its contents would have been capable of being perverted into a much stronger charge of promoting discontent amongst the slaves. Had I happened for instance to correspond with Smith, that alone would have hanged him.[97]

Tuesday, October 19th. 1824
Venerable Rowland Hill dined with me, aetat 80.[98]

Tuesday, November 30th. 1824
Sat with Hannah More about an hour and half, and she as animated as ever I knew her, quoting authors, naming people, etc., off about one after praying with her.[99]

1825

Saturday, January 1st. 1825
Our dear boys living in much harmony. What cause have I for gratitude, seeing my five children, my son's wife, and two grandchildren all round my table! Praise the Lord, O my soul.[100]

---

93. *Life*, v. pp. 213-214.
94. This was the last entry at this time, before he was confined to bed.
95. This entry reflected Wilberforce's preparation for his first public business he attempted after leaving his sick room on June 1st, 1824.
96. *Life*, v. p. 221.
97. Ibid., p. 222.
98. Ibid., p. 226.
99. Ibid., p. 227.
100. Ibid.

Monday, April 18[th.] 1825

I fear that I am wasting my precious time, and the night is coming fast with me. Oh may I strive to be ever abounding in the work of the Lord.[101] May he enable me to commence some useful work.[102]

Tuesday, July 12[th.] 1825

Oh may I only walk with God during my closing years, and then where is of little consequence.[103]

1826

Friday, February 3[rd.] 1826

Mr. and Mrs. W. came in the evening. How little did I improve the opportunity, though indeed I know not what could be done, but to show civility, and that I had no horns or tail.[104]

1826 12:35 Saty 7th Oct[r]

I have for many years kept only a Journal of Oly Events, my place & chief Employments the Weather &c. My eyes are indifft.[105] Alas.[106] Alas. My life is a sadly unprofitable one It quite grieves me to reflect upon it. This day I devote to devot[l] Exercises, fasting wo'd disable me from attendg witht distractn to prayer &c. But on acc[t] of my Eyes' State I must write but little, Alas. Alas. What Causes have I for deep Humiliatn for y[e] past & the present. O what deep remorse & Shame become me, for not havg turn'd my Parliamy Station to more Account. And yet on one of the points on which I blame myself, I really tried to get Chas Grant & another, at y[e] time proper[107] man, I think Chas. Long now Ld. Farnborough,[108] & I trust it was from Humility that I wish'd another to do it rather yn myself. But my Eveng devotns too much curtaild, & SS readg not duly or devotionally practis'd. My Servts spiritual Interests not duly attended to. In Hymn singing, & even family prayers not due spirituality & devotional feeling in conducting them. Dearest Rob[t] came in just now for Bickersteth on y[e] Sact,[109] what cause have I to be thankful

---

101. 1 Corinthians 15:58.

102. *Life*, v. p. 250.

103. Ibid., p. 249.

104. Ibid., p. 264.

105. MS Wilberforce e. 24, fo. 12.

106. MS Wilberforce e. 24, fo. 13.

107. Word here uncertain.

108. Charles Long (1760–1838) was created 1st Baron Farnborough of Bromley Hill Place in Kent, on 8 July, 1826. He was a close friend of William Pitt from their days together at Cambridge, becoming an M.P. in 1789. He held a number of government positions, including junior secretary to the Treasury (1791), Parliamentary Whip, and Lord of the Treasury (1804–1806). He was offered the Chancellorship of the Exchequer by Spencer Perceval but refused. Arts were his real passion and he became actively involved in promoting Britain's collections, including the purchase of the Elgin Marbles, and the founding of the National Gallery.

109. Edward Bickersteth (1786–1850), Dean of Lichfield, evangelical leader and theological writer, friend of Thomas Chalmers (1780–1847), and a great admirer of the 1843 Disruption. Bickersteth was a central figure in the creation of the Evangelical Alliance (1846), and through his

for Him. I have been readg over old Entries in former Books, in a 4to Book beginning wth 1804 at pages 66-71 &c. I go to prayer, 12:50.[110]

1:25

O[111] What[112] Cause for deep Humiliat[n], or rather for bitter remorse, for not havg more peace & still more, more Joy in believing.[113] I doubt not God wo'd have given it me abundantly, & perhaps intensely, if I had prayed more earnestly & striven more earnestly, to bring down & to retain, large measures of the H. Sp[t.] O let me not be lukewarm, an Object of my Saviour's disgust & lothing.[114] I trust I have not in me the real foundatn or Root of lukewarmness, Self-Satisfaction & Complacency. O no! yet let me not acquiesce in my low Estate, because of the promise to y[e] Contrite, but let me strive earnestly to grow in Grace & faith & Love & Heavenly-Mindedness. May my Zeal also increase. I have been looking a little over Benson's Life of Fletcher.[115] What a Man was there??! O may I be enabled to copy his Example a little. How merciful, how gracious is God to me, in giving me a blessed Interval between my public labours & y[e] Grave. O may I use it profitably &c. Lord help me to be a Blessing to Others as well as to advance in my own Soul. Ps[m] 71 is very applicable to my Case, espec[ly] v.14, 15,16 & O what Cause have I to apply to myself v.19.[116] Let me look into my pocket Books for 1824 or 5, for Causes for thankfulness. O Who has so many & so great! Praise the Lord O my soul. O may my Gratitude be more warm & constant.[117]

1827

Tuesday, October 23, 1827

A delightful morning. Walked out and saw the most abundant dew-drops sparkling in the sunbeams on the gazon. How it calls forth the devotional feelings in the morning when the mind is vacant from

---

work as secretary for the Church Missionary Society, he did much to encourage the growth and cohesion of evangelical Anglicans. He was also strongly anti-Catholic, as shown in his *Progress of Popery* (1836), and *The Divine Warning* (1844). The work Wilberforce was probably referring to was his *A Treatise on the Lord's Supper: Designed as a Guide and Companion to the Holy Communion*, in two parts by Rev. Edw. Bickersteth (London, 1825).

110. MS Wilberforce e. 24, fo. 13.

111. Ibid.

112. MS Wilberforce e. 24, fo. 14.

113. Romans 15:13.

114. Revelation 3:16.

115. Joseph Benson (1749–1821), Methodist minister, apologist and leader during the days of John Wesley. He was an Anglican and sought ordination, but after being refused Anglican ordination he became a Methodist. He served as headmaster of Selina, Countess of Huntingdon's college in Trefeca, Wales, but was fired when he sided with John Wesley against her on theology. He was president of the Methodist Conference in 1805 and 1809, and edited the 'Methodist Magazine' from 1803–1821. His life of Revd. John William Fletcher that Wilberforce here refers to, was published in 1804.

116. 'Your righteousness, God, reaches to the heavens, you who have done great things. Who is like you, God?'

117. MS Wilberforce e. 24, fo. 15. The next page begins with, 'Heads of my Life – for my Children's Use –. 'Heads' is written over another word. On the rear cover is written, 'Private Religious To be read by dearest B. only –'. This is the end of MS Wilberforce e. 24.

worldly business, to see all nature pour forth, as it were, its song of praise to the great Creator and Preserver of all things! I love to repeat Psalms civ. ciii. cxlv. etc. at such a season.[118]

Undated, 1827

I must record the truth, I seldom have found myself more unspiritual, more indisposed to prayer, than after my party had left me.[119] I could not somehow raise my mind to heavenly objects, alas, and so it has been partly this morning also. Is it that the society of an able worldly man is hereby indicated to be unsafe to me? I had a sort of struggle about inviting him, as if intimating the wish to be acquainted with an irreligious man, was showing too great a deference for talent. Is it as a punishment that I have since felt so cold and wandering in my mind? I would not be nervous and superstitious, but I ought to watch and keep my heart with all diligence. O let me deal honestly with myself. Let me give up, however entertaining, even however instructive, whatever it seems the intimation of God that I should relinquish. O Lord, cause me to be so full of love, and zeal, and grateful loyalty, and child-like affection for my Savior, that I may love them that love Thee; and may I thus become more in my tempers and frames of mind an inhabitant of heaven.[120]

1828

Tuesday, June 10, 1828

Lavington.[121] All my descendants met around the board – *mine,* of whom above forty years ago, when a bachelor in 1788, Dr. Warren declared that I had not stamina to last three weeks. Praise the Lord, O my soul.[122]

Thursday, October 9, 1828

Quite overpowered by the Hallelujah Chorus in the Messiah,[123] a flood of tears ensued, and the impression on my mind remained through the day.[124]

---

118. *Life*, v. p. 284.

119. Wilberforce recorded this after reflecting about an incident many years earlier, after he had then received, 'a very clever and entertaining man.' *Life*, v. p. 292.

120. *Life*, v. pp. 292-293.

121. Lavington is a name given to several English villages and towns, including East Lavington and West Lavington in west Sussex, West Lavington and Market Lavington both in Wiltshire, and Lavington in Lincolnshire, which is also referred to as Lenton. If Wilberforce is here referring to the latter, it is mentioned as far back as the *Domesday Book* as 'Lavintone', and is a small village in Lincolnshire, approximately 7 miles from Grantham. It is also associated with the site of the lost medieval settlement of Little Lavington, one half mile to the north-east.

122. *Life*, v. p. 301.

123. George Frederic Handel (1685–1759) composed the 'Messiah' between 22 August, 1741 and 14 September, 1741 in London. It is an English-language oratorio, with a scriptural text compiled from the King James Bible. It was first performed in Dublin on 13 April, 1742, with its London premiere almost a year later. It has become one of the most well known and most frequently performed choral works in Western music.

124. *Life*, v. p. 285.

1829

Sunday, February 15, 1829

This evening I expounded on the Epistle, 'So run that y[e.] may obtain, etc. lest I should be a castaway.'[125] The second lesson this very evening is 1 Cor. iv., in which St. Paul relates his labor and sufferings. And could pains be required by HIM, O then, my soul, strive, to him that overcometh only, the promise is assured.

My future state should now be my grand, indeed-comparatively speaking, my sole concern. God's kind providence has granted to me a residue of life after its business is over. I know I must be near death, perhaps very near it. I believe that on the state in which death finds me, will depend my eternal condition; and even though my state may now be such as to produce a humble hope that I am safe, yet by a wise improvement of my time, I may augment my eternal happiness, besides enjoying delightful communion with God in the interval. Let me then make the improvement of my soul the first grand business of my life, attending also to the good of others, if possible both by my pen, and conversation, and social intercourse.[126]

Wednesday, July 29, 1829

How striking is the change of fifty years, then Samuel Smith[127] and I travelled as bachelors, and now he has a house full of descendants; and I also have five children and a grandchild living, besides a daughter and sweet little grandson gone, I humbly trust, to a better world. Praise the Lord, O my soul. My dear, and I trust imparadised, child's birthday.[128]

1830

Sunday, February 21, 1830

Sunday, very cold and strong wind, so at home read some of the Church service. Evening, I expounded on Gal. iv. 6, second lesson; an exquisitely pregnant text. Blessed be God, not harassed by Williams's business all day,[129] but enabled to keep my mind filled with better things than those of this world, and felt goodwill towards poor Williams himself. I well remember

---

125. 1 Corinthians 9:27.

126. *Life*, v. pp. 323-324.

127. Samuel Smith (1754–1834), M.P.

128. *Life*, v. p. 319.

129. Rev. Theodore Williams (1785–1875), a Jamaican-born minister, vicar of Hendon, Middlesex (1812–1875), opposed Wilberforce's plan to build a chapel close to his house in Highwood Hill. He wrote a very critical letter to Wilberforce and published an attack that Wilberforce was only doing it for financial gain. Williams was adamantly opposed, too, to the Church Commissioner's granting the proposed new church a district. Wilberforce records meeting with Williams on 27 May, 1829, and records that Williams was very rude. On 5 June Wilberforce published an 'Address to the Parish of Hendon' in response to Williams's attacks. The delays Williams caused meant that though St. Paul's Chapel at Mill Hill would be built, it would be consecrated a few days after Wilberforce's death.

what Fenelon says, that we should remember that the grace of God may change the heart of him whom you may conceive most opposed to him.[130]

Undated, 1830
The 43rd Psalm is just now my delight, and the 71st.[131]

---

130. *Life*, v. p. 308.
131. Ibid., p. 311.

The Spiritual Reflections
of
William Wilberforce

1831–1833

William Wilberforce 1831–1833

This final period of Wilberforce's life is marked with increasing health problems, made all the worse when in 1832, Wilberforce suffers the sad loss of his recently married daughter Elizabeth. He was well enough the following April to address an anti-slavery meeting in Maidstone, but soon after he went into terminal decline, later becoming virtually immobile. His final days were spent at 44, Cadogan Place, London, the home of his cousin Lucy Smith. But even in his final week of life, Wilberforce still remained his own harshest critic,

> God has always disposed people to treat me so kindly, and with such attention! Popularity is certainly a dangerous thing … the antidote is chiefly in the feeling one has; how very differently they would regard me, if they knew me really![1]

Wilberforce rarely traveled to the capital in his later days, but he arrived in July 1833, planning to stay but a day or two. Once in London however, Wilberforce clearly knew he was ailing, for when a friend visited and asked, 'Well! how are you?' Wilberforce did not hesitate, 'I am like a clock which is almost run down.'[2] On July 22, just a week before his passing, he was visited by a party of children, 'What a delightful thing it is to think how many inhabitants are being trained up there for heaven! For when the means of grace are used, one does see, I think, that God so very greatly, one may say universally, blesses them.' When another friend came by also during that final week Wilberforce said to him 'How thankful should I be that I am not lying in severe pain, as so many are! Certainly, not to be able to move about is a great privation to me; but then I have so many comforts, and above all, such kind friends - and to that you contribute.'[3] After a family member had also visited at that time, he left a very intimate portrait of Wilberforce's demeanour, both physically and spiritually,

---

1. *Life*, 2nd ed. (London, 1839), v. p. 368.
2. Ibid.
3. Ibid., pp. 368-9.

At this time I arrived in London to see him, and was much struck by the signs of his approaching end. His usual activity was totally suspended by a painful local disorder, which prevented him from walking. The morning of Friday (July 26th) was pleasant, and I assisted before his breakfast to carry him in a chair to the steps in front of the house, that he might enjoy the air for a few moments. Here he presented a most striking appearance, looking forth with calm delight upon trees and grass, the freshness and vigour of which contrasted with his own decay. It was nearly his last view of God's works in this their lower manifestation. 'The doors' were soon to be 'shut in the streets, and those that look out of the windows to be darkened.'[4]

The same family member also related how unusually affectionate Wilberforce was at this time, for he received,

with great cheerfulness the visits of many old associates, from whom he had long been separated. The last words which I heard from him related to one of these, whose religious opinions he had for many years lamented. "How truly amiable he is, yet I can never see him without the deepest pain!" On Friday afternoon [July 26] I left him with the intention of preparing to receive him, on the following Tuesday [July 30], not knowing that before that time that he was to be a "partaker of the inheritance of the saints in light."[5]

As Wilberforce's sons reflected on their father's illness and subsequent passing, they commented that, 'It was altogether a striking combination of circumstances that he should have come to London at that time - to die. Yet had it been otherwise,' his sons remarked, 'his funeral could hardly have presented the circumstances, which made it the fit termination of such a life.'[6] Upon receiving the news that the Bill for the Abolition of Slavery had successfully passed its Readings in the House, and that 'his country was willing to redeem itself from the national disgrace at any sacrifice,' Wilberforce responded with his immortal words, 'Thank God that I should have lived to witness a day in which England is willing to give twenty millions sterling for the Abolition of Slavery.'[7]

On the evening of that Friday, July 26, it appeared Wilberforce had recovered to such a degree, there was every reason to believe he would be well enough to leave London in just three days as he originally had planned. Friday evening with family and friends gathered around him, Wilberforce made the following remarks,

I do declare that, the delight I have in feeling that there are a few people whose hearts are really attached to me, is the very highest I have in this world. And as far as the present state is concerned, what more could any man wish at the close of life, than to be attended by

---

4. Ibid., p. 369.

5. *Life*, 2nd ed. (London, 1839), v. pp. 369-70.

6. Ibid., p. 370.

7. Ibid.

his own children, and his own wife, and all treating him with such uniform kindness and affection?[8]

That same evening his son recorded of his father,

> He speaks very little as if looking forward to future happiness; but he seems more like a person in the actual enjoyment of heaven within: he hardly speaks of any one subject except to express his sense of thankfulness, and what cause he feels for gratitude. This is the case even in speaking of the things which try him most.[9]

That following morning the recovery appeared to continue. When an old servant took him out in a wheelchair, 'he talked with more than usual animation, and the fervency with which he offered up the family prayer was particularly noticed.'[10] Any recovery however was very short-lived, for just that very same evening, everyone present noticed his weakness had returned, except now in a very distressing manner. Then on the Sunday things deteriorated even further as he began to suffer memory loss, together with a succession of fainting fits, the latter being something he had only fairly recently started to experience.

However during a period of relative lucidity that same evening he was able to say, 'I am in a very distressed state,' to which someone close replied, 'Yes but you have your feet on the Rock.' To that Wilberforce responded, 'I do not venture to speak so positively; but I hope I have.' At three o'clock the following morning and after a single groan, his sons recorded that William Wilberforce 'entered into that world where pain and doubt are forever at an end.' It was the morning of Monday, July 29th, 1833 and Wilberforce was aged 73 years and 11 months.

Thomas Macaulay wrote that on his death bed,

> Wilberforce owned that he enjoyed life much, and that he had a great desire to live longer. Strange in a man who had, I should have said, so little to attach him to this world, and so firm a belief in another – in a man with a ruined fortune, a weak spine, a worn out stomach, a vixen wife, and a reprobate son ... Yesterday evening [the day after Wilberforce's death] I called at the house in Cadogan Place where the body is lying. It was deserted. Mrs. Wilberforce had gone into the country. Henry was out. Samuel was not yet come. And this great man, so popular, so much worshipped, was left to strangers and servants within thirty-six hours after his death.[11]

Wilberforce had written in his will only two years earlier, that he wished to be buried 'without the smallest pomp which in such a case seems to me to be preposterous and unseemly' in the Stephen family vault in Stoke Newington Churchyard, where his daughter and sister

---

8. Ibid., p. 371.

9. Ibid.

10. Ibid.

11. George O. Trevelyan, *The Life and Letters of Lord Macaulay*, 2 vols. (London: Longmans, Green, and Co. 1876), ii. p. 86.

had already been laid to rest.[12] Wilberforce's wishes on this however were supposedly not known until afterwards, for within just hours of Wilberforce's death, Henry Brougham, the Lord Chancellor, sent the following letter to Henry, Wilberforce's youngest son, as the only child who was with his father when he died,

> To the Rev. H.W. Wilberforce
>
> We the undersigned members of both Houses of parliament, being anxious upon public grounds to show our respect for the memory of the late William Wilberforce, and being also satisfied that public honours can never be more fitly bestowed than upon such benefactors of mankind, earnestly request that he may be buried in Westminster Abbey; and that we, and others who may agree with us in these sentiments, may have permission to attend his funeral.

Brougham added that he was 'authorized to add that nearly all the members of both Houses of Parliament would have joined, had the time allowed,' and subsequently a request in the same terms was duly signed by almost one hundred members of all parties in the House of Commons. Wilberforce's family soon agreed to the request they had received and the funeral was set for Saturday, 3 August. When that day came, one of Wilberforce's friends wrote that, 'You will like to know that as I came towards it down the Strand, every third person I met going about their ordinary business was in mourning.' Eye-witnesses reported that Westminster Abbey 'was thronged with the most respectable persons.'

When the procession reached the Abbey it was joined by members of Parliament who were already in attendance. Public business was suspended and the Speaker of the House of Commons, the Lord Chancellor, one Prince and other notable figures acted as the pall-bearers. Then followed Wilberforce's sons, other relatives, and then a number of his close friends. The Minister who was then in residence at Westminster, providentially one of Wilberforce's few surviving college friends, met it at the Minster gate and after a short service, Wilberforce's body was laid to rest in the north transept, close to the resting places of Pitt, Fox, and Canning.[13]

Soon after, a subscription was opened among Wilberforce's friends in London to place his statue in Westminster Abbey, close to his resting place. It was unveiled in 1840 and bears a lengthy epitaph part of which reads,

> To the memory of William Wilberforce ... Eminent as he was in every department of public labour, and a leader in every work of charity ... his name will ever be specially identified with those exertions which, by the blessing of God, removed from England the guilt of the African slave trade, and prepared the way for the abolition

12. Ibid., ii. pp. 289-92.
13. *Life*, v. pp. 376-7.

of slavery in every colony of the empire: in the prosecution of these objects he relied, not in vain, on God; but in the progress he was called to endure great obloquy and great opposition: he outlives, however, all enmity ... he died not unnoticed or forgotten by his country: the Peers and Commons of England, with the Lord Chancellor at their head, in solemn procession from their respective houses, carried him to his fitting place among the mighty dead around, here to repose: till, through the merits of Jesus Christ, his only Redeemer and Saviour, (whom, in this life and in his writings he had desired to glorify), he shall rise in the resurrection of the just.

At meetings held in both York and Hull in 1833, similar calls were made to commemorate the life and labors of William Wilberforce. Both cities saw their respective memorials come to fruition two years later. In York a decision was taken to establish a benevolent institution for the indigent blind in Wilberforce's name, with funds to be raised by public donation and subscription. As a result the Yorkshire School for the Blind, also known at the Wilberforce School for the Blind, was opened in King's Manor, York, in 1835. Today The Wilberforce Trust carries on the work by offering support, training and care services for people with sight loss, and provides supported accommodation in York and Tadcaster.

Hull's desire for some similar form of permanent memorial took shape at a public meeting, held in Hull on 12 August, 1833, at which many local citizens voiced their admiration, pride and thanks for Wilberforce's life and achievements,

> This meeting contemplates with the warmest admiration the splendid career, during the period of half a century, of our late townsman, William Wilberforce who, while he exhibited in private life all those virtues which spring forth from the cordial reception of Christian principles, in public life declined every scheme of personal aggrandizement ... it would not be creditable to the character of the town, which justly glories in having been the birthplace of such a man, and in having first sent him into Parliament, to suffer him to sink into his grave without raising some lasting monument of its veneration and affection for his memory.

The foundations for the Wilberforce Monument in Hull were laid August 1, 1834, the same day the abolition of slavery in the British Colonies took effect. The monument consisted of a ninety-foot Greek Doric column, upon which sat a twelve-foot statue of Wilberforce, the whole being fixed in place 12 November, 1835. The base declares that it was 'erected by voluntary subscription' to commemorate Hull's world-famous son. It was built at a cost of £1,250, the equivalent of almost $230,000 in 2021. In 1903 Hull City Corporation purchased Wilberforce's birthplace with the similar intent, that of honoring his memory in the city. So on the anniversary of Wilberforce's birthday in 1906, 25 High Street, Hull, was opened as a museum, and in the very room where it is known Wilberforce was born, a plaque was mounted that reads, 'Statesman, orator, philanthropist, saint.'

In July 1933, the City of Hull planned to commemorate both the centenary of Wilberforce's passing together with the passing of the Bill for the Abolition of the Slavery. The celebration opened with a commemoration service at Hull's Holy Trinity Church, to which the Lord Mayor and Corporation, members of the Wilberforce family and representatives of the various public bodies of Hull all marched in grand procession, led by the Archbishop of York, and preserved for posterity on film by British Pathé News..

The following day autographed letters, books, paintings and slave relics relating to Wilberforce were displayed at the Library and the Mortimer Galleries. That evening a civic reception for the Wilberforce family was held in the Guildhall. During the week, several other events also occurred, including a radio play entitled, 'William Wilberforce,' performed by the Hull Playgoers Society; a ceremonial civic tribute at the Wilberforce Monument in the city centre; and a presentation by Oxford History Professor Richard Coupland, on 'The Life and Work of Wilberforce.'

The Monument in Hull had stood for a century on its original site on Monument Bridge at Princes Dock, in the center of the City. But when a new road layout was being proposed for the area, a new home for the column was sought. There were many competing proposals, but in 1935 it was deconstructed, and moved to its present position on Wilberforce Drive, outside of Hull College near Queen's Gardens, at a cost of £1,500, the equivalent of $150,000 in 2021.

Hull suffered very badly during World War Two, due mainly to its being an important port city, with 95% of its buildings suffering some degree of bomb damage, with many being completely destroyed. Wilberforce House was almost lost forever, when on May 7 and 8, 1941, in the midst of the Blitz, Hull became a raging inferno. Almost 200 German aircraft attacked the city, dropping 29,000 incendiary and high-explosive bombs. John Coletta, a volunteer with the Auxiliary Fire Service, was awarded the George Medal for his part in saving the museum after it became encircled in flames in those attacks. Eric Lockwood, an Air Raid Precautions warden and an eye-witness, testified that he was in 'no doubt that Wilberforce House was saved as a result' of Coletta's actions, which displayed 'complete disregard for his own safety.' After the war, Coletta donated the medal to the museum, where it still remains on display.

Numerous events also occurred in 1959 (the 200th anniversary of his birth) and in 1983 (the 150th anniversary of his death, events focused on inspiring civic pride in Wilberforce's memory. These ranged from Church services and processions, to carnivals and music performances. These were followed in 2013 when the William Wilberforce Monument Fund was established. The aim was to raise funds to restore the monument to its original location in Hull, and also to pay for the lighting of the Monument by 2017, the year Hull would become European City of Culture.

In recent years there have also been a number of local organizations that have championed Wilberforce's legacies and carried out work in his name: Hull University's Wilberforce Institute for the Study of Slavery and Emancipation (WISE), situated next to the Wilberforce museum, exists to conduct ground-breaking research concerning instances of slavery in the modern world, and seeks to influence to policy and practice both nationally and internationally. The annual Freedom Festival, which attracts almost 150,000 visitors every year, is built on 'the foundations of Wilberforce's legacy.' Wilberforce remains an instrumental figure in the city of his birth, just as he has been for the last two hundred years.[14]

There have also been many developments further afield. In 1994, National Museums Liverpool opened the Transatlantic Slavery Gallery, the first of its kind in the world. Interest and attendance was so great that on 23 August 2007, Liverpool then opened the International Slavery Museum. The date was significant, being both Slavery Remembrance Day, but 2007 being the bicentenary of Abolition. The museum is situated in Liverpool's Albert Dock, only yards from the dry docks where eighteenth-century slave trading ships were repaired and fitted out.

In March 2015, when the Modern Slavery Act of the UK received Royal Assent, Kevin Hyland OBE was appointed as the UK's first Independent Anti-Slavery Commissioner. His role is to spearhead Britain's response to modern slavery by seeking to identify increasing numbers of such victims and referring them for support, while in tandem, to prosecute and convict increasing numbers of traffickers and slave masters. As Hyland himself stated,

> Modern slavery is a growing crime, a grave abuse and a gross injustice. Tackling it brings multiple challenges, but no challenge serves as an excuse to permit this trade in human life. Criminals promise people a better life, but once the bait is taken so too is their freedom. It is unacceptable that this persists, but it is also unacceptable for us to do nothing about it.[15]

This was followed in July 2020, when the Deputy Secretary-General of the UN issued a press release detailing the 'Moral Imperative' to end modern slavery and human trafficking,

> This is 2020. Centuries have passed since the end of the transatlantic slave trade. Yet more than 40.3 million people remain victims of modern slavery – 5 in every 1,000 people in the world … Modern slavery is a blight in our world that we must eradicate … Ending modern slavery and human trafficking would have significant payoffs for society at large. But above all, it is a moral imperative and our common responsibility.[16]

---

14. See http://museumshull.blogspot.com/2019/10/commemorating-wilberforce-legacies-in.html.

15. www.antislaverycommissioner.co.uk/about-the-commissioner/the-commissioner.

16. www.un.org/press/en/2020/dsgsm1431.doc.html.

Academic research has also been active, especially in the past decade, working to identify the persons and businesses that profited from the slave trade. The research is especially bringing to light present day companies and figures that can be shown to have benefited from the trade. Historians at Lancaster University UK, for example, have just been awarded a new £1 million research grant to examine, for the first time, the entire population of 6,500 investors in the transatlantic slave trade. The aim of the project will be to provide new insights on the extensive networks of individuals that tied Britain's economy to Atlantic slavery. Principal Investigator on the project Professor Pettigrew said, 'Britain's ability to confront her colonial past and post-colonial present depends upon the provision of high-quality data. This project will supply that need.'

> The life and labours of William Wilberforce continue to be honored, by those numerous organizations that have taken his name as they seek to operate by similar principles and aims, including Wilberforce University, America's oldest private, historically black University founded in 1856; The Colson Center's annual Wilberforce Weekend, an annual gathering to equip Christians in Christian worldview and cultural renewal. Regarded as the flagship event of the Colson Center, the weekend features world-class speakers, networking of Christian leaders, a reunion of Colson Center constituents and the recognition of a Christian leader with the Wilberforce Award; The Wilberforce School, Princeton, NJ, founded in 2005, 'to provide a distinctively Christian prep. school education characterized by academic excellence and joyful discovery within a classical framework.' The school was named after William Wilberforce, 'the great British statesman that lead [sic] the campaign in England to abolish the slave trade ... Our school was founded to cultivate students who are equipped to be leaders like Wilberforce.' In 2008, the US Congress even honored Wilberforce when it passed the William Wilberforce Trafficking Victims Protection Reauthorization Act (2008).

*Thank God, that I should have lived to witness
a day in which England is willing to give twenty
millions sterling for the abolition of slavery.*

William Wilberforce, 1833

1831

Saturday, January 1, 1831

A packet from Hull, enclosing letters of mine from Pocklington School rather too much in the style of the religious letters of that day, and (astonishing!) asking my leave to publish them. As I cannot doubt my having expressed the sentiments and feelings of my heart, I am sensibly impressed with a sense of the dreadful effects of the efforts afterwards used but too successfully to wean me from all religion, and to cherish the love of pleasure and the love of glory in the opening bud of youth.[1]

Undated, 1831

He will not suffer me to be disgraced in my old age. What gives me repose in all things, is the thought of their being his appointment. I doubt not that the same God who has in mercy ordered so many events for so long a course of time, will never fail to overrule all things both for my family and myself.

I can scarce understand why my life is spared so long, except it be to show that a man can be as happy without a fortune as with one.[2] What thanks do I owe to God that my declining strength appears likely not to be attended with painful diseases, but rather to lessen gradually and by moderate degrees! How good a friend God is to me! When I have any complaint it is always so mitigated and softened as to give me scarcely any pain. Praise the Lord, O my soul. I have had a feverish night, or rather a dreamy and disturbed one, but no headache or pain, D.G. What thanks do I owe to my gracious and kind heavenly Father![3]

Seldom have I felt anything so deeply. My hard heart quite confounded and overpowered. But I go to prayer. How thankful should I be to be spared such trials, my strength not being equal to them! I humbly commit myself unto him, who surely has given me reason to say, 'goodness and mercy have followed me all my days.'[4] O let me commit myself to him who has ever poured forth on me his mercies with so lavish a hand, 'God is love,'[5] that how can I doubt he will strengthen me for any cross he may see fit to lay on me. But, O Lord, 'if it be possible, let this cup pass from me.'[6] Oh may I be able to add, from the heart, 'nevertheless, not as I will, but as Thou wilt.'[7]

Meditating more on God as the Creator and Governor of the universe. Eighty millions of fixed stars, each as large at least as our

---

1. *Life*, i. p. 6.
2. This was recorded after recovering from a brief illness, *Life*, v. p. 326.
3. *Life*, v. pp. 334-335.
4. Psalm 23:6. This entry was recorded when one of Wilberforce's friends endured a painful operation.
5. 1 John 4:8.
6. Matthew 26:39.
7. Luke 22:42. This entry was recorded when Wilberforce himself was threatened with a similar attack. *Life*, v. p. 335.

sun. Combine the considerations hence arising with the madness and guilt of sin as setting up our will against that of God. Combine with it Christ's unspeakable mercy and love, and that of God in Christ.[8]

1832

Wednesday, April 4, 1832

Like the finest summer day. The air singularly mild and balmy, and not a leaf stirring. S. engaged in at a cottage reading. R. drove me out in the pony-chaise; which very pleasant. Much affected this evening by my own reflections. Alas, I am an unprofitable servant, but God's mercy and Christ's love are inconceivably great, his ways (thank God) not as our ways.[9]

1833

Wilberforce's final days

Saturday, July 6, 1833

Wilberforce was taken ill, quite suddenly, while sitting at dinner. A doctor was sent for and Wilberforce managed to get to bed. Though he was suffering from severe giddiness and sickness, he said,

> I have been thinking of the great mercy of God in trying me with illness of this kind, which, though very distressing, is scarcely to be called pain, rather than with severe suffering, which my bodily constitution could hardly bear.

When the doctor attendant came Wilberforce said,

> Thank God, I am not losing my faculties.

Upon being told that he could not easily go through a problem in arithmetic or geometry, he answered,

> I think I could go through the Asses' Bridge. Let me see.

He began, and would immediately correct himself if he omitted anything. His sons state that his attendant did of course, attempt to stop him. About eight o'clock, on being asked how he felt, Wilberforce answered,

> What cause have I for thankfulness! I have been all day almost as comfortable as if I had been pretty well. I have slept a good deal, and I have so many people who are kind to me. I am sure I feel deeply my servants' attention.'

---

8. *Life*, v. pp. 335-336.
9. *Life*, v. pp. 336-337.

Alluding to a remedy which was provided for some present discomfort, he burst out repeatedly into exclamations on the goodness of God in these little things, providing means to remedy the various inconveniences of sickness. To this subject he several times recurred, with the remark,

> How ungrateful men are in not seeing the hand of God in all their comforts! I am sure it greatly adds to our enjoyment to trace his hand in them.

Soon after he said,

> What is that text, 'He hath hid pride from man?'[10] I was thinking how God had taught him the folly of pride, because the most beautiful and delicate woman, and the proudest man, of the highest birth and station, who was never approached but with deference and formality, is exposed to exactly the same infirmities of this body of our humiliation that I am.

He was repeating from memory Psalm 51, and asked his son to look what came next after verse 11. He was told it was, 'Take not Thy Holy Spirit from me.'[11]

> Oh give me the comfort of Thy help again. It is very odd, I thought it had been 'Restore unto me the joy of Thy salvation.'[12] Do look what it is in the Bible Version.

It was found just as he said.

> What a very remarkable passage! It seems like an anticipation of the privileges of the new dispensation.

He spoke much of the delight which he had in the affection and care of his wife and children.

> Think what I should have done had I been left; as one hears of people quarrelling and separating. 'In sickness and in health' was the burden, and well has it been kept.

At that moment his wife came in and Wilberforce exclaimed,

> I was just praising you.

Those present at this time say, that except in his remark about pride, there was hardly a word he uttered that was not a bursting forth of praise. For example,

> What cause it is for thankfulness that I never suffer from headache.[13]

---

10. Job 33:17.
11. Psalm 51:11.
12. Psalm 51:12.
13. *Life*, v. p. 359.

Sunday Morning half-past eight, July 7, 1833

Remember, my dear H. that it is Sunday morning, and all our times here are very short. I am sure the manner of my dismissal, as far as it has yet gone, has been most gracious. I have not had so much time here for reading Scripture as I wish, hut I rejoice at having laid in a knowledge of it when I was stronger. I hope you always take care of that. From our familiarity with it, we do not feel about the Scripture at all as we should do, if we were to hear for the first time that there was a communication from God to man.

Think of our Savior coming down from heaven, and, when one feels what a little pain is, submitting to all that he endured; having the nails roughly driven through his hands. To be sure the thought of our Savior's sufferings is so amazing, so astonishing, I am quite overwhelmed. Next to the horrible driving of the nails, I have thought most of his being given over to the insults of the Roman soldiery, when one thinks what brutal fellows they were. His sufferings were not alleviated as mine are by the kindness of those about him. I have been thinking of that delightful text, which has often comforted me, 'Be careful for nothing, etc.'[14]

He actually went on as far as 'The peace of God shall keep your hearts and minds through Christ Jesus.'

To be sure, it is the same Almighty power which enables him to watch over all the world, every creature, beast, bird, or insect, and to attend to all the concerns of every individual.[15]

Sunday 4 oClock, July 7, 1833

I am a poor creature today, I cannot help thinking if some of the people who saw me swaggering away on the hustings at York could see me now, how much they would think me changed. What a mercy to think that these things do not come by chance, but are the arrangements of infinite wisdom! When I think how many poor people are suffering, without the luxuries that I possess, and the kind friends I have about me, I am quite ashamed of my comforts."[16]

Sunday 5 oClock, July 7, 1833

I cannot help thinking there was some mistake about my medicine; but it does not matter. There is nothing sinful in it.

Toussaint Louverture[17] was mentioned in the evening.

I sent word to Sir Walter Scott that he had not at all done justice to that part of his History, (of Buonaparte,) and he replied, that if I would

---

14. Philippians 4:6.

15. *Life*, v. pp. 360-361.

16. Ibid., p. 361.

17. Francois-Dominique Toussaint Louverture (1743–1803), a former slave who became the best-known leader of the slave revolt in St. Domingue, an event sometimes referred to as the Haitian Revolution of 1791. He was proclaimed governor for life, an act opposed by Napoleon (it being a French colony), with Louverture being forced to resign and being deported to France, where he died soon after. His name is also sometimes spelt L'ouverture.

point anything out to him, he would willingly alter it. I wanted dear
Stephen to do it, but he did not. I am very sorry for it, but it must
be known sooner or later. To be sure to make a treaty of amity and
friendship with a man, and then have him and his family seized and
sent on shipboard, and finally to the Chateau of Joux[18] ... And then a
veil is drawn over it. None knows what happened. What a story there
will be there, when this world shall give up its dead! It was something
like the case of the Duc D'Enghien,[19] but worse.[20]

Sunday 11 oClock, July 7, 1833

I feel more comfortable than I have done for I know not how long. Never
had a man such cause for thankfulness as I have, and above all, that I
have so many, many kind friends to do everything for me. My own son,
and my own wife. I am quite ashamed of my comforts when I think of
him who had not where to lay his head.[21]

Tuesday 4 oClock, July 9, 1833

Upon reading some of Cecil's remarks he said,

Nothing can be more opposite than that spirit of the present day,
which shows itself for instance in the pride of literature, to the spirit
of Christianity. Compare this bold, independent, daring spirit, with
the beatitudes. 'Blessed are the poor in spirit. Blessed are they that
mourn. Blessed are the meek.'[22] Nothing surely can be so contrary to
what ought to be the spirit of a creature who feels in himself the seeds
of corruption. Miss. Hannah More told me that towards the end of
Johnson's life, if he was asked how he was, he would answer, 'rather
better, I thank my God through Jesus Christ.' And so to whatever
he was asked.

His friend, Joseph John Gurney, who happened to be passing through
Bath, two days afterwards, on July 11th. paid him a visit which Gurney
himself records:

When I arrived at the house on the South Parade[23] which he then
occupied, I found that he had been suffering severely from a bilious
attack; and his lady, whose attentions to him were most tender and
unremitting, appeared to be in low spirits on his account. Still there
then appeared no reason to apprehend the near approach of death.
I was introduced to an apartment upstairs, where I found the veteran

---

18. Chateau de Joux or Fort de Joux, is a castle/fort, in La Cluse-et-Mijoux in the French Jura
mountains. It is especially remembered, as Wilberforce here notes in his Journal, as the place where
Louverture was imprisoned and later died on 7 April, 1803.

19. Louis Antoine Henri de Bourbon (1772–1804), Duke of Enghien, a relative of the French
Bourbon monarchs. Wilberforce's entry is here alluding to the fact that the Duke was executed for
aiding Britain and plotting against France, with European nobility being shocked and dismayed at
his being shot in the moat of the Chateau de Vincennes, as related in Alexandre Dumas' *The Last
Cavalier* (1869).

20. *Life*, v. pp. 361-362.

21. Ibid., p. 362.

22. Matthew 5:3.

23. William Wilberforce lived at 7, South Parade, Bath.

Christian reclining on a sofa, with his feet wrapped in flannel; and his countenance bespeaking increased age since I had last seen him, as well as much delicacy. He received me with the warmest marks of affection, and seemed to be delighted by the unexpected arrival of an old friend. I had scarcely taken my seat beside him before ... it seemed given me to remind him of the words of the psalmist, "Although y^e. have lien among the pots, yet shall y^e. be as the wings of a dove covered with silver, and her feathers with yellow gold,"[24] and I freely spoke to him of the good and glorious things, which, as I believed, assuredly awaited him in the kingdom of rest and peace. In the meantime the illuminated expression of his furrowed countenance, with his clasped and uplifted hands, were indicative of profound devotion and holy joy.

Soon afterwards he unfolded his own experience to me in a highly interesting manner. He told me that the text on which he was then most prone to dwell, and from which he was deriving peculiar comfort, was a passage in the Epistle to the Philippians, 'Be careful for nothing, but in everything by prayer and supplication, with thanksgiving, let your requests be made known unto God; and the peace of God which passeth all understanding shall keep your hearts and minds through Jesus Christ.'[25] While his frail nature was shaking, and his mortal tabernacle seemed ready to be dissolved, this 'peace of God' was his blessed and abundant portion.

The mention of this text immediately called forth one of his bright ideas, and led to a display, as in days of old, of his peculiar versatility of mind. 'How admirable,' said he, 'are the harmony and variety of St. Paul's smaller Epistles! You might well have given an argument upon it in your little work on evidence. The Epistle to the Galatians contains a noble exhibition of doctrine. That to the Colossians is a union of doctrine and precept, showing their mutual connection and dependence; that to the Ephesians, is seraphic; that to the Philippians, is all love. With regard to myself,' he added, 'I have nothing whatsoever to urge, but the poor Publican's plea, "God be merciful to me a sinner."'[26] These words were expressed with peculiar feeling and emphasis, and have since called to my remembrance his own definition of the word mercy, 'kindness to those that deserve punishment.' What a lesson may we derive from such an example! It may awfully remind us of the apostle's question, 'If the righteous scarcely be saved, where shall the sinner and ungodly appear?'[27]

A few days later, Wilberforce spoke the following words to his son,

You must all join with me in praying that the short remainder of my life may be spent in gaining that spirituality of mind which will fit me for heaven. And there I hope to meet all of you.[28]

---

24. Psalm 68:13.
25. Philippians 4:7.
26. Luke 18:13.
27. 1 Peter 4:18.
28. *Life*, v. pp. 362-365.

Saturday, July 20, 1833

My private prayers are much the same as those in the family, pardon and grace. Tonight particularly with regard to the week past. Perhaps I have been wrong in not praying more with others. But I never felt that I could open my heart with perfect freedom and sincerity, and the idea of doing otherwise in praying to Almighty God ... Now I own many good men use expressions which I cannot use, for instance, about their own corruption. I HOPE no man on earth has a stronger sense of sinfulness and unworthiness before God than I. But they speak as if they did not feel the wish to do the will of God, and I am sure I cannot say that. Now S. in his prayers often uses expressions of that kind, which quite amaze me in a man so sincere as he is.[29]

Saturday, July 27, 1833

On the Saturday, alluding apparently to his sickness, he said,

"I am in a very distressed state."

He was answered, 'Yes, but you have your feet on the Rock', to which he replied,

"I do not venture to speak so positively, but I hope I have."

After this expression of humble trust, 'with but one groan, he entered into that world where pain and doubt are forever at an end. He died at three o'clock in the morning of Monday, July 29th, aged 73 years and 11 months.'[30]

---

29. Ibid., p. 367.
30. Ibid., p. 373.

The Autobiography
of
William Wilberforce

Autobiography of William Wilberforce

I was Born Augt. 24, 1759 at Hull. Probably at about Seven attended the Grammar School with Satchell on my shoulder, having all my meals at home. When I had been at School about a year I believe, Joseph Milner succeeded therein in Hull School. I used occasionally to go to my Grandfather at Ferriby, 8 Miles off by the Humber side. In May 1768 a general Election in which my Father supported Mr. Weddell, who elected with Lord Rt. Manners. Soon after the Election my Father died & some months after, my Mother had a most long & dangerous Fever. In the Autumn I went with my aunt Smith to Nottingham & afterwards with their eldest Son to London to live with my Uncle Wilberforce my Father's elder & only Brother & his Lady, John Thornton's Sister, never any Children. After some time spent in enquiries I was placed at Mr. Chalmer's School at Putney where about 25 to 30 Boys, Lodgers, a very few being Parlour Boarders at about treble common price the staple of the School being a foundation for Charity Children of the place, of whom about 30 or 40 in a Gallery, no intercourse between us. This an academy, Chalmers a Scotchman & a better kind of Man, with a Scotch Usher, fitted Boys for business & for larger Schools. Latin, French, Writing, Arithmetic & a very little Greek. Many West-Indians placed there by Colonists Agents, Vanderpools, Hinvilles, Days &c.

At Home with my Uncle & Aunt in the Holydays, at Wimbledon Common & St. James' Place, almost every Summer visiting my Mother & Grand Father. Continued here till 72 or 73 when my Mother hearing I had become a Methodist, came up to London to ascertain the Fact & finding it true took me down to Hull almost heartbroken. A new School looked out. Mr. Skinner's thought of, where the St. Johns & Chaplin, 400 pounds for Annum. At length placed at Pocklington, Mr. Baskett, who had recently married Miss Waddington, having 3 children by a former, the two oldest about my own age. This an endowed Grammar School. The Master a fellow of St. John's College, an elegant tho' not deep Scholar & of gentlemanly mind & manners. I had a very good Room to myself.

There I staid till Oct. 1776, going in the Holydays to my Mother's at Hull & occasionally going to visit my Grandfather who died (I think) in 76, when I admitted of St. John's College Cambridge & went to reside in Octr. The Holy days, the Winter especially, utter idleness & dissipation; uninterrupted series, Sundays excepted of Suppers (Tea & Cards at Six, Supper Nine, port between 11 & 12. Singing &c. I a great Singer), Cards, assemblies, Concerts, Plays, and for Two Last Years with the Girls all the Morning, religion gradually wearing away till quite gone. At College introduced immediately to Genl. Smith, Tighe, Ashe & Macdonald (Irish) &c. Gisborne also, soon eventually drawing off from each other, he living entirely with Babington, I alas! with the wickedest & most ire [then paper torn] then often abhorring, the drinking &c. in which a party.

At length quite sick of the Society, took to the sober dissipation of Card playing & occasional dining & supping, chiefly with Fellows & Tutors. Never prest to attend Lectures, at which scarcely ever present & perfectly idle except studying the Classics for College Examination for credit sake & a little general English Literature. My Grandfather died I believe just when I went to College, my Uncle in 77 or 78. I had a perfect command of money. In the Winter came occasionally to London visiting Robert Smith or Uncle Smith but chiefly at Hull in Winter Vacations where same Dissipation as before & some Corps of Militia always quartered in the Town, the Officers increased the Dissipation. In 1778 the Nottingham Militia under Lord G. Sutton (Major Cartwright Gould Thoroton &c.). In 1779 the Suffolk Militia under Lord Euston now Duke of Grafton (containing Woodley Heigh found dead on his knees, Middleton &c.), Lord G. Sutton, Major Cartwright Gould Thoroton &c.

But in 79 Winter I a good deal in London attending the Gallery, for began now to think of becoming Member for Hull & in the Spring & Summer of 1780 canvassing in & about London, Poplar, Wapping, Redrift, Blackwall & afterwards going about canvassing Hull Voters. Election early in Septr., resting on my being of Age 24th. Augt. Preceding. Lord R. Manners, David Hartley, the old Members & myself Candidates. My numbers the sum of both theirs precisely & the worthy Freemen taking their Two and Four Guineas & the London Voters costing above Ten Pounds a man between Two and Three Hundred of them, the Election cost me 8 or 9,000 L. Great Riot, D. Hartley & Sir G. Saville's Lodgings broke open in the Night & they escaping over the Roof. Lord Robert, my Colleague.

Parlt. met in Novr. & I resolved to be no party man. Pitt elected about Xtmas. Sir James Lowther writing him a most handsome Letter offering a Seat. He residing in Lincolns Inn as a Lawyer. Goostry's Club soon formed of about 25 of us chiefly M.P.'s, all youngsters just entering into Life. The House Pall Mall, the back Rooms looking into Kings Place. Pitt, Pratt, Euston, Eliot, H. Andrews St. John, poor Bridgeman, Morris Robinson, Lord Graham, Bankes, came from Italy late in the Winter. Bob Smith, Lord George Cavendish, Tom. Steele, Genl. Smith,

Grenville, Lord Duncannon, Calthorpe, Apsley, C Lennox, Pepper Arden, and thro' me Edwards, now Sir G Noel, after a time Wyndham. I soon after chose to Brooks, Whites, Bootle's, Miles & Evan's &c. but Goostry's the staple. Pitt supping there every night during a whole winter. I think Charles Long.

In 1782 March, Lord North thrown out, at Duchess of Devonshire's Ball first introduced to the Prince of Wales. Invited, while Ministry forming, to a Meeting at Tommy Townsends. Fox awkwardly bringing out that Lord Shelbourne only had seen the King, in short Jealousy between Foxites & Shelburnites manifested, tho' for a time suppressed. Lord Rockingham Premier, Shelburne Secretary of State. I dined with Lord Rockingham on the 4th of June, he died shortly after. N.B. Foxe's memorable declaration that a stroke of Providence could not disunite them. In a few days Lord Shelburne Premier, Pitt accepted Chancelorship of Exchequer just turned Twenty Three, May 28th. Preceding. Fox resigning & declaring they could not have kept together if Lord Rockingham had lived. Eliot, Lord of Treasury & also Graham. Apsley I think Admiralty. Parliament prorogued & meeting again. I in Summer at my House on the Lakes, Rairig, which took the year before & enjoyed greatly, boating, riding, & alas! carding at home & at Rydal, Sir H. Fleming's where I sometimes supped, riding back at Midnight. St Andrew St John with Mr. _____ months together – Mother & Sister also & College Friends occasionally.

About Novr., Burkes Report of address Speech ridiculing the address, gravely answered by Pitt, great impression. Towards Xtmas provisional articles signed with America & Parliament adjourned to give time to negotiate for general Peace, which made when Parliament reassembled about Feby. I seconded Address and Coalition being formed, address negative & censure carried. Pitt's famous Speech on second day's debate (first day's not so good), spake Three hours at Four in the morning, stomach disordered & actually holding Solomon's Porch Door open with One Hand while vomiting during Fox's Speech, to whom He was to reply. Coalition Ministry, Duke of Portland Premier, Lord John Cavendish C. of Exchequer, Pitt returned to the Law. In Easter Holy days of 1781, visited young Genl. Smith at Chilton near Hungerford. Pitt, St. John, &c. and myself. In 1782 Easter, all went to Brighton & violent Wind & Rain coming on, drove off to Bath, where Corporation dining & Jolities. Lived at York House. Clear Bill. Pitt going the Western Circuit & entertaining Circuiters, Ickell &c. (2 about this last Ward). In Spring down to Mr. Bowles, Play, Aston, with Edwards, returned to London same night.

In autumn of 83, Pitt, Eliot & I went to Rheims for above Six Weeks. Thence to Paris & Fontainbleau. At Rheims, Peter Thellusson who, by Bob Smith's Request gave us Letters having only Maitre Epicier for Correspondent, we supposed to be Imposters. Archbishop sens de Laguise to make all out, who reported favorably, we invited to dinner by Archbishop (Perigord) & even to make his House our own. Two nephews Bozon & Archamber dined & supped with the Wine Merchant who rich and gave us excellent Champagne. M. de Chetel the Chief (2 Prefect) of Town, had been in England or had English connexions in the Douglas Cause buss. Lord Camden (Pratt) & Euston & Ricketts at Paris & went to Fontainbleau for four Days, where the Court was & dining and Suppings with some or other of the Ministers where Marie Antoinette was every Evening. M. de Comte Vergennes, Breteuil, Princess de Lamballe. Charles Ellis a great favorite of the Queen. At Paris dined one day with Lafayette to meet Dr. Franklin. Pitt sounded thro' Walpole & Lord Camden for Made'lle Necker afterwards Madame Stael. Pitt first knew Rose at Paris who travelled with Lord Thurlowe, who afterwards abhorred him.

Returned to England in Nov. & secret plottings, the King groaning under the Ministry that had been imposed on him. Provision for Prince of Wales difference, when Ministry gave up the measure rather than their places. Afterwards Fox's India Bill (in 1782 first knew Fox well, he giving us dinners twice or thrice very pleasant & unaffected.), which thrown out. Lord Temple's Fracas & long interregnum. At length Pitt Prime Minister about Feby. or March 1784 & House of Commons civil dissension. At last Mutiny Bill passed & Parliament dissolved.

The News of Dissolution came from Pitt via Letter received while speaking at the great Meeting in the Castle Yard at York, whither I had gone down not having I believe a single acquaintance except very slightly the Revd. Mr. Mason the Poet. Wonderful meeting for order & fair hearing, immense body of freeholders present, Lord Fitzwilliam, J. Cavendish, Surry, Carlisle &c. &c. After the meeting to a grand publick dinner at the York Tavern (the Foxites at Blewetts), & in the Evening after dinner when they all half tipsey, I made up a quarrel which had broken out between Associators and non-associators, Wigs & Tories: Wigs Lord Effingham & Tories West Riding Clothiers. This confirmed the disposition to propose my Candidate which had begun to be brought about at dinner among all ranks. Sawney Morritt, my old Steward Renard. I supped with Miss Morritts. Sawney, &c. there, sat late. Next morning meeting at Tavern of all our friends speechified again, settled that all the Gentlemen & Merchants should separately sound their Neighborhoods & came with the result to the County Meeting about a week afterwards.

Meanwhile I went to Hull, where re-elected by a large Majority tho' some angry at the idea County – settled in the Chair. Great meeting for Nomination in a long room between Courts. Speakers mounted on a Table. I replying to Lawyer Hill of Tadcaster, solomonated with Duncombe & Weddell & Fuljambre by the Rockinghamites, Fuljambre having been elected a few weeks before on his Uncle, Sir G. Saville resigned. Dunscombe & I meanwhile going together canvassing by Doncaster. First saw old & Harewood then Mr. Lascelles, at Ferrybridge not seeing a single <u>friendly</u> House all the week (on the returns to the Nomination Meeting our promises 3 or 4 to me) Rotherham, Jos. Walker,

Sheffield, honest Edmonds Worseborough, insight of Lord Fitzwilliam yet our Friend, Barnsley, Wakefield, Leeds, Bradford, Halifax, Huddersfield. Every where received with tumultuous. Returning to York, evening before Election & freeholders came in for the morrow's, when a message from Blewitts that our opponent resigned, Duncombe & I elected.

Next day riding & speechifying. (Nights of York meeting, first became acquainted with dear Burgh), shortly after to Hull where took up my Sister & drove for quiet & recreation to Teignmouth in Devon. Parlt. being to meet in May. At Teignmouth first knew Matthew Martin, Sir James Wright, &c. & after a while the Parlt. having a Lodging in Town as before & my House at Wimbledon (which inherited from my Uncle buying off Aunt's Term & during the Spring my young friends spending much time with me. Pitt for near 3 month slept almost every night there & I turning all the Garretts into nice little Rooms contrived to give 8 or 9 Beds).

Session over, went I think to Rayrigg, Burlington, Scarborough, York Races, where sung &c. and towards Autumn took my Mother & Sister & Bessy Smith abroad, also dear Milner having previously asked Burgh who declined. Milner & I travelling Tete a Tete in my chaise. The Ladies & Bloodworth & Bessy Smith's maid in a coach, Dixon with us. Called on my Uncle Martin Bird at Fontainebleau & took up Mary Bird. They associating with the Widow Beauharmor's afterwards Barras' Companion & the Empress Josephine. We went on to Lyons, thence by the Rhone 5 days without a Cloud (in Octr.) to Avignon in a barge. Thence resuming our Carriage to Marseilles, where saw George Ellis, stayed ten days, thence by Toulon to Nice. There had a Villa before entering the Town an orange garden between us and the Mediterranean Sea. Staid till 3d. Feby. 1785, when Milner & I to Paris & Calais & Dover. The number of English at that time resident at Nice was so great that there were at one time at an assembly given by the Duke & Duchess of Gloster between 90 & 100 of our Countrymen, among others the late Duke and Duchess of Gloster & the present Duke then a short little Boy. Lord Gambrel, Sir John Colpoys, Capt. Waghorne & seven other naval men.

Sir - - - then having the Command of the Mediterranean, the Natives were in general a wretched state, several of them however poor Nobility & there were nightly Card Parties at the different Houses & a great deal of Gambling. The only respectable young Person was the Chevalier Navel, Son of the Count de St. Andrew, Governor of Nice. The Chevalier spoke English extremely well & was a great friend of Mr. Frederick North now Lord Guildford, who also was at Nice in a very nervous state & giving entire credit to the pretense of the Animal Magnetisers. The chief operator M. Tanlay tried his skill upon Milner & myself, but neither of us felt anything, oweing perhaps to our incredulity. North on the contrary, was said to fall down on entering a room in which they practised upon him & to one he maintained that the Magnetizers could affect the human Frame when in another room & even at a distance &

the subject not being aware of their proceedings. There was an English apothecary, or rather I believe a Foreigner who had been long in England & spoke our language thoroughly, named Farradi. The poor fellow was disliked among the Natives, but was a favorite among the English. He afterwards I understood, bought a Patent of Nobility, but taking part in the Revolution, on a change of the ruling power of the day, he was soon after executed.

The climate was so delightful that many times during the month of January we carried our cold meat into some of the beautiful recesses of the mountains & rocks by which the place is surrounded on the land side, & dined in the open air as we should have in the Summer. But I believe this was a local, as I understood that after we left the place, on the 3d. of Feby., the weather became inclement, so bad was it in the neighborhood, that the snow continued all the rest of our journey to London. As I was anxious to return to the discharge of my Parliamentary duties, having been elected member for Yorkshire the preceding year, Milner & I, attended by Dixon as a courier, made the best of our way, setting out in the morning before it was light & travelling till after dark. The wretched Inns in which we had to take up our quarters, not being likely to afford any meat, we used to buy it where it was to be had during the day, carry it along with us, & when we came to our Inn at night, make it into soup with the addition of Pearl Barley, Onions &c. Not a morsel of Bread could we eat as it was all sour (indeed Milner & I never tasted Bread but twice on the Continent in both our expeditions). No wine, except now & then a little Frontiniac, no Brandy, no butter or cheese. In short, none of those things which in England we should deem indispensable for our comfort or even our health.

On my arrival in London, not having provided myself with Lodgings, I took up my quarters for a short time under the roof of Mr. Pitt in Downing Street, one of whose maid Servants seeing a Collection of 40 or 50 Letters on a chair, some opened others un-opened, conceiving them to be waste paper, threw them all unread into the fire. I dreaded the effect on my reputation in Yorkshire but happily no bad consequence ensued. About the end of the following June, Milner & I again set out on our return to meet the Ladies of our party at Genoa. They having come to us thither from Nice in a felacea. After remaining about a week in that fine City, we proceeded to Turin & thence over Mnt. Cennis to Geneva. Thence we proceeded to Lausanne, Vevey, Berne, the Lakes of Shun & Brientz, halting at the Paradise of Interlacken to Zurich, & Schaffhausen, & the falls of the Rhine, & by Basil & Strasburgh to Meritz, where we embarked on board a Vessel & sailed down to Cologne. There we resumed our carriages and proceeded to Spa. After passing about a Month amid that curious assemblage from all parts of Europe, which used then to meet at Spa, we returned to England thro' Liege, Brussels, Antwerp & Calais.

Very soon after the commencement of the first of these Continental Expeditions, Dr. Milner and I began occasionally to employ our Tete a Tete, in the discussion of religious topics, & during the latter part especially of this second Tour, we discussed them with augmented interest. Yet I am ashamed to confess, that tho' my understanding assented to Dr. Milner's religious opinions which were of the kind commonly termed evangelical, the hearts of neither of us were suitably affected. At length however, I began to think what folly & madness it was to go on as I was living.

I fully believed the truth of the divine declaration, that pardoning mercy & sanctifying grace were to be obtained by all who should sincerely implore them, in the name & for the sake of our great Mediator. I set myself therefore to obtain them as it is due to my late dear friend to declare, that tho' full of levity on all other subjects, he never expressed himself otherwise that with the utmost seriousness on every religious topic, & all he said to me tended to augment my dispensation to attend in earnest to the one thing needful. I therefore began to prosecute the work with the utmost seriousness, & for several months to make it the grand object of my thoughts & endeavors.

From the time of our return to England, several months elapsed before the meeting of Parliament. I divided my time between my house at Wimbledon & London, which I used to quarter myself at one of the Adelphi Hotels, as most conveniently situated for attending the various places of worship in the metropolis. Not long after my return to England, I had renewed my acquaintance with the Rev. Jn. Newton who when I was a Boy, I had visited when travelling with my Uncle & Aunt in our Journey into Yorkshire. I now profited much from his friendly Counsel, & in particular he enforced upon me the propriety of not relinquishing, in the degree I was disposed to do, the Society of my friends. I therefore went over to Mr. Pitt's & staid with him a few days. I was strongly impressed with a sense of its being incumbent on me, to perform my Parliamentary duties with increased diligence & conscientiousness. I therefore attended the House with great punctuality.

I took a House in Old Palace Yard & as soon as I conveniently could, I sold my House at Wimbledon. Meanwhile reports of all sorts were circulated concerning me & more particularly it was rumored that I was deranged. These reports however gave me no uneasiness. I was sure to live them down by a course of tolerable usefulness & consistency. When Parliament rose, I hastened to my Mother & Sister who were at Scarboro' with Mrs. Sykes, & as they had heard of the change that had taken place in my sentiment, they were prepared for great Eccentricities & were agreeably surprised by finding me at least as reasonable as before, & of course endeavoring to render my altered views more acceptable to them, by my increased attention & kindness, nor were my endeavors unsuccessful. I soon heard of the satisfaction with which Mr. Sykes had spoken to my Mother of my present disposition & demeanour, & I never can forget with what affectionate earnestness she parted from us, entreating with many tears and interest in my Prayers. From

Scarborough, if I mistake not, we went to Halifax & my Uncle Smith (Smith, Samuel) & staid many weeks.

No sooner had the great change which I have mentioned taken place in my views, than deeply lamenting my idleness at College, & for the last 7 or 8 years, I deemed it to be my duty to redeem the time & prosecute the studies I ought to have cultivated in my earlier years. I spent the greater part of my Parliamentary Recess, at the House of one friend or another, where I could have the command of my time & enjoy just as much Society as would be desireable for maintaining my spirits, & enabling me to continue my labors with cheerfulness & comfort. During one Summer I was at Mr. Sam. Smith's & at Wilford, another at the House of my old Tutor & Friend, the Revd. Wm. Cookson at Fawcett Norfolk. The living of Fawcett Norfolk had been given to Mr. Cookson by Sir R. Hill, who by the will of his ancestor, was bound to nominate to this & several other livings in his Gift some fellows of St. John's College, Cambridge.

This condition rendered the patronage so little desireable to him, that he was glad not long after to sell the whole of it. Some years before he had in vain wished to nominate his brother Rowland to one of the Livings, the college refusing to elect him a fellow. Mr. Cookson not long after was recommended thro' Dr. Arnold, formerly Tutor of St. John's College, who had been Tutor to the present King as Duke of York, to fill the same important trust, in conjunction with the Revd. Mr. Hughes, over the Duke of Cumberland Ernest, _____ the gestures, & Cambridge especially. Dr. Fisher the late Bishop of Salisbury, had previously, thro' the same recommendation, been appointed Tutor to Prince Edward, afterwards Duke of Kent. They lived at a House on Kew Green. It is affecting to relate that Poor Dr. Arnold not long after, became deranged. He was placed with a relation of the same name who had a House for the reception of Patients in those unhappy circumstances.

After a few years Dr. Arnold's faculties became impaired, & for many years before his death, he was in a state of idiotcy. He was a man of very superior parts but of a very nervous temperament. This used to display itself sometimes in nervous terrors, & it was supposed that his derangement was much promoted by the feverish anxiety with which he was looking forward to the gratification of his ambitions. Dr. Cookson in reward of his services, was made a Canon of Windsor & afterwards clerk of the _____ & I believe in sight of his Canonry, he afterwards obtained the Living of the beautiful Village of Bunfield in Windsor Forest, where he died a few years ago, after a long & very painful illness. He was a man of a good understanding but of solid rather than showy talents, and of a very amiable temper & real Integrity & kindness of Heart.

I spent the greater part of several of our Summer Recesses at Mr. Gisborne's, Yoxall Lodge in Needwood Forest, & afterwards at Mr. Babington's Rothley Temple near Leicester. No sooner had the change in my views become known to John Thornton Esqr., than observing to me that I should probably wish for occasional Retirement, he desired me to accept of a room in his House, & consider it as my own coming

& going at Pleasure without thinking it necessary to notice him more than should be convenient or agreeable. Mr. Thornton was allied to me both by relationship & family Connexion, & in his early youth he had been under the protection of my Grandfather, from whose friendly Counsel he declared himself to have considerably profited. My aunt Wilberforce being his Sister, I often used to be at his House during my residence under my Uncle's Roof, & I became familiarly tho' not intimately acquainted with the various members of his family.

There were Three Sons, Samuel, Robert & Henry, a Lone Daughter soon after married to Viscount Balgonie afterward Earl of Melville. Mr. Thornton's Character is so well known, that it is scarcely necessary to delineate it, it may be useful however, to state that it was by living with great simplicity of Intention & conduct in the habits & practice of a Xtian Life, more especially by devoting large Sums annually to various charitable purposes, both of a publick & private nature, that without any superiority of understanding or knowledge, he rendered his Name illustrious in the view of all the more respectable part of his Contemporaries. He had a Counting House in London, & a handsome Villa at Clapham with unusually large grounds behind. Mrs. Thornton tho' a Woman of good understanding, had somewhat of a turn to the splendid in all particulars. She was the daughter of a respectable mercantile family of the Name of Watson at Hull.

It is to the honor of Mr. Thornton, to state that he anticipated the disposition & pursuits of the succeeding Generation. He devoted himself principally to the relieving of the spiritual necessities of his fellow-Creatures, & to the promotion of the cause of Religion both in his own & in other Countries. A Considerable Sum He devoted to the purchase of Livings & he used to assist pious Clergymen, both to enable them to live in comfort in their own families, & to practice a useful hospitality. His person & habits were remarkably simple. His dinner hour at Clapham was Two oClock. He commonly attended publick worship at some Church or Chapel of the Establishment several Evenings in the week, & used often to sit up to a late Hour in his own study, which was at the Top of the house engaged in religious exercises.

I think it was about the year 1787 that I commenced my enquiries concerning the African Coast & the nature and effects of the Slave Trade. The publick Attention had been pretty generally turned to that subject, & Meetings naturally took place of those who were interested in the cause. Hence I soon became acquainted with Mr. Clarkson, whose attainment of a prize at Cambridge given by Dr. Peck, and to the best composition on the subject of the Slave Trade, had turned his active mind to that Object, & interested in his warm feelings in the sufferings of the wretched victims of avarice, whose wrongs had so long remained un-noticed. Several of us met at Breakfast at Sir C. Middleton's, I think at Mr. Bonnett Langston's, & I am sure also at my own house.

At first the African Merchants gave me information freely, but I found them full of error & prejudice. I then began to talk the matter over with Pitt & Grenville, & at length I well remember after a conversation in the open air, at the root of an old Tree at Holwood, just above the steep descent to the Valley of Keston, I resolved by their advice to give notice in the House, of my intention to bring the subject forward. It is somewhat worthy of attention, as indicative of the providential impulses by which we are led into particular lines of Conduct, that as early as 1780 or 81, I had been strongly interested for the West Indian Slaves, & in a Letter to my friend Gordon, who was going out to the West Indies, I expressed my determination or at least my hope, that some time or other, I should redress the wrongs of those wretched & degraded Beings. At length about March 1788, I was seized with a serious illness, & was for some time in danger. After a time, it pleased God that I became convalescent tho' by no means fully recovered. I was ordered to Bath, but I well remember previously obtaining from Mr. Pitt, a promise that if anything should happen to me, he would himself undertake the management of the business. About this time, I recollect the first formation of a connection with a Gentleman, whose friendship was a benefit & a pleasure to me for many succeeding years. I mean the late Mr. Grant, from whom I received a Letter signed by himself & three other friends of whom Mr. Udney was one, requesting me to interest myself in the religious Interests of British India.

Being ordered to relax with a view to my complete recovery, I gladly availed myself of an opportunity of taking my old House at Rairig for the Summer, & there accordingly I went with the Dean of Carlisle, my Mother & Sister joining us from Hull, the kindness manifested to me by Lord Carrington during this illness, as well as the friendly attention of Lord Muncaster I must ever remember with gratitude. It was in this Summer that we visited Lord Muncaster, & the Dean & I passed a few days with the Duchess of Gordon at Low Wood & Keswick. It was in the Autumn of this year, that we were alarmed by the first known derangement of the late King. Parliament was soon afterwards called together, & Mr. Fox was sent for & returned in the utmost extremity of haste from Italy. A Committee was formed of which I was one for examining the King's Physicians, & afterwards a second Committee, the eagerness of the opposition strikingly its own purpose. Meanwhile I brought forward the abolition of the Slave Trade, & an examination of witnesses commenced first at the Bar of the House, & afterwards in a Committee upstairs. By the advice of Mr. Pitt & Lord Grenville, I drew up & laid on the Table of the House, a number of propositions that contained the whole of our case, stating the number of slaves annually taken from Africa, the incurable guilt & cruelty inherent in the traffic, together with proofs drawn from accounts of the population of the Islands, that the stock of Negroes then in the Colonies could be maintained without fresh importations, while the continuance of the traffic introduced many uncompensated evils, & above all prevented the institution of a Commerce with Africa for her internal productions, & perpetuated the barbarism & darkness of these ill-fated regions of the Globe.

It has been stated I think by Mr. Belsham, in his History of George the 3d., that this was a highly injudicious proceeding, & that I ought to have availed myself of the favorable feelings toward our case which were then generally prevalent, whereas by my dilatory course I suffered them to die away, while self Interest sure and steady to its purpose, remained ready to exert its powers as policy should prescribe. But Mr. B. should have remembered that tho' a resolution condemning the Slave Trade in general might have been obtained, it was only thro' the medium of an Act of Parliament, that such a resolution could be carried into effect, & He should have borne in mind that the slow & cautious policy our of Legislative system, so excellent for the most parts in its effect, tho' in this & in some new instances to be regretted, gives the opponent of every measure at the least nine or ten, & in the case of a warm or dexterous partisan, many more stations for drawing up their array & visiting its progress. Of these opportunities, our opponents would doubtless have availed themselves, & the enquiry into this large & complicated subject, which actually lasted for great part of 3 Sessions of Parliament, would have been just as long, if the petitions from the African Traders & West India Merchants had been met on our part merely by our Bill itself, & not by the propositions which embodied our case, & manifested it to be no less consistent with policy than it was enforced by Justice & humanity. Will it be said that the House of Commons having passed a resolution condemning the Slave Trade, would have felt itself bound by what was due to consistency, or by feelings of consistency?

We know from experience too well, how little weight to assign to this Consideration. What Resolution could be more positive than that which was past in 1792, which drew from Mr. Pitt the remark that the sentence of death was passed, & that in 4 years the Sentence would assuredly be executed, yet 4 years after 4 years passed away, without the slightest apparent consciousness of the obligations that had been contracted, & it may be truly affirmed that the resolution had not the smallest influence in producing at last the long protracted abolition. I believe it was in 1789 not 88, that the examination into the African Slave Trade & the state of the West Indies as connected with it was carried on, first at the Bar of the House, & afterwards by a select Committee, where at first we mustered pretty strong on both sides, but the numbers gradually declined & at length there was but about 4 or 5, & latterly 2 or 3 on each side to carry on the Contest. Mr. Matthew Montague & still more Mr. Wm. Smith were my steady Coadjutors. The Members for Liverpool & Bristol, & Mr. Hanley a West India Proprietor formerly Attorney Genl. In St. Christopher's were our most constant opponents. Before the examination commenced, I laid the whole case before the House in a Long speech, in which I stated the Injustice & cruelty with all the various horrors of the Trade in Africa: the protracted agonies of the middle Passage, & above all the proof that the slave Trade had been the main obstacle to the communication of Xtian Truth & social Civilization to those vast & populous Regions. I then detailed the various abominations of the West India System, arguing that they would have been sufficient to account for a great annual decrease in the number of the slaves in our colonies, whereas in point of fact the decrease was but small & appeared for several years, to have been gradually diminishing.

I shewed that the reforming the various abuses of the system, would more than suffice for destroying the causes of the decrease & ensuring a future increase in the numbers, & still more so in the effective force of the slave population, while the gradual & progressive amelioration of the Condition of the slaves would improve their moral Character, & rendering them fit to enjoy with advantage to themselves, the civil rights & priviledges of freemen, would gradually raise that oppressed & degraded portion of our fellow Creatures, into the respectable state of a free peasantry. Finally I proved, that so far from its being true as had been contended, that the abolition would be ruinous to the Marine of the Country, our Commerce & Manufactures, that it would ultimately be beneficial to them all, substituting for our present limited Trade with Africa a legitimate Commerce to that Country, which might gradually introduce our manufactures into the interior, & diffuse them throughout the vast regions of that immense & hitherto unexplored Continent, & that so far from its being true as was most confidently predicted, that the Abolition must prove fatal to the Town of Liverpool, & even to the Manufacturers of Lancashire, that her spacious Docks and Warehouses would be untenanted, & her populous Streets become a Desert, that she would remain uninjured to carry on a bloodless & honest Commerce, all my assertions were flatly contradicted.

The Africans were represented as a set of Inferior Beings, unworthy of the name of Men, & intended at best by the Almighty to be Hewers of Wood & Drawers of Water for their fellow Creatures. That they were so incurably indolent, that all hopes of getting them to labour for their subsistence were illusory. That the Slave Trade afforded the means of saving the Lives annually, of vast Numbers of Negroes who would otherwise be put to death, & that in this & various other ways, the Slave Trade was quite a Blessing to Africa, that the middle Passage which was afterwards proved but too surely to verify my declaration that it contained the greatest amount of suffering ever condensed into the smallest space, was declared to be a scene of enjoyment, quite a party of pleasure. The Slaves in the West-Indies were declared to be in the best possible state. Governors of Islands & Admirals on the Station were brought to prove that in the West Indies for the first time, absolute power was not abused tho' in circumstances more likely to produce abuses, & it was maintained by the most respectable West-Indian Proprietors & Merchants, that the Abolition of the Slave Trade would infallibly produce the ruin of the West Indian Islands, & with them that of the Commerce & Revenues of the Mother Country, but that happily it would be utterly impossible to prevent the illicit importation of Negroes to any amount which the necessities of the Islands might require.

It is useful to look back upon such cases, as those in which it was attempted to prove that the wealth & industry of a great Nation, were founded on a basis of Injustice & Cruelty, & in which prejudices & fallacies obtained credit for a time which have been since universally exploded, as contrary alike to truth to reason & experience, A still more striking Lesson to the same effect was afforded in an early period of the Controversy. Some of our principal Supporters, one of whom was the late venerable & benevolent Sir Wm. Dolben, were led by curiosity to inspect with their own eyes, the slave Ship then fitting out in the River Thames. This was when the Spring was far advanced, & when despairing of making any progress during the existing Session, the enquiry & discussion were by mutual consent, put off till the next year. But Sir W. D. & his Friends, came back to the House of Commons with a description which produced one universal feeling of pity, shame & indignation.

In particular it appeared, that notwithstanding the Confidence with which it had been maintained, that self interest alone would suffice for securing kind treatment to the wretched victims of their Avarice, it was found that they were crowded into a space so small, as greatly to aggravate the poor Creatures' bodily sufferings. They were stowed on platforms between the Decks, & while they often had not room to lie on their backs, considerable numbers commonly perished during a short Voyage, & when any infectious disease broke out among them, the mortality became prodigious. At once it was resolved that enormities like these, should not be suffered to exist during the short period which had been then conceded to the Slave Trade (for which it was then supposed the Legislature would tolerate the existence of the Slave Trade), a Bill accordingly was proposed which was passed by a great Majority, but not without the fiercest opposition & more especially the delegates from Liverpool adduced the most respectable evidence, to prove that the proposed limitation of the number of Slaves to be carried in a given space, & the other allowances for the well being & comfort of the human Cargoe, would infallibly produce the utter ruin of the traffic.

The House of Commons however, was deaf to their remonstrances & the regulations were established by Law, & a few years only had elapsed, when it was universally conceded that they were not only beneficial to the Slaves, but profitable to the Merchant by the diminished mortality that took place, & the improved health of the Survivors. The Labors of the Commee as was stated above, continued till about March 1791, when the vast mass of evidence having been printed, I brought forward my Motion for the Abolition, grounding myself on the evidence reported to the House, superadded to the Contents of a vast volume partly of oral Testimony, partly of various documents reported from the privy Council. To make myself completely master of this great Mass of

Materials was no easy Task, & the better to secure the necessary quiet uninterrupted by other avocations, I retired with my documents & a few friends who kindly gave me their assistance, to Mrs. Bouverie's beautiful place of Teston, now Barham Court, from which after a few Weeks, I removed to another House of hers in Surry, Betsworth, a residence scarcely less lovely & desireable.

It may be as well to mention the close friendship that from Childhood had subsisted between Mrs. Bouverie & the Lady of Sir Ch. Middleton. In the Ladies' early youth, when Capt. Middleton proposed to his future Lady, then Miss Gambier, it was stated to him, that if he married the one he must take both, accordingly they ever after lived together. In the Winter, living at Capt., afterwards Sir Ch. Middleton's, & in the Summer, at one of the Seats of Mrs. Bouverie's, for the most part at Teston. Sir Ch. M. conducted the cultivation of a large farm of Mrs. B's. at their joint expence, & ultimately with great profit, tho' 13 years had elapsed before it had repaid the Sum expended on it. Sir C. M. bought a considerable landed property in the neighborhood and Mrs. B., who during her whole Life, enjoyed the Comforts of domestick Life with the dearest friend of her youth, lived with Sir C. M. in one unbroken course of the most attached friendship & unreserved Confidence.

Many years before her death, she had made him fully acquainted with the intended disposition of her property. It was large, & there were some of the Estates to which she conceived some of the relatives of her deceased Brother, from whom her Fortune was desired, might reasonably expect to succeed on the ordinary principles observed in the disposal of family property, she bequeathed Three of these Estates, (two of them at least, if not all the Three having Houses on them), to some one or other of the Bouveries. The Teston property it had been long settled, sh'd be left to Lord Barham, & indeed his Land & Hers were there so intermingled, & such Large Sums belonging to both had been expended upon them indiscriminately, that it would have been difficult if not impossible, to come to any accurate settlement, had it been necessary to separate the Property between the Two & assign to each his respective share. Lord B., being aware that the Three Estates above mentioned were to pass to the Mr. Bouveries, was necessarily delicate in his Conduct with relation to them.

I remember an instance of this kind in which his conduct appeared inexplicable to the Steward who superintended the management of all the properties. He had been urging on Lord B. for some time, to cut down some timber on one of the estates, alledging that it was losing value every year. Lord B. continually refused but wd. not explain his motive. The fact was that knowing that the property was bequeathed to Mr. Bouverie, Lord B. wished it to be conveyed to him without having suffered the slightest diminution in value. It ought likewise to be stated that the value of Mrs. Bouverie's landed property, was greatly increased by Lord Barham's management, & the 13 years had elapsed before the Capital invested in the Hop Farm was replaced, that Farm afterwards bccamc a source of great profit, & the uncertainty commonly supposed to be inevitable to the Cultivation of Hops, was in a great measure done away by the excellent Method that was pursued, for securing the plants from being injured by Wind & by other particulars of good management.

A regular account was kept of all the transactions in conducting the business of the Farm, directions being given what was to be done each day, how the stock to be disposed of, how the Cattle & Horses to be employed, & another Account was kept of what had actually been done, which was daily sent to Lord Barham when he was absent, & tho' he was deeply interested in agricultural pursuits, & tho' his Farm was perhaps the most beautiful Specimen in the Kingdom of the Ferme ounce,[1] it ought to be stated to his Honor, that when in an Official Situation at the Admiralty, which as he thought, rendered it desireable that he should be constantly on the spot for many months together, I rather believe for near a year, he never once visited Teston. Indeed Mr. Pitt tho' not personally attached to him, has more than once acknowledged to me that he thought him the best man of business he ever knew.

But the united forces of the African Merchants proved too powerful for us this year. Pains were taken to interest the Country in the question, & great numbers of petitions were sent up to both Houses, praying for the immediate abolition of the Slave Trade. All parties appeared determined to use their utmost efforts. The West Indians, many of whom were closely connected with Scotland, secured the good offices of Mr. Dundas afterward Lord Melville, for the question not being brought forward by a member of Government, & the Judgement of the Administration not having been taken upon it, every official man was at liberty to act as he saw fit, & here it may be proper to enter into some explanation on this head. Mr. Pitt's enemies having called in question his sincerity as a friend of the abolition, but certainly without any just ground, tho' not without plausibility, especially in the Instance of those who are unacquainted with the actual practice of Parliament.

It is the established System, that all Official Men are to vote with their Principal, but notwithstanding the systematick support of a Ministry which has resulted from systematick opposition to him, the Minister is not considered as being entitled to require the votes of the inferior Members of Government, except on political Questions, or those in which the credit or stability of the Government be fairly supposed to be in some measure at stake. For instance, when Mr. Pitt brought forward his measure for improving the poor Laws, many of his warmest political adherents opposed his measure, without its being supposed by any one, that they were less attached to him than before. In short, what shall & what shall not be a Govt. Question, is not an arbitrary arrangement, nor is it dependent on the Minster's Will, it turns in fact on the answer to thc qucstion, Is thc crcdit or stability of an administration at stake?

---

1. The meaning of Ferme ounce is uncertain.

In the instance therefore of my Motion for abolishing the Slave Trade, every one was perfectly at liberty to vote as he should see fit. It was in no sense a party Question. Yet it must be owned, that the Question considered in relation either to the commercial Interests of the Country, or to the personal security of a large mass of its population, was of great importance, & there is the more reason to regret the narrow view that was taken of it, because it prevented Governments taking the measure (as they ought to have done), into their own hands & associating it as they must have done, with a plan for improving the Condition of the Negro Slaves, & gradually transmuting them into a free Peasantry. Unhappily this just view of the case was not taken, a circumstance which if I mistake not, the West Indians will have reason deeply to deplore. In consequence, the Question was considered as of a moral Nature, grounded on justice & humanity, on the Laws of God & the rights of Man, & here it should be remarked, tho' it is too commonly forgotten, that, except a very few who were directly interested by their property, or their political situation from the places they represented in Parliament, our opponents professed to concur with us in design, to have the same object in view as ourselves but to adopt a more moderate more prudent, & as they contended, more effectual method of accomplishing our common purpose. Thus it was that they whose principles or feelings, or regard for the principles of their assumed Character, could not avowedly oppose us were our more dangerous and fatal enemies. Under these impressions however, men took their Ground & having chosen their side, they could not quit it without self-condemnation, as well as inconsistency.

Never did Mr. Pitt feel more warmly or enforce his arguments with more convincing reasoning or more impressive eloquence. I well remember the day after he had made his celebrated speech in 1792, (when at the close of the second day's debate, the vote for gradual abolition was carried against the comparatively small minority, tho' united force, both of African & West Indians), Mr. Wyndham who had no love for Mr. Pitt, telling me that he had walked from the House thro' the Park on the preceding Morning, with Mr. Fox & Mr. Grey for the House did not separate till between 8 & 9 oClock. They had all agreed that his Speech was one of the most extraordinary displays of eloquence they had ever witnessed, "For the last half Hour, he really seemed inspired."

The War soon after broke out & under an idea of executing his declared purpose of not making peace with France without indemnity for the past, & security for the future, he was seduced by Mr. Dundas, then the War Minister, into West Indian Expeditions, more especially into an attack on the Great Colony of St. Domingo, an enterprize which after an immense expenditure of blood & treasure, terminated in our giving up to Toussaint 12,000 black Troops who had served us faithfully. Afterwards he was led also into the conquest of the Dutch settlement in Guiana, & tho' he never ceased, both in publick & private to speak strongly & warmly in favour of the abolition, yet it must be confessed that other questions & other interests occupied more his thoughts & feelings. Once indeed under the impulse of an indignant feeling, when we had been defeated towards the close of a Session, he declared that on the following year he would himself bring the measure forward. I forget how it was that this Intention was not realized. I can truly however declare, that he never manifested any unwillingness to consult with me in the best method, of proceeding with a view to the carrying of our question, & never produced in my mind, any suspicions of lukewarmness in his opinion or feelings on the question, & I must add that I believe the same impression was always felt by my friend Mr. Wm. Smith, one of the oldest & most zealous friends of our measure, who however being in open opposition & more especially feeling most affectionate veneration for the person & political principles of Mr. Fox, was not likely to regard Mr. Pitt or his measures with any partiality.

(The autobiography was dictated by Wilberforce and written down by an amanuensis. It cannot be stated with any real certainty exactly when he dictated it, but some of the details he refers within the document do indicate that must have been dictating at some point after 1807. In his Diary *Life*, i. p. viii, it indicates there that he dictated it, 'late in life.' Where words were unable to be deciphered then a line has been inserted to denote that, apart from that nothing has been changed from how this document was originally written.)

Reflections on Psalm 40
by
William Wilberforce

1828

Reflections on Psalm 40
by William Wilberforce – 1828

Mr. Wilberforce
Jan 2 1828
Psm 40

To our blessed Saviour, David was considered as a Type & Forerunner of Jesus Christ. Our Saviour was to sit upon the Spiritual Throne of David. But at the same time that parts of it have been in this applied to our blessed Saviour; yet other parts speak plainly of David's own case being not applicable to the case of our Saviour, especially when it says, that "his sins have taken such hold of him that he is not able to look up." As the Psalm is applicable to David himself, so it is also to any Christians in the same circumstances, for it is one of the excellencies of the book of Psalms that it is applicable to all Christians in every age, & has been the blessed means of calling out the devout affections of the people of God in all countries & ages where they have enjoyed the blessings of a Revelation. "I waited patiently for the Lord & he inclined unto me & heard my cry." "He brought me up also out of the horrible pit, out of the miry clay, & set my feet upon a rock & established my goings and he hath put a new song into my mouth, even praise unto our God."

All deliverances should produce gratitude. When we have been experiencing the goodness of God, have been delivered by him from dangers & sufferings, & injuries, we should then have our hearts raised to the giver of all good in gratitude & thanksgiving. It is a sad part of human nature to be forgetful of God when we are enjoying his mercies. The Israelites were warned against it, but "when thou hast eaten & art full thou forgot God." We might have said, "what? Forget him <u>then</u>?" Yes. Such is our sad tendency & therefore we should watch ourselves when we are living in the regular enjoyment of the comforts of life, & have nothing to diversify the external place in which God has placed us; for we are too apt to consider only the <u>extraordinary</u> work, the things that make a change in our condition, & to forget the blessings of the even

439

current of life which is gradually bringing the Christian to the Haven of everlasting light & peace & joy. May we have in our own experience a new song put into our Mouths even of praise to God.

There are none to whom this is more applicable than to those who ~~after they~~ have turned to God to true repentance, after feeling almost overwhelmed by a sense of sin, & of the ingratitude with which they have requited so many mercies; who look to that Saviour, whose sacrifice has made atonement for sin – when a man has been sinking into the very depths of despair from his guilt & misery, <u>then</u> to receive the assurance of pardon & mercy and not only so; for the criminal might Well rejoice in a reprieve when expecting execution, but God does infinitely <u>more</u> – he not only forgives his enemies, but receives them into the number of his <u>children</u> & offers them a happiness & joy which are above any conceptions we can form of them. Seeing such instances as these in The case of others, as well as experiencing the same ourselves, should have the effect of making us observe the dealings of God with us & see how they affect us, "Many shall see it & fear & shall trust in the Lord."

It should lead us to put our trust in God under all circumstances, to adore his infinite goodness, mercy & love. There is a danger lest from our being acquainted with the truths of Christianity from our childhood, we should not feel as if we heard them for the first time. There is a sort of indifference about them perfectly wonderful, as if the deliverance to be experienced by the death of Christ, the being rescued from Hell, & admitted to Heaven, were a <u>common</u> thing, & a <u>common</u> mercy – yet it is a Mercy so great that imagination falls short of every thing approaching to it, & extorts from us the exclamation, "Thy ways are not as our ways, not thy thoughts as our thoughts." "Blessed is that Man who maketh the Lord his trust, & respecteth not the proud, nor such as turn aside to lies." "Many O Lord, my God, are thy wonderful works which thou hast done, & thy thoughts which are to us ward. They cannot be reckoned up in order unto thee – If I would declare & speak of them, they are 'more than can be remembered.'"

How true is this, our whole lives are one continual succession of mercies. We are incessantly receiving blessings from the hand of that very God whom we too often forget, but truly <u>his</u> thoughts to us ward, thoughts of mercy, kindness, forbearance, long suffering are <u>astonishing</u>, such as we cannot conceive, much less express. In fact nothing is more astonishing than to compare with Christianity all the human ideas of religion that ever were devised, where they are strangers to the knowledge of the Christian Revelation, to consider what were the thoughts and speculations of Men as to the means of atoning for sin. For there is a sort of natural feeling in Man that there is a great Being, to whom he has not sufficiently paid attention. In many places there are some traces of this feeling: There is a religion of fear, fear of the greatness & power of some invisible Being, which power they are sensible of in Storms & Tempests, Thunder & Lightning.

These external tokens of invisible <u>power</u>, gave them a sort of awe of that Being who exerted it. But <u>no</u> human imagination ever conceived the <u>Love</u> of God, or had an adequate notion of his moral character. It is <u>Christianity</u> that tells us, "God is Love," and relates that astonishing fact, the greatest mercy of all, his Sending his only Son to die for us Men & for our Salvation. "He sent not his Son into the world to condemn the world, but that the world through him might be saved."

Select Bibliography

Primary Sources

Clarkson, Thomas, A*n Essay on the Slavery and Commerce of the Human Species, particularly the African.* (London, 1786).

_____, *Strictures on a Life of William Wilberforce.* (London: Longman, Orme, Brown, Green & Longmans, 1838).

Doddridge, Philip, *The Rise and Progress of Religion in the Soul.* (London, 1744).

Harford, John Scandrett, *Recollections of William Wilberforce, Esq.* 2nd edition. (London: Longman, Green, Longman, Roberts & Green, 1865).

Milner, Mary, *The Life of Dr. Isaac Milner, DD, FRS.* (London and Cambridge, 1842).

Morris, Caspar, *The Life of William Wilberforce: Compiled from the Memoir published by his sons, and from other sources.* (New York, 1857).

Newton, John, *An Authentic Narrative of Some Interesting Particulars in the Life of (John Newton).* (London, 1764).

Newton, John, *Thoughts upon the African Slave Trade*, 2nd ed. (London, 1788).

Southey, Charles C. (ed.), *The Life and Correspondence of the late Robert Southey*, 6 vols. (London: Longman, Brown, Green and Longmans, 1849–50).

Trevelyan, George O., *The Life and Letters of Lord Macaulay*, 2 vols. (London: Longmans, Green, and Co. 1876).

Wilberforce, Reginald, *Life of Samuel Wilberforce, Bishop of Oxford and Winchester.* (London, 1888).

Wilberforce, Robert Isaac and Samuel, *The Life of William Wilberforce*, 5 vols. (London: John Murray, 1838).

Wilberforce, Samuel, *Life of William Wilberforce.* (London: John Murray, 1868).

Wilberforce, William, *A Practical View of the Prevailing Religious System of Professed Christians in the Higher and Middle Classes ... contrasted with Real Christianity.* (London: T. Cadell, 1797).

_____, *Letter on the Abolition of the Slave Trade; Addressed to the Freeholders and Other Inhabitants of Yorkshire.* (London: T. Cadell, 1807).

_____, *A Letter to his Excellency the Prince of Talleyrand Perigord &c. &c. &c. on the subject of The Slave Trade*, by William Wilberforce, ESQ., M.P. (1814).

_____, 'A Recommendation of Richard Baxter's *Saints' Rest'.* (Wilberforce wrote the recommendation for an 1814 edition of Baxter's work.)

_____, *An Appeal to the Religion, Justice, and Humanity of the Inhabitants of the British Empire on Behalf of the Negro Slaves in the West Indies.* (London: J. Hatchard, 1823).

_____, 'An Introductory Essay for John Witherspoon's *Essay on Justification'.* (This appeared in an 1840 edition of Witherspoon's work.)

_____, *A Journey to the Lake District from Cambridge, 1779,* ed. C. E. Wrangham. (Stocksfield, Northumberland: Oriel Press, 1983).

Family Prayers by the Late William Wilberforce, edited by his son, Robert Isaac Wilberforce, 6th ed. (London: J. Hatchard & Son, 1837).

The Correspondence of William Wilberforce, eds. Robert Isaac and Samuel Wilberforce, 2 vols. (London: John Murray, 1840).

Private Papers of William Wilberforce, Collected and edited by Anna M. Wilberforce. (London: T. F. Unwin, 1897).

Amazing Dad: Letters from William Wilberforce to his Children, ed. Stephanie Byrd. (Maitland, FL: Xulon Press, 2010).

Secondary Sources

Alexander, William, *The Witness of the Psalms to Christ and Christianity.* (London: John Murray, 1877).

Anonymous, *The Slaves Champion, or The Life, Deeds, and Historical Days of William Wilberforce. Written in Commemoration of his Birthday. By the Author of 'The Popular Harmony of the Bible,' &c.*

To which is Appended An Account of the Keeping of the Twenty-Fifth Birthday of Freedom. (London: Seeleys, 1859).

Ashwell, A.R. and Wilberforce, R.G., *The Life of the Right Reverend Samuel Wilberforce, DD.* (New York, 1883).

Atkins, Gareth, 'Wilberforce and his Milieux: The Worlds of Anglican Evangelicalism c. 1780–1830', Ph.D. Thesis (Cambridge, 2009).

Baehr, Ted, et al., *The Amazing Grace of Freedom: The Inspiring Faith of William Wilberforce.* (Green Forest, AR: New Leaf Press, 2007).

Bayne, Peter, *Men Worthy to Lead.* (London: Simpkin, Marshall, Hamilton, Kent & Co., 1890).

Beauregard, John, *William Wilberforce, 1759–1833: An Annotated Author and Subject Bibliography.* (Wenham, MA: Gordon College, 2003).

Bebbington, David W., *Evangelicalism in Modern Britain: A History from the 1730s to the 1980s* (London: Unwin Hyman Ltd., 1989).

Bebbington, Eileen, *A Patterned Life: Faith, History, and David Bebbington.* (Eugene, OR: Wipf & Stock, 2014).

Belmonte, Kevin, 'William Wilberforce: The Making of an Evangelical Reformer'. MA Thesis (Gordon-Conwell Theological Seminary, MA, 1995).

_____, *365 Days with Wilberforce: A collection of daily readings from the writings of William Wilberforce.* (Leominster UK: Day One, 2006).

_____, *A Journey through the Life of William Wilberforce: the Abolitionist who changed the face of a Nation.* (Leominster, UK: Day One 2007).

_____, *William Wilberforce: A Hero for Humanity.* (Grand Rapids, MI: Zondervan, 2007).

Boyle, J. R., *Wilberforce House, High Street, Hull: A Memoir and a Memorial.* (Hull, 1896, reprinted by Malet Lambert High School, Hull, 1985).

Bradley, Ian, *The Call to Seriousness: The Evangelical Impact on the Victorians.* (New York: Macmillan Publishing Co. Inc., 1976).

Brown, F. K., *Fathers of the Victorians: The Age of Wilberforce.* (Cambridge: CUP, 1961).

Buxton, Travers, *William Wilberforce: The Story of a Great Crusade.* (London: Religious Tract Society, n.d.).

Carey, Brycchan, 'William Wilberforce's Sentimental Rhetoric: Parliamentary Reportage and the Abolition Speech of 1789', *The Age of Johnson: A Scholarly Annual,* 14 (2003), 281-305.

Clapham Antiquarian Society, *Clapham and the Clapham Sect.* (Clapham: 1927).

Colquhoun, John Campbell, *William Wilberforce, His Friends and Times.* (London: Longmans, Green, Reader, and Dyer, 1866).

Conroy, Carolyn, *Homage to the Emancipator: Hull and the William Wilberforce Monument.* (Hull: William Wilberforce Monument Fund, 2014).

Cormack, Patrick, *Wilberforce, The Nation's Conscience.* (London: Pickering, 1983).

Coupland, Reginald, *Wilberforce: A Narrative.* (Oxford: The Clarendon Press, 1923).

Cowie, Leonard W., *William Wilberforce, 1759–1833, A Bibliography.* (London: Greenwood Press, 1992).

Deverell, Liz and Watkins, Gareth, *Wilberforce and Hull.* (Kingston-upon-Hull: Kingston Press, 2000).

Everett, Betty S., *Freedom Fighter: The Story of William Wilberforce, the British Parliamentarian who Fought to Free Slaves.* (London: CLC, 1994).

Feltham, John, *A Guide to all the Watering and Sea-Bathing Places, for 1813.* (London: Longman, Hurst, Rees, Orme, and Brown, 1813).

Fendall, Lon, *William Wilberforce: Abolitionist, Politician, Writer.* (Uhrichsville, OH: Barbour Books, 2002).

Forster, E. M., *Marianne Thornton: A Domestic Biography.* (London: Edward Arnold, 1956).

Furneaux, Robin, *William Wilberforce.* (London: Hamish Hamilton, 1974).

Guinness, Os, *Character Counts: Leadership Qualities in Washington, Wilberforce, Lincoln and Solzhenitsyn.* (Grand Rapids: Baker Books, 1999).

Gurney, Joseph John, *Familiar Sketch of the Late William Wilberforce.* (Norwich: Josiah Fletcher, 1838).

Hague, William, *William Wilberforce: The Life of the Great Anti-Slave Trade Campaigner.* (London: HarperPress, 2007).

Hancock, Christopher, 'The "Shrimp" who Stopped Slavery'. *Christian History,* Issue 53 (Vol. XVI, No. 1).

Holzmann, John, *William Wilberforce: Britain's Great Emancipator.* (Littleton, CO: Avyx, 2014).

Jackson, Gordon, *Hull in the Eighteenth Century: A Study in Economic and Social History.* (London, New York, and Toronto: OUP, 1972).

Jenkins, Wilfred J., *William Wilberforce: A Champion of Freedom.* (London: Epworth Press, 1932).

Lawson, John, *A Town Grammar School through Six Centuries: A History of Hull Grammar School against its Local Background.* (London: OUP, 1963).

Lawson, Steven J., *Holman Old Testament Commentary: Psalms 76-150.* (Nashville: B&H Academic, 2004).

Lean, Garth, *God's Politician: William Wilberforce's Struggle.* (London: Darton, Longman and Todd, 1980).

Meacham, Standish, *Henry Thornton of Clapham.* (Cambridge, MA: Harvard University Press, 1964).

Melaas-Swanson, Barbara J., 'The Life and Thought of the Very Reverend Dr. Isaac Milner and his contribution to the Evangelical Revival in England'. Ph.D. Thesis (Durham University, 1993).

Metaxas, Eric, *Amazing Grace.* (New York: HarperCollins, 2007).

———, *7 Men and the Secret of their Greatness.* (Nashville: Nelson Books, 2016).

Michael, Charles D., *The Slave and his Champions.* (London: S. W. Partridge, n.d.).

Patten, John A., *These Remarkable Men: The Beginnings of a World Enterprise.* (London: Lutterworth Press, 1945).

Piper, John, *Amazing Grace in the Life of William Wilberforce.* (Wheaton, IL: Crossway, 2006).

———, *The Roots of Endurance: Invincible Perseverance in the Lives of John Newton, Charles Simeon, and William Wilberforce* (Wheaton, IL: Crossway Books, 2006).

Pollock, John, *Wilberforce.* (London: Constable and Company, 1977).

———, *William Wilberforce: A Man Who Changed His Times.* (London: The Trinity Forum, 2006).

———, *Abolition! Newton, the ex-slave trader, and Wilberforce, the little liberator.* (Leominster, UK: 2007).

Price, Thomas, *A Memoir of William Wilberforce,* 2nd American Ed. (Boston: Light & Stearns, 1836).

Pym, Dorothy, *Battersea Rise.* (London: Jonathan Cape, 1934).

Redman, Melody, 'Heroes 12: William Wilberforce', Nucleus, the student journal of the Christian medical fellowship 44, No.1 (January 2014): 32-34.

Sheahan, J. J., *History of the Town and Port of Kingston-upon-Hull,* 2nd ed. (Beverley, 1866).

Silvester, James, *William Wilberforce, Christian Liberator: A Centenary Biography.* (London: Mitre Press, 1934).

Smith, Gary Scott, *Duty and Destiny: The Life and Faith of Winston Churchill.* (Grand Rapids, MI: Wm. B. Eerdmans, 2021).

Stanhope, Earl, *Life of the Right Honourable William Pitt,* 3 vols. 2nd ed. (London: John Murray, 1862).

Stetson, Charles P., *Creating the Better Hour: Lessons from William Wilberforce.* (Macon, GA: Stroud and Hall, 2007).

_____, *The British Abolitionists and their Influence, with a Survey of their Writings.* (Front Royal, VA: Essentials in Education, Inc., 2009).

Stott, Anne, *Wilberforce Family and Friends.* (New York: Oxford University Press, Inc., 2012).

Stoughton, John, *William Wilberforce.* (London: Hodder & Stoughton, 1880).

Thomas, Hugh, *The Slave Trade: The Story of the Atlantic Slave Trade 1440-1870.* (New York: Simon & Schuster, 1997).

Tompkins, Stephen, *William Wilberforce: A Biography.* (Grand Rapids, MI: Eerdmans, 2007).

Van Dyke, Henry, *The Story of the Psalms.* (New York, 1887).

Wilberforce, Yvette, *William Wilberforce, An Essay.* Foreword by C. E. Wrangham. (Privately Printed, 1967).

Wildridge, T. Tindall, *The Wilberforce Souvenir, A Little Sketch Book, in which Pen and Pencil Record, without elaboration, things Worthy to be Remembered in connection with William Wilberforce.* (Hull: M. C. Peck, 1884, reprinted by Malet Lambert High School, Hull, 1983).

Williamson, Mark, *William Wilberforce: Achieving the Impossible.* (Milton Keynes: Authentic Media, 2014).

Wolffe, John, *The Expansion of Evangelicalism: The Age of Wilberforce, More, Chalmers, and Finney.* (Nottingham: IVP, 2006).

By the same author

Hearts Aflame

Cuori Ardenti

Clouds of Heaven

The Prayers and Meditations of Susanna Wesley

The Passionate Preacher

God's Polished Arrow

Hearts Aflame (Braille edition)

The Prayers and Meditations of Susanna Wesley (Chinese edition)

The Blessing of God

God's Polished Arrow (Braille edition)

M'Cheyne's Sermons on Hebrews

M'Cheyne's Sermons from the New Testament

M'Cheyne's Sermons from the Old Testament

The Glory and Honor of God

The Unpublished Sermons of Jonathan Edwards

The Diary of Andrew Fuller

The Glory and Honor of God (Korean edition)

Index of People and Places

K

Kent, Duke of.......348, 367, 385, 426
Keston 73, 79, 126-7, 428
Keswick...428
Kettering...........347-8, 347n275, 352
Kimber, John................ 164, 164n99,
193, 213, 214

L

Lafayette, Marquis de 49, 223,
223n472, 422
Lambridge 280-5
Lancashire....................................430
Langston, Bonnett...................... 427
Langston, Stephen.......358, 358n341
Lansdown, Lord.......................... 354
Lascelles, Henry 335n194, 422
'Launchers'................. 33, 192-3, 230,
231n510, 284
Lavater, Johann....180, 180n210, 194
Lavington 393, 393n121
Leeds 345-6, 356, 423
Leeds, Duchess of........................ 279
Leicester............345, 345n266, 326-7
Leighton, Robert..........176, 176n186,
177, 197, 241, 273
Lennox, C. 421
Leveson, Lord Granville............. 354
Liege 424
Lillingston, Abraham
Spooner 232, 232n518,
258n663, 272, 273n767, 282
Lindsey, Theophilus 50, 97
Liverpool 74, 405, 429-31
Locke, John.................................... 65
London.............. 26, 28, 44-51, 59-60,
74, 88, 105, 116, 142,
168-9, 190, 218, 225, 283,
283n833, 285, 314, 317,
399-402, 419-21, 424-5
Adelphi..................63, 63n39, 425
Barnet 345, 345n268
Battersea Rise 38, 79,
105n160, 132, 132n353, 154-8,
160, 162-9, 171-85, 191, 192-3,
194-5, 196-202, 203-7, 216-21,
222-3, 224, 237-8, 260, 285
Bootle's 421
British
Institution...... 350-1, 350n296
Brompton Grove.......389, 389n88
Brooks.......................................421

Broomfield House 235-7,
235n535, 238, 251-7, 261,
263, 268-75, 271n750
Clapham, ... 79, 105, 122-5, 129,
141-2, 150-1, 250-1, 427
Downing Street 424
Freemasons' Tavern 385
Goostry's Club.................... 420-1
Hampstead............................. 160
House of Commons 49, 61n26,
73, 74, 89, 106, 244n590,
251n625, 296, 311, 318n73,
346, 351-2, 351n303, 366-7,
385, 402, 422, 429, 431
House of Lords 103n148,
104n154, 227n494,
296, 319, 327
Hyde Park........... 30, 308n20, 385
Kensington Gore......97n103, 343,
343n245, 376-7, 383-4
Kew 95, 95n89, 426
King's Arms Yard... 111, 111n208,
116, 117n253, 127-9, 193-4
Lambeth 350, 350n294
Lock Hospital 91, 91n51, 94,
94n76, 96, 102, 106, 117,
162, 166, 207, 242, 262,
274n774, 344, 389
Miles & Evan's 421
Newgate Prison 366, 382
Royal Observatory 95, 95n90
Old Palace Yard......103, 103n148,
116-22, 117n253, 124, 125-6,
134, 149-50, 161-2, 163, 166,
170-1, 172, 174, 177, 178,
190-1, 192, 193, 195-6, 201,
202-7, 217, 218-20, 223-4,
225-9, 232-3, 240-4, 246-50,
260-3, 264-8, 285-8, 425
Parliament........ 39, 48-9, 74-7, 83,
139-40, 296, 304-6, 309,
327, 333, 347, 365-9,
373-4, 381, 387, 402-3,
421-2, 424-6, 428-9,
433-4
Putney...........................45, 47, 419
Scotch Church 367, 377,
377n34
Shooting Hill 143, 254
St. Antholin's 58, 58n7
St. Bartholomew's
Hospital............. 234, 234n528

Scripture References